Readings in
Managerial
Psychology

Edited by
Harold J.
Leavitt
and
Louis R.
Pondy

Readings in Managerial Psychology

Second Edition

The University of Chicago Press
Chicago and London

The University of Chicago Press, Chicago 60637
The University of Chicago Press, Ltd., London
© 1964, 1973 by The University of Chicago
All rights reserved. Published 1964. Second Edition 1973
Printed in the United States of America
International Standard Book Number:
0–226–46984–0 (clothbound)
Library of Congress Catalog Card Number: 72–96499

73 74 75 76 77
1 2 3 4 5 6 7 8 9 10

HAROLD J. LEAVITT is now the Walter Kilpatrick Professor of
Organizational Behavior and Psychology in the Graduate School
of Business, Stanford University. He is the author of *Managerial
Psychology*, 3d ed. (University of Chicago Press, 1972), editor of
The Social Science of Organizations, and coeditor of *New
Perspectives in Organizational Research*. LOUIS R. PONDY .
currently professor of business administration at the University of
Illinois (Urbana), has also taught at Duke University and at the
University of Pittsburgh. He has been involved as a researcher
and as a consultant to the federal government on health systems
and health manpower problems. He is on the editorial board of
the *Administrative Science Quarterly*, and has contributed
numerous articles to scholarly publications .
[1973]

Contents

1

**People as Individuals
The Integration of Thought
and Feeling**

2

3

**Collections of Individuals
Group Processes**

4

People in Complex Systems Formal Organizations

Preface

The preface to the first edition of this book started this way:

> This book is intended for managers in business and in-
> dustrial organizations and for students of management.
> But we hope that public administrators, university ad-
> ministrators, and executives in other organizations will
> also find it relevant and applicable to their problems,
> for one of the biases of our point of view is that the
> same broad classes of managerial problems are to be
> found in organizations of several different types.
>
> We intend this to be a practical book, practical in the
> sense that the reader will find some new and better ways
> to think about certain problems than he did before. It
> may, therefore, seem surprising that only a few of the
> articles deal directly with management as such. The ma-
> jority are drawn from the many sciences of behavior and
> were *not* written especially for students of management.
>
> The inclusion of such "non-practical" articles in a
> "practical" book reflects another bias—that manage-
> ment is increasingly becoming a set of skills which can
> be taught and learned, instead of an art which is inborn
> or gleaned *only* through long experience (though experi-
> ence is still a good tool). Many useful techniques and
> methods of management find their source or their sup-
> port in social science research. The articles selected
> summarize and give perspective to much of this
> research.
>
> We have designed this book to be fact-oriented rather
> than value oriented. Each of the articles provides either
> some new information on or some systematic presenta-
> tion of how and why people behave as they do in orga-
> nizations, not how they *ought* to behave. We do not pur-
> port to tell the manager what goals to pursue or even
> how to pursue whatever goals he has. What we have
> tried to do is collect some papers that describe alterna-

tive approaches to management, their costs and implications.

Most of the emphasis is on problems of the management of people—as individuals, as members of small face-to-face groups, and as participants in larger, less personal, formal organizations. But especially in considering large organizational problems, we have included some papers that emphasize problems of structure and technology as well as problems of people.

We are willing to leave *most* of what we said in the 1964 preface about as it is. We continue to believe that these readings are just about as relevant for public or other non-business managers as for managers in business firms. In fact, since 1964 the dividing line between organizations in the private and public sectors has become even hazier than it seemed then.

And we still intend this to be a practical book, one which will be helpful in solving problems ranging from management of the individual employee all the way through designing large complex organizations. And we still have drawn most of the articles in the book from the underlying behavioral sciences rather than directly from applied journals of management. Moreover, the main structure of the book has remained unchanged. Part 1 still deals with the individual, part 2 with pairs of individuals, part 3 with small groups, and part 4 with large complex organizations.

But there are several changes: Although the main thrust of the book is still fact-oriented, we have included this time more papers which directly raise important value issues; and we have also shown more concern for the organization-environment relationship.

We have also made an extra effort this time to select articles which are well written and easily readable, and to avoid as much as possible those which are heavily laden with technical jargon.

Of the forty-six papers in this revised edition, only ten are holdovers from the first edition and thirty-six are new. A new chapter on attitudes and beliefs has been added to part 1. In part 2, the chapter on power has been expanded considerably. Part 3 has gone through a major restructuring, with a new chapter dealing primarily with sensitivity training, and an expanded chapter on group conflict. In part 4, a new chapter on the relationship between the organization and its environment has been added. Also the chapters on decision making and technological aspects of formal organizations have been combined, with updated empirical data on the impact of computers on organizational decision making. Cutting across the major parts of the book, new material on cognitive styles has been added to chapter 2 (the paper by Leavitt and Doktor) and in chapter 11 (the paper by March). And ethical issues are raised more explicitly than before in the papers by Lovell on the human use of personality tests (chapter 4), by Milgram on obedience and disobedience to authority (chapter 6) and in Lakin's paper on sensitivity training (chapter 9).

A "contingency" theme surfaced repeatedly in several parts of the book, a view that there is no one best way of dealing with people in organizations. Thus, in chapter 5. Hall and Whyte stress the ways in which effective communication varies from culture to culture; and in chapter 7, Morse and Lorsch argue for the effectiveness of democratic leadership in ill-structured situations, but for more bureaucratic forms in stable, well-defined situations. In chapter 11, Lawrence and Lorsch, Emery and Trist, and March, and in chapter 14, Bennis, all share the view that complex, uncertain, unstructured organizational environments require more open and adaptive organizational structures.

One other change from the first edition is worth mentioning. We have considerably expanded our editorial commentaries at the beginning of each chapter in this edition. These introductory comments are designed to provide a road map for the reader to help give him perspective on each article within each chapter and each chapter within the major parts of the book. Sometimes they provide a little additional information which was not covered in the articles themselves. The commentaries are somewhat more critical this time, too. We hope that this provides a more stimulating and helpful introduction to each of the chapters.

Those familiar with the third edition of Leavitt's *Managerial Psychology* will notice that this *reader* roughly parallels it in its general structure. The similarity is intentional so that the two books can be used together by those who choose to.

H.J.L.
L.R.P.

1

**People as Individuals:
The Integration of
Thought and Feeling**

1

Motivation: The Driving Force

Introduction

Part 1 of this book puts the spotlight on the individual human being. In subsequent parts we shall consider how individuals interact with one another, how they behave in small groups, and how large complex organizations affect their behavior.

But first, in the four chapters that make up part 1, we want to take a good look at the person himself, examining successively the motivation of human beings, their thinking and problem-solving behavior, the processes of perception and attitude formation, and finally considering the problem of assessing the whole man.

One important common thread running throughout these first four chapters is the notion that one's behavior is jointly influenced by his internal state and by the pressures of his environment.

In chapter 1, we examine *motivation,* a concept presumably reflecting an important internal state of man.

The concept of motivation was invented by social scientists to explain the connections between the individual's environment and his behavior. Motivation is a patchwork concept (indeed a collection of other concepts, like feelings, needs, goals, and drives) designed to account for the individual's tendency to respond differently to the same stimulus at different times and for different individuals' tendencies to respond differently to the same stimulus.

Chapter 1 consists of four papers. Two of them, by Maslow and Herzberg, espouse particular theories of human motivation. The other two papers, by Hunt and Hill and by Lawler, compare and integrate different theories of motivation and examine evidence about those theories.

Maslow argues, as do many other theorists, that people tend to engage in those activities they believe will satisfy unfulfilled needs. But he also proposes that the important human needs are arranged in a sort of hierarchy. If two or

3

more needs, for example, the needs for love and for esteem, are relatively unsatisfied, Maslow argues, the person will engage in behavior aimed at satisfying the more fundamental of the needs, in this case the love needs, according to Maslow's theory. But, when two different patterns of behavior are available to a person, and both can satisfy the person's most salient need, Maslow's theory does *not* very well account for how the person chooses one behavior rather than the other.

Both Maslow and Herzberg consider the conditions that generate need satisfaction, but Herzberg makes the additional distinction that dissatisfaction is an emotional state of its own, not merely the opposite of satisfaction.

Herzberg, in brief, proposes that a given piece of behavior may be either an intrinsic factor (that is, it may serve as a source of satisfaction in and of itself), or an extrinsic factor (that is, as a source of relief from dissatisfaction). The behaviors which provide intrinsic satisfaction he calls *motivators,* and those which provide relief from dissatisfaction he calls *hygiene factors.* He then goes on to argue that the only reliable way to motivate employees to be productive is to provide them with intrinsically satisfying jobs, that is, with motivators. Using extrinsic controls (his hygiene factors) like the promise of promotion, or the threat of dismissal, or better rest rooms, requires continual application to be effective, and even then may not be very reliable. Herzberg has coined the term "job enrichment" to describe the process of designing such intrinsically satisfying jobs that provide the opportunity for personal growth. (The reader should pay particular attention to the careful distinction he makes between job enrichment and an older concept, job enlargement.)

The paper by Hunt and Hill provides an excellent summary and comparison of the Maslow and Herzberg views. Of particular interest is the parallel Hunt and Hill draw between Maslow's lower order needs and Herzberg's hygiene factors on the one hand and Maslow's higher order needs and Herzberg's motivators on the other hand. They claim that the empirical evidence in support of either Maslow's or Herzberg's theories is neither very extensive nor very solid. However, not all psychologists agree with their conclusions. For a different and more positive interpretation of the empirical evidence bearing on Herzberg's Motivation-Hygiene theory, the reader may wish to consult Whitsett and Winslow.[1] And

1. D. A. Whitsett and E. K. Winslow, "An Analysis of Studies Critical of the Motivation-Hygiene Theory," *Personnel Psychology* 20, no. 4 (Winter 1967): 391–415.

other direct tests of the job enrichment hypothesis which provide positive support are also available.[2]

Hunt and Hill go on to summarize a third view of motivation (espoused by Vroom and others) which attempts to establish an explicit connection between the individual's goals, the rewards which he perceives, and his level of performance. Vroom takes explicit account of a person's *choice* among alternative paths to goals. If the only path to a person's goal of respect from his colleagues is to be productive, then he is likely to be productive. If, on the other hand, one has available several possible ways to earn the esteem of his colleagues (for example, to take the leadership role in organizing a local labor union), then (1) it is far from certain that the person will choose the route of high productivity, and (2) it may be possible to analyze the situation so as to predict (with reasonable probability) his likely choice.

As Lawler points out in his paper, an employee could thus be influenced to increase his productivity in any one of several ways: by increasing his subjective probability (his own belief) that effort will lead to high performance; by increasing the employee's subjective probability that a high level of performance will be rewarded; or by closing off alternative ways of reaching his goal, whether that goal be higher income, personal satisfaction, or whatever. Lawler's view is consistent with and in fact derives in part from the work of Vroom. In addition, Lawler makes use of Herzberg's distinction between horizontal job enlargement (providing employees a greater variety of jobs to do), and vertical job enlargement (providing the employees with more control and responsibility for the activities in which they are engaged). Lawler goes on to argue that the employee will be motivated to be more productive only when both horizontal and vertical job enlargement are present, and he presents some evidence in support of his position.

As the reader will see, chapter 1 is mostly concerned with the problem of motivation as it relates to productivity. However, the positions presented here can also provide a basis for analysis of motivation in other settings, like the motivation for creativity, or for participation in group activity, or for education.

Some other important motivational questions are also con-

2. W. J. Paul, Jr., K. B. Robertson, and Frederick Herzberg, "Job Enrichment Pays Off," *Harvard Business Review,* March–April 1969, pp. 61–78; Robert N. Ford, *Motivation through the Work Itself* (New York: American Management Association, 1970).

sidered in these papers. For instance, where do people get their motives and how do they develop? Maslow considers these issues to some extent, but they are also covered in more detail in chapter 3 in the article by Sandra and Daryl Bem and in the papers in chapter 4 by McClelland and Downs.

In going through this chapter, the reader may also want to be aware of the following underlying ideas that are implicitly shared by almost all students of motivation:

1. People tend to concentrate their energies on only a few of their needs at a time.

2. Except in pathological cases, people seldom seek *total* satisfaction of their needs. They tend to shoot for goals which are adequate or good enough, or better-than-now, rather than for the best of all possible worlds.

3. When a person's goals are set higher than his ability to achieve them, or when he encounters several needs which are mutually inconsistent, feelings of frustration or internal conflict will result. These feelings in turn tend to generate offbeat behavior, like withdrawal from uncomfortable situations or "irrational" aggression against some otherwise neutral target.

4. Don't expect rationality and consistency in human motives. People want some things they think they shouldn't want, or say they don't want, or don't know they want. There is a logic to motivational *processes* in general but *not* a simple consistent logic in each person's head to account for his goals and his choices. If you insist on demanding from others a logical and "reasonable" accounting for their wants and needs, you are likely to bring forth a mixture of rationalizations, guilt, and anger.

A Theory of Human Motivation
A. H. Maslow

Dynamics of the Basic Needs

The "Physiological" Needs

The needs that are usually taken as the starting point for motivation theory are the so-called physiological drives. Two recent lines of research make it necessary to revise our customary notions about these needs: first, the development of the concept of homeostasis, and, second, the finding that appetites (preferential choices among foods) are a fairly efficient indication of actual needs or lacks in the body.

Homeostasis refers to the body's automatic efforts to maintain a constant, normal state of the blood stream. Cannon[1] has described this process for (1) the water content of the blood, (2) salt content, (3) sugar content, (4) protein content, (5) fat content, (6) calcium content, (7) oxygen content, (8) constant hydrogen-ion level (acid-base balance), and (9) constant temperature of the blood. Obviously this list can be extended to include other minerals, the hormones, vitamins, and so on.

Young in a recent article[2] has summarized the work on appetite in its relation to body needs. If the body lacks some chemical, the individual will tend to develop a specific appetite or partial hunger for that food element.

Thus it seems impossible as well as useless to make any list of fundamental physiological needs for they can come to almost any number one might wish, depending on the degree of specificity of description. We cannot identify all physiological needs as homeostatic. That sexual desire, sleepiness, sheer activity, and maternal behavior in animals are homeo-

Abridged from A. H. Maslow, "A Theory of Human Motivation," *Psychological Review* 50 (1943): 370–96. Copyright 1943 by the American Psychological Association, and reproduced by permission.
    1. W. B. Cannon, *Wisdom of the Body* (New York: Norton, 1932).
    2. P. T. Young, "The Experimental Analysis of Appetite," *Psychological Bulletin* 38 (1941): 129–64.

static, has not yet been demonstrated. Furthermore, this list would not include the various sensory pleasures (tastes, smells, tickling, stroking) which are probably physiological and which may become the goals of motivated behavior.

In a previous paper[3] it has been pointed out that these physiological drives or needs are to be considered unusual rather than typical because they are isolable and because they are localizable somatically. That is to say, they are relatively independent of each other, of other motivations and of the organism as a whole, and, in many cases, it is possible to demonstrate a localized, underlying somatic base for the drive. This is true less generally than has been thought (exceptions are fatigue, sleepiness, maternal responses), but it is still true in the classic instances of hunger, sex, and thirst.

It should be pointed out again that any of the physiological needs and the consummatory behavior involved with them serve as channels for all sorts of other needs as well. The person who thinks he is hungry may actually be seeking more for comfort or dependence than for vitamins or proteins. Conversely, it is possible to satisfy the hunger need in part by other activities such as drinking water or smoking cigarettes. In other words, these physiological needs are only relatively isolable.

Undoubtedly these physiological needs are the most prepotent of all needs. What this means specifically is that, in the human being who is missing everything in life in an extreme fashion, it is most likely that the major motivation would be the physiological needs rather than any others. A person who is lacking food, safety, love, and esteem would most probably hunger for food more strongly than for anything else.

If all the needs are unsatisfied, and the organism is then dominated by the physiological needs, all other needs may become simply nonexistent or be pushed into the background. It is then fair to characterize the whole organism by saying simply that it is hungry, for consciousness is almost completely preempted by hunger. All capacities are put into the service of hunger-satisfaction, and the organization of these capacities is almost entirely determined by the one purpose of satisfying hunger. The receptors and effectors, the intelligence, memory, habits, all may now be defined simply as hunger-gratifying tools. Capacities that are not useful for this purpose lie dormant or are pushed into the

3. A. H. Maslow, "A Preface of Motivation Theory," *Psychosomatic Medicine* 5 (1943): 85–92.

background. The urge to write poetry, the desire to acquire an automobile, the interest in American history, the desire for a new pair of shoes are, in the extreme case, forgotten or become of secondary importance. For the man who is extremely and dangerously hungry, no other interests exist but food. He dreams food, he remembers food, he thinks about food, he emotes only about food, he perceives only food, and he wants only food. The more subtle determinants that ordinarily fuse with the physiological drives in organizing even feeding, drinking, or sexual behavior, may now be so completely overwhelmed as to allow us to speak at this time (but *only* at this time) of pure hunger drive and behavior, with the one unqualified aim of relief.

Another peculiar characteristic of the human organism when it is dominated by a certain need is that the whole philosophy of the future tends also to change. For our chronically and extremely hungry man, utopia can be defined very simply as a place where there is plenty of food. He tends to think that, if only he is guaranteed food for the rest of his life, he will be perfectly happy and will never want anything more. Life itself tends to be defined in terms of eating. Anything else will be defined as unimportant. Freedom, love, community feeling, respect, philosophy, may all be waved aside as fripperies which are useless, since they fail to fill the stomach. Such a man may fairly be said to live by bread alone.

It cannot possibly be denied that such things are true, but their *generality* can be denied. Emergency conditions are, almost by definition, rare in the normally functioning peaceful society. That this truism can be forgotten is due mainly to two reasons. First, rats have few motivations other than physiological ones, and since so much of the research upon motivation has been made with these animals, it is easy to carry the rat-picture over to the human being. Second, it is too often not realized that culture itself is an adaptive tool, one of whose main functions is to make the physiological emergencies come less and less often. In most of the known societies, chronic extreme hunger of the emergency type is rare rather than common. In any case, this is still true in the United States. The average American citizen is experiencing appetite rather than hunger when he says, "I am hungry." He is apt to experience sheer life-and-death hunger only by accident and then only a few times through his entire life.

Obviously a good way to obscure the "higher" motivations, and to get a lopsided view of human capacities and human nature, is to make the organism extremely and chronically hungry or thirsty. Anyone who attempts to make an emergency picture into a typical one and who will measure all of man's goals and desires by his behavior during extreme physiological deprivation is certainly being blind to many things. It is quite true that man lives by bread alone— when there is no bread. But what happens to man's desires when there *is* plenty of bread and when his belly is chronically filled?

At once other (and "higher") needs emerge and these, rather than physiological hungers, dominate the organism. And when these in turn are satisfied, again new (and still "higher") needs emerge, and so on. This is what we mean by saying that the basic human needs are organized into a hierarchy of relative prepotency.

One main implication of this phrasing is that gratification becomes as important a concept as deprivation in motivation theory, for it releases the organism from the domination of a relatively more physiological need, permitting thereby the emergence of other more social goals. The physiological needs, along with their partial goals, when chronically gratified cease to exist as active determinants or organizers of behavior. They now exist only in a potential fashion in the sense that they may emerge again to dominate the organism if they are thwarted. But a want that is satisfied is no longer a want. The organism is dominated and its behavior organized only by unsatisfied needs. If hunger is satisfied, it becomes unimportant in the current dynamics of the individual.

This statement is somewhat qualified by a hypothesis to be discussed more fully later, namely, that it is precisely those individuals in whom a certain need has always been satisfied who are best equipped to tolerate deprivation of that need in the future; furthermore, those who have been deprived in the past will react to current satisfactions differently from the one who has never been deprived.

The Safety Needs

If the physiological needs are relatively well gratified, there then emerges a new set of needs, which we may categorize roughly as the safety needs. All that has been said of the physiological needs is equally true, although in lesser degree, of these desires. The organism may equally well be wholly dominated by them. They may serve as the almost exclusive organizers of behavior, recruiting all the capacities of the organism in their service, and we may then fairly describe the whole organism as a safety-seeking mechanism. Again we may say of the receptors, the effectors, of the intellect and the other capacities that they are primarily safety-seeking tools. Again, as in the hungry man, we find that the dominating goal is a strong determinant not only of his current world-outlook and philosophy but also of his philosophy of the future. Practically everything looks less important than safety (even sometimes the physiological needs which being satisfied, are now underestimated). A man, in this state, if it is extreme enough and chronic enough, may be characterized as living almost for safety alone.

Although in this paper we are interested primarily in the needs of the adult, we can approach an understanding of his safety needs perhaps more efficiently by observation of infants and children, in whom these needs are much more simple and obvious. One reason for the clearer appearance of the threat or danger reaction in infants is that they do not inhibit this reaction at all, whereas adults in our society have been taught to inhibit it at all costs. Thus even when adults do feel their safety to be threatened, we may not be able to see this on the surface. Infants will react in a total fashion and as if they were endangered, if they are disturbed or dropped suddenly, startled by loud noises, flashing light, or other unusual sensory stimulation, by rough handling, by general loss of support in the mother's arms, or by inadequate support.[4]

In infants we can also see a much more direct reaction to bodily illnesses of various kinds. Sometimes these illnesses seem to be immediately and per se threatening and seem to make the child feel unsafe. For instance, vomiting, colic, or other sharp pains seem to make the child look at the whole world in a different way. At such a moment of pain, it may be postulated that, for the child, the appearance of the whole world suddenly changes from sunniness to darkness, so to speak, and becomes a place in which anything at all might happen, in which previously stable things have suddenly become unstable. Thus a child who because of some bad food is taken ill may, for a day or two, develop fear, nightmares, and a need for protection and reassurance never seen in him before his illness.

Another indication of the child's need for safety is his pref-

---

4. As the child grows up, sheer knowledge and familiarity as well as better motor development make these "dangers" less and less dangerous and more and more manageable. Throughout life it may be said that one of the main conative functions of education is this neutralizing of apparent dangers through knowledge, e.g., I am not afraid of thunder because I know something about it.

erence for some kind of undisrupted routine or rhythm. He seems to want a predictable, orderly world. For instance, injustice, unfairness, or inconsistency in the parents seems to make a child feel anxious and unsafe. This attitude may be not so much because of the injustice per se or any particular pains involved, but rather because this treatment threatens to make the world look unreliable or unsafe or unpredictable. Young children seem to thrive better under a system which has at least a skeletal outline of rigidity, in which there is a schedule of a kind, some sort of routine, something that can be counted upon, not only for the present, but also far into the future. Perhaps one could express this more accurately by saying that the child needs an organized world rather than an unorganized or unstructured one.

The central role of the parents and the normal family setup are indisputable. Quarreling, physical assault, separation, divorce, or death within the family may be particularly terrifying. Also parental outbursts of rage or threats of punishment directed to the child, calling him names, speaking to him harshly, shaking him, handling him roughly, or actual physical punishment sometimes elicit such total panic and terror in the child that we must assume more is involved than the physical pain alone. While it is true that in some children this terror may represent also a fear of loss of parental love, it can also occur in completely rejected children, who seem to cling to the hating parents more for sheer safety and protection than because of hope of love.

Confronting the average child with new, unfamiliar, strange, unmanageable stimuli or situations will too frequently elicit the danger or terror reaction, as, for example, getting lost or even being separated from the parents for a short time, being confronted with new faces, new situations, or new tasks, the sight of strange, unfamiliar, or uncontrollable objects, illness, or death. Particularly at such times, the child's frantic clinging to his parents is eloquent testimony to their role as protectors (quite apart from their roles as food-givers and love-givers).

From these and similar observations, we may generalize and say that the average child in our society usually prefers a safe, orderly, predictable, organized world which he can count on and in which unexpected, unmanageable, or other dangerous things do not happen and in which, in any case, he has all-powerful parents who protect and shield him from harm.

That these reactions may so easily be observed in children

is in a way a proof of the fact that children in our society feel too unsafe (or, in a word, are badly brought up). Children who are reared in an unthreatening, loving family do *not* ordinarily react as we have described above.[5] In such children the danger reactions are apt to come mostly to objects or situations that adults too would consider dangerous.[6]

The healthy, normal, fortunate adult in our culture is largely satisfied in his safety needs. The peaceful, smoothly running, "good" society ordinarily makes its members feel safe enough from wild animals, extremes of temperature, criminals, assault and murder, tyranny, and so on. Therefore, in a very real sense, they no longer have any safety needs as active motivators. Just as a sated man no longer feels hungry, a safe man no longer feels endangered. If we wish to see these needs directly and clearly we must turn to neurotic or near-neurotic individuals, and to the economic and social underdogs. In between these extremes, we can perceive the expressions of safety needs only in such phenomena as, for instance, the common preference for a job with tenure and protection, the desire for a savings account, and for insurance of various kinds (medical, dental, unemployment, disability, old age).

Other broader aspects of the attempt to seek safety and stability in the world are seen in the very common preference for familiar rather than unfamiliar things, or for the known rather than the unknown. The tendency to have some religion or world-philosophy that organizes the universe and the men in it into some sort of satisfactorily coherent, meaningful whole is also in part motivated by safety-seeking. Here too we may list science and philosophy in general as partially motivated by the safety needs (we shall see later that there are also other motivations to scientific, philosophical, or religious endeavor).

Otherwise the need for safety is seen as an active and dominant mobilizer of the organism's resources only in emer-

5. M. Shirley, "Children's Adjustments to a Strange Situation," *Journal of Abnormal and Social Psychology* 37 (1942): 201–17.

6. A "test battery" for safety might be confronting the child with a small exploding firecracker or with a bewhiskered face, having the mother leave the room, putting him upon a high ladder, giving him a hypodermic injection, having a mouse crawl up to him, and so on. Of course I cannot seriously recommend the deliberate use of such "tests," for they might very well harm the child being tested. But these and similar situations come up by the score in the child's ordinary day-to-day living and may be observed. There is no reason why these stimuli should not be used with, for example, young chimpanzees.

gencies, e.g., war, disease, natural catastrophes, crime waves, societal disorganization, neurosis, brain injury, chronically bad situation.

Some neurotic adults in our society are, in many ways, like the unsafe child in their desire for safety, although in the former it takes on a somewhat special appearance. Their reaction is often to unknown, psychological dangers in a world that is perceived to be hostile, overwhelming, and threatening. Such a person behaves as if a great catastrophe were almost always impending, i.e., he is usually responding as if to an emergency. His safety needs often find specific expression in a search for a protector, or a stronger person on whom he may depend, or perhaps a *Führer*.

The neurotic individual may be described in a slightly different way with some usefulness as a grown-up person who retains his childish attitudes toward the world. That is to say, a neurotic adult may be said to behave "as if" he were actually afraid of a spanking or of his mother's disapproval or of being abandoned by his parents or of having his food taken away from him. It is as if his childish attitudes of fear and threat reaction to a dangerous world had gone underground and, untouched by the growing up and learning processes, were now ready to be called out by any stimulus that would make a child feel endangered and threatened.[7]

The neurosis in which the search for safety takes its clearest form is in the compulsive-obsessive neurosis. Compulsive-obsessives try frantically to order and stabilize the world so that no unmanageable, unexpected, or unfamiliar dangers will ever appear.[8] They hedge themselves about with all sorts of ceremonials, rules, and formulas so that every possible contingency may be provided for and so that no new contingencies may appear. They are much like the brain-injured cases, described by Goldstein,[9] who manage to maintain their equilibrium by avoiding everything unfamiliar and strange and by ordering their restricted world in such a neat, disciplined, orderly fashion that everything in the world can be counted upon. They try to arrange the world so that anything unexpected (dangers) cannot possibly occur. If, through

7. Not all neurotic individuals feel unsafe. Neurosis may have at its core a thwarting of the affection and esteem needs in a person who is generally safe.
8. A. H. Maslow and B. Mittelmann, *Principles of Abnormal Psychology* (New York: Harper & Bros., 1941).
9. K. Goldstein, *The Organism* (New York: American Book Co., 1939).

no fault of their own, something unexpected does occur, they go into a panic reaction as if this unexpected occurrence constituted a grave danger. What we can see only as a none-too-strong preference in the healthy person, e.g., preference for the familiar, becomes a life-and-death necessity in abnormal cases.

The Love Needs

If both the physiological and the safety needs are fairly well gratified, then there will emerge the love and affection and belongingness needs, and the whole cycle already described will repeat itself with this new center. Now the person will feel keenly, as never before, the absence of friends or a sweetheart or a wife or children. He will hunger for affectionate relations with people in general, namely, for a place in his group, and he will strive with great intensity to achieve this goal. He will want to attain such a place more than anything else in the world and may even forget that once, when he was hungry, he sneered at love.

In our society the thwarting of these needs is the most commonly found core in cases of maladjustment and more severe psychopathology. Love and affection, as well as their possible expression in sexuality, are generally looked upon with ambivalence and are customarily hedged about with many restrictions and inhibitions. Practically all theorists of psychopathology have stressed thwarting of the love needs as basic in the picture of maladjustment. Many clinical studies have therefore been made of this need and we know more about it perhaps than any of the other needs except the physiological ones.[10]

One thing that must be stressed at this point is that love is not synonymous with sex. Sex may be studied as a purely physiological need. Ordinarily sexual behavior is multidetermined, that is to say, determined not only by sexual but also by other needs, chief among which are the love and affection needs. Also not to be overlooked is the fact that the love needs involve both giving *and* receiving love.[11]

The Esteem Needs

All people in our society (with a few pathological exceptions)

10. Maslow and Mittelmann, *Principles of Abnormal Psychology.*
11. For further details see A. H. Maslow, "The Dynamics of Psychological Security-Insecurity," *Character and Personality* 10 (1942): 331–44, and J. Plant, *Personality and the Cultural Pattern* (New York: Commonwealth Fund, 1937), chap. 5.

have a need or desire for a stable, firmly based, (usually) high evaluation of themselves, for self-respect, or self-esteem, and for the esteem of others. By firmly based self-esteem, we mean that which is soundly based upon real capacity, achievement, and respect from others. These needs may be classified into two subsidiary sets. These are, first, the desire for strength, for achievement, for adequacy, for confidence in the face of the world, and for independence and freedom.[12] Second, we have what we may call the desire for reputation or prestige (defining it as respect or esteem from other people), recognition, attention, importance, or appreciation.[13] These needs have been relatively stressed by Alfred Adler and his followers, and have been relatively neglected by Freud and the psychoanalysts. More and more today, however, there is appearing widespread appreciation of their central importance.

Satisfaction of the self-esteem need leads to feelings of self-confidence, worth, strength, capability, and adequacy, of being useful and necessary in the world. But thwarting of these needs produces feelings of inferiority, of weakness, and of helplessness. These feelings in turn give rise to either basic discouragement or else compensatory or neurotic trends. An appreciation of the necessity of basic self-confidence and an understanding of how helpless people are without it, can be easily gained from a study of severe traumatic neurosis.[14]

The Need for Self-Actualization

Even if all these needs are satisfied, we may still often (if not always) expect that a new discontent and restlessness will

12. Whether or not this particular desire is universal we do not know. The crucial question, especially important today, is, "Will men who are enslaved and dominated inevitably feel dissatisfied and rebellious?" We may assume on the basis of commonly known clinical data that a man who has known true freedom (not paid for by giving up safety and security but rather built on the basis of adequate safety and security) will not willingly or easily allow his freedom to be taken away from him. But we do not know that this is true for the person born into slavery. The events of the next decade should give us our answer. See discussion of this problem in E. Fromm, *Escape from Freedom* (New York: Farrar & Rinehart, 1941), chap. 5.

13. Perhaps the desire for prestige and respect from others is subsidiary to the desire for self-esteem or confidence in one's self. Observation of children seems to indicate that this is so, but clinical data give no clear support of such a conclusion.

14. A. Kardiner, *The Traumatic Neuroses of War* (New York: Hoeber, 1941). For more extensive discussion of normal self-esteem, as well as for reports of various researches, see A. H. Maslow, "Dominance, Personality, and Social Behavior in Women," *Journal of Social Psychology* 10 (1939): 3–39.

soon develop, unless the individual is doing what he is fitted for. A musician must make music, an artist must paint, a poet must write, if he is to be ultimately happy. What a man *can* be, he *must* be. This need we may call self-actualization.

This term, first coined by Kurt Goldstein, is being used in this paper in a much more specific and limited fashion. It refers to the desire for self-fulfillment, namely, to the tendency for one to become actualized in what one is potentially. This tendency might be phrased as the desire to become more and more what one is, to become everything that one is capable of becoming.

The specific form that these needs take will of course vary greatly from person to person. In one individual it may be expressed maternally, as the desire to be an ideal mother, in another athletically, in still another aesthetically, in the painting of pictures, and in another inventively in the creation of new contrivances. It is not necessarily a creative urge, although in people who have any capabilities for creation it will take this form.

The clear emergence of these needs rests upon prior satisfaction of the physiological, safety, love, and esteem needs. We shall call people who are satisfied in these needs, basically satisfied people, and it is from these that we may expect the fullest (and healthiest) creativeness.[15] Since, in our society, basically satisfied people are the exception, we do not know much about self-actualization, either experimentally or clinically. It remains a challenging problem for research.

The Preconditions for the Basic Need Satisfactions

There are certain conditions which are immediate prerequisites for the basic need satisfactions. Danger to these is reacted to almost as if it were a direct danger to the basic needs themselves. Such conditions as freedom to speak, freedom to do what one wishes so long as no harm is done to others, freedom to express one's self, freedom to investigate

---

15. Clearly creative behavior, like painting, is like any other behavior in having multiple determinants. It may be seen in "innately creative" people whether they are satisfied or not, happy or unhappy, hungry or sated. Also, it is clear that creative activity may be compensatory, ameliorative, or purely economic. It is my impression (as yet unconfirmed) that it is possible to distinguish the artistic and intellectual products of basically satisfied people from those of basically unsatisfied people by inspection alone. In any case, here too we must distinguish, in a dynamic fashion, the overt behavior itself from its various motivations or purposes.

and seek for information, freedom to defend one's self, justice, fairness, honesty, orderliness in the group are examples of such preconditions for basic need satisfactions. Thwarting in these freedoms will be reacted to with a threat or emergency response. These conditions are not ends in themselves but they are *almost* so, since they are so closely related to the basic needs, which are apparently the only ends in themselves. These conditions are defended because without them the basic satisfactions are quite impossible, or, at least, very severely endangered.

If we remember that the cognitive capacities (perceptual, intellectual, learning) are a set of adjustive tools, which have, among other functions, that of satisfaction or our basic needs, then it is clear that any danger to them, any deprivation or blocking of their free use, must also be indirectly threatening to the basic needs themselves. Such a statement is a partial solution of the general problems of curiosity, the search for knowledge, truth, and wisdom, and the ever persistent urge to solve the cosmic mysteries.

We must therefore introduce another hypothesis and speak of degrees of closeness to the basic needs, for we have already pointed out that *any* conscious desires (partial goals) are more or less important as they are more or less close to the basic needs. The same statement may be made for various behavior acts. An act is psychologically important if it contributes directly to satisfaction of basic needs. The less directly it so contributes, or the weaker this contribution is, the less important this act must be conceived to be from the point of view of dynamic psychology. A similar statement may be made for the various defense or coping mechanisms. Some are very directly related to the protection or attainment of the basic needs, others are only weakly and distantly related. Indeed, if we wished, we could speak of more basic and less basic defense mechanisms and then affirm that danger to the more basic defenses is more threatening than danger to less basic defenses (always remembering that this is so only because of their relationship to the basic needs).

The Desires to Know and to Understand

So far, we have mentioned the cognitive needs only in passing. Acquiring knowledge and systematizing the universe have been considered as, in part, techniques for the achievement of basic safety in the world, or, for the intelligent man, expressions of self-actualization. Also freedom of inquiry and expression have been discussed as preconditions of satisfactions of the basic needs. True though these formulations may be, they do not constitute definitive answers to the question as to the motivation role of curiosity, learning, philosophizing, experimenting, and so on. They are, at best, no more than partial answers.

This question is especially difficult because we know so little about the facts. Curiosity, exploration, desire for the facts, desire to know may certainly be observed easily enough. The fact that they often are pursued even at great cost to the individual's safety is an earnest of the partial character of our previous discussion. In addition, the writer must admit that, though he has sufficient clinical evidence to postulate the desire to know as a very strong drive in intelligent people, no data are available for unintelligent people. It may then be largely a function of relatively high intelligence. Rather tentatively, then, and largely in the hope of stimulating discussion and research, we shall postulate a basic desire to know, to be aware of reality, to get the facts, to satisfy curiosity, or as Wertheimer phrases it, to see rather than to be blind.

This postulation, however, is not enough. Even after we know, we are impelled to know more and more minutely and microscopically, on the one hand, and, on the other, more and more extensively in the direction of a world philosophy, religion, and so on. The facts that we acquire, if they are isolated or atomistic, inevitably get theorized about, and either analyzed or organized or both. This process has been phrased by some as the search for "meaning." We shall then postulate a desire to understand, to systematize, to organize, to analyze, to look for relations and meanings.

Once these desires are accepted for discussion, we see that they too form themselves into a small hierarchy in which the desire to know is prepotent over the desire to understand. All the characteristics of a hierarchy of prepotency that we have described above seem to hold for this one as well.

We must guard ourselves against the too easy tendency to separate these desires from the basic needs we have discussed above, i.e., to make a sharp dichotomy between "cognitive" and "conative" needs. The desire to know and to understand are themselves conative, i.e., have a striving character, and are as much personality needs as the "basic needs" we have already discussed.[16]

16. M. Wertheimer, unpublished lectures at the New School for Social Research.

Further Characteristics of the Basic Needs

The Degree of Fixity of the Hierarchy of Basic Needs

We have spoken so far as if this hierarchy were a fixed order but actually it is not nearly as rigid as we may have implied. It is true that most of the people with whom we have worked have seemed to have these basic needs in about the order that has been indicated. However, there have been a number of exceptions.

1. There are some people in whom, for instance, self-esteem seems to be more important than love. This most common reversal in the hierarchy is usually due to the development of the notion that the person who is most likely to be loved is a strong or powerful person, one who inspires respect or fear and who is self-confident or aggressive. Therefore, such people who lack love and seek it, may try hard to put on a front of aggressive, confident behavior. But essentially they seek high self-esteem and its behavior expressions more as a means-to-an-end than for its own sake; they seek self-assertion for the sake of love rather than for self-esteem itself.

2. There are other, apparently innately creative people in whom the drive to creativeness seems to be more important than any other counterdeterminant. Their creativeness might appear as self-actualization released not by basic satisfaction but in spite of lack of basic satisfaction.

3. In certain people the level of aspiration may be permanently deadened or lowered. That is to say, the less prepotent goals may simply be lost and may disappear forever, so that the person who has experienced life at a very low level, i.e., chronic unemployment, may continue to be satisfied for the rest of his life if only he can get enough food.

4. The so-called "psychopathic personality" is another example of permanent loss of the love needs. There are people who, according to the best data available,[17] have been starved for love in the earliest months of their lives and have simply lost forever the desire and the ability to give and to receive affection (as animals lose sucking or pecking reflexes that are not exercised soon enough after birth).

5. Another cause of reversal of the hierarchy is that when a need has been satisfied for a long time, this need may be underevaluated. People who have never experienced chronic hunger are apt to underestimate its effects and to look upon food as a rather unimportant thing. If they are dominated by

17. D. M. Levy, "Primary Affect Hunger," *American Journal of Psychiatry* 94 (1937): 643–52.

a higher need, this higher need will seem to be the most important of all. It then becomes possible, and indeed does actually happen, that they may, for the sake of this higher need, put themselves into the position of being deprived in a more basic need. We may expect that after a long-time deprivation of the more basic need there will be a tendency to reevaluate both needs so that the more prepotent need will actually become consciously prepotent for the individual who may have given it up very lightly. Thus, a man who has given up his job rather than lose his self-respect, and who then starves for six months or so, may be willing to take his job back even at the price of losing his self-respect.

6. Another partial explanation of *apparent* reversals is seen in the fact that we have been talking about the hierarchy of prepotency in terms of consciously felt wants or desires rather than of behavior. Looking at behavior itself may give us the wrong impression. What we have claimed is that the person will *want* the more basic of two needs when deprived in both. There is no necessary implication here that he will act upon his desires. Let us say again that there are many determinants of behavior other than needs and desires.

7. Perhaps more important than all these exceptions are the ones that involve ideals, high social standards, high values, and the like. With such values people become martyrs; they will give up everything for the sake of a particular ideal, or value. These people may be understood, at least in part, by reference to one basic concept (or hypothesis) which may be called "increased frustration-tolerance through early gratification." People who have been satisfied in their basic needs throughout their lives, particularly in their earlier years, seem to develop exceptional power to withstand present or future thwarting of these needs simply because they have strong, healthy character structure as a result of basic satisfaction. They are the "strong" people who can easily weather disagreement or opposition, who can swim against the stream of public opinion, and who can stand up for the truth at great personal cost. It is just the ones who have loved and been well loved and who have had many deep friendships who can hold out against hatred, rejection or persecution.

I say all this in spite of the fact that there is a certain amount of sheer habituation which is also involved in any full discussion of frustration tolerance. For instance, it is likely that those persons who have been accustomed to relative starvation for a long time are partially enabled thereby to withstand food deprivation. What sort of balance must be made between these two tendencies, of habituation on the one hand, and of past satisfaction breeding present frustration tolerance on the other hand, remains to be worked out by further research. Meanwhile we may assume that they are both operative, side by side, since they do not contradict each other. In respect to this phenomenon of increased frustration tolerance, it seems probable that the most important gratifications come in the first two years of life. That is to say, people who have been made secure and strong in the earliest years tend to remain secure and strong thereafter in the face of whatever threatens.

Degrees of Relative Satisfaction

So far, our theoretical discussion may have given the impression that these five sets of needs are somehow in a stepwise, all-or-none relationship to one another. We have spoken in such terms as the following: "If one need is satisfied, then another emerges." This statement might give the false impression that a need must be satisfied 100 percent before the next need emerges. In actual fact, most members of our society who are normal are partially satisfied in all their basic needs and partially unsatisfied in all their basic needs at the same time. A more realistic description of the hierarchy would be in terms of decreasing percentages of satisfaction as we go up the hierarchy of prepotency. For instance, if I may assign arbitrary figures for the sake of illustration, it is as if the average citizen is satisfied perhaps 85 percent in his physiological needs, 70 percent in his safety needs, 50 percent in his love needs, 40 percent in his self-esteem needs, and 10 percent in his self-actualization needs.

As for the concept of emergence of a new need after satisfaction of the prepotent need, this emergence is not a sudden, saltatory phenomenon but rather a gradual emergence by slow degrees from nothingness. For instance, if prepotent need A is satisfied only 10 percent then need B may not be visible at all. However, as this need A becomes satisfied 25 percent, need B may emerge 5 percent; as need A becomes satisfied 75 percent, need B may emerge 90 percent; and so on.

Unconscious Character of Needs

These needs are neither necessarily conscious nor unconscious. On the whole, however, in the average person, they are more often unconscious. It is not necessary at this point to overhaul the tremendous mass of evidence which indicates the crucial importance of unconscious motivation. It would by now be expected, on a priori grounds alone, that unconscious motivations would on the whole be rather more important than the conscious motivations. What we have called the basic needs are very often largely unconscious although they may, with suitable techniques and with sophisticated people, become conscious.

The Role of Gratified Needs

It has been pointed out above several times that our higher needs usually emerge only when more prepotent needs have been gratified. Thus gratification has an important role in motivation theory. Apart from this, however, needs cease to play an active determining or organizing role as soon as they are gratified.

What this means, for example, is that a basically satisfied person no longer has the needs for esteem, love, safety, and so on. The only sense in which he might be said to have them is in the almost metaphysical sense that a sated man has hunger or a filled bottle has emptiness. If we are interested in what *actually* motivates us and not in what has, will, or might motivate us, then a satisfied need is not a motivator. It must be considered for all practical purposes simply not to exist, to have disappeared. This point should be emphasized because it has been either overlooked or contradicted in every theory of motivation I know.[18] The perfectly healthy, normal, fortunate man has no sex needs or hunger needs, or needs for safety or for love or for prestige or for self-esteem, except in stray moments of quickly passing threat. If we were to say otherwise, we should also have to aver that every man had all the pathological reflexes, e.g., Babinski, etc., because if his nervous system were damaged, these would appear.

It is such considerations as these that suggest the bold postulation that a man who is thwarted in any of his basic needs may fairly be envisaged simply as a sick man. This is a fair parallel to our designation as "sick" of the man who lacks vitamins or minerals. Who is to say that a lack of love is less important than a lack of vitamins? Since we know the pathogenic effects of love starvation, who is to say that we are invoking value-questions in an unscientific or illegitimate way, any more than the physician does who diagnoses and

18. Note that acceptance of this theory necessitates basic revision of the Freudian theory.

treats pellagra or scurvy? If I were permitted this usage, I should then say simply that a healthy man is primarily motivated by his needs to develop and actualize his fullest potentialities and capacities. If a man has any other basic needs in any active, chronic sense, then he is simply an unhealthy man. He is as surely sick as if he had suddenly developed a strong salt-hunger or calcium hunger.[19]

If this statement seems unusual or paradoxical the reader may be assured that this is only one among many such paradoxes that will appear as we revise our ways of looking at man's deeper motivations. When we ask what man wants of life, we deal with his very essence.

Summary

1. There are at least five sets of goals which we may call basic needs. These are briefly physiological, safety, love, esteem, and self-actualization. In addition, we are motivated by the desire to achieve or maintain the various conditions upon which these basic satisfactions rest and by certain more intellectual desires.

2. These basic goals are related to one another, being arranged in a hierarchy of prepotency. This means that the most prepotent goal will monopolize consciousness and will tend of itself to organize the recruitment of the various capacities of the organism. The less prepotent needs are minimized, even forgotten or denied. But when a need is fairly well satisfied, the next prepotent ("higher") need emerges, in turn to dominate the conscious life and to serve as the center of organization of behavior, since gratified needs are not active motivators.

Thus man is a perpetually wanting animal. Ordinarily the satisfaction of these wants is not altogether mutually exclusive but only tends to be. The average member of our society is most often partially satisfied and partially unsatisfied in all of his wants. The hierarchy principle is usually empirically observed in terms of increasing percentages of nonsatisfaction as we go up the hierarchy. Reversals of the

19. If we were to use the "sick" in this way, we should then also have to face squarely the relations of man to his society. One clear implication of our definition would be that (1) since a man is to be called sick who is basically thwarted, and (2) since such basic thwarting is made possible ultimately only by forces outside the individual, the (3) sickness in the individual must come ultimately from a sickness in the society. The "good" or healthy society would then be defined as one that permitted man's highest purposes to emerge by satisfying all his prepotent basic needs.

average order of the hierarchy are sometimes observed. Also it has been observed that an individual may permanently lose the higher wants in the hierarchy under special conditions. There are not only ordinarily multiple motivations for usual behavior but, in addition, many determinants other than motives.

3. Any thwarting or possibility of thwarting of these basic human goals, or danger to the defenses which protect them or to the conditions upon which they rest, is considered to be a psychological threat. With a few exceptions, all psychopathology may be partially traced to such threats. A basically thwarted man may actually be defined as a "sick" man.

4. It is such basic threats which bring about the general emergency reactions.

5. Certain other basic problems have not been dealt with because of limitations of space. Among these are (a) the problem of values in any definitive motivation theory, (b) the relation between appetites, desires, needs, and what is "good" for the organism, (c) the etiology of the basic needs and their possible derivation in early childhood, (d) redefinition of motivational concepts, i.e., drive, desire, wish, need, goal, (e) implication of our theory for hedonistic theory, (f) the nature of the uncompleted act, of success and failure, and of aspiration-level, (g) the role of association, habit, and conditioning, (h) relation to the theory of interpersonal relations, (i) implications for psychotherapy, (j) implication for theory of society, (k) the theory of selfishness, (l) the relation between needs and cultural patterns, (m) the relation between this theory and Allport's theory of functional autonomy. These as well as certain other less important questions must be considered as motivation theory attempts to become definitive.

One More Time: How Do You Motivate Employees?
Frederick Herzberg

How many articles, books, speeches, and workshops have pleaded plaintively, "How do I get an employee to do what I want him to do?"

The psychology of motivation is tremendously complex, and what has been unraveled with any degree of assurance is small indeed. But the dismal ratio of knowledge to speculation has not dampened the enthusiasm for new forms of snake oil that are constantly coming on the market, many of them with academic testimonials. Doubtless this article will have no depressing impact on the market for snake oil, but since the ideas expressed in it have been tested in many corporations and other organizations, it will help—I hope—to redress the imbalance in the aforementioned ratio.

"Motivating" with KITA

In lectures to industry on the problem, I have found that the audiences are anxious for quick and practical answers, so I will begin with a straightforward, practical formula for moving people.

What is the simplest, surest, and most direct way of getting someone to do something? Ask him? But if he responds that he does not want to do it, then that calls for a psychological consultation to determine the reason for his obstinacy. Tell him? His response shows that he does not understand you, and now an expert in communication methods has to be brought in to show you how to get through to him. Give him a monetary incentive? I do not need to remind the reader of the complexity and difficulty involved in setting up and administering an incentive system. Show him? This means a costly training program. We need a simple way.

Every audience contains the "direct action" manager who shouts, "Kick him!" And this type of manager is right. The surest and least circumlocuted way of getting someone to do something is to kick him in the pants—give him what might be called the KITA.

There are various forms of KITA, and here are some of them:

Negative Physical KITA. This is a literal application of the term and was frequently used in the past. It has, however, three major drawbacks: (1) it is inelegant; (2) it contradicts the precious image of benevolence that most organizations cherish; and (3) since it is a physical attack, it directly stimulates the automatic nervous system, and this often results in negative feedback—the employee may just kick you in return. These factors give rise to certain taboos against negative physical KITA.

The psychologist has come to the rescue of those who are no longer permitted to use negative physical KITA. He has uncovered infinite sources of psychological vulnerabilities and the appropriate methods to play tunes on them. "He took my rug away"; "I wonder what he meant by that"; "the boss is always going around me"—these symptomatic expressions of ego sores that have been rubbed raw are the result of application of:

Negative Psychological KITA. This has several advantages over negative physical KITA. First, the cruelty is not visible; the bleeding is internal and comes much later. Second, since it affects the higher cortical centers of the brain with its inhibitory powers, it reduces the possibility of physical backlash. Third, since the number of psychological pains that a person can feel is almost infinite, the direction and site possibilities of the KITA are increased many times. Fourth, the person administering the kick can manage to be above it all and let the system accomplish the dirty work. Fifth, those who practice it receive some ego satisfaction (one-up-manship), whereas they would find drawing blood abhorrent. Finally, if the employee does complain, he can always be accused of being paranoid, since there is no tangible evidence of an actual attack.

Now, what does negative KITA accomplish? If I kick you in the rear (physically or psychologically), who is motivated? *I* am motivated; *you* move! Negative KITA does not lead to motivation, but to movement. So:

Positive KITA. Let us consider motivation. If I say to you, "Do this for me or the company, and in return I will give you a reward, an incentive, more status, a promotion, all the quid pro quos that exist in the industrial organization," am I motivating you? The overwhelming opinion I receive from management people is, "Yes, this is motivation."

I have a year-old Schnauzer. When it was a small puppy and I wanted it to move, I kicked it in the rear and it moved. Now that I have finished its obedience training, I hold up a dog biscuit when I want the Schnauzer to move. In this instance, who is motivated—I or the dog? The dog wants the biscuit, but it is I who want it to move. Again, I am the one who is motivated, and the dog is the one who moves. In this instance all I did was apply KITA frontally; I exerted a pull instead of a push. When industry wishes to use such positive KITAs, it has available an incredible number and variety of dog biscuits (jelly beans for humans) to wave in front of the employee to get him to jump.

Why is it that managerial audiences are quick to see that negative KITA is *not* motivation, while they are almost unanimous in their judgment that positive KITA *is* motivation? It is because negative KITA is rape, and positive KITA is seduction. But it is infinitely worse to be seduced than to be raped; the latter is an unfortunate occurrence, while the former signifies that you were a party to your own downfall. This is why positive KITA is so popular: it is a tradition; it is in the American way. The organization does not have to kick you; you kick yourself.

Myths about Motivation

Why is KITA not motivation? If I kick my dog (from the front or the back), he will move. And when I want him to move again, what must I do? I must kick him again. Similarly, I can charge a man's battery, and then recharge it, and recharge it again. But it is only when he has his own generator that we can talk about motivation. He then needs no outside stimulation. He *wants* to do it.

With this in mind, we can review some positive KITA personnel practices that were developed as attempts to instill "motivation":

1. *Reducing Time Spent at Work*. This represents a marvelous way of motivating people to work—getting them off the job! We have reduced (formally and informally) the time spent on the job over the last fifty or sixty years until we are finally on the way to the "6½-day weekend." An interesting variant of this approach is the development of off-hour recreation programs. The philosophy here seems to be that those

who play together, work together. The fact is that motivated people seek more hours of work, not fewer.

2. *Spiraling Wages.* Have these motivated people? Yes, to seek the next wage increase. Some medievalists still can be heard to say that a good depression will get employees moving. They feel that if rising wages don't or won't do the job, perhaps reducing them will.

3. *Fringe Benefits.* Industry has outdone the most welfare-minded of welfare states in dispensing cradle-to-the-grave succor. One company I know of had an informal "fringe benefit of the month club" going for a while. The cost of fringe benefits in this country has reached approximately 25 percent of the wage dollar, and we still cry for motivation.

People spend less time working for more money and more security than ever before, and the trend cannot be reversed. These benefits are no longer rewards; they are rights. A six-day week is inhuman, a ten-hour day is exploitation, extended medical coverage is a basic decency, and stock options are the salvation of American initiative. Unless the ante is continuously raised, the psychological reaction of employees is that the company is turning back the clock.

When industry began to realize that both the economic nerve and the lazy nerve of their employees had insatiable appetites, it started to listen to the behavioral scientists who, more out of a humanist tradition than from scientific study, criticized management for not knowing how to deal with people. The next KITA easily followed.

4. *Human Relations Training.* Over thirty years of teaching and, in many instances, of practicing psychological approaches to handling people have resulted in costly human relations programs and, in the end, the same question: How do you motivate workers? Here, too, escalations have taken place. Thirty years ago it was necessary to request, "Please don't spit on the floor." Today the same admonition requres three "please's before the employee feels that his superior has demonstrated the psychologically proper attitudes toward him.

The failure of human relations training to produce motivation led to the conclusion that the supervisor or manager himself was not psychologically true to himself in his practice of interpersonal decency. So an advanced form of human relations KITA, sensitivity training, was unfolded.

5. *Sensitivity Training.* Do you really, really understand yourself? Do you really, really, really trust the other man? Do you really, really, really, really cooperate? The failure of sen-

sitivity training is now being explained, by those who have become opportunistic exploiters of the technique, as a failure to really (five times) conduct proper sensitivity training courses.

With the realization that there are only temporary gains from comfort and economic and interpersonal KITA, personnel managers concluded that the fault lay not in what they were doing, but in the employee's failure to appreciate what they were doing. This opened up the field of communications, a whole new area of "scientifically" sanctioned KITA.

6. *Communications*. The professor of communications was invited to join the faculty of management training programs and help in making employees understand what management was doing for them. House organs, briefing sessions, supervisory instruction on the importance of communication, and all sorts of propaganda have proliferated until today there is even an International Council of Industrial Editors. But no motivation resulted, and the obvious thought occurred that perhaps management was not hearing what the employees were saying. That led to the next KITA.

7. *Two-Way Communication*. Management ordered morale surveys, suggestion plans, and group participation programs. Then both employees and management were communicating and listening to each other more than ever, but without much improvement in motivation.

The behavioral scientists began to take another look at their conceptions and their data, and they took human relations one step further. A glimmer of truth was beginning to show through in the writings of the so-called higher-order-need psychologists. People, so they said, want to actualize themselves. Unfortunately, the "actualizing" psychologists got mixed up with the human relations psychologists, and a new KITA emerged.

8. *Job Participation*. Though it may not have been the theoretical intention, job participation often became a "give them the big picture" approach. For example, if a man is tightening 10,000 nuts a day on an assembly line with a torque wrench, tell him he is building a Chevrolet. Another approach had the goal of giving the employee a *feeling* that he is determining, in some measure, what he does on his job. The goal was to provide a *sense* of achievement rather than a substantive achievement in his task. Real achievement, of course, requires a task that makes it possible.

But still there is no motivation. This led to the inevitable conclusion that the employees must be sick, and therefore to the next KITA.

9. *Employee Counseling*. The initial use of this form of KITA in a systematic fashion can be credited to the Hawthorne experiment of the Western Electric Company during the early 1930s. At that time, it was found that the employees harbored irrational feelings that were interfering with the rational operation of the factory. Counseling in this instance was a means of letting the employees unburden themselves by talking to someone about their problems. Although the counseling techniques were primitive, the program was large indeed.

The counseling approach suffered as a result of experiences during World War II, when the programs themselves were found to be interfering with the operation of the organization; the counselors had forgotten their role of benevolent listeners and were attempting to do something about the problems that they heard about. Psychological counseling, however, has managed to survive the negative impact of World War II experiences and today is beginning to flourish with renewed sophistication. But, alas, many of these programs, like all the others, do not seem to have lessened the pressure of demands to find out how to motivate workers.

Since KITA results only in short-term movement, it is safe to predict that the cost of these programs will increase steadily and new varieties will be developed as old positive KITAs reach their satiation points.

Hygiene vs. Motivators

Let me rephrase the perennial question this way: How do you install a generator in an employee? A brief review of my motivation-hygiene theory of job attitudes is required before theoretical and practical suggestions can be offered. The theory was first drawn from an examination of events in the lives of engineers and accountants. At least sixteen other investigations, using a wide variety of populations (including some in the Communist countries), have since been completed, making the original research one of the most replicated studies in the field of job attitudes.

The findings of these studies, along with corroboration from many other investigations using different procedures, suggest that the factors involved in producing job satisfaction (and motivation) are separate and distinct from the factors that lead to job dissatisfaction. Since separate factors need to be considered, depending on whether job satisfaction or job dissatisfaction is being examined, it follows that these two feelings are not opposites of each other. The opposite of job satisfaction is not job dissatisfaction but, rather, *no* job satisfaction; and, similarly, the opposite of job dissatisfaction is not job satisfaction, but *no* job dissatisfaction.

Stating the concept presents a problem in semantics, for we normally think of satisfaction and dissatisfaction as opposites—i.e., what is not satisfying must be dissatisfying, and vice versa. But when it comes to understanding the behavior of people in their jobs, more than a play on words is involved.

Two different needs of man are involved here. One set of needs can be thought of as stemming from his animal nature —the built-in drive to avoid pain from the environment, plus all the learned drives which become conditioned to the basic biological needs. For example, hunger, a basic biological drive, makes it necessary to earn money, and then money becomes a specific drive. The other set of needs relates to that unique human characteristic, the ability to achieve and, through achievement, to experience psychological growth. The stimuli for the growth needs are tasks that induce growth; in the industrial setting, they are the *job content*. Contrariwise, the stimuli inducing pain-avoidance behavior are found in the *job environment*.

The growth or *motivator* factors that are intrinsic to the job are achievement, recognition for achievement, the work itself, responsibility, and growth or advancement. The dissatisfaction-avoidance or *hygiene* (KITA) factors that are extrinsic to the job include company policy and administration, supervision, interpersonal relationships, working conditions, salary, status, and security.

A composite of the factors that are involved in causing job satisfaction and job dissatisfaction, drawn from samples of 1,685 employees, is shown in figure 1. The results indicate that motivators were the primary cause of satisfaction, and hygiene factors the primary cause of unhappiness on the job. The employees, studied in twelve different investigations, included lower-level supervisors, professional women, agricultural administrators, men about to retire from management positions, hospital maintenance personnel, manufacturing supervisors, nurses, food handlers, military officers, engineers, scientists, housekeepers, teachers, technicians, female assemblers, accountants, Finnish foremen, and Hungarian engineers.

They were asked what job events had occurred in their work that had led to extreme satisfaction or extreme dissatisfaction on their part. Their responses are broken down in the figure into percentages of total "positive" job events and

Factors characterizing 1,844
events on the job that led to
extreme dissatisfaction
Percentage frequency

Factors characterizing 1,753
events on the job that led to
extreme satisfaction
Percentage frequency

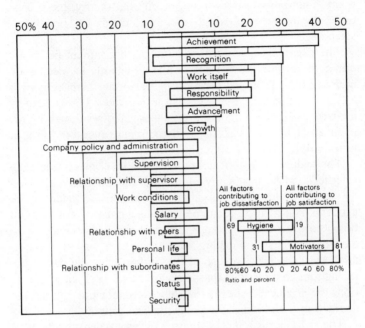

Fig. 1. Factors Affecting Job Attitudes, as Reported in Twelve Investigations

of total "negative" job events. (The figures total more than 100 percent on both the "hygiene" and "motivators" sides because often at least two factors can be attributed to a single event; advancement, for instance, often accompanies assumption of responsibility.)

To illustrate, a typical response involving achievement that had a negative effect for the employee was, "I was unhappy because I didn't do the job successfully." A typical response in the small number of positive job events in the Company Policy and Administration grouping was, "I was happy because the company reorganized the section so that I didn't report any longer to the guy I didn't get along with."

As the lower right-hand part of the figure shows, of all the factors contributing to job satisfaction, 81 percent were motivators. And of all the factors contributing to the employees' dissatisfaction over their work, 69 percent involved hygiene elements.

Eternal Triangle

There are three general philosophies of personnel management. The first is based on organizational theory, the second on industrial engineering, and the third on behavioral science.

The organizational theorist believes that human needs are either so irrational or so varied and adjustable to specific situations that the major function of personnel management is to be as pragmatic as the occasion demands. If jobs are organized in a proper manner, he reasons, the result will be the most efficient job structure, and the most favorable job attitudes will follow as a matter of course.

The industrial engineer holds that man is mechanistically oriented and economically motivated and his needs are best met by attuning the individual to the most efficient work process. The goal of personnel management therefore should be to concoct the most appropriate incentive system and to design the specific working conditions in a way that facilitates the most efficient use of the human machine. By structuring jobs in a manner that leads to the most efficient operation, the engineer believes that he can obtain the optimal organization of work and the proper work attitudes.

The behavioral scientist focuses on group sentiments, attitudes of individual employees, and the organization's social and psychological climate. According to his persuasion, he emphasizes one or more of the various hygiene and motivator needs. His approach to personnel management generally emphasizes some form of human relations education, in the hope of instilling healthy employee attitudes and in organizational climate which he considers to be felicitous to human values. He believes that proper attitudes will lead to efficient job and organizational structure.

There is always a lively debate as to the overall effectiveness of the approaches of the organizational theorist and the industrial engineer. Manifestly they have achieved much. But the nagging question for the behavioral scientist has been: What is the cost in human problems that eventually cause more expense to the organization—for instance, turnover, absenteeism, errors, violation of safety rules, strikes, restriction of output, higher wages, and greater fringe benefits? On the other hand, the behavioral scientist is hard put to document much manifest improvement in personnel management using his approach.

The three philosophies can be depicted as a triangle, as is done in figure 2, with each persuasion claiming the apex angle. The motivation-hygiene theory claims the same angle as industrial engineering, but for opposite goals. Rather than rationalizing the work to increase efficiency, the theory suggests that work be *enriched* to bring about effective utilization of personnel. Such a systematic attempt to motivate employees by manipulating the motivator factors is just beginning.

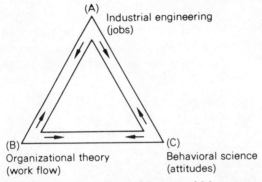

Fig. 2. "Triangle" of Philosophies of Personnel Management

The term *job enrichment* describes this embryonic movement. An older term, job enlargement, should be avoided because it is associated with past failures stemming from a misunderstanding of the problem. Job enrichment provides the opportunity for the employee's psychological growth, while job enlargement merely makes a job structurally bigger. Since scientific job enrichment is very new, this article only suggests the principles and practical steps that have recently emerged from several successful experiments in industry.

Job Loading

In attempting to enrich an employee's job, management often succeeds in reducing the man's personal contribution, rather than giving him an opportunity for growth in his accustomed job. Such an endeavor, which I shall call horizontal job loading (as opposed to vertical loading, or providing motivator factors), has been the problem of earlier job enlargement programs. This activity merely enlarges the meaninglessness of the job. Some examples of this approach, and their effect, are:

1. Challenging the employee by increasing the amount of production expected of him. If he tightens 10,000 bolts a

day, see if he can tighten 20,000 bolts a day. The arithmetic involved shows that multiplying zero by zero still equals zero.

2. Adding another meaningless task to the existing one, usually some routine clerical activity. The arithmetic here is adding zero to zero.

3. Rotating the assignment of a number of jobs that need to be enriched. This means washing dishes for a while, then washing silverware. The arithmetic is substituting one zero for another zero.

4. Removing the most difficult parts of the assignment in order to free the worker to accomplish more of the less challenging assignments. This traditional industrial engineering approach amounts to subtraction in the hope of accomplishing addition.

These are common forms of horizontal loading that frequently come up in preliminary brainstorming sessions on job enrichment. The principles of vertical loading have not all been worked out as yet, and they remain rather general, but I have furnished seven useful starting points for consideration in table 1.

Table 1
Principles of Vertical Job Loading

Principle	Motivators Involved
A. Removing some controls while retaining accountability	Responsibility and personal achievement
B. Increasing the accountability of individuals for own work	Responsibility and recognition
C. Giving a person a complete natural unit of work (module, division, area, and so on)	Responsibility, achievement, and recognition
D. Granting additional authority to an employee in his activity; job freedom	Responsibility, achievement, and recognition
E. Making periodic reports directly available to the worker himself rather than to the supervisor	Internal recognition
F. Introducing new and more difficult tasks not previously handled	Growth and learning
G. Assigning individuals specific or specialized tasks, enabling them to become experts	Responsibility, growth, and advancement

A Successful Application

An example from a highly successful job enrichment experiment can illustrate the distinction between horizontal and vertical loading of a job. The subjects of this study were the stockholder correspondents employed by a very large corporation. Seemingly, the task required of these carefully selected and highly trained correspondents was quite complex and challenging. But almost all indexes of performance and job attitudes were low, and exit interviewing confirmed that the challenge of the job existed merely as words.

A job enrichment project was initiated in the form of an experiment with one group, designated as an achieving unit, having its job enriched by the principles described in table 1. A control group continued to do its job in the traditional way. (There were also two "uncommitted" groups of correspondents formed to measure the so-called Hawthorne Effect —that is, to gauge whether productivity and attitudes toward the job changed artificially merely because employees sensed that the company was paying more attention to them in doing something different or novel. The results for these groups were substantially the same as for the control group, and for the sake of simplicity I do not deal with them in this summary.) No changes in hygiene were introduced for either group other than those that would have been made anyway, such as normal pay increases.

The changes for the achieving unit were introduced in the first two months, averaging one per week of the seven motivators listed in table 1. At the end of six months the members of the achieving unit were found to be outperforming their counterparts in the control group, and in addition indicated a marked increase in their liking for their job. Other results showed that the achieving group had lower absenteeism and, subsequently, a much higher rate of promotion.

Figure 3 illustrates the changes in performance, measured in February and March, before the study period began, and at the end of each month of the study period. The shareholder service index represents quality of letters, including accuracy of information, and speed of response to stockholders' letters of inquiry. The index of a current month was averaged into the average of the two prior months, which means that improvement was harder to obtain if the indexes of the previous months were low. The "achievers" were performing less well before the six-month period started, and their performance service index continued to decline after the

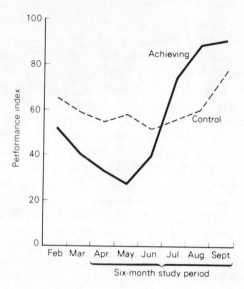

Fig. 3. Shareholder Service Index in Company Experiment (three-month cumulative average)

introduction of the motivators, evidently because of uncertainty over their newly granted responsibilities. In the third month, however, performance improved, and soon the members of this group had reached a high level of accomplishment.

Figure 4 shows the two groups' attitudes toward their job, measured at the end of March, just before the first motivator was introduced, and again at the end of September. The cor-

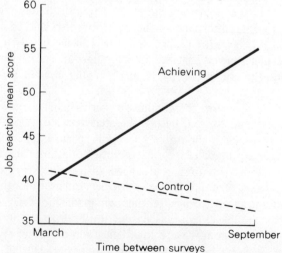

Fig. 4. Changes in Attitudes toward Tasks in Company Experiment (changes in mean scores over six-month period)

respondents were asked sixteen questions, all involving motivation. A typical one was, "As you see it, how many opportunities do you feel that you have in your job for making worthwhile contributions?" The answers were scaled from 1 to 5, with 80 as the maximum possible score. The achievers became much more positive about their job, while the attitude of the control unit remained about the same (the drop is not statistically significant).

How was the job of these correspondents restructured? Table 2 lists the suggestions made that were deemed to be horizontal loading, and the actual vertical loading changes that were incorporated in the job of the achieving unit. The capital letters under "Principle" after "Vertical Loading" refer to the corresponding letters in table 1. The reader will note that the rejected forms of horizontal loading correspond closely to the list of common manifestations of the phenomenon enumerated under "Job Loading."

Steps to Job Enrichment

Now that the motivator idea has been described in practice, here are the steps that managers should take in instituting the principle with their employees:

1. Select those jobs in which (a) the investment in industrial engineering does not make changes too costly, (b) attitudes are poor, (c) hygiene is becoming very costly, and (d) motivation will make a difference in performance.

2. Approach these jobs with the conviction that they can be changed. Years of tradition have led managers to believe that the content of the jobs is sacrosanct and the only scope of action that they have is in ways of stimulating people.

3. Brainstorm a list of changes that may enrich the jobs, without concern for their practicality.

4. Screen the list to eliminate suggestions that involve hygiene, rather than actual motivation.

5. Screen the list for generalities, such as "give them more responsibility," that are rarely followed in practice. This might seem obvious, but the motivator words have never left industry; the substance has just been rationalized and organized out. Words like "responsibility," "growth," "achievement," and "challenge," for example, have been elevated to the lyrics of the patriotic anthem for all organizations. It is the old problem typified by the pledge of allegiance to the flag being more important than contributions to the country —of following the form, rather than the substance.

6. Screen the list to eliminate any *horizontal* loading suggestions.

Table 2
Enlargement vs. Enrichment of Correspondents' Tasks in Company Experiment

Horizontal Loading Suggestions (Rejected)	Vertical Loading Suggestions (Adopted)	Principle
Firm quotas could be set for letters to be answered each day, using a rate which would be hard to reach.	Subject matter experts were appointed within each unit for other members of the unit to consult with before seeking supervisory help. (The supervisor had been answering all specialized and difficult questions.)	G
The women could type the letters themselves, as well as compose them, or take on any other clerical functions.	Correspondents signed their own names on letters. (The supervisor had been signing all letters.)	B
All difficult or complex inquiries could be channeled to a few women so that the remainder could achieve high rates of output. These jobs could be exchanged from time to time.	The work of the more experienced correspondents was proofread less frequently by supervisors and was done at the correspondents' desks, dropping verification from 100 percent to 10 percent. (Previously, all correspondents' letters had been checked by the supervisor.)	A
The women could be rotated through units handling different customers, and then sent back to their own units.	Production was discussed, but only in terms such as "a full day's work is expected." As time went on, this was no longer mentioned. (Before, the group had been constantly reminded of the number of letters that needed to be answered.)	D
	Outgoing mail went directly to the mailroom without going over supervisors' desks. (The letters had always been routed through the supervisors.)	A
	Correspondents were encouraged to answer letters in a more personalized way. (Reliance on the form-letter approach had been standard practice.)	C
	Each correspondent was held personally responsible for the quality and accuracy of letters. (This responsibility had been the province of the supervisor and the verifier.)	B, E

7. Avoid direct participation by the employees whose jobs are to be enriched. Ideas they have expressed previously certainly constitute a valuable source for recommended changes, but their direct involvement contaminates the process with human relations *hygiene* and, more specifically, gives them only a *sense* of making a contribution. The job is to be changed, and it is the content that will produce the motivation, not attitudes about being involved or the challenge inherent in setting up a job. That process will be over shortly, and it is what the employees will be doing from then on that will determine their motivation. A sense of participation will result only in short-term movement.

8. In the initial attempts at job enrichment, set up a controlled experiment. At least two equivalent groups should be chosen, one an experimental unit in which the motivators are systematically introduced over a period of time, and the other one a control group in which no changes are made. For both groups, hygiene should be allowed to follow its natural course for the duration of the experiment. Pre- and postinstallation tests of performance and job attitudes are necessary to evaluate the effectiveness of the job enrichment program. The attitude test must be limited to motivator items in order to divorce the employee's view of the job he is given from all the surrounding hygiene feelings that he might have.

9. Be prepared for a drop in performance in the experimental group the first few weeks. The changeover to a new job may lead to a temporary reduction in efficiency.

10. Expect your first-line supervisors to experience some anxiety and hostility over the changes you are making. The anxiety comes from their fear that the changes will result in poorer performance for their unit. Hostility will arise when the employees start assuming what the supervisors regard as their own responsibility for performance. The supervisor without checking duties to perform may then be left with little to do.

After a successful experiment, however, the supervisor usually discovers the supervisory and managerial functions he has neglected, or which were never his because all his time was given over to checking the work of his subordinates. For example, in the R&D division of one large chemical company I know of, the supervisors of the laboratory assistants were theoretically responsible for their training and evaluation. These functions, however, had come to be performed in a routine, unsubstantial fashion. After the job enrichment program, during which the supervisors were not merely passive observers of the assistants' performance, the supervisors actually were devoting their time to reviewing performance and administering thorough training.

What has been called an employee-centered style of supervision will come about not through education of supervisors, but by changing the jobs that they do.

Concluding Note

Job enrichment will not be a one-time proposition, but a continuous management function. The initial changes, however, should last for a very long period of time. There are a number of reasons for this:

1. The changes should bring the job up to the level of challenge commensurate with the skill that was hired.
2. Those who have still more ability eventually will be able to demonstrate it better and win promotion to higher-level jobs.
3. The very nature of motivators, as opposed to hygiene factors, is that they have a much longer-term effect on employees' attitudes. Perhaps the job will have to be enriched again, but this will not occur as frequently as the need for hygiene.

Not all jobs can be enriched, nor do all jobs need to be enriched. If only a small percentage of the time and money that is now devoted to hygiene, however, were given to job enrichment efforts, the return in human satisfaction and economic gain would be one of the largest dividends that industry and society have ever reaped through their efforts at better personnel management.

The argument for job enrichment can be summed up quite simply: If you have someone on a job, use him. If you can't use him on the job, get rid of him, either via automation or by selecting someone with lesser ability. If you can't use him and you can't get rid of him, you will have a motivation problem.

The New Look in Motivational Theory for Organizational Research
J. G. Hunt and
J. W. Hill

During the last few years the treatment of motivation with respect to industrial and other formal organizations has more often than not been in terms of models by Maslow or Herzberg.[1] Where theories are apparently so thoroughly accepted, one naturally assumes a fairly substantial amount of data leading to empirical verification. However, as we shall show, there is relatively little empirical evidence concerning Maslow's theory; and while there are many studies bearing on Herzberg's theory, it remains controversial. After comparing these two approaches and reviewing their present status, we will describe a newer motivation theory developed by Vroom, which is similar to those developed by Atkinson et al. and Edwards in experimental psychology, and Peak, Rosenberg, and Fishbein in social psychology.[2] It is our contention, on both theoretical and empirical grounds, that Vroom's theory, more than Maslow's or Herzberg's, is in line with the thinking of contemporary psychologists and indus-

Reproduced by permission of the Society for Applied Anthropology from *Human Organization* 28, no. 2 (1969): 100–109.

1. A. H. Maslow, *Motivation and Personality* (New York: Harper and Row, 1954); idem, "A Theory of Human Motivation," *Psychological Review* 50 (1943): 370–96; idem, *Eupsychian Management* (Homewood, Ill.: Irwin-Dorsey, 1965); F. Herzberg, B. Mausner, and B. B. Snyderman, *The Motivation to Work* (New York: Wiley, 1959); F. Herzberg, *Work and the Nature of Man* (Cleveland, Ohio: World Publishing Co., 1966), pp. 130–31; V. H. Vroom, *Work and Motivation* (New York: Wiley, 1964).

2. J. W. Atkinson, J. R. Bastian, R. W. Earl, and G. H. Litwin, "The Achievement Motive, Goal Setting, and Probability Preferences," *Journal of Abnormal and Social Psychology* 60 (1960): 27–36; W. Edwards, "Behavior Decision Theory," in *Annual Review of Psychology* (Palo Alto, Calif: Annual Reviews Inc., 1961), pp. 473–99; H. Peak, "Attitude and Motivation," *Nebraska Symposium on Motivation* (Lincoln, Neb.: University of Nebraska Press, 1955), pp. 148–84; M. Rosenberg, "Cognitive Structure and Attitudinal Affect," *Journal of Abnormal and Social Psychology* 53 (1956): 367–72; M. Fishbein, "An Operational Definition of Belief and Attitude," *Human Relations* 15 (1962): 35–43.

trial sociologists and is the best yet developed for organizational use.

The Maslow Model

Maslow's theory hypothesizes five broad classes of needs arranged in hierarchical levels of prepotency so that when one need level is satisfied, the next level is activated. The levels are: (1) physiological needs; (2) security or safety needs; (3) social, belonging, or membership needs; (4) esteem needs further subdivided into esteem of others and self-esteem including autonomy; and (5) self-actualization or self-fulfillment needs.

The original papers present very little empirical evidence in support of the theory and no research at all that tests the model in its entirety. Indeed, Maslow argues that the theory is primarily a framework for future research. He also discusses at length some of the limitations of the model and readily admits that these needs may be unconscious rather than conscious. While Maslow discusses his model and its limitations in detail, a widely publicized paper by McGregor gives the impression that the model can be accepted without question and also that it is fairly easy to apply.[3] In truth, the model is difficult to test, which is probably why there are so few empirical studies to either prove or refute the theory.

Porter provides the most empirical data concerning the model.[4] At the conscious level he measures all except the physiological needs. His samples are based only on managers, but they cover different managerial levels in a wide range of business organizations in the United States and thirteen other countries. Porter's studies have a number of interesting findings, but here we are primarily concerned with two: (1) in the United States and Britain (but not in the other twelve countries) there tends to be a hierarchical satisfaction of needs as Maslow hypothesizes; and (2) regardless of country or managerial level there is a tendency for those needs which managers feel are most important to be least satisfied.

A study by Beer of female clerks provides additional data

3. D. McGregor, "Adventure in Thought and Action," *Proceedings of the Fifth Anniversary Convocation of the School of Industrial Management, Massachusetts Institute of Technology* (Cambridge, Massachusetts: Massachusetts Institute of Technology, 1957), pp. 23–30.

4. L. W. Porter, *Organizational Patterns of Managerial Job Attitudes* (New York: American Foundation for Management Research, 1964). See also M. Haire, E. Ghiselli, and L. W. Porter, *Managerial Thinking: An International Study* (New York: Wiley, 1966), especially chaps. 4 and 5.

concerning the model.[5] He examines the relationship between participative and considerate or human relations–oriented supervisory leadership styles and satisfaction
of needs. He also goes one step further and argues that need
satisfaction, as such, does not necessarily lead to motivation.
Rather, motivation results only from need satisfaction which
occurs in the process of task-oriented work. He reasons that a
participative leadership style should meet this condition since
it presumably allows for the satisfaction of the higher order
needs (self-actualization, autonomy, and esteem). Beer found
that workers forced to arrange needs in a hierarchy (as
required by his ranking method) tend to arrange them as
predicted by Maslow. He also found that self-actualization,
autonomy, and social needs were most important, while esteem and security needs were least important, although his
method (unlike Porter's) did not allow a consideration of the
relationship between importance and need satisfaction. Interestingly enough, there was no significant relationship between
need satisfaction and Beer's measure of motivation nor between any of the leadership style dimensions and motivation.
There were, however, significant relationships between leadership style dimensions and need satisfaction. Beer concludes
that the model has questionable usefulness for a theory of industrial motivation although it may provide a fairly reliable
measurement of the a priori needs of industrial workers.

We have found only three studies that systematically consider the Maslow theory in terms of performance.[6]

The first of these, by Clark, attempts to fit a number of
empirical studies conducted for different purposes into a
framework which provides for progressive activation and satisfaction of needs at each of the hierarchical levels. The
findings are used to make predictions concerning productivity, absenteeism, and turnover as each need level is activated and then satisfied. While the article does not explicitly
test the Maslow model, it is highly suggestive in terms of hypotheses for future research that might relate the theory to
work group performance.

5. M. Beer, *Leadership, Employee Needs, and Motivation*
(Columbus, Ohio: Bureau of Business Research, Ohio State University,
1966).
6. J. V. Clark, "Motivation in Work Groups: A Tentative View,"
Human Organization 19 (1960): 199–208; E. E. Lawler and L. W.
Porter, "The Effect of Performance on Job Satisfaction," *Industrial
Relations* 7, no. 1 (1967): 20–28; L. W. Porter and E. E. Lawler, *Managerial Attitudes and Performance* (Homewood, Ill.: Irwin-Dorsey,
1968), pp. 148, 150.

A second study, by Lawler and Porter, correlates satisfaction of managers' needs (except physiological) with rankings of their performance by superiors and peers. All correlations are significant but low, ranging from 0.16 to 0.30. Lawler and Porter conclude that satisfaction of higher order needs is more closely related to performance than satisfaction of lower order needs. However, the differences are not very great and they are not tested for significance. For example, correlations of superior ratings for the lower order security and social needs are 0.21 and 0.23, while for the higher order esteem, autonomy, and self-actualization needs they are 0.24, 0.18, and 0.30. Peer correlations are similar. Thus, unlike Lawler and Porter, we conclude that in this study the correlations for lower order needs are about the same as for higher order needs.

A more recent Porter and Lawler investigation seems to provide additional support for their earlier findings by showing that higher order needs accounted for more relationships significant at the 0.01 level than lower order needs. However, they do not report correlations between these needs and performance and so we cannot evaluate their conclusion as we did for their earlier study.

The Herzberg Model

A second frequently mentioned motivational model is that proposed by Herzberg and his associates in 1959.[7] They used a semistructured interview technique to get respondents to recall events experienced at work which resulted in a marked improvement or a marked reduction in their job satisfaction. Interviewees were also asked, among other things, how their feelings of satisfaction or dissatisfaction affected their work performance, personal relationships, and well-being. Content analysis of the interviews suggested that certain job characteristics led to job satisfaction, while *different* job characteristics led to job dissatisfaction. For instance, job achievement was related to satisfaction while working conditions were related to dissatisfaction. Poor conditions led to dissatisfaction, but good conditions did not necessarily lead to satisfaction. Thus, satisfaction and dissatisfaction are not simple opposites. Hence a two-factor theory of satisfaction is needed.

The job content characteristics which produced satisfaction were called "motivators" by Herzberg and his associates

7. Herzberg, Mausner, and Snyderman, *The Motivation to Work.*

because they satisfied the individual's need for self-actualization at work. The job environment characteristics which led to dissatisfaction were called "hygienes" because they were work-supporting or contextual rather than task-determined and hence were analogous to the "preventative" or "environmental" factors recognized in medicine. According to this dichotomy, motivators include achievement, recognition, advancement, possibility of growth, responsibility, and work itself. Hygienes, on the other hand, include salary; interpersonal relations with superiors, subordinates, and peers; technical supervision; company policy and administration; personal life; working conditions; status; and job security.

There is considerable empirical evidence for this theory. Herzberg himself, in a summary of research through early 1966, includes ten studies of seventeen populations which used essentially the same method as his original study.[8] In addition, he reviews twenty more studies which used a variety of methodologies to test the two-factor theory. Of the studies included in his review, those using his critical incident method generally confirm the theory. Those using other methods give less clear results, which Herzberg acknowledges but attempts to dismiss for methodological reasons. At least nine other studies, most of which have appeared since Herzberg's 1966 review, raise even more doubts about the theory.[9]

While it is beyond the scope of the present article to consider these studies in detail, they raise serious questions as to whether the factors leading to satisfaction and dissatisfaction

8. Herzberg, *Work and the Nature of Man,* chaps. 7, 8. See also K. Davis, *Human Relations at Work,* 3d ed. (New York: McGraw-Hill, 1967), pp. 32–36; R. J. Burke, "Are Herzberg's Motivators and Hygienes Unidimensional?" *Journal of Applied Psychology* 50 (1966): 217–221.

9. For a review of six of these studies as well as a report on their own similar findings see M. D. Dunnette, J. P. Campbell, and M. D. Hakel, "Factors Contributing to Job Satisfaction and Job Dissatisfaction in Six Occupational Groups," *Organizational Behavior and Human Performance* 2 (1967): 143–74. See also C. L. Hulin and P. A. Smith, "An Empirical Investigation of Two Implications of the Two-Factor Theory of Job Satisfaction," *Journal of Applied Psychology* 51 (1967): 396–402; C. A. Lindsay, E. Marks, and L. Gorlow, "The Herzberg Theory: A Critique and Reformulation," *Journal of Applied Psychology* 51 (1967): 330–39. This latter study and one by J. R. Hinrichs and L. A. Mischkind, "Empirical and Theoretical Limitations of the Two-Factor Hypothesis of Job Satisfaction," *Journal of Applied Psychology* 51 (1967): pp. 191–200, are especially useful for suggesting possible reformulations and extensions of the theory which may help overcome some the objections voiced in the studies mentioned above.

are really different from each other. A number of the studies show that certain job dimensions appear to be more important for *both* satisfaction and dissatisfaction. Dunnette, Campbell, and Hakel, for example, conclude from these and also from their own studies that Herzberg is shackled to his method and that achievement, recognition, and responsibility seem important for both satisfaction *and* dissatisfaction, while such dimensions as security, salary, and working conditions are less important.[10] They also raise by implication an issue concerning Herzberg's methodology which deserves further comment. That is, if data are analyzed in terms of percentage differences between groups, one result is obtained; if they are analyzed in terms of ranks within groups, another result occurs. The first type of analysis is appropriate for identifying factors which account for differences between events (as Herzberg did in his original hypothesis). The second type of analysis is appropriate if we want to know the most important factors within the event categories (which is what Herzberg claims he was doing). Analyzing the findings of Dunnette and his colleagues by the first method, we confirm Herzberg's theory; but if we rank the findings within categories, as Dunnette et al. also did, we find no confirmation. If we want to know whether "achievement" is important in job satisfaction we must look at its relative rank among other factors mentioned in the events leading to satisfaction, not whether it is mentioned a greater percentage of the time in satisfying events than in dissatisfying events. This distinction in analytical methods was discussed several years ago by Viteles and even earlier by Kornhauser.[11]

We conclude that any meaningful discussion of Herzberg's theory must recognize recent negative evidence even though the model seems to make a great deal of intuitive sense. Much the same can be said of Maslow's theory.

Further Considerations in Using the Maslow and Herzberg Theories

Putting aside for the moment the empirical considerations presented by the two models, it is instructive to compare them at the conceptual level suggested in figure 1. While the figure shows obvious similarities between the Maslow and Herzberg models, there are important differences as well.

---

10. Dunnette, Campbell, and Hakel, "Factors Contributing to Job Satisfaction," pp. 169–73.

11. M. S. Viteles, *Motivation and Morale in Industry* (New York: Norton, 1953), chap. 14; A. Kornhauser, "Psychological Studies of Employee Attitudes," *Journal of Consulting Psychology* 8 (1944): 127–43.

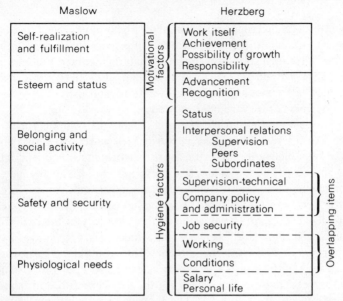

Fig. 1. Maslow's Need-Priority Model Compared with Herzberg's Motivation-Hygiene Model

Adapted from K. Davis, *Human Relations at Work* (New York: McGraw-Hill, 1967), p. 37.

Where Maslow assumes that any need can be a motivator if it is relatively unsatisfied, Herzberg argues that only the higher order needs serve as motivators and that a worker can have unsatisfied needs in both the hygiene and motivator areas simultaneously. One might argue that the reason higher order needs are motivators is that lower order needs have essentially been satisfied. However, Herzberg presents some evidence that even in relatively low-level blue collar and service jobs, where presumably lower order needs are less well satisfied, the higher order needs are still the only ones seen by the workers as motivators.[12]

Another important consideration is the relationship of these models to the accomplishment of organizational objectives. Even if there were unequivocal empirical support for the theories, there is need to translate the findings into usable incentives for promoting such objectives as superior performance, lower turnover, lower absenteeism, and so on. If not, they are of little use to industrial organizations. As indicated earlier, there is relatively little evidence empirically relating Maslow's model to performance, or even to psychological well-being. Furthermore, the one Lawler and Porter study

12. Herzberg, *Work and the Nature of Man,* chaps. 7–9.

seems to show that satisfaction of higher and lower order needs are about equally related to performance, although their later investigation suggests that the former are more strongly related to performance than the latter. But we cannot tell for sure because correlations and differences between correlations are not reported.

Similarly, although Herzberg asked his respondents for effects of job events on their performance, he reports only two studies which attempt to measure performance independent of the respondent's estimate. These seem to show the performance is favorably influenced as more "motivators" are provided in the job.[13] However, insufficient data are presented to permit evaluation of the adequacy of the experimental design and performance measures. A study by Friedlander and Walton that considered employee turnover used a modification of Herzberg's technique and found that employees' reasons for staying on the job were different from their reasons for leaving.[14] The reasons for staying would be called "motivators" while those for leaving were "hygiene" factors.

We conclude that Herzberg's two-factor theory *may* be related to turnover and performance; but present studies are subject to serious criticisms. And we could find only two empirical investigations which related Maslow's model to any of these outputs.

In addition, it should be noted that neither model adequately handles the theoretical problem of some kind of linkage by which individual need satisfaction is related to the achievement of organizational objectives. Given the present formulation, it is entirely possible that there can be need satisfaction which is *not necessarily* directed toward the accomplishment of organizational goals. For example, an important organizational objective might be increased production, but workers might conceivably receive more need satisfaction from turning out a higher quality product at a sacrifice in quantity. They might also be meeting their social needs through identification with a work group with strong sanctions against "rate busting."

Finally, neither of these theories as they stand can really handle the problem of individual differences in motivation. Maslow, for example, explains that his model may not hold

13. Ibid., chap. 8.
14. F. Friedlander and E. Walton, "Positive and Negative Motivations toward Work," *Administrative Science Quarterly* 9 (1964): 194–207.

for persons with particular experiences. His theory is therefore nonpredictive because data that do not support it can be interpreted in terms of individual differences in previous need gratification leading to greater or lesser prepotency of a given need category.[15] Herzberg, in similar fashion, describes seven types of people differentiated by the extent to which they are motivator or hygiene seekers, or some combination of the two, although he never relates these differences empirically to actual job performance. We turn then to a model which explicitly recognizes these issues and appears to offer great potential for understanding motivation in organizations.

The Vroom Model

Brayfield and Crockett as long ago as 1955 suggested an explicit theoretical linkage between satisfaction, motivation, and the organizational goal of productivity. They said:

> It makes sense to us to assume that individuals are motivated to achieve certain environmental goals and that the achievement of these goals results in satisfaction. Productivity is seldom a goal in itself but is more commonly a means to goal attainment. Therefore, . . . we might expect high satisfaction and high productivity to occur together when productivity is perceived as a path to certain important goals and when these goals are achieved.[16]

Georgopoulos, Mahoney, and Jones provide some early empirical support for this notion in their test of the "path-goal hypothesis."[17] Essentially, they argue that an individual's motivation to produce at a given level depends upon his particular needs as reflected in the goals toward which he is moving *and* his perception of the relative usefulness of productivity behavior as a path to attainment of these goals. They qualify this, however, by saying that the need must be sufficiently high, no other economical paths must be avail-

15. It should be noted that the Porter and Lawler research reported above extends the Maslow model by providing an explicit linkage between need satisfaction and performance and also implicitly recognizes individual motivational differences. To do these things, their research makes use of Vroomian concepts discussed in the next section.

16. A. H. Brayfield and W. H. Crockett, "Employee Attitudes and Employee Performance," *Psychological Bulletin* 52 (1955): 416.

17. B. S. Georgopoulos, G. M. Mahoney, and N. W. Jones, "A Path-Goal Approach to Productivity," *Journal of Applied Psychology* 41 (1957): 345–53.

able to the individual, and there must be a lack of restraining practices.

More recently, Vroom has developed a motivational model which extends the above concepts and is also related to earlier work of experimental and social psychologists.[18] He defines motivation as a "process governing choices, made by persons or lower organisms, among alternative forms of voluntary activity."[19] The concept is incorporated in figure 2, which depicts Vroom's model graphically. Here, the individual is shown as a role occupant faced with a set of alternative

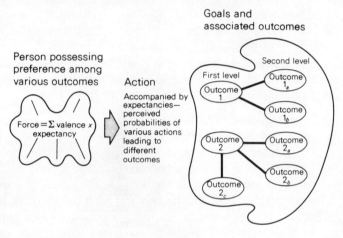

Fig. 2. Vroom's Motivational Model

Adapted from M. D. Dunnette. "The Motives of Industrial Managers," *Organizational Behavior and Human Performance* 2 (1967):178. (Copyright, Academic Press, Inc.)

"first-level outcomes." His preference choice among these first-level outcomes is determined by their expected relationship to possible "second-level outcomes."

Two concepts are introduced to explain the precise method of determining preferences for these first-level outcomes. These concepts are *valence* and *instrumentality*. Valence refers to the strength of an individual's desire for a particular outcome. Instrumentality indicates an individual's perception of the relationship between a first-level outcome and a

18. This section is based especially on discussions in Vroom, *Work and Motivation,* chap. 2 and 7. See also J. Galbraith and L. L. Cummings, "An Empirical Investigation of the Motivational Determinants of Task Performance: Interactive Effects between Instrumentality—Valence and Motivation—Ability," *Organizational Behavior and Human Performance* 2 (1967): 237–57.
19. Vroom, *Work and Motivation,* p. 6.

second-level outcome or, in other words, the extent to which a first-level outcome is seen as leading to the accomplishment of a second-level outcome.

Valence is measured by instructing workers to rank important individual goals in order of their desirability, or they may rate goals on Likert-type scales. Instrumentality can be measured by rating scales which involve perceived differences in the direction and strength of relationships between various first- and second-level outcomes. Important goals of industrial workers often cited in the empirical behavioral science literature are promotion, pay, pleasant working conditions, and job security. The goals can be ranked by individual workers in terms of their desirability. The resulting scores are measures of valence. In addition, each individual can be instructed to indicate on an appropriate scale the likelihood that a certain job behavior, e.g., high productivity, will lead to each of the four goals described. This score is the instrumental relationship between productivity and a specified goal. Obviously there are alternative methods of measurement available for the concepts; we will leave these for a more detailed discussion later.

Vroom expresses the valence of a first-level outcome to a person "as a monotonically increasing function of an algebraic sum of the products of the valences of all [second-level] outcomes and his conceptions of its instrumentality for the attainment of the [second-level] outcomes."[20]

For example, assume that an individual desires promotion and feels that superior performance is a very strong factor in achieving that goal. His first-level outcomes are then superior, average, or poor performance. His second-level outcome is promotion. The first-level outcome of high performance thus acquires a positive valence by virtue of its expected relationship to the preferred second-level outcome of promotion. Assuming no negative second-level outcomes associated with high performance and no other first-level outcomes that contribute to promotion, we expect motivation toward superior performance because promotion is important and superior performance is seen as instrumental in its accomplishment. Or, to put it in Vroom's terms, performance varies directly with the product of the valence of the reward (promotion) and the perceived instrumentality of performance for the attainment of the reward.

An additional concept in Vroom's theory is *expectancy*. This is a belief concerning the likelihood that a particular ac-

20. Ibid., p. 17.

tion or effort will be followed by a particular first-level outcome and can be expressed as a subjective probability
ranging from 0 to 1. Expectancy differs from instrumentality
in that it relates *efforts* to first-level outcomes where instrumentality relates first- and second-level outcomes to each
other. Vroom ties this concept to his previous one by stating,
"the force on a person to perform an [action] is a monotonically increasing function of the algebraic sum of the
products of the valences of all [first-level] outcomes and the
strength of his expectancies that the [action] will be followed
by the attainment of these outcomes."[21] "Force" here is similar to our concept of motivation.

This motivational model, unlike those discussed earlier,
emphasizes individual differences in motivation and makes
possible the examination of very explicit relationships between motivation and the accomplishment of organizational
goals, whatever these goals may be. Thus instead of assuming
that satisfaction of a specific need is likely to influence organizational objectives in a certain way, we can find out how
important to the employees are the various second-level outcomes (worker goals), the instrumentality of various first-
level outcomes (organizational objectives) for their attainment, and the expectancies that are held with respect to the
employees' ability to influence the first-level outcomes.

Empirical Tests of Vroom's Model

Vroom has already shown how his model can integrate many
of the empirical findings in the literature on motivation in
organizations.[22] However, because it is a relatively recent
development, empirical tests of the model itself are just
beginning to appear. Here we shall consider four such investigations.

In the first study, Vroom is concerned with predicting the
organizational choices of graduating college students on the
basis of their instrumentality-goal index scores.[23] These
scores reflect the extent to which membership in an organization was perceived by the student as being related to the
acquisition of desired goals. According to the theory, the
chosen organization should be the one with the highest instrumentality-goal index. Ratings were used to obtain preferences for fifteen different goals and the extent to which these

21. Ibid., p. 18.
22. Ibid.
23. V. H. Vroom, "Organizational Choice: A Study of Pre- and Post-
decision Processes," *Organizational Behavior and Human Performance*
1 (1966): 212–25.

goals could be attained through membership in three different organizations. These two ratings were thus measures of the valences of second-level outcomes and the instrumentality of organizational membership for attainment of these outcomes, respectively. The instrumentality-goal index was the correlation between these two measures. But Vroom's theory also involves consideration of expectancy, i.e., how probable is it that the student can become a member of a particular organization. The choice is not his alone but depends upon whether he is acceptable to the organization. A rough measure of expectancy in this study was whether or not the student had received an offer by the organization. If he had received an offer, expectancy would be high; if not, it would be low. The results show that, considering only organizations from which offers of employment were actually received, 76 percent of the students chose the organization with the highest instrumentality-goal index score. The evidence thus strongly supports Vroom's theory.

The next study, by Galbraith and Cummings, utilizes the model to predict the productivity of operative workers.[24] Graphic rating scales were used to measure the instrumentality of performance for five goals—money, fringe benefits, promotion, supervisor's support, and group acceptance. Similar ratings were used for measuring the desirability of each of the goals for the worker. The authors anticipated that a worker's expectation that he could produce at a high level would have a probability of one because the jobs were independent and productivity was a function of the worker's own effort independent of other human or machine pacing. Figure 3 outlines the research design.

Multiple regression analysis showed that productivity was significantly related positively to the instrumentality-goal interactions for supervisor support and money, and there was an almost significant ($p < 0.10$) relationship with group acceptance. The other factors did not approach significance and the authors explain this lack of significance in terms of the situational context. That is, fringe benefits were dependent not so much on productivity as on a union/management contract, and promotion was based primarily on seniority. Thus the instrumentality of productivity for the attainment of these goals was low and the model would predict no relationship. The Galbraith and Cummings study thus supports Vroom's contention that motivation is related to productivity in those situations where the acquisition of desired goals is dependent

24. Galbraith and Cummings, "An Empirical Investigation," pp. 237–57.

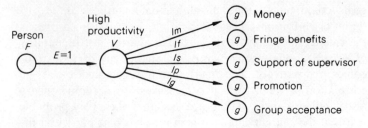

Fig. 3. Individual Goals and Productivity as Measured by Vroom's Model in One Industrial Plant

g = Desirability of a particular outcome (rating).
I = Instrumentality of production for particular outcomes (rating of relationship).
E = Expectancy (= 1 here because worker sets own pace and is assumed to be capable of high productivity).
V = (Valence) the sum of the cross products of instrumentality and g.
F = (Force) expectancy times the valence of productivity.
Productivity = Objective measures of amount of production in relation to the production standard.

Based on data from J. Galbraith and L. L. Cummings. See footnote 23.

upon the individual's production and not when desired outcomes are contingent on other factors.

A third study is that of Hill relating a model similar to Vroom's to behavior in a utility company.[25] Hill's model is based upon Edward's subjective expected utility maximization theory of decision making.[26] Here one given a choice between alternatives A and/or B will select that alternative which maximizes his subjective expected utility or expected value. If the outcomes associated with action A are more desirable than those associated with B, and their probability of occurrence is greater than or equal to those associated with B, then an individual will choose behavior A over behavior B. The basic concepts are subjective expectation and subjective utility or valence. Expectation and utility are multiplicatively related and can be measured by the same techniques used to test Vroom's theory. Where a relationship is found between Subjective Expected Utility (SEU) and overt behavior, it can be interpreted as support for Vroom.

The behavior considered in Hill's study is that of job bid-

25. J. W. Hill, "An Application of Decision Theory to Complex Industrial Behavior" (dissertation, Wayne State University, Detroit, Michigan, 1965).
26. Edwards, "Behavioral Decision Theory," pp. 473–99.

ding. This behavior is encountered in organizations that post descriptions of job openings on employee bulletin boards and encourage qualified employees to "bid" (apply) for them. Here records were kept of the number of bids made over a three-year period by groups of semiskilled electrical repairmen matched in learning ability, seniority in grade, and age. The men were asked about the consequences of bidding and not bidding on the next higher grade job, and rated the consequence on a seven-point scale of desirability and a similar scale of probability of occurrence. Bidders were those who had bid three or more times during that time.

Fourteen different SEU indices were computed from interview data to determine the relative validity of each in predicting bidding behavior. Typical of these indices were: (1) the sums of the cross products of expectation and utility for the positive consequences of bidding ($\Sigma \overset{+}{SEU}$); (2) the same score for the negative consequences of bidding ($\Sigma \overset{-}{SEU}$); and (3) the cross products of the *mean* expectation and utility scores for positive and negative consequences $\left(\dfrac{\Sigma \overset{+}{SEU}}{N}, \dfrac{\Sigma \overset{-}{SEU}}{N} \right)$. In addition to these SEU indices, two traditional attitudinal and motivational measures were used. Semantic differential scales measured each subject's respective evaluation of bidding and the next higher grade job and each subject's need for achievement was obtained.[27]

It was hypothesized that: (1) there would be a positive correlation between the SEU indices and bidding; and (2) the SEU indices would be more highly related to bidding behavior than the traditional measures.

We do not discuss relationships for all of the indices here but do consider results for one of the more comprehensive indices and those from multiple regression analysis. This index is the algebraic sum of the cross products of the positive and negative consequences of bidding minus the same score for not bidding for each individual. The correlation of this index with bidding was 0.26, $p < 0.05$ for a one-tailed test. The correlations between the two semantic differential scales and

27. For discussions of these measures see C. Osgood, G. Suci, and P. Tannenbaum, *The Measurement of Meaning* (Urbana, Ill.: University of Illinois Press, 1957); A. L. Edwards, *Personal Preference Schedule Manual* (New York: Psychological Corporation, 1959).

bidding were -0.09 and -0.25, respectively. Neither of these is significant for a one-tailed test predicting a positive correlation. The correlation between need for achievement and bidding was a nonsignificant 0.17. A multiple regression analysis determined the relative contribution of the SEU indices to the prediction of bidding. A variable was selected for analysis on the basis of its relationship to the criterion and its intercorrelation with the other predictors. The multiple correlation for bidding and seven selected variables was 0.61, $p < 0.05$. This correlation included four SEU indices, all of which had higher beta weights than the semantic differentials or need for achievement. Thus these variables accounted for more variance in the criterion than did the traditional attitudinal and motivational measures. Both hypotheses were therefore confirmed. This study adds support to the usefulness of this type of model in the study of motivation.

Finally, Lawler and Porter report a study that attempts to relate managerial attitudes to job performance rankings by superiors and peers.[28] In it, 145 managers from five different organizations completed questionnaires concerning seven kinds of rewards, and their expectations that different kinds of behavior would lead to these rewards. The expectations and the ratings of the importance of instrumentality and valence, respectively, were combined multiplicatively to yield multiple correlations which were significantly related to supervisor and peer rankings of the manager's effort to perform his job well. The correlations were higher with effort to perform the job than with the rankings of job performance. Lawler and Porter predicted this result because they reasoned that job performance is influenced by variables other than motivation, e.g., by ability and role perceptions. Of course, Vroom's model is not a behavioral theory but one of motivation only. Motivation is not going to improve performance if ability is low or role perceptions are inaccurate. Vroom's model explains how goals influence effort and that is exactly the relationship found by Lawler and Porter.

Conclusion

Taken together, the four studies discussed in the previous section seem to show that Vroom's model holds great promise for predicting behavior in organizations. There still remain some unanswered questions. We do not know all of the goals

28. E. E. Lawler and L. W. Porter, "Antecedent Attitudes of Effective Managerial Performance," *Organizational Behavior and Human Performance* 2 (1967): 122–42.

that have positive valence in a work situation. We do not know how much of a difference in force is necessary before one kind of outcome is chosen over another. Nor do we know what combination of measures yields the best prediction in a given situation. The answers to these and other questions await further research.

One more point should perhaps be made concerning the four studies and their measurement of Vroom's concepts. While it is true that all of them used subjective measures, the model can in fact be tested with more objective devices. Instrumentality can be inferred from organization practices, expectations can be manipulated by instructions, and goals can be inferred from observed approach and avoidance behaviors. Of course, all of these techniques require assumptions concerning their relationship to the worker's subjective perceptions of the situation; but the model is certainly not bound to the methods of measurement used so far. In fact, Vroom specifies in considerable detail the different kinds of techniques that might be used to test his model.[29]

More work must be done before we can make any statements concerning the overall validity of Vroom's model. But the rigor of his formulation, the relative ease of making the concepts operational, and the model's emphasis on individual differences show considerable promise. We are also encouraged by the results of relatively sophisticated studies testing the theory. We believe it is time for those interested in organizational behavior to take a more thoroughly scientific look at this very complex subject of industrial motivation, and Vroom's model seems a big step in that direction.

29. Vroom, *Work and Motivation*, chap. 2.

Job Design and Employee Motivation
Edward E. Lawler III

The psychological literature on employee motivation contains many claims that changes in job design can be expected to produce better employee job performance. Very few of these claims, however, are supported by an explanation of why changes in job design should be expected to affect performance except to indicate that they can affect employee motivation. Thus, I would like to begin by considering the WHY question with respect to job design and employee performance. That is, I want to focus on the reasons for expecting changes in job design to affect employee motivation and performance. Once this question is answered, predictions will be made about the effects on performance of specific changes in job design (e.g., job enlargement and job rotation).

A Theory of Motivation

Basic to any explanation of why people behave in a certain manner is a theory of motivation. As Jones[1] has pointed out, motivation theory attempts to explain "how behavior gets started, is energized, is sustained, is directed, is stopped and what kind of subjective reaction is present in the organism." The theory of motivation that will be used to understand the effects of job design is "expectancy theory." Georgopoulos, Mahoney, and Jones, Vroom,[2] and others have recently stated expectancy theories of job performance. The particular expectancy theory to be used in this paper is based upon this earlier work and has been more completely described else-

Reprinted from *Personnel Psychology* 22 (1969): 426–35, by permission of the publisher and author.

1. M. R. Jones, ed., *Nebraska Symposium on Motivation* (Lincoln, Nebr.: Nebraska University Press, 1959).
2. B. S. Georgopoulos, G. M. Mahoney, and M. N. Jones, "A Path-goal Approach to Productivity," *Journal of Applied Psychology* 41 (1957): 345–53; V. H. Vroom, *Work and Motivation* (New York: John Wiley & Sons, 1964).

where.[3] According to this theory, an employee's motivation to perform effectively is determined by two variables. The first of these is contained in the concept of an effort-reward probability. This is the individual's subjective probability that directing a given amount of effort toward performing effectively will result in his obtaining a given reward or positively valued outcome. This effort-reward probability is determined by two subsidiary subjective probabilities: the probability that effort will result in performance and the probability that performance will result in the reward. Vroom refers to the first of these subjective probabilities as an expectancy and to the second as an instrumentality.

The second variable that is relevant here is the concept of reward value or valence. This refers to the individual's perception of the value of the reward or outcome that might be obtained by performing effectively. Although most expectancy theories do not specify why certain outcomes have reward value, for the purpose of this paper I would like to argue that the reward value of outcomes stems from their perceived ability to satisfy one or more needs. Specifically relevant here is the list of needs suggested by Maslow that includes security needs, social needs, esteem needs, and self-actualization needs.

The evidence indicates that, for a given reward, reward value and the effort-reward probability combine multiplicatively in order to determine an individual's motivation. This means that if either is low or nonexistent then no motivation will be present. As an illustration of this point, consider the case of a manager who very much values getting promoted but who sees no relationship between working hard and getting promoted. For him, promotion is not serving as a motivator, just as it is not for a manager who sees a close connection between being promoted and working hard but who doesn't want to be promoted. In order for motivation to be present, the manager must both value promotion and see the relationship between his efforts and promotion. Thus, for an individual reward or outcome the argument is that a multiplicative combination of its value and the appropriate effort-reward probability is necessary. However, an individual's motivation is influenced by more than one outcome. Thus, in order to determine an individual's motivation it is

3. E. E. Lawler and L. W. Porter, "Antecedent Attitudes of Effective Managerial Performance," *Organizational Behavior and Human Performance* 2 (1967): 122–42; L. W. Porter and E. E. Lawler, *Managerial Attitudes and Performance* (Homewood, Ill.: Irwin-Dorsey, 1968).

necessary to combine data concerned with a number of different outcomes. This can be done for an individual worker by considering all the outcomes he values and then summing the products obtained from multiplying the value of these outcomes to him by their respective effort-reward probabilities.

According to this theory, if changes in job design are going to affect an individual's motivation they must either change the value of the outcomes that are seen to depend upon effort, or positively affect the individual's beliefs about the probability that certain outcomes are dependent upon effort. The argument in this paper is that job design changes can have a positive effect on motivation, because they can change an individual's beliefs about the probability that certain rewards will result from putting forth high levels of effort. They can do this because they have the power to influence the probability that certain rewards will be seen to result from good performance, not because they can influence the perceived probability that effort will result in good performance. Stated in Vroom's language, the argument is that job design changes are more likely to affect the instrumentality of good performance than to affect the expectancy that effort will lead to performance.

Before elaborating on this point, it is important to distinguish between two kinds of rewards. The first type are those that are extrinsic to the individual. These rewards are part of the job situation and are given by others. Hence, they are externally mediated and are rewards that can best be thought of as satisfying lower order needs. The second type of rewards are intrinsic to the individual and stem directly from the performance itself. These rewards are internally mediated since the individual rewards himself. These rewards can be thought of as satisfying higher order needs such as self-esteem and self-actualization. They involve such outcomes as feelings of accomplishment, feelings of achievement, and feelings of using and developing one's skills and abilities. The fact that these rewards are internally mediated sets them apart from the extrinsic rewards in an important way. It means that the connection between their reception and performance is more direct than is the connection between the reception of externally mediated rewards and performance. Hence, potentially they can be excellent motivators because higher effort-reward probabilities can be established for them than can be established for extrinsic rewards. They also have the advantage that for many people rewards of this nature have a high positive value.

Job content is the critical determinant of whether employees believe that good performance on the job leads to feelings of accomplishment, growth, and self-esteem; that is, whether individuals will find jobs to be intrinsically motivating. Job content is important here because it serves a motive arousal function where higher order needs are concerned and because it influences what rewards will be seen to stem from good performance. Certain tasks are more likely to arouse motives like achievement and self-actualization, and to generate, among individuals who have these motives aroused, the belief that successful performance will result in outcomes that involve feelings of achievement and growth. It is precisely because changes in job content can affect the relationship between performance and the reception of intrinsically rewarding outcomes that it can have a strong influence on motivation and performance.

There appear to be three characteristics which jobs must possess if they are to arouse higher order needs and to create conditions such that people who perform them will come to expect that good performance will lead to intrinsic rewards. The first is that the individual must receive meaningful feedback about his performance. This may well mean the individual must himself evaluate his own performance and define the kind of feedback that he is to receive. It may also mean that the person may have to work on a whole product or a meaningful part of it. The second is that the job must be perceived by the individual as requiring him to use abilities that he values in order for him to perform the job effectively. Only if an individual feels that his significant abilities are being tested by a job can feelings of accomplishment and growth be expected to result from good performance. Several laboratory studies have in fact shown that, when people are given tasks they see as testing their valued abilities, greater motivation does appear.[4] Finally, the individual must feel he has a high degree of self-control over setting his own goals and over defining the paths to these goals. As Argyris[5] points out, only if this condition exists will people experience psychological "success" as a result of good performance.

Thus, it appears that the answer to the *why* question can be found in the ability of job design factors to influence em-

4. Thelma G. Alper, "Task-orientation vs. Ego-orientation in Learning and Retention," *American Journal of Psychology* 38 (1946): 224–38; Elizabeth G. French, "Some Characteristics of Achievement Motivation," *Journal of Experimental Psychology* 50 (1955): 232–36.
5. C. Argyris, *Integrating the Individual and the Organization* (New York: John Wiley & Sons, 1964).

ployees' perceptions of the probability that good performance will be intrinsically rewarding. Certain job designs apparently encourage the perception that it will, while others do not. Because of this, job design factors can determine how motivating a job will be.

Job Design Changes

Everyone seems to agree that the typical assembly line job is not likely to fit any of the characteristics of the intrinsically motivating job. That is, it is not likely to provide meaningful knowledge of result, test valued abilities, or allow self-control. Realizing this, much attention has been focused recently on attempts to enlarge assembly line jobs, and there is good reason to believe that enlarging assembly line jobs can lead to a situation where jobs are more intrinsically motivating. However, many proponents of job enlargement have failed to distinguish between two different kinds of job enlargement. Jobs can be enlarged on both the horizontal dimension and the vertical dimension. The horizontal dimension refers to the number and variety of the operations that an individual performs on the job. The vertical dimension refers to the degree to which the job holder controls the planning and execution of his job and participates in the setting of organization policies. The utility man on the assembly line has a job that is horizontally but not vertically enlarged, while the worker who Argyris[6] suggests can participate in decision making about his job while he continues to work on the assembly line, has a vertically but not a horizontally enlarged job.

The question that arises is, what kind of job enlargement is necessary if the job is going to provide intrinsic motivation? The answer, that is suggested by the three factors that are necessary for a task to be motivating, is that jobs must be enlarged both vertically and horizontally. It is hard to see, in terms of the theory, why the utility man will see more connection between performing well and intrinsic rewards than will the assembly line worker. The utility man typically has no more self-control, only slightly more knowledge of results, and only a slightly greater chance to test his valued abilities. Hence, for him, good performance should be only slightly more rewarding than it will be for the individual who works in one location on the line. In fact, it would seem that jobs can be overenlarged on the horizontal dimension so that they

6. Ibid.

will be less motivating than they were originally. Excessive horizontal enlargement may well lead to a situation where meaningful feedback is impossible, and where the job involves using many additional abilities that the worker does not value. The worker who is allowed to participate in some decisions about his work on the assembly line can hardly be expected to perceive that intrinsic rewards will stem from performing well on the line. His work on the line still is not under his control, he is not likely to get very meaningful feedback about it, and his valued abilities still are not being tested by it. Thus, for him it is hard to see why he should feel that intrinsic rewards will result from good performance.

On the other hand, we should expect that a job which is both horizontally and vertically enlarged will be a job that motivates people to perform well. For example, the workers Kuriloff [7] has described, who make a whole electronic instrument, check and ship it, should be motivated by their jobs. This kind of job does provide meaningful feedback, it does allow for self-control, and there is a good chance that it will be seen as testing valued abilities. It does not, however, guarantee that the person will see it as testing his valued abilities since we don't know what the person's valued abilities are. In summary, then, the argument is that if job enlargement is to be successful in increasing motivation, it must be enlargement that affects both the horizontal and the vertical dimensions of the job. In addition, individual differences must be taken into consideration in two respects. First and most obviously, it must only be tried with people who possess higher order needs that can be aroused by the job design and who, therefore, will value intrinsic rewards. Second, individuals must be placed on jobs that test their valued abilities.

Let me now address myself to the question of how the increased motivation, that can be generated by an enlarged job, will manifest itself in terms of behavior. Obviously, the primary change that can be expected is that the individual will devote more effort to performing well. But will this increased effort result in a higher quality work, higher productivity, or both? I think this question can be answered by looking at the reasons we gave for the job content being able to affect motivation. The argument was that it does this by affecting whether intrinsic rewards will be seen as coming

7. A. H. Kuriloff, *Reality in Management* (New York: McGraw-Hill, 1966).

from successful performance. It would seem that high quality work is indispensable if most individuals are to feel they have performed well and are to experience feelings of accomplishment, achievement, and self-actualization. The situation is much less clear with respect to productivity. It does not seem at all certain that an individual must produce great quantities of a product in order to feel that he has performed well. In fact, many individuals probably obtain more satisfaction from producing one very high quality product than they do from producing a number of lower quality products.

There is a second factor which may cause job enlargement to be more likely to lead to higher work quality than to higher productivity. This has to do with the advantages of division of labor and mechanization. Many job enlargement changes create a situation in which, because of the losses in terms of machine assistance and optimal human movements, people actually have to put forth more energy in order to produce at the pre–job enlargement rate. Thus, people may be working harder but producing less. It seems less likely that the same dilemma would arise in terms of work quality and job enlargement. That is, if extra effort is devoted to quality after job enlargement takes place, the effort is likely to be translated into improved quality. This would come about because the machine assistance and other features of the assembly line jobs are more of an aid in bringing about high productivity than they are in bringing about high quality.

The Research Evidence

There have been a number of studies that have attempted to measure the effects of job enlargement programs. These were examined to determine if the evidence supports the contention stated previously that both horizontal and vertical job enlargement are necessary if intrinsic motivation is to be increased. Also sought was an indication of whether the effects of any increased motivation were more likely to result in higher quality work than in high productivity.

In the literature search, reports of ten studies where jobs had been enlarged on both the horizontal and the vertical dimensions were found. Table 1 presents a brief summary of the results of these studies. As can be seen, every study shows that job enlargement did have some positive effect since every study reports that job enlargement resulted in higher quality work. However, only four out of ten studies report that job enlargement led to higher productivity. This

Table 1

Research Study[a]	Higher Quality	Higher Productivity
Biggane and Stewart (1963)	Yes	No
Conant and Kilbridge (1965)	Yes	No
Kilbridge (1960)		
Davis and Valfer (1965)	Yes	No
Davis and Werling (1960)	Yes	Yes
Elliot (1953)	Yes	Yes
Guest (1957)	Yes	No
Kuriloff (1966)	Yes	Yes
Marks (1954)	Yes	No
Rice (1953)	Yes	Yes
Walker (1950)	Yes	No

[a]J. F. Biggane and P. A. Stewart, *Job Enlargement: A Case Study,* Research Series, no. 25, Bureau of Labor and Management, State University of Iowa (Iowa City, Iowa 1963); E. H. Conant and M. D. Kilbridge, "An Interdisciplinary Analysis of Job Enlargement: Technology, Costs, and Behavioral Implications," *Industrial and Labor Relations Review* 18 (1965): 377–95; M. D. Kilbridge, "Reduced Costs through Job Enlargement: A Case," *Journal of Business* 33 (1960): 357–62; L. E. Davis and E. S. Valfer, "Intervening Responses to Changes in Supervisor Job Designs," *Occupational Psychology* 39 (1965): 171–89; L. E. Davis and R. Werling, "Job Design Factors," *Occupational Psychology* 34 (1960): 109–32; J. D. Elliot, "Increasing Office Productivity through Job Enlargement," in *The Human Side of the Office Manager's Job,* A. M. A. Office Management Series, no. 134 (New York, 1953), pp. 5–15; R. H. Guest, "Job Enlargement: A Revolution in Job Design," *Personnel Administration* 20 (1957): 9–16; A. H. Kuriloff, *Reality in Management* (New York: McGraw-Hill, 1966); A. R. N. Marks, "An Investigation of Modifications of Job Design in an Industrial Situation and Their Effects on Some Measures of Economic Productivity" (Ph.D. dissertation, University of California, Berkeley, 1954); A. K. Rice, "Productivity and Social Organization in an Indian Weaving Shed," *Human Relations* 6 (1953): 297–329; C. R. Walker, "The Problem of the Repetitive Job," *Harvard Business Review* 28 (1950): 54–59.

provides support for the view that the motivational effects produced by job enlargement are more likely to result in higher quality work than in higher productivity.

There are relatively few studies of jobs enlarged only on either the horizontal or the vertical dimension so that it is difficult to test the prediction that both kinds of enlargement are necessary if motivation is to be increased. There are a few studies which have been concerned with the effects of horizontal job enlargement,[8] while others have stressed its advantages. However, most of these studies have been con-

8. C. R. Walker and R. H. Guest, *The Man on the Assembly Line* (Cambridge, Mass.: Harvard University Press, 1952).

cerned with its effects on job satisfaction rather than its effects on motivation. None of these studies appears to show that horizontal enlargement tends to increase either productivity or work quality. Walker and Guest, for example, talk about the higher satisfaction of the utility men but they do not report that they work harder. Thus, with respect to horizontal job enlargement, the evidence does not lead to rejecting the view that it must be combined with vertical in order to increase production.

The evidence with respect to whether vertical job enlargement alone can increase motivation is less clear. As Argyris[9] has pointed out, the Scanlon plan has stressed this kind of job enlargement with some success. However, it is hard to tell if this success stems from people actually becoming more motivated to perform their own job better. It is quite possible that improvements under the plan are due to better overall decision making rather than to increased motivation. Vroom[10] has analyzed the evidence with respect to the degree to which participation in decision making per se leads to increased motivation. This evidence suggests that vertical job enlargement can lead to increased motivation when it leads to the employees' committing themselves to higher production goals.

Perhaps the crucial distinction here is whether the participation involves matters of company policy or whether it involves matters directly related to the employees' work process. Participation of the former type would seem much less likely to lead to increased motivation than would participation of the latter type. Thus, it seems to be crucial to distinguish between two quite different types of vertical job enlargement, only one of which leads to increased motivation. Considered together, the evidence suggests that, of the two types of job enlargement, vertical is more important than horizontal. Perhaps this is because it can lead to a situation in which subjects feel their abilities are being tested and where they can exercise self-control even though horizontal enlargement does not take place. Still, the evidence, with respect to situations where both types of enlargement have been jointly installed, shows that much more consistent improvements in motivation can be produced by both than can be produced by vertical alone.

9. Argyris, *Integrating the Individual.*
10. Vroom, *Work and Motivation.*

Summary

It has been argued that, when a job is structured in a way that makes intrinsic rewards appear to result from good performance, then the job itself can be a very effective motivator. In addition, the point was made that, if job content is to be a source of motivation, the job must allow for meaningful feedback, test the individual's valued abilities, and allow a great amount of self-control by the job holder. In order for this to happen, jobs must be enlarged on both the vertical and horizontal dimensions. Further, it was predicted that job enlargement is more likely to lead to increased product quality than to increased productivity. A review of the literature on job enlargement generally tended to confirm these predictions.

2

Mind: The Organizing Force

Introduction

While chapter 1 was concerned with man as an emotional animal, the four papers in chapter 2 deal with the reasoning side of man, with the ways he thinks, solves problems, and makes decisions. In a sense, thinking and problem solving are ways of dealing with the world hypothetically and symbolically and to some extent logically. This chapter is intended as a reminder that while much of our behavior is a product of subconscious, often impulsive forces, much of it also emerges from conscious calculation and analysis. Some key underlying ideas the reader may want to keep in mind include the following:

1. Man's capacity for thought, his intelligence, is some function (not yet fully understood) of *both* his genetic inheritance and also his physical, psychological, and social environment. This is the central point of the paper by Morton Hunt, who marshals persuasive evidence in support of his position.

2. Although we human beings often intend to behave rationally, limitations in our capacities for memory and information processing leave us only limitedly rational. We are just not good enough computers to be able to consider all alternative solutions to our problems, are unable to trace out all the consequences, even of those alternatives we do consider, and usually we are unable to specify our goals with sufficient precision to make a unique choice of the very best possible alternative. These limitations on man's cognitive capacities carry extremely important implications for decision making and policy formulation in large complex organizations. Some of these implications are traced out in the paper by Charles Lindblom. In addition, Lindblom does a nice job of comparing and contrasting the styles of decision making implied by certain suprarational models of man, on the one hand, and the models of man as a limited reasoner on the other.

3. Most of the research on thinking has dealt with the process by which people *solve* problems. But the process by which people *find* problems, that is, the process by which they decide *which* problems to work on, is a relatively neglected area of research. The paper by Pounds on "The Process of Problem Finding" represents one of the few thoughtful pieces of work in this area. Pounds proposes that people decide they have found a problem when the existing situation is out of kilter with some internally held model or some external prototype of the situation.

4. People don't all use the same "cognitive styles" or languages of thought. When we think about thinking we usually have in mind the manipulation of symbols. But a looser cognitive mode, an "iconic" mode, seems often to be used in many perceptive and creative acts of thought. Thought can occur at a raw sensory level in which problems and solutions are merely experienced in a holistic sense rather than in a tight logical sense. These ideas are discussed in the paper by Leavitt and Doktor, and are picked up again in the paper by March, "The Technology of Foolishness," in part 4.

The reader may also want to consider for himself how these four articles relate to one another. For example, if, as Leavitt and Doktor argue, human beings do indeed progress from sensory modes of thought through iconic and symbolic modes, then perhaps Hunt's argument about the effects of environment on intelligence must be altered slightly. Not only does the person become more intelligent in a one-dimensional sense, but he also develops a capacity to think in different cognitive languages. Intelligence tests typically measure mostly one's capacity to think symbolically but perhaps we need to develop better means for assessing his capacity for sensory and imagic thought as well. Or consider the complementarities between the ideas presented by Pounds and by Lindblom. Lindblom argues that much decision making is incremental, building from a base of current practice. Similarly, Pounds argues that one of the places an organization finds its problems to be solved is in its own past history. Pounds thus seems to treat the process of problem finding as incremental, too.

There are a great many other recent ideas about thinking and problem solving which could not be represented in chapter 2. One such idea has to do with cognitive balance. People seem to have a need for internal consistency among their perceptions, attitudes, and beliefs. In their desire for such cognitive balance, people seem to have a tendency to deny what is true, or actually to falsify truths in order to avoid having to live with inconsistent thought patterns. The concept of cognitive balance will turn up in chapter 3, however.

A second important idea is that people are so overwhelmed with inputs from their environment, that they must select which stimuli to attend to and which stimuli to ignore. Social psychologists refer to this as a process of selective perception. On the one hand it prevents the person from becoming overwhelmed with information; but, obviously, on the other hand it gives him an incomplete picture of his environment. The basis for selectively perceiving the world may derive from habits of thought developed early in life, or may be affected by current motivation. In any case the process of selective perception represents an important phenomenon which cannot be ignored if we are to understand the thinking side of man. These issues receive more detailed consideration, however, in the paper by Hastorf, Schneider, and Polefka in the next chapter.

The Intelligent Man's Guide to Intelligence
Morton Hunt

As if there weren't enough controversy in our time, people are now fighting about *intelligence*—not the CIA type but the kind that *Webster's Dictionary* defines as: "the faculty of understanding; the capacity to know or apprehend." What could be debatable about that? Listen:

Sir Charles Snow, the eminent British novelist and scientist —and a liberal—says in March 1969 that the astonishing disproportion of Jews among Nobel Prize winners and other outstandingly intelligent groups suggests that "there [is] something in the Jewish gene-pool which produces talent on quite a different scale from, say, the Anglo-Saxon gene-pool." For this, he draws a fierce barrage of criticism from non-Jews and Jews—many of *them* liberals—who call his suggestion "benign racism" and a "mirror image" of Nazi racist theories.

The Los Angeles City Council, following the lead of New York City and Washington, D. C., votes in early 1969 to eliminate I. Q. testing from the lower grades of public schools. The cause: pressure by militant Negroes and other disadvantaged people, who regard I. Q. testing as one of Whitey's tricks to keep them out of college and the better schools. They have some odd bedfellows: The John Birch Society has been attacking I. Q. testing for years, on the ground that it is an effort by Big Government to control the minds of Americans.

Psychologist Arthur Jensen, of the University of California at Berkeley, publishes a long, dense, scholarly paper in the *Harvard Educational Review,* using statistical methods to show that heredity is far more responsible than environment for differences in tested intelligence and suggesting that this may account for most of the fifteen-point difference between average white and Negro I. Q. scores. Dozens of newspapers and magazines find this article "inflammatory" and "incendiary." In the staid, academic pages of the *Harvard Educational Review,* various scholars and educators term his article "mischievous" and "unforgivable" and label him a "high priest of racism." At Berkeley, his office is picketed by the SDS, black students try to disrupt his classes and his safety is threatened via mail and phone.

In October 1969 physicist William Shockley, of Stanford University, arises to deliver an address to a National Academy of Sciences meeting held at Dartmouth College. Shockley, a Nobel Prize winner as coinventor of the transistor, wants the academy to support research on the inheritance of intelligence. As soon as he is introduced, some forty Negro students begin clapping loudly—and keep it up for ninety minutes, until Shockley and the administrative staff call the meeting off.

A militant social-reform group named American Psychologists for Social Action circulates an anti-Jensen, anti-I. Q.-testing petition. One of the more vocal members of the organization, Dr. Martin Deutsch, of New York University, tells me: "There's no scientific definition of intelligence at this time. It's a convenient label for certain kinds of behavior; but I suspect that, in actual fact, the thing itself doesn't really exist."

Intelligence doesn't exist? What's he talking about? Don't we all *know* it exists? Even when we were children, we could tell which kids around us were smart and which were dumb. As adults, we have a fair idea, after a few minutes of conversation, whether a new acquaintance is bright or stupid and, after spending some time with any person, we *know* which he is. But our everyday experiences of intelligence do not tell us exactly what it is; they do not even prove its existence.

However, we have more than everyday experiences to go by; indeed, in the past sixty-six years, no subject in all of psychology has been so extensively researched and put to practical use as has intelligence. Each year, millions of I. Q. tests are given to school children, college students, draftees, and job applicants. Articles, monographs, and books on new research in intelligence appear at the rate of one a day. Current research concerns a wide variety of topics: the development of many new kinds of tests; the relationship of intelligence scores to social class, to ethnic origins, to the time and place of testing, and even to the sex of the tester; the chemistry of the brain; problem-solving ability in pigeons, rats, cats, dogs, WASPs, and Negroes; and such arcana as the representation of the structure of intellect by a three-dimensional matrix. Dr. Deutsch must be wrong; some of these people must know *something* about the subject.

And they do; the trouble is that they disagree about the meaning of most of what they know. Incompatible theories of intelligence exist in embarrassing profusion. The oldest was formulated half a century ago by English psychologist Charles Spearman, who noted that many mental abilities are statistically correlated: a person who does well in vocabulary is likely to do well in arithmetic, pencil-and-paper mazes, and so on; a person who does poorly in one of them is likely to do poorly in the others. To Spearman, this clearly suggested that an unseen general intelligence, or *g,* lay behind the various specific abilities, or *s's*, and made all the scores go one way or the other. But what was *g* itself? Spearman could only suggest that it was the ability to perceive relationships or connections between things.

Most psychologists accepted *g* as a reality; a number of them, in fact, set about improving upon, and complicating, Spearman's basic theory. Louis Thurstone, of the University of Chicago, an authority on intelligence, and others found "group factors" common to bunches of *s's*—higher than *s's*, but still subordinate to *g*. Raymond Cattell, now with the University of Illinois, and various others found not one but two kinds of *g;* one provides the brain power for routine learned abilities such as vocabulary, another provides the brain power for less teachable and more complex abilities such as abstract reasoning. Some psychologists eventually decided that *g* doesn't really explain anything and that the theory might as well be junked. J. P. Guilford and his students at the University of Southern California identified many highly specialized mental abilities—more than eighty, at last count—and organized them into a kind of three-dimensional structure, in which all are of equal merit and there is no overriding unseen "pure" intelligence. The brilliant Swiss psychologist Jean Piaget has, meanwhile, ignored practically the entire business of *g, s,* I. Q., and testing; instead, he has studied intelligence as a living, growing thing and described its functions in the various stages of the mind's development.

Those are some of the theories at the present time. Each answers some questions, raises others, ignores yet others. But not all is chaos. There are two distinct sides in the intelligence war and, on nearly every debated issue, psychologists are in one camp or the other. The two are those old classic opposites, nature versus nurture, heredity versus environment, instinct versus experience—the very same polarization of views that exists in the field of animal-behavior studies, between the instinct-oriented ethologists and the developmentalists. (See "Man and Beast," *Playboy,* July 1970.)

Hereditarians think that intelligence is essentially based on the individual's brain structure and chemistry, and hence is largely predetermined by his genetic make-up. Environmentalists think intelligence consists primarily of acquired or learned abilities to understand, to think and to solve problems; they consider it largely determined by experience.

Many adherents of one side or the other, however, are repelled by the company they find themselves in: hereditarians by racists who maintain that the Negro is an inferior species of human being; environmentalists' by those liberals who refuse even to consider genetic knowledge. As a result, psychologists often equivocate. One distinguished member of this discipline, who publicly is a convinced environmentalist, privately told me, "Arthur Jensen has done us a real service —we needed to pin down the genetic contribution." But Jensen himself, having argued at great length in print that racial I. Q. differences are largely inherited, states that he has never labeled Negro intelligence "inferior."

Some hard facts do, nevertheless, exist and are generally accepted. They are nearly all derived from I. Q. testing; for despite its limitations, it is still the only means we have of measuring intelligence. To date, no one has observed the actual phenomenon of thought taking place in the brain, nor seen any record of its having occurred. Physiologists know a fair amount about the brain—that it weighs about three pounds in the adult; that thought takes place in the cortex, a paint-thin outer layer of gray matter consisting of some 12 billion nerve cells, or neurons; that each neuron is almost, but not completely, connected to many other neurons at contact points called synapses; and that remembering, learning, and problem solving involve the transmission of electrical impulses through the cells. At present, it is thought that the cell, when excited, produces a chemical, acetylcholine, that permits the electrical impulse to pass across the gap at the synapse to the next cell, exciting it, in turn; the moment the message has passed, however, another chemical, cholinesterase, destroys the acetylcholine and ends the transmission —all this within 4/10,000ths of a second.

A group of researchers at the University of California at Berkeley have been rearing bright rats and stupid rats, chop-

ping off their heads and chemically analyzing their brains—
and finding different ratios of acetylcholine to cholinesterase
in the brains of the two strains. It may be that one ratio
makes for faster transmission than the other: that is, faster
thinking. But this still leaves many questions unanswered.
Where and how is information stored and how is it drawn
upon in the thinking process? Why are some men superb
thinkers in some areas, such as music and mathematics, but
not in others? Why have we never found any indication,
under the microscope, of the "memory trace"—the record of
permanent change due to learning or experience? Why is
there no perceptible difference between the neurons of a genius and those of an idiot, those of the learned man and of
the ignoramus, those of the dominant (operative) half of the
brain and of the subordinate (unused) half?

But if we cannot yet observe intelligence directly, at least
we can observe its effects in the form of intelligent behavior.
This is why testing has been the principal source of information on the subject. It began sixty-six years ago, when the
Ministry of Public Instruction in Paris commissioned psychologist Alfred Binet to design a test that would identify in
advance the children who lacked the capacity to follow the
regular curriculum and who should, therefore, be put in
special schools. Binet's test consisted of numerous tasks and
questions that graded those perceptual, verbal, arithmetical,
and reasoning abilities necessary for success in school; yet, it
seemed obvious to him, and to most other psychologists, that
he was measuring not only achievement but overall intelligence.

Known in its various American revisions as the Stanford-
Binet, it is still the most widely used individual intelligence
test, although there are at least forty others in print, including the well-known Wechsler-Bellevue test. All of them,
however, are unsuited to large-scale use because they have
to be given to one person at a time. Group tests, therefore, in
which the subjects read questions to themselves and check off
multiple-choice answers, have become a big business; there
are close to two hundred of them in print, with the Otis-
Lennon Mental Ability Test (used in many schools) and the
Armed Forces Qualification Test the best-known.

Originally, Binet scored each tested child as to his mental
age, depending on how far the child got in the test compared
with other children. But since a bright child might have a
mental age of ten when he was only eight—and a dull one a
mental age of ten when he was chronologically twelve—the
important figure was the *ratio* between mental age and chron-

ological age; this ratio was his intelligence quotient, or I. Q.
For the bright eight-year-old, it would be $\frac{10}{8}$ (x 100 to get rid
of decimals), or 125; for the dull twelve-year-old, it would be
$\frac{10}{12}$ x 100, or about 83.

The tasks in all I. Q. tests are arranged in the order of
their increasing difficulty. In the Stanford-Binet, for instance,
three-year-olds are asked to do simple things such as building
a bridge with three blocks or copying a circle. The four-year-
old begins to get simple verbal and reasoning problems, such
as "Why do we have cars?" or "Father is a man, mother is a
——." The ten-year-old, in the Otis-Lennon test, has to do
much more advanced reasoning, involving questions such as
this:

> The opposite of *easy* is:
> hard slow tiresome simple short

or this:

> Which number should come next in this series?
>   2   3   5   6   8   9   ?

or this:

Reproduced from Otis-Lennon Mental Ability Test. Copyright ©
1967 by Harcourt Brace Jovanovich, Inc. Reproduced by permission.

Questions for teenagers and adults are, naturally, even
harder and call upon anywhere from seven different mental
abilities to scores of them. In The Psychological Corporation's Multi-Aptitude Test, which is much like other tests of
general intelligence, there are, for instance, items testing
verbal ability, such as:

> What word *means most nearly the same as* IMBUE:
> distort refute abstain inoculate allege

Others deal with quantitative (arithmetic) reasoning, such as:

> Find the rule according to which this number series is
> formed, and write the next *two* numbers of the series:
>   5 − 7 10 − 14 19 − 25 —— ——

Still others deal with abstract reasoning, such as:
These four figures are alike in some way:

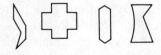

Which one of these five goes with the previous four?

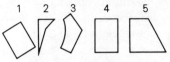

1   2   3   4   5

("Inoculate" comes closest in meaning to imbue; the rule for the number series is—the difference gets larger by one each time, but also the sign changes every other time, hence the last two numbers are 32 and −40; figure 3 is the only one that goes with the set of four because it alone has more than four angles.)

Using various I. Q. tests, psychologists have learned that intelligence is "normally" distributed in the general population—that is, the great majority of people have I. Q.s of 100, give or take a few points. More than two-thirds have I. Q.s between 85 and 115; less than 3 percent score under 70 and less than 3 percent score 130 or above. The former are the mentally retarded; the latter are the gifted.

Such statistics are helpful as guides to planning the size of the school system, institutions for the mentally retarded, manpower needs, and the like. More important, they enable us to ask what makes for intelligence; for when we find out what kinds of people are at the upper end and at the lower end of the I. Q. curve, we may begin looking for cause-and-effect relationships. For instance, most of the people at the high end are in the higher socioeconomic strata of society and most of those at the low end are in lower and impoverished ones. Hereditarians, by and large, think that intelligent persons make their way to the upper levels, unintelligent ones remain behind or sink in the scale. Environmentalists feel that children of poverty—and especially of minority groups —never have a chance to develop their intelligence and that, moreover, I. Q. tests are built on middle-class values and do not give a fair picture of the talents of the poor.

Equally indisputable are facts about the average I. Q. of various ethnic groups—and equally moot are the explanations offered. Scots in the British Isles and Jews in America have higher average I. Q.s than the populations around them (Jews, for instance, run five to eight I. Q. points above the average of non-Jews in their same social and economic positions). Americans of northern-European origin average somewhat higher than those of southern-European origin. Oriental children, in some West Coast school surveys, come out consistently higher than white children. Why? Innate superiority? Social factors making for greater striving? The particular cultural tradition or kind of family life in which the child is reared? Every possible view has some adherents and some supporting data.

I. Q. is, as might be expected, as good a predictor of success in life as it is in school. The distinguished psychologist Lewis Terman followed a number of highly gifted children through decades of their lives; as a group, they turned out to be uncommonly successful in terms of career, social position, creative output, health, marriage, and similar criteria. More generally, people with high I. Q.s tend to have careers of high social status and, indeed, careers that tend to require high I. Q.s: Ph.D.s have a median I. Q. close to 140; accountants, 128; lawyers, 127; salesmen and managers of retail stores, 116; auto mechanics, 102; farmers, 94; and teamsters, 89. (These are only averages; some farmers have scored as high as 147, some accountants as low as 94.)

The field of intelligence studies is full of curiosa of this sort. Here is a sampling:

Despite all the clichés concerning the mental dullness of the criminal population, it seems to have about the same intelligence as the population at large.

Males are consistently more intelligent than females, but only by a negligible amount—and only beyond the onset of adolescence; in childhood, girls score slightly higher than boys. In adulthood, though women score a little lower overall, they definitely surpass men in vocabulary and verbal fluency as well as straight memory; men are superior in arithmetical reasoning, mechanical aptitude, and spatial relationships.

Leadership among children, and probably among adults, is correlated with high I. Q., but only up to a point. When a person is thirty or more points brighter than most of the people in his group, he does not become a leader; it's anybody's guess why not. (There have been notable exceptions, however; Jefferson was evidently a highly intelligent man, and so were Churchill and Woodrow Wilson, among others.)

Of all the measured similarities between man and wife, such as economic background, education, and the like, the highest correlation is that of intelligence; spouses are even more alike in intelligence than brothers and sisters. Love evidently can't grow or survive where one lover is painfully dumb, or the other objectionably smart.

The first-born child in a family is likely to be brighter than the last-born child by a little over three points. The difference could be due to the better intra-uterine or other bio-logical advantages of being first in line; it might, however, be due to the greater attention and training first-borns get from their parents.

Not all children of high-I. Q. parents are bright and not all children of low-I. Q. parents are dumb; in fact, on the average, children are part way between their parents' level and the average of the whole population.

Creativity is not an automatic accompaniment of high I. Q.; in fact, some creative people have modest I. Q.s. A high I. Q. *is* essential for creativity in nuclear physics, mathematics, and architecture; but numerous studies have shown that among painters, sculptors, and designers, the correlation between creativity and intelligence is, oddly enough, zero or even slightly negative. (This does not mean that highly creative artists are stupid; rather, they are all fairly intelligent, but among them the *more* creative are not necessarily the *more* intelligent.)

Twins average four to seven I. Q. points lower than singly born children. The psychological explanation: They get less individual attention from their parents. The biological explanation: They had less room in the womb, hence got a poorer start.

Children born of incestuous matings between brothers and sisters, or parents and their own children, have, on the average, considerably depressed I. Q.s, plus an inordinate number of physical ailments. The genetic explanation: inbreeding increases the chance of inheriting the same recessive hidden defects from both parents, in which case they become dominant. The environmental explanation: incestuous connections are most common among people of extremely poor social position and defective home life, both of which cripple the offspring. Perhaps both genetics and environment play a part. But in Japan, where cousin marriages are perfectly acceptable and occur in all classes, the children of such marriages average eight I. Q. points below children of comparable noncousin marriages. Here, at least, there is no choice of alternative explanations—only the genetic makes sense.

Such is the more-or-less solid ground in intelligence; all the rest is a slough of conflicting data and contradictory hypotheses. Environmentalists hold that intelligence tests do not measure "innate" intelligence, because there is no such thing. Dr. Alexander Wesman, director of the Test Division of The Psychological Corporation, maintains, "Intelligence is the summation of the learning experiences of the individual;

that's what the tests measure and that's all they measure. It is possible that some people do have a greater neurological potential for learning than others, but I haven't yet seen it proved or disproved—least of all by the existing intelligence tests." Others are completely skeptical. Says Dr. Jack Victor of the Institute for Developmental Studies at New York University: "Intelligence tests measure a variety of subskills, but whether these, taken together, really equal intelligence is highly debatable. The subskills are real, but intelligence may be a fictitious concept, a convenient label with which to refer to a number of disparate traits."

Hereditarians, however, insist that the tests do measure something innate and very real—an over-all potential capacity to learn, to recall, to discriminate, to think, and to solve problems—and that this capacity deserves the name of intelligence. They admit that in most I. Q. tests, it is expressed through learned materials; but they insist that the "neurological substrate"—the individual's nervous structure and biochemistry—largely determines the ease with which he learns them and the effectiveness with which he uses them.

Variations in the neurological substrate are obvious enough, if one compares different species of animal. The brain of the worm is almost nonexistent, while that of the rat is well developed; the worm can learn only the simplest mazes; the rat, highly complex ones. But even within any given species, there are inherited differences in skeletal and body type, in excitability, in blood type, in hair color and the shape of the features, in the sensitivity to various pathogens; how could there not also be differences in the innate responsiveness and educability of the brain? Thus far, they have not been anatomically identified, but their presence is felt by every animal trainer and every teacher: puppies of a given breed, children from very similar backgrounds, do not learn with equal ease or apply their training with equal success. In cloud chambers, physicists study unseen particles by means of the trails of droplets that condense along the paths they take; in I. Q. testing, psychologists study unseen innate intelligence by means of its effects on verbal, arithmetical, and logical performance.

Some hereditarians go further; they argue that it *is* possible to measure "pure" or innate intelligence directly by omitting verbal and other culturally loaded materials and building tests around designs and shapes so familiar to persons of all classes and all cultures that learning is of no consequence. One such "culture-fair" test was constructed by

Dr. Cattell (he of the two-*g* theory); it uses problems such as these:

Which one of these is different from the other four?

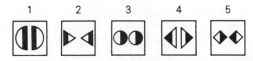

Which of the figures on the right goes in the missing square on the left?

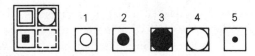

(Number 3 is different from the other four. Figure 2 goes into the missing square.)

Dr. Cattell says that in countries as different as the U. S., India and Taiwan, his test has yielded quite comparable results, indicating that it is unaffected by culture and is, indeed, measuring innate intelligence.

The environmentalists maintain that such tests, even if they are really culture-fair, measure only very special abilities rather than the broad sweep of intelligence. Says J. P. Guilford (he of the three-dimensional matrix of eighty or more mental abilities), "In ruling out verbal tests, probably the most important aspects of intelligence have been lost." The Psychological Corporation used to publish Dr. Cattell's test, but gave it up, and Dr. Wesman explains: "We came to the conclusion that although such a test may use learnings common to different cultures and subcultures, it ignores the relevance of those learnings to survival and success. That being the case, it can hardly provide an adequate measure of intelligence."

But even if the standard I. Q. tests are the best measures of intelligence now available, and even if they do measure something genuine, those measurements are very frequently distorted by variables in the testing process. Taking a test, for instance, is more productive of anxiety for some people than for others, and anxiety decreases problem-solving ability, When Negro children from impoverished homes take an I. Q. test under the supervision of a neatly dressed white examiner, they are very likely to feel strange, awkward, and uneasy—and consequently do not do as well as they might. Recently, psychologist Irwin Katz, of the Graduate Center at

New York University, deceived black students taking an I. Q. test into thinking they were being tested merely in eye-hand coordination. Freed of anxiety, they registered significantly higher I. Q.s—and did better when the test giver was white than when he was black. Katz's explanation: Well aware of the low opinion most whites have of black intellectual ability, the black's motivation to do well on the I.Q. test was low. But when the test was disguised as something else, the desire to do well took over and scores improved. And the challenge to do well in the eyes of the white examiner was greater than for one of their own.

The Katz study is backed up by the findings of British psychologist Peter Watson, who tested black West Indian students in a London working-class neighborhood. When the test was identified as an I. Q. test, scores dropped by ten points. Watson is convinced that the variation can account for the average fifteen points by which blacks fall behind whites in I. Q. tests—the basis for the claim that whites are, genetically speaking, superior intellectually to blacks. Interestingly enough, both Watson and Katz admit that heredity no doubt contributes to intelligence—but that the science of genetics is not advanced enough to state precisely how much. (Incidentally, even Arthur Jensen has reported that Negro children, when they feel at ease with the examiner, will score eight to ten points higher on an I. Q. test.)

Most important in the Negro subculture, when it comes to the matter of I. Q. testing, is the fact that grammar and vocabulary in common use are markedly different from those in white middle-class society. Moreover, Negro mothers in the more disadvantaged levels of society are not explainers, as are white middle-class mothers. Negro children may, in consequence, simply be unacquainted with the words, the grammatical usages, and many of the elemental concepts (such as categorization) that are needed to think about the questions asked. A social worker in Watts satirically constructed the "Chitling Test"—a mock I. Q. test using only words and problems familiar to the Negro poor—and few middle-class whites who saw it could answer most of the questions correctly. So, too, a French-Canadian guide might score moronic on verbal ability and abstract reasoning, yet completely outclass his examiner at out-thinking wild animals or surviving in a midwinter storm.

For these and similar reasons, many of the findings of researchers on intelligence are contradicted by the findings of others. It is not just a matter of varying interpretations of the data; it is a matter of two or more studies of the same subject yielding different and even opposite findings.

Take the matter of intelligence and age. Various early studies indicated that it declines steadily from early adulthood onward. In the thirties, for instance, researchers tested almost everybody in one New England town and found that the older the adults were, the lower they scored on reasoning ability. But whenever particular persons are tested and retested over a period of years, they show no such decline before the onset of senility; indeed, in one study a number of people were retested in middle age with an intelligence test they had taken thirty years earlier in college and got *better* scores in everything except arithmetic.

Just as bewildering is the case of our rapidly growing national intelligence. During World War II, a large group of average soldiers took a test much like one given soldiers in World War I; if the 1917 standards for computing I. Q. had been used on their raw scores, they would have come out an average of fifteen points higher than the World War I soldiers. The rise has continued: since the end of World War II, raw scores have gone up half as much again. What are we to think? Are the bright outbreeding the dull? Are we better informed because of improvements in education? Or have we merely become test-sophisticated; that is, skilled at getting better scores—but not any more intelligent than we were?

Assuming higher I. Q. scores would mean more than mere test-taking skill, the big question is: Can intensive education significantly increase the I. Q. in low-scoring children? Project Head Start, the nationwide Federally funded program of nursery-school experience for poor children, did not appreciably raise the school performance of the children involved—the I. Q. gains of five to ten points frequently reported for Head Start children did not hold up after the first year of regular school. But other efforts at compensatory education have used other techniques, and with more success: Colleagues of Dr. Deutsch at the Institute for Developmental Studies at New York University claim that their intensive-education experiments with small groups of New York City Negro children have resulted in average I. Q. gains of nearly eight points in a year of three-hours-per-day schooling. Whether these gains will endure is not yet known; to judge by some similar experiments, once the children return to ordinary classrooms, the discouraging milieu of Negro slum life may make them lose interest in schooling and cause them to drop back.

Such preschool compensatory programs are designed to bring the underprivileged up to par with the rest of American society, but could early education also benefit those who already have normal advantages? Some experts think so and certain experiments in which preschool children have been taught to read and to use typewriters lend credence to their arguments.

But equally eminent psychologists, including Jean Piaget and the late Arnold Gesell, have been convinced that children cannot grasp certain problems until their neural organization is ready—and that the maturation of the neural system cannot be accelerated. In a typical Piaget test, when children under seven see water poured from a short, wide glass into a tall, thin one, they think it has become "more." Even though they can be persuaded to *say* that it is the same, they cannot be taught to *feel* that it is the same. Beyond the age of seven, however, they become educable on the matter. Similarly, though it takes a good deal of effort, children can be taught to read a year or two before first grade; but those who are not taught until several years later catch on so rapidly and easily that they soon are abreast of the early learners, and often have a more positive and joyous feeling about reading.

These are only facets of the unanswered central question: Is the individual's intelligence primarily a product of his perceptions, experiences, and the influence of other persons upon him, or is his intelligence primarily determined by his genotype, the unique mixture of genes he has inherited from his father and mother?

Time and research have amassed impressive evidence on both sides. A very few examples will give some idea how thoroughly convincing each argument is, and how hopelessly contradictory they appear to be.

First, evidence for the supermacy of environment:

In Israel, children of European-Jewish origin have an average I. Q. of 105, while those of Oriental-Jewish origin (Yemenities and other Mideastern Jews) have an average I. Q. of only 85, or borderline normal. But when both groups of children are brought up in a kibbutz, where they spend most of their time in communal nurseries run by dedicated nurses, both groups—according to informal reports by some observers—end up with an average I. Q. of 115.

Some thirty years ago in Iowa, a small group of mentally retarded year-old orphans was experimentally placed in a hospital ward for feeble-minded women. In an orphanage, the children had had a minimum of individual attention; in the hospital, they were "adopted" by the feeble-minded women, who fed and bathed them, played with them, and talked to them. In less than two years, their average I. Q. leaped from 64 to 94 and all had become good prospects for adoption. By the age of six, all were in adoptive homes, where they made small additional gains averaging two I. Q. points. Many years later, a follow-up found that they were almost all living normal married lives and that their own children had an average I. Q. of 105.

Gypsy and canal-boat children in England, and Appalachian and Negro children in the U. S., have normal or near-normal I. Q.s when very young but drift downward thereafter. All four groups get a normal amount of stimulation at the infant level, but in childhood and the teens suffer "stimulus deprivation," because of their impoverished homes, their barren cultural surroundings, and their poor school experiences. A number of studies show marked I. Q. losses for these various groups, averaging twenty to thirty points between their preschool years and their late teens.

To the environmentalists scores of such studies seem proof positive that I. Q. is not genetically fixed and does not follow an inevitable course of development as do such traits as skin color and blood type.

Now, evidence for the supremacy of the genotype:

First, recall what we learned earlier about the offspring of cousin marriages: Their average I. Q. is eight points lower than that of other children in their own socioeconomic class. The phenomenon has no explanation other than the matching up of recessive genetic defects inherited from both sides.

Even when socioeconomic factors are reversed, Negro children do not surpass or even equal whites: Negro children born of parents in the *highest* of four socioeconomic groupings (the professional-managerial) average nearly four I. Q. points below white children born of parents in the *lowest* of the four groupings (unskilled labor). The over-all socioeconomic status of American Indian children is as poor (and perhaps poorer) as that of Negro children, yet the Indian children average seven or eight I. Q. points higher.

Unrelated children reared in the same home ought to have very similar I. Q.s if environment were the dominant factor in intellectual development. But their I. Q.s show a correlation only half as large as that between real siblings *reared in different homes*. Similarly, the I. Q.s of foster children correlate more closely with those of their biological parents than with those of their foster parents.

Identical twins have exactly the same complement of

genes; when they are reared together, therefore, both their genotypes and their environments are substantially identical. Nor surprisingly, the correlation between their I. Q.s is very high: Various studies report it close to the 90 percent mark. In a few score of known cases, however, identical twins have been separated soon after birth and adopted into different homes; if environment were the major factor in determining their I. Q.s, the correlation should drop almost to zero but, in fact, it remains very high. Even in different environments, identical twins grow up far more alike in I. Q. than ordinary twins reared in the same home.

Scores of such studies seem proof positive to hereditarians that biological endowment is a far more significant determinant of the intelligence of the individual than is environmental influence. They will admit, if pressed, that environment does affect mental development for good or ill in measurable ways, but having said so, they do their best to minimize its role, arguing that it accounts for 20 percent or less of the variance in I. Q. scores.

It seems obvious that one point of view must be correct, the other incorrect; but what seems obvious is not necessarily true. Most human phenomena are neither wholly good nor wholly bad, nor is a single doctrinaire explanation usually wholly true or wholly false. The truth lies not just in the middle but in a synthesis of the two sides. And so it is in the matter of intelligence. A unifying synthesis does exist.

It begins, as the noted psychologist I. I. Gottesman, of the University of Minnesota, points out, with the recognition that intelligence is not a lump sum, to which heredity contributes so many I. Q. points and environment the rest. The genotype and the environment do not *add up,* they *interact*—and the result is not a sum but a product.

But if we cannot separate the two interacting factors, at least we can ask how much difference it makes to modify one while keeping the other constant. We can ask, "Given any one genotype, how much can we modify the I. Q. by changing the environment?" And we can ask, "Given any one environment, how great are the variations heredity yields within it?"

As yet, there are no relevant research data that settle these questions for human I. Q.—but answers do exist for animals. Groups of genetically bright and gentically dull rats were reared in "restricted," "natural," and "enriched" environments, and then tested on maze-solving ability; various breeds of dogs were reared both indulgently and strictly, and then tested for their ability to obey a difficult command (not to eat). In both cases, the relative contributions of heredity and of environment varied for each combination of breed and rearing. For some breeds, changing the environment made little difference, while for others, it made a lot; and, conversely, within some environments, differences in heredity didn't amount to much, while within others, differences in heredity assumed considerable proportions.

Professor Gottesman believes that these results will prove to apply to human I. Q. and will make sense of what seem to be major contradictions in existing data. He offers the following diagram (from *Handbook of Mental Deficiency,* edited by N. Ellis) by way of illustrating the varying interactions (all of them speculative at this point) among a series of different environments and four hypothetical genotypes.

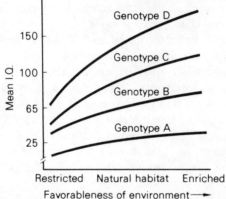

For genotype A, which might represent Mongolism, the "reaction range" is very narrow; that is, its various interactions with environments ranging from the worst to the best are all much alike, with a difference of only 50 percent or so between lowered and highest. For genotype D, which might represent hereditary genius, the reaction range is very broad; that is, its interactions with environments ranging from the worst to the best are very dissimilar, with a difference of some 300 percent between lowest and highest. Genotypes B and C are more nearly average and cover intermediate ranges.

Thus, it is clear that there is not one answer, not two answers, but a number of answers to the nature-nurture problem. It is clear, too, that both sides of the old argument have been right, and wrong, at the same time. For it is true that intelligence is the sum total of what has been learned—if we add: *learned by a given mind, which can utilize its experiences only within its own biological limits.* And it is also true that intelligence is a trait carried by the individual's genotype —if we add: *as it develops in the environment available to it.*

Applying this approach to the subject, we can make sense of many of the seeming contradictions in the existing findings. The contradictory results, for instance, of the intensive schooling of low-scoring children is not surprising: We have many genotypes being tested in many varied environments—and without anything like scientific control of either. Jewish children of two different backgrounds and I. Q. levels wind up, in a kibbutz, rising to the same higher level of I. Q.—but perhaps their genotypes were not really as dissimilar as one might suppose from their external traits. Negro and white children in the same schools, and even in the same socioeconomic class, remain widely separated, the Negro children being distinctly lower in I. Q.—but perhaps their environments were not really as similar as one might imagine. Negro and white children, even in the same schools and in the same socioeconomic class, do not actually have the same environment if, by environment, we mean the totality of the individual's experiences. Growing up black in a white society *feels* so different from growing up white in that society, even when class and income are equal, that we cannot fairly ascribe the remaining 10- or 11- point difference in I. Q. to heredity.

If Negroes were ever to experience thoroughgoing equality —social, economic, and emotional—the average Negro I. Q. would very likely rise: perhaps only a little, still remaining distinctly below that of the white; perhaps enough for the two to coincide; perhaps enough to outstrip the white. We can't predict the outcome at this point, for blacks in America have never achieved genuine equality. Until they do, both those who say it will make no appreciable difference and those who are positive that all races have equal mental gifts are being demagogic in proclaiming as scientific fact ideologies that may be based on political sentiment.

What is tragic is that they are both serving vicious ends while pursuing noble ones. Jensen and the behavioral geneticists are carrying on legitimate and potentially very important research, but some of them—Jensen, in particular—have unscientifically extended their tentative and speculative findings into firm and fixed policy recommendations. Jensen, for instance, in urging special schooling for many

Negroes on the basis of their supposedly irremediable inferiority, is going far beyond anything his own work justifies. Deutsch and other environmentalists, on the other hand, are also doing important research, but most of them are so powerfully moved by their own egalitarian feelings and their desire to help the underprivileged that they have tried to block the publiciation of pro-Jensenist papers and condemned all further research on the genetics of intelligence on the ground that whatever information it yielded would be "irrelevant" and "inflammatory."

Yet scientific inquiry and democratic progress are not, or at least need not be, antithetical. If the synthesis that resolves the nature-nurture controversy could be heard over the din of ideological battle, it might bring the two into harmonious alliance. Men did not learn to fly by ignoring gravity or denying that it existed but by learning the laws of aerodynamics and overcoming gravity. Men will make the most of their intelligence neither by denying the role of genetics nor by denigrating the importance of environment but by learning all they can about both and about the interaction of the two—and then applying the knowledge so as to give every man in society the maximum opportunity to develop his own potential.

The Science of
"Muddling Through"
Charles E. Lindblom

Suppose an administrator is given responsibility for formulating policy with respect to inflation. He might start by trying to list all related values in order of importance, e. g., full employment, reasonable business profit, protection of small savings, prevention of a stock market crash. Then all possible policy outcomes could be rated as more or less efficient in attaining a maximum of these values. This would of course require a prodigious inquiry into values held by members of society and an equally prodigious set of calculations on how much of each value is equal to how much of each other value. He could then proceed to outline all possible policy alternatives. In a third step, he would undertake systematic comparison of his multitude of alternatives to determine which attains the greatest amount of values.

In comparing policies, he would take advantage of any theory available that generalized about classes of policies. In considering inflation, for example, he would compare all policies in the light of the theory of prices. Since no alternatives are beyond his investigation, he would consider strict central control and the abolition of all prices and markets on the one hand and elimination of all public controls with reliance completely on the free market on the other, both in the light of whatever theoretical generalizations he could find on such hypothetical economies. Finally, he would try to make the choice that would in fact maximize his values.

An alternative line of attack would be to set as his principal objective, either explicitly or without conscious thought, the relatively simple goal of keeping prices level. This objective might be compromised or complicated by only a few other goals, such as full employment. He would in fact disregard most other social values as beyond his present in-

Reprinted from the *Public Administration Review* 19, no. 2 (1959): 78–88, by permission of the author and the American Society for Public Administration.

terest, and he would for the moment not even attempt to rank the few values that he regarded as immediately relevant. Were he pressed, he would quickly admit that he was ignoring many related values and many possible important consequences of his policies.

As a second step, he would outline those relatively few policy alternatives that occurred to him. He would then compare them. In comparing his limited number of alternatives, most of them familiar from past controversies, he would not ordinarily find a body of theory precise enough to carry him through a comparison of their respective consequences. Instead he would rely heavily on the record of past experience with small policy steps to predict the consequences of similar steps extended into the future.

Moreover, he would find that the policy alternatives combined objectives or values in different ways. For example, one policy might offer price level stability at the cost of some risk of unemployment; another might offer less price stability but also less risk of unemployment. Hence, the next step in his approach—the final selection—would combine into one the choice among values and the choice among instruments for reaching values. It would not, as in the first method of policy making, approximate a more mechanical process of choosing the means that best satisfied goals that were previously clarified and ranked. Because practitioners of the second approach expect to achieve their goals only partially, they would expect to repeat endlessly the sequence just described, as conditions and aspirations changed and as accuracy of prediction improved.

By Root or by Branch

For complex problems, the first of these two approaches is of course impossible. Although such an approach can be described, it cannot be practiced except for relatively simple problems and even then only in a somewhat modified form. It assumes intellectual capacities and sources of information that men simply do not possess, and it is even more absurd as an approach to policy when the time and money that can be allocated to a policy problem is limited, as is always the case. Of particular importance to public administrators is the fact that public agencies are in effect usually instructed not to practice the first method. That is to say, their prescribed functions and constraints—the politically or legally possible —restrict their attention to relatively few values and relatively few alternative policies among the countless alternatives that might be imagined. It is the second method that is practiced.

Curiously, however, the literatures of decision making, policy formulation, planning, and public administration formalize the first approach rather than the second, leaving public administrators who handle complex decisions in the position of practicing what few preach. For emphasis I run some risk of overstatement. True enough, the literature is well aware of limits on man's capacities and of the inevitability that policies will be approached in some such style as the second. But attempts to formalize rational policy formulation—to lay out explicitly the necessary steps in the process—usually describe the first approach and not the second.[1]

The common tendency to describe policy formulation even for complex problems as though it followed the first approach has been strengthened by the attention given to, and successes enjoyed by, operations research, statistical decision theory, and systems analysis. The hallmarks of these procedures, typical of the first approach, are clarity of objective, explicitness of evaluation, a high degree of comprehensiveness of overview, and, wherever possible, quantification of values for mathematical analysis. But these advanced procedures remain largely the appropriate techniques of relatively small-scale problem solving where the total number of variables to be considered is small and value problems restricted. Charles Hitch, head of the Economics Division of RAND Corporation, one of the leading centers for application of these techniques, has written:

> I would make the empirical generalization from my experience at RAND and elsewhere that operations research is the art of sub-optimizing, i.e., of solving some lower-level problems, and that difficulties increase and our special competence diminishes by an order of magnitude with every level of decision making we attempt to ascend. The sort of simple explicit model which operations researchers are so proficient in using can certainly reflect most of the significant factors influencing traffic control on the George Washington Bridge, but the proportion of the relevant reality which

1. James G. March and Herbert A. Simon similarly characterize the literature. They also take some important steps, as have Simon's other recent articles to describe a less heroic model of policy making. See *Organizations* (New York: John Wiley & Sons, 1958), p. 137.

we can represent by any such model or models in studying, say, a major foreign-policy decision, appears to be almost trivial.[2]

Accordingly, I propose in this paper to clarify and formalize the second method, much neglected in the literature. This might be described as the method of *successive limited comparisons*. I will contrast it with the first approach, which might be called the rational-comprehensive method.[3] More impressionistically and briefly—and therefore generally used in this article—they could be characterized as the "branch method" and "root method," the former continually building out from the current situation, step-by-step and by small degrees; the latter starting from fundamentals anew each time, building on the past only as experience is embodied in a theory, and always prepared to start completely from the ground up.

Let us put the characteristics of the two methods side by side in simplest terms.

Rational-Comprehensive (*Root*)	*Successive Limited Comparisons* (*Branch*)
1*a*. Clarification of values or objectives distinct from and usually prerequisite to empirical analysis of alternative policies.	1*b*. Selection of value goals and empirical analysis of the needed action are not distinct from one another but are closely intertwined.
2*a*. Policy-formulation is therefore approached through means-end analysis: First the ends are isolated, then the means to achieve them are sought.	2*b*. Since means and ends are not distinct, means-end analysis is often inappropriate or limited.
3*a*. The test of a "good" policy is that it can be shown to	3*b*. The test of a "good" policy is typically that various

2. "Operations Research and National Planning—a Dissent," *Operations Research* 5 (October 1957): 718. Hitch's dissent is from particular points made in the article to which his paper is a reply; his claim that operations research is for low-level problems is widely accepted.

For examples of the kind of problems to which operations research is applied see C. W. Churchman, R. L. Ackoff, and E. L. Arnoff, *Introduction to Operations Research* (New York: John Wiley & Sons, 1957); and J. F. McCloskey and J. M. Coppinger, eds., *Operations Research for Management*, vol. 2 (Baltimore: Johns Hopkins Press, 1956).

3. I am assuming that administrators often make policy and advise in the making of policy and am treating decision making and policy making as synonymous for purposes of this paper.

be the most appropriate means to desired ends.	analysts find themselves directly agreeing on a policy (without their agreeing that it is the most appropriate means to an agreed objective).

4a. Analysis is comprehensive; every important relevant factor is taken into account.	4b. Analysis is drastically limited:
	  i) Important possible outcomes are neglected.
	  ii) Important alternative potential policies are neglected.
	  iii) Important affected values are neglected.

5a. Theory is often heavily relied upon.	5b. A succession of comparisons greatly reduces or eliminates reliance on theory.

Assuming that the root method is familiar and understandable, we proceed directly to clarification of its alternative by contrast. In explaining the second, we shall be describing how most administrators do in fact approach complex questions, for the root method, the "best" way as a blueprint or model, is in fact not workable for complex policy questions, and administrators are forced to use the method of successive limited comparisons.

Intertwining Evaluation and Empirical Analysis (1b)

The quickest way to understand how values are handled in the method of successive limited comparisons is to see how the root method often breaks down in *its* handling of values or objectives. The idea that values should be clarified, and in advance of the examination of alternative policies, is appealing. But what happens when we attempt it for complex social problems? The first difficulty is that on many critical values or objectives, citizens disagree, congressmen disagree, and public administrators disagree. Even where a fairly specific objective is prescribed for the administrator, there remains considerable room for disagreement on subobjectives. Consider, for example, the conflict with respect to locating public housing, described in Meyerson and Banfield's study of the Chicago Housing Authority[4]—

4. Martin Meyerson and Edward C. Banfield, *Politics, Planning, and the Public Interest* (Glencoe, Ill.: Free Press, 1955).

disagreement which occurred despite the clear objective of providing a certain number of public housing units in the city. Similarly conflicting are objectives in highway location, traffic control, minimum wage administration, development of tourist facilities in national parks, or insect control.

Administrators cannot escape these conflicts by ascertaining the majority's preference, for preferences have not been registered on most issues; indeed, there often *are* no preferences in the absence of public discussion sufficient to bring an issue to the attention of the electorate. Furthermore, there is a question of whether intensity of feeling should be considered as well as the number of persons preferring each alternative. By the impossibility of doing otherwise, administrators often are reduced to deciding policy without clarifying objectives first.

Even when an administrator resolves to follow his own values as a criterion for decisions, he often will not know how to rank them when they conflict with one another, as they usually do. Suppose, for example, that an administrator must relocate tenants living in tenements scheduled for destruction. One objective is to empty the buildings fairly promptly, another is to find suitable accommodation for persons displaced, another is to avoid friction with residents in other areas in which a large influx would be unwelcome, another is to deal with all concerned through persuasion if possible, and so on.

How does one state even to himself the relative importance of these partially conflicting values? A simple ranking of them is not enough; one needs ideally to know how much of one value is worth sacrificing for some of another value. The answer is that typically the administrator chooses—and must choose—directly among policies in which these values are combined in different ways. He cannot first clarify his values and then choose among policies.

A more subtle third point underlies both the first two. Social objectives do not always have the same relative values. One objective may be highly prized in one circumstance, another in another circumstance. If, for example, an administrator values highly both the dispatch with which his agency can carry through its projects *and* good public relations, it matters little which of the two possibly conflicting values he favors in some abstract or general sense. Policy questions arise in forms which put to administrators such a question as: Given the degree to which we are or are not already achieving the values of dispatch and the values of good public relations, is it worth sacrificing a little speed for a happier clientele, or is it better to risk offending the clientele so that we can get on with our work? The answer to such a question varies with circumstances.

The value problem is, as the example shows, always a problem of adjustments at a margin. But there is not practicable way to state marginal objectives or values except in terms of particular policies. That one value is preferred to another in one decision situation does not mean that it will be preferred in another decision situation in which it can be had only at great sacrifice of another value. Attempts to rank or order values in general and abstract terms so that they do not shift from decision to decision end up by ignoring the relevant marginal preferences. The significance of this third point thus goes very far. Even if all administrators had at hand an agreed set of values, objectives, and constraints, and an agreed ranking of these values, objectives, and constraints, their marginal values in actual choice situations would be impossible to formulate.

Unable consequently to formulate the relevant values first and then choose among policies to achieve them, administrators must choose directly among alternative policies that offer different marginal combinations of values. Somewhat paradoxically, the only practicable way to disclose one's relevant marginal values even to oneself is to describe the policy one chooses to achieve them. Except roughly and vaguely, I know of no way to describe—or even to understand—what my relative evaluations are for, say, freedom and security, speed and accuracy in governmental decisions, or low taxes and better schools than to describe my preferences among specific choices that might be made between the alternatives in each of the pairs.

In summary, two aspects of the process by which values are actually handled can be distinguished. The first is clear: evaluation and empirical analysis are intertwined; that is, one chooses among values and among policies at one and the same time. Put a little more elaborately, one simultaneously chooses a policy to attain certain objectives and chooses the objectives themselves. The second aspect is related but distinct: the administrator focuses his attention on marginal or incremental values. Whether he is aware of it or not, he does not find general formulations of objectives very helpful and in fact makes specific marginal or incremental comparisons. Two policies, X and Y, confront him. Both promise the same degree of attainment of objectives $a, b, c, d,$ and e. But X promises him somewhat more of f than does Y, while Y promises him somewhat more of g than does X. In choosing between them, he is in fact offered the alternative of a marginal or incremental amount of f at the expense of a marginal or incremental amount of g. The only values that are relevant to his choice are these increments by which the two policies differ; and, when he finally chooses between the two marginal values, he does so by making a choice between policies.[5]

As to whether the attempt to clarify objectives in advance of policy selection is more or less rational than the close intertwining of marginal evaluation and empirical analysis, the principal difference established is that for complex problems the first is impossible and irrelevant, and the second is both possible and relevant. The second is possible because the administrator need not try to analyze any values except the values by which alternative policies differ and need not be concerned with them except as they differ marginally. His need for information on values or objectives is drastically reduced as compared with the root method; and his capacity for grasping, comprehending, and relating values to one another is not strained beyond the breaking point.

Relations between Means and Ends (2b)

Decision making is ordinarily formalized as a means-ends relationship: means are conceived to be evaluated and chosen in the light of ends finally selected independently of and prior to the choice of means. This is the means-ends relationship of the root method. But it follows from all that has just been said that such a means-ends relationship is possible only to the extent that values are agreed upon, are reconcilable, and are stable at the margin. Typically, therefore, such a means-ends relationship is absent from the branch method, where means and ends are simultaneously chosen.

Yet any departure from the means-ends relationship of the root method will strike some readers as inconceivable. For it will appear to them that only in such a relationship is it possible to determine whether one policy choice is better or worse than another. How can an administrator know whether he has made a wise or foolish decision if he is without prior values or objectives by which to judge his decisions? The answer to this question calls up the third distinctive difference between root and branch methods: how to decide the best policy.

5. The line of argument is, of course, an extension of the theory of market choice, especially the theory of consumer choice, to public policy choices.

The Test of "Good" Policy (3b)

In the root method, a decision is "correct," "good," or "rational" if it can be shown to attain some specified objective, where the objective can be specified without simply describing the decision itself. Where objectives are defined only through the marginal or incremental approach to values described above, it is still sometimes possible to test whether a policy does in fact attain the desired objectives; but a precise statement of the objectives takes the form of a description of the policy chosen or some alternative to it. To show that a policy is mistaken one cannot offer an abstract argument that important objectives are not achieved; one must instead argue that another policy is more to be preferred.

So far, the departure from customary ways of looking at problem solving is not troublesome, for many administrators will be quick to agree that the most effective discussion of the correctness of policy does take the form of comparison with other policies that might have been chosen. But what of the situation in which administrators cannot agree on values or objectives, either abstractly or in marginal terms? What then is the test of "good" policy? For the root method, there is no test. Agreement on objectives failing, there is no standard of "correctness." For the method of successive limited comparisons, the test is agreement on policy itself, which remains possible even when agreement on values is not.

It has been suggested that continuing agreement in Congress on the desirability of extending old age insurance stems from liberal desires to strengthen the welfare programs of the federal government and from conservative desires to reduce union demands for private pension plans. If so, this is an excellent demonstration of the ease with which individuals of different ideologies often can agree on concrete policy. Labor mediators report a similar phenomenon: the contestants cannot agree on criteria for settling their disputes but can agree on specific proposals. Similarly, when one administrator's objective turns out to be another's means, they often can agree on policy.

Agreement on policy thus becomes the only practicable test of the policy's correctness. And for one administrator to seek to win the other over to agreement on ends as well would accomplish nothing and create quite unnecessary controversy.

If agreement directly on policy as a test for "best" policy seems a poor substitute for testing the policy against its objectives, it ought to be remembered that objectives themselves have no ultimate validity other than they are agreed upon. Hence agreement is the test of "best" policy in both methods. But where the root method requires agreement on what elements in the decision constitute objectives and on which of these objectives should be sought, the branch method falls back on agreement wherever it can be found.

In an important sense, therefore, it is not irrational for an administrator to defend a policy as good without being able to specify what it is good for.

Noncomprehensive Analysis (4b)

Ideally, rational-comprehensive analysis leaves out nothing important. But it is impossible to take everything important into consideration unless "important" is so narrowly defined that analysis is in fact quite limited. Limits on human intellectual capacities and on available information set definite limits to man's capacity to be comprehensive. In actual fact, therefore, no one can practice the rational-comprehensive method for really complex problems, and every administrator faced with a sufficiently complex problem must find ways drastically to simplify.

An administrator assisting in the formulation of agricultural economic policy cannot in the first place be competent on all possible policies. He cannot even comprehend one policy entirely. In planning a soil bank program, he cannot successfully anticipate the impact of higher or lower farm income on, say, urbanization—the possible consequent loosening of family ties, the possible consequent need for revisions in social security and further implications for tax problems arising out of new federal responsibilities for social security and municipal responsibilities for urban services. Nor, to follow another line of repercussions, can he work through the soil bank program's effects on prices for agricultural products in foreign markets and consequent implications for foreign relations, including those arising out of economic rivalry between the United States and the USSR.

In the method of successive limited comparisons, simplification is systematically achieved in two principal ways. First, it is achieved through limitation of policy comparisons to those policies that differ in relatively small degree from policies presently in effect. Such a limitation immediately reduces the number of alternatives to be investigated and also drastically simplifies the character of the investigation of each. For it is not necessary to undertake fundamental inquiry into an alternative and its consequences; it is necessary only to study those respects in which the proposed alternative and its consequences differ from the status quo. The empirical comparison of marginal differences among alternative policies that differ only marginally is, of course, a counterpart to the incremental or marginal comparison of values discussed above.[6]

Relevance as Well as Realism

It is a matter of common observation that in Western democracies public administrators and policy analysts in general do largely limit their analyses to incremental or marginal differences in policies that are chosen to differ only incrementally. They do not do so, however, solely because they desperately need some way to simplify their problems; they also do so in order to be relevant. Democracies change their policies almost entirely through incremental adjustments. Policy does not move in leaps and bounds.

The incremental character of political change in the United States has often been remarked. The two major political parties agree on fundamentals; they offer alternative policies to the voters only on relatively small points of difference. Both parties favor full employment, but they define it somewhat differently; both favor the development of water power resources, but in slightly different ways; and both favor unemployment compensation, but not the same level of benefits. Similarly, shifts of policy within a party take place largely through a series of relatively small changes, as can be seen in their only gradual acceptance of the idea of governmental responsibility for support of the unemployed, a change in party positions beginning in the early thirties and culminating in a sense in the Employment Act of 1946.

Party behavior is in turn rooted in public attitudes, and political theorists cannot conceive of democracy's surviving in the United States in the absence of fundamental agreement on potentially disruptive issues, with consequent limitation of policy debates to relatively small differences in policy.

Since the policies ignored by the administrator are politically impossible and so irrelevant, the simplification of analysis achieved by concentrating on policies that differ only

6. A more precise definition of incremental policies and a discussion of whether a change that appears "small" to one observer might be seen differently by another is to be found in my "policy Analysis," *American Economic Review* 48 (June 1958): 298.

incrementally is not a capricious kind of simplification. In addition, it can be argued that, given the limits on knowledge within which policy makers are confined, simplifying by limiting the focus to small variations from present policy makes the most of available knowledge. Because policies being considered are like present and past policies, the administrator can obtain information and claim some insight. Nonincremental policy proposals are therefore typically not only politically irrelevant but also unpredictable in their consequences.

The second method of simplification of analysis is the practice of ignoring important possible consequences of possible policies, as well as the values attached to the neglected consequences. If this appears to disclose a shocking shortcoming of successive limited comparisons, it can be replied that, even if the exclusions are random, policies may nevertheless be more intelligently formulated than through futile attempts to achieve a comprehensiveness beyond human capacity. Actually, however, the exclusions, seeming arbitrary or random from one point of view, need be neither.

Achieving a Degree of Comprehensiveness

Suppose that each value neglected by one policy-making agency were a major concern of at least one other agency. In that case, a helpful division of labor would be achieved, and no agency need find its task beyond its capacities. The shortcomings of such a system would be that one agency might destroy a value either before another agency could be activated to safeguard it or in spite of another agency's efforts. But the possibility that important values may be lost is present in any form of organization, even where agencies attempt to comprehend in planning more than is humanly possible.

The virtue of such a hypothetical division of labor is that every important interest or value has its watchdog. And these watchdogs can protect the interests in their jurisdiction in two quite different ways: first, by redressing damages done by other agencies; and, second, by anticipating and heading off injury before it occurs.

In a society like that of the United States in which individuals are free to combine to pursue almost any possible common interest they might have and in which government agencies are sensitive to the pressures of these groups, the system described is approximated. Almost every interest has its watchdog. Without claiming that every interest has a sufficiently powerful watchdog, it can be argued that our system often can assure a more comprehensive regard for the values of the whole society than any attempt at intellectual comprehensiveness.

In the United States, for example, no part of government attempts a comprehensive overview of policy on income distribution. A policy nevertheless evolves, and one responding to a wide variety of interests. A process of mutual adjustment among farm groups, labor unions, municipalities and school boards, tax authorities, and government agencies with responsibilities in the fields of housing, health, highways, national parks, fire, and police accomplishes a distribution of income in which particular income problems neglected at one point in the decision processes become central at another point.

Mutual adjustment is more pervasive than the explicit forms it takes in negotiation between groups; it persists through the mutual impacts of groups upon one another even where they are not in communication. For all the imperfections and latent dangers in this ubiquitous process of mutual adjustment, it will often accomplish an adaptation of policies to a wider range of interests than could be done by one group centrally.

Note, too, how the incremental pattern of policy making fits with the multiple pressure pattern. For when decisions are only incremental—closely related to known policies, it is easier for one group to anticipate the kind of moves another might make and easier too for it to make correction for injury already accomplished.[7]

Even partisanship and narrowness, to use pejorative terms, will sometimes be assets to rational decision making, for they can doubly insure that what one agency neglects, another will not; they specialize personnel to distinct points of view. The claim is valid that effective rational coordination of the federal administration, if possible to achieve at all, would require an agreed set of values[8]—if "rational" is defined as the practice of the root method of decision making. But a high degree of administrative coordination occurs as each agency adjusts its policies to the concerns of the other agencies in the process of fragmented decision making I have just described.

7. The link between the practice of the method of successive limited comparisons and mutual adjustment of interests in a highly fragmented decision-making process adds a new facet to pluralist theories of government and administration.

8. Herbert Simon, Donald W. Smithburg, and Victor A. Thompson, *Public Administration* (New York: Alfred A. Knopf, 1950), p. 434.

For all the apparent shortcomings of the incremental approach to policy alternatives with its arbitrary exclusion coupled with fragmentation, when compared to the root method, the branch method often looks far superior. In the root method, the inevitable exclusion of factors is accidental, unsystematic, and not defensible by any argument so far developed, while in the branch method the exclusions are deliberate, systematic, and defensible. Ideally, of course, the root method does not exclude; in practice it must.

Nor does the branch method necessarily neglect long-run considerations and objectives. It is clear that important values must be omitted in considering policy, and sometimes the only way long-run objectives can be given adequate attention is through the neglect of short-run considerations. But the values omitted can be either long-run or short-run.

Succession of Comparisons (5b)

The final distinctive element in the branch method is that the comparisons, together with the policy choice, proceed in a chronological series. Policy is not made once and for all; it is made and remade endlessly. Policy making is a process of successive approximation to some desired objectives in which what is desired itself continues to change under reconsideration.

Making policy is at best a very rough process. Neither social scientists nor politicians nor public administrators yet know enough about the social world to avoid repeated error in predicting the consequences of policy moves. A wise policy maker consequently expects that his policies will achieve only part of what he hopes and at the same time will produce unanticipated consequences he would have preferred to avoid. If he proceeds through a *succession* of incremental changes, he avoids serious lasting mistakes in several ways.

In the first place, past sequences of policy steps have given him knowledge about the probable consequences of further similar steps. Second, he need not attempt big jumps toward his goals that would require predictions beyond his or anyone else's knowledge, because he never expects his policy to be a final resolution of a problem. His decision is only one step, one that if successful can quickly be followed by another. Third, he is in effect able to test his previous predictions as he moves on to each further step. Lastly, he often can remedy a past error fairly quickly—more quickly than if policy proceeded through more distinct steps widely spaced in time.

Compare this comparative analysis of incremental changes with the aspiration to employ theory in the root method. Man cannot think without classifying, without subsuming one experience under a more general category of experiences. The attempt to push categorization as far as possible and to find general propositions which can be applied to specific situations is what I refer to with the word "theory." Where root analysis often leans heavily on theory in this sense, the branch method does not.

The assumption of root analysts is that theory is the most systematic and economical way to bring relevant knowledge to bear on a specific problem. Granting the assumption, an unhappy fact is that we do not have adequate theory to apply to problems in any policy area, although theory is more adequate in some areas—monetary policy, for example—than in others. Comparative analysis, as in the branch method, is sometimes a systematic alternative to theory.

Suppose an administrator must choose among a small group of policies that differ only incrementally from each other and from present policy. He might aspire to "understand" each of the alternatives—for example, to know all the consequences of each aspect of each policy. If so, he would indeed require theory. In fact, however, he would usually decide that, *for policy-making purposes,* he need know, as explained above, only the consequences of each of those aspects of the policies in which they differed from one another. For this much more modest aspiration, he requires no theory (although it might be helpful, if available), for he can proceed to isolate probable differences by examining the differences in consequences associated with past differences in policies, a feasible program because be can take his observations from a long sequence of incremental changes.

For example, without a more comprehensive social theory about juvenile delinquency than scholars have yet produced, one cannot possibly understand the ways in which a variety of public policies—say on education, housing, recreation, employment, race relations, and policing—might encourage or discourage delinquency. And one needs such an understanding if he undertakes the comprehensive overview of the problem prescribed in the models of the root method. If, however, one merely wants to mobilize knowledge sufficient to assist in a choice among a small group of similar policies —alternative policies on juvenile court procedures, for example—he can do so by comparative analysis of the results of similar past policy moves.

Theorists and Practitioners

This difference explains—in some cases at least—why the

administrator often feels that the outside expert or academic problem solver is sometimes not helpful and why they in turn often urge more theory on him. And it explains why an administrator often feels more confident when "flying by the seat of his pants" than when following the advice of theorists. Theorists often ask the administrator to go the long way round to the solution of his problems, in effect ask him to follow the best canons of the scientific method, when the administrator knows that the best available theory will work less well than more modest incremental comparisons. Theorists do not realize that the administrator is often in fact practicing a systematic method. It would be foolish to push this explanation too far, for sometimes practical decision makers are pursuing neither a theoretical approach nor successive comparisons, nor any other systematic method.

It may be worth emphasizing that theory is sometimes of extremely limited helpfulness in policy making for at least two rather different reasons. It is greedy for facts; it can be constructed only through a great collection of observations. And it is typically insufficiently precise for application to a policy process that moves through small changes. In contrast, the comparative method both economizes on the need for facts and directs the analyst's attention to just those facts that are relevant to the fine choices faced by the decision maker.

With respect to precision of theory, economic theory serves as an example. It predicts that an economy without money or prices would in certain specified ways misallocate resources, but this finding pertains to an alternative far removed from the kind of policies on which administrators need help. Yet it is not precise enough to predict the consequences of policies restricting business mergers, and this is the kind of issue on which the administrators need help. Only in relatively restricted areas does economic theory achieve sufficient precision to go far in resolving policy questions; its helpfulness in policy making is always so limited that it requires supplementation through comparative analysis.

Successive Comparison as a System

Successive limited comparisons is, then, indeed a method or system; it is not a failure of method for which administrators ought to apologize. Nonetheless, its imperfections, which have not been explored in this paper, are many. For example, the method is without a built-in safeguard for all relevant values, and it also may lead the decision maker to overlook excellent policies for no other reason than that they are not suggested by the chain of successive policy steps leading up to the present. Hence, it ought to be said that under this method, as well as under some of the most sophisticated variants of the root method—operations research, for example—policies will continue to be as foolish as they are wise.

Why then bother to describe the method in all the above detail? Because it is in fact a common method of policy formulation, and is, for complex problems, the principal reliance of administrators as well as of other policy analysts.[9] And because it will be superior to any other decision-making method available for complex problems in many circumstances, certainly superior to a futile attempt at superhuman comprehensiveness. The reaction of the public administrator to the exposition of method doubtless will be less a discovery of a new method than a better acquaintance with an old. But by becoming more conscious of their practice of this method, administrators might practice it with more skill and know when to extend or constrict its use. (That they sometimes practice it effectively and sometimes not may explain the extremes of opinion on "muddling through," which is both praised as a highly sophisticated form of problem solving and denounced as no method at all. For I suspect that in so far as there is a system in what is known as "muddling through," this method is it.)

One of the noteworthy incidental consequences of clarification of the method is the light it throws on the suspicion an administrator sometimes entertains that a consultant or adviser is not speaking relevantly and responsibly when in fact by all ordinary objective evidence he is. The trouble lies in the fact that most of us approach policy problems within a

9. Elsewhere I have explored this same method of policy formation as practiced by academic analysts of policy ("Policy Analysis," *American Economic Review,* vol. 48). Although it has been here presented as a method for public administrators, it is no less necessary to analysts more removed from immediate policy questions, despite their tendencies to describe their own analytical efforts as though they were the rational-comprehensive method with an especially heavy use of theory. Similarly, this same method is inevitably resorted to in personal problem solving, where means and ends are sometimes impossible to separate, where aspirations or objectives undergo constant development, and where drastic simplification of the complexity of the real world is urgent if problems are to be solved in the time that can be given to them. To an economist accustomed to dealing with the marginal or incremental concept in market processes, the central idea in the method is that both evaluation and empirical analysis are incremental. Accordingly I have referred to the method elsewhere as "the incremental method."

framework given by our view of a chain of successive policy choices made up to the present. One's thinking about appropriate policies with respect, say, to urban traffiic control is greatly influenced by one's knowledge of the incremental steps taken up to the present. An administrator enjoys an intimate knowledge of his past sequences that "outsiders" do not share, and his thinking and that of the "outsider" will consequently be different in ways that may puzzle both. Both may appear to be talking intelligently, yet each may find the other unsatisfactory. The relevance of the policy chain of succession is even more clear when an American tries to discuss, say, antitrust policy with a Swiss, for the chains of policy in the two countries are strikingly different and the two individuals consequently have organized their knowledge in quite different ways.

If this phenomenon is a barrier to communication, an understanding of it promises an enrichment of intellectual interaction in policy formulation. Once the source of difference is understood, it will sometimes be stimulating for an administrator to seek out a policy analyst whose recent experience is with a policy chain different from his own.

This raises again a question only briefly discussed above on the merits of like-mindedness among government administrators. While much of organization theory argues the virtues of common values and agreed organizational objectives, for complex problems in which the root method is inapplicable, agencies will want among their own personnel two types of diversification: administrators whose thinking is organized by reference to policy chains other than those familiar to most members of the organization and, even more commonly, administrators whose professional or personal values or interests create diversity of view (perhaps coming from different specialties, social classes, geographical areas) so that, even within a single agency, decision making can be fragmented and parts of the agency can serve as watchdogs for other parts.

The Process of
Problem Finding
William F. Pounds

Introduction

As a result of research efforts over the past twenty years, a number of extremely effective analytical techniques are currently available for the solution of management problems. Linear programming is used routinely in the specification of optimum cattle feeds and fertilizers. Decision rules based on inventory models form the basis for production and inventory control systems in a wide variety of manufacturing companies. Simulation is evolving from a means for doing research on complex managerial problems to a process which can provide useful information to managers on a real-time basis.

Like other technological changes, these methods raise a number of social and organizational issues within the organizations which use them, but their net contribution is no longer seriously in doubt. As a result, in most large organizations and in many smaller ones, operating managers either are aware of these methods or have ready access to help and advice in their application.

But the manager's job is not only to solve well-defined problems. He must also identify the problems to be solved. He must somehow assess the cost of analysis and its potential return. He must allocate resources to questions before he knows their answers. To many managers and students of management, the availability of formal problem solving procedures serves only to highlight those parts of the manager's job with which these procedures do *not* deal: problem

Reprinted with the permission of the author and publisher from William F. Pounds, "The Process of Problem Finding," *Industrial Management Review* 11 (1969): 1–19. © 1969 by the Industrial Management Review Association; all rights reserved.

Research for this paper was supported in part by a grant from NASA. The author gratefully acknowledges the many contributions of Professor E. H. Bowman to all phases of this study and particularly those he made to the planning and execution of the company study.

identification, the assignment of problem priority, and the allocation of scarce resources to problems. These tasks, which must be performed without the benefit of a well-defined body of theory, may be among the most critical of the manager's decision-making responsibilities.

This paper is concerned primarily with the first of these tasks—problem identification. It reviews some research rele-decision rules which are easy to teach and execute and easy to improve through analysis, simulation, or experimentation. study of the process by which managers in a successful industrial organization define their problems. Because this research was stimulated in part by an interest in the relationship between the so-called new techniques of management and what might be called traditional managerial behavior, similarities between these two modes of management which are suggested both by the theory and the empirical evidence are briefly noted.

Background

Prior to 1945, our understanding of most cognitive tasks within industrial organizations was not much better than our understanding of the process of problem finding is today. Inventory levels were maintained, production schedules were determined, and distribution systems were designed by individuals who, through years of experience, had learned ways to get these jobs done. With few exceptions these individuals were not explicit about how they performed these tasks and, as a result, training for these jobs was a slow process and the development and testing of new procedures was difficult indeed.

So it is with the process of problem finding today. All managers have discovered ways to maintain a list of problems that can occupy their working hours—and other hours as well. They frequently find it difficult, however, to be explicit about the process by which their problems are selected. Consequently, the development of improved problem finding procedures is difficult.

Since 1945, however, some progress has been made in understanding certain cognitive tasks in the areas of production and inventory control. Decisions rules have been derived from mathematical models of particular tasks, and in a number of cases these rules have performed as well as or better than the complex intuitive process they have replaced. The significant fact about these developments for this discussion is not, however, the economic impact of such rules, although it has been significant. Rather, it is the implication that the essential processes by which important decisions are made may be carried out satisfactorily by simple explicit decision rules which are easy to teach and execute and easy to improve through analysis, simulation, or experimentation.

Of course it is possible to discount these accomplishments by saying that inventory decisions were always rather simple ones to make. The validity of such arguments, however, seems suspiciously dependent on knowledge of what has been accomplished and on a lack of knowledge of inventory systems.

It is true, however, that mathematical analysis has been able only to suggest decision rules for a wide variety of managerial tasks. These tasks, including the definition of problems, seem to require symbols and analytical procedures not readily represented by standard mathematical forms. Some other means for discovering the decision rules by which such tasks are performed is clearly required.

Some progress in this direction has already been made. Encouraged both by the success of the analytical approach to decision problems, and by the availability of large digital computers, Newell, Simon, and others have been studying human decision behavior since the early 1950s. They have focused their attention primarily on tasks which would facilitate the development of a methodology for approaching decision situations not readily describable in mathematical terms. They have considered the decision processes involved in proving theorems in symbolic logic[1] and plane geometry.[2] They have considered decision processes involved in playing games like chess[3] and checkers.[4] They have worked on the assembly line balancing problem[5] and on trust investment.[6]

1. A. Newell, J. C. Shaw, and H. A. Simon, "Empirical Explorations of the Logic Theory Machine," *Proceedings of the Western Joint Computer Conference* (February 1957), pp. 218–30.

2. H. L. Gelernter, "Realization of a Geometry Theorem Proving Machine," *UNESCO Conference on Information Processing Proceedings* (1959).

3. A. Newell, J. C. Shaw, and H. A. Simon, "Chess-Playing Programs and the Problem of Complexity," *IBM Journal of Research and Development,* October 1958, pp. 320–35.

4. A. L. Samuel, "Some Studies in Machine Learning, Using the Game of Checkers," *IBM Journal of Research and Development* July 1959, pp. 210–30.

5. F. M. Tonge, *A Heuristic Program for Assembly-Line Balancing* (Englewood Cliffs, N. J.: Prentice-Hall, 1962).

6. G. P. Clarkson, *Portfolio Selection: A Simulation of Trust Investment* (Englewood Cliffs, N. J.: Prentice-Hall, 1962).

The relevance of this research to problem finding can perhaps best be illustrated by considering the work on chess.

Research on Chess

Chess is a game with rules simple enough for almost anyone to learn and yet complex enough that even the largest computer cannot play it by working out the consequences of all possible moves. Chess is a game of strategy in which individual moves can not always be evaluated without considering future moves. Chess moves are inconvenient to describe in mathematical terms and few people can be explicit about how they play chess. For these reasons and several others, chess was an attractive medium in which to attempt to unravel human decision processes that could not be modeled mathematically.

Three aspects of the work on chess playing behavior are relevant to this discussion. First, simple explicit decision rules were discovered which make for very good chess play. This result has been tested by programming computers with such rules and observing the quality of play which resulted in response to the play of human experts. Second, the decision rules for chess playing were derived from observations, interviews, and the writings of chess masters. Thus, it is not necessary that simple, explicit decision rules be derived from mathematical or theoretical considerations. They can be abstracted from humans who have themselves never systematically considered the process of their own decision making. And, third, the decision rules by which humans play chess appear to be separable into three rather distinct classes: rules for defining alternative moves, rules for evaluating alternative moves, and rules for choosing a move from among evaluated alternatives. H.A. Simon has called these three classes of behavior intelligence, design, and choice, respectively,[7] and on the basis of his work both on chess and other decision making situations has concluded that the process of intelligence or alternative definition is the key to effective behavior.

The work on chess and other complex tasks does not directly suggest how managers go about finding and defining the problems to which they devote their time. It does suggest, however, that tasks of this same order of complexity may be understood through careful observation of and abstraction

7. H. A. Simon, *The New Science of Management Decision* (New York: Harper and Brothers, 1960).

from the behavior of human experts. It further suggests that, if useful insights into managerial problem finding can be gained, they may contribute significantly to managerial effectiveness.

An Empirical Study of Managerial Problem Finding

Since it was possible to gain useful insights into the process by which humans play chess by observing experts, it seemed likely that insights into the process of managerial problem finding might be derived from careful observation of successful managers. Arrangements were made therefore to interview, observe, and interrogate about fifty executives in a decentralized operating division of a large technically based corporation, which will be referred to as the Southern Company.

The study consisted of four relatively distinct activities. First, interviews were conducted during which executives were asked to describe the problems they faced and the processes by which they had become aware of these problems. Second, observations were made of meetings during which problems were identified, discussed, and sometimes solved. Third, investigations were made of the source and disposition of several specific problems. And, fourth, a questionnaire was devised and administered to each executive who participated in the study.

As data began to accumulate from each of these activities, it became clear that a major objective of the study would be to discover some level of abstraction which would preserve what seemed to be essential details of the managerial situations being observed and at the same time provide a structure which would convert isolated anecdotes into data from which some generalizations might be drawn. This structure will be described in the following pages together with some of the observations it explains. Observations made outside this particular study will also be reported.

Theoretical Structure

Like any number of other industrial tasks, the process of management can be viewed as the sequential execution of elementary activities. In describing their own work, executives find it easy to think and talk in terms of elementary activities like making out the production schedule, reading the quality control report, visiting a customer, etc. The attractive feature of this view of managerial work is that elementary tasks can be defined at almost any level of detail. Clearly the task of preparing a production schedule is itself made up of more elementary tasks like collecting data on orders and labor availability, which are themselves made up of even more elementary activities. On the other hand, one can aggregate elements like production scheduling into larger units of analysis like managing production.

A choice of some level of abstraction cannot be avoided. For purposes of this study, the level chosen was that which the managers themselves used in describing their activities. Thus, even at the theoretical level, advantage was taken of the fact that the managers' language had evolved as a useful means for processing information about their jobs.

Elements of managerial activity will be referred to as *operators*. An operator transforms a set of input variables into a set of output variables according to some predetermined plan. For example, the operator "lay out a production schedule" takes machine capacities, labor productivities, product requirements, and other input variables and yields man, product, machine, and time associations covering some appropriate period of time. Since the action of an operator produces an effect which is more or less predictable, operators are frequently named for their effect on the environment. The operator "lay out production schedule" changes the production organization from one with no schedule to one with a schedule. The operator "hire qualified lathe operator" changes the size of the work force.[8]

The word "problem" is associated with the difference between some existing situation and some desired situation. The problem of reducing material cost, for example, indicates a difference between the existing material cost and some desired level of material cost. The problems of hiring qualified engineers and of reducing finished goods inventories similarly define differences to be reduced. Because problems are defined by differences and operators can be executed to reduce differences, strong associations are formed between problems and operators. The problem of devising a production schedule can ordinarily be "solved" by applying the operator "lay out production schedule." The problem of "increasing sales volume" can sometimes be "solved" by applying the operator "revise advertising budget." Since operator selection is triggered by the difference to be reduced, the

8. Because this paper is concerned primarily with problem finding, the process of operator selection and execution will not be discussed. The definitions are included only to complete the description of the theoretical structure.

process of problem finding is the process of defining differences. Problem solving, on the other hand, is the process of selecting operators which will reduce differences.

The manager defines differences by comparing what he perceives to the output of a *model* which predicts the same variables. A difference might be defined by comparing an idle machine to a production schedule which implies high machine utilization. In this case, the production schedule is the model used to define a difference. A difference might be defined by comparing a 10 percent reject rate in a department to a budgeted rate of two percent. In this case, the budget is the model. A difference might be defined by comparing available data to those required for a special report. The problem of understanding problem finding is therefore eventually reduced to the problem of understanding the models which managers use to define differences.

It should be noted that the theoretical framework proposed here has drawn on ideas discussed by Miller, Galanter, and Pribram,[9] who in turn refer to some basic work by Newell, Shaw, and Simon.[10] Figure 1 presents a flow chart of the process described in this section and, for comparison, the structures proposed by others.

Managerial Models for Problem Finding

Historical Models

On the assumption that recent past experience is the best estimate of the short-term future, managers maintain a wide variety of models based on the continuity of historical relationships: April sales exceed March sales by 10 percent; Department X runs 5 percent defective product; the cost of making item Y is $10.50 per thousand; the lead time on that raw material is three weeks, etc. Because the manager's world is complex and these models tend to be simple, discrepancies frequently arise between the models' predictions and what actually takes place. Such discrepancies are a major source of problems to which managers devote their time. Why is our inventory account drifting out of line? Why is our reject rate so high this week? What has happened to make so many deliveries late? What can be done to reverse this trend in absenteeism? Why is our safety record suddenly so good? All

9. G. A. Miller, E. Galanter, and K. H. Pribram, *Plans and the Structure of Behavior* (New York: Henry Holt & Co., 1960).

10. A. Newell, J. C. Shaw, and H. A. Simon, "Report on a General Problem-Solving Program," *Proceedings of the ICIP*, June 1960; reprinted in *Computers and Automation*, July 1960, as "A General Problem-Solving Program for a Computer."

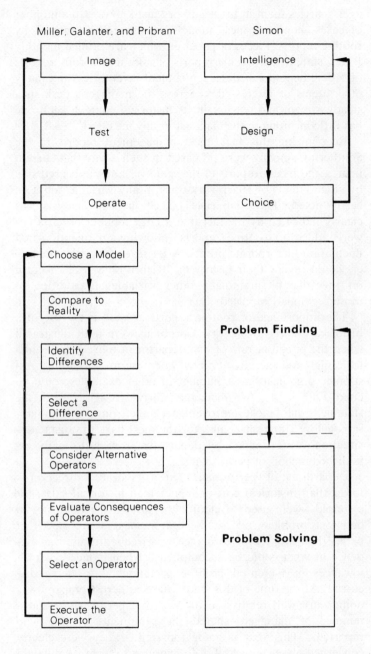

Fig. 1. Flow Chart of Managerial Behavior

these problems and a host of others like them are triggered by discrepancies from historical models and can keep a manager and his organization busy all day every day.

For the most part these models are nonexplicit. The manager "carries them in his head" or "just knows." In a number of cases, however, these models are strongly supported by routine reports. Pieces of paper on which are printed monthly P & L statements, weekly reports of sales totals, daily reports of orders behind schedule, semiannual inventories, and many other items of interest flow across the manager's desk in a steady stream and, except in its historical context, each one has little meaning to the manager or anyone else.[11]

Recognizing this fact, most management reports in the Southern Company were prepared in such a way that current figures and recent reports of the same variables appeared side by side. Trends or sharp variations in any variable could be easily noted. The confidence placed in such analysis was clearly indicated by the fact that a large number of variables were added to routine reports following an unanticipated fluctuation in corporate profits. After several months, managers could review their history of "Return on Sales," "Return on Investment," and many other variables in addition to those previously reported.

The importance of routine reports as well as the use of a historical model to identify a problem were both illustrated when the rejection rate of one department moved past a historic high and thereby attracted attention to the Quality Assurance organization. A number of other examples could be cited. Out of fifty-two managers, forty-two agreed with the statement that "most improvements come from correcting unsatisfactory situations." and, for the most part, unsatisfactory situations were defined by departures from historically established models of performance.

Departures of performance in a favorable direction— lower than historical cost or higher than historical sales, for example—were used to modify the historical model, not to define a problem per se. Several managers reported that better-than-average performance was frequently used as evidence of what could be accomplished when reduced cost allowances or increased profit expectations were being discussed. At the time of this study, the Southern Company was doing very well relative to its own past performance and a number of managers shared the sentiments of one who reported. "This year is going too well." They were clearly concerned about their ability to continue to meet what would become a new historical standard. Several were already working on that problem-to-be.

11. Budgets, which can also provide context for such data, are discussed in the next section.

Besides serving as triggers for corrective and innovative problem solving, historical models are used extensively in the process of devising plans for future operations. These plans are in turn converted into budget objectives, and the budget objectives can sometimes serve as models which trigger managerial problem solving. Because of the complex process by which they are devised, managerial planning models will be discussed separately from the more straightforward historical ones.

Planning Models

Managers in the Southern Company devoted substantial amounts of time to planning future operations. Detailed projections of operating variables for the coming year and less detailed projections for the coming five years were presented annually to corporate officers by each product department manager. When approved, perhaps after some modification, these projections were used periodically to evaluate managerial performance, and for other purposes as well.

In view of the importance attributed to planning by the Southern Company, it might be expected that planning models would constitute an important part of the problem finding process. In fact they did not. Historical models were more influential on managerial behavior than planning models. To understand why, it is necessary to examine both the function of planning models and the process by which they were devised.

Among other things, plans are organizationally defined limits of managerial independence. So long as the manager is able to perform at least as well as his plan requires, he expects, and is normally granted, the right to define his problems as he sees fit. That is to say, as long as meeting his plan does not itself constitute a problem, the manager can use other criteria for defining his problems. If, however, he is unable to perform as well as he planned, he can expect to attract the attention of higher levels of management and to receive substantial assistance in problem identification. In other words, he will lose, perhaps only temporarily, the right to manage. One product manager put the matter this way, "The best way to remain in charge is to be successful." Other managers strongly supported this position. Success was defined relative to the predictions of the planning model.

In view of the fact that unfavorable deviatons in performance were far more undesirable to managers than favorable deviations, it is not surprising that planning models were not simple descriptions of what the managers expected would happen. On the contrary, planning models represented the minimum performance the manager could reasonably expect if several of his plans failed or were based on the minimum organizational expectations of managerial performance, whichever was higher. Planning models were in general very conservatively biased historical models. For the most part these biases in plans were not injected surreptitiously. After approving a manager's plan, upper-level managers always inquired about how he would deal with various contingencies. At this point the manager would reveal some but usually not all of his "hedges" against uncertainty. If he could report a number of conservative estimates and contingent plans to back up the plan being proposed, this was viewed as highly desirable.

In aggregating department plans, further "adjustments" were made which led the plan to depart from expectations. In some cases, these adjustments shifted expected profits from one department to another to "make the package look OK." In other cases, already conservative departmental estimates were "rounded down" to cover contingencies further. Some of these adjustments were made explicit at higher levels.

Even with all its conservative biases, the division's plan still exceeded the corporation's minimum profit and volume expectations. It is not surprising, therefore, that the planning model was a far less important source of management problems than historical models. Extrapolations of past performance simply implied much higher levels of performance than the planning model called for. Only in those cases (not observed) where the corporate expectations required improvements over historical trends would one expect planning models to be important in the process of problem finding.

Other Peoples' Models

Some models which define problems for the manager are maintained by other people. A customer whose model of product quality is violated by the product he receives may notify the manager of the producing organization of this fact and thereby define a problem for him. A higher level manager may lack information to complete an analysis and this discrepancy can define a problem for a lower level manager. An employee may need a decision on vacation policy and his request will define a problem for his supervisor. A basic function of an organization structure is to channel problems which are identified by its various members to individuals especially qualified to solve them. Managers as well as other members of the organization do not always work on problems defined by their own models.

In the Southern Company, invitations to attend meetings, requests to prepare reports, and requests for projects of various kinds whether made by superiors, subordinates, or peers were rarely questioned by managers as appropriate ways to spend their time. While it was sometimes easy to get vehement testimony as to the uselessness of many of these activities, the behavior of managers clearly indicated the strong influence of other people's models. One reason for the influence of these models may be the cost to the manager of doubting them. Any attempt to validate each request made on him could easily imply a heavier workload on the manager than the simple execution of the work requested. In addition, by providing "good service" the manager builds (or at least many managers believe they build) a store of goodwill among other managers toward his own requests.

During the course of the company study, several clear examples of the influence of these models were observed. In a series of interviews, managers were asked to specify the problems currently faced by them and their organizations. Most of them mentioned from five to eight problems. Later in the same interview, each manager was asked to describe in broad terms his own activities for the previous week. In reviewing the data from these interviews as they were collected, it was noted that no manager had reported any activity which could be directly associated with the problems he had described.

In order to be sure that this result was not due to some semantic problem, this point was discussed with several managers—in some cases during the first interview with them and in other cases as a follow-up question. One manager found the point both accurate and amusing. He smiled as he replied, "That's right. I don't have time to work on *my* problems—I'm too busy." Another manager took a different tack in agreeing with the general conclusion. He replied rather confidentially, "I don't really make decisions. I just work here." In further discussion with a number of managers, the power of other peoples' models was repeatedly indicated. The influence of these models was also noted in the case of a rather involved project which was observed in some detail.

The Plant Engineering Department, using a quite different model, decided to look at the desirability of revising the management of the company's twenty-one fork trucks.

Besides scheduling and other operating questions which were investigated by people within the Engineering Department, studies of the contract under which the trucks were leased and an economic evaluation of leasing versus buying trucks were also felt to be required. The manager of plant engineering called representatives of the comptroller's organization and the Legal Department to a meeting in which the project was discussed in some detail. This discussion clearly indicated that the project was risky both from the point of view of economic payoff and political considerations. The representatives accepted their tasks, however, and in due course their studies were completed. In neither case did the studies take much time, but the assumption that it was the job of the Accounting Department and the Legal Department to serve the Plant Engineering Department was clear. A problem found by someone in the organization carries with it substantial influence over the problems on which other parts of the organization will work.

Even clearer evidence of the power of other peoples' models was the time devoted by all the managers in the Southern Company to the preparation of reports "required" by higher management. These reports ranged in their demands on managerial time from a few minutes in the case of a request for routine information to several man months of work on the preparation of a plan for the coming year's operations. In reply to the question, "If you were responsible for the whole company's operations would you require more, the same, or less planning?" four managers responded that they would require more planning, thirty-two said the same amount of planning, and sixteen replied less. For many managers the expectations of the organization were consistent with their own ideas of the time required for effective planning. For a number of others, however, the influence of other people was clear.

In discussing these models as a source of problems, it is difficult to avoid a negative connotation due to the widely held ethic which values individual problem definition. Two points are worth emphasizing. First, the study was conducted to find out how managers do define their problems—not how they should do so—although that, of course, may be a long-term objective of this work. Second, both the organization and the individuals described here would, by almost any standards, be judged to be highly successful and this fact should be included in any attempt to evaluate their behavior.

Because historical, planning, and other peoples' models

require almost no generalization to make them relevant to particular events of interest to the manager, and because these three types of models can easily generate more problems than the manager can reasonably hope to deal with, it is not surprising, perhaps, that models requiring somewhat more generalization are less important elements of the process of problem finding. It is true, however, that on occasion managers draw on experiences other than their own to define problems for themselves and their organizations.

Extraorganizational Models

Trade journals which report new practices and their effects in other organizations can sometimes define useful areas for managerial analysis. Customers frequently serve the same function by reporting the accomplishments of competitors in the area of price, service, and/or product quality. General Motors is known for its practice of ranking the performance measures of a number of plants producing the same or similar products and making this information available to the managers of these facilities. The implication is strong in these comparisons that problems exist in plants where performance is poor relative to other plants.

In using all such extraorganizational models to define intraorganizational problems, the manager must resolve the difficult question of model validity. "Is the fact that our West Coast plant has lower maintenance costs relevant to our operations? After all, they have newer equipment." "Is the fact that our competitor is lowering its price relevant to our pricing policy? After all, our quality is better." There are enough attributes in any industrial situation to make it unlikely indeed that any extraorganizational model will fit the manager's situation perfectly. Judgments on the question of model validity must frequently be made by operating managers.

In the Southern Company one clear case was observed where two extraorganizational models were employed in an attempt to define a problem. A member of the Plant Engineering Department attended a meeting of an engineering society at which a technique called "work sampling" was discussed in the context of several successful applications in other plants. This model of a current engineering practice, which had not been employed by his department, led this man to consider the problem of finding an application for work sampling in the Southern Company. Clearly if this technique could be successfully applied, it would reduce the difference between his department and his extraorganizational model. A few days later this engineer noticed an idle, unattended fork truck in one of the manufacturing shops and he immediately thought that an analysis of fork truck operations might be the application he was looking for. He discussed this idea with his supervisors and they agreed that the project should be undertaken.

Because of the lack of direct responsibility for fork trucks, Plant Engineering was aware from the beginning of the project that its primary task would be to convince the product departments that their fork trucks indeed constituted a problem. To provide the department managers with evidence on this point, in addition to the internal work sampling study, a survey of fork truck operations was made in six nearby plants engaged in similar manufacturing operations. The explicit purpose of the survey was to define a basis (an extraorganizational model) on which internal fork truck operations could be evaluated.

The six-company survey yielded in part the following results:

1. The number of trucks operated ranged from six to fifty, with an average of twenty-one—same as Southern Company;

2. Utilizations ranged from fifty percent to seventy-one percent, with an average of sixty-three percent—eighteen and five tenths percent higher than Southern Company;

3. Responsibility for trucks was centralized in all six companies—contrary to Southern Company:

4. Trucks were controlled through dispatching or scheduling in five of the six companies (some used radio control)—contrary to Southern Company;

5. All companies owned rather than leased their trucks—contrary to Southern Company;

6. All companies performed their own maintenance of their trucks—contrary to Southern Company;

7. Three companies licensed their drivers, and assigned them full time to driving—contrary to Southern Company.

The fact that the surveyed companies on the average operated the same number of trucks as the Southern Company was clearly cited as evidence supporting the validity of this extraorganizational model.

Because the six-company survey and the work sampling study had defined the problem in aggregate terms, the analysis and recommendations proceeded at this level. The Plant

Engineering Department decided to make their recommendation on the basis of an overall utilization of 60 percent (the average utilization found in the six company survey) which implied a reduction of five trucks. They then looked at their work sampling data and reallocated trucks among departments to bring individual truck utilization figures as close to 60 percent as possible. The recommended reallocation in fact supplied a saving of five trucks. The recommendation went on to suggest that Product Departments "compensate [for this reduction in trucks] by establishing sharing arrangements between departments."

The recommendation also proposed "permanent [full time] licensed drivers" instead of production workers operating the trucks on an *ad hoc* basis as part of their regular duties. As a result of a study which had indicated that leasing was preferable to buying the fork trucks, no change in ownership or maintenance was proposed. The annual savings anticipated from the recommended changes amounted to $7,250.

It is interesting to note that the recommendations themselves constituted problems for the Product Department managers. The task of "establishing sharing arrangements among departments" had not been resolved by the study and remained a thorny problem. The task of transferring qualified production workers to full-time truck driving duties involved not only complex problems of morale and labor relations but also economic trade-offs not evaluated by the study. The task of redefining departmental work procedures to relate to centrally controlled truck services was similarly unresolved. In return for these problems, the seven product department managers could expect to share in an annual savings of $7,250. Their response to the recommendation was less than enthusiastic. They agreed, after some bargaining, to return one truck to the leasing company but were not willing to pursue the matter any further.

Despite this rather negative conclusion, it is interesting to note that most managers considered the fork truck study a success. The validity of using the extraorganizational model derived from the survey as a means of defining the problem was never questioned and an evaluation of the existing policy on this basis was considered well justified.

A more complicated use of extraorganizational models occurred in the case of several managers who had had personal experience in other organizations. In several situations they used this experience to define intraorganizational problems by emphasizing the personal element of this experience as evidence of its validity and by de-emphasizing (or not mentioning) where this experience was gained.

Extraorganizational models have a natural disadvantage as sources of problems because of the question of model validity which can always be raised against them. When extraorganizational experience agrees with local experience (historical model), it is seen as valid, but since it agrees with the local experience, it defines no problem. When extraorganizational experience disagrees with local experience and might therefore define a problem, the discrepancy itself raises the question of model validity. This attribute of extraorganizational models may serve to explain the fact that they were a relatively weak source of management problems in the Southern Company. Out of fifty-two managers, forty-seven agreed with the statement: "Most of our new ideas are generated within the company."

In the case of new organizations, of course, historical models are not available and extraorganizational models become more influential. One such situation was observed in the Southern Company. A promising new product was moving from the latter stages of development into the early stages of production and sales. A new product department was formed on an informal basis and the standard procedures of accounting data collection and reporting were instituted. No one expected the new department to be profitable immediately but after some months an executive at the product group level used a model not based on the history of the new department but one based on the performance of other departments to define a problem. He described the process this way:

> The numbers [on the monthly reports] were horrifying. I asked for a report and I got fuzzy answers that I didn't believe so I said, "Fellows, I'm taking over the right to ask questions."
>
> In asking questions I found I could pick holes in their analysis of the situation. Everything was loose.
>
> I analyzed their orders and found that with their overhead they couldn't make money.
>
> The department was reorganized.

In new organizations, extraorganizational models can be powerful sources of management problems.

Some Normative Questions

The principal objective of this study was to find a relatively simple theoretical structure to explain the process of problem finding used by the managers at the Southern Company, and the set of four models just described represents that structure. These models, which range from ones maintained by other members of the organization, through simple historical and planning models, to those which apply the experience of other organizations to local situations, have been tested against the rather massive sample of data collected at the Southern Company and have been found sufficient to explain all these observations. That is to say, it is possible to trace all the observed behavior back to differences defined by one of these four classes of models. To this extent the study was successful.

But observations like these, even after abstraction into a theoretical structure, are only observations. They do not suggest the consequences of using other kinds of models or using these same models with different frequencies. They do not suggest how managers might behave more effectively than they do. Isolated observations cannot define differences. Observations must be compared to a model before normative questions can be answered.

One way to generate such comparisons would be to conduct comparative studies within and among a number of organizations. One could then answer such questions as: "Are these same models used by unsuccessful managers? If so, how can the difference in performance be explained? If not, what models are used? Do managers in other organizations use these models with different frequencies or under different circumstances? Are there systematic differences in the use of these models at different levels of the organization?" All such questions could be answered by careful study of several organizations or several levels of the same organization and these extraorganizational models might serve to suggest management improvements. Until such studies are completed, however, the only models which can be used to evaluate the behavior observed in the Southern Company are some which were not used there.

Scientific Models

When compared to models used in the physical and social sciences for quite similar purposes, the models used by the managers in the Southern Company (and elsewhere) are almost startling in their naïveté. In the same company, electrical engineers explicitly used quite complex theoretical models to help them define problems associated with the design of a relatively simple electronic control system.

Similarly, mechanical engineers employed a variety of quite general theories in the design of new high speed production equipment. In neither of these cases did the engineers base their predictions on their own experience except in a very general sense. They quite confidently applied theories derived from the observations of others and the equipment which resulted from their work required relatively little redesign after construction. Managers, on the other hand, based their expectations on relatively small samples of their own experience. Their rather simple theories, as has already been noted, yielded rather poor predictions, and managers therefore spent a substantial amount of time solving either their own problems or those defined by others.

The behavior of scientists (an extraorganizational model) suggests that there is an alternative to this rather frantic approach to a complex world. When discrepancies arise between a model and the environment, one can undertake to improve the model rather than change the environment. In fact, a scientist might even go so far as to suggest that, until one has a fairly reliable model of the environment, it is not only foolish but perhaps even dangerous to take action when its effect cannot be predicted.

If carried to an extreme, of course, the scientist's tendency to search for better models of the world as it is would leave no time for taking action to change it, and it seems unlikely that this allocation of time and talent would be an appropriate one for the operating manager. In the Southern Company, it must be remembered, those managers who based their actions on very simple models which took very little time to construct were judged to be quite successful by their organization.

On the other hand, the increasing use by managers of more sophisticated modeling techniques like those mentioned earlier in this paper may suggest that the balance between model building and action taking is shifting. A number of companies now base changes in distribution systems, production and inventory control systems, quality control systems, advertising allocation systems, and so on, on the predictions of relatively complex models which are based on substantial bodies of theory and empirical evidence. To the extent that these models fail to describe events which take place, they, like the simpler models they replace, can serve to define problems. To the extent that these more complete models take into account events which the manager cannot, or prefers not to, control, these models can serve to protect the manager from problems on which he might otherwise waste his energy.

While it may be true that these more explicit scientific models will gradually replace simple intuitive models, several reasons suggest that the change will take some time. First, many operating managers today find the language of the new techniques foreign, despite increasing attempts to change this situation through training. Second, the new techniques often involve even more generalization than extraorganizational models, and honest questions of model validity will tend to delay their widespread use. And third, the process of problem finding currently used will perpetuate itself simply by keeping managers so busy that they will find little time to learn about and try these new methods of problem finding.

More important than any of these reasons, however, may be one which, curiously, has been created by the advocates of management science. In most, it not all, of the literature describing them, model building techniques are described as means for solving management problems. In their now classical book on operations research, Churchman, Ackoff, and Arnoff, for example, suggest model building as a step which should follow "formulating the problem."[12] The process by which the problem should be formulated, however, is left totally unspecified—and this is where managers as well as students of management frequently report their greatest difficulty. They can see the process by which these techniques can solve problems but they cannot see how to define the problems.

The theory which has been proposed here suggests that problem definition cannot precede model construction. It is impossible to know, for example, that a cost is too high unless one has some basis (a model) which suggests it might be lower. This basis might be one's own experience, the experience of a competitor, or the output of a scientific model. Similarly, one cannot be sure that his distribution costs will be reduced by linear programming until a model is constructed and solved which suggests that rescheduling will lower costs. The imperfections of an inventory system are revealed only by comparing it to some theoretical model; they cannot be defined until after the model has been built. The logical inconsistency which suggests that problems must be clearly defined in order to justify model construction is

---

12. C. W. Churchman, R. L. Ackoff, and E. L. Arnoff, *Introduction to Operations Research* (New York: John Wiley & Sons, 1957).

very likely an important reason that scientific models will
only slowly be recognized by operating managers as important aids in the definition of their problems.

Despite their current disadvantages, the so-called new
techniques of model building are, as has already been noted,
making significant contributions to management effectiveness. They represent, therefore, not only a means for
evaluating current managerial behavior but also a new class
of models which can be used by managers to define their
problems.

The Problem of Model Selection

The study of managers in the Southern Company indicates
that concepts like image and intelligence which have been
proposed to explain the process of problem finding can be
made somewhat more operational. A rather small set of
model classes has been defined which constitutes sufficient
stimuli to trigger a fairly large sample of managerial behavior. This is not to say that future observations may not indicate the need for additional model classes or that future
work is not required to make the process of managerial
model building even more operational and testable. The
study of the Southern Company represents perhaps only an
encouraging start at understanding an important and little
understood area of management.

Even with these initial insights, however, it is possible to
see where major theoretical gaps still exist. Chief among
these is the problem of model selection. As has already been
noted, the requests of other people are sufficient to define a
full-time job for many managers. The problem of investigating and taking corrective action on discrepancies from
historical trends can keep any manager busy all the time. The
construction of extraorganizational and/or scientific models
and the actions which they trigger are similarly time-consuming. Even after the manager has constructed the models
he will use to define his problems, he must somehow select
from among the differences which are simultaneously defined
by these models. Personal requests, historical discrepancies,
extraorganizational ideas, and the stimuli of scientific models
do not in general define differences one at a time. The choice
of the discrepancy to attend to next may be as important a
process as the construction of the models which define them.
It seems clear, however, that we must understand the process
by which differences are defined before we can worry

seriously about understanding the process of selecting from among them. The study in the Southern Company, therefore, largely ignored the priority problem and concentrated on difference definitions only.

It is impossible, however, to observe managers at work without getting some rough ideas about how they deal with the priority problem. Telephone calls, for example, are very high priority stimuli. A ringing telephone will interrupt work of virtually every kind. This priority rule is complicated sometimes by an intervening secretary but many managers pride themselves on always answering their own phone. One manager reported that he always worked on problems which would "get worse" before he worked on static problems. Thus, he dealt with a problem involving a conflict between a foreman and a troublesome employee before pressing forward on a cost reduction program.

Perhaps the most explicit priorities in the Southern Company were established by means of deadlines. Most problems defined by other members of the organization carried with them a time at which, or by which, the request should be satisfied. Certain reports were due monthly, a fixed number of working days after the end of the preceding month. Meetings were scheduled at stated times. Annual plans were required on a specified date. While a number of such requests might face a manager simultaneously, they almost never would have the same deadline and by this means the manager could decide which to do when. The fact that most problems triggered by other people's models carried deadlines may explain why these problems seemed to be given so much attention. When asked to indicate "Which problems do you usually get to first, time deadline, big payoff or personal interest?" forty-three out of fifty-two managers indicated time deadline.

From a theoretical point of view, one could consider the flow of problems through an organization as analogous to the flow of jobs through a job shop and perhaps apply some of the theories which have been developed there to understand and perhaps prescribe the process of priority assignment. Managers, for example, must trade off relative lateness of their tasks with the duration of the tasks just as a foreman loading machines in a machine shop. Once the problem definition is well understood it would appear that some theory is already available to structure the process of assigning problem priorities. The array of models used by and available to managers suggests that an understanding of the process by which problems are defined will not constitute a complete theory of problem finding. A process which assigns priorities to a set of simultaneously defined problems remains to be specified.

Personal Growth, Laboratory Training, Science, and All That: A Shot at a Cognitive Clarification

Harold J. Leavitt and Robert Doktor

In the "old" days, the forties, laboratory trainers did battle with conservative scientists and educators. The trainers claimed to be breaking new ground in the realm of insightful experiential learning; the conservatives claimed that the T-Groupers were fooling around with unscientific mystique.

In the sixties, Argyris,[1] a veteran laboratory trainer, takes on the personal growth people; in the pages of this *Journal* he champions science, implying (we felt) that the existential, body movement, personal growth "stuff" is unscientific foolishness.

This tripartite debate—traditional "old" psychological science vs. old-fashioned laboratory training vs. personal growth laboratory training—is usually argued in the pages of this *Journal* in clinical, laboratory-training language, especially by the laboratory trainers. The *JABS* discussion among Argyris[2] and others follows the same pattern, with the issues ranging across childhood constraints on masturbation to adult attitudes toward authority and with great emphasis on anxiety and defensiveness as factors limiting the capacity of individuals to experience the world.

But another language for bonding many of the issues together may be much more cognitive—out of the tradition of Piaget and more recently derivative of Bruner, Olver, and Greenfield.[3] One can reread that issue of *JABS* and translate a large part of it from clinical, psychoanalytic, and existential terminology into developmental-cognitive terminology and end up with what looks like a moderately simple, but highly

Reproduced by special permission from *The Journal of Applied Behavioral Science* 6, no. 2 (1970): 173–79, copyright 1970 by the NTL Institute for Applied Behavioral Science.

1. C. Argyris, "On the Future of Laboratory Education," *J. Appl. Behav. Sci.* 3, no. 2 (1967): 153–83.
2. Ibid.
3. J. Bruner, R. Olver, and P. Greenfield, *Studies in Cognitive Growth* (New York: Wiley, 1966).

explanatory, set of ideas. This is not, incidentally, to propose that there is a full trade-off between the two approaches; only that a large portion of the problem(s) can be novelly and fruitfully looked at from this cognitive point of view.

Bruner, following Piaget, shows empirically that as children develop, they proceed through three grossly successive, but overlapping stages. The first is an enactive stage in which the meaning of things is mediated primarily by sensory-motor processes, often largely kinesthetic. The child learns by touching, feeling, handling. Things are how they feel. The child then moves into an ikonic stage which is perceptual-imagic in nature. Now the child begins to understand through the use of perceptual imagery in any sensory mode. He imagines how things feel, how they smell, or how they look. And he problem-solves by manipulating images of things rather than by dealing tactually or sensorially with the things themselves. A third stage, which apparently begins around age seven in Western society, is symbolic. The child begins to use symbols to stand for things, and to understand by manipulating symbols, largely words and numbers.

While these three developmental stages occur successively, the degree to which symbolic behavior appears, when it appears, and the extent to which it dominates seem to be a function of environmental variables—like education and interactions with other symbol-users. Rural Mexican children of a given age, for example, use the symbolic mode less often and less sophisticatedly than counterpart Mexican children in city schools. Since most symbols are so clearly man-made (in this verbal-mathematical sense), it is understandable that they are likely to be much more highly culturally dependent than ikonic or enactive tools.

If we now do some even freer elaboration upon this interpretation of the Bruner et al. model, several ideas begin to fall into place. Consider first the possibility that we can use these modes in our search for interpersonal meanings as well as the meanings for things and consider that any person can be more or less "sophisticated" in any mode—that each mode has depth as well as breadth, as it were. So just as one person has a larger verbal vocabulary than another or a larger vocabulary in mathematics, he may also have a wider range of touches or physical feelings than another—as, for example, blind persons are purported to have. And the ikonic vocabulary of persons may show comparable variance, too. One person may be able directly to perceive in some experience of the world, e.g., a painting, a much wider and more differentiated range of things than some others.

But in the course of events we tend, let us suppose, in one society, or family, or profession, to learn a larger vocabulary in one of those modes than in the others. If we become mathematicians, we probably learn a very large symbolic vocabulary, and conceivably we may remain relatively mute ikonically or enactively. It may be possible for great men, exposed to rich environments, to become sophisticated in all three modes. Perhaps traditional education emphasizes the symbolic more than the others (though we have not entirely neglected physical education in our schools).

More than "vocabulary" or semantic richness is involved here. More than alternative modes or languages with which to give meaning to things. *Grammars* and *syntaxes* differ as well, between and within modes.

Consider, for example, mathematics, a symbolic language. The grammar of mathematics, the rules for relating symbols to one another, are relatively constrained and rigid. There are *right* and *wrong* ways. But what of ikonic grammar? The grammar of the abstract painter or of the sensitively perceiving T-Group trainer? The rules for relating parts in the ikonic mode may be far less fixed, far more open. Even portrait painters may internalize a vocabulary of noses, but where and how they relate them to eyes is not so tightly or grammatically constrained—not these days. And for nonrepresentational abstract painting the rules are verbally very loose. Classical ballet, largely enactive, was grammatically tight. Not so modern dance. And so on. Finally, T-Group trainers have, it often seems, almost entirely private grammars, finding meaning in what they perceive through some private heuristic rules derived from their own personal experiential histories.

We may therefore expect (a) a greater variety of interpretations of the meaning of things in one area of activity than another, and (b) more frequently original or "creative" products where rules are loose than where they are tight. It may be probabilistically less likely that one can be original in plumbing than in modern dancing—though both are quite enactive.

Developmentally these three modes are sequentially ordered. The symbolic mode develops later than the other two. There is therefore an implication of a hierarchy. Indeed we would argue that the *symbolic mode* is a mode of higher order, permitting greater abstraction and communication of concepts than the others, more efficient in dealing with a modern techno-symbolic world. Even the most "clinical" of clinicians tend to use symbols to describe or generalize their perceptions—which is to argue that while vocabularies and grammatical rules may occur in any mode, we generally utilize the symbolic mode both to try to order and to communicate relationships among perceptions or sensory feelings.

We would suggest too that for the "feel" to go beyond the instantaneously felt and forgotten, for the experienced trainer to see things this time that look like things he saw before, and to reach for an intervention likely to work, he needs an "executive program" of some kind—some sort of constrained, ruled rationality. Otherwise he behaves randomly. At the moment, symbols are very useful for the construction of such governing programs.

Finally, consider again, originality or creativity. Can they not *(since we are now describing a product as well as a process)* occur in any mode? A largely enactive-creative product may be a piece of sculpture, a new surgical technique, or a dance. An ikonic-creative product may be a painting or a new set of sounds or perhaps an interpersonal insight. A symbolic-creative product may be a scientific theory or a new construction principle. But in that symbolic realm the grammatical constraints are usually tighter; the probability of a creative (seen by the relevant world as novel and useful) outcome is smaller. In ticktacktoe it is hard to be creative—the rules are too tight. In a verbal-symbolic game like *Scrabble* it is somewhat easier. In a game of *Let's Paint an Abstract,* it is easier still to do something original—but harder perhaps for the world to evaluate its originality. A new solution to a theorem in symbolic logic is easy to tab as original but much less likely to occur than an unusual sculpture. Not that arts always have loose grammars. Classical ballet does not. How easy is it to be a *creative* ballerina? Deciding what is "really" creative in contemporary, grammatically loose art or music causes nightmares for judges, in part because there are many candidates; and there are many candidates in part because the grammars are loose. The really creative mathematician is easier to spot, but the candidates are few.

Incidentally, nothing rules out a mix of modes. The architect probably *has* to play the symbolic-ikonic game. The old-time jazz musician (not the composer) probably is enactive-ikonic. He probably plays using tactile and auditory cues, and reacts to his playing ikonically. But a composer, one would guess, might *either* put symbols together and then listen to the sounds (symbolic-ikonic) or imagine the sounds and then write the symbols (ikonic-symbolic), or both.

Back to the laboratory training debate. Argyris now appears to be at the interface of the ikonic and symbolic modes. He wants people to develop ikonic interpersonal vocabularies, but he wants these responses and perceptions translated into the symbolic mode—written down in books, with symbolically expressed rules and relationships. The nonlaboratory "traditional" scientific types (with their silly old values about research standards) do not even want to treat the experiential as part of the game until *after* it has been symbolized. Whereas the new left wing is enactive. When they "feel," they mean *feel*. They do not mean "perceive" or "imagine." They are satisfied, apparently, to develop in people large enactive vocabularies without very tight grammatical rules. If for them there is to be translation, it need be only to or from the ikonic, not necessarily even into or from the symbolic mode.

Hence perhaps we should expect very little *written* theory from the personal growth people; perhaps there will be an increasing rejection of "theory" sessions and such cognitive language in laboratory training, if we interpret rightly Robert Tannenbaum's[4] plea to Chris to come and feel it, to believe it.

Incidentally, that anxiety should be high when we try to get symbolic people to behave ikonically or enactively is neither surprising nor unexplainable. Anxiety usually accompanies movement from the certain into the uncertain, from the realm in which we are skilled and knowledgeable into new areas in which we expect ourselves to be awkward and perhaps entirely unable to fulfill our needs. Youngsters are anxious when we try to get them into the water for the first time; so are dogs and cats. Students are anxious when they first try to apply an unfamiliar mathematical method to an important problem. Symbolic people are anxious when playing charades. Enactive or ikonic sensitivity trainers exhibit anxiety (do they not?) in symbolic discussions with "hard science" types.

So we see these enactive developments in laboratory training as one kind of effort to generate vocabulary in the enactive mode. The belief that expansion of such vocabulary will make us more whole or more human or more something does not send us. The belief that some things for some people are more readily communicated in one vocabulary than another does sound reasonable. So does the idea, which we

4. R. Tannenbaum, "Reactions to Chris Argyris," *J. Appl. Behav. Sci.* 3, no. 2 (1967): 205–6.

do not believe was expressed in the aforementioned *JABS* dialogue, that if we force people to communicate or experience in vocabularies unfamiliar to them, they will perforce be less able to build defenses. The man who "intellectualizes" defensively when symbolically (verbally) confronted with his own behavior may be too *un*facile in another mode to defend himself against an unwelcome confrontation presented in that mode. But that apparent teaching advantage of thus catching a man when he has no vocabulary for defense sounds like a transient one. When one becomes really savvy about the body movement method, he should be able to fend and parry in that mode, too. The army psychiatrists who used to parade the recruits around nude to get their defenses down would have their problems with the recruit who was a confirmed nudist.

Finally, the implicit proposal (which sometimes accompanies the personal growth view) that man is "too" symbolic seems nonsensical. To argue that man will be bigger if he is able to experience in several modes is not nonsensical. But to suggest that man's wondrous capacity to symbolize and his exploitation of it through science and literature makes him *less* human is to have things a little backwards, is it not?

Perhaps we can learn some new things in other than symbolic modes. But our guess is that the real richness of exploitation will come in two ways: First it will come when we can translate readily from one mode to another; when we can do a much less halting job of saying what we feel, or feeling what others say, or visualizing mathematics, or verbalizing dancing, or learning to swim enactively by perceiving or symbolizing the swimming process. And second, we would also guess (old-fashionedly) that the job is much bigger than just vocabulary building in the enactive and ikonic modes. We also need to develop some grammars in those modes, and the grammars may end up in the symbolic as a master mode.

3

Perceptions,
Attitudes, and Beliefs

Introduction

Most readers are probably familiar with culture shock. In a few hours we can fly from a Western culture to the Orient and are immediately beset with a host of new sights and smells and customs. The shock part of culture shock seems to come from our initial inability to straighten out and simplify this jungle of new stimulation.

Because human beings are unable to cope with massive numbers of discrete inputs from the outside world, they need to find ways of simplifying, filtering, stabilizing, and classifying their information about the world. This chapter is about those simplifying, filtering, stabilizing, and classifying processes.

Consider the following statements: "A woman's place is in the home." "Smoking pot won't lead to using the hard stuff." "Whites don't have soul." "People should be objective in dealing with others on the job, and not let personal considerations enter into their decisions." "It's not right for public employees to strike." Each of those statements expresses an attitude either about some factual matter or about rights and wrongs. Each of those attitudes, true or not, justified or not, helps its holder to simplify part of the world. The woman who believes that her place *is* in the home doesn't have to spend time deciding which career to pursue. The person who believes that pot won't lead to harder stuff will find it easier to decide whether or not to accept the offer of a stick. Attitudes (and stereotypes and values), by simplifying and categorizing chunks of the world, enable one to deal more easily with it. But while simplifying, our attitudes may also partially blind us; for some of the simplification is brought about by filtering out some of what is really out there. And there is no guarantee that the filter will only filter out the irrelevant facts.

This chapter is about attitudes and perceptions, about how

attitudes are formed, how they influence our behavior, and how we can change them, and how and why what we perceive may be different from what is really there. Like needs and motivations, attitudes are a state of mind. But whereas needs and motives provide the driving force for behavior, attitudes provide the *premises* for behavior. They play a vital role both in influencing our perceptions and providing cues for behavior. Indeed attitudes provide the meeting place of the emotional and the reasoning sides of people.

But where do we get our attitudes? As the paper on "Training the Woman to Know Her Place" by Sandra and Daryl Bem makes clear, some of our most powerful attitudes, our very deeply held beliefs and values, are initiated during our early childhood and perhaps even during infancy. When one of us told his four-year-old daughter that he was a teacher, she could only giggle incredulously. Both of her nursery school teachers had been women. How could her daddy be a teacher? A month or so later, in response to a question about what she wanted to be when she grew up, she mentioned nursing. When her daddy asked why she wouldn't want to be a doctor instead of a nurse, she voiced disbelief. Only boys became doctors. As each of us grows up, we are told by a thousand different sources what is true and what is good.

Once formed, attitudes are slow to change, for two important reasons: First, because our attitudes are useful to us. They help to filter our perceptions of the world and thereby keep us comfortable. We tend not to perceive those things which contradict our beliefs and values. But if contradictory facts and values are filtered out, how can new facts and new values find their way in? How can we change? Either slowly, or through such strong attacks from the world that our filters break down; and by some other means, too.

A second reason attitudes don't change very rapidly is that they hang together in a more or less consistent structure and thereby support one another. Some people who are prejudiced against blacks quote biblical scripture in support of their position. Frequently these people are Bible-belt fundamentalists. To change their racial attitudes might also require changing their religious beliefs about the infallibility of the Bible and the Word of God. Instead of the chain being no stronger than its weakest link, the attitude structure seems to be no weaker than its strongest belief. When the Chinese Communists brainwashed American POWs during the Korean War, one of their strategies was to undermine the

POW's entire system of beliefs. But to do this successfully, they had to remove any social support provided by each POW's buddies and even by the system of military rank. Thus, as Hastorf, Schneider, and Polefka point out in their paper in this chapter, attitudes have structure, stability, and meaning.

The brief selection by Zimbardo and Ebbesen on motivation research demonstrates how knowledge about the structure and dynamics of attitudes can be used to induce people to give blood, to buy cigarettes, to fly a particular airline's jets, and perhaps to induce behaviors of less commercial varieties. The point of their brief paper is that perceptive filters can be bypassed, and once bypassed, behavior can be influenced and attitudes changed.

The final selection in this chapter, by Erich Fromm, considers a particular attitude, the bureaucratic attitude, as a character trait. Fromm defines the bureaucratic attitude as a state of mind in which people are dealt with as if they were *things*. This is an attitude about the relationship between man and organization that pervades most of the world. Like the attitudes about women, the bureaucratic attitude is a nonconscious ideology of which most of us are only dimly aware. Fromm goes on to argue, and we agree, that much inhumanity in organizations results from this deeply held attitude. There are other important attitudes about organizations that are nearly as important. Consider, for example, attitudes about our obligation to accept authority, about a fair day's work for a fair day's pay, about loyalty to the organization, about the virtue of success in climbing the organizational ladder, and so on. The reader can go on to identify many more such implicit attitudes.

This set of papers is about such attitudes, their origins, development, and change; and about how they affect and are affected by the process of perception.

Training the Woman to Know Her Place: The Power of a Nonconscious Ideology

Sandra L. Bem and Daryl J. Bem

In the beginning God created the heaven and the earth.
. . . And God said, Let us make man in our image, after
our likeness; and let them have dominion over the fish
of the sea, and over the fowl of the air, and over the
cattle, and over all the earth. . . . And the rib, which the
Lord God had taken from man, made he a woman and
brought her unto the man. . . . And the Lord God said
unto the woman, What is this that thou has done? And
the woman said, The serpent beguiled me, and I did eat.
. . . Unto the woman He said, I will greatly multiply thy
sorrow and thy conception; in sorrow thou shalt bring
forth children; and thy desire shall be to thy husband,
and he shall rule over thee. (Gen. 1, 2, 3)

And lest anyone fail to grasp the moral of this story, Saint
Paul provides further clarification:

> For a man . . . is the image and glory of God; but the
> woman is the glory of the man. For the man is not of the
> woman, but the woman of the man. Neither was the
> man created for the woman, but the woman for the man.
> (1 Cor. 11)

> Let the woman learn in silence with all subjection.
> But I suffer not a woman to teach, nor to usurp author-
> ity over the man, but to be in silence. For Adam was
> first formed, then Eve. And Adam was not deceived, but
> the woman, being deceived, was in the transgression.
> Notwithstanding, she shall be saved in childbearing, if

they continue in faith and charity and holiness with sobriety. (1 Tim. 2)

And lest it be thought that only Christians have this rich
heritage of ideology about women, consider the morning
prayer of the Orthodox Jew:

Blessed art Thou, oh Lord our God, King of the Universe, that I was not born a gentile.
Blessed art Thou, oh Lord our God, King of the Universe, that I was not born a slave.
Blessed art Thou, oh Lord our God, King of the Universe, that I was not born a woman.

Or the Koran, the sacred text of Islam:

Men are superior to women on account of the
qualities in which God has given them preeminence.

Because they think they sense a decline in feminine "faith,
charity, and holiness with sobriety," many people today jump
to the conclusion that the ideology expressed in these pas-
sages is a relic of the past. Not so. It has simply been obscured by an equalitarian veneer, and the ideology has now
become nonconscious. That is, we remain unaware of it
because alternative beliefs and attitudes about women go
unimagined. We are like the fish who is unaware that his environment is wet. After all, what else could it be? Such is the
nature of all nonconscious ideologies. Such is the nature of
America's ideology about women. For even those Americans
who agree that a black skin should not uniquely qualify its
owner for janitorial or domestic service continue to act as if
the possession of a uterus uniquely qualifies *its* owner for
precisely that.

Consider, for example, the 1968 student rebellion at
Columbia University. Students from the radical left took over
some administration buildings in the name of equalitarian
principles which they accused the university of flouting. Here
were the most militant spokesmen one could hope to find in
the cause of equalitarian ideals. But no sooner had they occupied the buildings than the male militants blandly turned
to their sisters-in-arms and assigned them the task of
preparing the food, while they—the menfolk—would presumably plan further strategy. The reply these males received
was the reply they deserved, and the fact that domestic tasks
behind the barricades were desegregated across the sex line
that day is an everlasting tribute to the class consciousness of
the ladies of the left.

But these conscious coeds are not typical, for the nonconscious assumptions about a woman's "natural" talents (or lack of them) are at least as prevalent among women as they are among men. A psychologist named Philip Goldberg[1] demonstrated this by asking female college students to rate a number of professional articles from each of six fields. The articles were collated into two equal sets of booklets, and the names of the authors were changed so that the identical article was attributed to a male author (e.g., John T. McKay) in one set of booklets and to a female author (e.g., Joan T. McKay) in the other set. Each student was asked to read the articles in her booklet and to rate them for value, competence, persuasiveness, writing style, and so forth.

As he had anticipated, Goldberg found that the identical article received significantly lower ratings when it was attributed to a female author than when it was attributed to a male author. He had predicted this result for articles from professional fields generally considered the province of men, like law and city planning, but to his surprise, these coeds also downgraded articles from the fields of dietetics and elementary school education when they were attributed to female authors. In other words, these students rated the male authors as better at everything, agreeing with Aristotle that "we should regard the female nature as afflicted with a natural defectiveness." We repeated this experiment informally in our own classrooms and discovered that male students show the same implicit prejudice against female authors that Goldberg's female students showed. Such is the nature of a nonconscious ideology!

It is significant that examples like these can be drawn from the college world, for today's students have challenged the established ways of looking at almost every other issue, and they have been quick to reject those practices of our society which conflict explicitly with their major values. But as the above examples suggest, they will find it far more difficult to shed the more subtle aspects of a sex-role ideology which—as we shall now attempt to demonstrate—conflicts just as surely with their existential values as any of the other societal practices to which they have so effectively raised objection. And as we shall see, there is no better way to appreciate the power of a society's nonconscious ideology than to examine it within the framework of values held by that society's avant-garde.

1. P. Goldberg, "Are Women Prejudiced against Women?" *Transaction* 5 (April 1968): 28–30.

Individuality and Self-Fulfillment

The dominant values of today's students concern personal growth on the one hand, and interpersonal relationships on the other. The first of these emphasizes individuality and self-fulfillment; the second stresses openness, honesty, and equality in all human relationships.

The values of individuality and self-fulfillment imply that each human being, male or female, is to be encouraged to "do his own thing." Men and women are no longer to be stereotyped by society's definitions. If sensitivity, emotionality, and warmth are desirable human characteristics, then they are desirable for men as well as for women. (John Wayne is no longer an idol of the young, but their pop-art satire.) If independence, assertiveness, and serious intellectual commitment are desirable human characteristics, then they are desirable for women as well as for men. The major prescription of this college generation is that each individual should be encouraged to discover and fulfill his own unique potential and identity, unfettered by society's presumptions.

But society's presumptions enter the scene much earlier than most people suspect, for parents begin to raise their children in accord with the popular stereotypes from the very first. Boys are encouraged to be aggressive, competitive, and independent, whereas girls are rewarded for being passive and dependent.[2] In one study, six-month-old infant girls were already being touched and spoken to more by their mothers while they were playing than were infant boys. When they were thirteen months old, these same girls were more reluctant than the boys to leave their mothers; they returned more quickly and more frequently to them; and they remained closer to them throughout the entire play period. When a physical barrier was placed between mother and child, the girls tended to cry and motion for help; the boys made more active attempts to get around the barrier.[3] No one knows to what extent these sex differences at the age of thirteen months can be attributed to the mothers' behavior at the age of six months, but it is hard to believe that the two are unconnected.

As children grow older, more explicit sex-role training is

2. H. Barry III, M. K. Bacon, and I. L. Child, "A Cross-cultural Survey of Some Sex Differences in Socialization," *Journal of Abnormal and Social Psychology* 55 (1957): 327–32; R. R. Sears, E. E. Maccoby, and H. Levin, *Patterns of Child Rearing* (Evanston, Ill.: Row, Peterson, 1957).

3. S. Goldberg and M. Lewis, "Play Behavior in the Year-old Infant: Early Sex Differences," *Child Development* 40 (1969): 21–31.

introduced. Boys are encouraged to take more of an interest in mathematics and science. Boys, not girls, are given chemistry sets and microscopes for Christmas. Moreover, all children quickly learn that mommy is proud to be a moron when it comes to mathematics and science, whereas daddy knows all about these things. When a young boy returns from school all excited about biology, he is almost certain to be encouraged to think of becoming a physician. A girl with similar enthusiasm is told that she might want to consider nurse's training later so she can have "an interesting job to fall back upon in case—God forbid—she ever needs to support herself." A very different kind of encouragement. And any girl who doggedly persists in her enthusiasm for science is likely to find her parents as horrified by the prospect of a permanent love affair with physics as they would be by the prospect of an interracial marriage.

These socialization practices quickly take their toll. By nursery school age, for example, boys are already asking more questions about how and why things work.[4] In first and second grade, when asked to suggest ways of improving various toys, boys do better on the fire truck and girls do better on the nurse's kit, but by the third grade, boys do better regardless of the toy presented.[5] By the ninth grade, 25 percent of the boys, but only 3 percent of the girls, are considering careers in science or engineering.[6] When they apply for college, boys and girls are about equal on verbal aptitude tests, but boys score significantly higher on mathematical aptitude tests—about sixty points higher on the College Board examinations, for example.[7] Moreover, girls improve their mathematical performance if problems are reworded so that they deal with cooking and gardening, even though the abstract reasoning required for their solutions remains the same.[8] Clearly, not just ability, but motivation too, has been affected.

4. M. E. Smith, "The Influence of Age, Sex, and Situation on the Frequency of Form and Functions of Questions Asked by Preschool Children," *Child Development* 3 (1933): 201–13.

5. E. P. Torrance, *Guiding Creative Talent* (Englewood Cliffs, N. J.: Prentice-Hall, 1962).

6. J. C. Flanagan, "Project Talent," unpublished manuscript; cited by J. Kagan, "Acquisition and Significance of Sex Typing and Sex Role Identity," in M. L. Hoffman and L. W. Hoffman, eds., *Review of Child Development Research* (New York: Russell Sage Foundation, 1964), 1: 137–67.

7. R. Brown, *Social Psychology* (New York: Free Press, 1965), p. 162.

8. G. A. Milton, *Five Studies of the Relation between Sex Role Identification and Achievement in Problem Solving,* Technical Report no. 3, Department of Industrial Administration, Department of Psychology, Yale University, December 1958.

But these effects in mathematics and science are only part of the story. A girl's long training in passivity and dependence appears to exact an even higher toll from her overall motivation to achieve, to search for new and independent ways of doing things, and to welcome the challenge of new and unsolved problems. In one study, for example, elementary school girls were more likely to try solving a puzzle by imitating an adult, whereas the boys were more likely to search for a novel solution not provided by the adult.[9] In another puzzle-solving study, young girls asked for help and approval from adults more frequently than the boys; and, when given the opportunity to return to the puzzles a second time, the girls were more likely to rework those they had already solved, whereas the boys were more likely to try puzzles they had been unable to solve previously.[10] A girl's sigh of relief is almost audible when she marries and retires from the outside world of novel and unsolved problems. This, of course, is the most conspicuous outcome of all: the majority of American women become full-time homemakers. Such are the consequences of a nonconscious ideology.

But why does this process violate the values of individuality and self-fulfillment? It is *not* because some people may regard the role of homemaker as inferior to other roles. That is not the point. Rather, the point is that our society is managing to consign a large segment of its population to the role of homemaker solely on the basis of sex just as inexorably as it has in the past consigned the individual with a black skin to the role of janitor or domestic. It is not the quality of the role itself which is at issue here, but the fact that in spite of their unique identities, the majority of America's women end up in the *same* role.

Even so, however, several arguments are typically advanced to counter the claim that America's homogenization of its women subverts individuality and self-fulfillment. The three most common arguments invoke, respectively, (1) free will, (2) biology, and (3) complementarity.

1. The free will argument proposes that a twenty-one-year-old woman is perfectly free to choose some other role if she cares to do so; no one is standing in her way. But this argument conveniently overlooks the fact that the society which has spent twenty years carefully marking the woman's ballot

9. J. W. McDavid, "Imitative Behavior in Preschool Children," *Psychological Monographs,* vol. 73, whole no. 486 (1959).
10. V. J. Crandall and A. Rabson, "Children's Repetition Choices in an Intellectual Achievement Situation Following Success and Failure," *Journal of Genetic Psychology* 97 (1960): 161–68.

for her has nothing to lose in that twenty-first year by pretending to let her cast it for the alternative of her choice. Society has controlled not her alternatives, but her motivation to choose any but one of those alternatives. The so-called freedom to choose is illusory and cannot be invoked to justify the society which controls the motivation to choose.

2. The biological argument suggests that there may really be inborn differences between men and women in, say, independence or mathematical ability. Or that there may be biological factors beyond the fact that women can become pregnant and nurse children which uniquely dictate that they, but not men, should stay home all day and shun serious outside commitment. Maybe female hormones really are responsible somehow. One difficulty with this argument, of course, is that female hormones would have to be different in the Soviet Union, where one-third of the engineers and 75 percent of the physicians are women. In America, women constitute less than 1 percent of the engineers and only 7 percent of the physicians.[11] Female physiology *is* different, and it may account for some of the psychological differences between the sexes, but America's sex-role ideology still seems primarily responsible for the fact that so few women emerge from childhood with the motivation to seek out any role beyond the one that our society dictates.

But even if there really were biological differences between the sexes along these lines, the biological argument would still be irrelevant. The reason can best be illustrated with an analogy.

Suppose that every black American boy were to be socialized to become a jazz musician on the assumption that he has a "natural" talent in that direction, or suppose that his parents should subtly discourage him from other pursuits because it is considered "inappropriate" for black men to become physicians or physicists. Most liberal Americans, we submit, would disapprove. But suppose that it *could* be demonstrated that black Americans, *on the average,* did possess an inborn better sense of rhythm than white Americans. Would *that* justify ignoring the unique characteristics of a *particular* black youngster from the very beginning and specifically socializing him to become a musician? We don't think so. Similarly, as long as a woman's socialization does not nurture her uniqueness, but treats her only as a member

11. N. D. Dodge, *Women in the Soviet Economy* (Baltimore: The Johns Hopkins Press, 1966).

of a group on the basis of some assumed *average* characteristic, she will not be prepared to realize her own potential
in the way that the values of individuality and self-fulfillment
imply she should.

The irony of the biological argument is that it does not
take biological differences seriously enough. That is, it fails
to recognize the range of biological differences between individuals within the same sex. Thus, recent research has
revealed that biological factors help determine many personality traits. Dominance and submissiveness, for example,
have been found to have large inheritable components; in
other words, biological factors *do* have the potential for partially determining how dominant or submissive an individual,
male or female, will turn out to be. But the effects of this biological potential could be detected only in males.[12] This
implies that only the males in our culture are raised with
sufficient flexibility, with sufficient latitude given to their biological differences, for their "natural" or biologically determined potential to shine through. Females, on the other
hand, are subjected to a socialization which so ignores their
unique attributes that even the effects of biology seem to be
swamped. In sum, the biological argument for continuing
America's homogenization of its women gets hoisted with its
own petard.

3. Many people recognize that most women do end up as
full-time homemakers because of their socialization and that
these women do exemplify the failure of our society to raise
girls as unique individuals. But, they point out, the role of the
homemaker is not inferior to the role of the professional
man: it is complementary but equal.

This argument is usually bolstered by pointing to the joys
and importance of taking care of small children. Indeed,
mothers *and* fathers find childrearing rewarding, and it is certainly important. But this argument becomes insufficient
when one considers that the average American woman now
lives to age seventy-four and has her *last* child at about age
twenty-six; thus, by the time the woman is thirty-three or so,
her children all have more important things to do with their
daytime hours than to spend them entertaining an adult
woman who has nothing to do during the second half of her
life span. As for the other "joys" of homemaking, many writers[13] have persuasively argued that the role of the home-

12. I. I. Gottesman, "Heritability of Personality: A Demonstration,"
Psychological Monographs, vol. 77, whole no. 572 (1963).
13. B. Friedan, *The Feminine Mystique* (New York: Norton, 1963).

maker has been glamorized far beyond its intrinsic worth. This charge becomes plausible when one considers that the average American homemaker spends the equivalent of a man's working day, 7.1 hours, in preparing meals, cleaning house, laundering, mending, shopping, and doing other household tasks. In other words, 43 percent of her waking time is spent in activity that would command an hourly wage on the open market well below the federally-set minimum for menial industrial work.

The point is not how little she would earn if she did these things in someone else's home, but that this use of time is virtually the same for homemakers with college degrees and for those with less than a grade school education, for women married to professional men and for women married to blue-collar workers. Talent, education, ability, interests, motivations: all are irrelevant. In our society, being female uniquely qualifies an individual for domestic work.

It is true, of course, that the American homemaker has, on the average 5.1 hours of leisure time per day, and it is here, we are told, that each woman can express her unique identity. Thus, politically interested women can join the League of Women Voters; women with humane interests can become part-time Gray Ladies; women who love music can raise money for the symphony. Protestant women play Canasta; Jewish women play Mah-Jongg; brighter women of all denominations and faculty wives play bridge; and so forth.

But politically interested *men* serve in legislatures; *men* with humane interests become physicians or clinical psychologists; *men* who love music play in the symphony; and so forth. In other words, why should a woman's unique identity determine only the periphery of her life rather than its central core?

Again, the important point is not that the role of homemaker is necessarily inferior, but that the woman's unique identity has been rendered irrelevant. Consider the following "predictability test." When a boy is born, it is difficult to predict what he will be doing twenty-five years later. We cannot say whether he will be an artist, a doctor, or a college professor because he will be permitted to develop and to fulfill his own unique potential, particularly if he is white and middle-class. But if the newborn child is a girl, we can usually predict with confidence how she will be spending her time twenty-five years later. Her individuality doesn't have to be considered; it is irrelevant.

The socialization of the American male has closed off certain options for him too. Men are discouraged from developing certain desirable traits such as tenderness and sensitivity just as surely as women are discouraged from being assertive and, alas, "too bright." Young boys are encouraged to be incompetent at cooking and child care just as surely as young girls are urged to be incompetent at mathematics and science.

Indeed, one of the errors of the early feminist movement in this country was that it assumed that men had all the goodies and that women could attain self-fulfillment merely by being like men. But that is hardly the utopia implied by the values of individuality and self-fulfillment. Rather, these values would require society to raise its children so flexibly and with sufficient respect for the integrity of individual uniqueness that some men might emerge with the motivation, the ability, and the opportunity to stay home and raise children without bearing the stigma of being peculiar. If homemaking is as glamorous as the women's magazines and television commercials portray it, then men, too, should have that option. Even if homemaking isn't all that glamorous, it would probably still be more fulfilling for some men than the jobs in which they now find themselves.

And if biological differences really do exist between men and women in "nurturance," in their inborn motivations to care for children, then this will show up automatically in the final distribution of men and women across the various roles: relatively fewer men will choose to stay at home. The values of individuality and self-fulfillment do not imply that there must be equality of outcome, an equal number of men and women in each role, but that there should be the widest possible variation in outcome consistent with the range of individual differences among people, regardless of sex. At the very least, these values imply that society should raise its males so that they could freely engage in activities that might pay less than those being pursued by their wives without feeling that they were "living off their wives." One rarely hears it said of a woman that she is "living off her husband."

Thus, it is true that a man's options are limited by our society's sex-role ideology, but as the "predictability test" reveals, it is still the woman in our society whose identity is rendered irrelevant by America's socialization practices. In 1954, the United States Supreme Court declared that a fraud and hoax lay behind the slogan "separate but equal." It is unlikely that any court will ever do the same for the more subtle motto that successfully keeps the woman in her place: "complementary but equal."

Interpersonal Equality

> Wives, submit yourselves unto your own husbands, as
> unto the Lord. For the husband is the head of the wife,
> even as Christ is the head of the church; and he is the
> savior of the body. Therefore, as the church is subject
> unto Christ, so let the wives be to their own husbands in
> everything. (Eph. 5)

As this passage reveals, the ideological rationalization that
men and women hold complementary but equal positions is a
recent invention of our modern "liberal" society, part of the
equalitarian veneer which helps to keep today's version of the
ideology nonconscious. Certainly those Americans who value
open, honest, and equalitarian relationships generally are
quick to reject this traditional view of the male-female relationship; and, an increasing number of young people even
plan to enter "utopian" marriages very much like the following hypothetical example:

> Both my wife and I earned Ph.D. degrees in our re-
> spective disciplines. I turned down a superior academic
> post in Oregon and accepted a slightly less desirable
> position in New York where my wife could obtain a
> part-time teaching job and do research at one of the sev-
> eral other colleges in the area. Although I would have
> preferred to live in a suburb, we purchased a home near
> my wife's college so that she could have an office at
> home where she would be when the children returned
> from school. Because my wife earns a good salary, she
> can easily afford to pay a maid to do her major house-
> hold chores. My wife and I share all other tasks around
> the house equally. For example, she cooks the meals,
> but I do the laundry for her and help her with many of
> her other household tasks.

Without questioning the basic happiness of such a marriage or its appropriateness for many couples, we can legitimately ask if such a marriage is, in fact, an instance of interpersonal equality. Have all the hidden assumptions about the
woman's "natural" role really been eliminated? Has the
traditional ideology really been exorcised? There is a very
simple test. If the marriage is truly equalitarian, then its
description should retain the same flavor and tone even if the
roles of the husband and wife were to be reversed:

> Both my husband and I earned Ph.D. degrees in our
> respective disciplines. I turned down a superior aca-

demic post in Oregon and accepted a slightly less desirable position in New York where my husband could obtain a part-time teaching job and do research at one of the several other colleges in the area. Although I would have preferred to live in a suburb, we purchased a home near my husband's college so that he could have an office at home where he would be when the children returned from school. Because my husband earns a good salary, he can easily afford to pay a maid to do his major household chores. My husband and I share all other tasks around the house equally. For example, he cooks the meals, but I do the laundry for him and help him with many of his other household tasks.

It seems unlikely that many men or women in our society would mistake the marriage *just* described as either equalitarian or desirable, and thus it becomes apparent that the ideology about the woman's "natural" role nonconsciously permeates the entire fabric of such "utopian" marriages. It is true that the wife gains some measure of equality when her career can influence the final place of residence, but why is it the unquestioned assumption that the husband's career solely determines the initial set of alternatives that are to be considered? Why is it the wife who automatically seeks the part-time position? Why is it *her* maid instead of *their* maid? Why *her* laundry? Why *her* household tasks. And so forth throughout the entire relationship.

The important point here is not that such marriages are bad or that their basic assumptions of inequality produce unhappy, frustrated women. Quite the contrary. It is the very happiness of the wives in such marriages that reveals society's smashing success in socializing its women. It is a measure of the distance our society must yet traverse toward the goals of self-fulfillment and interpersonal equality that such marriages are widely characterized as utopian and fully equalitarian. It is a mark of how well the woman has been kept in her place that the husband in such a marriage is often idolized by women, including his wife, for "permitting" her to squeeze a career into the interstices of their marriage as long as his own career is not unduly inconvenienced. Thus is the white man blessed for exercising his power benignly while his "natural" right to that power forever remains unquestioned.

Such is the subtlety of a nonconscious ideology!

A truly equalitarian marriage would permit both partners to pursue careers or outside commitments which carry equal weight when all important decisions are to be made. It is here, of course, that the "problem" of children arises. People often assume that the woman who seeks a role beyond home and family would not care to have children. They assume that if she wants a career or serious outside commitment, then children must be unimportant to her. But of course no one makes this assumption about her husband. No one assumes that a father's interest in his career necessarily precludes a deep and abiding affection for his children or a vital interest in their development. Once again America applies a double standard of judgment. Suppose that a father of small children suddenly lost his wife. No matter how much he loved his children, no one would expect him to sacrifice his career in order to stay home with them on a full-time basis—*even if he had an independent source of income.* No one would charge him with selfishness or lack of parental feeling if he sought professional care for his children during the day. An equalitarian marriage simply abolishes this double standard and extends the same freedom to the mother, while also providing the framework for the father to enter more fully into the pleasures and responsibilities of child rearing. In fact, it is the equalitarian marriage which has the most potential for giving children the love and concern of two parents rather than one.

But few women are prepared to make use of this freedom. Even those women who have managed to finesse society's attempt to rob them of their career motivations are likely to find themselves blocked by society's trump card: the feeling that the raising of the children is their unique responsibility and—in time of crisis—ultimately theirs alone. Such is the emotional power of a nonconscious ideology.

In addition to providing this potential for equalized child care, a truly equalitarian marriage embraces a more general division of labor which satisfies what might be called "the roommate test." That is, the labor is divided just as it is when two men or two women room together in college or set up a bachelor apartment together. Errands and domestic chores are assigned by preference, agreement, flipping a coin, given to hired help, or—as is sometimes the case—left undone.

It is significant that today's young people, many of whom live this way prior to marriage, find this kind of arrangement within marriage so foreign to their thinking. Consider an analogy. Suppose that a white male college student decided to room or set up a bachelor apartment with a black male friend. Surely the typical white student would not blithely assume that his black roommate was to handle all the domestic chores. Nor would his conscience allow him to do so even in the unlikely event that his roommate would say: "No, that's okay. I like doing housework. I'd be happy to do it." We suspect that the typical white student would still not be comfortable if he took advantage of this offer, if he took advantage of the fact that his roommate had been socialized to be "happy" with such an arrangement. But change this hypothetical black roommate to a female marriage partner, and somehow the student's conscience goes to sleep. At most it is quickly tranquilized by the thought that "she is happiest when she is ironing for her loved one." Such is the power of a nonconscious ideology.

Of course, it may well be that she *is* happiest when she is ironing for her loved one.

Such, indeed, is the power of a nonconscious ideology!

Person Perception
Albert H. Hastorf,
David J. Schneider, and
Judith Polefka

The Perceptual Process

Both philosophers and psychologists have long been in-
trigued with the nature of the human perceptual process. One
explanation for their interest is that man is naturally curious
about his contact with the outside world and wonders how his
experiences are caused and to what degree they reflect the
world accurately. Beyond general curiosity, the reason for the
interest stems from an apparent paradox, the basis of which
lies in the difference between the nature of our experiences
and our knowledge of how those experiences are caused.

Anyone who takes the trouble to think about and to
describe his own experiences usually finds himself
overwhelmed with both their immediacy and their structure.
One's experience of the world is dominated by objects which
stand out in space and which have such attributes as shape,
color, and size. The immediacy of such experiences becomes
obvious if one closes his eyes, turns his head in a new direction, and then opens his eyes again. A structured world of objects is immediately present in awareness, without delay and
without any consciousness of interpretative or inferential activity. The world appears to be given to us in experience. Yet
a casual analysis of these events indicates a very different
state of affairs.

You have opened your eyes and you experience a blue
vase about six inches high situated on a table. The vase appears to be at a certain distance, and its shape and color are
equally clear. Let us remind ourselves of the causal events
that are involved. Light waves of a certain wavelength are
reflected off the vase. Some of them impinge on the retina of
your eye, and if enough retinal cells are irritated, some visual
nerves will fire and a series of electrical impulses will be

Abridged by permission from A. H. Hastorf, D. J. Schneider, and J.
Polefka, *Person Perception* (Reading, Mass.: Addison-Wesley, 1970).

carried through the sensory apparatus, including the subcortical centers, and will finally arrive at the cortex. This description paints a picture of a very indirect contact with the world: light waves to retinal events to sensory nerve events to subcortical events and finally to cortical events, from which visual experiences result. What is especially important is that this causal description reveals a very different picture than does our naïve description of experience. (This causal description led a famous German physiologist to remark that "we are aware of our nerves, not of objects.") Thus we have a conflict between our everyday-life experiences of objects together with their properties and an analysis of how these experiences come to exist. The notion of the existence of an "objective observer" who sees the world accurately because he has had no past experience or is disinterested is patently false. If such a person did exist, we would have to predict that he would not see a structured, stable, and meaningful world.

In summary, our past experiences and purposes play an absolutely necessary role in providing us with knowledge of the world that has structure, stability, and meaning. Without them, events would not make sense. With them, our perceptions define a predictable world, an orderly stage for us to act on.

The Perception of People

Let us now turn our attention to two very crucial facets of our experience of other people. The first is that we perceive them as *causal agents*. They are potential causes of their behavior. They may intend to do certain things, such as attempting to cause certain effects; and because we see them as one source of their actions, we consider them capable of varying their behavior to achieve their intended effects. (This position was formulated by Heider.)[1] Our perception of others' intentionality leads us next to organize the behavior of other people into intent-act-effect segments which form perceptual units. We infer the intentions of another; but we go further. If we perceive a particular intent on several occasions, we are prone to perceive the other as having an enduring personality characteristic. A person who seems to intend to hurt others much of the time will be quickly labeled as hostile. Our verbal label now becomes more abstract

1. F. Heider, "Social Perception and Phenomenal Causality," *Psych. Rev.* 51 (1944): 358–74; idem, *The Psychology of Interpersonal Relations* (New York: Wiley, 1958).

because we are categorizing the person according to a characteristic which endures over time.

Second, we perceive other people as similar to ourselves. Hence we are pushed to infer that they possess attributes which, unlike size and behavior, we cannot observe directly but which we are aware of in ourselves. In particular, we perceive others to possess emotional states; we see them as feeling angry, happy, or sad. On some occasions these experiences are of fleeting or temporary states; however, if we perceive them often enough in a person, we code or label that person as having that state as an enduring characteristic; e.g., chronically sad people are depressed.

We can now take a brief look at how our three attributes of experience (structure, stability, and meaning) relate to the perception of people.

Our experiences of other people are structured. Just as we create structure in the inanimate world by categorizing stimuli into objects and their attributes, so we create order in the world of people by categorizing them and their behavior. The number of ways that we can categorize people is overwhelmingly large; we can go well beyond any of the possible schemata for inanimate objects. The dictionary, for example, contains thousands of trait names describing ways in which we can perceive people as different. Often we use categories which have been functional in the past. The football coach will employ very different categories for perceiving members of the freshman class than will the dean of students or a professor of physics.

Dornbush et al.[2] demonstrated that our past experiences and our present motives affect the categories we use when they explored the categorizing activities of ten- and eleven-year-old children at a summer camp. Children who had lived together in the same tent for two or three weeks were requested in an interview situation to describe their tent mates. The interviewer carefully avoided stipulating any categories; he asked the children to "tell me about——." The interviews were then coded in order to classify the categories the children had employed in describing one another. An example of a category is "neatness." A statement was classified in this category if it described the other person as being either neat or sloppy. The authors were primarily in-

2. S. M. Dornbush et al., "The Perceiver and Perceived: Their Relative Influence on Categories of Interpersonal Perception," *Journal of Pers. and Soc. Psych.* 1 (1965): 434–40.

terested in category usage, not in where the person was placed within the category.

Especially pertinent to our thesis is a comparison of the categorization employed by a common perceiver of different stimuli with the categorization by two different perceivers of a common-stimulus person. The category overlap was greatest when one perceiver described two different children (57 percent); the overlap for two different perceivers describing the same stimulus person was smaller (45 percent) and not very different from the overlap obtained (38 percent) when the descriptions of two different perceivers, each describing a different person, were compared. The last figure was interpreted as the amount of overlap created by a common culture. These data imply that the perceiver plays a dominant role in selecting the characteristics of other people to be observed (and described). He does not passively record the attributes of the other person, but selects and organizes his perceptions in terms of categories which are particularly useful to him.

However, we should be very cautious in designating an individual described by two perceivers as "a common-stimulus person." It is highly likely that when one person interacts with different people on different occasions, he is really not the same stimulus person. His behavior will vary as a function of the situation, which includes the nature of the other participants. This fact is an example of the complexity of both social interaction and person perception. How you categorize and perceive me will influence how you behave toward me, and your behavior, in turn, will influence how I behave. Our point, for the moment, is to stress the role the selecting and categorizing activities of the perceiver play in *creating* his perceptions of the other and in producing structure in his world of other people.

Our experiences of other people have stability. The behaviors engaged in by another person vary widely over even brief periods of time; thus the interpersonal acts of another provide as continually varying a stimulus as the size of his body provides the retina when he walks across a room. Were we to perceive as discrete all the acts of another person, our experiential world would be as rapidly changing and unstable as our experience of his size if that were dependent merely on the size of the retinal image. The stability in our experience of other people seems to be produced by processes analogous to those involved in the constancies in perception. We search to perceive the invariant properties of other people.

In perceiving attributes of another person, we focus not on his behavior, which is ever-changing, but on more invariant characteristics, namely, his intents and purposes. Since these invariant properties cannot be perceived directly, our search for invariance is centered on discovering functional relationships between behavior-effect sequences, which are observable, and intentions, which are not. For example, suppose that another person shoves you in the hall, verbally abuses you in a class, and criticizes your friends in private. The behaviors and the contexts in which they are expressed differ, but the same end is achieved: the other person hurts you. Yet the effect is an invariant function of the behavior and the context, just as proximal size is an invariant function of object size and distance. In the attribution to him of the intent to hurt you, an invariance will have been achieved. Whenever we can assume that the person had the ability to produce the behaviors and hence the effects, when we can assume that he was the cause of what occurred, we tend to attribute to him the intent of producing the effect. This attribution of intent provides us with knowledge which will make our future interactions with the person more predictable.

Should we observe the same person behaving in a similar manner toward others, we go further and attribute to him the dispositional property of desiring to hurt other people; we consider him hostile or aggressive. This attribution of a dispositional property to another results again from the search for invariance. If we can classify a person according to certain traits or concepts, we can increase the predictability of our interpersonal world. An aggressive person will act to hurt not only us but others as well. We can predict his behavior in a wide variety of situations. It is also possible that such inferences about enduring dispositions will lead us into dramatic misperceptions. It is very disruptive for us to perceive as failing a person we "know" to be capable and to be trying hard. This is especially true if we have some strong loyalty to or identification with him.

Our experiences of other persons are meaningful. We see other people as organized entities, and nearly always their behavior makes sense. Nonetheless, the behavior of others does confuse and puzzle us on occasion. It is probably a good guess that if a person is consistently puzzling to us, our inability to make sense of him leads us to avoid further interactions with him. No wonder the behavior of most of the people we "know" makes sense!

What are the processes by which we develop these organized perceptions of others as meaningful entities? First, as already pointed out, we organize their behavior into intent-act-effect units, and that procedure not only enables us to develop some behavioral organization but also permits and even pushes us to develop some hypotheses covering the enduring intents and dispositions or personality traits. Second, meaning derives from the fact that other people are similar to one another and to ourselves. We all share a certain number of important characteristics; we all behave, think, and feel; and some of the structured meanings we experience derive from the assumption that other people are like us. The assumption of similarity—"That's the way I would feel"—can lead to assumed relationships between both behaviors and intents. Even though the process may not be conscious, we often operate as follows: "I engage in behavior *A* and also in behavior *B;*" therefore, "if he engages in behavior *A,* then he must also engage in behavior *B.*" The same operation would apply to intents and feelings. This process is one of the sources of what we shall later call *implicit personality theory;* it produces assumptions about relationships between personality traits in other people, so that knowing some things about a person permits us to infer other things. The process does not imply that the inferences are necessarily correct, however.

Finally, meaning derives from familiarity. When we have coded a person's behavior in a similar way a number of times and have made the same inferences about the causes of the behavior, then meaning and the feeling of understanding may result. This is especially true when we perceive that certain traits are correlated. A behavior is familiar not only in that we have seen it before but also in that it implies other behaviors. Implicit personality theories, the assumed correlations between traits which we carry around in our heads, are generalizations from behavior we may have observed in ourselves and one or two other persons. Once we have acquired these theories, we can then apply them as a general rule. The process is identical to that which produces a phenomenon usually called *group stereotypes*.

One way in which we simplify the complex world of other people is to organize them into groups. We talk of Germans, Jews, and Italians; of college students, policemen, even of little old ladies in tennis shoes; and we attribute certain characteristics to all members of each group. On reflection, we are all perfectly willing to grant that college students come in all different shapes and sizes and with very different orientations toward the world; yet we still find ourselves classifying people into groups and then imputing certain characteristics to the members of the groups. We neglect both situational pressures and disconfirming evidence in our push to categorize a person according to his group membership.

Our impressions of another person are also a form of stereotype; we abstract certain aspects of his behavior, organize them around certain dispositions, and develop a picture of the person. This process permits the development of meaning in our experience of other persons. It can also restrict our awareness of some of another's behavior. Group and individual stereotypes do create stability and meaning; but they may well do it at the risk of inaccuracy.

Motivation Research: For Hidden Motives, a Hidden Persuader
Philip Zimbardo and Ebbe B. Ebbesen

Ernest Dichter, the author of *Handbook of Consumer Motivations*[1] provides the keynote statement for us: "No successful advertising can ignore the stable, enduring attitudes of the consumer public. Since attitudes affect the way a product is seen, affect the very perception of facts, facts alone cannot combat hostile attitudes."[2]

An entire industry, called motivational research, has developed from the assumptions that consumers respond to appeals which tap the irrational, emotional, and unconscious aspects of self. This business uses a clinical, personality-oriented approach coupled with Gestalt psychology (which stresses the perceptual organization processes). The reactions of small groups of consumers to a specific product are studied intensively with depth interviews, projective tests, and free association tests. On the basis of these data and theoretical insights, motivation researchers claim that they can change the perception of potential consumers toward a product, alter attitudes toward it, and most important, get people to buy it. For businessmen, this is the only relevant criterion: does an advertising campaign result in increased sales? The reader might want to read Vance Packard's *Hidden Persuaders* for interesting examples and an evaluation of this approach.

Some of the problems worked on by people in motivation research are: how to get people to give blood to the Red Cross, how to design a one-minute television commercial with maximum impact, and how to increase airline ticket sales. Let us briefly examine how they do it.

Abridged by permission from Philip Zimbardo and Ebbe B. Ebbesen, *Influencing Attitudes and Changing Behavior* (Reading, Mass.: Addison-Wesley, 1969).

1. Ernest Dichter, *Handbook of Consumer Motivations* (New York: McGraw-Hill, 1964).
2. Ibid., p. 396.

It's Like Giving Blood

The appeal once made by the Red Cross to the patriotism of potential donors proved to be a dismal failure. This was because abstract, ideological principles rarely motivate immediate, concrete action. Using the skillful techniques of motivation research, it was determined that giving blood arouses many unconscious anxieties, especially with men, by whom it is equated with giving away part of their virility and strength. "There is a similarity between sacrifice, masochism, and feminine submission," says Dichter.[3]

If this is so, then information about the rapid regeneration of blood, or references to national emergencies will not be heard by the anxious individual. Even if he acknowledges the truth of the facts, they will only raise the level of anxious conflict. While they increase his tendency to think about giving blood, they leave unchanged his unconscious tendency to avoid the threatening act. To get a man to give blood, then, it is vital to make him feel more masculine, to prove that he has so much virility he can afford to give away a little, and to make him personally proud of any suffering (for example, by giving him a pin in the form of a white drop of blood, the equivalent of a wounded soldier's Purple Heart Medal).

The relevance of this example to the issue of changing prejudiced attitudes based upon unconscious motives requires no comment other than that, in this particular instance, the recommended persuasive tactics did, in fact, result in a sudden, dramatic increase in blood donations to the Red Cross.

It's Like Giving . . .

If there is only a brief opportunity to expose a product, then (using the psychological principles of closure, the Zeigarnik effect, and active rehearsal) the way to design an advertisement for that time spot is to require the audience to concentrate on the task, to complete the task, and to rehearse the message *after* the direct exposure to it. Abbreviations like L.S.M.F.T. (*Lucky Strike Means Fine Tobacco*) are designed to meet these goals. Even more effective are the T.V. ads for *Salem* cigarettes in which the audience first learns a simple catchy musical refrain: "You can take *Salem* out of the country, *but* [pause] you can't take the country out of *Salem*." Then at the end of the commercial, only the first part

---

3. Ibid., p. 463.

is sung, "You can take *Salem* out of the country, *but.* . . ." The listener will himself complete the pattern in order to gain closure. In so doing, he actively repeats the message.

An approach to the motivation underlying consumer attitudes can generate either specific tactics or a general strategy or approach. When a rationally designed advertising campaign to increase airplane ticket sales stressed the speed of the company's new jets, and described how quickly a businessman could get to city *X,* sales declined. Analysis revealed that this appeal stimulated guilt, because it described how fast a husband and father could get away from his family, perhaps for fun as well as business. On the basis of depth interviews, the appeal was changed to, "In only——hours you can *return* from your business trip in city *X* to your family." Sales rose sharply.

If the product being sold door-to-door by the Avon "ding-dong" salesladies were not skin beauty products, but rather a more tolerant attitude toward people whose skin color differs from the housewife, could we use these consumer motivation techniques to reduce prejudice and discrimination? It is worth considering.

Thoughts on
Bureaucracy
Erich Fromm

The problem I want to deal with can in a way be expressed
under the heading, "The Human Side of Management." You
are perhaps aware that one could express the same problem
in a different way and speak of the "managerial problem of
humanity." That sounds quite unusual, because most work in
this field has been expressed in the former terms. For instance, Mayo's book is titled, *The Human Problems of an Industrial Civilization,*[1] rather than "The Industrial Problem of
Man." The question is obviously what is the subject. Is man
the subject and the aim of all social arrangements, including
those of management? Then we should speak of the indus-
trial-managerial problem of man. If management and
production are the subject and the end of all social arrangements, then, indeed, we should speak of the human problem
of management.

There is a good deal of literature in the field of industrial
psychology which seems to assume a kind of preestablished
harmony between man and management; the assumption is
that *what is good for management is good for man, and what
is good for man is good for managed institutions.* In saying
this I am by no means minimizing the importance and great
merits of the literature on industrial psychology. I am sure
you are familiar with it, and I do not have to quote any
names or titles. And, indeed, I believe that in the field of industrial psychology a great deal has been found that is very
valuable, and not only valuable but important in making it
possible to further the understanding of what managers call

Reprinted by permission of the author and of The Institute of Management Sciences from *Management Science* 16, no. 12 (August 1970):
B699–B705.
1. Elton Mayo (New York: Macmillan Co., 1933); reprinted by
Division of Research, Harvard Business School, Boston, Massachusetts,
1946.

"the human problem." But I should still like to propose that the assumption of a preestablished harmony between man and management is not necessarily correct; that by making this assumption we are really evading the issue. We have to ask ourselves: *what if the interest of management and that of man is not harmonious?* What would we decide if something were better for man but worse for the process of production from the standpoint of maximal profit and the expansion of the enterprise?

I do not think we can evade this choice. As things are, the vast majority of Americans, not only in managerial groups but people in general, believe that what matters most is production, profit, and efficiency; that if certain humanitarian measures are good for man without adversely affecting these highest goals, then one might employ such measures. But if there is any conflict, one should stress the side of efficiency, rather than that of man. If one takes this position then, indeed, one narrows considerably the range of one's thinking, and the possibility of creating alternative styles of management. What I am suggesting is the necessity of recognizing the potential conflict between the two interests, hence the existence of a choice.

The great problem is: *What is "good" for man?*

The terms self-expression, spontaneity, and expression of potentialities have beome very fashionable; these are all words which have a meaning, but they are generally used vaguely, and they have become clichés. We must go beyond the clichés in popular literature and conversation and try to be precise; i.e., to know what is meant by these words in the context of our knowledge of man.

I contend that man is a system that can be studied like any other system. That is true whether we speak of man's body or whether we speak of his mind; and even this division is wrong, because we are really referring only to two different aspects of the same system. I need not remind you that if we speak of a living system we speak of something that is coherent, where the whole determines the part, where every change in one part implies a change in every other part; that system-thinking is not a linear form of thinking relating to cause and effect, but thinking about a totality, about a dynamic process; that the question "what is *the* cause" is meaningless, because there is no single "cause"; that one has to understand the whole system, with its hundreds of different aspects and its subsystems; that one has to go around it and look at it from all sides; that one has to find out in what particular way this system dysfunctions, and only then can one determine whether the dysfunction is still curable.

I might add that in speaking of systems we also speak of forces that move, and not of static entities put together in a mechanical way which can be changed as, let us say, parts of a machine can be changed. Such a science dealing with the "system man" is developing. Perhaps it started with Spinoza. It was greatly advanced by Freud. To be sure, it still is only a crude model of a system, but I believe that only to the extent that managers or, in general, people who try to understand society or a large enterprise, take the System Man as seriously as they take the system economics, the system technology, and so on, can they meaningfully talk about *human* ends in relation to the aims and ends of the managerial process.

I should like to mention one example, one of many that could be given. I choose this example because it constitutes one of the crucial aspects of our managerial society and, I believe, embodies one of the options we have. And that is the problem of bureaucracy, the problem of the bureaucrat. What is bureaucracy? What is a bureaucrat?

We know in the first place that bureaucratic management exists today in practically all large organizations, whether they are in industry or government, whether they pertain to education, health, or religion. All large organizations are managed in a bureaucratic way. And that is true not only for the so-called capitalist countries, but it holds true just as well, or more so, for the so-called communist countries— especially the Soviet Union, where the bureaucratic method is heavier and more old-fashioned, more conservative than it is in a highly-advanced capitalist country like the United States. But basically I think one can define contemporary capitalism and what the Russians call "socialism" as *bureaucratic-technological industrialism,* although they differ with regard to certain political and economic features.

It is obvious that bureaucracy is by no means a new discovery; one need only think, for example, of the bureaucratic system as it existed in ancient Egypt. Lewis Mumford pointed out in his splendid book *The Myth of the Machine,* that the technical achievements of the Egyptian society would not have been possible without their bureaucratic organization, which was so thorough and so complete that Mumford speaks of it as a "megamachine." That is to say, not in the usual sense of a machine, but in the sense that society itself is made into a machine of which each person becomes a part.

Another old bureaucracy is the Roman Catholic Church; one finds at the present time that the oppositionist movement within the Church is to a large extent a protest against bureaucracy. Clearly, in speaking about bureaucracy we are referring to a phenomenon that is not new; it is not a phenomenon of the nineteenth or twentieth centuries, but one which has adapted itself to the particular requirements of our society and its own needs for management in a bureaucratic way.

What would be a general definition of the bureaucratic method? There are many definitions and much has been written about bureaucracy. I remind all those who are interested in this especially of the work of Max Weber, which gave a great impetus to the study of bureaucracy in the United states. Let me suggest a very simple definition: *bureaucracy is a method of managing in which people are dealt with as if they were things*.

I do not have to dwell on the obvious advantages of bureaucratic management from the standpoint of economic efficiency. All textbooks and the popular literature are full of praise for bureaucratic management to such an extent that most people believe that there is no other possible way of managing a highly complex human system. Obviously the advantages of bureaucratic methods are very great (even though the disadvantages are seldom recognized) and I take them very seriously. And I *have* to take them very seriously if I suggest the possibility that one could have an industrial society that is not built on the bureaucratic form of management.

But what I want to speak about mainly is not bureaucracy as a problem of organization but as a human problem. The question is whether we can speak of bureaucracy as a character trait, a mentality or an "attitude"? We do speak about a pedantic or stingy character, and we know what we mean by that. Can one speak also about a bureaucratic character, of a bureaucratic way of behaving, relating, and being? I hope you will not mind if I now speak very much as a psychoanalyst about an empirical problem of characterology about the problem, *what is the bureaucratic attitude as a character trait?*

Perhaps I should begin with a preliminary remark. When I speak about the bureaucratic attitude I am referring to character, rather than behavior. This difference itself is an important one, but it would require a detour to really explain the difference between a *behavior trait* and a *character trait*. However, I should like to give one example, at least, to explain what I have in mind.

If you see a man who is behaving in a courageous way you might say "he has courage." That is a description of behavior. This behavior can be defined in the sense of a man's risking life and freedom for the sake of a certain aim in which he believes. But if you ask what the various possible motivations behind courage are, then you find that the motivations can be entirely different. What we usually like to think of as courage is the courageous behavior of those people who are so dedicated to an ideal and so free of egotism that they are willing to risk their lives for the sake of a fellowman, an ideal or a group. There are quite a few of whom this can be said, but there are many others who behave courageously for different motives, e.g., out of vanity, the desire to be admired. Others behave courageously because they have—consciously or unconsciously—suicidal tendencies and they do not care whether they live or die; in fact unconsciously they may want to die. And there are others who behave courageously simply because they lack the imagination to see danger. Now all this behavior is usually classified in terms of "courage" as a *behavior* trait; but if you compare the man who has a deep faith and dedication to an aim and the suicidal man, and the vain man, and the stupid man, then you can see that underneath this overt behavior trait you deal with entirely different forms of character. In fact, if you study the behavior more exactly you will find that even the behavior is not the same. For instance, a "suicidal" officer will be excellent in a certain situation in which reckless tactics are useful. But in general he would be very dangerous for his troops because he would not be sufficiently interested in life to avoid actions that a responsible officer should not initiate. The same holds true for the vain man, and so on. In other words, an analysis of the behavior would show that in accordance with different unconscious motivations, the behavior differs also.

If you ask how one can discover the differences in motivations, especially the unconscious ones, then I will have to refer you to the science of man, and particularly to psychoanalysis. It is possible to discover these unconscious data from dreams, one can discover them from facial expressions, from the minute observation of what is said, from the language that is used; people do not have to be put on the couch in order to discover what character type they are. In fact, any good observer of men—which certainly applies to most effective managers—knows a great deal, not about the behavior but about the character of another person, simply by observation. One does not have to be a psychologist in order to be interested in perceiving more than just how the other person behaves at the moment, but in what is behind his overt behavior; that is to say, in the question, how will this man behave not only now, but tomorrow?

Let us be still more specific and describe what goes on between two people and how they relate to each other. Take as an example the situation between a teacher and a student. Compare the teacher while he is teaching with the same teacher while he is examining his students. These are two entirely different human situations. When I am teaching a student I am related to him; I am in tune with him. He is not an object sitting over there while I put something in him. I am in the process of teaching; I am sensitive to him; I am responsive to him; and if I am not, then I am not a good teacher. If the same student comes to me in the situation of an examination I am transformed into a mixture of policeman, judge, and bureaucrat. Because at that moment my duty is no longer that of responding to him, teaching him, being his ally, but that of watching him—even suspiciously, even to the point of finding out his tricks, finding out how he tries to deceive me. Suddenly the human relationship as it existed while I was teaching is transformed into an inhuman relationship in which he becomes an "object" to me. I watch him as I would watch a machine, or an instrument. I am no longer giving. I myself become a machine over here, and he is a machine over there; the machine *I* tries to find what goes on in the other machine. In fact, you could have two machines watching each other in that way—but this is not a human relationship. You find the same problem in the attitude of an executive to his employee. It is not a question of being "nice" and "friendly," or harsh and cruel, but the fact that due to the bureaucratic structure of the relationship the employee is a "thing," an object like any other part of the enterprise, and he is experienced like a thing, in an impersonal alienated and essentially inhuman fashion. Another example of bureaucrats are judges; they are people who act in a bureaucratic fashion, and if a judge were not to act thusly, how could he ever tell a man "I determine that you shall be executed on this or that day."? No human being fully related to another human being could ever say this except in hate. But if the defendant is not experienced as a human being but as an object of the judicial machine, then, of course, it is easy to say it.

Another interesting example of bureaucratic attitudes are nurses, who often relate to the patient as a "case," a thing they control—even with the best of intentions—but not to a person. The patient *is* an appendectomy, or a neurotic, or whatever the case may be. There are a number of investigations which show that the nurse's attitude makes a significant difference in the patient's chances of recovery. Studies have been made of postoperative patients who have been taken care of by "regular" nurses, and others who have been taken care of by nurses with special talent for an affectionate, responsive attitude to the patient as a *person*. The number of those who had postoperative complications were about three times as great with the "regular" nurse than they were with the "special" nurse. This is not a sentimental story from the *Reader's Digest* about "the good nurse," but a very well-documented study which simply shows what a difference it makes for a sick person if he is handled bureaucratically or humanly.

Many psychoanalysts and psychiatrists act bureaucratically. One of the favorite expressions of a bureaucratic response by a psychiatrist is the word "hmmm." The patient is "encouraged" to continue, the analyst wants to show that he is listening and not asleep; the word "hmmm" is deeply noncommittal, it does not even commit the analyst to much of an effort; it is, as I see it, a bureaucratic stimulus with no particular response expected.

The essential point of bureaucratic behavior is that the other person becomes a thing, and in watching him in a detached attitude, I become a thing myself. A technical philosophical expression for this is: the person becomes *reified*. He also becomes petrified; that is to say, deeply frightened, even though he may not be aware of the degree of this fright. In this bureaucratic, nonresponsive situation the person involved becomes very lonely. This loneliness leads to deep suffering—again without the suffering being necessarily conscious. Man is not made to be without genuine human contact with his fellowman. And if he puts himself in the position of the "observer" or the "object" (and do not forget that the words "object" and "objection" have the same root), an inhuman relationship is established even if superficially it is a friendly one; it is manipulative, as many courses in "human relations" teach it.

We can differentiate between two kinds of bureaucratic attitudes which I am sure you will all identify immediately. One is the *friendly bureaucrat*. His "friendliness," nevertheless, does not alter the fact that the other person is an "object" to him, just as he can be friendly to his car and to other things he uses. These friendly bureaucrats usually have a friendly disposition, or they fake it, because it is in the nature of their particular position and method of management that they have to appear to be friendly.

Quite different from the friendly, though indifferent bureaucrat is the *authoritarian-sadistic bureaucrat* who is somewhat more old-fashioned. I had an experience with one such individual the other day—I still travel by train, as my last-ditch battle against the American railroad companies. I went to Pennsylvania Station to buy a ticket to Mexico, and the man behind the ticket window told me that as of the end of that year the Pullman service from St. Louis to Laredo would be discontinued, and he said, *"I'm glad about it.* I'm really glad about it." Then he added, "All that work, such a difficult ticket to make out!" (The difficult work is caused by not having a printed ticket, but having to write a ticket from here to St. Louis and from St. Louis to Mexico City.) This is the sadistic-authoritarian bureaucrat. Here was a man about fifty-five years of age; so he has been working for the railroads for thirty years. By discontinuing passenger travel his own job will be slowly abolished. He has grown up in this activity, and yet he is glad about its destruction. He is also so passive that even the small amount of activity involved in writing out a more difficult ticket then the usual ones is to him only a disagreeable chore. Another example is the face of the man behind the ticket window when three customers are still waiting and he puts his shade down and you can sometimes observe that slightly sadistic smile: this smile makes it clear that the man is not merely acting according to the rules, but that his *character* is that of a sadistic bureaucrat. If that same man were in a Fascist regime he might commit acts of great cruelty because he has a sadistic-authoritarian character that is satisfied by having other people submitted to his power and being able to see them being hurt, humiliated, and frustrated.

The friendly bureaucrat is the more modern type of bureaucrat, the one who has learned to "oil" people so that they work with less friction. The older type of bureaucrat, the authoritarian character, is more often to be found in conservative enterprises like railroads, shipping, post offices, law courts, and so on.

But in spite of these differences between the "friendly" and the "authoritarian-sadistic" bureaucrat, they have one important quality in common: that they relate themselves to the other person as to a thing, as to an object—that they do not experience the other as a person and hence relate themselves to him without empathy or compassion.

I want to add that one must consider that the way people behave in their work situation, whether it is in business, in a hospital, or in a university, carries over to the way in which they behave in the other spheres of life. The often discussed idea, that work will very soon be more or less abolished is, I think, rather fantastic; we will continue to live with work—even though much less—for a long time to come; the way in which people relate to their fellowman in work will determine the way in which they relate to their fellowman outside of work. Therefore the work relationship itself will remain of utmost importance for the character of the relationships they have to other people.

The question is whether a nonbureaucratic, humanistic, man-centered form of management is possible.

This is a very complex and difficult question which I cannot discuss here. (I have discussed it at length elsewhere.)[2] I only want to state this: first, I believe that nonbureaucratic humanist management is possible. Second, the methods of such management are not easy to find, but the problem is not more difficult than space travel. Third, such methods will be found only if one is convinced (a) that the present bureaucratic spirit is inhospitable to life, joy, independence, love, compassion, meaningful human relations, real intimacy, and sharing between people, and (b) that if one does not change the bureaucratic methods into humanist ones, the result will be increasing loneliness, boredom, aggressiveness, competition, consumption—from cars to sex, liquor, and drugs—and cruelty as the result of a lack of compassion. Fourth, that one can convince oneself of the real damage caused by bureaucratic behavior by studying the "System Man," and what it is that increases or decreases his optimal functioning as a human being. Economic and social planning is blind if the Science of Man is not integrated into the science of management and social planning.

2. For instance in *The Sane Society* (New York: Holt, Rinehart and Winston, 1955); and *The Revolution of Hope* (New York: Harper and Row, 1968).

Personality and Its Assessment

Introduction

Our first three chapters stressed some general ideas about human behavior, about what we humans share. In only a few instances have the articles suggested that people differ in important ways. This chapter focuses chiefly on these differences among people, particularly those attributes that make up what we call personality. The papers also consider some different ways of measuring or assessing personality, and some of the ethical issues involved in personality testing.

One aim of personality theory is to explain why different people behave differently in the same situation or when exposed to the same stimulus. Our first three chapters argued that a person's behavior is influenced by his motivations, his thought processes, and his attitudes. The whole man's "personality" is made up of all three of these internal states. But that particular personality is largely conditioned by that particular person's particular set of experiences in his environment. So it is not surprising that different people should end up with widely different personalities. And since personality affects behavior, it is not surprising either that once the personality begins to take shape, different people begin to respond very differently to the same inputs from the environment.

The number and kinds of personality categories defined by different theories of personality is somewhat arbitrary. The paper by McClelland identifies three "types" of personality (or really three patterns of motives which differ among people), depending upon relative strengths of the person's need for achievement, need for affiliation, or need for power. The paper by Downs, on the other hand, identifies five types of bureaucratic personalities. Two of these are purely self-interested: *climbers,* who consider power, income, and prestige as their most important goals or motives; and *conservers,* who value convenience, security, and risk-aversion. The other three types in Downs's perspective are all in the broad category of people who mix pure self-interest with altruistic loyalty to some larger values: zealots, who are committed to relatively narrow concepts, like ecological protection; advocates, who feel loyalty to a broader set of functions or to some administrative unit of the organization; and finally statesmen, whom Downs sees as bureaucratic types loyal to society as a whole, with no particular loyalties to specific ideas or administrative units.

But classifying types of personalities is only a small part of the job. We must also explain how they got that way, how to identify them, and how to predict each type's probable response to a given situation.

The development of personality has been touched upon before. Downs's article makes clear that personality types are not fixed forever. He points out, for example, that as people grow older, they tend to change from climbers to conservers. McClelland's article suggests that the relative strengths of people's needs are formed in large part by the social standards carried to them through parents and teachers, and through other socializing mechanisms while they are growing up.

On measurement and on the relationship between personality type and behavior, consider the McClelland position: Using sketchy data (which might also be explained by many other hypotheses) he makes the rather heroic assertion that the economic development of nations is predictable from knowledge of the level of need for achievement in the population. He estimates need for achievement by analysis of the content of children's stories prevalent in the society when the current adult population was in its childhood. Although some people would consider McClelland's hypothesis as bordering on the fanciful, it is, nevertheless, a most intriguing one, basically arguing that economic development in a nation is a function of its people's entrepreneurial attitudes.

Downs, in explaining the behavior exhibited by each of his five bureaucratic types, is both more specific and more limited in scale than McClelland. Downs argues that since the primary motivation of *climbers* is to increase their power, income, and prestige, they will attempt to do this by jumping from job to job as better opportunities open up, by aggrandizing their current positions, and by seeking to expand the functions over which they have authority. On the other hand, *conservers* will be much more likely to form defensive coalitions with others to protect their own current functions.

Downs carries out a comparable analysis of the behavior of each of the other three types as well. His system seems to be particularly well suited to understanding individual behavior within large complex organizations.

If any one of these approaches to personality is to be useful to us in our day-to-day behavior, we will need some means of identifying the categories into which to slot particular people. And that takes us immediately to the issue of tests and testing, with all the technical and ethical questions that accompany that issue. Formal personality tests administered by a trained psychologist are not always necessary, of course. Day-to-day assessment and categorization of others is both possible and commonplace. We all do it, but much more as an art than a science. It requires a good third ear, an ability to distill a great deal out of a few samples of another person's behavior and an ability to get at the underlying motivations which drive him and at the underlying abilities which suit him for one job or another.

But assessment is not limited to on-the-spot evaluation. Formal tests exist which help in assessing most aspects of personality. They range from pencil-and-paper, multiple-choice tests to "projective" techniques, in which the person is asked to respond to some ambiguous stimulus, as in the famous Rorschach ink-blot tests.

McClelland describes his use of such projective techniques for assessing the strength of a person's achievement motivation.

A different kind of issue is whether using tests to assess the personality types constitutes a violation of human autonomy and an invasion of privacy. Victor Lovell's very provocative paper, "The Human Use of Personality Tests," explores these issues in detail. As he points out, personality tests may be used in many ways: to research into the nature of personality; to advise a person on job choice; to help an individual's personal adjustment; or to assess the capacities and characters of people in order to assign them to particular jobs. These issues are very much alive right now, especially in relation to the use of tests in employment of minorities. Lovell's article goes right at those problems.

**Business Drive and
National Achievement**
David C. McClelland

What accounts for the rise in civilization? Not external resources (i.e., markets, minerals, trade routes, or factories) but the entrepreneurial spirit which exploits those resources —a spirit found most often among businessmen.

Who is ultimately responsible for the pace of economic growth in poor countries today? Not the economic planners or the politicians but the executives whose drive (or lack of it) will determine whether the goals of the planners are fulfilled.

Why is Russia developing so rapidly that—if it continues its present rate of growth—it will catch up economically with the most advanced country in the world, the United States, in twenty-five or thirty years? Not, as the USSR claims, because of the superiority of its Communist system, but because, by hook or by crook, it has managed to develop a stronger spirit of entrepreneurship among executives than we have today in the United States.

How can foreign aid be most efficiently used to help poor countries develop rapidly? Not by simply handing money over to their politicians or budget makers but by using it in ways that will select, encourage, and develop those of their business executives who have a vigorous entrepreneurial spirit or a strong drive for achievement. In other words: *invest in a man, not just in a plan.*

What may be astonishing about some of these remarks is that they come from a college professor, and not from the National Association of Manufacturers. They are not the defensive drum rattlings of an embattled capitalist but are my conclusions, based on nearly fifteen years of research, as a strictly academic psychologist, into the human motive that

Reprinted from the *Harvard Business Review*, July–August 1962, pp. 99–112, by permission of the author and the publisher. © 1962 by the President and Fellows of Harvard College; all rights reserved.

appears to be largely responsible for economic growth—research which has recently been summarized in my book, *The Achieving Society*.[1]

Since I am an egghead from way back, nothing surprises me more than finding myself rescuing the businessman from the academic trash heap, dusting him off, and trying to give him the intellectual respectablility that he has had a hard time maintaining for the last fifty years or so. For the fact is that the businessman has taken a beating, not just from the Marxists, who pictured him as a greedy capitalist, and the social critics, who held him responsible for the Great Depression of the 1930s, but even from himself, deep in his heart.

One of the queerest ironies of history, as John Kenneth Galbraith points out in *The Affluent Society*,[2] is that in a sense Marx won his case with his sworn enemies, the capitalists. Marx loudly asserted that they were selfish and interested only in profits. In the end many agreed. They accepted the Marxist materialistic view of history. The modern businessman, says Galbraith, "suspects that the moral crusade of reformers, do-gooders, liberal politicians, and public servants, all their noble protestations notwithstanding, are based ultimately on self-interest. 'What,' he inquires, 'is their gimmick?' "[3]

If not only the Marxists, but Western economists, and even businessmen themselves, end up assuming that their main motive is self-interest and a quest for profit, it is small wonder that they have had a hard time holding their heads high in recent years.

But now the research I have done has come to the businessman's rescue by showing that everyone has been wrong, that it is *not* profit per se that makes the businessman tick but a strong desire for achievement, for doing a good job. Profit is simply one measure among several of how well the job has been done, but it is not necessarily the goal itself.

The Achievement Goal

But what exactly does the psychologist mean by the "desire for achievement"? How does he measure it in individuals or in nations? How does he know that it is so important for economic growth? Is it more important for businessmen to have this desire than it is for politicians, bishops, or generals?

1. Princeton, N. J.: D. Van Nostrand Co., 1961.
2. Boston: Houghton Mifflin Co., 1958.
3. Ibid., p. 71.

These are the kinds of questions which are answered at great length and with as much scientific precision as possible in my book. Here we must be content with the general outline of the argument, and develop it particularly as it applies to businessmen.

To begin with, psychologists try to find out what a man spends his time thinking and daydreaming about when he is not under pressure to think about anything in particular. What do his thoughts turn to when he is by himself or not engaged in a special job? Does he think about his family and friends, about relaxing and watching TV, about getting his superior off his back? Or does he spend his time thinking and planning how he can "sell" a particular customer, cut production costs, or invent a better steam trap or toothpaste tube?

If a man spends his time thinking about doing things better, the psychologist says he has a concern for achievement. In other words, he cares about achievement or he would not spend so much time thinking about it. It he spends his time thinking about family and friends, he has a concern for affiliation; if he speculates about who is boss, he has a concern for power, and so on. What differs in my approach from the one used by many psychologists is that my colleagues and I have not found it too helpful simply to *ask* a person about his motives, interests, and attitudes. Often he himself does not know very clearly what his basic concerns are—even more often he may be ashamed and cover some of them up. So what we do is to try and get a sample of his normal waking thoughts by asking him just to tell a few stories about some pictures.

Stories within Stories

Let us take a look at some typical stories written by United States business executives. These men were asked to look briefly at a picture—in this case, a man at a worktable with a small family photograph at one side—and to spend about five minutes writing out a story suggested by the picture. Here is a very characteristic story:

> The engineer is at work on Saturday when it is quiet and he has taken time to do a little daydreaming. He is the father of the two children in the picture—the husband of the woman shown. He has a happy home life and is dreaming about some pleasant outing they have had. He is also looking forward to a repeat of the incident which is now giving him pleasure to think about.

He plans on the following day, Sunday, to use the afternoon to take his family for a short trip.

Obviously, no achievement-related thoughts have come to the author's mind as he thinks about the scene in the picture. Instead, it suggests spending time pleasantly with his family. His thought runs along *affiliative* lines. He thinks readily about interpersonal relationships and having fun with other people. This, as a matter of fact, is the most characteristic reaction to this particular picture. But now consider another story:

> A successful industrial designer is at his "work bench" toying with a new idea. He is "talking it out" with his family in the picture. Someone in the family dropped a comment about a shortcoming in a household gadget, and the designer has just "seen" a commercial use of the idea. He has picked up ideas from his family before—he is "telling" his family what a good idea it is, and "confidentially" he is going to take them on a big vacation because "their" idea was so good. The idea will be successful, and family pride and mutual admiration will be strengthened.

The author of this story maintains a strong interest in the family and in affiliative relationships, but has added an achievement theme. The family actually has helped him innovate—get a new idea that will be successful and obviously help him get ahead. Stories which contain references to good new ideas, such as a new product, an invention, or a unique accomplishment of any sort, are scored as reflecting a concern for achievement in the person who writes them. In sum, this man's mind tends to run most easily along the lines of accomplishing something or other. Finally, consider a third story:

> The man is an engineer at a drafting board. The picture is of his family. He has a problem and is concentrating on it. It is merely an everyday occurrence—a problem which requires thought. How can he get that bridge to take the stress of possible high winds? He wants to arrive at a good solution of the problem by himself. He will discuss the problem with a few other engineers and make a decision which will be a correct one—he has the earmarks of competence.

The man who wrote this story—an assistant to a vice-president, as a matter of fact—notices the family photograph, but that is all. His thoughts tend to focus on the problem that the engineer has to solve. In the scant five minutes allowed, he even thinks of a precise problem—how to build a bridge that will take the stress of possible high winds. He notes that the engineer wants to find a good solution by himself, that he goes and gets help from other experts and finally makes a correct decision. These all represent different aspects of a complete achievement sequence—defining the problem, wanting to solve it, thinking of means of solving it, thinking of difficulties that get in the way of solving it (either in one's self or in the environment), thinking of people who might help in solving it, and anticipating what would happen if one succeeded or failed.

Each of these different ideas about achievement gets a score of $+1$ in our scoring system so that the man in the last incident gets a score of $+4$ on the scale of concern or need for achievement (conventionally abbreviated to n Achievement). Similarly, the first man gets a score of -1 for his story, since it is completely unrelated to achievement, and the second man a score of $+2$ because there are two ideas in it which are scorable as related to achievement.

Each man usually writes six such stories and gets a score for the whole test. The coding of the stories for "achievement imagery" is so objective that two expert scorers working independently rarely disagree. In fact, it has recently been programed for a high-speed computer that does the scoring rapidly, with complete objectivity, and fairly high accuracy. What the score for an individual represents is the frequency with which he tends to think spontaneously in achievement terms when that is not clearly expected of him (since the instructions for the test urge him to relax and to think freely and rapidly).

Thinking Makes It So

What are people good for who think like this all the time? It doesn't take much imagination to guess that they might make particularly good business executives. People who spend a lot of their time thinking about getting ahead, inventing new gadgets, defining problems that need to be solved, considering alternative means of solving them, and calling in experts for help should also be people who in real life *do* a lot of these things or at the very best are readier to do them when the occasion arises.

I recognize, of course, that this is an assumption that

requires proof. But, as matters turned out, our research produced strong factual support. Look, for instance, at figure 1. It shows that in three countries representing different levels and types of economic development managers or executives scored considerably higher on the average in achievement thinking than did professionals or specialists of comparable education and background. Take the two democratic countries shown there:

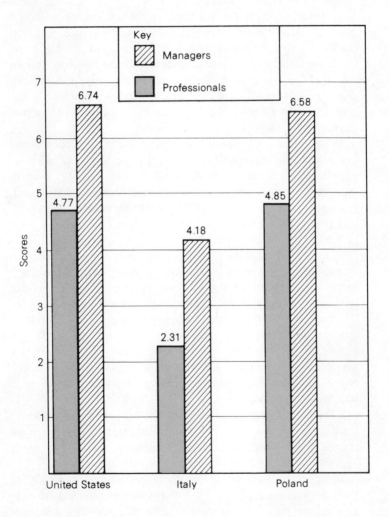

Fig. 1. Average *n* Achievement Scores of Managers and Professionals in Three Countries

In the United States the comparison was between matched pairs of unit managers and specialists of the same position level, age, educational background, and length of service in the General Electric Company. The managers spent more of their time in the test writing about achievement than the specialists did.

The same was true of middle-level executives from various companies in Italy when contrasted with students of law, medicine, and theology who were roughly of the same intelligence level and social background.

In other words it takes a concern for achievement to be a manager in a foreign country like Italy, for instance, just as it does in the United States. It is worth nothing in passing, however, that the level of achievement thinking among Italian managers is significantly lower than it is among American managers—which, as will be shown later, quite probably has something to do with the lower level and rate of economic development in Italy.

What about a Communist country? The figures for Poland are interesting, because (1) the level of concern for achievement is about what it is in the United States, and (2) even in businesses owned and operated by the state, as in Poland, managers tend to have a higher concern for achievement than do other professionals.

Another even more striking result, not shown in figure 1, is the fact that there is *no real difference* between the average *n* Achievement score of managers working for the United States government (9.3) and those in United States private business generally (8.90). Apparently, a manager working for the Bureau of Ships in the Department of the Navy spends as much time thinking about achievement as his counterpart in Ford or Sears, Roebuck; government service does not weaken his entrepreneurial spirit. Whether he is able to be as effective as he might be in private business is another matter, not touched on here.

Careful quantitative studies of the prevalence of achievement concern among various types of executives also yield results in line with what one would expect. Thus, sales managers score higher than other types of managers do.

In general, more successful managers tend to score higher than do less successful managers (except in government service where promotion depends more on seniority). The picture is clear in small companies, where the president tends to score higher than his associates. In large companies, the picture is a little more complicated. Men in the lowest salary brackets (earning less than $20,000 a year) definitely have the lowest average n Achievement scores, while those in the next bracket up ($20,000 to $25,000 a year) have the highest average n Achievement level. Apparently an achievement concern helps one get out of the ranks of the lowest paid into a higher income bracket. But from there on, the trend fades. Men in the highest income brackets have a somewhat lower average concern for achievement, and apparently turn their thoughts to less achievement-oriented concerns. Possibly these men are doing well enough to relax a little.

Businessmen and Achievement

Businessmen usually raise either one of two questions at this point:

1. "Where can I get this test for n Achievement? It sounds like a good way of picking young executives!"

2. "Why is this concern for achievement specific to being a success as a business manager? What about other types of achievement? Why isn't the entrepreneurial spirit necessary for success as an opera star, a preacher, a great teacher, or a great scientist?"

The answer to the first question, unfortunately, is simple: no practicable, marketable test for assessing achievement concern exists as yet. The method of measurement we have been using is too sensitive, too easily influenced by the social atmosphere surrounding the people who take the test, to give reliable individual results. Under carefully controlled conditions it works adequately to distinguish large groups of people like managers versus professionals, but it is not yet useful for individual selection. What we have here is a theoretical, scientific "breakthrough," not a practicable working device.

The second question is harder to answer but it takes us further in the direction of understanding exactly what kind of a person it is who spends a lot of his time thinking about achievement. To begin with, the facts are clear: many important types of professionals (doctors, lawyers, priests, or research scientists) fail to score on the average as high as business executives, yet clearly their work is in every sense as much of an achievement as the businessman's. How come?

Let us consider a particular case for a moment—that of the research scientist. Certainly his work represents an important achievement, for he is the one who often makes the breakthrough on which new technological and economic advances depend. Shouldn't he be thinking about defining a problem, doing a good job of solving it, getting help from experts, and so on?

Yet, when we tested a number of such scien-

tists—including several outstanding Nobel prize winners—
we found, somewhat to our surprise, that they were not
unusually high in *n* Achievement but rather tended to be
average. Then it occurred to us that having a very high concern for achievement might make a person unsuitable for
being a research scientist. Why? Simply because in research a
man must often work for what may become very long periods
of time without any knowledge of how well he is doing. He
may not even know if he is on the right track for as much as
five or ten years. But a man with a high need for achievement
likes to know quickly whether he is accomplishing anything
and quite possibly would become frustrated by the lack of
feedback in basic science as to whether he is getting anywhere. He would then more likely move into an area such as
management where results are more tangible. On the other
hand, the research scientist obviously needs *some* achievement concern, or he is not likely to want to engage in his occupation at all.

Characteristics of Achievers

Considerations like these focus attention on what there is
about the job of being a business entrepreneur or executive
that should make such a job peculiarly appropriate for a man
with a high concern for achievement. Or, to put it the other
way around, a person with high *n* Achievement has certain
characteristics which enable him to work best in certain
types of situations that are to his liking. An entrepreneurial
job simply provides him with more opportunities for making
use of his talents than do other jobs. Through careful empirical research we know a great deal by now about the man with
high *n* Achievement, and his characteristics do seem to fit
him unusually well for being a business executive.
Specifically:

1. *To begin with, he likes situations in which he takes personal responsibility for finding solutions to problems.* The
reason is obvious. Otherwise, he could get little personal
achievement satisfaction from the successful outcome. No
gambler, he does not relish situations where the outcome
depends not on his abilities and efforts but on chance or
other factors beyond his control. For example:

Some business-school students in one study played a game
in which they had to choose between two options, in each of
which they had only one chance in three of succeeding. For
one option they rolled a die and if it came up, say, a 1 or a 3
(out of six possibilities), they won. For the other option they
had to work on a difficult business problem which they knew

only one out of three people had been able to solve in the time allotted.

Under these conditions, the men with high n Achievement regularly chose to work on the business problem, even though they knew the odds of success were statistically the same as for rolling the dice.

To men strong in achievement concern, the idea of winning by chance simply does not produce the same achievement satisfaction as winning by their own personal efforts. Obviously, such a concern for taking personal responsibility is useful in a business executive. He may not be faced very often with the alternative of rolling dice to determine the outcome of a decision, but there are many other ways open to avoid personal responsibility, such as passing the buck, or trying to get someone else (or a committee) to take the responsibility for getting something done.

The famed self-confidence of a good executive (which actually is related to high achievement motivation) is also involved here. He thinks it can be done if *he* takes responsibility, and very often he is right because he has spent so much time thinking about how to do it that he does it better.

2. *Another characteristic of a man with a strong achievement concern is his tendency to set moderate achievement goals and to take "calculated risks."* Again his strategy is well suited to his needs, for only by taking on moderately difficult tasks is he likely to get the achievement satisfaction he wants. If he takes on an easy or routine problem, he will succeed but get very little satisfaction out of his success. If he takes on an extremely difficult problem, he is unlikely to get any satisfaction because he will not succeed. In between these two extremes, he stands the best chance of maximizing his sense of personal achievement.

The point can be made with the children's game of ring toss, some variant of which we have tried out at all ages to see how a person with high n Achievement approaches it. To illustrate:

The child is told that he scores when he succeeds in throwing a ring over a peg on the floor, but that he can stand anywhere he pleases. Obviously, if he stands next to the peg, he can score a ringer every time; but if he stands a long distance away, he will hardly ever get a ringer.

The curious fact is that the children with high concern for achievement quite consistently stand at moderate distances from the peg where they are most apt to get achievement satisfaction (or, to be more precise, where the decreasing probability-of-success curve crosses the increasing satisfaction-from-success curve). The ones with low *n* Achievement, on the other hand, distribute their choices of where to stand quite randomly over the entire distance. In other words, people with high *n* Achievement prefer a situation where there is a challenge, where there is some real risk of not succeeding, but not so great a risk that they might not overcome it by their own efforts.

Again, such a characteristic would seem to suit men unusually well for the role of business entrepreneur. The businessman is always in a position of taking calculated risks, of deciding how difficult a given decision will be to carry out. If he is too safe and conservative, and refuses to innovate, to invest enough in research or product development or advertising, he is likely to lose out to a more aggressive competitor. On the other hand, if he invests too much or overextends himself, he is also likely to lose out. Clearly, then, the business executive should be a man with a high concern for achievement who is used to setting moderate goals for himself and calculating carefully how much he can do successfully.

Therefore, we waste our time feeling sorry for the entrepreneur whose constant complaints are that he is overworking, that he has more problems than he knows how to deal with, that he is doomed to ulcers because of overwork, and so on. The bald truth is that if he has high *n* Achievement, he loves all those challenges he complains about. In fact, a careful study might well show that he creates most of them for himself. He may talk about quitting business and living on his investments, but if he did, he might then *really* get ulcers. The state of mind of being a little overextended is precisely the one he seeks, since overcoming difficulties gives him achievement satisfaction. His real problem is that of keeping the difficulties from getting *too* big for him, which explains in part why he talks so much about them because it is a nagging problem for him to keep them at a level he can handle.

3. *The man who has a strong concern for achievement also wants concrete feedback as to how well he is doing.* Otherwise how could he get any satisfaction out of what he had done? And business is almost unique in the amount of feedback it provides in the form of sales, cost, production, and profit figures. It is really no accident that the symbol of the businessman in popular cartoons is a wall chart with a line on it going up or down. The businessman sooner or later knows how well he is doing; salesmen will often know their success

from day to day. Furthermore, there is a concreteness in the knowledge of results which is missing from the kind of feedback professionals get.

Take, for example, the teacher as a representative professional. His job is to transmit certain attitudes and certain kinds of information to his students. He does get some degree of feedback as to how well he has done his job, but results are fairly imprecise and hardly concrete. His students, colleagues, and even his college's administration may indicate that they like his teaching, but he still has no real evidence that his students have *learned* anything from him. Many of his students do well on examinations, but he knows from past experience that they will forget most of that in a year or two. If he has high *n* Achievement and is really concerned about whether he has done his job well, he must be satisfied with sketchy, occasional evidence that his former pupils did absorb some of his ideas and attitudes. More likely, however, he is not a person with high *n* Achievement and is quite satisfied with the affection and recognition that he gets for his work which gratify other needs that he has.

The case of the true entrepreneur is different. Suppose he is a book publisher. He gets a manuscript and together with his editors decides that it is worth publication. At time of issuance, everyone is satisfied that he is launching a worthwhile product. But then something devastatingly concrete happens —something far more definite than ever happens to a teacher —namely, those monthly sales figures.

Obviously not everyone likes to work in situations where the feedback is so concrete. It can prove him right, but it also can prove him wrong. Oddly enough, the person with high *n* Achievement has a compelling interest to know whether he was right or wrong. He thrives and is happier in this type of situation than he is in the professional situation.

Two further examples from our research may make the point clearer. Boys with high *n* Achievement tend to be good with their hands, to like working in a shop or with mechanical or electrical gadgets. What characterizes such play again is the concrete feedback it provides as to how well a person is doing. If he wires up an electric circuit and then throws the switch, the light either goes on or it does not. Knowledge of results is direct, immediate, and concrete. Boys with high *n* Achievement like this kind of situation, and while some may go on to become engineers, others often go into business where they can continue getting this kind of concrete feedback.

What Money Means

In business, this feedback comes in the form of money, in costs and profits that are regularly reported. It is from this simple fact that the confusion between the so-called profit motive and the achievement motive has arisen in the minds of both Marxist and classical economists. For, in the typical case, a concern for profit in a capitalist economy does *not* mean that the businessman is primarily interested in money for its own sake. Rather, this concern is merely the *symptom* of a strong achievement concern, since profitability in a capitalist economy provides the best and simplest measure of success. It provides the same sort of concrete knowledge of achievement that a person with high n Achievement seeks all the time. Research findings clearly support this analysis. If you simple offer a person with high n Achievement a larger money reward for doing a certain task, he doesn't do any better than he did without the prize. In fact, he tends to do a little worse because the money makes him nervous. Not so the person with low n Achievement; he works harder when he has a chance of taking some money away from a situation. The money in and of itself means more to him than it does to the person with high n Achievement.

Of course, it follows that concrete measures of achievement other than money could be devised by other types of economic systems to satisfy the entrepreneurial spirit. Something like this has apparently happened in Communist states like Poland and Russia, where plant managers work under a fairly rigid quota system which demands that they make their quotas—or else! In the free enterprise system a businessman must make his profit—or else. The psychological effects, so far as the achievement motive is concerned, are apparently pretty much the same. In both systems the manager gets feedback in concrete terms as to how well he is doing. If he has high n Achievement, he is more likely to live and survive under such a challenge.

While these three characteristics of people with a strong concern for achievement—the desire for personal responsibility, the tendency to set moderate achievement goals, and the need for concrete feedback of results—are the most important, there are some other minor characteristics possessed by these people which tend to suit them for an entrepreneurial job. They like to travel, they are willing to give up one bird in the hand to get two in the bush, and they prefer experts to friends as working partners. But to discuss any of these in detail would take us far afield.

Achieving Nations

If the theory underlying the experiments with determining n Achievement in individuals is correct, then what is true for groups of individuals might well prove true for nations. Does a high achievement concern herald a nation's rise? Let's take a look at the facts.

Naturally, tests of individual businessmen in particular countries would not prove very much about the influence of achievement concern on the nation's success. However, we figured that by coding popular literature of past and present, we could get a rough estimate of the strength of the concern for achievement in a given country at a given time period. So we took samples from various time periods of a wide variety of the most popular imaginative literature we could find—poems, songs, plays—and scored them for n Achievement just as we had scored the simple stories written by individuals.

When we plotted the number of achievement ideas per hundred lines sampled in a given time period against economic indexes for the same time period, we got two curves that showed a very interesting relationship to each other. Normally, we found, a high level of concern for achievement is followed some fifty years or so later by a rapid rate of economic growth and prosperity. Such was certainly the case in ancient Greece and in Spain in the late Middle Ages. Furthermore, in both cases a decline in achievement concern was followed very soon after by a decline in economic welfare. The relationship between the two curves is shown most dramatically in figure 2, which plots the data for the three-hundred-year time span from Tudor times to the Industrial Revolution in England.

There were two waves of economic growth in this time period, one smaller one around 1600 and a much larger one around 1800 at the beginning of the Industrial Revolution. Each wave was preceded by a wave of concern for achievement reflected in popular literature, a smaller one prior to the growth spurt around 1600 and a larger one prior to the Industrial Revolution.

What clearer evidence could one ask for? What people are concerned about determines what they do, and what they do determines the outcome of history!

Present Confirms Past

In modern nations, too, the picture is very much the same. Children's stories used in public school textbooks proved to be the most standardized form of popular literature that we could get from a large number of different countries. As a matter of fact, the simple, imaginative stories that every country uses to teach its children to read are very similar in format to the stories produced by individuals when we test them as described earlier, particularly if one concentrates as we did on second-, third-, and fourth-grade readers, where normally political influences are quite unimportant. The stories could be coded quite easily by the standard *n* Achievement scoring system.

Growth rates had to be estimated from the only figures available that could be trusted on such a wide variety of countries—namely, the figures showing electric power consumption—but there is ample evidence to show that electricity consumed is probably the best single available index of gross national income in modern times.

The *n* scores, when compared with the subsequent rates of

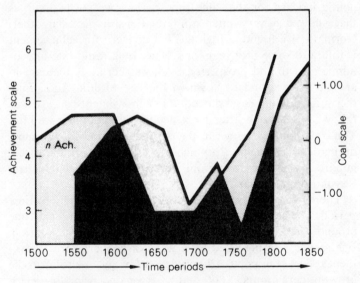

Fig. 2. How Achievement Thinking Expressed in English Literature Predicts the Rate of Industrial Growth Fifty Years Later.
Note: Achievement thinking (*n* Ach.) = Mean number of achievement images per 100 lines.
Rate of industrial growth = Rate of gain in coal imports at London, as deviations from average trend (standard deviation units).

economic growth for various countries, confirm the findings of the historical studies to a surprising extent. The higher the *n* Achievement level in the children's readers around 1925, the more rapid the subsequent rate of economic growth. (For twenty-two countries, the correlation was actually a substantial .53.) Furthermore, the higher the *n* Achievement level in a country's children's readers around 1950, the more rapid its rate of growth between 1952–58. In fact, of twenty countries above average in *n* Achievement in 1950, thirteen (or 65 percent) showed a rapid rate of economic growth in 1952–58. Whereas, of nineteen low in *n* Achievement, only five (or 26 percent) achieved a rapid rate of growth.

Prediction Possibilities

How meaningful are these findings, especially when one realizes the crudity of the data? In a certain sense, the cruder one admits the data to be, the more remarkable the findings appear. After all, the data suggest that one could have got a pretty good line on the economic future of various countries by studying its stories for children in 1925—regardless of a major depression, a world war, and a host of other political and economic factors.

Is it possible that we have stumbled on a way of predicting the future course of history? And from such an almost laughable source—stories for children—rather than the serious pronouncements of statesmen, generals, and economists? How is it possible?

The best interpretation of such findings would appear to run something as follows. The stories tell us what is on the minds of significant elites in the country, what these influential persons tend to think about most naturally, when they are "off guard," so to speak, and not under any particular pressure to think one thing or another. In this sense, the stories are exactly analogous to the ones written for us by individuals. If you ask a man whether he is interested in achievement, the chances are that he will tell you that of course he is. Similarly, if you were to ask a country's leaders whether they wanted their nation to forge ahead, they would find it unpatriotic to say no. But, regardless of what such leaders say in public, the stories in the children's readers of many nations will show whether their people's thoughts turn naturally to achievement or to matters other than achievement.

Here is an illustration. Take a simple story theme like one in which some children are building a boat. Such themes are frequently borrowed by one culture from another and appear in several different readers, but the way they are embroidered may be quite different and quite revealing. For example:

In Country A, an *achievement*-oriented country, the emphasis is on making the boat, on constructing something that will work, and not sink or tip over in a strong wind.

In Country B, the emphasis may be on *affiliation,* on the fun that the children have in playing together to sail their boat. Here little may be said about the details of constructing a seaworthy craft and much about the personal interaction of the children.

In Country C, the story may center on *power,* and describe how the children were organized to produce the boat. One boy might set himself up as a leader, coordinating the work of the other children and telling them what to do.

Apparently, what comes most readily to the minds of these authors—whether concepts of achievement, affiliation, or power—reflects sufficiently well what is on the minds of key people in the country. And not only will these concepts seem natural and pleasing to the readers of these stories but will determine what they spend their time doing in the years to come. Thus, if the stories stress achievement, it means that an entrepreneurial spirit is abroad in the land. It indicates that many key people are thinking in achievement terms even when they do not need to.

In a nation, a strong achievement orientation affects particularly the business or economic sector of the population. And if the entrepreneurial types are strongly motivated to do well, they apparently succeed in getting the economy moving at a faster rate. So the children's stories are a symptom of the quality or "drive" of the entrepreneurial sector of an economy.

Rising and Falling Nations

With this in mind it is interesting to look at scores for particular countries—if only to make a better guess as to where to invest one's money! A generation ago, the North European countries, particularly Sweden and England, were very high in *n* Achievement, but both have fallen in the 1950s to well below average. Is it just a coincidence that one hears reports of stagnation or "maturity" in both economies? Are England's present difficulties the fault of outside circumstances, or do these difficulties stem from the fact that its citizens have lost their achievement drive? For some reason, the Central European countries—France, Germany, and Russia —were all low in achievement concern in 1925, but by the 1950s all had increased sharply.

The case of Russia is particularly critical for us. How does the United States stand in achievement motivation as compared to the USSR? According to a historical study, achievement concern in the United States increased regularly from 1800 to around 1890 but has decreased more or less regularly since, although there is a possibility that the decline has leveled off in the past thirty years. We are still above average and, in fact, were at approximately the same level as Russia in 1950, although we were probably on the way down while they were certainly on the way up.

From the point of view of this analysis, the argument whether a socialist or a free enterprise system is the better way of stimulating an economy has been based on a false premise all along. Americans claimed that the success of their economy resulted, naturally, from the free enterprise system. Then, when the Soviet Union scored successes in outer space and in other fields, the Russians immediately claimed these great economic and technological achievements stemmed from the superiority of their system.

Both contentions may well be wrong. Economic success and technological development depend on achievement motivation, and the rapid rate of Russian economic growth is due to an increase in her achievement concern just as ours was a generation or so earlier. There are other issues involved in comparing the two social systems, of course, but so far as this particular issue is concerned it has been misunderstood by both sides.

Need for Acceptance

There is one final question that must be answered before we move on. Is it possible that achievement motivation will be aroused in *any* nation which comes in contact with modern technology and sees vividly the opportunity for a better life? Can't achievement motivation be "borrowed" or assimilated from one nation to another? Are there not good illustrations of countries in which need for achievement has risen as they see more and more clearly the possibilities of growing and developing into modern, economically advanced nations? Are we just describing the "revolution of rising expectations" in fancy psychological jargon?

Opportunity is part of the story, of course. It does arouse people to act, but it arouses precisely those who have some need for achievement *already*. The soil must be ready for the seeds, if they are to grow. After all, many countries have been in touch with Western technology for generations—for example, the Islamic nations around the Mediterranean; yet they have been very slow to respond to the possibilities of a better life clearly presented to them all this time.

Consider, for example, a nation like Nigeria, which

provides a good illustration of how opportunity and motivation must interact. Nigeria is essentially a federation of three regions, each of which is dominated by a different cultural group. Only one of these groups—the Yoruba—is known to be very high in need for achievement. In fact, long before the Yoruba had much contact with the West, this tribe was noted for its skill and interest in trade and native financial transactions. An indication of the validity of the achievement theory is shown by the fact that the Yoruba tribe, when exposed to new opportunities, produced a much stronger and more successful economic response than did the other tribes—as would be predicted. The regional bank operated by the Yoruba is in a much sounder position, for example, than the other two regional banks in Nigeria.

Opportunity challenges those who are achievement-oriented. Like two other groups high in n Achievement, American Jews and American Catholics between the ages of thirty-five and forty-five (John F. Kennedy, for instance), the Yoruba reacted vigorously to develop economic opportunities as they became available. Exposure to economic and technological opportunities did not produce as vigorous a response from groups lower in n Achievement in Nigeria any more than a similar exposure has done through the years to similar low n Achievement groups in the United States.

What Can We Do?

Is it inevitable that the achievement concern shown by United States citizens should continue to decline? Must we fade out in time as all other civilizations have in the past? Not if we understand what is happening and take steps to change it. Not if we move decisively and quickly to influence the sources of achievement concern in individuals and in our nation.

What are those sources? Clearly, not race or climate—those traditional external explanations of the superior energies of some nations. For Russia's n Achievement level has increased decisively since 1925, while Sweden's and England's have dropped. Certainly there have been no equally decisive changes in the gene pools or the climates of those nations in that time period.

In fact, external factors are usually unimportant, though occasionally they may play a role, as they have in helping to create generally high levels of n Achievement in immigrant countries like the United States, Canada, and Australia. Such nations tended to attract immigrants higher in n Achievement, because:

1. They drew their population initially from countries that were higher in achievement concern than those from which the Latin American countries drew.

2. They provided a haven for many persecuted religious minorities whose achievement concern was very strong.

3. They did not provide as many opportunities for getting rich quick as did Mexico and Peru, for example, with their plentiful supplies of gold and silver.

In short, countries like the United States were lucky. The barrier to migration was so formidable that primarily those with high *n* Achievement climbed it.

Historians have sometimes claimed that it was the great frontier in the United States that provided the challenge and stimulus to development. Nonsense. Great frontiers have existed and still exist in many South American countries without eliciting a similar response. It was the achievement-oriented immigrants to America who regarded the frontier as a challenge to be overcome. It was not the frontier that made them achievement-oriented. Opportunities, like new frontiers, always exist, but it takes a certain kind of person to see them and believe he can exploit them.

While our distance from Europe, our tolerance for religious minorities, our good fortune in drawing immigrants initially from countries high in *n* Achievement tended to insure that we got more citizens with high achievement motivation, our later restrictive immigration policies have drastically reduced our chances of continuing to receive such people. These policies continue to give preference to immigrants from the North European countries, whose achievement drive has dropped significantly, and to restrict immigration from other countries where the *n* Achievement has been rising sharply. It would be a tragic irony of history if in an endeavor to protect ourselves, we managed to shut off the supply of that entrepreneurial spirit that made our country great!

Sources of Achievement

Where does strong achievement motivation come from? Values, beliefs, ideology—these are the really important sources of a strong concern for achievement in a country. Studies of the family have shown, for instance, that for a boy three factors are important in producing high *n* Achievement—parents' high standard of achievement, warmth and encouragement, and a father who is not dominating and authoritarian. Here is a typical study that reveals this fact:

A group of boys were blindfolded and asked to stack irregularly shaped blocks on top of each other with their left hands, at home in front of their parents. Separately, the mothers and fathers were asked how high they thought their sons could stack the blocks. Both parents of a boy with high *n* Achievement estimated that their boys should do better; they expected more of him than did the parents of a boy with low *n* Achievement. They also encouraged him more and gave him more affection and reward while he was actually doing the task. Finally, the father of boys with high *n* Achievement directed the behavior of their sons much less when they were actually stacking the blocks; that is, they told them less often to move their hands this way or that, to try harder, to stop jiggling the table, and so forth, than did the fathers of boys with low *n* Achievement.

Other studies have shown that fathers must be respected by their sons; but after the boy is capable of achieving something for himself, his father must stop directing every step he takes if the boy is to develop a strong concern for achievement.

In a sense, however, these family studies only push the question further back. Where did the parents get their standards? Why do some emphasize achievement and affectionately reward self-reliance? Because, very simply, they themselves believe in achievement for their family or for their political, social, or religious group. For one reason or another they are caught up in some great wave of achievement ideology.

One of the paradoxes of history is that often the achievement concern was not itself initially directed toward business or economics. For instance, the two great waves of achievement concern in the history of England shown in figure 2 were each associated with waves of Protestant reform or revival, whose explicit aims were not secular but strictly religious. The Methodists, for example, in the second wave of the English Protestant revival, stressed religious perfection in this life; yet even John Wesley recognized with some puzzlement that devout Methodists tended to get rich, a fact which he considered a handicap in attaining religious perfection.

But now we can understand what happened. The strong concern for Christian perfection in this world tended to produce an achievement orientation in Methodist parents and their sons that turned the boys toward business because, as we have shown above, an achievement concern is most easily satisfied in business. In our day, it is the secular religions of nationalism and communism that have placed the highest emphasis on achievement and tended to create higher levels of *n* Achievement in underdeveloped and Communist countries. Communism lays the same claims to superiority as a means of salvation that Christianity once did. However wrong we may feel it to be, we must recognize that it tends to create a strong atmosphere of achievement that has important consequences for economic growth.

The Achievement Challenge

If we are to compete successfully with Russia in the economic sphere, we must develop an achievement ideology at least as strong as hers. If we are to help poor countries develop rapidly and become self-reliant, we must recognize that the first order of priority lies in fostering the enterpreneurial spirit in those countries, not in simply providing them with material capital or in meeting their physical needs.

Oddly enough, a businessman knows this about his own company. He knows that in the final analysis it is the spirit in the company that counts most—the entrepreneurial drive of the executives, the feeling of all that they are working together to achieve a common goal: it is not "hardware" that counts in the long run—the size and slickness of the plant, or the money in the bank. These assets will melt away like snow in a hot sun without the proper achievement orientation in the company. Knowing this, the wise executive acts accordingly. He is concerned to keep the achievement orientation of the company alive by talking about its aims, by setting moderate but realizable goals for himself and his associates, by assigning personal responsibility, by making sure that people know how well they are doing, by selecting executives with high *n* Achievement or by developing it in those who need it.

What is true for a business is also true for a country, but this is not widely recognized. And we must realize that it is important to foster the achieving spirit not only at home but abroad if we are to be effective as a nation. American foreign policy is currently based on two main strategies: *(a)* the provision of political freedom and *(b)* material aid. Both are excellent goals, but they are not enough. How long would a company last if its chief goals were freedom from interference by others and freedom from want? It needs positive, specific goals such as a more effective marketing program, or a strict cost reduction program; something dynamic is necessary to keep a company—and a country—alive and growing.

Over and over again we have failed to learn the lesson that political freedom without a strong drive for progress is empty and impossible to maintain for long. China was politically free under Chiang Kai-shek, but it lacked the dynamic of a really self-sacrificing achievement effort until it was taken over by the Communists. Unless we learn our lesson and find ways of stimulating that drive for achievement under freedom in poor countries, the Communists will go on providing it all around the world. We can go on building dikes to maintain freedom and impoverishing ourselves to feed and arm the people behind those dikes, but only if we develop the entrepreneurial spirit in those countries will we have a sound foreign policy. Only then can they look after their own dikes and become economically self-sufficient.

Compare India and China, for example. Despite newspaper reports to the contrary, economic experts assure us that China is developing much more rapidly economically today than is India. Why? Is it because the West has given less material help to India than the Communist world has to China? Probably not. Is it because there is less political freedom in India than in China? Certainly not. Yet if the keystones of our foreign aid policy are the insuring of political freedom and the granting of economic aid, these measures are clearly not doing very well as far as developing India is concerned. Russia has apparently exported something more important to China—namely, an achievement dynamic that has galvanized the whole country. There is absolutely no evidence that this dynamic needs to be associated with regimentation and lack of personal freedom as it is in China, for the United States had this dynamic once, still has quite a lot of it, and could export it more effectively—if we really tried.

Hard to Export

Actually, we have been hampered in exporting our achievement dynamic, not only by a misguided emphasis on material as opposed to motivational factors, but also by a laudable desire to avoid appearing superior. When Americans travel and discover how poor people are in many countries and how inferior their political institutions appear to be to ours, they often either withdraw in horror into their own American enclaves and become "ugly Americans" or they remember their college anthropology and become cultural relativists, deciding that after all there is some good in all ways of life and we must not impose ours on other people. Neither of these reactions is very intelligent. For the fact is that all poor countries are going to modernize and want to modernize.

They refuse to remain quaint, impoverished specimens for the anthropologist to study.

How can we help provide such countries with an achievement dynamic without seeming to impose it on them? One simple way is to sell them on *their own country* and *its* possibilities, not on *ours*. It may sound absurd to say that our job is to help sell the Tanganyikans on Tanganyika or the Mexicans on Mexico, but the fact is that in many of these countries most of the people have never even heard of the nation of which they are citizens, and know little or nothing about the possibilities for a better life that they may have at home.

In other words, our job really is to do what Americans have been so good at doing—creating wants, selling a people on their future, making them believe in their own achievement.

Our other difficulty is organizational. Somewhere along the line we decided that federal funds for foreign aid must be spent by federal employees, usually in the form of grants or loans to be doled out by federal employees in other countries. This is a natural enough policy, because foreign relations are sensitive matters, but there is nothing inevitable about it. In fact, there is considerable evidence that aid channeled through nonofficial or private agencies is much more welcome in many countries and also less expensive.

Private organizations in the United States have had a long record of useful service abroad. Why should their resources not be increased by federal grants so that they can do their job even more effectively and on a larger scale? Why do new federal agencies have to be created all the time to try to hire people away from such groups when they are already organized to do a good job? Why must the Peace Corps compete for scarce specialists, whom it is currently having trouble recruiting? Why couldn't it make grants to organizations which already have such specialists on their staffs and instruct them to expand their efforts abroad?

Often such organizations can do a better job because they are not official representatives of Uncle Sam. They would certainly be more welcome in countries like Mexico, which will not accept Peace Corps volunteers because as United States employees they have political significance. What if some of these organizations are religious, when we believe in the separation of church and state? This is true, of course, but *all* Russians sent abroad are "religious" Communists. Can we really object to helping a few Christians go abroad, particularly if they are not official representatives of our government?

Conclusion

Our biggest challenge is to find some way to harness the enormous potential of American business to help develop poor countries. Why should creeping federalism continue to spawn new agencies for providing economic assistance to foreign countries when such agencies already exist under private ownership in the United States? For example, if Brazil needs a new electric power system somewhere, why should our government not help by working out a contract, complete with all the necessary credits or loans, with one of our own light and power companies? Aid, in other words, would be on a company-to-company basis rather than on a government-to-government basis. In the long run, it would probably prove to be cheaper and more efficient. More important, the achievement orientation of our business executives could make itself felt in various ways in the newly developing companies abroad.

This idea has many complexities which need to be worked out—some of which are dealt with in *The Achieving Society*— but basically it is designed to harness some of the enormous reserves of achievement ideology and skill in American business to the gargantuan task of developing poor countries. Money is not enough. Drive and enthusiasm are needed. Ways of locating and exporting these resources must be found.

If there is one thing that all this research has taught me, it is that men can shape their own destiny, that external difficulties and pressures are not nearly so important in shaping history as some people have argued. It is how people respond to those challenges that matters, and how they respond depends on how strong their concern for achievement is. So the question of what happens to our civilization or to our business community depends quite literally on how much time tens of thousands or even millions of us spend thinking about achievement, about setting moderate achievable goals, taking calculated risks, assuming personal responsibility, and finding out how well we have done our job. The answer is up to us.

Inside Bureaucracy: Five Types of Bureaucrats
Anthony Downs

The Motivation of Officials

Officials as "Utility Maximizers"

All the agents in our theory—officials, politicians, citizens, bureau clients, and so on—are assumed to be *utility maximizers*. Economists use the concept of *utility* as a sort of mental currency that decisionmakers use in arriving at choices among things that have no obvious "lowest common denominator." In other words, a man implicitly assigns certain "utility ratings" to the results of possible acts which express the preference he has for those acts. He then compares utilities among various acts, and chooses the act, or the combination of acts, that gives him the most total utility. Thus he maximizes his utility.

However, assuming that officials maximize utility is not enough to predict their behavior. Utility maximization really means the rational pursuit of one's goals. Therefore, in order to predict what officials will do, we must know their goals.

General Motives of Officials

We assume that all officials have multiple goals drawn from a certain overall set of possible goals listed below. Different types of officials may be motivated by different subsets of this overall set:

Power. This can include power within the bureau or outside it.

Money income.

Prestige.

Convenience. This is expressed by a resistance to changes in behavior that increase personal effort, and willingness to accept those that reduce personal effort.

Abridged from chaps. 8 and 9 of Anthony Downs, *Inside Bureaucracy* (New York: Little, Brown and Co., 1967), by permission of the publisher and RAND Corporation. Copyright © 1967 by The RAND Corporation.

Security. This is defined as a low probability of future losses in power, income, prestige, or convenience.

Personal loyalty. This is personal allegiance to either the official's own work-group, his bureau as a whole, a larger organization containing the bureau (the government if he is in a government bureau), or the nation.

Pride in proficient performance of work.

Desire to serve the public interest. "The public interest" is here defined as what each official believes the bureau ought to do to best carry out its social function. Thus we are not positing the existence of any single objective version of the public interest, but only many diverse personal opinions concerning it.

Commitment to a specific program of action. Some men become so attached to a particular policy that it becomes a significant motive per se in determining their behavior (an example might be Billy Mitchell and the military use of aircraft).

The first five goals (power, money income, prestige, convenience, and security) can be considered "pure" manifestations of self-interest. Loyalty may be either partly self-interested or almost wholly altruistic, depending upon the object. Pride in proficiency is also a "mixed" motive. Desire to serve the public interest is almost purely altruistic. Commitment to a program is ambiguous since it could be caused solely by personal identification (self-interest), or solely by conviction concerning the objective importance of the program (altruism), or by both. Thus the "utility functions" of the officials in our theory are made up of both self-interested and altruistic goals.

A Typology of Officials

Types of Officials

Although there are nine different motives in the "bureaucrat's utility function" described above, not all officials are influenced to the same degree by each motive. In theory, an infinite number of different relative weight combinations can be formed from these motives. However, in this study we will concentrate on five such combinations. Each will be considered typical of a certain kind of official, and these five types of officials will form an important part of our analysis.

Admittedly, these "ideal types" are oversimplified. Every man pursues a great many goals. Furthermore, utility maximizers actually trade off among their many goals as their relative values change, but some of the officials in our theory sacrifice everything else for one or two goals. Finally, no small number of "ideal types" can encompass the bewildering variety of personalities and characters encountered in the real world. Nevertheless, we believe use of these five abstractions will provide significant insights into the way bureaus actually behave.

The five types of officials in our theory and the values they exhibit are defined as follows:

Purely self-interested officials are motivated almost entirely by goals that benefit themselves rather than their bureaus or society as a whole. There are two types of such officials:

1. *Climbers* consider power, income, and prestige as nearly all-important in their value structures.

2. *Conservers* consider convenience and security as nearly all-important. In contrast to climbers, conservers seek merely to retain the amount of power, income, and prestige they already have, rather than to maximize them.

Mixed-motive officials have goals that combine self-interest and altruistic loyalty to larger values. The main differences among the three types of mixed-motive officials is the breadth of the larger values to which they are loyal.

1. *Zealots* are loyal to relatively narrow policies or concepts, such as the development of nuclear submarines. They seek power both for its own sake and to effect the policies to which they are loyal. We shall call these their *sacred policies*.

2. *Advocates* are loyal to a broader set of functions or to a broader organization than zealots. They also seek power because they want to have a significant influence upon policies and actions concerning those functions or organizations.

3. *Statesmen* are loyal to society as a whole, and they desire to obtain the power necessary to have a significant influence upon national policies and actions. They are altruistic to an important degree because their loyalty is to the "general welfare" as they see it. Therefore, statesmen closely resemble the theoretical bureaucrats of public administration textbooks.

Climbers: The Road Upward

General Motivation

Because each climber seeks to maximize his own power, income, and prestige, he always desires more of these goods.

There are three basic ways he can pursue this ambition:

1. He can be promoted to a higher rank within the bureau's hierarchy.

2. He can increase the power, income, or prestige associated with his existing job or rank.

3. He can shift to a new and more satisfactory job outside the bureau (or in such a "distant" part of the hierarchy that the shift does not really constitute a promotion but a new job).

We will refer to these techniques as *promotion, aggrandizement,* and *jumping.*

Normally, promotion is more satisfactory to climbers than aggrandizement. The range of variation in power, income, and prestige among different levels in the hierarchy is much greater than the range available at any one level. Although the limitations of each position can often be evaded on informal levels by a forceful individual, the official description of duties usually acts as a powerful check on possibilities for aggrandizement.

Paths to Promotion

By definition, bureaus seek to promote men who have done or are likely to do a good job in their organizational roles. But because a bureau has no markets, its members cannot be directly appraised in terms of their contribution to the ultimate value of its output. Therefore, an official can win promotion only by following one or both of two lines of action.

First, he can please his superiors. True, an official can antagonize one immediate superior without necessarily jeopardizing his chances of promotion, but he cannot antagonize a high percentage of those whose reports influence the promoting authority.

Second, he can score well on whatever objective standards are used for appraising his promotional qualifications. This means attending the right schools, getting good test grades, acquiring experience in the right jobs, and so on.

In our theory, aggrandizement is defined as increasing the amount of power, income, and prestige attached to a given position. An official can achieve this by doing more than the previous officeholder did, doing the same things better, or both. The available scope for aggrandizement by doing the same things better depends upon how badly his predecessor did them, and the total scope of the office itself. The Air Force Chief of Staff has such a wide span of responsibilities that no man can do the job "perfectly"; hence, there is plenty of room for his successors to improve on his performance.

However, it is usually possible to accomplish much greater aggrandizement by adding new functions to the job than it is by doing established ones more efficiently. There are two reasons for this. First, there are definite and narrow limits on the functions assigned to most positions. Even "perfect" discharge of the described responsibilities would not increase the power or status of the officeholder very significantly.

Second, it is normally much easier for an official to increase his total power by adding more people to his formal control than by increasing his actual control over the people already assigned to him.

Almost any attempt by an official to enlarge his functions requires him to request more money. Climbers, therefore, tend to aggravate the struggle for resources which is constantly occurring within every bureau. If the bureau can enlarge its total appropriations, it can allow some of its parts to expand without imposing losses on other parts. Therefore, members of every bureau have a strong incentive to react to change by attempting to increase their overall appropriations rather than by rearranging their existing allocations. This tends to bring each bureau into conflict with all others under the same central appropriations agency (such as Congress).

Climbers seek to aggrandize in ways that will create the least effective resistance. Therefore, a climber will try to make use of the following procedures:

He will seek to acquire specific functions not now performed by anyone else, particularly by anyone in his bureau. Therefore, climbers are strongly motivated to invent new functions for their bureaus, especially functions not performed elsewhere. This causes many climbers to spend at least some time operating outside of their bureaus in order to manufacture support for this aggrandizement.

If a climber cannot aggrandize by creating wholly new functions, he will seek to "capture" functions performed by persons whose power of resistance is low. This means his selection of functional areas in which to expand will be influenced just as much by power considerations as by any logical linkage with his present role.

Every climber has strong incentives not to economize unless he can use at least some of the savings to finance an expansion of his functions. If he merely turns savings back into the appropriations agency, it might reduce his next year's appropriation.

Jumping

The more opportunities a given official has to advance himself (or even just retain his present rank) by jumping to other organizations, the less control can be exercised over him by the organization he is now in, other things being equal. Conversely, the fewer opportunities for jumping he has, the more control it can exercise over him.

Certain skills normally provide more opportunities to jump than others. For example, computer programmers and lawyers currently have a wide choice of alternative jobs in our society, whereas customs inspectors have specialized knowledge usable in only one or two organizations. In fact, various skills could conceivably be arranged along a spectrum ranging from almost wholly jump-oriented occupations at one extreme to almost wholly non-jumping at the other.

Most of the skills near the jump-oriented end of this spectrum provide opportunities for individuals to create reputations for themselves independent of their organizations; these skills are professions. Professions develop their own quality standards and media of expressions. In fact, some analysts of bureaus consider professionals as a separate bureaucratic type because each is more strongly influenced by his occupation than his organization. However, in our typology, professionals can be considered highly jump-oriented climbers. The relative freedom from control by large organizations enjoyed by jump-oriented climbers ultimately stems from either or both of the following conditions: First, some skills can be practiced by individuals operating outside of any large organizations. Examples are psychiatrists and lawyers. Second, during some historical period, the demand for certain skills rises much faster than the supply of those who possess them, partly because long training periods make supply relatively inelastic in the short run. Hence organizations requiring specialists with these skills act as latent alternatives for similar specialists in other organizations.

Both of these conditions are conducive to high job mobility. This in turn produces rapid turnover in the organizations employing such persons, a strong orientation among them toward activities occurring outside their organizations, and a willingness of top-level bureau officials to tolerate such external orientation and to create an atmosphere of generally loose control over these specialists in order to keep them.

The above reasoning implies that bureaus may have to organize and operate those internal sections staffed by highly jump-oriented specialists differently from those staffed by "locked-in" specialists. The former group may demand more autonomy, hence more decentralized controls, than the latter.

Conservers: Holding On to What You've Got

General Motivation

Conservers seek to maximize their security and convenience. Since we have defined security as maintaining one's present level of power, income, and prestige, maximizing security really means holding on to all these "goods" already possessed. Maximizing convenience means reducing one's efforts to the minimum possible level.

Conservers, therefore, have an asymmetrical attitude toward change. On one hand, they strongly oppose any losses in their existing power, income, and prestige. On the other hand, they do not particularly desire more of these "goods."[1] In part, this relative indifference to gain occurs because they are not basically as ambitious or avaricious as climbers. In part, it occurs because they do not believe they have much chance of receiving significant gains in power, income, and prestige. Hence both their underlying values and their expectations contribute to their net belief that negative change would be very bad, but positive change would not be very good.

As a result, conservers tend to be biased against any change in the status quo. It might harm them greatly and cannot do them much good. The only changes they strongly favor are those that reduce either their effort and inconvenience or the probability that any additional future changes will threaten their security.

Conservers may differ from climbers in their basic personalities, their expectations, or both. The basic personalities of some people naturally incline them to be conservers. This group includes people who are timorous, self-effacing, extremely cautious, plagued by inferiority feelings, or just indifferent about their occupations.[2] Others are conservers because of a combination of personal traits and expectations. The group includes people of mediocre abilities whose past failures have erased any optimism they may once have had

1. See Leonard Reissman, "A Study of Role Conception in Bureaucracy," *Social Forces* 27 (1949): 305–10.
2. Classification of "indifferents" as conservers is based upon the analysis in Robert Presthus, *The Organizational Society* (New York: Alfred A. Knopf, 1962), chap. 7. Presthus divides "organization men" into three classes. His *upward-mobiles* are analogous to our *climbers* and his *indifferents* form a subcategory of our *conservers*. However, his third group—*ambivalents*—have no analog in our theory.

about future prospects. Still other people are conservers mainly because of their expectations rather than their person- alities. This group includes competent persons technically barred from improving their positions by age, seniority, or other unchangeable traits.

How Officials Become Conservers

Some officials are conservers from the first day they join the bureau, even if they enter at the lowest possible level. Their "conserver-ism" results from the basic personalities or expec- tations they bring with them, as explained above. This ac- counts for the widespread presence of conservers at the very lowest levels of bureaus, even among new recruits.

However, not all conservers are born that way; some are made within the bureau itself.

Climbers are likely to become conservers whenever they believe there is only a very low probability that they can gain further promotions, significantly aggrandize their existing positions, or jump to a better job elsewhere.

The longer any official remains in a given position, the more likely he is to become a conserver. Long tenure in a given job may imply several things: the job-holder has little ability and therefore a low expectation of promotion; he is ineligible for further promotion because of some unchange- able factor; he is "over-due" for a promotion because he has marginal abilities—in which case he does not want to do any- thing that might "rock the boat"; or he is a fanatic zealot whose radical views have alienated his superiors. In the first three cases, he is likely to be a conserver already. In the last case, prolonged frustration is likely eventually to weaken his enthusiasm and encourage him to "blend into the landscape" by becoming a conserver.

The older any official is, the more likely he is to become a conserver. As he gets older, his chances for really substantial future advancement or achievement of any kind are reduced unless he is at the very top of the hierarchy. Also, the great efforts required in taking the initiative are more difficult for older men.

Except for the few officials in the "mainstream" of promo- tion to the very top, the longer an official remains within a bureau, the more likely he is to become a conserver. The longer an official has been in a bureau, the more he has been exposed to the difficulties and frustrations of trying to change its behavior; hence the less optimistic he is likely to be about achieving future changes. Also, the longer he has failed to get into the "mainstream" leading to the top, the less expectation he has of getting there in the future.

The more authority and responsibility an official has—the closer he is to the top—the more likely he is to become a conserver if he is not still in the "mainstream" of further promotion and he has strong job security. As an official acquires more and more power, income, prestige, and influence over policy, the probability rises that changes in the status quo will reduce his stock of these "goods" instead of increasing it. Therefore, he is likely to devote more energy to hanging onto what he's got than to getting still more.

These conclusions add up to the "Law of Increasing Conserverism." *In every bureau, there is an inherent pressure upon the vast majority of officials to become conservers in the long run.*

Why Conservers Stick to the Rules

Decision making is inherently a risky process because decisions can prove wrong, unpopular, or both. We have already seen that conservers are basically change avoiders because they fear the risks of losing power, income, and prestige. Hence we can also view them as risk avoiders. This implies that they try to escape responsibility for making decisions. However, the duties of most officials force them to make decisions constantly. This seems to pose a dilemma to conservers, but they have devised an ingenious way of simultaneously making decisions and avoiding the responsibility for doing so.

This consists of rigidly applying the rules of procedure promulgated by higher authorities. Instead of "playing it by ear" and adapting the rules to fit particular situations, many conservers eschew even the slightest deviation from written procedures unless they obtain approval from higher authority. Thus, rigid rule-following acts as a shield protecting them from being blamed for mistakes by their superiors, and even from having to obey any orders that conflict with "the book." This attitude of rigidity, plus the delays involved in obtaining official rulings for unusual situations, create the conditions that have become stereotyped as "the bureaucratic mentality" and "red tape."

Extreme rigidity in following rules also allows many conservers to perform their jobs without becoming emotionally involved with either the problems of their clients or the proper performance of their social functions. In bureaus that deal with clients who have severe personal problems (such as police departments or mental hospitals), strong emotional involvement or identification with individual clients can be highly destructive to an official's psychological balance. Also, the primary interests of many officials lie in their avocational pursuits rather than their bureau jobs, toward which they are largely indifferent.

Mixed-motive Officials, Their Similarities and Differences

Their Conceptions of the Public Interest

By definition, mixed-motive officials seek goals connected with the public interest to some extent, since they are partly motivated by altruistic loyalty. However, because no single conception of the public interest can be unequivocally identified as "the one best" version, each official pursues the public interest as he himself perceives it. As a result, there are nearly as many different conceptions as there are people thinking about it.

We believe, however, that variations in officials' operational conceptions of the public interest produce definite patterns related to other characteristics of these officials. An official's *operational conception* of the public interest is the one he actually uses in making decisions related to his job, as opposed to the one he might cite in a philosophic discussion. These conceptions vary concerning both their breadth of focus and their stability of contents.

Some officials act as though pursuit of the public interest means promotion of very specific policy goals (such as development of the Multi-Lateral Force) regardless of the antagonism they encounter or the particular positions they occupy. Hence their conceptions are narrow in focus and stable in content both in time and under varying circumstances. We classify such officials as *zealots*.

Other officials act as though pursuit of the public interest means promotion of very broad policy goals (such as promoting peace through strength) which they try to use as guidelines for decision making regardless of the particular positions they occupy. Their conceptions are therefore broad in focus but also quite stable in content. These officials are *statesmen*.

However, a majority of mixed-motive officials act as though pursuit of the public interest means promotion of goals closely connected with the fortunes of the particular offices they happen to hold. By this we do not refer to their pursuit of self-interest goals, but to their truly altruistic loyalty to the organizations in which they are situated. Thus, their operational conceptions of the public interest vary in breadth of focus and are flexible in content both in time and under various circumstances. These officials are *advocates*.

Their Psychological Predispositions

These variations in mixed-motive officials' operational conceptions of the public interest are closely linked to differing psychological predispositions. All three types are idealistic in nature, in contrast to purely self-interested officials. Also, all three types are relatively optimistic in temperament, since they believe that their pursuit of the public interest actually benefits society. But in other respects, they differ markedly.

Zealots are much more optimistic than the other two types, and are extraordinarily energetic and aggressive. These traits are evidenced by their willingness to promote their sacred policies in the face of seemingly overwhelming obstacles. Moreover, because they are "inner directed" in character, they continue to promote their own views even when most of their colleagues and associates—including their superiors—vehemently disagree with them. Many seem to relish conflict situations, even when vastly outnumbered. In fact, because of their "gadfly" roles in bureaus, many zealots develop an aggressive outspokenness that irritates most other types of officials. Finally, they are fanatically loyal to their sacred policies, which they promote at every opportunity, no matter what official position they occupy or what circumstances they are in.

Advocates are basically optimistic, and normally quite energetic. However, they are considerably more "other directed" in character than zealots; hence they are strongly subject to influence by their superiors, equals, and subordinates. Nevertheless, they are often quite aggressive in pressing for what they believe best suits their organizations. Thus they are willing to engage in conflict if they are supported by their colleagues, but are not likely to be "loners" like many zealots. We will analyze the factors that influence the breadth of focus and stability of contents of their loyalties later in this chapter.

Statesmen vary in energy from extreme laziness to hyperactivity. Lazy statesmen espouse very broad views but undertake little action; they make good critics but poor achievers. Statesmen are inclined to be philosophical and academic because their broad viewpoints often conflict with their narrow operational responsibilities. This causes frequent frustration and explains why statesmen are somewhat less optimistic than advocates or zealots. They are mainly "inner directed" in character, and therefore can persist in maintaining a generalized outlook even when their responsibilities are quite particular. However, they do not like conflict situations and seek to reconcile clashes of particular viewpoints through compromises based upon their broad general loyalties.

The Human Use of Personality Tests: A Dissenting View
Victor R. Lovell

During the past ten years, public resentment of personality testing has become increasingly evident.[1] Testimony has been given on the abuse of personality tests before the Senate Subcommittee on Constitutional Rights[2] and the House Special Subcommittee on Invasion of Privacy of the Committee on Government Operations.[3] It seems evident that unless psychologists concerned with personality assessment voluntarily restrict their own activities in some fashion, they will soon be subject to legal restrictions. At this writing, one bill to set up such restrictions has already been introduced into the House of Representatives.[4]

The response of psychologists to this outcry has usually been to attribute it to public ignorance or political extremism.[5] I think we have been somewhat fatuous in this

Reprinted from *American Psychologist,* May 1967, pp. 383–93. Copyright 1967 by the American Psychological Association, and reproduced by permission of the publisher and author.

I am indebted to my colleague, Norman S. Ciddan, for the benefit of numerous clarifying discussions on the problems with which this paper is concerned.

1. M. Amrine, "The 1965 Congressional Inquiry into Testing: A Commentary," *American Psychologist* 20 (1965): 859–70; J. T. Dailey, "Emotional Criticisms of Testing" (Paper read at a joint meeting of the American Educational Research Association and the National Council on Measurement in Education, Chicago, February 1963); M. L. Gross, *The Brain Watchers* (New York: Random House, 1962); B. Hoffman, *The Tyranny of Testing* (New York: Crowell-Collier, 1962); V. Packard, *The Naked Society* (New York: McKay, 1964); W. Whyte, *The Organization Man* (New York: Simon & Schuster, 1956).

2. "Testimony before the Senate Subcommittee on Constitutional Rights of the Committee on the Judiciary," *American Psychologist* 20 (1965): 888–954.

3. "Testimony before the House Special Subcommittee on Invasion of Privacy of the Committee on Government Operations," *American Psychologist* 20 (1965): 955–88.

4. R. F. Doktor, "Testing: The Heat Is on in Congress," *California State Psychologist* 7 (1966): 3.

5. Amrine, "The 1965 Congressional Inquiry"; Dailey, "Emotional Criticisms of Testing"; F. L. Vance, "Work of the APA Committee on Psychological Assessment in Relation to Public Concern about Testing," *American Psychologist* 20 (1965): 873–74.

matter. In my opinion, the protests we have heard, however ill-informed and inarticulate they have been, are directed at misuses of psychology which are quite real and very serious, to which our vested interests have blinded us.

Fundamentally, I think the issue is one of reconciling three divergent interests: *(a)* the public's right to privacy; *(b)* the social scientist's freedom of inquiry; and *(c)* the personnel worker's right to determine fitness for employment. Solutions, insofar as they have been proposed, have usually taken the direction of *restricting test content*. I do not think this tack can ever lead to any resolution of the basic conflicts involved.

The problem with restricting content is twofold. First, as is always the case with censorship, one does not know how to go about laying down concrete guidelines. Second, to do so will not offer adequate protection to the public, nor to the social scientist, nor to the personnel worker. Even if items dealing with sex, politics, and religion are deleted from personality inventories, the respondent's private thoughts are still likely to be probed. *Any* restriction of content is clearly an incursion on freedom of inquiry. Finally, determination of job qualifications may require the use of threatening stimuli, as, for example, when candidates for work in hospitals are given concept-formation tests involving pictures of horrible wounds.

An alternative to restricting content is to *restrict function*. Specifically, I am going to propose that certain kinds of tests should not be used in certain ways. I will lay down concrete guidelines for this proposal by arguing that certain kinds of "contracts" between assessors and respondents should be outlawed.

Basically, personality testing is used for two very different purposes, which I shall call the *personnel function* and the *client function*. I define the former as applying to situations where there is a potential conflict of interest between assessor and respondent, and the latter as applying to situations where there is not. The personnel function usually involves decisions about hiring, promotion, and termination. The client function usually involves providing services to the respondent. There are, however, important exceptions to these generalizations.

Where testing is purely for research purposes, we have the client function, except in situations where research subjects are coerced, deceived, or when their test results are not considered to be confidential, in which case we have the personnel function. The latter would include all research enterprises where participation by subjects is not voluntary. Testing serves a personnel function in all service situations where the respondent is not free to accept or reject services (as when he is committed to a mental hospital), or where he must qualify for them in some way other than by being able to pay for them (as when he is applying for welfare benefits).

Three Test Contracts

Whether a particular assessment situation involves the client function or the personnel function becomes apparent when we examine the test contract involved. By "test contract," I mean whatever is understood between assessor and respondent. This involves some extension of the sense of "contract," since the term is usually restricted to voluntary agreements, and assessment often involves involuntary elements.

Suppose we should administer a personality inventory to a group of incoming freshmen at a college or university, and suppose the following message were to appear printed on the first inside page of the booklet which contains the test items:

To the Respondent:

We are asking you these questions because we really want to know what you think, and how you feel, and because we are convinced that it will contribute to your education in some small way for you to ask them of yourself.

The information we are asking you to give will be used in one or both of two ways. First, it may contribute to our research on the process of higher education and the character of youth in our contemporary world. Second, it may be used to help provide you with psychological services during your college career, if you should decide that you require them. It will not be used by others to make decisions about you, although it may contribute to helping you make your own decisions more effectively.

If you take this inventory, the information you give us will be held in the strictest confidence. It will not be made available without your express permission (written, signed, and in our judgment uncoerced) to administrators, faculty members, parents, prospective employers, or anyone else except those on your campus whose primary obligation is to provide you with mental health or counseling services, or to do unbiased research in the social sciences.

When you take the inventory, we would like you to enter into a contract with us: *You don't try to fool us and we don't try to fool you.* The appropriate response to an item in this inventory is the one which you feel in your heart to be honest; the inappropriate one is the one which you know is not. If you do not feel that you can accept these terms, we would prefer that you did not take the inventory, for without this contract you will be wasting both your time and ours.

Since the inventory contains material which is personal and controversial, you should think carefully before deciding to take it. If you should decide not to, we shall understand and respect your decision.

If you do decide to take the inventory, we wish you a pleasant and provocative exercise in self-discovery. We hope that this experience will move you a little closer to that intimate self-knowledge which has always been one of the primary goals of higher education.

Good luck!

Signed,
(the test authors)

We shall call this message the *client contract*.

Now suppose instead this message appears:

To the Respondent:

Because of the complexity of the technical considerations involved, and the limited space available here, it is not possible for us to explain to you the nature of this psychological assessment. We assure you that it is being done for sound reasons, and that nothing is being demanded of you capriciously.

The information you give us will be used in many very important ways. It will become a part of your permanent academic record. It may influence critical decisions which others will have to make about your career. It will be made available in various forms to administrators, faculty members, parents, prospective employers, and others who have a vital interest in your character and your welfare.

Make your test responses as honestly as you can. It will not be in your best interest to do otherwise. If you should try to slant your answers so as to make a more favorable impression than is justified, this will become apparent to us when we score your test, and will reflect badly upon you.

Be conscientious and be careful!

Signed,
(the test authors)

We shall call this message the *strong personnel contract*.

Finally, consider a third message:

To the Respondent:

Because of the complexity of the technical considerations involved, the limited space available here, and the uses to which the material is to be put, it is not possible for us to explain to you the nature of this psychological assessment. We assure that it is being done for sound reasons, and that nothing is being demanded of you capriciously.

The information which we will gain from this test will be used in many very important ways. It will become a part of your permanent academic record. It may influence critical decisions which others will have to make about your career. It will be made available in various forms to administrators, faculty-members, prospective employers, parents, and others who have a vital interest in your character and your welfare.

You may try to slant your test answers so as to create a favorable impression. We will take this into consideration when we score your test. Your ability to create a favorable impression is of great interest to us, for it is likely to contribute much to your success or failure in a great many life situations. If you don't want to play this game with us, you can probably get away with refusing to take this test, if you really want to push it. We will try to make it as hard as possible for you to do so, because our boss wants you tested, and we work for him, and not for you.

We have to live too!

Signed,
(the test authors)

We shall call this message the *weak personnel contract*.

Test Contracts and Test Standardization

The three examples given above represent the major alternatives available to the psychologist when he administers a personality assessment program. For the sake of brevity, the research contract and the counseling contract have been fused into one. It should be clear that current practice seldom involves making the nature of the situation explicit to the respondent. Typically, in the kind of situation alluded to above, the freshman class would be herded into an auditorium at some time during a crowded "orientation week," handed the test materials, and told to follow the simple instructions printed thereon. If someone should object, it is likely to be communicated to him that he is a troublemaker who has no business questioning the wisdom of professional people who obviously have only his best interests at heart.

The first point I should like to make is that, both as individuals involved in the administration of assessment programs, and, I am convinced, eventually as a profession, we must choose between the alternatives suggested above, and we must make them explicit to the respondent. If we do not, we shall not be able to validate our assessment instruments in any very broad and profound fashion, because we shall not be able to maintain standard and uniform testing conditions. No matter what validation data we may have about our hypothetical personality inventory, if these data have been gathered under the client contract, we shall have difficulty making valid inferences about the meaning of test scores acquired under conditions where a personnel contract was involved. Further, if the testing actually serves a personnel function, the effect of personnel decisions will probably be a feeding back of information into the respondent population, which will alter the relationship of test variables with critical nontest variables; that is to say, people will become test wise and validity will vanish. For a discussion of the relationship between test validity and test situations, see Sarason.[6]

It has traditionally been argued that where the message making explicit the testing contract (or lack of such) is withheld, the respondent will make his own idiosyncratic interpretation of the situation, and that this interpretation, as manifested in his responses, will be indicative of broad and enduring traits of character in which the assessor is interested. While this argument is based on what is perhaps one of the most profound ideas in psychological assessment, its specific application to the *assessment contract* is naïve and wrongheaded. This is because most situations in which per-

6. S. B. Sarason, "The Test-Situation and the Problem of Prediction," *Journal of Clinical Psychology* 6 (1950): 387–92.

sonality tests are administered are in fact highly structured. The respondent may be expected to infer the rules and goals of the game from the context in which it is played, even if they are not articulated by the assessors. In other words, variance due to interpretation of the test contract is probably mostly situational, rather than individual, in its determination.

If a man is applying for a job, and we give him a test, he does not need to be told that the success of his application is contingent on his responses (although present ethical standards state that he should be). He reasonably assumes that we would not do it if it were not good business, and he knows that the task at hand is to decide whether or not to hire him. If we in fact tested the job applicant for some other purpose, such as to decide where in the organization he might best be placed, we would run some danger of defeating ourselves, for our validity data would probably be based on the responses of men already placed, rather than on job applicants.

In the freshman testing situation described above, the respondent has spent a good deal of time during the past weeks providing information for various administrative records. Further, he has just spent the past year providing information to admissions officers, on the basis of which various critical decisions about his life have been made. It is unlikely to make much difference if a client contract is in fact the intention of the assessors. Even if independent psychological services exist on the campus, he will not come to the conclusion that they do, and he will infer a personnel contract.

I hold that eventually we must choose among the client contract, the strong personnel contract, and the weak personnel contract, not only for specific instruments and specific assessment programs, but also as a profession, for all "personality tests." This is because each time any one of us administers a personality test, he is participating in the creation of a cultural institution. Which test contract is understood by the respondent depends not only upon what cues are present in the testing situation, nor upon the immediate institutional context which surrounds it, but also upon the respondent's general understanding of the legitimate functions of personality assessment in his society. If one looks at what is said about personality tests, one gets the impression that, outside the private practice of psychology, with individual clients, the weak personnel contract is fast becoming normative, both from the point of view of the lay public, and from the point of view of professional psychologists. If we do not make the decision, it will be made for us as a result of the institutional processes in which we are involved. I am concerned lest it be already too late for a rational and considered choice to be possible.

If the reader has followed the argument thus far, three questions are likely to come to mind. First, what sort of contract with the respondent is most consistent with the ethical practice of psychology? Second, what sort of contract is most likely to lead in the long run to the valid measurement of personality? And third, what contract will allow us to offer the community the broadest range of psychological services?

In the remainder of this essay, I shall argue for a client contract on all three counts. I shall further take the view that our three questions cannot ultimately be considered independently from one another, because ethics, science, and services are all outcomes of a single activity, and this activity is one of many interdependent components of a unitary social process. One cannot do something ethically, if one cannot do it at all. We cannot use our personality tests to provide psychological services if we are unable to construct valid measures. And, as I have already tried to suggest comparing sample contracts, the validity of our tests is not independent of our ethics, because our ethics supply the social context in which our tests are administered and in which they are validated.

Test Contracts and Ethics

In its public manifestos, the profession of psychology is firmly committed to political democracy, civil liberties, and the dignity of the individual. In practice, we sometimes violate these commitments, on behalf of bureaucratic or commercial interests. I do not believe that the strong personnel contract has any place in a free society, and I think that its occasional appearance is psychology's unique contribution to creeping totalitarianism in our times.

The strong personnel contract flatly denies the respondent's right to privacy. It proposes that kind of total surveillance of the individual which is characteristic of police states. Further, the strong personnel contract reeks with paternalism. It suggests total supervision as well as total surveillance. Finally, it creates the conditions for mutual suspicion and distrust among men. It invokes the possibility that deceit, if successful, may be richly rewarded, while at the same time threatening dire consequences if it is not.

The weak personnel contract might be considered ethically marginal. It is not a clear-cut invasion of privacy. It neither demands truth, nor threatens falsehood. Surveillance is more limited to that which is directly relevant, for to the degree to which the goal of the respondent's task is made clear, the test could be considered a work sample. Like the strong personnel contract, however, it is paternalistic (perhaps "maternalistic" would be more exact). It implies that those in positions of authority need not account to the public for their actions, and that their decisions must be taken on faith. Finally, the weak personnel contract, if received sufficiently often, will contribute in some small part to undermining the foundations of democratic process, for the efficacy of that process depends upon the authentic confrontation by the citizenry of each other, in order that their collective will may be determined. Since the weak personnel contract promises to reward conformity, it may discourage the articulation of loyal opposition, if it is true that what is learned in social situations is widely generalized.

The client contract protects the right to privacy, for it guarantees confidentiality, specifies the limits of confidence, and invites the respondent to decline to take the test if this is not satisfactory. It leaves him in a good position to make his decision, since it states the nature of the assessment, and indicates the possible benefits of making the choice to participate. Finally, it attempts to promote the kind of human relationships which contribute to harmonious living in a free and open community.

Although Messick suggests that "We should be especially careful not to let it be inferred that any change in our standards for psychological assessment necessarily reflects a general admission of past guilt,"[7] both the strong and the weak personnel contracts are quite permissible under present APA Ethical Standards, which simply state that:

> The psychologist who asks that an individual reveal personal information in the course of interviewing, testing, or evaluation, or who allows such information to be divulged to him, does so only after making certain that the responsible person is fully aware of the purpose of the interview, testing or evaluation and of the ways in which the information may be used.[8]

7. S. Messick, "Personality Measurement and the Ethics of Assessment," *American Psychologist* 20 (1965): 137.
8. American Psychological Association, "Ethical Standards of Psychologists," *American Psychologist* 18 (1963): 56–60, principle 7d, p. 57.

This is analogous to the legal principle which demands that the accused be informed that anything he says may be held against him, but the analogy is not carried out consistently. The accused may not decline to testify against himself. His psychological interrogator need obtain no search warrant in order to examine his psyche.

Privacy and Duplicity

Two related ethical themes arise when the proper use of personality tests is considered: *privacy* and *duplicity*. If the assessor is bound by no constraints in his invasions of the former, then the respondent is sure to react with the latter, and the assessor must outwit him by the use of *counter-duplicity*. This is a particularly messy business, because the respondent is not typically asked to testify as to objective matters of fact, but rather to the status of his attitudes, impulses, memories, emotions, and so forth. Because of this, his testimony cannot be independently corroborated. It may be examined for its internal consistency, but this is not relevant in the way that it would be, say in a legal situation, because consistency is not necessarily a property of attitudes, impulses, memories, emotions, etc.

It is sometimes suggested that this impasse may be resolved scientifically, rather than ethically. We need only investigate duplicity as a behavioral phenomenon, and when we have come to understand it, our subjects will not be able to deceive us. This line of thought springs from the notion that social science can function outside the social contract, without reference to moral concepts. All experimenters have moral commitments, however, just as all experimenters are either male or female, and I think it reasonable to expect the former to be as much involved in determining the behavior of subjects as the latter.

Once the respondent and the assessor have entered into a contract which permits them to deceive each other, it is difficult to see how any operational meaning can be given to the notion of duplicity. In order to investigate duplicity, the assessor must have some way of determining its presence or absence, but this requires that the declarations of the respondent be in some way corroborated, and we have seen that it is not clear how this is to be done. Even if the responses of the subject are recorded under conditions where it is believed that he is not aware of being observed, the authenticity of his behavior will be hard to establish, because this belief may be mistaken, and the observer is involved in a social game which leaves him no way to check up on himself.

However, even though duplicity is neither observed nor understood, administration of personality tests accompanied by a personnel contract might make it possible to validly predict some very critical events in which someone had a legitimate interest. The question of whether it is likely that this *can* be done will be taken up at a later point. The question at hand is whether it *should* be done.

Those who think it should often espouse what might be called the "hired-gun ethic." Duplicity in human relations, particularly in the presentation of one's own character to others, seems to be a common and pervasive characteristic of human society in general and personnel situations in particular. As long as this sort of thing is going to go on, the game might as well be played as well as possible by all concerned. It is not the business of professional psychologists either to rebel against the human condition, or to make policy for their employers. A similar defense is usually given by scientists and technicians involved in the design and production of war machines intended for the destruction of human property and human life.

Another kind of cold war could result. Some psychologists will make it their business to devise ever more complex and subtle ways of tricking their unwilling victims into revealing themselves. Others will offer their services as coaches to the respondent, to help him outwit the assessor. It is difficult to see how the enterprise of measuring individual differences could survive such a social holocaust, or how the individual would retain a voice in the conduct of his society. Actually, the orthodox version of the hired-gun ethic usually assumes that it is ethical for the psychologist to help the personnel worker to deceive the respondent, but not vice versa. The reasons for this bias are commercial, not ethical. So far, respondent coaching has been by nonpsychologists.[9]

In a nation where private enterprise is the dominant form of economic organization, it may be argued that while public agencies may be restricted, private institutions should be allowed to handle their personnel problems as they see fit, and therefore that professional psychologists who are employed by them should feel free to help them do so. A little thought should convince one that this is not so. Under our present system, hiring and firing practices are regulated by ethics and by legislation, just as working conditions are. To deny that this is as it should be would be to argue, for ex-

9. C. Alex, *How to Beat Personality Tests* (New York: Arc, 1965); Whyte, *The Organization Man.*

ample, that personnel workers should be able to tap the telephone lines of job applicants, or inject them with truth serums.

Ethics, Prejudice, and Paternalism

It is sometimes argued that the use of personality tests in selection is equalitarian in effect, if not libertarian in method. The advent of abilities tests as selection devices contributed a great deal to the leveling of barriers to social mobility in our society. It tended to make advancement more dependent on merit, and less on privilege. It has been claimed that personality tests, if used in the same fashion, may do the same. I think it is more likely that they will have the opposite effect. The correlation between personality traits and demographic variables such as social class, caste, and religious persuasion is well known.

Suppose a personality inventory contained the following item: I am a Negro.   (T)   (F)
As social scientists, we know that this item would be a valid predictor of all sorts of critical social outcomes in which the personnel worker has a legitimate interest, such as whether or not the respondent's conduct is likely to be criminal. However, we also know that the validity of the item would depend upon the operation of social forces the existence of which most of us deplore. Few of us would use this item if we could, because we would recognize that to do so would help perpetuate those social forces. Our prediction would be self-fulfilling, and contribute to the maintenance of barriers to social mobility. Yet it is probable that whenever we use personality tests in selection, we capitalize upon, and perpetuate, all sorts of prejudices, more subtle, less well understood, and perhaps more profound and in the very long run even more destructive than those regarding race. No matter how inclined we might be to use brute empiricism with our prediction problems, federal law would prohibit us from using the item above. However, for the most part, the choice of what test content to use for what assessment purpose is presently left to our own discretion, as well as the use we make of such. I suggest that we should exercise discretion, before this choice is taken away from us by a justifiably resentful public.

It is often pointed out that effective selection may protect the respondent from being put in a situation where he will fail, or where he will be uncomfortable. If the information necessary to do this must be extracted from him without his consent, is it not doing him a service to extract it? The trouble with this view is that it presupposes a paternalistic view of society which seems hardly compatible with the democratic values to which we are committed. In order to afford the respondent this kind of "protection," someone else has to decide what is good for him. In some areas, it makes sense to do this. A doctor does not usually feel the need to ask permission to save a patient's life; he assumes that the patient wants to live. But in the area of physical well-being there are norms with which it can be safely assumed that almost everyone will agree. In the area of emotional well-being there are no such norms.

Test Contracts and Test Validity

Our grandiosity in assuming that we can measure people who we can safely assume do not wish to be measured barely conceals our manifest failure, at least up to now, to measure nonintellective personality traits at all. I suspect that there is some kind of connection between the two. Would a physiologist attempt to measure basal metabolism without the cooperation of his subject? Why should we think we can do better?

The public seems well informed of the basic principles underlying the use of personality tests in personnel work, including the rather crude devices presently in existence for the detection of faking.[10] This has been true for some time now.[11] I think it likely, as Whyte suggests, that the general nature of the game is understood intuitively even by unsophisticated respondents. The vast body of "hard data" in existence on dissimulation is probably irrelevant here, since almost all of it has been collected in totally artificial situations.

What is ethical is usually what is practical when one takes a broad view of things. We guarantee complete confidentiality to our clients in psychotherapy because we know that if we did not do so, they would not trust us and we would not obtain the kind of communication from them which we require in order to effectively provide this service. I believe that something of this sort applies to the relationship between validity and contract in personality testing.

What kind of test contract will tend to maximize overall validity? This, of course, is an "empirical question," but if it

10. Alex, *How to Beat Personality Tests.*
11. Whyte, *The Organization Man.*

is approached in the hammer-and-tongs fashion which the term often implies when used by psychologists, the results could well be disastrous. If we gave our hypothetical personality inventory to three different groups of freshmen from the same class, each with a different one of our three contracts printed in the test booklet, we might then proceed to examine its validity under the three conditions, relative to various prediction problems. However, even if our consciences permitted us to conduct such an experiment, and we were able to obtain administrative approval for it, we might run some danger of precipitating a student revolt. In any case, we would create an atmosphere on the campus which would make validity data collected there subsequently somewhat difficult to interpret.

Nevertheless, let us suppose that as a profession we embark on a program of research of the sort alluded to above. I doubt that after ten or fifteen years of this sort of thing we will be much closer to resolving the issue on so-called empirical grounds than we are right now. We will have accumulated another one of those vast and diffuse bodies of literature which have become so common of late. Even those of us working in the immediate area will not have time to read it all. Everyone who has taken a stand on the issue will find ways to produce results consistent with his position. Everyone who has not will be unable to digest the data and make up his mind.

Investigations of this kind are fruitless because they rest on an outmoded and wrongheaded notion of what validity is. They are addressed to no legitimate theoretical issue. They proliferate, not because one finding leads to others which can be reconciled with it in more general terms, but because one finding provokes the production of others which are interesting only because they can be made to appear inconsistent with it, or with each other. The proper dialectic of science is not advanced. Such research programs regard validity solely in terms of predictive power, without taking predictive scope into consideration.

To decide the issue at hand in light of the outcome of some set of particular predictive ventures would be to make the implausible assumption that there exists some general solution which would be true for all test variables, all criterion variables, all populations, and all combinations thereof. It would be to treat a methodological bias as if it were a theoretical model. Moreover, the decision would have to be based on investigations limited by the marginal level of validity characteristic of most existent personality measures.

If the empirical question be approached in a less concretistic fashion, I believe that there are good empirical grounds for choosing the client contract, in order to facilitate the development of valid procedures for personality assessment. All of our psychological theories contain propositions, well supported by empirical evidence, to the effect that when an organism is in danger, its behavior becomes less variable and less complex. Such behavior may not lend itself to the enterprise of differentiating between organisms.

Learning theory tells us that when organisms are placed on a reinforcement schedule their behavior becomes less variable. Cognitive theory informs us that when an organism is exposed to the threat of punishment or to induced conflict, dedifferentiation of the cognitive structure and isolation of its components is the result. Social psychology tells us that when the status of human beings is in jeopardy, their behavior will be characterized by rigid and pervasive conformity to norms which are perceived as associated with its maintenance. Psychoanalytic theory holds that the threat of ego damage evokes anxiety, and that anxiety produces repression and constriction, which prevent expression and articulation of the whole personality. All of these propositions seem to suggest that the threat and coercion involved in personnel contracts will tend to mitigate against the measurement of individual differences, where honesty is required of the subject.

Good psychological theory, therefore, would seem to predict that under many conditions, with many variables, the effect of test administration involving personnel contracts will be to restrict the dispersion of the test variables, while at the same time increasing their intercorrelation, an effect which we would expect in general to render them less useful in the prediction of external criteria. To specify for which test variables, which criterion variables, and under exactly what conditions this will be so is the task of the theorist. Because this task is part of a process which is never complete, the issue at hand can never be summarily "settled" empirically, although it may always be further investigated, if other considerations do not dictate otherwise.

In terms of common sense, what is being suggested here is that we will obtain more information from people if we trust them and they trust us. This thesis is in good accord with the accumulated wisdom of the Judeo-Christian heritage. To hold that it will be true for all people, all situations, and all kinds of information would indeed be naïve. It is both normative and descriptive in intent, for as a prediction, it is likely to be self-fulfilling. I do not think it naïve to suggest that, for our profession, there is a presumption that it is the most viable game, both scientifically and socially.

Those who do personality research are often concerned lest if the option to refuse to take a personality test is made explicit and available, and is as a result often accepted, the generality of their findings will suffer. Potential respondents who decline to be tested will surely be different from those who do not, in ways that are important to us as scientists. I do not think that the truth of this can be disputed, but I think that it is often felt to have implications which it does not, namely, that opportunity for empirical inquiry is seriously diminished. Offering potential respondents the option of refusing to be tested will enable us to record and search for correlates of this behavior. An imaginative investigator who has a clear understanding of the theoretical questions and practical applications to which he has addressed himself will be able to use the data to achieve his goals. The loss involved in making the population tested more highly selected may not seem so great when we recall that most of the populations we test are already highly selected. Furthermore, we will now administer an additional "test," namely the acceptance or rejection of the assessment itself. We psychologists sometimes involve ourselves in an interesting paradox: On one hand we claim that our understanding of human nature will contribute to the "control" of human behavior, while on the other we demand that the control of human behavior be handed over to us in order that we may accomplish our ends.

A New Ethical Standard

It should be clear from what has already been said that I am proposing a considerable restriction of the uses to which certain kinds of mental tests may be put. The client contract is clearly appropriate to different assessment goals from those of the personnel contract. What will be the effect of this restriction on our capacity to provide psychological services? In order to discuss this question it is necessary to specify exactly what restrictions I advocate.

Up to now I have used the term "personality test." Although this more or less accords with popular usage, it is a misnomer, because all mental tests are properly speaking tests of personality. The kinds of tests I mean this discussion to refer to might best be called tests of character, virtue, psychopathology, and the like. The kinds of tests I do not mean to include under this rubric are tests of ability, aptitude, achievement, proficiency, and their ilk, where what is assessed is a work capacity or a work sample. In the remainder of this paper, I shall refer to the former as *tests of character,* and to the latter as *tests of capacity.*

A test of capacity is one for which there are criteria for deciding which responses are correct and which responses are incorrect, which are independent of the respondent, and of which the respondent is properly informed. By "correct responses" I mean those which will be rewarded; by "incorrect responses" those which will be punished. In testing for capacity, the respondent is told that he is to be evaluated, given an understanding of what is to constitute success and what failure, and success and failure are determined by norms which are external to him, be they subjective, as in an essay examination, or objective, as in an intelligence test. A test of character is one for which there are no criteria for deciding which responses are correct and which responses are not, or one for which the criteria of "correctness" are norms which are relative to the respondent, i.e., when the respondent is told that the "correct" answer is the "honest" one. Tests of character involve the recording of behavior under conditions where the assessor has not defined success and failure for the respondent, or under conditions where the assessor has defined success and failure for the respondent only in terms of the authenticity of self-report.

Personality inventories and projective techniques usually involve tests of character. Tests of capacity are most often concerned with ability, skills, problem solving, learning, the production of specified mechanical outputs, and so forth. But none of this is necessarily so, because the definition given above is independent of the nature of the test stimuli. A personality inventory becomes a test of capacity if the respondent is instructed to give the responses which will make a good impression on some particular class of people, and his protocol is scored for its correspondence with some reasonable determination of what responses do in fact make a good impression on this class. An intelligence test becomes a test of character if the respondent is asked not to solve problems but rather to indicate which kinds of problems he prefers and which he does not. It is still a test of character if the respondent is asked to solve problems, but his protocol is scored for his style of problem solving, rather than for the merit of his solutions. A person perception test is a test of capacity if it is scored for accuracy; if it is scored in terms of preferences for certain response categories, regardless of the appropriateness of these categories to actual persons, it is a test of character.

Whether a test involves character or capacity depends upon what the respondent is told to do, and upon how response categories are defined by the assessor when he scores the test protocol.

Tests of *social stimulus value,* in which the respondent is not identical with the person assessed, fall into a third category. Letters of recommendation, ratings of others, sociometric data, and so forth, are neither tests of capacity nor tests of character with respect to the person recommended, rated, or chosen. *With respect to the respondent,* they may be either tests of capacity or of character, depending upon the nature of his contract with the assessor.

One may determine whether a test is one of character or of capacity by asking if the respondent can "fake good." The notion of representing oneself as *better than one is* is never applicable to tests of capacity, but always applicable to tests of character. The latter are motivationally labile in a way that the former are not.

A moment's reflection should reveal that this distinction is independent not only of test content, but also of the construct which is measured. If intelligence is measured by the success of problem-solving activity, as it usually is, we have a test of capacity. But if it is measured, as it occasionally is, by the tendency to claim attitudes characteristic of successful problem solvers, then we have a test of character. If flexibility is measured by some kind of self-report device, then it is measured by a test of character. But if it is measured by success in a problem-solving situation, then it is measured by a test of capacity.

If the administration of a personality inventory involves the client contract or the strong personnel contract, as given earlier, the inventory is a test of character, because the respondent is asked to give an honest self-report. The interesting thing about the weak personnel contract is that it is a mixed bag. In terms of the distinction between character and capacity it is neither fish nor fowl. The question of whether a correct response is to be defined in terms of internal or external norms is left ambiguous. The accused is properly informed that what he says may be used against him, but he does not know how. If the task assigned the respondent were solely to make a good impression, and the persons to be impressed were indicated, and the scoring of the test were based in some way on the actual attitudes of these persons towards the test items, then we would have a *pure* test of capacity; otherwise we would not.

It may be objected that the categories of character and capacity may not be mutually exclusive. The weak personnel contract may make the inventory *both* a test of character and of capacity, since it is suggested that a correct response may be defined either with reference to internal or to external norms. The nature of the situation where the categories seem to overlap is perplexing, because the distinction involves what the respondent is asked to do, and it is not clear what he is being asked to do when he is told that his responses will be evaluated in terms of potentially conflicting norms. My inclination is to argue that under such conditions, we have a test of character, rather than of capacity, because if it is not clear what the respondent has been asked to do, then he has not been asked to do anything in particular.

The distinction between tests of character and tests of capacity is similar to that made by Cronbach[12] between *tests of typical performance* and *tests of maximal performance,* and to that made by Wallace[13] between *response predisposition* and *response capability*. The principal difference is that the categories used here are based solely on the nature of the test instructions and the test scoring, while those used by Cronbach and Wallace have reference also to theoretical constructs.

My position is that tests of character should never be used for any kind of personnel function, whether it be selection or placement. They should be used only for unbiased research, subject to the restrictions implicit in the client function, and to provide psychological services in situations where the assessor's first professional loyalty is to the respondent. I have argued this position on ethical grounds and on scientific grounds. I shall now consider what effect its implementation might have on the marketing of psychological services.

Ethics and Psychological Services

I should first like to reemphasize a point which has already been made. Our capacity to provide assessment services cannot be discussed independently of the validity, present and future, of our assessment procedures, nor of the ethical standards which are to be applied to these procedures. We cannot provide services with invalid instruments. It is likely

12. L. J. Cronbach, *Essentials of Psychological Testing,* 2d ed. (New York: Harper, 1960).

13. J. Wallace, "An Abilities Conception of Personality: Some Implications for Personality Measurement," *American Psychologist* 21 (1966): 132–38.

that we shall not be allowed to offer services if our ethics offend the public. Bills to restrict the activity of psychological testing have been appearing in our state legislatures for some time. They appeal to a variety of political groups for a variety of reasons, and are capable of attracting widespread support.

I have tried to define the sort of assessment procedure which must be restricted as narrowly as possible. In principle, the personnel psychologist is not to be enjoined from measuring any construct, nor from using any kind of test content. Essentially, all that must be given up is the demand for a certain kind of contract with the respondent, one which I doubt that much sense can be made of anyway, either in a legalistic or a scientific way. In practice, the personnel psychologist will not be able to measure constructs involving the notions of self-report or spontaneous behavior. I doubt that this is a real limitation; I think that the logic of such constructs dictates that they cannot be measured in personnel settings anyway, because of the likelihood that spontaneous or authentic behavior may be penalized. Many writers on the subject have reached similar conclusions. Cronbach,[14] for example, says:

> Complete frankness cannot be anticipated in any situation where the subject will be rewarded or punished for his response. Some degree of reward and punishment is implicit in any institutional use of tests, such as clinical diagnosis or employee selection. Honest self-examination can be hoped for only when the tester is helping the subject solve his own problems, and even then the subject may have a goal for which he wishes the support of the counselor's authority, which biases his response.

I would not go so far as to endorse the suspicion, suggested by the last phrase, that the notion of "honest self-examination" can have no place at all in our psychological constructs. Rather, my position is that the only way to escape from this dilemma is to make it clear in our testing contracts whether or not we intend to reward and punish, and if we do so intend, to indicate which response classes are to be rewarded and which punished, and then to try to the best of our ability to keep the contract, and that the only way to do this is to uniformly confront our potential respondents as a profession with some simple and broad ethical commitment. I think that

14. Cronbach, *Essentials of Psychological Testing,* p. 454.

if we do this we can become involved with constructs in which the concept of authenticity plays a part, while if we do not we shall of necessity close off many possible areas of research and service. I do not mean that we can produce interpersonal processes in which self-deception and the need to deceive others will not play a part; dynamic psychology dictates otherwise. I mean that we can only give operational value to such notions as authenticity and honest self-examination by creating situations where the integrity of interpersonal processes is protected by a particular kind of ethical structure, such as we have with regard to the processes of counseling and psychotherapy.

By restricting the activities of the personnel psychologist and in some cases those of the research psychologist, I believe we will act to protect the integrity of a variety of other psychological services, such as counseling and psychodiagnosis. These enterprises are simpler and more profound if we have the trust of our clients. Service-oriented research will also be facilitated if psychological assessors are trusted by their subjects. The counseling service might even be extended. Institutions which formerly depended only upon the personnel process to assign persons to places might employ private counseling psychologists who would report only to the candidate, and who would guarantee complete confidentiality to him. Self-selection and self-placement could then contribute to personnel decisions at the option of the candidate.

2

Individuals in Interaction: Communication and Influence

5

On Listening and Being Heard

Introduction

Throughout the four chapters in part 1 our focus has been on the individual human being. In the three chapters of part 2 our attention shifts to the process of *interaction between* individuals, especially the process by which one person tries to influence another. Several approaches to influence are discussed in these three chapters, including the use of formal authority, the use of power tactics and manipulative strategies, and other procedures which place reliance on more collaborative persuasion. But all these approaches to influence require as a precondition some kind of communication between the people involved. This first chapter of part 2 therefore deals specifically with communication processes.

The two papers that comprise this short chapter both carry a simple central theme: a particular message conveys much more than its words alone seem to contain. A corollary theme is that important messages are often conveyed by other means than the written or spoken word.

The words we say and how we say them affect the climate of a particular communication and, in fact, of longer relationships between people. Sometimes our messages generate a defensive climate; sometimes a supportive one. If a defensive climate develops, the person on the receiving end is likely to behave as though he had been backed into a corner. He may attack, he may attempt to withdraw from the situation, and almost certainly he will fail to hear accurately the manifest message being transmitted. On the other hand, if we can establish a supportive climate around our messages to other people, we are much more likely to bring about an accurate and full exchange of information; and indeed to maintain a problem-solving flavor to the situation, rather than one of competition and fear.

There are many easy ways to create a defensive climate. One is to make sure our listener sees us as being his evaluator, as attempting to control or proscribe his actions. Another is to communicate a feeling of our superiority in the relationship; or to treat him as an object rather than as another person; or to provide the impression that all we say and do has been carefully and strategically planned in advance. Almost any of these will generate defensiveness.

On the other hand, if we are able, in our direct communication with others, to describe rather than evaluate, to behave spontaneously more than strategically, empathetically more than neutrally, and to demonstrate openness rather than convinced certainty; then we are more likely to create a more supportive climate in which we can convey our thoughts more accurately.

One irony is that by consciously training ourselves to create supportive climates, we may violate the value of spontaneity! If our "spontaneity" is planned or at least is perceived that way by our listener, the reaction is likely to be defensive.

One more comment: no matter what the nature of the communication, defensiveness is more likely to arise when there are real status differences between communicators—when the communication is between child and parent, student and teacher, subordinate and boss, or in any other relationship where there is a difference in authority. It is not surprising therefore that distortions in communication occur very frequently up and down the organizational hierarchy.

These are some of the issues raised by Gibb in his readable paper on "Defensive Communication." But note that the findings reported in his paper derive from research on organizations in the *American* society. They may not apply elsewhere or at other times in history. Egalitarian behavior by a superior toward a subordinate in an organization in a Far Eastern culture might generate more confusion than comfort, therefore appearing more threatening to the subordinate than supportive. Hall and Whyte make this point with several examples in the second paper of this chapter. Not only do attitudes about authority differ from culture to culture, but so do attitudes about time, space, the display of emotion, and the meaning of touching other people.

Some of these cultural differences are only differences in the meanings assigned to common symbols. For example, the North American gesture for "okay," made of forming a circle with the thumb and index finger, carries an entirely different and quite insulting connotation in Latin America. One of us, during a trip to Brazil, discovered this difference to his horror after the damage had been done.

But it is fairly easy to learn the local meanings of such specific symbols and gestures. It is much more difficult to learn the meaning associated not with specific actions but with whole patterns of behavior. In the Hall and Whyte piece on intercultural communication the reader will find many pithy examples. But we would like to add a postscript to their article. Despite the homogenizing influences of television and the other mass media, there are still significant cultural differences in the meanings of words and behavioral patterns *within* the United States, even between organizations. Not only is the ghetto vocabulary different from the suburban one; but almost every occupational and professional group, indeed almost every social group, develops a verbal and behavioral jargon of its own. So that the same English word can have two very different meanings in two related discussion groups, and representatives of the two groups may not discover the difference for quite some time. For example, in most of the social and physical sciences the word "model" means "abstract representation." But in the very closely related field of academic medicine, the word model typically means "prototype," that is, a working demonstration rather than some abstraction. This very subtle difference, in the meaning of one word, lying unknown, delayed for several days the resolution of a problem in a research team of our acquaintance made up jointly of management scientists and academic physicians.

The rough rules of thumb that seem to emerge from all this are these: If you want to increase your chances of influencing someone in your direction, (a) keep two-way communication channels open by avoiding actions that generate a defensive climate, and (b) watch out for the hidden pitfalls of unrecognized intercultural differences.

Defensive Communication
Jack R. Gibb

One way to understand communication is to view it as a people process rather than as a language process. If one is to
make fundamental improvement in communication, he must
make changes in interpersonal relationships. One possible
type of alteration—and the one with which this paper is concerned—is that of reducing the degree of defensiveness.

Definition and Significance

"Defensive behavior" is behavior which occurs when an individual perceives threat or anticipates threat in the group. The
person who behaves defensively, even though he also gives
some attention to the common task, devotes an appreciable
portion of his energy to defending himself. Besides talking
about the topic, he thinks about how he appears to others,
how he may be seen more favorably, how he may win, dominate, impress, or escape punishment, and/or how he may
avoid or mitigate a perceived or an anticipated attack.

Such inner feelings and outward acts tend to create
similarly defensive postures in others; and, if unchecked, the
ensuing circular response becomes increasingly destructive.
Defensive behavior, in short, engenders defensive listening,
and this in turn produces postural, facial, and verbal cues
which raise the defense level of the original communicator.

Defensive arousal prevents the listener from concentrating
upon the message. Not only do defensive communicators
send off multiple value, motive, and affect cues, but also
defensive recipients distort what they receive. As a person
becomes more and more defensive, he becomes less and less
able to perceive accurately the motives, the values, and the
emotions of the sender. The writer's analyses of tape
recorded discussions revealed that increases in defensive be-

Reprinted from the *Journal of Communication* 11, no. 3 (September
1961): 141–48, by permission of the author and the publisher.

havior were correlated positively with losses in efficiency in communication.[1] Specifically, distortions became greater when defensive states existed in the groups.

The converse also is true. The more "supportive" or defense reductive the climate the less the receiver reads into the communication-distorted loadings which arise from projections of his own anxieties, motives, and concerns. As defenses are reduced, the receivers become better able to concentrate upon the structure, the content, and the cognitive meanings of the message.

Categories of Defensive and Supportive Communication

In working over an eight-year period with recordings of discussions occurring in varied settings, the writer developed the six pairs of defensive and supportive categories presented in table 1. Behavior which a listener perceives as possessing any

Table 1

Categories of Behavior Characteristic of Supportive and Defensive Climates in Small Groups

Defensive Climates	*Supportive Climates*
1. Evaluation	1. Description
2. Control	2. Problem orientation
3. Strategy	3. Spontaneity
4. Neutrality	4. Empathy
5. Superiority	5. Equality
6. Certainty	6. Provisionalism

of the characteristics listed in the left-hand column arouses defensiveness, whereas that which he interprets as having any of the qualities designated as supportive reduces defensive feelings. The degree to which these reactions occur depends upon the personal level of defensiveness and upon the general climate in the group at the time.[2]

Evaluation and Description

Speech or other behavior which appears evaluative increases defensiveness. If by expression, manner of speech, tone of

1. J. R. Gibb, "Defense Level and Influence in Small Groups," in *Leadership and Interpersonal Behavior,* ed. L. Petrullo and B. M. Bass (New York: Holt, Rinehart & Winston, 1961), pp. 66–81.

2. J. R. Gibb, "Sociopsychological Processes of Group Instruction," in *The Dynamics of Instructional Groups,* ed. N. B. Henry (Fifty-ninth Yearbook of the National Society for the Study of Education, part 2, 1960), pp. 115–35.

voice, or verbal content the sender seems to be evaluating or judging the listener, then the receiver goes on guard. Of course, other factors may inhibit the reaction. If the listener thinks that the speaker regards him as an equal and is being open and spontaneous, for example, the evaluativeness in a message will be neutralized and perhaps not even perceived. This same principle applies equally to the other five categories of potentially defense-producing climates. The six sets are interactive.

Because our attitudes toward other persons are frequently, and often necessarily, evaluative, expressions which the defensive person will regard as nonjudgmental are hard to frame. Even the simplest question usually conveys the answer that the sender wishes or implies the response that would fit into his value system. A mother, for example, immediately following an earth tremor that shook the house, sought for her small son with the question: "Bobby, where are you?" The timid and plaintive "Mommy, I didn't do it" indicated how Bobby's chronic mild defensiveness predisposed him to react with a projection of his own guilt and in the context of his chronic assumption that questions are full of accusation.

Anyone who has attempted to train professionals to use information-seeking speech with neutral affect appreciates how difficult it is to teach a person to say even the simple "Who did that?" without being seen as accusing. Speech is so frequently judgmental that there is a reality base for the defensive interpretations which are so common.

When insecure, group members are particularly likely to place blame, to see others as fitting into categories of good or bad, to make moral judgments of their colleagues, and to question the value, motive, and affect loadings of the speech which they hear. Since value loadings imply a judgment of others, a belief that the standards of the speaker differ from his own causes the listener to become defensive.

Descriptive speech, in contrast to that which is evaluative, tends to arouse a minimum of uneasiness. Speech acts which the listener perceives as genuine requests for information or as material with neutral loadings is descriptive. Specifically, presentations of feelings, events, perceptions, or processes which do not ask or imply that the receiver change behavior or attitude are minimally defense-producing. The difficulty in avoiding overtone is illustrated by the problems of news reporters in writing stories about unions, Communists, Negroes, and religious activities without tipping off the "party" line of the newspaper. One can often tell from the opening words in a news article which side the newspaper's editorial policy favors.

Control and Problem Orientation

Speech which is used to control the listener evokes resistance. In most of our social intercourse someone is trying to do something to someone else—to change an attitude, to influence behavior, or to restrict the field of activity. The degree to which attempts to control produce defensiveness depends upon the openness of the effort, for a suspicion that hidden motives exist heightens resistance. For this reason attempts of nondirective therapists and progressive educators to refrain from imposing a set of values, a point of view, or a problem solution upon the receivers meet with many barriers. Since the norm is control, noncontrollers must earn the perceptions that their efforts have no hidden motives. A bombardment of persuasive "messages" in the fields of politics, education, special causes, advertising, religion, medicine, industrial relations, and guidance has bred cynical and paranoidal responses in listeners.

Implicit in all attempts to alter another person is the assumption by the change agent that the person to be altered is inadequate. That the speaker secretly views the listener as ignorant, unable to make his own decisions, uninformed, immature, unwise, or possessed of wrong or inadequate attitudes is a subconscious perception which gives the latter a valid base for defensive reactions.

Methods of control are many and varied. Legalistic insistence on detail, restrictive regulations and policies, conformity norms, and all laws are among the methods. Gestures, facial expressions, other forms of nonverbal communication, and even such simple acts as holding a door open in a particular manner are means of imposing one's will upon another and hence are potential sources of resistance.

Problem orientation, on the other hand, is the antithesis of persuasion. When the sender communicates a desire to collaborate in defining a mutual problem and in seeking its solution, he tends to create the same problem orientation in the listener; and, of greater importance, he implies that he has no predetermined solution, attitude, or method to impose. Such behavior is permissive in that it allows the receiver to set his own goals, make his own decisions, and evaluate his own progress—or to share with the sender in doing so. The exact methods of attaining permissiveness are not known, but they must involve a constellation of cues, and they certainly go beyond mere verbal assurances that the communicator has no hidden desires to exercise control.

Strategy and Spontaneity

When the sender is perceived as engaged in a stratagem involving ambiguous and multiple motivations, the receiver becomes defensive. No one wishes to be a guinea pig, a role player, or an impressed actor, and no one likes to be the victim of some hidden motivation. That which is concealed, also, may appear larger than it really is, with the degree of defensiveness of the listener determining the perceived size of the suppressed element. The intense reaction of the reading audience to the material in the *Hidden Persuaders* indicates the prevalence of defensive reactions to multiple motivations behind strategy. Group members who are seen as "taking a role," as feigning emotion, as toying with their colleagues, as withholding information, or as having special sources of data are especially resented. One participant once complained that another was "using a listening technique" on him!

A large part of the adverse reaction to much of the so-called human relations training is a feeling against what are perceived as gimmicks and tricks to fool or to "involve" people, to make a person think he is making his own decision, or to make the listener feel that the sender is genuinely interested in him as a person. Particularly violent reactions occur when it appears that someone is trying to make a stratagem appear spontaneous. One person has reported a boss who incurred resentment by habitually using the gimmick of "spontaneously" looking at his watch and saying, "My gosh, look at the time—I must run to an appointment." The belief was that the boss would create less irritation by honestly asking to be excused.

Similarly, the deliberate assumption of guilelessness and natural simplicity is especially resented. Monitoring the tapes of feedback and evaluation sessions in training groups indicates the surprising extent to which members perceive the strategies of their colleagues. This perceptual clarity may be quite shocking to the strategist, who usually feels that he has cleverly hidden the motivational aura around the "gimmick."

This aversion to deceit may account for one's resistance to politicians who are suspected of behind-the-scenes planning to get his vote; to psychologists whose listening apparently is motivated by more than the manifest or content-level interest in his behavior, or to the sophisticated, smooth, or clever person whose "oneupmanship" is marked with guile. In training groups the role-flexible person frequently is resented because his changes in behavior are perceived as strategic maneuvers.

Conversely, behavior which appears to be spontaneous and free of deception is defense reductive. If the communicator is seen as having a clean id, as having uncomplicated motivations, as being straightforward and honest, and as behaving spontaneously in response to the situation, he is likely to arouse minimal defense.

Neutrality and Empathy

When neutrality in speech appears to the listener to indicate a lack of concern for his welfare, he becomes defensive. Group members usually desire to be perceived as valued persons, as individuals of special worth, and as objects of concern and affection. The clinical, detached, person-is-an-object-of-study attitude on the part of many psychologist-trainers is resented by group members. Speech with low affect that communicates little warmth or caring is in such contrast with the affect-laden speech in social situations that it sometimes communicates rejection.

Communication that conveys empathy for the feelings and respect for the worth of the listener, however, is particularly supportive and defense reductive. Reassurance results when a message indicates that the speaker identifies himself with the listener's problems, shares his feelings, and accepts his emotional reactions at face value. Abortive efforts to deny the legitimacy of the receiver's emotions by assuring the receiver that he need not feel bad, that he should not feel rejected, or that he is overly anxious, though often intended as support giving, may impress the listener as lack of acceptance. The combination of understanding and empathizing with the other person's emotions with no accompanying effort to change him apparently is supportive at a high level.

The importance of gestural behavioral cues in communicating empathy should be mentioned. Apparently spontaneous facial and bodily evidences of concern are often interpreted as especially valid evidence of deep-level acceptance.

Superiority and Equality

When a person communicates to another that he feels superior in position, power, wealth, intellectual ability, physical characteristics, or other ways, he arouses defensiveness. Here, as with the other sources of disturbance, whatever arouses feelings of inadequacy causes the listener to center upon the affect loading of the statement rather than upon the cognitive elements. The receiver then reacts by not hearing the message, by forgetting it, by competing with the sender, or by becoming jealous of him.

The person who is perceived as feeling superior communicates that he is not willing to enter into a shared problem-solving relationship, that he probably does not desire feedback, that he does not require help, and/or that he will be likely to try to reduce the power, the status, or the worth of the receiver.

Many ways exist for creating the atmosphere that the sender feels himself equal to the listener. Defenses are reduced when one perceives the sender as being willing to enter into participative planning with mutual trust and respect. Differences in talent, ability, worth, appearance, status, and power often exist, but the low defense communicator seems to attach little importance to these distinctions.

Certainty and Provisionalism

The effects of dogmatism in producing defensiveness are well known. Those who seem to know the answers, to require no additional data, and to regard themselves as teachers rather than as coworkers tend to put others on guard. Moreover, in the writer's experiment, listeners often perceived manifest expressions of certainty as connoting inward feelings of inferiority. They saw the dogmatic individual as needing to be right, as wanting to win an argument rather than solve a problem, and as seeing his ideas as truths to be defended. This kind of behavior often was associated with acts which others regarded as attempts to exercise control. People who were right seemed to have low tolerance for members who were "wrong"—i.e., who did not agree with the sender.

One reduces the defensiveness of the listener when he communicates that he is willing to experiment with his own behavior, attitudes, and ideas. The person who appears to be taking provisional attitudes, to be investigating issues rather than taking sides on them, to be problem solving rather than debating, and to be willing to experiment and explore tends to communicate that the listener may have some control over the shared quest or the investigation of the ideas. If a person is genuinely searching for information and data, he does not resent help or company along the way.

Conclusion

The implications of the above material for the parent, the teacher, the manager, the administrator, or the therapist are fairly obvious. Arousing defensiveness interferes with communication and thus makes it difficult—and sometimes impossible—for anyone to convey ideas clearly and to move effectively toward the solution of therapeutic, educational, or managerial problems.

Intercultural Communication: A Guide to Men of Action
Edward T. Hall and William Foote Whyte

How can anthropological knowledge help the man of action in dealing with people of another culture? We shall seek to answer that question by examining the process of intercultural communication.

Anthropologists have long claimed that a knowledge of culture is valuable to the administrator. More and more people in business and government are willing to take this claim seriously, but they ask that we put culture to them in terms they can understand and act upon.

When the layman thinks of culture, he is likely to think in terms of (1) the way people dress, (2) the beliefs they hold, and (3) the customs they practice—with an accent upon the esoteric. Without undertaking any comprehensive definition, we can concede that all three are aspects of culture, and yet point out that they do not get us very far, either theoretically or practically.

Dress is misleading, if we assume that differences in dress indicate differences in belief and behavior. If that were the case, then we should expect to find people dressed like ourselves to be thinking and acting like ourselves. While there are still peoples wearing "colorful" apparel quite different from ours, we find in many industralizing societies that the people with whom we deal dress much as we do—and yet think and act quite differently.

Knowledge of beliefs may leave us up in the air because the connections between beliefs and behavior are seldom obvious. In the case of religious beliefs, we may know, for example, that the Mohammedan must pray to Allah a certain number of times a day and that therefore the working day must provide for praying time. This is important, to be sure, but the point is so obvious that it is unlikely to be overlooked

Reproduced with the permission of the Society for Applied Anthropology from *Human Organization* 19, no. 1 (1960): 5–12.

by anyone. The administrator must also grasp the less dramatic aspects of everyday behavior, and here a knowledge of beliefs is a very imperfect guide.

Customs provide more guidance, providing we do not limit ourselves to the esoteric and also search for the pattern of behavior into which a given custom fits. The anthropologist, in dealing with customary behavior, is not content with identifying individual items. To him, these items are not miscellaneous. They have meaning only as they are fitted together into a pattern.

But even assuming that the pattern can be communicated to the administrator, there is still something important lacking. The pattern shows how the people act—when among themselves. The administrator is not directly concerned with that situation. Whatever background information he has, he needs to interpret to himself how the people act *in relation to himself*. He is dealing with a cross-cultural situation. The link between the two cultures is provided by acts of communication between the administrator, representing one culture, and people representing another. If communication is effective, then understanding grows with collaborative action. If communication is faulty, then no book knowledge of culture can assure effective action.

This is not to devalue the knowledge of culture that can be provided by the anthropologist. It is only to suggest that the point of implementation of the knowledge must be in the communication process. Let us therefore examine the process of intercultural communication. By so doing we can accomplish two things: (A) Broaden knowledge of ourselves by revealing some of our own unconscious communicative acts. (B) Clear away heretofore almost insurmountable obstacles to understanding in the cross-cultural process. We also learn that communication, as it is used here, goes far beyond words and includes many other acts upon which judgments are based of what is transpiring and from which we draw conclusions as to what has occurred in the past.

Culture affects communication in various ways. It determines the time and timing of interpersonal events, the places where it is appropriate to discuss particular topics, the physical distance separating one speaker from another, the tone of voice that is appropriate to the subject matter. Culture, in this sense, delineates the amount and type of physical contact, if any, which convention permits or demands, and the intensity of emotion which goes with it. Culture includes the relationship of *what is said to what is meant*—as when "no" means "maybe" and "tomorrow" means "never." Culture, too, determines whether a given matter—say, a business contract—should be initially discussed between two persons or hacked out in a day-long conference which includes four or five senior officials from each side, with perhaps an assist from the little man who brings in the coffee.

These are important matters which the businessman who hopes to trade abroad ignores at his peril. They are also elusive, for every man takes his own culture for granted. Even a well-informed national of another country is hard put to explain why, in his own land, the custom is thus-and-so rather than so-and-thus; as hard put, indeed, as you would probably be if asked what is the "rule" which governs the precise time in a relationship that you begin using another man's first name. One "just knows." In other words, you do not know and cannot explain satisfactorily because you learn this sort of thing unconsciously in your upbrnging, in your culture, and you take such knowledge for granted. Yet the impact of culture on communication can be observed and the lessons taught.

Since the most obvious form of communication is by language, we will first consider words, meanings, voice tones, emotions, and physical contact; then take up, in turn, the cultural impact of time, place, and social class relations on business situations in various lands. Finally, we will suggest what the individual administrator may do to increase his effectiveness abroad, and what students of culture may do to advance this application of anthropology.

Beyond Language

Americans are often accused of not being very good at language, or at least not very much interested in learning foreign languages. There is little evidence that any people are inherently "better" at languages than any other, given the opportunity and incentive to learn. The West and Central European who has since childhood been in daily contact with two or three languages learns to speak them all, and frequently to read and write them as well. Under similar conditions, American children do the same. Indeed, a not uncommon sight on the backroads of Western Europe is a mute, red-faced American military family lost on a Sunday drive while the youngest child, barely able to lisp his own English, leans from the window to interpret the directions of some gnarled farmer whose dialect is largely unintelligible to most of his own countrymen.

We should not underestimate the damage our lack of language facility as a nation has done to our relations all over the world. Obviously, if you cannot speak a man's language, you are terribly handicapped in communicating with him.

But languages can be learned and yet most, if not all, of the disabling errors described in this article could still be made. Vocabulary, grammar, even verbal facility are not enough. Unless a man understands the subtle cues that are implicit in language, tone, gestures, and expression, he will not only consistently misinterpret what is said to him, but he may offend irretrievably without knowing how or why.

Do They Mean What They Say?

Can't you believe what a man says? We all recognize that the basic honesty of the speaker is involved. What we often fail to recognize, however, is that the question involves cultural influences that have nothing to do with the honesty or dependability of the individual.

In the United States we put a premium on direct expression. The "good" American is supposed to say what he means and to mean what he says. If, on important matters, we discover that someone spoke deviously or evasively, we would be inclined to regard him thereafter as unreliable if not out-and-out dishonest.

If some other cultures, the words and their meanings do not have such a direct connection. People may be more concerned with the emotional context of the situation than with the meaning of particular words. This leads them to give an agreeable and pleasant answer to a question when a literal, factual answer might be unplesant or embarrassing.

This situation is not unknown in our culture, of course. How many times have you muttered your delighted appreciation for a boring evening. We tern this simple politeness and understand each other perfectly.

On the other hand, analogous "polite" behavior on a matter of factory production would be incomprehensible. An American businessman would be most unlikely to question another businessman's word if he were technically qualified and said that his plant could produce 1,000 gross of widgets a month. We are "taught" that it is none of our business to inquire too deeply into the details of his production system. This would be prying and might be considered an attempt to steal his operational plans.

Yet this cultural pattern has trapped many an American into believing that when a Japaense manufacturer answered a direct question with the reply that he could produce 1,000 gross of widgets, he meant what he said. If the American had been escorted through the factory and had seen quite clearly that its capacity was, at the most, perhaps 500 gross of widgets per month, he would be likely to say to himself: "Well, this fellow probably has a brother-in-law who has a factory who can make up the difference. He isn't telling the whole story because he's afraid I might try to make a better deal with the brother-in-law. Besides, what business is it of mine, so long as he meets the schedule?"

The cables begin to burn after the American returns home and only 500 gross of widgets arrive each month.

What the American did not know was that in Japanese culture one avoids the direct question unless the questioner is absolutely certain that the answer will not embarrass the Japanese businessman in any way whatsoever. In Japan for one to admit being unable to perform a given operation or measure up to a given standard means a bitter loss of face. Given a foreigner who is so stupid, ignorant, or insensitive as to ask an embarrassing question, the Japanese is likely to choose what appears to him the lesser of two evils.

Americans caught in this cross-cultural communications trap are apt to feel doubly deceived because the Japanese manufacturer may well be an established and respected member of the business community.

Excitable People?

Man communicates not by words alone. His tone of voice, his facial expressions, his gestures all contribute to the infinitely varied calculus of meaning. But the confusion of tongues is more than matched by the confusion of gesture and other culture cues. One man's nod is another man's negative. Each culture has its own rich array of meaningful signs, symbols, gestures, emotional connotatoins, historical references, traditional responses, and—equally significant—pointed silences. These have been built up over the millennia as (who can say?) snarls, growls, and love murmurs gathered meaning and dignity with long use, to end up perhaps as the worn coinage of trite expression.

Consider the Anglo-Saxon tradition of preserving one's calm. The American is taught by his culture to suppress his feelings. He is conditioned to regard emotion as generally bad (except in weak women who can't help themselves) and a stern self-control as good. The more important a matter, the more solemn and outwardly dispassionate he is likely to be. A cool head, granite visage, dispassionate logic—it is no accident that the Western story hero consistently displays these characteristics.

In the Middle East it is otherwise. From childhood, the Arab is permitted, even encouraged to express his feelings without inhibition. Grown men can weep, shout, gesture expressively and violently, jump up and down—and be admired as sincere.

The modulated, controlled Anglo-Saxon is likely to be regarded with suspicion—he must be hiding something, practicing to deceive.

The exuberant and emotional Arab is likely to disturb the Anglo-Saxon, cause him to writhe inwardly with embarrassment—for isn't this childish behavior? And aren't things getting rather our of hand?

Then, again, there is the matter of how loudly one should talk.

In the Arab world, in discussions among equals, the men attain a decibel level that would be considered aggressive, objectionable, and obnoxious in the United States. Loudness connotes strength and sincerity among Arabs; a soft tone implies weakness, deviousness. This is so "right" in the Arab culture that several Arabs have told us they discounted anything heard over the "Voice of America" because the signal was so weak!

Personal status modulates voice tone, however, even in Arab society. The Saudi Arab shows respect to his superior —to a sheik, say—by lowering his voice and mumbling. The affluent American may also be addressed in this fashion, making almost impossible an already difficult situation. Since in the American culture one unconsciously "asks" another to raise his voice by raising one's own, the American speaks louder. This lowers the Arab's tone more and increases the mumble. This triggers a shouting response in the American —which cues the Arab into a frightened "I'm not being respectful enough" tone well below audibility.

They are not likely to part with much respect for each other.

To Touch or Not to Touch?

How much physical contact should appropriately accompany social or business conversation?

In the United States we discourage physical contact, particularly between adult males. The most common physical contact is the handshake and, compared to Europeans, we use it sparingly.

The handshake is the most detached and impersonal form

of greeting or farewell in Latin America. Somewhat more friendly is the left hand placed on another man's shoulder during a handshake. Definitely more intimate and warm is the *double abrazo* in which two men embrace by placing their arms around each other's shoulders.

These are not difficult conventions to live with, particularly since the North American can easily permit the Latin American to take initiative in any form of contact more intimate than the handshake. Far more difficult for the North American to learn to live with comfortably are the less stylized forms of physical contact such as the hand on one's arm during conversation. To the North American this is edging toward what in his culture is an uncomfortable something—possibly sexual—which inhibits his own communication.

Yet there are cultures which restrict physical contact far more than we do. An American at a cocktail party in Jave tripped over the invisible cultural ropes which mark the boundaries of acceptable behavior. He was seeking to develop a business relationship with a prominent Javanese and seemed to be doing very well. Yet, when the cocktail party ended, so apparently did a promising beginning. For the North American spent nearly six months trying to arrange a second meeting. He finally learned, through pitying intermediaries, that at the cocktail party he had momentarily placed his arm on the shoulder of the Javanese—and in the presence of other people. Humiliating! Almost unpardonable in traditional Javanese etiquette.

In this particular case, the unwitting breach was mended by a graceful apology. It is worth noting, however, that a truly cordial business relationship never did develop.

The Five Dimensions of Time

If we peel away a few layers of cultural clothing, we begin to reach almost totally unconscious reactions. Our ideas of time, for example, are deeply instilled in us when we are children. If they are contradicted by another's behavior, we react with anger, not knowing exactly why. For the businessman, five important temporal concepts are: appointment time, discussion time, acquaintance time, visiting time, and time schedules.

Anyone who has traveled abroad or dealt at all extensively with non-Americans learns that punctuality is variously interpreted. It is one thing to recognize this with the mind; to adjust to a different kind of *appointment time* is quite another.

In Latin America, you should expect to spend hours waiting in outer offices. If you bring your American interpretation of what constitutes punctuality to a Latin-American office, you will fray your temper and elevate your blood pressure. For a forty-five-minute wait is not unusual—no more than a five-minute wait would be in the United States. No insult is intended, no arbitrary pecking order is being established. If, in the United States, you would not be outraged by a five-minute wait, you should not be outraged by the Latin American's forty-five-minute delay in seeing you. The time pie is differently cut, that's all.

Further, the Latin American doesn't usually schedule individual appointments to the exclusion of other appointments. The informal clock of his upbringing ticks more slowly and he rather enjoys seeing several people on different matters at the same time. The three-ring circus atmosphere which results, if interpreted in the American's scale of time and propriety, seems to signal him to go away, to tell him that he is not being properly treated, to indicate that his dignity is under attack. Not so. The clock on the wall may look the same but it tells a different sort of time.

The cultural error may be compounded by a further miscalculation. In the United States, a consistently tardy man is likely to be considered undependable, and by our cultural clock this is a reasonable conclusion. For you to judge a Latin American by your scale of time values is to risk a major error.

Suppose you have waited forty-five minutes and there is a man in his office, by some miracle alone in the room with you. Do you now get down to business and stop "wasting time"?

If you are not forewarned by experience or a friendly advisor, you may try to do this. And it would usually be a mistake. For in the American culture, *discussion* is a means to an end: the deal. You try to make your point quickly, efficiently, neatly. If your purpose is to arrange some major affairs, your instinct is probably to settle the major issues first, leave the details for later, possibly for the technical people to work out.

For the Latin American, the discussion is a part of the spice of life. Just as he tends not to be overly concerned about reserving you your specific segment of time, he tends not as rigidly to separate business from nonbusiness. He runs it all together and wants to make something of a social event out of what you, in your culture, regard as strictly business.

The Latin American is not alone in this. The Greek businessman, partly for the same and partly for different reasons, does not lean toward the "hit-and-run" school of business behavior, either. The Greek businessman adds to the social element, however, a feeling about what length of discussion time constitutes good faith. In America, we show good faith by ignoring the details. "Let's agree on the main points. The details will take care of themselves."

Not so the Greek. He signifies good will and good faith by what may seem to you an interminable discussion which includes every conceivable detail. Otherwise, you see, he cannot help but feel that the other man might be trying to pull the wool over his eyes. Our habit, in what we feel to be our relaxed and friendly way, of postponing details until later smacks the Greek between the eyes as a maneuver to flank him. Even if you can somehow convince him that this is not the case, the meeting must still go on a certain indefinite—but, by our standards, long—time or he will feel disquieted.

The American desire to get down to business and on with other things works to our disadvantage in other parts of the world, too; and not only in business. The head of a large, successful Japanese firm commented: "You Americans have a terrible weakness. We Japanese know about it and exploit it every chance we get. You are impatient. We have learned that if we just make you wait long enough, you'll agree to anything."

Whether this is literally true or not, the Japanese executive singled out a trait of American culture which most of us share and which, one may assume from the newspapers, the Russians have not overlooked, either.

By *acquaintance time* we mean how long you must know a man before you are willing to do business with him.

In the United States, if we know that a salesman represents a well-known, reputable company, and if we need his product, he may walk away from the first meeting with an order in his pocket. A few minutes' conversation to decide matters or price, delivery, payment, model of product—nothing more is involved. In Central America, local custom does not permit a salesman to land in town, call on the customer, and walk away with an order, no matter how badly your prospect wants and needs your product. It is traditional there that you must see your man at least three times before you can discuss the nature of your business.

Does this mean that the South American businessman does not recognize the merits of one product over another? Of course it doesn't. It is just that the weight of tradition presses him to do business within a circle of friends. If a product he needs is not available within his circle, he does not go outside it so much as he enlarges the circle itself to include a new friend who can supply the want. Apart from his cultural need to "feel right" about a new relationship, there is the logic of his business system. One of the realities of his life is that it is dangerous to enter into business with someone over whom you have no more than formal, legal "control." In the past decades, his legal system has not always been as firm as ours and he has learned through experience that he needs the sanctions implicit in the informal system of friendship.

Visiting time involves the question of who sets the time for a visit. George Coelho, a social psychologist from India, gives an illustrative case. A U.S. businessman received this invitation from an Indian businessman: "Won't you and your family come and see us? Come anytime." Several weeks later, the Indian repeated the invitation in the same words. Each time the American replied that he would certainly like to drop in—but he never did. The reason is obvious in terms of our culture. Here "come anytime" is just an expression of friendliness. You are not really expected to show up unless your host proposes a specific time. In India, on the contrary, the words are meant literally—that the host is putting himself at the disposal of his guest and really expects him to come. It is the essence of politeness to leave it to the guest to set a time at his convenience. If the guest never comes, the Indian naturally assumes that he does not want to come. Such a misunderstanding can lead to a serious rift between men who are trying to do business with each other.

Time schedules present Americans with another problem in many parts of the world. Without schedules, deadlines, priorities, and timetables, we tend to feel that our country could not run at all. Not only are they essential to getting work done, but they also play an important role in the informal communication process. Deadlines indicate priorities and priorities signal the relative importance of people and the processes they control. These are all so much a part of our lives that a day hardly passes without some reference to them. "I have to be there by 6:30." "If I don't have these plans out by 5:00 they'll be useless." "I told J. B. I'd be finished by noon tomorrow and now he tells me to drop everything and get hot on the McDermott account. What do I do now?"

In our system, there are severe penalties for not completing work on time and important rewards for holding to schedules. One's integrity and reputation are at stake.

You can imagine the fundamental conflicts that arise when

we attempt to do business with people who are just as strongly oriented away from time schedules as we are toward them.

The Middle Eastern peoples are a case in point. Not only is our idea of time schedules no part of Arab life but the mere mention of a deadline to an Arab is like waving a red flag in front of a bull. In his culture, your emphasis on a deadline has the emotional effect on him that his backing you into a corner and threatening you with a club would have on you.

One effect of this conflict of unconscious habit patterns is that hundreds of American-owned radio sets are lying on the shelves of Arab radio repair shops, untouched. The Americans made the serious cross-cultural error of asking to have the repair completed by a certain time.

How do you cope with this? How does the Arab get another Arab to do anything? Every culture has its own ways of bringing pressure to get results. The usual Arab way is one which Americans avoid as "bad manners." It is needling.

An Arab businessmen whose car broke down explained it this way:

> First, I go to the garage and tell the mechanic what is wrong with my car. I wouldn't want to give him the idea that I didn't know. After that, I leave the car and walk around the block. When I come back to the garage, I ask him if he has started to work yet. On my way home from lunch I stop in and ask him how things are going. When I go back to the office I stop by again. In the evening, I return and peer over his shoulder for a while. If I didn't keep this up, he'd be off working on someone else's car.

If you haven't been needled by an Arab, you just haven't been needled.

A Place for Everything

We say that there is a time and place for everything, but compared to other countries and cultures we give very little emphasis to place distinctions. Business is almost a universal value with us; it can be discussed almost anywhere, except perhaps in church. One can even talk business on the church steps going to and from the service. Politics is only slightly more restricted in the places appropriate for its discussion.

In other parts of the world, there are decided place restrictions on the discussion of business and politics. The American who is not conscious of the unwritten laws will offend if he abides by his own rather than by the local rules.

In India, you should not talk business when visiting a man's home. If you do, you prejudice your chances of ever working out a satisfactory business relationship.

In Latin America, although university students take an active interest in politics, tradition decrees that a politician should avoid political subjects when speaking on university grounds. A Latin American politician commented to anthropologist Allan Holmberg that neither he nor his fellow politicians would have dared attempt a political speech on the grounds of the University of San Marcos in Peru—as did Vice-President Nixon.

To complicate matters further, the student body of San Marcos, anticipating the visit, had voted that Mr. Nixon would not be welcome. The University Rector had issued no invitation, presumably because he expected what did, in fact, happen.

As a final touch, Mr. Nixon's interpreter was a man in full military uniform. In Latin American countries, some of which had recently overthrown military dictators, the symbolism of the military uniform could hardly contribute to a cordial atmosphere. Latin Americans need no reminder that the United States is a great military power.

Mr. Nixon's efforts were planned in the best traditions of our own culture: he hoped to improve relations through a direct, frank, and face-to-face discussion with students—the future leaders of their country. Unfortunately, this approach did not fit in at all with the culture of the host country. Of course, elements hostile to the United States did their best to capitalize upon this cross-cultural misunderstanding. However, even Latin Americans friendly to us, while admiring the Vice-President's courage, found themselves acutely embarrassed by the behavior of their people and ours in the ensuing difficulties.

Being Comfortable in Space

Like time and place, differing ideas of space hide traps for the uninformed. Without realizing it, almost any person raised in the United States is likely to give an unintended snub to a Latin American simply in the way we handle space relationships, particularly during conversations.

In North America, the "proper" distance to stand when talking to another adult male you do not know well is about two feet, at least in a formal business conversation. (Naturally, at a cocktail party, the distance shrinks, but anything under eight to ten inches is likely to provoke an apology or an attempt to back up.)

To a Latin American, with his cultural traditions and habits, a distance of two feet seems to him approximately what five feet would to us. To him, we seem distant and cold. To us, he gives an impression of pushiness.

As soon as a Latin American moves close enough for him to feel comfortable, we feel uncomfortable and edge back. We once observed a conversation between a Latin and a North American which began at one end of a forty-foot hall. At intervals we noticed them again, finally at the other end of the hall. This rather amusing displacement had been accomplished by an almost continual series of small backward steps on the part of the American, trying unconsciously to reach a comfortable talking distance, and an equal closing of the gap by the Latin American as he attempted to reach his accustomed conversation space.

Americans in their offices in Latin America tend to keep their native acquaintances at our distance—not the Latin American's distance—by taking up a position behind a desk or typewriter. The barricade approach to communication is practiced even by old hands in Latin America who are completely unaware of its cultural significance. They know only that they are comfortable without realizing that the distance and equipment unconsciously make the Latin American uncomfortable.

How Class Channels Communication

We would be mistaken to regard the communication patterns which we observe around the world as no more than a miscellaneous collection of customs. The communication pattern of a given society is part of its total culture pattern and can only be understood in that context.

We cannot undertake here to relate many examples of communication behavior to the underlying culture of the country. For the businessman, it might be useful to mention the difficulties in the relationship between social levels and the problem of information feedback from lower to higher levels in industrial organizations abroad.

There is in Latin America a pattern of human relations and union-management relations quite different from that with which we are familiar in the United States. Everett Hagen of MIT has noted the heavier emphasis upon line authority and the lesser development of staff organizations in

Latin American plants when compared with North American counterparts. To a much greater extent than in the United States, the government becomes involved in the handling of all kinds of labor problems.

These differences seem to be clearly related to the culture and social organization of Latin America. We find there that society has been much more rigidly stratified than it has with us. As a corollary, we find a greater emphasis upon authority in family and the community.

This emphasis upon status and class distinction makes it very difficult for people of different status levels to express themselves freely and frankly in discussion and argument. In the past, the pattern has been for the man of lower status to express deference to his superior in any face-to-face contact. This is so even when everyone knows that the subordinate dislikes the superior. The culture of Latin America places a great premium upon keeping personal relations harmonious on the surface.

In the United States, we feel that it is not only desirable but natural to speak up to your superior, to tell the boss exactly what you think, even when you disagree with him. Of course, we do not always do this, but we think that we should, and we feel guilty if we fail to speak our minds frankly. When workers in our factories first get elected to local union office, they may find themselves quite self-conscious about speaking up to the boss and arguing grievances. Many of them, however, quickly learn to do it and enjoy the experience. American culture emphasizes the thrashing-out of differences in face-to-face contacts. It de-emphasizes the importance of status. As a result, we have built institutions for handling industrial disputes on the basis of the local situation, and we rely on direct discussion by the parties immediately involved.

In Latin America, where it is exceedingly difficult for people to express their differences face-to-face and where status differences and authority are much more strongly emphasized than here, the workers tend to look to a third party—the government—to take care of their problems. Though the workers have great difficulty in thrashing out their problems with management, they find no difficulty in telling government representatives their problems. And it is to their government that they look for an authority to settle their grievances with management.

Status and class also decide whether business will be done on an individual or a group basis.

In the United States, we are growing more and more accustomed to working as members of large organizations. Despite this, we still assume that there is no need to send a delegation to do a job that one capable man might well handle.

In some other parts of the world, the individual cannot expect to gain the respect necessary to accomplish this purpose, no matter how capable he is, unless he brings along an appropriate number of associates.

In the United States, we would rarely think it necessary or proper to call on a customer in a group. He might well be antagonized by the hard sell. In Japan—as an example—the importance of the occasion and of the man is measured by whom he takes along.

This practice goes far down in the business and government hierarchies. Even a university professor is likely to bring one or two retainers along on academic business. Otherwise people might think that he was a nobody and that his affairs were of little moment.

Even when a group is involved in the U.S., the head man is the spokesman and sets the tone. This is not always the case in Japan. Two young Japanese once requested an older American widely respected in Tokyo to accompany them so that they could "stand on his face." He was not expected to enter into the negotiation; his function was simply to be present as an indication that their intentions were serious.

Adjustment Goes Both Ways

One need not have devoted his life to a study of various cultures to see that none of them is static. All are constantly changing and one element of change is the very fact that U.S. enterprise enters a foreign field. This is inevitable and may be constructive if we know how to utilize our knowledge. The problem is for us to be aware of our impact and to learn how to induce changes skillfully.

Rather than try to answer the general question of how two cultures interact, we will consider the key problem of personnel selection and development in two particular intercultural situations, both in Latin cultures.

One U.S. Company had totally different experiences with "Smith" and "Jones" in the handling of its labor relations. The local union leaders were bitterly hostile to Smith, whereas they could not praise Jones enough. These were puzzling reactions to higher management. Smith seemed a fair-minded and understanding man; it was difficult to fathom how anyone could be bitter against him. At the same time, Jones did not appear to be currying favor by his generosity in giving away the firm's assets. To management, he seemed to be just as firm a negotiator as Smith.

The explanation was found in the two men's communication characteristics. When the union leaders came in to negotiate with Smith, he would let them state their case fully and freely—without interruption, but also without comment. When they had finished, he would say, "I'm sorry. We can't do it." He would follow this blunt statement with a brief and entirely cogent explanation of his reasons for refusal. If the union leaders persisted in their arguments, Smith would paraphrase his first statement, calmly and succinctly. In either case, the discussion was over in a few minutes. The union leaders would storm out of Smith's office complaining bitterly about the cold and heartless man with whom they had to deal.

Jones handled the situation differently. His final conclusion was the same as Smith's—but he would state it only after two or three hours of discussion. Furthermore, Jones participated actively in these discussions, questioning the union leaders for more information, relating the case in question to previous cases, philosophizing about labor relations and human rights and exchanging stories about work experience. When the discussion came to an end, the union leaders would leave the office, commenting on how warmhearted and understanding he was, and how confident they were that he would help them when it was possible for him to do so. They actually seemed more satisfied with a negative decision from Jones than they did with a hard-won concession from Smith.

This was clearly a case where the personality of Jones happened to match certain discernible requirements of the Latin American culture. It was happenstance in this case that Jones worked out and Smith did not, for by American standards both were top-flight men. Since a talent for the kind of negotiation that the Latin American considers graceful and acceptable can hardly be developed in a grown man (or perhaps even in a young one), the basic problem is one of personnel selection in terms of the culture where the candidate is to work.

The second case is more complicated because it involves much deeper intercultural adjustments. The management of the parent U.S. company concerned had learned—as have the directors of most large firms with good-sized installations overseas—that one cannot afford to have all of the top and middle-management positions manned by North Americans. It is necessary to advance nationals up the overseas-management ladder as rapidly as their abilities permit. So the nationals have to learn not only the technical aspects of their jobs but also how to function at higher levels in the organization.

Latin culture emphasizes authority in the home, church, and community. Within the organization this produces a built-in hesitancy about speaking up to one's superiors. The initiative, the acceptance of responsibility which we value in our organizations had to be stimulated. How could it be done?

We observed one management man who had done a remarkable job of building up these very qualities in his general foremen and foremen. To begin with, he stimulated informal contacts between himself and these men through social events to which the men and their wives came. He saw to it that his senior North American assistants and their wives were also present. Knowing the language, he mixed freely with all. At the plant, he circulated about, dropped in not to inspect or check up, but to joke and to break down the great barrier that existed in the local traditions between authority and the subordinates.

Next, he developed a pattern of three-level meetings. At the top, he himself, the superintendents, and the general foremen. At the middle level, the superintendents, general foremen, and foremen. Then the general foremen, foremen, and workers.

At the top level meeting, the American management chief set the pattern of encouraging his subordinates to challenge his own ideas, to come up with original thoughts. When his superintendents (also North Americans) disagreed with him, he made it clear that they were to state their objections fully. At first, the general foremen looked surprised and uneasy. They noted, however, that the senior men who argued with the boss were encouraged and praised. Timorously, with great hesitation, they began to add their own suggestions. As time went on, they more and more accepted the new convention and pitched in without inhibition.

The idea of challenging the boss with constructive new ideas gradually filtered down to the second and third level meetings. It took a lot of time and gentle handling, but out of this approach grew an extraordinary morale. The native general foremen and foremen developed new pride in themselves, accepted new responsibilities, even reached out for more. They began to work to improve their capacities and to look forward to moving up in the hierarchy.

Conformity or Adjustment?

To work with people, must we be just like them? Obviously not. If we try to conform completely, the Arab, the Latin American, the Italian, whoever he might be, finds our behavior confusing and insincere. He suspects our motive. We are expected to be different. But we are also expected to respect and accept the other people as they are. And we may, without doing violence to our own personalities, learn to communicate with them by observing the unwritten patterns they are accustomed to.

To be aware that there are pitfalls in cross-cultural dealings is the first big step forward. And to accept the fact that our convictions are in no respect more eternally "right" than someone else's is another constructive step.

Beyond these:

1. We can learn to control our so-called frankness in a culture which puts a high value on maintaining pleasant surface relations.

2. We can avoid expressing quick decisions when their utterance without a long period of polite preparation would show disrespect.

3. We can be on the lookout for the conversation patterns of nationals of whatever country we are in and accustom ourselves to closer quarters than we are used to. (This is uncomfortable at first but understanding the reason why it is important helps greatly.)

4. Where the situation demands it, we can learn to express our emotions more freely—most people find this rather exhilarating.

5. We can try to distinguish between the organizational practices which are really necessary to effectiveness and those that we employ from habit because they happen to be effective in the United States.

Research for Organizational Effectiveness

We have outlined a point of view the individual can seek to apply in order to increase his own effectiveness. Valuable as they may be, we must recognize the limitations of an individual approach. Since each family transported overseas represents an investment of between $25,000 and $100,000 per year to the organization, the losses involved in poor selection or inadequate training can be enormous.

While no ready-made answers are now available, research can serve the organization both in *selection* and *training* of personnel.

It would be a mistake to assume that the ideal training program would fit just any administrator effectively into any given culture. We must assume that some personalities will fit more readily than others. By the time man reaches adulthood, his personality is rather solidly formed, and basic changes are difficult if not impossible to induce. It is therefore important to work to improve the selection process so that men with little chance of fitting into a foreign culture will not be sent where they are bound to fail.

Our Latin American case of Smith and Jones is relevant here. One who had observed Smith in his native setting should have been able to predict that he would not be effective in handling labor relations in Latin America. However, that statement is based upon the hindsight observation that there was a very obvious lack of fit between Smith's personality and the cultural requirements of his job. It remains for research men to devise schemes of observation and testing which will enable personnel men to base their selections upon criteria of personality *and* culture.

To what extent can training improve the effectiveness of individuals in intercultural communication? Training of men in overseas operations is going on all the time. So far as we know, little of it currently deals with the considerations outlined in this article. Until organizations are prepared to develop training along these lines—and support research on the effects of such training—we shall not know to what extent intercultural communications can be improved through training.

We do not mean to give the impression that behavioral scientists already have the knowledge needed regarding intercultural communication. What we have presented here is only a demonstration of the importance of the topic. We have not presented a systematic analysis of the problems of communication from culture A to culture B. We have just said in effect: "These are some of the things that are important. Watch out for them."

What more is needed? In the first place, the problem calls for a new emphasis in anthropological research. In the past, anthropologists have been primarily concerned with the *internal* pattern of a given culture. In giving attention to intercultural problems, they have examined the impact of one culture upon another. Very little attention has been given to the actual communication process between representatives of different cultures.

Much could be learned, for example, if we observed North Americans in interaction with people of another culture. We would want also to be able to interview both parties to the interaction to study how A was interpreting B and how B was interpreting A. In this way we might discover points of friction and miscommunication whose existence we now do not even suspect. Such studies, furthermore, would provide systematic knowledge much more useful than the fragments provided in this article.

6

Power and Manipulation: Over and under the Table

Introduction

There are five papers in this chapter, which makes it the biggest chapter in the book. This reflects our belief that the topics of power and manipulation are of extreme importance in understanding behavior in organizations. They are important because the display of power and the widespread use of manipulative strategies usually reflects either an inefficient organizational design or the presence of latent conflict among the organization members. Moreover, widespread use of power tactics and manipulative methods may just plain make working life painful and lonely for many organizational members.

The organizational issue is not altruism versus self-interest. Two hundred years ago Adam Smith alleged that the only dependable human motive was self-interest; and that assertion still seems an appropriate one. Instead, we believe the central issue in organizational design is to provide means by which members may further their self-interest while furthering the interests of the organization and of one another. This internal organizational problem, as one industrial slogan puts it, is "to do good while doing well."

Some of the papers in this chapter deal directly with the specific tactics used by individuals for succeeding in business. The papers by Mechanic and Strauss are of particular interest because they describe the power tactics used by people in organizations who have little or no formal authority.

Some of the papers also raise important ethical questions even as they describe tactics and behavior involved in the use of power. The paper by Martin and Sims is particularly worth noting in this respect.

It says: "This is what we have seen successful men do." It leaves to the reader the question: "Shall I (or do I) do the same? If so, are such behaviors (1) right, (2) necessary, (3) perhaps even *self-destructive?*"

A third theme struck in these papers is best articulated in the article by Zaleznik, who seeks for the sources and origins of such behavior. Zaleznik, using a psychologic-analytic orientation, argues that much of the power-political behavior that we observe in organizations can be traced back to excessive dependency in infancy and childhood.

The impressive and somewhat depressing research described by Milgram raises still another dimension of the problem of power tactics. Milgram looks at the receiving end of power—at obedience, describing his now classic experiments showing the extraordinary degree to which ordinary humans will obey even when the orders do not come from a very legitimate source, and even when the obedient acts appear to be physically hurting and endangering their fellow humans. Perhaps any of us who are turned off by power and manipulative tactics must consider not just the user of such tactics but the propensity of most of us to accept and obey them.

One of the distinguishing characteristics of power tactics and manipulative strategies is that they aim primarily at securing *overt,* often short-run compliance by others, rather than longer-term attitude change. A second distinguishing characteristic is that power and manipulation are often aimed at modifying the dominant relations among people in the organization, typically at changing the pecking order or reinforcing it. For example, Strauss cites numerous ways in which purchasing agents attempt to exert more control over engineering design and production scheduling departments. And Mechanic argues that "lower participants" attempt to exert countervailing power over the formal hierarchy by monopolizing information about their jobs. So such tactics, even though they're bad for the whole system, look functional and purposive for particular segments of the organization. But they probably appear more functional to the "local" department in some organizations than in others, because some organizations are so rigid that almost any other less drastic methods of influence are doomed to fail. The only recourse to advancing your self-interest in such organizations may be to engage in power politics.

Power Tactics
Norman H. Martin and
John Howard Sims

Executives—whether in business, government, education, or
the church—have power and use it. They maneuver and manipulate in order to get a job done and, in many cases, to
strengthen and enhance their own position. Although they
would hate the thought and deny the allegation, the fact is
that they are politicians. "Politics," according to one of the
leading authorities in this complex and facinating field, "is
. . . concerned with relationships of control or of influence.
To phrase the idea differently, politics deals with human
relationships of superordination and subordination, of dominance and submission, of the governors and the governed."[1]
In this sense, everyone who exercises power must be a politician.

It is true, as many others have pointed out in different connections, that we in this country have an instinctive revulsion
against the term "power." It carries immoral connotations for
us, despite the definitions of men like R. H. Tawney, the economic historian, who divorces it from any ethical attributes
by calling it simply "the capacity of an individual or group of
individuals to modify the conduct of other individuals or
groups in the manner which he desires, and to prevent his
own conduct from being modified in the manner which he
does not."[2]

Furthermore, though we glorify ambition in the abstract,
we frown on its practice and are distressed at the steps which
must be taken if ambition is to be translated into actual advancement. Thus when power is coupled with ambition, we
shy away and try to pretend that neither really exists.

Reprinted from the *Harvard Business Review,* November–December
1956, pp. 25–29, by permission of the authors and the publisher. © 1956
by the President and Fellows of Harvard College; all rights reserved.
1. V. O. Key Jr., *Politics, Parties and Pressure Groups,* 2d ed. (New
York: Thomas Y. Crowell Co., 1948), p. 3.
2. R. H. Tawney, *Equality,* 4th ed. (London: George Allen & Unwin,
Ltd., 1952), p. 175.

But the fact is that we use power and exercise our ambitions just the same—troubled though we may be by the proverbial New England conscience which "doesn't prevent you from doing anything—it just keeps you from enjoying it!"

The complexity of the problem is increased when we recall that the real source of power is not the superior but the subordinate. Men can only exercise that power which they are allowed by other men—albeit their positions are buttressed by economic, legal, and other props. The ultimate source of power is the group; and a group, in turn, is made up of people with consciousness and will, with emotion and irrationality, with intense personal interests and tenaciously held values.

The human being resists being treated as a constant. Knowledge, reason, and technical know-how will not suffice as means of control but give way to the arts of persuasion and inducement, of tactics and maneuver, of all that is involved in interpersonal relationships. Power cannot be given; it must be won. And the techniques and skills of winning it are at the same time the methods of employing it as a medium of control. This represents the political function of the power-holder.

In such a light, we see why the successful functioning and advancement of the executive is dependent, not only on those aspects of an enterprise which are physical and logical, but on morale, teamwork, authority, and obedience—in a word, on the vast intricacy of human relationships which make up the political universe of the executive.

The real question then becomes: How can power be used most effectively? What are some of the political stratagems which the administrator must employ if he to carry out his responsibilities and further his career? This is an area that has carefully been avoided by both students and practitioners of business—as if there were something shady about it. But facts are facts, and closing our eyes to them will not change them. Besides, if they are important facts, they should be brought into the open for examination.

Accordingly, we present here some of the first stage of a fairly extensive investigation of just how the executive functions in his political-power environment. We have searched the biographies of well-known leaders of history, from Alexander to Roosevelt; we have explored the lives of successful industrialists like Rockefeller and Ford; and we have interviewed a number of contemporary executives.

There follows an account of certain tactics which we have

found to be practiced by most men whose success rests on ability to control and direct the actions of others—no doubt, raw and oversimplified when reduced to a few black-and-white words, but for this very reason more likely to be provocative. With further refinement, these generalizations will serve as hypotheses in the succeeding stages of our research, but in the meantime we present them to businessmen to look at openly and objectively—to ask, "Do we not use just such techniques frequently?" and, if so, to ponder, "How can we best operate in this particular area, for our own interest as managers and for the good of people under us?"

Taking counsel. The able executive is cautious about how he seeks and receives advice. He takes counsel only when he himself desires it. His decisions must be made in terms of his own grasp of the situation, taking into account the views of others when he thinks it necessary. To act otherwise is to be subject, not to advice, but to pressure; to act otherwise too often produces vacillation and inconsistency.

Throwing a question to a group of subordinates is all too often interpreted as a delegation of power, and the executive may find himself answered with a decision instead of counsel. He must remember that he, not the group under him, is the responsible party. If an executive allows his subordinates to provide advice when he does not specifically call for it, he may find himself subject, not only to pressure, but to conflicting alignments of forces within his own ranks. A vague sort of policy which states, "I am always ready to hear your advice and ideas on anything," will waste time, confuse issues, dilute leadership, and erode power.

Alliances. In many respects, the executive system in a firm is composed of complexes of sponsor-protégé relationships.[3] For the protégé, these relationships provide channels for advancement; for the sponsor, they build a loyal group of followers. A wise administrator will make it a point to establish such associations with those above and below him. In the struggles for power and influence that go on in many organizations, every executive needs a devoted following and close alliances with other executives, both on his own level and above him, if he is to protect and to enhance his status and sphere of influence.

Alliances should not be looked upon, however, merely as a

3. See Norman H. Martin and Anselm S. Strauss, "Patterns of Mobility within Industrial Organizations," *Journal of Business,* April 1956, p. 101.

protective device. In addition, they provide ready-made systems of communication, through which the executive can learn firsthand how his decisions are being carried out, what unforeseen obstacles are being encountered, and what the level of morale in the organization is at any moment.

Maneuverability. The wise executive maintains his flexibility, and he never completely commits himself to any one position or program. If forces beyond his control compel a major change in company policy, he can gracefully bend with the wind and cooperate with the inevitable, thus maintaining his status.

An executive should preserve maneuverability in career planning as well. He ought never to get in a situation that does not have plenty of escape hatches. He must be careful, for instance, that his career is not directly dependent on the superior position of a sponsor. He should provide himself with transferable talents, and interfirm alliances, so that he will be able to move elsewhere if the conditions in his current organization become untenable.

Communication. During recent years emphasis has been placed on the necessity for well-dredged channels of communication which run upward, downward, and sideways. Top management should supply its subordinates with maximum information, according to this theory; subordinates, in turn, must report fully to their chiefs.

It is possible, however, that executives have been oversold on maximizing the flow of information. It simply is not good strategy to communicate everything one knows. Instead, it may often be advantageous to withhold information or to time its release. This is especially true with reference to future plans—plans which may or may not materialize; it is also valid in the case of information that may create schism or conflict within the organization; and it is prudent when another executive is a threat to one's own position. Furthermore, information is an important tactical weapon, and should be considered as such.

It would appear, then, that executives should be concerned with determining "who gets to know what and when" rather than with simply increasing the flow. Completely open communication deprives the executive of the exclusive power of directing information which should be his.

Compromising. The executive should accept compromise as a means of settling differences with his tongue in his cheek. While appearing to alter his view, he should continue to press forward toward a clear-cut set of goals. It is frequently necessary to give ground on small matters, to delay, to move off tangents, even to suffer reverses in order to retain power for future forward movement. Concessions, then, should be more apparent than real.

Negative timing. The executive is often urged to take action with which he is not in agreement. Sometimes pressure for such action arises from the expectations of subordinates, the influence of his associates with his superiors, the demands of custom and tradition, or other sources he would be unwise to ignore.

To give in to such demands would be to deny the executive's prerogative; to refuse might precipitate a dangerous crisis, and threaten his power. In such situations the executive may find it wise to use what might be called the technique of "negative timing." He initiates action, but the process of expedition is retarded. He is considering, studying, and planning for the problem; there are difficulties to be overcome and possible ramifications which must be considered. He is always *in the process* of doing something but never quite does it, or finally he takes action when it is actually too late. In this way the executive escapes the charge of dereliction, and at the same time the inadvisable program "dies on the vine."

Self-dramatization. Most vocal communication in which an executive engages—whether with his superiors, his colleagues, or his subordinates—is unpremeditated, sincere, spontaneous. His nonvocal communication—the impression projected by his posture, gestures, dress, or facial expressions—is commonly just as natural.

But executives would do well to reexamine this instinctive behavior, for many of them are overlooking an important political stratagem. The skill of the actor—whose communication is "artistic" as opposed to "natural"—represents a potential asset to an administrator. Dramatic art is a process by which selections from reality are chosen and arranged by the artists for the particular purpose of arousing the emotions, of convincing, of persuading, of altering the behavior of the audience in a *planned direction.*

The actor's purpose is no different from that of the manager who wants to activate his subordinates in certain specific directions—to secure a certain response from those with whom he communicates. The actor's peculiar gift is in deliberately shaping his own speech and behavior to accomplish his purpose. The element of chance, the variable of the unknown, is diminished, if not removed; and rehearsal with some foreknowledge of what is to occur takes place. The *how* of communicating is considered as well as the *what*.

Of course, this is no easy task. The effectiveness of the actor's performance depends on his ability to estimate what will stimulate the audience to respond. And once he makes his choices, he must be able to use them skillfully. His voice and body must be so well disciplined, so well trained, that the images he chooses may be given life. The question is, How can an executive acquire the skill of artistic communication? How can he learn to dramatize himself?

The development of sharper powers of observation is the first step. Having witnessed effective communication—whether a TV drama or an actual meeting of the board of directors—the executive should try to determine what made it effective. He should pay attention to *how* a successful man handled himself, not what he said or did. Formal classes can provide the executive with control over his voice —its pitch, tone, color, speed, diction; training can do the same for his body—gesture, posture, and mime. Most important, the executive should seize any opportunity to gain actual experience in putting such skills to work, in amateur theatricals or "role-playing" sessions.

It would be foolish to deny that such skills cannot be entirely learned; to some extent they depend on the unknowns of flair, talent, and genius. But such an acknowledgment does not excuse the executive from making an effort, for the range of possible improvement is very great.

Confidence. Related to, but not identical with, self-dramatization is the outward appearance of confidence. Once an executive has made a decision, he must look and act decided. In some instances genuine inner conviction may be lacking, or the manager may find it difficult to generate the needed dynamics. The skillful executive who finds himself in such a situation will either produce the effect of certainly or postpone any contact with his associates in order to avoid appearing in an unfavorable light.

Thus, the man who constantly gives the impression of knowing what he is doing—even if he does not—is using his power and increasing it at the same time.

Always the boss. Warm personal relations with subordinates have sometimes been considered the mark of a good executive. But in practice an atmosphere of social friendship interferes with the efficiency of an operation and acts to limit the power of the manager. Personal feelings should not be a basis for action—either negative or positive. The executive should never permit himself to be so committed to a subordinate as a friend that he is unable to withdraw from this personal involvement and regard the man objectively as an element in a given situation.

Thus, a thin line of separation between executive and subordinate must always be maintained. The situation should be one of isolation and contact—of the near and far—of marginality. No matter how cordial he may be, the executive must sustain a line of privacy which cannot be transgressed; in the final analysis, he must always be the boss. If we assume, then, that the traditional "open-door" policy of the modern executive is good strategy, we must always ask the question: "How far open?"

The foregoing discussion will undoubtedly raise questions, and even indignation, in the minds of some readers. In the last two decades, the finger of censure has often been pointed at the interpersonal relations in the management of industrial organizations, questioning whether they are harmonious with a democratic society and ideology.[4] Executives have been urged to adopt practices and programs aimed at "democratizing" their businesses. Perhaps they have even developed a sense of guilt from the realization of their own position of authority and that they cannot be completely frank, sincere, honest, and aboveboard in their interpersonal relations. We live in an era of "groupiness"; we are bombarded with admonitions which insist that everyone who is participating in an enterprise should have a part in the management of it.

In the light of such a trend even the terminology used in this article—"power," "maneuver," "tactics," "techniques"—appears disturbing when set down in black and white. But in fact it is neither immoral nor cynical to recognize and describe the actual daily practices of power. After all, sweeping them under the rug—making believe that they are not actually part of the executive's activity—does not cause them to vanish. Open and honest discussion of the political aspects in the administrator's job exposes these stratagems to the constructive spotlight of knowledge. They exist; therefore, we had better take a look at them and see what they are really like.

As we delve deeper into the study of political tactics in business management, the contrast with modern human relations theory and practice will stand out in ever-sharper relief.

---

4. See Thomas C. Cochran, "Business and the Democratic Tradition," *Harvard Business Review*, March–April 1956, p. 39.

Mutual confidence, open communication, continuing consultation and participation by subordinates, friendship, and an atmosphere of democracy seem hard to reconcile with much of the maneuvering and power plays that go on in the nation's offices and factories every day.

Yet businessmen must develop some rationale of executive behavior which can encompass the idealism of democracy and the practicality of politics—and, at the same time, be justified in terms of ultimate values. If they do not, they will feel like hypocrites as the day-to-day operation of their offices clashes with their speeches before women's clubs. The old cliché that "business is business" is no longer satisfying to the general public nor to the executive himself.

One way to try to fit human relations theory and political tactics together is to state that the means or ways of exercising power are neutral. In and of themselves, they have no moral value. They take on moral qualities only in connection with the ends for which they are used. Power can be used for good or ill according to this theory, and we should have the courage and knowledge to use it wisely. Conscious, deliberate, and skilled use of executive power means responsible use of power. If men in the past have employed power for evil ends, that is unfortunate; it is just as true that other men, if they had made use of business politics in an effective fashion, might have been a greater force for good.

The difficulty with this line of thought lies in the well-known pitfalls inherent in the timeless means-ends controversy. In real life, what are means and what are ends? Can you achieve good ends by bad means? If the way one man conducts his relationship with another has no moral implications, what human activity does have moral significance?

Others may take the position that "so long as my general philosophy is sound and moral, the specific actions I have to take in the course of my job don't matter." But one may question the validity of a philosophy of life that breaks down every time it comes into contact with reality.

Still another formula could be found in the statement, "The good of the company comes before that of an individual. If I have to violate moral codes and democratic principles in dealing with one man, that is too bad for him. But I cannot allow any single person to overshadow the interests of all our other employees, stockholders, and customers." The skeptical listener might then raise the issue of collectivism versus individualism, and ask whether the general welfare really overrides the worth and dignity of the individual. Can we build a society on the idea of the individual's importance if we violate the principle whenever it interferes with what we consider to be the good of the group?

There are, of course, other approaches, but they too are fraught with internal contradictions. The riddle, then, remains unsolved; the conflict between the use of power and the principles of democracy and enlightened management is unrelieved. Businessmen, who face this paradox every day in countless situations, cannot avoid the responsibility of explaining or resolving it. If a viable philosophy of management is to be developed, they must contribute their ideas— for the sake of their own peace of mind, if nothing else.

If this article succeeds in getting more businessmen to do some thinking along this line, then it will have served its purpose.

Power and Politics in Organizational Life
Abraham Zaleznik

There are few business activities more prone to a credibility gap than the way in which executives approach organizational life. A sense of disbelief occurs when managers purport to make decisions in rationalistic terms while most observers and participants know that personalities and politics play a significant if not an overriding role. Where does the error lie? In the theory which insists that decisions should be rationalistic and nonpersonal? Or in the practice which treats business organizations as political structures?

Whatever else organizations may be (problem-solving instruments, sociotechnical systems, reward systems, and so on), they are political structures. This means that organizations operate by distributing authority and setting a stage for the exercise of power. It is no wonder, therefore, that individuals who are highly motivated to secure and use power find a familiar and hospitable environment in business.

At the same time, executives are reluctant to acknowledge the place of power both in individual motivation and in organizational relationships. Somehow, power and politics are dirty words. And in linking these words to the play of personalities in organizations, some managers withdraw into the safety of organizational logics.

As I shall suggest in this article, frank recognition of the importance of personality factors and a sensitive use of the strengths and limitations of people in decisions on power distributions can improve the quality of organizational life.

Political Pyramid

Organizations provide a power base for individuals. From a

Reprinted by permission of the publishers from Edward C. Bursk and Timothy B. Blodgett, *Developing Executive Leaders* (Cambridge, Mass.: Harvard University Press), copyright 1971 by the President and Fellows of Harvard College.

purely economic standpoint, organizations exist to create a surplus of income over costs by meeting needs in the marketplace. But organizations also are political structures which provide opportunities for people to develop careers and therefore provide platforms for the expression of individual interests and motives. The development of careers, particularly at high managerial and professional levels, depends on accumulation of power as the vehicle for transforming individual interests into activities which influence other people.

Scarcity and Competition

A political pyramid exists when people compete for power in an economy of scarcity. In other words, people cannot get the power they want just for the asking. Instead, they have to enter into the decisions on how to distribute authority in a particular formal organization structure. Scarcity of power arises under two sets of conditions:

1. Where individuals gain power in absolute terms at someone else's expense.

2. Where there is a gain comparatively—not literally at someone else's expense—resulting in a relative shift in the distribution of power.

In either case, the psychology of scarcity and comparison takes over. The human being tends to make comparisons as a basis for his sense of self-esteem. He may compare himself with other people and decide that his absolute loss or the shift in proportional shares of authority reflects an attrition in his power base. He may also compare his position relative to others against a personal standard and feel a sense of loss. This tendency to compare is deeply ingrained in people, especially since they experience early in life the effects of comparisons in the family where—in an absolute sense— time and attention, if not love and affection, go to the most dependent member.

Corporate acquisitions and mergers illustrate the effects of both types of comparisons. In the case of one merger, the president of the acquired company resigned rather than accept the relative displacement in rank which occurred when he no longer could act as a chief executive officer. Two vice-presidents vied for the position of executive vice-president. Because of their conflicting ambitions, the expedient of making them equals drove the competition underground, but not for long. The vice-president with the weaker power base soon resigned in the face of his inability to consolidate a workable definition of his responsibilities. His departure resulted in increased power for the remaining vice-president and the gradual elimination of "rival camps" which had been covertly identified with the main contenders for power.

The fact that organizations are pyramids produces a scarcity of positions the higher one moves in the hierarchy. This scarcity, coupled with inequalities, certainly needs to be recognized. While it may be humane and socially desirable to say that people are different rather than unequal in their potential, nevertheless executive talent is in short supply. The end result should be to move the more able people into the top positions and to accord them the pay, responsibility, and authority to match their potential.

On the other side, the strong desires of equally able people for the few top positions available means that someone will either have to face the realization of unfulfilled ambition or have to shift his interest to another organization.[1]

Constituents and Clients

Besides the conditions of scarcity and competition, politics in organizations grows out of the existence of constituencies. A superior may be content himself with shifts in the allocation of resources and consequently power, but he represents subordinates who, for their own reasons, may be unhappy with the changes. These subordinates affirm and support their boss. They can also withdraw affirmation and support, and consequently isolate the superior with all the painful consequences this entails.

While appointments to positions come from above, affirmation of position comes from below. The only difference between party and organizational politics is in the subtlety of the voting procedure. Consider:

In a large consumer products corporation, one division received almost no capital funds for expansion while another division, which had developed a new marketing approach for products common to both, expanded dramatically. The head of the static division found his power diminished considerably, as reflected in how seriously his subordinates took his efforts at influence (e.g., in programs to increase the profit return from existing volume).

He initiated one program after another with little support from subordinates because he could not make a claim for capital funds. The flow of capital funds in this corporation

1. See my article, "The Management of Disappointment," *Harvard Business Review*, November–December 1967, p. 59.

provided a measure of power gains and losses in both an absolute and a relative sense.

Power and Action

Still another factor which heightens the competition for power that is characteristic of all political structures is the incessant need to use whatever power one possesses. Corporations have an implicit "banking" system in power transactions. The initial "capitalization" which makes up an individual's power base consists of three elements:

1. The quantity of formal authority vested in his position relative to other positions.

2. The authority vested in his expertise and reputation for competence (a factor weighted by how important the expertise is for the growth areas of the corporation as against the historically stable areas of its business).

3. The attractiveness of his personality to others (a combination of respect for him as well as liking, although these two sources of attraction are often in conflict).

This capitalization of power reflects the total esteem with which others regard the individual. By a process which is still not too clear, the individual internalizes all of the sources of power capital in a manner parallel to the way he develops a sense of self-esteem. The individual knows he has power, assesses it realistically, and is willing to risk his personal esteem to influence others.

A critical element here is the risk in the uses of power. The individual must perform *and* get results. If he fails to do either, an attrition occurs in his power base in direct proportion to the doubts other people entertained in their earlier appraisals of him.

What occurs here is an erosion of confidence which ultimately leads the individual to doubt himself and undermines the psychological work which led him in the first place to internalize authority as a prelude to action. (While, as I have suggested, the psychological work that an individual goes through to consolidate his esteem capital is a crucial aspect of power relations, I shall have to reserve careful examination of this problem until a later date. The objective now is to examine from a political framework the problems of organizational life.)

What distinguishes alterations in the authority structure from other types of organizational change is their direct confrontation with the political character of corporate life.

Such confrontations are real manipulations of power as compared with the indirect approaches which play on ideologies and attitudes. In the first case, the potency and reality of shifts in authority have an instantaneous effect on what people do, how they interact, and how they think about themselves. In the second case, the shifts in attitude are often based on the willingness of people to respond the way authority figures want them to; ordinarily, however, these shifts in attitude are but temporary expressions of compliance.

One of the most common errors executives make is to confuse compliance with commitment. Compliance is an attitude of acceptance when a directive from an authority figure asks for a change in an individual's position, activities, or ideas. The individual complies or "goes along" usually because he is indifferent to the scope of the directive and the changes it proposes. If compliance occurs out of indifference, then one can predict little difficulty in translating the intent of directives into actual implementation.[2]

Commitment, on the other hand, represents a strong motivation on the part of an individual to adopt or resist the intent of a directive. If the individual commits himself to a change, then he will use his ingenuity to interpret and implement the change in such a way as to assure its success. If he decides to fight or block the change, the individual may act as if he complies but reserve other times and places to negate the effects of directives. For example:

In one large company, the top management met regularly for purposes of organizational planning. The executives responsible for implementing planning decisions could usually be counted on to carry them out when they had fought hard and openly in the course of reaching such decisions. When they seemed to accept a decision, giving all signs of compliance, the decision usually ended up as a notation in the minutes. Surface compliance occurred most frequently when problems involved loyalties to subordinates.

In one instance, a division head agreed to accept a highly regarded executive from another division to meet a serious manpower shortage in his organization. When the time came to effect the transfer, however, this division general manager refused, with some justification, on the grounds that bringing someone in from outside would demoralize his staff. He used compliance initially to respond to the problem of "family"

2. See Chester Barnard, *The Function of the Executive* (Cambridge, Mass.: Harvard University Press, 1938), p. 167.

loyalties to which he felt committed. Needless to say, the existence of these loyalties was the major problem to be faced in carrying out organizational planning.

Compliance as a tactic to avoid changes and commitment as an expression of strong motivation in dealing with organizational problems are in turn related to how individuals define their interests. In the power relations among executives, the so-called areas of common interest are usually reserved for the banalities of human relationships. The more significant areas of attention usually force conflicts of interest, especially competition for power, to the surface.

Interest Conflicts

Organizations demand, on the one hand, cooperative endeavor and commitment to common purposes. The realities of experience in organizations, on the other hand, show that conflicts of interest exist among people who ultimately share a common fate and are supposed to work together. What makes business more political and less ideological and rationalistic is the overriding importance of conflicts of interest.

If an individual (or group) is told that his job scope is reduced in either absolute or proportional terms for *the good corporation,* he faces a conflict. Should he acquiesce for the idea of common good or fight in the service of his self-interest? Any rational man will fight (how constructively depends on the absence of neurotic conflicts and on ego strength). His willingness to fight increases as he comes to realize the intangible nature of what people think is good for the organization. And, in point of fact, his willingness may serve the interests of corporate purpose by highlighting issues and stimulating careful thinking before the reaching of final decisions.

Secondary Effects

Conflicts of interest in the competition for resources are easily recognized, as, for example, in capital budgeting or in allocating money for research and development. But these conflicts can be subjected to bargaining procedures which all parties to the competition validate by their participation.

The secondary effects of bargaining do involve organizational and power issues. However, the fact that these power issues *follow* debate on economic problems rather than *lead* it creates a manifest content which can be objectified much more readily than in areas where the primary considerations are the distributions of authority.

In such cases, which include developing a new formal organization structure, management succession, promotions, corporate mergers, and entry of new executives, the conflicts of interest are severe and direct simply because there are no objective measures of right or wrong courses of action. The critical question which has to be answered in specific actions is: Who gets power and position? This involves particular people with their strengths and weaknesses and a specific historical context in which actions are understood in symbolic as well as rational terms. To illustrate:

A large corporation, General Motors in fact, inadvertently confirmed what every seasoned executive knows: that coalitions of power to overcome feelings of rivalry and the play of personal ambitions are fragile solutions. The appointment of Edward Cole to the presidency followed by Semon Knudsen's resignation shattered the illusion that the rational processes in business stand apart or even dominate the human emotions and ties that bind men to one another. If any corporation prides itself on rationality, General Motors is it. To have to experience so publicly the inference that major corporate life, particularly at the executive levels, is not so rational after all, can be damaging to the sense of security people get from belief in an idea as it is embodied in a corporate image.

The fact that Knudsen subsequently was discharged from the presidency of Ford (an event I shall discuss later in this article) suggests that personalities and the politics of corporations are not so much aberrations as conditions of life in large organizations.

But just as General Motors wants to maintain an image, many executives prefer to ignore what this illustration suggests: that organizations are political structures which feed on the psychology of comparison. To know something about the psychology of comparison takes us into the theory of self-esteem in both its conscious manifestations and its unconscious origins. Besides possibly enlightening us in general and giving a more realistic picture of people and organizations, there are some practical benefits in such knowledge. These benefits include:

Increased freedom to act more directly; instead of trying to "get around" a problem, one can meet it.

Greater objectivity about people's strengths and limitations, and, therefore, the ability to use them more honestly as well as effectively.

More effective planning in organizational design and in distribution of authority; instead of searching for the "one best solution" in organization structure, one accepts a range of alternatives and then gives priority to the personal or emotional concerns that inhibit action.

Power Relations

Organizational life within a political frame is a series of contradictions. It is an exercise in rationality, but its energy comes from the ideas in the minds of power figures the content of which, as well as their origins, are only dimly perceived. It deals with sources of authority and their distribution; yet it depends in the first place on the existence of a balance of power in the hands of an individual who initiates actions and gets results. It has many rituals associated with it, such as participation, democratization, and the sharing of power; yet the real outcome is the consolidation of power around a central figure to whom other individuals make emotional attachments.

Faulty Coalitions

The formal organization structure implements a coalition among key executives. The forms differ, and the psychological significance of various coalitions also differs. But no organization can function without a consolidation of power in the relationship of a central figure with his select group. The coalition need not exist between the chief executive and his immediate subordinates or staff. It may indeed bypass the second level as in the case of presidents of the United States who do not build confident relationships within their cabinets, but instead rely on members of the executive staff or on selected individuals outside the formal apparatus.

The failure to establish a coalition within the executive structure of an organization can result in severe problems, such as paralysis in the form of inability to make decisions and to evaluate performance, and infighting and overt rivalry within the executive group.

When a coalition fails to develop, the first place to look for causes is the chief executive and his problems in creating confident relationships. The causes are many and complex, but they usually hinge around the nature of the chief executive's defenses and what he needs to avoid as a means of alleviating stress. For example:

The "palace revolt," which led to Semon Knudsen's departure from Ford Motor Company, is an illustration of the failure in the formation of a coalition. While it is true that Henry Ford II named Knudsen president of the company, Knudsen's ultimate power as a newcomer to an established power structure depended on forming an alliance. The particular individual with whom an alliance seemed crucial was Lee Iacocca. For some reason, Knudsen and Iacocca competed for power and influence instead of using cooperatively a power base to which both contributed as is the case with most workable coalitions. In the absence of a coalition, the alternate postures of rivalry and battle for control erupted. Ford ultimately responded by weighing his power with one side over the other.

As I have indicated, it is not at all clear why in Knudsen's case the coalition failed to develop. But in any failure the place to look is in the personalities of the main actors and in the nature of their defenses which make certain coalitions improbable no matter how strongly other realities indicate their necessity.

But defensiveness on the part of a chief executive can also result in building an unrealistic and unworkable coalition, with self-enforced isolation which is its consequence. One of the most frequently encountered defensive maneuvers which leads to the formation of unrealistic coalitions or to the isolation of the chief executive is the fear of rivalry.

A realistic coalition matches formal authority and competence with the emotional commitments necessary to establish and maintain the coalition. The fear of rivals on the part of chief executives, or the jealousy on the part of subordinates of the chief executive's power, can at the extreme result in paranoid distortions. People become suspicious of one another, and through selective perceptions and projections of their own fantasies create a world of plots and counterplots.

The displacement of personal concerns onto substantive material in decision making is potentially the most dangerous form of defensiveness. The need for defenses arises because people become anxious about the significance of evaluations within existing power coalitions. But perhaps even more basic is the fear and the rivalry to which all coalitions are susceptible given the nature of investments people make in power relations. While it is easy to dismiss emotional reactions like these as neurotic distortions, their prevalence and impact deserve careful attention in all phases of organizational life.

Unconscious Collusions

All individuals and consequently groups experience areas of stress which mobilize defenses. The fact that coalitions embody defensive maneuvers on those occasions where stress goes beyond the usual level of tolerance is not surprising. An even more serious problem, however, occurs when the main force that binds men in a structure is the need to defend against or to act out the conflicts which individuals cannot tolerate alone.

Where coalitions represent the aggregation of power with conscious intention of using the abilities of members for constructive purposes, collusions represent predominance of unconscious conflict and defensive behavior. In organizational life, the presence of collusions and their causes often becomes the knot which has to be unraveled before any changes can be implemented.

The collusion of latent interests among executives can become the central theme and sustaining force of an organization structure of top management. For a collusion to take hold, the conflicts of the "power figure" have to be communicated and sensed by others as an overriding need which seeks active expression in the form of a theme. The themes vary just as do the structures which make a collusion. Thus one common theme is the need to control; another is the need to be admired and idealized; and still another is the need to find a scapegoat to attack in response to frustrations in solving problems.

If people could hold on to and keep within themselves areas of personal conflict, there would be far fewer collusions in organizational life. But it is part of the human condition for conflicts and needs to take over life situations. As a result, we find numerous instances of collusions controlling the behavior of executives. To illustrate:

A multidivisional corporation found itself with a revolution on its hands. The president was sensitive to the opinions of a few outside board members representing important stockholder interests. He was so concerned that he would be criticized by these board members, he demanded from vice-presidents full information on their activities and complete loyalty to him. Over a period of years, he moved divisional chief executives to corporate headquarters so he could assure himself of their loyalty. Other executives joined in to gratify the president's need for control and loyalty.

The result of this collusion, however, was to create a schism between headquarters and field operations. Some of the staff members in the field managed to inform the board members of the lack of attention to and understanding of field problems. Discontent grew to such an extent that the board placed the president on early retirement.

Subsequently, the new president, with the support of the board, decentralized authority and appointed new division heads who were to make their offices in divisional headquarters with full authority to manage their respective organizations. One of the lingering problems of the new president was to dissolve the collusion at headquarters without wholesale firing of vice-presidents.

Just as power distributions are central to the tasks of organizational planning, so the conservation of power is often the underlying function of collusions. Thus:

A manufacturing vice-president of a medium-sized company witnessed over a period of fifteen years a procession of changes in top management and ownership. He had managed to retain his job because he made himself indispensable in the management of the factory.

To each new top management, he stressed the importance of "home rule" as a means of assuring loyalty and performance in the plant. He also tacitly encouraged each supervisor to go along with whatever cliques happened to form and dominate the shop floor.

However, over time a gradual loss of competitive position, coupled with open conflict among cliques in the form of union disputes, led to the dismissal of the vice-president. None of his successors could reassert control over the shop, and the company eventually moved or liquidated many of the operations in this plant.

"Life Dramas"

Faulty coalitions and unconscious collusions, as I have illustrated, can result from the defensive needs of a chief executive. These needs, which often appear as a demand on others to bolster the self-esteem of the chief executive, are tolerated to a remarkable degree and persist for a long time before harmful effects become apparent to outside stockholders, bankers, or boards of directors which ultimately control the distributions of power in organizations. Occasionally, corporations undergo critical conflicts in organizational politics which cannot be ignored in the conscious deliberations which affect how power gets distributed or used.

Intertwined with the various expressions of power conflicts in organizations are three underlying "life dramas" deserving careful attention:

The *first* portrays stripping the powers of a *parental figure*.

The *second* portrays the predominance of *paranoid thinking*, where distortions of reality result from the surfacing of conflicts which formerly had been contained in collusions.

The *third* portrays a *ritualistic ceremonial* in which real power issues are submerged or isolated in compulsive behavior but at the cost of real problem solving and work.

Parental Figure

The chief executive in a business, along with the heads of states, religious bodies, and social movements, becomes an object for other people. The term "object" should be understood, in a psychological sense, as a person who is the recipient of strong emotional attachments from others. It is obvious that a chief executive is the *object* because he controls so many of the levers which ultimately direct the flow of rewards and punishments. But there is something to say beyond this obvious calculation of rewards and punishments as the basis for the emotional attachments between leader and led as *object* and *subject*.

Where a leader displays unusual attributes in his intuitive gifts, cultivated abilities, or deeper personal qualities, his fate as the *object* is governed by powerful emotions. I hesitate to use the word "charismatic" to describe such a leader, partially because it suggests a mystique but also because, in its reference to the "great" man as charismatic leader, it expands to superhuman proportions what really belongs to the psychology of everyday life.

What makes for strong emotional attachments is as much in the need of the *subject* as in the qualities of the *object*. In other words, the personalities of leaders take on proportions which meet what subordinates need and even demand. If leaders in fact respond with the special charisma that is often invested in them at the outset, then they are parties to a self-fulfilling prophecy. Of course, the qualities demanded have to be present in some nascent form ready to emerge as soon as the emotional currents become real in authority relationships.

The emotional attachments I am referring to usually contain mixtures of positive and negative feelings. If the current were only of one kind, such as either admiration or hostility, then the authority relationship would be simpler to describe as well as to manage. All too often, the way positive feelings blend into the negative sets off secondary currents of emotion which intensify the relationships.

On the one side, subordinates cannot help but have fantasies of what they would do if they held the number one position. Such fantasies, besides providing fleeting pleasures and helping one to regulate his ambitions, also provide channels for imaginative and constructive approaches to solving problems. It is only a short step from imagining what one would do as chief executive to explaining to the real chief executive the ideas which have been distilled from this flight into fantasy. If the chief executive senses envy in back of the thoughts, he may become frightened and choke off ideas which can be used quite constructively.

Critical episode: But suppose a situation arises where not one but several subordinates enjoy the same fantasy of being number one? Suppose also that subordinates feel deprived in their relationship with the chief executive? Suppose finally that facing the organization there are substantive problems which are more or less out of control. With these three conditions, and depending on the severity of the real problems besetting the enterprise, the stage is set for a collusion which, when acted out, becomes a critical episode of displacing the parental figure. To demonstrate:

In November 1967, the directors of the Interpublic Group, a $700 million complex in advertising and public relations, moved for the resignation of the leader and chief executive officer, Marion Harper, Jr. Briefly, Harper had managed over a period of 18 years to build the world's largest conglomerate in market services, advertising, and information on the base of a personally successful agency career. In expanding from this base, Harper made acquisitions, started new companies, and widened his orbit into international branches and companies.

As often happens, the innovator and creative person is careless in controlling what he has built so that financial problems become evident. In Harper's case, he appeared either unwilling or unable to recognize the seriousness of his financial problems and, in particular, the significance of allowing cash balances to go below the minimum required in agreements with lending institutions.

Harper seemed careless in another, even more telling, way. Instead of developing a strong coalition among his executive group, he relied on individual ties to him in which he clearly dominated the relationship. If any of the executives "crossed" him, Harper would exile the offender to one of the "remote" branches or place him on partial retirement.

When the financial problems became critical, the aggrieved executives who had once been dependent on Harper and then cast out, formed their own coalition, and managed to garner the votes necessary to, in effect, fire the head man. Although little information is available on the aftermath of this palace revolution, the new coalition had its own problems—which, one would reasonably judge, included contentions for power.

A cynic viewing this illustration of the demise of a parental figure could conclude that if one seeks to maintain power by dominance, then one had best go all the way. This means that to take some but not all of the power away from rebellious sons sets the stage for a cabal among the deprived. With a score to settle, they await only the right circumstances to move in and depose the aggressor.

While this cynical view has its own appeal, it ignores the deeper issues of why otherwise brilliant men fail to recognize the realistic needs for coalitions in the relationships of superior and subordinates. To answer this question, we would need to understand how powerful people operate with massive blind spots which limit vision and the ability to maneuver in the face of realistic problems.

The one purpose that coalitions serve is to guard against the effects of blind spots, since it is seldom the case that two people have identical limitations in their vision and ability to respond. The need to control and dominate in a personalistic sense is perhaps the most serious of all possible blind spots which can affect a chief executive, because he makes it difficult for people to help him, while creating grievances which sooner or later lead to attacks on him.

The unseating of a chief executive by a coalition of subordinates seldom reduces the emotional charge built up in the uncertain attachments to the ousted leader. A new head man has to emerge and establish a confident coalition. Until the contentions for power subside and the guilt reactions attached to deposing the leader dissolve, individuals remain. vulnerable to their own blind spots and unconscious reactions to striving for power.

The references to a parental figure in the preceding discussion may appear to exaggerate the meaning of power conflicts. In whatever ways it exaggerates, it also condenses a variety of truths about coalitions among executives. The chief executive is the central *object* in a coalition because he occupies a position analogous to parents in the family. He is at the nucleus of a political structure whose prototype is the family in which jealousy, envy, love, and hate find original impetus and expression.

It would be a gross error to assume that in making an analogy between the family and formal organizations the parental role is strictly paternal. There are also characteristics of the mother figure in certain types of chief executives and combinations of mother-father in the formation of executive coalitions.

Chief executives can also suffer from depersonalization in their roles and as a result become emotionally cold and detached. The causes of depersonalization are complex but, in brief, have some connections to the narrow definitions of rationality which exclude the importance of emotions in guiding communication as well as thought.

For the purpose of interpreting how defensive styles affect the behavior of leaders, there is some truth to the suggestion that the neutrality and lack of warmth characteristic of some leaders is a result of an ingrained fear of becoming the *object* for other people—for to become the *object* arouses fears that subordinates will become envious and compete for power.

Paranoid Thinking

This is a form of distortion in ideas and perception to which all human beings are susceptible from time to time. For those individuals who are concerned in their work with the consolidation and uses of power, the experience with suspiciousness, the attribution of bad motives to others, jealousy, and anxiety (characteristics of paranoid thinking), may be more than a passing state of mind.

In fact, such ideas and fantasies may indeed be communicated to others and may even be the main force which binds men into collusions. Organizational life is particularly vulnerable to the effects of paranoid thinking because it stimulates comparisons while it evokes anticipations of added power or fears of diminished power.

To complicate matters even more and to suggest just how ambiguous organizational decisions become, there may be some truth and substance in back of the suspicions, distrust, and jealousies which enflame thinking. Personality conflicts do affect decisions in allocating authority and responsibility, and an individual may not be distorting at all to sense that he had been excluded or denied an ambition based on some undercurrents in his relationships with others. To call these sensitivities paranoid thinking may itself be a gross distortion. But no matter how real the events, the paranoid potential is still high as a fallout of organizational life.

Paranoid thinking goes beyond suspiciousness, distrust, and jealousy. It may take the form of grandiose ideas and overestimation of one's power and control. This form of distortion leads to swings in mood from elation to despair, from a sense of omnipotence to helplessness. Again, when acted out, the search for complete control produces the tragedies which the initial distortions attempt to overcome. The tragedy of Jimmy Hoffa is a good case in point. Consider:

From all indications, Hoffa performed brilliantly as president of the teamsters' union. He was a superb organizer and bargainer, and in many ways a highly moral and even prudish man. There is little evidence to support allegations that he used his office to enrich himself.

Hoffa's troubles stemmed from his angry reactions when he could not get his way in managing the union's pension fund and from his relations with the government. In overestimating his power, Hoffa fell victim to the illusion that no controls outside himself could channel his actions. At this writing, Hoffa is serving a sentence in Lewisburg Penitentiary, having been found guilty of tampering with a jury.

It is interesting to note that Hoffa's successor delegated considerable authority to regional officers, a step that removed him from direct comparisons with Hoffa and served to cement a coalition of top officers in the teamsters.

Executives, too, can be victims of their successes just as much as of their failures. If past successes lead to the false sense of omnipotence which goes unchecked in, say, the executive's control of the board of directors, then he and his organization become the victims of changing times and competitive pressures along with the weakening in perception and reasoning which often accompanies aging.

One could speculate with some reason that paranoid distortions are the direct result of senility and the inability to accept the fact of death. While intellectually aware of the inevitability of death, gifted executives can sometimes not accept emotionally the ultimate in the limitations of power. The disintegration of personality in the conflict between the head and the heart is what we come to recognize as the paranoid potential in all forms of our collective relations.

Ritualistic Ceremonial

Any collective experience, such as organizational life with its capacity for charging the atmosphere in the imagery of power conflicts, can fall victim to rigidities. The rigidities I have in mind consist mainly of the formation and elaboration of structures, procedures, and other ceremonials which create the illusion of solving problems but in reality only give people something to act on to discharge valuable energies.

The best example of a ritualistic approach to real problems is the ever-ready solution of bringing people together in a committee on the naïve grounds that the exchange of ideas is bound to produce a solution. There are even fads and fashions to ritualism as in the sudden appearance of favorite words like "brainstorming" or "synergism."

It is not that bringing people together to discuss problems is bad. Instead, it is the naïve faith which accompanies such proposals, ultimately deflecting attention from where it properly belongs. Thus:

In one research organization, professionals faced severe problems arising from personal jealousies as well as differences of opinion on the correct goals and content for the research program. Someone would periodically suggest that the problems could not be solved unless people came together, preferably for a weekend away from the job, to share ideas and really get down to the "nitty-gritty" of the problem. (It is interesting to note that no one ever defines the "nitty-gritty.") The group would indeed follow such suggestions and typically end the weekend with a feeling of euphoria brought on by considerable drinking and a sumptuous meal.

The most concrete proposal for action was in the idea that the basic problem stemmed from the organization's increased size so that people no longer knew one another and their work. The solution which appeared, only shortly to disappear, was to publish a laboratory newsletter that would keep people abreast of their colleagues' newest ideas.

In a more general vein, ritualism can be invoked to deal with any real or fancied danger, with uncertainty, ambivalent attitudes, or a sense of personal helplessness. Rituals are used even in the attempt to manipulate people. That power relations in organization should become a fertile field for ritualism should not surprise anyone.

As I have tried to indicate, the problems of organizational life involve the dangers associated with losses of power; the uncertainties are legion especially in the recognition that there is no one best way to organize and distribute power, and yet any individual must make a commitment to some form of organization.

Ambivalent attitudes, such as the simultaneous experience of love and hate, are also associated with authority relationships, particularly in how superior-subordinate become the subject and object for the expression of dependency reactions. In addition, the sense of helplessness is particularly sensitized in the events which project gains and losses in power and status.

Finally, superior and subordinate in any power structure are constantly tempted to manipulate each other as a way of gaining control over one's environment, and the more so when there is a lack of confidence and credibility in the organization's efforts to solve problems in realistic ways.

The negative effects of ritualism are precisely in the expenditure of energy to carry out the rituals and also in the childlike expectation that the magic formulas of organizational life substitute for diagnosing and solving real problems. When the heads of organizations are unsure of the bases for the exercise of power and become defensive, the easy solution is to play for time by invoking rituals which may temporarily relieve anxiety.

Similarly, when executives fail to understand the structure and potential of the power coalitions they establish (either consciously or unconsciously), they increasingly rely on rituals to deflect attention away from their responsibilities. And, when leaders are timid men incapable of initiating or responding, the spontaneous reaction is to use people to act out rituals. Usually, the content and symbolism in the rituals provide important clues about the underlying defensiveness of the executive.

Obsessional leaders: The gravitational pull to ceremonials and magic is irresistible. In positions of power, obsessional leaders use in their public performances the mechanisms of defense which originate in their private conflicts. These defenses include hyper-rationality, the isolation of thought and feeling, reactive behavior in turning anger into moral righteousness, and passive control of other people as well as their own thought processes.

Very frequently, particularly in this day and age of psychologizing conflict, obsessive leaders "get religion" and try to convert others into some new state of mind. The use of sensitivity training with its attachment to "openness" and "leveling" in power relations seems to be the current favorite.

What these leaders do not readily understand is the fallacy of imposing a total solution for the problem of power relations where reality dictates at best the possibility of only partial and transient solutions. To force openness through the use of group pressure in T-groups and to expect to sustain this pressure in everyday life is to be supremely ritualistic.

People intelligently resist saying everything they think to other people because they somehow have a deep recognition that this route leads to becoming overextended emotionally and, ultimately, to sadistic relationships.

Intelligent uses of power: The choice fortunately is not between ritualistic civility and naïve openness in human relationships, particularly where power is concerned. In between is the choice of defining those partial problems which can be solved and through which bright people can learn something about the intelligent uses of power.

We should not lose sight of the basic lesson that people in positions of power differ from "ordinary" human beings mainly in their capacity to impose their personal defenses onto the stage of corporate life. Fortunately, the relationships are susceptible to intelligent management, and it is to the nature of this intelligence that I wish to address the conclusion of this article.

Coming Full Circle

The main job of organizational life, whether it concerns developing a new political pyramid, making new appointments to executive positions, or undergoing management succession at top levels, is to bring talented individuals into location for the legitimate uses of power. This is bound to be a highly charged event in corporate relationships because of the real changes in power distributions and the emotional reactions people experience along with the incremental gains and losses of power.

The demand, on the one hand, is for objectivity in assessing people and needs (as opposed to pseudorationality and rationalizing). This objectivity, on the other hand, has to be salvaged from the impact of psychological stresses which impel people to act out fantasies associated with power conflicts. The stresses of change in power relations tend to increase defensiveness to which counterreactions of rationalizing and of mythmaking serve no enduring purpose except perhaps to drive underground the concerns which make people react defensively in the first place.

Stylistic Biases

Thought and action in the politics of organizational life are subject to the two kinds of errors commonly found in practical life: the errors of omission and those of commission. It is both what people do and what they neglect to do that result in the negative effects of action outweighing the positive. But besides the specific errors of omission and commission (the tactical aspects of action), there are also the more strategic aspects which have to be evaluated. The strategic aspects deal both with the corporate aims and objectives and with the style of the leaders who initiate change.

In general, leaders approach change with certain stylistic biases over which they may not have too much control. There is a preferred approach to power problems which derives from the personality of the leader and his defenses as well as from the realities of the situation. Of particular importance as stylistic biases are the preferences for partial, as contrasted with total, approaches and the preferences for substance over form.

Partial vs. total: The partial approaches attempt to define and segregate problems which become amenable to solution by directive, negotiation, consensus, and compromise.

The total approaches usually escalate the issues in power relations so that implicitly people act as though it were necessary to undergo major conversions. The conversions can be directed toward personality structure, ideals, and beliefs, or toward values which are themselves connected to important aspects of personal experience.

When conversions become the end products of change, then one usually finds the sensitization of concerns over such matters as who dominates and who submits, who controls and who is being controlled, who is accepted and who is rejected. The aftermath of these concerns is the heightening of fantasy and defense at the expense of reality.

It may come as something of a disappointment to readers who are favorably disposed to psychology to consider the possibility that while organizations do have an impact on the attitudes of their constituent members, they cannot change personality structures or carry out therapeutic procedures. People may become more effective while working in certain kinds of organizations, but only when effectiveness is not dependent on the solution of neurotic conflict.

The advocates of total approaches seem to miss this point in their eagerness to convert people and organizations from one set of ideals to another. It becomes a good deal wiser, if these propositions are true, to scale down and make concrete the objectives that one is seeking to achieve.

A good illustration is in the attention given to decentralization of authority. Decentralization can be viewed in the image of conversion to certain ideals about who should have power and how this power should be used responsibly, or through an analytical approach to decide selectively where power is ill-placed and ill-used and to work on change at these locations. In other words, the theory of the partial approach to organizations asserts priorities and depends on good diagnostic observation and thought.

Substance vs. form: Leaders can also present a stylistic bias in their preference for substance or form. Substance, in the language of organizations, is the detail of goals and performance—that is, who has to do what with whom to meet specific objectives. Form directs attention to the relationship of "who to whom" and attempts to achieve goals by specifying how the people should act in relation to each other.

There is no way in which matters of form can be divorced from substance. But students of organization should at least be clear that attention to form *ahead of* substance threatens a person's sense of what is reasonable in undertaking actions. Attention to form may also present an implicit attack on one's conception of his independence and freedom from constraint.

Making form secondary to substance has another virtue: it can secure agreement on priorities without the need of predetermining who will have to give way in the ultimate give-and-take of the negotiations that must precede decisions on organization structure.

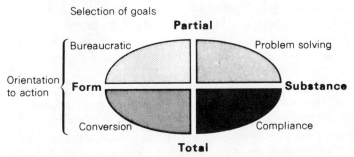

Fig. 1. Cognitive Management Styles in Organizational Life

The two dimensions of bias, shown in the figure 1 matrix, along with the four cells which result, clarify different executive approaches to power. The two dimensions define the executive's cognitive biases in: (I) selection of goals (partial vs. total), and (2) orientation toward action (form vs. substance).

In the *bureaucratic* approach—that is, partial goals and attachment to form as a mode of acting—the emphasis is on procedure and the establishment of precedent and rule to control the uses of power.

The appeal of this approach is its promise of certainty in corporate relationships and in the depersonalization of power. The weaknesses of the bureaucratic approach are too familiar to need detailing here. Its major defect, however, is its inability to separate the vital from the trivial. It more easily commands energy over irrelevant issues because the latent function of the bureaucratic approach is to bypass conflict.

My contention here is that few important problems can be attended to without conflict of ideas and interests. Eventually organizations become stagnant because the bureaucratic approaches seldom bring together power and the vital issues which together make organizations dynamic.

The *conversion* approach (total-form) is notable through the human relations and sensitivity training movements as well as ideological programs, such as the Scanlon Plan and other forms of participative management. The popularity of "management by objectives" bears some scrutiny as a conversion movement directed toward power figures.

Another "total" approach which differs from conversion in its emphasis on substance is *compliance* with the directives of the powerful leader. This is the arena of the authoritarian personality (in both the leader, who has the power, and in the led, who seek submission), for whom personal power gets expressed in some higher goal that makes it possible for ends to justify means. The ideals may, for example, be race, as with dictator Adolf Hitler, or religion, as with Father Charles Coughlin, a dictator-type of the depression. In business, the illustrations are of a technological variety as with Frederick Winslow Taylor's "scientific management" and Henry Ford's automobile and assembly line.

Almost any technology can assume the proportions of the total approach if it is advanced by a charismatic leader and has deep emotional appeal. This explains the popularity of "management information systems," "value analysis," and "program planning and budgeting" which lead to a belief that the system itself is based on order, rationality, and control; therefore, the belief in turn helps to counteract the fears of chaos and lack of control which make people willing to demand total dependence and compliance in power relations. The effects of this fear on how people seek to arrange power relations in business, government, and the community cannot be overestimated.

Problem-solving Approach

It should be perfectly obvious by now that my favored

approach to organizational life combines the biases in figure 1 of the partial substantive quadrant which I have designated "problem solving." From observation of competent business executives, we know it is precisely their ability to define problems worthy of thought and action and to use their organization to evolve solutions which characterize their style.

The contrary notion that executives are primarily caretakers, mediators, and seekers of consensus is more a myth than an accurate portrayal of how the competent ones attach themselves to power. To have power and not direct it to some substantive end that can be attained in the real world is to waste energy. The difficulties with the problem-solving approach are in risking power in favor of a substantive goal.

While there are no absolute right answers in problem solving, there are ways of evaluating the correctness of a program and plan. With a favorable average, the executive finds his power base enhanced and his ability to take risks increased.

The problem-solving approach to organization structure operates according to certain premises:

1. That organization structure is an instrument rather than an end. This means that a structure should be established or modified quickly instead of stringing out deliberations as though there actually exists a best and single solution for the problem of allocating power.

2. That organization structure can be changed but should not be tinkered with. This means that members of an executive organization can rely on a structure and can implement it without the uncertainty which comes from the constant modification of the organization chart.

3. That organization structure expresses the working coalition attached to the chief executive. In other words, the coalition has to be established de facto for the structure to mean anything. If the structure is out of line with the coalition, there will be an erosion of power and effectiveness. If no coalition exists in the minds of participants, putting it on paper in the form of an organization chart is nothing more than an academic exercise and a confusing one at that.

4. That organization structure represents a blend of people and job definitions, but the priority is in describing the structure to accommodate competent people. The reason for this priority lies in the fact that competent executives are hard to find. Therefore, as an action principle, one should ensure the effective uses of the scarcest resources rather than conform to some ideal version of power relations.

5. That organization structure is a product of negotiation and compromise among executives who hold semiautonomous power bases. The more the power base of an executive is his demonstrated competence, the greater his autonomy of power and therefore capacity to determine the outcome in the allocations of power.

The basic criticism of the problem-solving approach is in the danger of defining issues narrowly and ultimately undermining the moral and ethical basis of leadership. This criticism is valid, but as with so many problems in practical affairs, it can be overcome only by leaders who can see beyond the limits of immediate contingencies. In fact, I have tried to show throughout this article how the limitations of leaders, in both their cognitive and their emotional capacities, become the causes of power problems.

We have therefore come full circle in this analysis: because power problems are the effects of personality on structure, the solutions demand thinking which is free from the disabilities of emotional conflicts. This insight is often the margin between enduring with what exists or taking those modest steps which align competence with institutional authority in the service of human needs.

Some Conditions of Obedience and Disobedience to Authority
Stanley Milgram

The situation in which one agent commands another to hurt a third turns up time and again as a significant theme in human relations. It is powerfully expressed in the story of Abraham, who is commanded by God to kill his son. It is no accident that Kierkegaard,[1] seeking to orient his thought to the central themes of human experience, chose Abraham's conflict as the springboard to his philosophy.

War too moves forward on the triad of an authority which commands a person to destroy the enemy, and perhaps all organized hostility may be viewed as a theme and variation on the three elements of authority, executant, and victim.[2] We describe an experimental program, recently conducted at Yale University, in which a particular expression of this conflict is studied by experimental means.

Reprinted from *Human Relations,* vol. 18, no. 1 (1965), by permission of the author and of the original publisher, The Plenum Publishing Company, Ltd.

This research was supported by two grants from the National Science Foundation: NSF G-17916 and NSF G-24152. Exploratory studies carried out in 1960 were financed by a grant from the Higgins Funds of Yale University. The author is grateful to John T. Williams, James J. McDonough, and Emil Elges for the important part they played in the project. Thanks are due also to Alan Elms, James Miller, Taketo Murata, and Stephen Stier for their aid as graduate assistants. The author's wife, Sasha, performed many valuable services. Finally, a profound debt is owed to the many persons in New Haven and Bridgeport who served as subjects.

1. S. Kierkegaard, *Fear and Trembling* (1843), English ed. (Princeton, N.J.: Princeton University Press, 1941).

2. Consider, for example, J. P. Scott's analysis of war in his monograph on aggression:

"While the actions of key individuals in a war may be explained in terms of direct stimulation to aggression, vast numbers of other people are involved simply by being part of an organized society.

". . . For example, at the beginning of World War I an Austrian archduke was assassinated in Sarajevo. A few days later soldiers from all over Europe were marching toward each other, not because they were stimulated by the archduke's misfortune, but because they had been trained to obey orders." (Slightly rearranged from J. P. Scott, *Aggression* (Chicago: University of Chicago Press, 1958), p. 103.)

In its most general form the problem may be defined thus: if *X* tells *Y* to hurt *Z*, under what conditions will *Y* carry out the command of *X* and under what conditions will he refuse? In the more limited form possible in laboratory research, the question becomes: if an experimenter tells a subject to hurt another person, under what conditions will the subject go along with this instruction, and under what conditions will he refuse to obey? The laboratory problem is not so much a dilution of the general statement as one concrete expression of the many particular forms this question may assume.

One aim of the research was to study behavior in a strong situation of deep consequence to the participants, for the psychological forces operative in powerful and lifelike forms of the conflict may not be brought into play under diluted conditions.

This approach meant, first, that we had a special obligation to protect the welfare and dignity of the persons who took part in the study; subjects were, of necessity, placed in a difficult predicament, and steps had to be taken to ensure their well-being before they were discharged from the laboratory. Toward this end, a careful, postexperimental treatment was devised and has been carried through for subjects in all conditions.[3]

Terminology

If *Y* follows the command of *X* we shall say that he has obeyed *X*; if he fails to carry out the command of *X*, we shall say that he has disobeyed *X*. The terms *to obey* and *to dis-*

3. It consisted of an extended discussion with the experimenter and, of equal importance, a friendly reconciliation with the victim. It is made clear that the victim did not receive painful electric shocks. After the completion of the experimental series, subjects were sent a detailed report of the results and full purposes of the experimental program. A formal assessment of this procedure points to its overall effectiveness. Of the subjects, 83.7 percent indicated that they were glad to have taken part in the study; 15.1 percent reported neutral feelings; and 1.3 percent stated that they were sorry to have participated. A large number of subjects spontaneously requested that they be used in further experimentation. Four-fifths of the subjects felt that more experiments of this sort should be carried out, and 74 percent indicated that they had learned something of personal importance as a result of being in the study. Furthermore, a university psychiatrist, experienced in outpatient treatment, interviewed a sample of experimental subjects with the aim of uncovering possible injurious effects resulting from participation. No such effects were in evidence. Indeed, subjects typically felt that their participation was instructive and enriching. A more detailed discussion of this question can be found in S. Milgram, "Issues in the Study of Obedience: A Reply to Baumrind," *Amer. Psychol.* 19 (1964): 848–52.

obey, as used here, refer to the subject's overt action only, and carry no implication for the motive or experiential states accompanying the action.[4]

To be sure, the everyday use of the word *obedience* is not entirely free from complexities. It refers to action within widely varying situations, and connotes diverse motives within those situations: a child's obedience differs from a soldier's obedience, or the love, honor, and *obey* of the marriage vow. However, a consistent behavioral relationship is indicated in most uses of the term: in the act of obeying, a person does what another person tells him to do. Y obeys X if he carries out the prescription for action which X has addressed to him; the term suggests, moreover, that some form of dominance-subordination, or hierarchical element, is part of the situation in which the transaction between X and Y occurs.

A subject who complies with the entire series of experimental commands will be termed an *obedient* subject; one who at any point in the command series defies the experi-

4. *To obey* and *to disobey* are not the only terms one could use in describing the critical action of Y. One could say that Y is cooperating with X, or displays conformity with regard to X's commands. However, *cooperation* suggests that X agrees with Y's ends, and understands the relationship between his own behavior and the attainment of those ends. (But the experimental procedure, and, in particular, the experimenter's command that the subject shock the victim even in the absence of a response from the victim, preclude such understanding.) Moreover, cooperation implies status parity for the coacting agents, and neglects the asymmetrical, dominance-subordination element prominent in the laboratory relationship between experimenter and subject. *Conformity* has been used in other important contexts in social psychology, and most frequently refers to imitating the judgments or actions of others when no explicit requirement for imitation has been made. Furthermore, in the present study there are two sources of social pressure: pressure from the experimenter issuing the commands, and pressure from the victim to stop the punishment. It is the pitting of a common man (the victim) against an authority (the experimenter) that is the distinctive feature of the conflict. At a point in the experiment the victim demands that he be let free. The experimenter insists that the subject continue to administer shocks. Which act of the subject can be interpreted as conformity? The subject may conform to the wishes of his peer or to the wishes of the experimenter, and conformity in one direction means the absence of conformity in the other. Thus the word has no useful reference in this setting, for the dual and conflicting social pressures cancel out its meaning.

In the final analysis, the linguistic symbol representing the subject's action must take its meaning from the concrete context in which that action occurs; and there is probably no word in everyday language that covers the experimental situation exactly, without omissions or irrelevant connotations. It is partly for convenience, therefore, that the terms *obey* and *disobey* are used to describe the subject's actions. At the same time, our use of the words is highly congruent with dictionary meaning.

menter will be called a *disobedient* or *defiant* subject. As used in this report, the terms refer only to the subject's performance in the experiment, and do not necessarily imply a general personality disposition to submit to or reject authority.

Subject Population

The subjects used in all experimental conditions were male adults, residing in the greater New Haven and Bridgeport areas, aged twenty to fifty years, and engaged in a wide variety of occupations. Each experimental condition described in this report employed forty fresh subjects and was carefully balanced for age and occupational types. The occupational composition for each experiment was: workers, skilled and unskilled: 40 percent; white collar, sales, business: 40 percent; professionals: 20 percent. The occupations were intersected with three age categories (subjects in twenties, thirties, and forties, assigned to each condition in the proportions of 20, 40, and 40 percent respectively).

The General Laboratory Procedure

The focus of the study concerns the amount of electric shock a subject is willing to administer to another person when ordered by an experimenter to give the "victim" increasingly more severe punishment. The act of administering shock is set in the context of a learning experiment, ostensibly designed to study the effect of punishment on memory. Aside from the experimenter, one naïve subject and one accomplice perform in each session. On arrival each subject is paid $4.50. After a general talk by the experimenter, telling how little scientists know about the effect of punishment on memory, subjects are informed that one member of the pair will serve as teacher and one as learner. A rigged drawing is held so that the naïve subject is always the teacher, and the accomplice becomes the learner. The learner is taken to an adjacent room and strapped into an "electric chair."[5]

5. A more detailed account of the laboratory procedure can be found in S. Milgram, "Behavioral Study of Obedience," *J. Abnorm. Soc. Psychol.* 67 (1963): 371–78. A similar and independently evolved experimental procedure, employing a shock generator, victim, and learning task, was reported by Arnold H. Buss, *The Psychology of Aggression* (New York and London: John Wiley, 1961). Buss used the technique for studying aggression, not obedience, and did not make use of the fundamental measure employed in the present study: break-off points. His investigation promises to be a useful complement to the present research.

The naïve subject is told that it is his task to teach the learner a list of paired associates, to test him on the list, and to administer punishment whenever the learner errs in the test. Punishment takes the form of electric shock, delivered to the learner by means of a shock generator controlled by the naïve subject. The teacher is instructed to increase the intensity of electric shock one step on the generator on each error. The learner, according to plan, provides many wrong answers, so that before long the naïve subject must give him the strongest shock on the generator. Increases in shock level are met by increasingly insistent demands from the learner that the experiment be stopped because of the growing discomfort to him. However, in clear terms the experimenter orders the teacher to continue with the procedure in disregard of the learner's protest. Thus, the naïve subject must resolve a conflict between two mutually incompatible demands from the social field. He may continue to follow the orders of the experimenter and shock the learner with increasing severity, or he may refuse to follow the orders of the experimenter and heed the learner's pleas. The experimenter's authority operates not in a free field, but against ever-mounting countervailing pressures from the person being punished.

A few technical points need to be considered before the findings of the study are described. For the purpose of delivering shock, a simulated shock generator is used, with thirty clearly marked voltage levels that range from 15 to 450 volts (and each activated by one of thirty individual lever switches set in a horizontal line). The naïve subject is given a sample shock of 45 volts to convince him of the authenticity of the instrument. The generator bears verbal designations that range from "Slight Shock" to "Danger: Severe Shock."

The responses of the victim are standardized on tape, and each protest is coordinated to a particular voltage level on the shock generator. Starting with 75 volts the learner begins to grunt and moan. At 150 volts he demands to be let out of the experiment. At 180 volts he cries out that he can no longer stand the pain. At 300 volts he refuses to provide any more answers to the memory test, insisting that he is no longer a participant in the experiment and must be freed. In response to this last tactic, the experimenter instructs the naïve subject to treat the absence of an answer as equivalent to a wrong answer, and to follow the usual shock procedure. The experimenter reinforces his demand with the statement: "You have no other choice, you must go on!" (This imperative is used whenever the naïve subject tries to break off the experiment.) If the subject refuses to give the next higher level of shock, the experiment is considered at an end. A quantitative value is assigned to the subject's performance based on the maximum intensity shock he administered before breaking off. Thus any subject's score may range from zero (for a subject unwilling to administer the first shock level) to thirty (for a subject who proceeds to the highest voltage level on the board). For any particular subject and for any particular experimental condition the degree to which participants have followed the experimenter's orders may be specified with a numerical value, corresponding to the metric on the shock generator.

This laboratory situation gives us a framework in which to study the subject's reactions to the principal conflict of the experiment. Again, this conflict is between the experimenter's demands that he continue to administer the electric shock, and the learner's demands, which become increasingly more insistent, that the experiment be stopped. The crux of the study is to vary systematically the factors believed to alter the degree of obedience to the experimental commands, to learn under what conditions submission to authority is most probable, and under what conditions defiance is brought to the fore.

Pilot Studies

Pilot studies for the present research were completed in the winter of 1960; they differed from the regular experiments in a few details: for one, the victim was placed behind a silvered glass, with the light balance on the glass such that the victim could be dimly perceived by the subject.[6]

Though essentially qualitative in treatment, these studies pointed to several significant features of the experimental situation. At first no vocal feedback was used from the victim. It was thought that the verbal and voltage designations on the control panel would create sufficient pressure to curtail the subject's obedience. However, this was not the case. In the absence of protests from the learner, virtually all subjects, once commanded, went blithely to the end of the board, seemingly indifferent to the verbal designations ("Extreme Shock" and "Danger: Severe Shock"). This deprived us of an adequate basis for scaling obedient tendencies. A force had

6. S. Milgram, "Dynamics of Obedience: Experiments in Social Psychology," mimeographed report (Washington, D.C.: National Science Foundation, 25 January 1961).

to be introduced that would strengthen the subject's resistance to the experimenter's commands, and reveal individual differences in terms of a distribution of break-off points.

This force took the form of protests from the victim. Initially, mild protests were used, but proved inadequate. Subsequently, more vehement protests were inserted into the experimental procedure. To our consternation, even the strongest protests from the victim did not prevent all subjects from administering the harshest punishment ordered by the experimenter; but the protests did lower the mean maximum shock somewhat and created some spread in the subject's performance; therefore, the victim's cries were standardized on tape and incorporated into the regular experimental procedure.

The situation did more than highlight the technical difficulties of finding a workable experimental procedure: it indicated that subjects would obey authority to a greater extent than we had supposed. It also pointed to the importance of feedback from the victim in controlling the subject's behavior.

One further aspect of the pilot study was that subjects frequently averted their eyes from the person they were shocking, often turning their heads in an awkward and conspicuous manner. One subject explained: "I didn't want to see the consequences of what I had done." Observers wrote:

> Subjects showed a reluctance to look at the victim, whom they could see through the glass in front of them. When this fact was brought to their attention they indicated that it caused them discomfort to see the victim in agony. We note, however, that although the subject refuses to look at the victim, he continues to administer shocks.

This suggested that the salience of the victim may have, in some degree, regulated the subject's performance. If, in obeying the experimenter, the subject found it necessary to avoid scrutiny of the victim, would the converse be true? If the victim were rendered increasingly more salient to the subject, would obedience diminish? The first set of regular experiments was designed to answer this question.

Immediacy of the Victim

This series consisted of four experimental conditions. In each condition the victim was brought "psychologically" closer to the subject giving him shocks.

In the first condition (Remote Feedback) the victim was placed in another room and could not be heard or seen by the subject, except that, at 300 volts, he pounded on the wall in protest. After 315 volts he no longer answered or was heard from.

The second condition (Voice Feedback) was identical to the first except that voice protests were introduced. As in the first condition the victim was placed in an adjacent room, but his complaints could be heard clearly through a door left slightly ajar, and through the walls of the laboratory.[7]

The third experimental condition (Proximity) was similar to the second, except that the victim was now placed in the same room as the subject, and one and a half feet from him. Thus he was visible as well as audible, and voice cues were provided.

The fourth, and final, condition of this series (Touch-Prox-

7. It is difficult to convey on the printed page the full tenor of the victim's responses, for we have no adequate notation for vocal intensity, timing, and general qualities of delivery. Yet these features are crucial to producing the effect of an increasingly severe reaction to mounting voltage levels. (They can be communicated fully only by sending interested parties the recorded tapes.) In general terms, however, the victim indicates no discomfort until the 75-volt shock is administered, at which time there is a light grunt in response to the punishment. Similar reactions follow the 90- and 105-volt shocks, and at 120 volts the victim shouts to the experimenter that the shocks are becoming painful. Painful groans are heard on administration of the 135-volt shock, and at 150 volts the victim cries out, "Experimenter, get me out of here! I won't be in the experiment any more! I refuse to go on!" Cries of this type continue with generally rising intensity, so that at 180 volts the victim cries out, "I can't stand the pain," and by 270 volts his response to the shock is definitely an agonized scream. Throughout, he insists that he be let out of the experiment. At 300 volts the victim shouts in desperation that he will no longer provide answers to the memory test; and at 315 volts, after a violent scream, he reaffirms with vehemence that he is no longer a participant. From this point on, he provides no answers, but shrieks in agony whenever a shock is administered; this continues through 450 volts. Of course, many subjects will have broken off before this point.

A revised and stronger set of protests was used in all experiments outside the proximity series. Naturally, new baseline measures were established for all comparisons using the new set of protests.

There is overwhelming evidence that the great majority of subjects, both obedient and defiant, accepted the victims' reactions as genuine. The evidence takes the form of: (a) tension created in the subjects (see discussion of tension); (b) scores on "estimated pain" scales filled out by subjects immediately after the experiment; (c) subjects' accounts of their feelings in postexperimental interviews; and (d) quantifiable responses to questionnaires distributed to subjects several months after their participation in the experiments. This matter will be treated fully in a forthcoming monograph.

(The procedure in all experimental conditions was to have the naïve subject announce the voltage level before administering each shock, so that—independently of the victim's responses—he was continually reminded of delivering punishment of ever-increasing severity.)

imity) was identical to the third, with this exception: the victim received a shock only when his hand rested on a shockplate. At the 150-volt level the victim again demanded to be let free and, in this condition, refused to place his hand on the shockplate. The experimenter ordered the naïve subject to force the victim's hand onto the plate. Thus obedience in this condition required that the subject have physical contact with the victim in order to give him punishment beyond the 150-volt level.

Forty adult subjects were studied in each condition. The data revealed that obedience was significantly reduced as the victim was rendered more immediate to the subject. The mean maximum shock for the conditions is shown in figure 1.

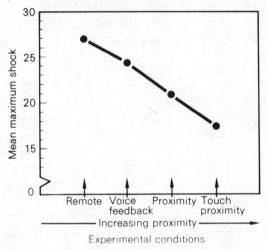

Fig. 1

Expressed in terms of the proportion of obedient to defiant subjects, the findings are that 34 percent of the subjects defied the experimenter in the Remote condition, 37.5 percent in Voice Feedback, 60 percent in Proximity, and 70 percent in Touch-Proximity.

How are we to account for this effect? A first conjecture might be that as the victim was brought closer the subject became more aware of the intensity of his suffering and regulated his behavior accordingly. This makes sense, but our evidence does not support the interpretation. There are no consistent differences in the attributed level of pain across the four conditions (i.e., the amount of pain experienced by the victim was estimated by the subject and expressed on a 14-point scale). But it is easy to speculate about alternative mechanisms:

Empathic cues. In the Remote and to a lesser extent the

Voice Feedback condition, the victim's suffering possesses an abstract, remote quality for the subject. He is aware, but only in a conceptual sense, that his actions cause pain to another person; the fact is apprehended, but not felt. The phenomenon is common enough. The bombardier can reasonably suppose that his weapons will inflict suffering and death, yet this knowledge is divested of affect, and does not move him to a felt, emotional response to the suffering resulting from his actions. Similar observations have been made in wartime. It is possible that the visual cues associated with the victim's suffering trigger empathic responses in the subject and provide him with a more complete grasp of the victim's experience. Or it is possible that the empathic responses are themselves unpleasant, possessing drive properties which cause the subject to terminate the arousal situation. Diminishing obedience, then, would be explained by the enrichment of empathic cues in the successive experimental conditions.

Denial and narrowing of the cognitive field. The Remote condition allows a narrowing of the cognitive field so that the victim is put out of mind. The subject no longer considers the act of depressing a lever relevant to moral judgment, for it is no longer associated with the victim's suffering. When the victim is close it is more difficult to exclude him phenomenologically. He necessarily intrudes on the subject's awareness since he is continuously visible. In the Remote conditions his existence and reactions are made known only after the shock has been administered. The auditory feedback is sporadic and discontinuous. In the Proximity conditions his inclusion in the immediate visual field renders him a continuously salient element for the subject. The mechanism of denial can no longer be brought into play. One subject in the Remote condition said: "It's funny how you really begin to forget that there's a guy out there, even though you can hear him. For a long time I just concentrated on pressing the switches and reading the words."

Reciprocal fields. If in the Proximity condition the subject is in an improved position to observe the victim, the reverse is also true. The actions of the subject now come under proximal scrutiny by the victim. Possibly, it is easier to harm a person when he is unable to observe our actions than when he can see what we are doing. His surveillance of the action directed against him may give rise to shame, or guilt, which may then serve to curtail the action. Many expressions of language refer to the discomfort or inhibitions that arise in face-to-face confrontation. It is often said that it is easier to criticize a man "behind his back" than to "attack him to his face." If we are in the process of lying to a person it is reputedly difficult to "stare him in the eye." We "turn away from others in shame" or in "embarrassment" and this action serves to reduce our discomfort. The manifest function of allowing the victim of a firing squad to be blindfolded is to make the occasion less stressful for him, but it may also serve a latent function of reducing the stress of the executioner. In short, in the Proximity conditions, the subject may sense that he has become more salient in the victim's field of awareness. Possibly he becomes more self-conscious, embarrassed, and inhibited in his punishment of the victim.

Phenomenal unity of act. In the Remote conditions it is more difficult for the subject to gain a sense of *relatedness* between his own actions and the consequences of these actions for the victim. There is a physical and spatial separation of the act and its consequences. The subject depresses a lever in one room, and protests and cries are heard from another. The two events are in correlation, yet they lack a compelling phenomenological unity. The structure of a meaningful act—*I am hurting a man*—breaks down because of the spatial arrangements, in a manner somewhat analogous to the disappearance of phi phenomena when the blinking lights are spaced too far apart. The unity is more fully achieved in the Proximity conditions as the victim is brought closer to the action that causes him pain. It is rendered complete in Touch-Proximity.

Incipient group formation. Placing the victim in another room not only takes him further from the subject, but the subject and the experimenter are drawn relatively closer. There is incipient group formation between the experimenter and the subject, from which the victim is excluded. The wall between the victim and the others deprives him of an intimacy which the experimenter and subject feel. In the Remote condition, the victim is truly an outsider, who stands alone, physically and psychologically.

When the victim is placed close to the subject, it becomes easier to form an alliance with him against the experimenter. Subjects no longer have to face the experimenter alone. They have an ally who is close at hand and eager to collaborate in a revolt against the experimenter. Thus, the changing set of spatial relations leads to a potentially shifting set of alliances over the several experimental conditions.

Acquired behavior dispositions. It is commonly observed that laboratory mice will rarely fight with their litter mates. Scott[8] explains this in terms of passive inhibition. He writes:

8. Scott, *Aggression.*

"By doing nothing under ... circumstances [the animal] learns to do nothing, and this may be spoken of as passive inhibition ... this principle has great importance in teaching an individual to be peaceful, for it means that he can learn not to fight simply by not fighting." Similarly, we may learn not to harm others simply by not harming them in everyday life. Yet this learning occurs in a context of proximal relations with others, and may not be generalized to that situation in which the person is physically removed from us. Or possibly, in the past, aggressive actions against others who were physically close resulted in retaliatory punishment which extinguished the original form of response. In contrast, aggression against others at a distance may have only sporadically led to retaliation. Thus the organism learns that it is safer to be aggressive toward others at a distance, and precarious to be so when the parties are within arm's reach. Through a pattern of rewards and punishments, he acquires a disposition to avoid aggression at close quarters, a disposition which does not extend to harming others at a distance. And this may account for experimental findings in the remote and proximal experiments.

Proximity as a variable in psychological research has received far less attention than it deserves. If men were sessile it would be easy to understand this neglect. But we move about; our spatial relations shift from one situation to the next, and the fact that we are near or remote may have a powerful effect on the psychological processes that mediate our behavior toward others. In the present situation, as the victim is brought closer to the man ordered to give him shocks, increasing numbers of subjects break off the experiment, refusing to obey. The concrete, visible, and proximal presence of the victim acts in an important way to counteract the experimenter's power and to generate disobedience.[9]

Closeness of Authority

If the spatial relationship of the subject and victim is relevant

9. Admittedly, the terms *proximity, immediacy, closeness,* and *salience-of-the-victim* are used in a loose sense, and the experiments themselves represent a very coarse treatment of the variable. Further experiments are needed to refine the notion and tease out such diverse factors as spatial distance, visibility, audibility, barrier interposition, etc.

The Proximity and Touch-Proximity experiments were the only conditions where we were unable to use taped feedback from the victim. Instead, the victim was trained to respond in these conditions as he had in experiment 2 (which employed taped feedback). Some improvement is possible here, for it should be technically feasible to do a proximity series using taped feedback.

to the degree of obedience, would not the relationship of subject to experimenter also play a part?

There are reasons to feel that, on arrival, the subject is oriented primarily to the experimenter rather than to the victim. He has come to the laboratory to fit into the structure that the experimenter—not the victim—would provide. He has come less to understand his behavior than to *reveal* that behavior to a competent scientist, and he is willing to display himself as the scientist's purposes require. Most subjects seem quite concerned about the appearance they are making before the experimenter, and one could argue that this preoccupation in a relatively new and strange setting makes the subject somewhat insensitive to the triadic nature of the social situation. In other words, the subject is so concerned about the show he is putting on for the experimenter that influences from other parts of the social field do not receive as much weight as they ordinarily would. This overdetermined orientation to the experimenter would account for the relative insensitivity of the subject to the victim, and would also lead us to believe that alterations in the relationship between subject and experimenter would have important consequences for obedience.

In a series of experiments we varied the physical closeness and degree of surveillance of the experimenter. In one condition the experimenter sat just a few feet away from the subject. In a second condition, after giving initial instructions, the experimenter left the laboratory and gave his orders by telephone; in still a third condition the experimenter was never seen, providing instructions by means of a tape recording activated when the subjects entered the laboratory.

Obedience dropped sharply as the experimenter was physically removed from the laboratory. The number of obedient subjects in the first condition (Experimenter Present) was almost three times as great as in the second, where the experimenter gave his orders by telephone. Twenty-six subjects were fully obedient in the first condition, and only 9 in the second (Chi square obedient vs. defiant in the two conditions, 1 d.f. $= 14.7$; $p < .001$). Subjects seemed able to take a far stronger stand against the experimenter when they did not have to encounter him face to face, and the experimenter's power over the subject was severely curtailed.[10]

Moreover, when the experimenter was absent, subjects

10. The third condition also led to significantly lower obedience than this first situation, in which the experimenter was present, but it contains technical difficulties that require extensive discussion.

displayed an interesting form of behavior that had not occurred under his surveillance. Though continuing with the experiment, several subjects administered lower shocks than were required and never informed the experimenter of their deviation from the correct procedure. (Unknown to the subjects, shock levels were automatically recorded by an Esterline-Angus event recorder wired directly into the shock generator; the instrument provided us with an objective record of the subjects' performance.) Indeed, in telephone conversations some subjects specifically assured the experimenter that they were raising the shock level according to instruction, whereas in fact they were repeatedly using the lowest shock on the board. This form of behavior is particularly interesting: although these subjects acted in a way that clearly undermined the avowed purposes of the experiment, they found it easier to handle the conflict in this manner than to precipitate an open break with authority.

Other conditions were completed in which the experimenter was absent during the first segment of the experiment, but reappeared at the point that the subject definitely refused to give higher shocks when commanded by telephone. Although he had exhausted his power via telephone, the experimenter could frequently force further obedience when he reappeared in the laboratory.

Experiments in this series show that the physical *presence* of an authority is an important force contributing to the subject's obedience or defiance. Taken together with the first experimental series on the proximity of the victim, it would appear that something akin to fields of force, diminishing in effectiveness with increasing psychological distance from their source, have a controlling effect on the subect's performance. As the victim is brought closer, the subject finds it harder to administer shocks to him. When the victim's position is held constant relative to the subject, and the authority is made more remote, the subject finds it easier to break off the experiment. This effect is substantial in both cases, but manipulation of the experimenter's position yielded the more powerful results. Obedience to destructive commands is highly dependent on the proximal relations between authority and subject.

Tensions

The description of final scores does not fully convey the character of the subjects' performance, and it would be useful to interrupt our reporting of quantitative relationships to remark on the subjects' general reaction to the situation.

One might suppose that a subject would simply break off or continue as his conscience and temperament dictated. Yet this is very far from what happened. There were powerful reactions of tension and emotional strain in a substantial proportion of the participants. Persons were observed to sweat, tremble, stutter, bite their lips, and groan as they found themselves increasingly implicated in the experimental conflict. Some sense of the subjects' mood can be gotten from a transcript of their remarks at break-off point. Here are the remarks of two defiant subjects:

> Is he banging? . . . Is he hurt out there? Well, I don't want to be responsible for anything that happens to him. No, I can't go on with it. I don't know whether he's all right or not. I mean he may have a heart condition or something; I wouldn't feel right doing it. He's banging for help. He's evidently in trouble or he wouldn't bang . . . I don't see any sense to this—to knocking him out or something. I just can't see it.
> *(Subject refuses to administer shocks)*
>
> [*Subject 0108*]

> The man is banging. He wants to get out . . . I'm sorry. If the man wants to get out, I'd just as soon stop . . . I don't want to administer any more [extremely excited] . . . I will gladly refund the check, but I will not harm this man . . . I'm sorry, I will not give him any more if he obviously wants to get out. There is no money in the world that will make me hurt another individual. [*Subject 010X*]

And here is a transcript from an obedient subject. He began the experiment calmly, but became increasingly tense as the experiment proceeded. After administering the 150-volt shock, he began to address the experimenter in agitated tones:

> *150 volts delivered.* You want me to keep going?
> *165 volts delivered.* That guy is hollering in there. There's a lot of them here. He's liable to have heart condition. You want me to go?
> *180 volts delivered.* He can't stand it! I'm not going to kill that man in there! You hear him hollering? He's hollering. He can't stand it. What if something happens to him? . . . I'm not going to get that man sick in there. He's hollering in there. You know what I mean? I mean I refuse to take responsibility. He's getting hurt in there. He's in there hollering. Too many left here. Geez, if he

gets them wrong. There's too many of them left. I mean who is going to take responsibility if anything happens to that gentleman?
[*The experimenter accepts responsibility.*]
All right.
195 volts delivered. You see he's hollering. Hear that. Gee, I don't know. [*The experimenter says: "The experiment requires that you go on."*]—I know it does, sir, but I mean—hugh—he don't know what he's in for. He's up to 195 volts.
210 volts delivered.
225 volts delivered.
240 volts delivered. Aw, no. You mean I've got to keep going up with the scale? No sir. I'm not going to kill that man! I'm not going to give him 450 volts! [*The experimenter says: "The experiment requires that you go on."*]—I know it does, but that man is hollering in there, sir . . .

Despite his numerous, agitated objections, which were constant accompaniments to his actions, the subject unfailingly obeyed the experimenter, proceeding to the highest shock level on the generator. He displayed a curious dissociation between word and action. Although at the verbal level he had resolved not to go on, his actions were fully in accord with the experimenter's commands. This subject did not want to shock the victim, and he found it an extremely disagreeable task, but he was unable to invent a response that would free him from *E*'s authority. Many subjects cannot find the specific verbal formula that would enable them to reject the role assigned to them by the experimenter. Perhaps our culture does not provide adequate models for disobedience.

One puzzling sign of tension was the regular occurrence of nervous laughing fits. In the first four conditions 71 of the 160 subjects showed definite signs of nervous laughter and smiling. The laughter seemed entirely out of place, even bizarre. Full-blown, uncontrollable seizures were observed for 15 of these subjects. On one occasion we observed a seizure so violently convulsive that it was necessary to call a halt to the experiment. In the postexperimental interviews subjects took pains to point out that they were not sadistic types and that the laughter did not mean they enjoyed shocking the victim.

In the interview following the experiment subjects were asked to indicate on a fourteen-point scale just how nervous or tense they felt at the point of maximum tension (figure 2).

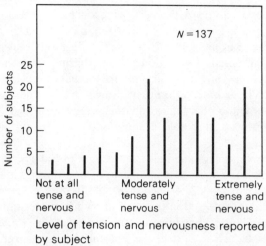

N = 137

Level of tension and nervousness reported by subject

Fig. 2 shows the self-reports on "tension and nervousness" for 137 subjects in the Proximity experiments. Subjects were given a scale with fourteen values ranging from "Not at all tense and nervous" to "Extremely tense and nervous." They were instructed: "Thinking back to that point in the experiment when you felt the most tense and nervous, indicate just how you felt by placing an X at the appropriate point on the scale." The results are shown in terms of mid-point values.

The scale ranged from "Not at all tense and nervous" to "Extremely tense and nervous." Self-reports of this sort are of limited precision, and at best provide only a rough indication of the subject's emotional response. Still, taking the reports for what they are worth, it can be seen that the distribution of responses spans the entire range of the scale, with the majority of subjects concentrated at the center and upper extreme. A further breakdown showed that obedient subjects reported themselves as having been slightly more tense and nervous than the defiant subjects at the point of maximum tension.

How is the occurrence of tension to be interpreted? First, it points to the presence of conflict. If a tendency to comply with authority were the only psychological force operating in the situation, all subjects would have continued to the end and there would have been no tension. Tension, it is assumed, results from the simultaneous presence of two or more incompatible response tendencies.[11] If sympathetic concern for the victim were the exclusive force, all subjects

11. N. E. Miller, "Experimental Studies of Conflict," in J. McV. Hunt, ed., *Personality and the Behavior Disorders* (New York: Ronald Press, 1944).

would have calmly defied the experimenter. Instead, there were both obedient and defiant outcomes, frequently accompanied by extreme tension. A conflict develops between the deeply ingrained disposition not to harm others and the equally compelling tendency to obey others who are in authority. The subject is quickly drawn into a dilemma of a deeply dynamic character, and the presence of high tension points to the considerable strength of each of the antagonistic vectors.

Moreover, tension defines the strength of the aversive state from which the subject is unable to escape through disobedience. When a person is uncomfortable, tense, or stressed, he tries to take some action that will allow him to terminate this unpleasant state. Thus tension may serve as a drive that leads to escape behavior. But in the present situation, even where tension is extreme, many subjects are unable to perform the response that will bring about relief. Therefore there must be a competing drive, tendency, or inhibition that precludes activation of the disobedient response. The strength of this inhibiting factor must be of greater magnitude than the stress experienced, else the terminating act would occur. Every evidence of extreme tension is at the same time an indication of the strength of the forces that keep the subject in the situation.

Finally, tension may be taken as evidence of the reality of the situations for the subjects. Normal subjects do not tremble and sweat unless they are implicated in a deep and genuinely felt predicament.

Background Authority

In psychophysics, animal learning, and other branches of psychology, the fact that measures are obtained at one institution rather than another is irrelevant to the interpretation of the findings, so long as the technical facilities for measurement are adequate and the operations are carried out with competence.

But it cannot be assumed that this holds true for the present study. The effectiveness of the experimenter's commands may depend in an important way on the larger institutional context in which they are issued. The experiments described thus far were conducted at Yale University, an organization which most subjects regarded with respect and sometimes awe. In postexperimental interviews several participants remarked that the locale and sponsorship of the study gave them confidence in the integrity, competence, and benign purposes of the personnel; many indicated that they would not have shocked the learner if the experiments had been done elsewhere.

This issue of background authority seemed to us important for an interpretation of the results that had been obtained thus far; moreover it is highly relevant to any comprehensive theory of human obedience. Consider, for example, how closely our compliance with the imperatives of others is tied to particular institutions and locales in our day-to-day activities. On request, we expose our throats to a man with a razor blade in the barber shop, but would not do so in a shoe store; in the latter setting we willingly follow the clerk's request to stand in our stockinged feet, but resist the command in a bank. In the laboratory of a great university, subjects may comply with a set of commands that would be resisted if given elsewhere. One must always question the relationship of obedience to a person's sense of the context in which he is operating.

To explore the problem we moved our apparatus to an office building in industrial Bridgeport and replicated experimental conditions, without any visible tie to the university.

Bridgeport subjects were invited to the experiment through a mail circular similar to the one used in the Yale study, with appropriate changes in letterhead, etc. As in the earlier study, subjects were paid $4.50 for coming to the laboratory. The same age and occupational distributions used at Yale, and the identical personnel, were employed.

The purpose in relocating in Bridgeport was to assure a complete dissociation from Yale, and in this regard we were fully successful. On the surface, the study appeared to be conducted by Research Associates of Bridgeport, an organization of unknown character (the title had been concocted exclusively for use in this study).

The experiments were conducted in a three-room office suite in a somewhat run-down commercial building located in the downtown shopping area. The laboratory was sparsely furnished, though clean, and marginally respectable in appearance. When subjects inquired about professional affiliations, they were informed only that we were a private firm conducting research for industry.

Some subjects displayed skepticism concerning the motives of the Bridgeport experimenter. One gentleman gave us a written account of the thoughts he experienced at the control board:

Should I quit this damn test? Maybe he passed out? What dopes we were not to check up on this deal. How do we know that these guys are legit? No furniture, bare walls, no telephone. We could of called the Police up or the Better Business Bureau. I learned a lesson tonight. How do I know that Mr. Williams [the experimenter] is telling the truth ... I wish I knew how many volts a person could take before lapsing into unconsciousness.

[*Subject 2412*]

Another subject stated:

I questioned on my arrival my own judgment [about coming]. I had doubts as to the legitimacy of the operation and the consequences of participation. I felt it was a heartless way to conduct memory of learning processes on human beings and certainly dangerous without the presence of a medical doctor.

[*Subject 2440 V*]

There was no noticeable reduction in tension for the Bridgeport subjects. And the subjects' estimation of the amount of pain felt by the victim was slightly, though not significantly, higher than in the Yale study.

A failure to obtain complete obedience in Bridgeport would indicate that the extreme compliance found in New Haven subjects was tied closely to the background authority of Yale University; if a large proportion of the subjects remained fully obedient, very different conclusions would be called for.

As it turned out, the level of obedience in Bridgeport, although somewhat reduced, was not significantly lower than that obtained at Yale. A large proportion of the Bridgeport subjects were fully obedient to the experimenter's commands (48 percent of the Bridgeport subjects delivered the maximum shock vs. 65 percent in the corresponding condition at Yale).

How are these findings to be interpreted? It is possible that if commands of a potentially harmful or destructive sort are to be perceived as legitimate they must occur within some sort of institutional structure. But it is clear from the study that it need not be a particularly reputable or distinguished institution. The Bridgeport experiments were conducted by an unimpressive firm lacking any credentials; the laboratory was set up in a respectable office building with title listed in the building directory. Beyond that, there was no evidence of benevolence or competence. It is possible that the *category* of institution, judged according to its professional function, rather than its qualitative position within that category, wins our compliance. Persons deposit money in elegant, but also in seedy-looking banks, without giving much thought to the differences in security they offer. Similarly, our subjects may consider one laboratory to be as competent as another, so long as it *is* a scientific laboratory.

It would be valuable to study the subjects' performance in other contexts which go even further than the Bridgeport study in denying institutional support to the experimenter. It is possible that, beyond a certain point, obedience disappears completely. But that point had not been reached in the Bridgeport office: almost half the subjects obeyed the experimenter fully.

Further Experiments

We may mention briefly some additional experiments undertaken in the Yale series. A considerable amount of obedience and defiance in everyday life occurs in connection with groups. And we had reason to feel in the light of many group studies already done in psychology that group forces would have a profound effect on reactions to authority. A series of experiments was run to examine these effects. In all cases only one naïve subject was studied per hour, but he performed in the midst of actors who, unknown to him, were employed by the experimenter. In one experiment (Groups for Disobedience) two actors broke off in the middle of the experiment. When this happened 90 percent of the subjects followed suit and defied the experimenter. In another condition the actors followed the orders obediently; this strengthed the experimenter's power only slightly. In still a third experiment the job of pushing the switch to shock the learner was given to one of the actors, while the naïve subject performed a subsidiary act. We wanted to see how the teacher would respond if he were involved in the situation but did not actually give the shocks. In this situation only three subjects out of forty broke off. In a final group experiment the subjects themselves determined the shock level they were going to use. Two actors suggested higher and higher shock levels; some subjects insisted, despite group pressure, that the shock level be kept low; others followed along with the groups.

Further experiments were completed using women as subjects, as well as a set dealing with the effects of dual, unsanctioned, and conflicting authority. A final experiment concerned the personal relationship between victim and subject. These will have to be described elsewhere, lest the present report be extended to monographic length.

It goes without saying that future research can proceed in

many different directions. What kinds of response from the victim are most effective in causing disobedience in the subject? Perhaps passive resistance is more effective than vehement protest. What conditions of entry into an authority system lead to greater or lesser obedience? What is the effect of anonymity and masking on the subject's behavior? What conditions lead to the subject's perception of responsibility for his own actions? Each of these could be a major research topic in itself, and can readily be incorporated into the general experimental procedure described here.

Levels of Obedience and Defiance

One general finding that merits attention is the high level of obedience manifested in the experimental situation. Subjects often expressed deep disapproval of shocking a man in the face of his objections, and others denounced it as senseless and stupid. Yet many subjects complied even while they protested. The proportion of obedient subjects greatly exceeded the expectations of the experimenter and his colleagues. At the outset, we had conjectured that subjects would not, in general, go above the level of "Strong Shock." In practice, many subjects were willing to administer the most extreme shocks available when commanded by the experimenter. For some subjects the experiment provides an occasion for aggressive release. And for others it demonstrates the extent to which obedient dispositions are deeply ingrained, and are engaged irrespective of their consequences for others. Yet this is not the whole story. Somehow, the subject becomes implicated in a situation from which he cannot disengage himself.

The departure of the experimental results from intelligent expectation, to some extent, has been formalized. The procedure was to describe the experimental situation in concrete detail to a group of competent persons, and to ask them to predict the performance of 100 hypothetical subjects. For purposes of indicating the distribution of break-off points judges were provided with a diagram of the shock generator, and recorded their predictions before being informed of the actual results. Judges typically underestimated the amount of obedience demonstrated by subjects.

In figure 3, we compare the predictions of forty psychiatrists at a leading medical school with the actual performance of subjects in the experiment. The psychiatrists predicted that most subjects would not go beyond the tenth shock level (150 volts; at this point the victim makes his first explicit

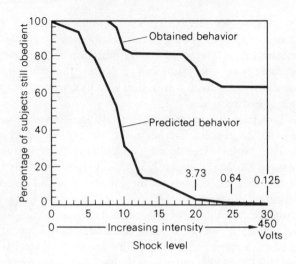

Fig. 3

demand to be freed). They further predicted that by the twentieth shock level (300 volts; the victim refuses to answer) 3.73 percent of the subjects would still be obedient; and that only a little over one-tenth of one per cent of the subjects would administer the highest shock on the board. But, as the graph indicates, the obtained behavior was very different. Sixty-two percent of the subjects obeyed the experimenter's commands fully. Between expectation and occurrence there is a whopping discrepancy.

Why did the psychiatrists underestimate the level of obedience? Possibly, because their predictions were based on an inadequate conception of the determinants of human action, a conception that focuses on motives in vacuo. This orientation may be entirely adequate for the repair of bruised impulses as revealed on the psychiatrist's couch, but as soon as our interest turns to action in larger settings, attention must be paid to the situation in which motives are expressed. A situation exerts an important press on the individual. It exercises constraints and may provide push. In certain circumstances it is not so much the kind of person a man is, as the kind of situation in which he is placed, that determines his actions.

Many people, not knowing much about the experiment, claim that subjects who go to the end of the board are sadistic. Nothing could be more foolish as an overall characterization of these persons. It is like saying that a person thrown into a swift-flowing stream is necessarily a fast swimmer, or that he has great stamina because he moves so rapidly relative to the bank. The context of action must always be considered. The individual, upon entering the laboratory, becomes integrated into a situation that carries its own momentum. The subject's problem then is how to become disengaged from a situation which is moving in an altogether ugly direction.

The fact that disengagement is so difficult testifies to the potency of the forces that keep the subject at the control board. Are these forces to be conceptualized as individual motives and expressed in the language of personality dynamics, or are they to be seen as the effects of social structure and pressures arising from the situational field?

A full understanding of the subject's action will, I feel, require that both perspectives be adopted. The person brings to the laboratory enduring dispositions toward authority and aggression, and at the same time he becomes enmeshed in a social structure that is no less an objective fact of the case. From the standpoint of personality theory one may ask: What mechanisms of personality enable a person to transfer responsibility to authority? What are the motives underlying obedient and disobedient performance? Does orientation to authority lead to a short-circuiting of the shame-guilt system? What cognitive and emotional defenses are brought into play in the case of obedient and defiant subjects?

The present experiments are not, however, directed toward an exploration of the motives engaged when the subject obeys the experimenter's commands. Instead, they examine the situational variables responsible for the elicitation of obedience. Elsewhere, we have attempted to spell out some of the structural properties of the experimental situation that account for high obedience, and this analysis need not be repeated here.[12] The experimental variations themselves represent our attempt to probe that structure, by systematically changing it and noting the consequences for behavior. It is clear that some situations produce greater compliance with the experimenter's commands than others. However, this does not necessarily imply an increase or decrease in the strength of any single definable motive. Situations producing the greatest obedience could do so by triggering the most powerful, yet perhaps the most idiosyncratic, of motives in each subject confronted by the setting. Or they may simply recruit a greater number and variety of motives in their service. But whatever the motives involved—and it is far from

12. Milgram, "Behavioral Study of Obedience."

certain that they can ever be known—action may be studied as a direct function of the situation in which it occurs. This has been the approach of the present study, where we sought to plot behavioral irregularities against manipulated properties of the social field. Ultimately, social psychology would like to have a compelling *theory of situations* which will, first, present a language in terms of which situations can be defined; proceed to a typology of situations; and then point to the manner in which definable properties of situations are transformed into psychological forces in the individual.[13]

Postscript

Almost a thousand adults were individually studied in the obedience research, and there were many specific conclusions regarding the variables that control obedience and disobedience to authority. Some of these have been discussed briefly in the preceding sections, and more detailed reports will be released subsequently.

There are now some other generalizations I should like to make, which do not derive in any strictly logical fashion from the experiments as carried out, but which, I feel, ought to be made. They are formulations of an intuitive sort that have been forced on me by observation of many subjects responding to the pressures of authority. The assertions represent a painful alteration in my own thinking; and since they were acquired only under the repeated inpact of direct observation, I have no illusion that they will be generally accepted by persons who have not had the same experience.

With numbing regularity good people were seen to knuckle under the demands of authority and to perform actions that were callous and severe. Men who are in everyday life responsible and decent were seduced by the trappings of authority, by the control of their perceptions, and by the uncritical acceptance of the experimenter's definition of the situation, into performing harsh acts.

What is the limit of such obedience? At many points we attempted to establish a boundary. Cries from the victim were inserted; not good enough. The victim claimed heart trouble; subjects still shocked him on command. The victim pleaded that he be let free, and his answers no longer registered on the signal box; subjects continued to shock him. At

---

13. My thanks to Professor Howard Leventhal of Yale for strengthening the writing in this paragraph.

the outset we had not conceived that such drastic procedures would be needed to generate disobedience, and each step was added only as the ineffectiveness of the earlier techniques became clear. The final effort to establish a limit was the Touch-Proximity condition. But the very first subject in this condition subdued the victim on command, and proceeded to the highest shock level. A quarter of the subjects in this condition performed similarly.

The results, as seen and felt in the laboratory, are to this author disturbing. They raise the possibility that human nature, or—more specifically—the kind of character produced in American democratic society, cannot be counted on to insulate its citizens from brutality and inhumane treatment at the direction of malevolent authority. A substantial proportion of people do what they are told to do, irrespective of the content of the act and without limitations of conscience, so long as they perceive that the command comes from a legitimate authority. If in this study an anonymous experimenter could successfully command adults to subdue a fifty-year-old man, and force on him painful electric shocks against his protests, one can only wonder what government, with its vastly greater authority and prestige, can command of its subjects. There is, of course, the extremely important question of whether malevolent political institutions could or would arise in American society. The present research contributes nothing to this issue.

In an article entitled "The Dangers of Obedience," Harold J. Laski wrote:

> Civilization means, above all, an unwillingness to inflict unnecessary pain. Within the ambit of that definition, those of us who heedlessly accept the commands of authority cannot yet claim to be civilized men. . . . Our business, if we desire to live a life not utterly devoid of meaning and significance, is to accept nothing which contradicts our basic experience merely because it comes to us from tradition or convention or authority. It may well be that we shall be wrong; but our self-expression is thwarted at the root unless the certainties we are asked to accept coincide with the certainties we experience. That is why the condition of freedom in any state is always a widespread and consistent skepticism of the canons upon which power insists.[14]

14. Harold J. Laski, "The Dangers of Obedience," *Harper's Monthly Magazine* 159 (June 1929): 1–10.

Sources of Power of Lower Participants in Complex Organizations
David Mechanic

It is not unusual for lower participants[1] in complex organizations to assume and wield considerable power and influence not associated with their formally defined positions within these organizations. In sociological terms they have considerable personal power but no authority. Such personal power is often attained, for example, by executive secretaries and accountants in business firms, by attendants in mental hospitals, and even by inmates in prisons. The personal power achieved by these lower participants does not necessarily result from unique personal characteristics, although these may be relevant, but results rather from particular aspects of their location within their organizations.

Informal versus Formal Power

Within organizations the distribution of authority (institutionalized power) is closely if not perfectly correlated with the prestige of positions. Those who have argued for the independence of these variables[2] have taken their examples from diverse organizations and do not deal with situations where power is clearly comparable.[3] Thus when Bierstedt argues that Einstein had prestige but no power, and the policeman power but no prestige, it is apparent that he is comparing categories that are not comparable. Generally persons

Reprinted from *Administrative Science Quarterly* 7, no. 3 (December 1962): 349–64, by permission of the author and the publisher.

1. The term "lower participants" comes from Amitai Etzioni, *A Comparative Analysis of Complex Organizations* (New York, 1961) and is used by him to designate persons in positions of lower rank: employees, rank-and-file, members, clients, customers, and inmates. We shall use the term in this paper in a relative sense denoting position vis-à-vis a higher-ranking participant.

2. Robert Bierstedt, "An Analysis of Social Power," *American Sociological Review* 15 (1950): 730–38.

3. Robert A. Dahl, "The Concept of Power," *Behavioral Science* 2 (1957): 201–15.

occupying high-ranking positions within organizations have more authority than those holding low-ranking positions.

One might ask what characterizes high-ranking positions within organizations. What is most evident, perhaps, is that lower participants recognize the right of higher-ranking participants to exercise power, and yield without difficulty to demands they regard as legitimate. Moreover, persons in high-ranking positions tend to have considerable access and control over information and persons both within and outside the organization, and to instrumentalities or resources. Although higher supervisory personnel may be isolated from the task activities of lower participants, they maintain access to them through formally established intermediary positions and exercise control through intermediary participants. There appears, therefore, to be a clear correlation between the prestige of positions within organizations and the extent to which they offer access to information, persons, and instrumentalities.

Since formal organizations tend to structure lines of access and communication, access should be a clue to institutional prestige. Yet access depends on variables other than those controlled by the formal structure of an organization, and this often makes the informal power structure that develops within organizations somewhat incongruent with the formally intended plan. It is these variables that allow work groups to limit production through norms that contravene the goals of the larger organization, that allow hospital attendants to thwart changes in the structure of a hospital, and that allow prison inmates to exercise some control over prison guards. Organizations, in a sense, are continuously at the mercy of their lower participants, and it is this fact that makes organizational power structure especially interesting to the sociologist and social psychologist.

Clarification of Definitions

The purpose of this paper is to present some hypotheses explaining why lower participants in organizations can often assume and wield considerable power which is not associated with their positions as formally defined within these organizations. For the purposes of this analysis the concepts "influence," "power," and "control" will be used synonymously. Moreover, we shall not be concerned with type of power, that is, whether the power is based on reward, punishment, identification, power to veto, or whatever.[4] Power will be defined as *any force that results in behavior that would not have occurred if the force had not been present.* We have defined power as a force rather than a relationship because it appears that much of what we mean by power is encompassed by the normative framework of an organization, and thus any analysis of power must take into consideration the power of norms as well as persons.

I shall also argue, following Thibaut and Kelley,[5] that power is closely related to dependence. To the extent that a person is dependent on another, he is potentially subject to the other person's power. Within organizations one makes others dependent upon him by controlling access to information, persons, and instrumentalities, which I shall define as follows:

a. Information includes knowledge of the organization, knowledge about persons, knowledge of the norms, procedures, techniques, and so forth.

b. Persons include anyone within the organization or anyone outside the organization upon whom the organization is in some way dependent.

c. Instrumentalities include any aspect of the physical plant of the organization or its resources (equipment, machines, money, and so on).

Power is a function not only of the extent to which a person controls information, persons, and instrumentalities, but also of the importance of the various attributes he controls.[6]

Finally, following Dahl,[7] we shall agree that comparisons of power among persons should, as far as possible, utilize comparable units. Thus we shall strive for clarification by attempting to oversimplify organizational processes; the goal is to set up a number of hypothetical statements of the rela-

---

4. One might observe, for example, that the power of lower participants is based primarily on the ability to "veto" or punish. For a discussion of bases of power, see John R. P. French, Jr., and Bertram Raven, "The Bases of Social Power," in D. Cartwright and A. Zander, eds., *Group Dynamics* (Evanston, Ill., 1960), pp. 607–23.

5. John Thibaut and Harold H. Kelley, *The Social Psychology of Groups* (New York, 1959). For a similar emphasis on dependence see Richard M. Emerson, "Power-Dependence Relationships," *American Sociological Review* 27(1962): 31–41.

6. Although this paper will not attempt to explain how access may be measured, the author feels confident that the hypotheses concerned with access are clearly testable.

7. Dahl, "The Concept of Power."

tionship between variables taken two at a time, "all other factors being assumed to remain constant."

A Classic Example

Like many other aspects of organizational theory, one can find a classic statement of our problem in Weber's discussion of the political bureaucracy. Weber indicated the extent to which bureaucrats may have considerable power over political incumbents, as a result, in part, of their permanence within the political bureaucracy, as contrasted to public officials, who are replaced rather frequently.[8] Weber noted how the low-ranking bureaucrat becomes familiar with the organization—its rules and operations, the work flow, and so on, which gives him considerable power over the new political incumbent, who might have higher rank but is not as familiar with the organization. While Weber does not directly state the point, his analysis suggests that bureaucratic permanence has some relationship to increased access to persons, information, and instrumentalities. To state the hypothesis suggested somewhat more formally:

H1 Other factors remaining constant, organizational power is related to access to persons, information, and instrumentalities.

H2 Other factors remaining constant, as a participant's length of time in an organization increases, he has increased access to persons, information, and instrumentalities.

While these hypotheses are obvious, they do suggest that a careful scrutiny of the organizational literature, especially that dealing with the power or counterpower of lower participants, might lead to further formalized statements, some considerably less obvious than the ones stated. This kind of hypothesis formation is treated later in the paper, but at this point I would like to place the discussion of power within a larger theoretical context and discuss the relevance of role theory to the study of power processes.

Implications of Role Theory for the Study of Power

There are many points of departure for the study of power processes within organizations. An investigator might view influence in terms of its sources and strategies; he might un-

8. Max Weber, "The Essentials of Bureaucratic Organization: An Ideal-Type Construction," in Robert Merton et al., *Reader in Bureaucracy* (Glencoe, Ill., 1952), pp. 18–27.

dertake a study of the flow of influence; he might concentrate on the structure of organizations, seeing to what extent regularities in behavior might be explained through the study of norms, roles, and traditions; and, finally, more psychologically oriented investigators might concentrate on the recipients of influence and the factors affecting susceptibility to influence attempts. Each of these points of departure leads to different theoretical emphases. For our purposes the most important emphasis is that presented by role theorists.

Role theorists approach the question of influence and power in terms of the behavioral regularities which result from established identities within specific social contexts like families, hospitals, and business firms. The underlying premise of most role theorists is that a large proportion of all behavior is brought about through socialization within specific organizations, and much behavior is routine and established through learning the traditional modes of adaptation in dealing with specific tasks. Thus the positions persons occupy in an organization account for much of their behavior. Norms and roles serve as mediating forces in influence processes.

While role theorists have argued much about vocabulary, the basic premises underlying their thought have been rather consistent. The argument is essentially that knowledge of one's identity or social position is a powerful index of the expectations such a person is likely to face in various social situations. Since behavior tends to be highly correlated with expectations, prediction of behavior is therefore possible. The approach of role theorists to the study of behavior within organizations is of particular merit in that it provides a consistent set of concepts which is useful analytically in describing recruitment, socialization, interaction, and personality, as well as the formal structure of organizations. Thus the concept of role is one of the few concepts clearly linking social structure, social process, and social character.

Many problems pertaining to role theory have been raised. At times it is not clear whether role is regarded as a real entity, a theoretical construct, or both. Moreover, Gross has raised the issue of role consensus, that is, the extent to which the expectations impinging upon a position are held in common by persons occupying reciprocal positions to the one in question.[9] Merton has attempted to deal with inevitable

9. Neal Gross, Ward S. Mason, and Alexander W. McEachern, *Explorations in Role Analysis* (New York, 1958).

inconsistencies in expectations of role occupants by introducing the concept of role-set which treats differences in expectations as resulting, in part, from the fact that any position is differently related to a number of reciprocal positions.[10] Furthermore, Goffman has criticized role theory for its failure to deal adequately with commitment to roles[11]—a factor which Etzioni has found to be related intimately to the kind of power exercised in organizations.[12] Perhaps these various criticisms directed at role theory reflect its importance as well as its deficiencies, and despite the difficulties involved in role analysis, the concept of role may prove useful in various ways.

Role theory is useful in emphasizing the extent to which influence and power can be exercised without conflict. This occurs when power is integrated with a legitimate order, when sentiments are held in common, and when there are adequate mechanisms for introducing persons into the system and training them to recognize, accept, and value the legitimacy of control within the organization. By providing the conditions whereby participants within an organization may internalize the norms, these generalized rules, values, and sentiments serve as substitutes for interpersonal influence and make the workings of the organization more agreeable and pleasant for all.

It should be clear that lower participants will be more likely to circumvent higher authority, other factors remaining constant, when the mandates of those in power, if not the authority itself, are regarded as illegitimate. Thus as Etzioni points out, when lower participants become alienated from the organization, coercive power is likely to be required if its formal mandates are to be fulfilled.[13]

Moreover, all organizations must maintain control over lower participants. To the extent that lower participants fail to recognize the legitimacy of power, or believe that sanctions cannot or will not be exercised when violations occur, the organization loses, to some extent, its ability to control their behavior. Moreover, in-so-far as higher participants can create the impression that they can or will exert sanctions above their actual willingness to use such sanctions, control over lower participants will increase. It is usually to the ad-

10. Robert Merton, "The Role-Set: Problems in Sociological Theory," *British Journal of Sociology* 8 (1957): 106–20.

11. Erving Goffman, *Encounters* (Indianapolis, Ind., 1961), pp. 85–152.

12. Etzioni, *A Comparative Analysis.*

13. Ibid.

vantage of an organization to externalize and impersonalize controls, however, and if possible to develop positive sentiments toward its rules.

In other words, an effective organization can control its participants in such a way as to make it hardly perceivable that it exercises the control that it does. It seeks commitment from lower participants, and when commitment is obtained, surveillance can be relaxed. On the other hand, when the power of lower participants in organizations is considered, it often appears to be clearly divorced from the traditions, norms, and goals and sentiments of the organization as a whole. Lower participants do not usually achieve control by using the role structure of the organization, but rather by circumventing, sabotaging, and manipulating it.

Sources of Power of Lower Participants

The most effective way for lower participants to achieve power is to obtain, maintain, and control access to persons, information, and instrumentalities. To the extent that this can be accomplished, lower participants make higher-ranking participants dependent upon them. Thus dependence together with the manipulation of the dependency relationship is the key to the power of lower participants.

A number of examples can be cited which illustrate the preceding point. Scheff, for example, reports on the failure of a state mental hospital to bring about intended reform because of the opposition of hospital attendants.[14] He noted that the power of hospital attendants was largely a result of the dependence of ward physicians on attendants. This dependence resulted from the physician's short tenure, his lack of interest in administration, and the large amount of administrative responsibility he had to assume. An implicit trading agreement developed between physicians and attendants, whereby attendants would take on some of the responsibilities and obligations of the ward physician in return for increased power in decision-making processes concerning patients. Failure of the ward physician to honor his part of the agreement resulted in information being withheld, disobedience, lack of cooperation, and unwillingness of the attendants to serve as a barrier between the physician and a ward full of patients demanding attention and recognition. When the attendant withheld cooperation, the physician had difficulty in making a graceful entrance and departure from the ward, in

14. Thomas J. Scheff, "Control over Policy by Attendants in a Mental Hospital," *Journal of Health and Human Behavior* 2 (1961): 93–105.

handling necessary paper work (officially his responsibility), and in obtaining information needed to deal adequately with daily treatment and behavior problems. When attendants opposed change, they could wield influence by refusing to assume responsibilities officially assigned to the physician.

Similarly, Sykes describes the dependence of prison guards on inmates and the power obtained by inmates over guards.[15] He suggests that although guards could report inmates for disobedience, frequent reports would give prison officials the impression that the guard was unable to command obedience. The guard, therefore, had some stake in ensuring the good behavior of prisoners without use of formal sanctions against them. The result was a trading agreement whereby the guard allowed violations of certain rules in return for cooperative behavior. A similar situation is found in respect to officers in the Armed Services or foremen in industry. To the extent that they require formal sanctions to bring about cooperation, they are usually perceived by their superiors as less valuable to the organization. For a good leader is expected to command obedience, at least, if not commitment.

Factors Affecting Power

Expertise

Increasing specialization and organizational growth has made the expert or staff person important. The expert maintains power because high-ranking persons in the organization are dependent upon him for his special skills and access to certain kinds of information. One possible reason for lawyers obtaining many high governmental offices is that they are likely to have access to rather specialized but highly important means to organizational goals.[16]

We can state these ideas in hypotheses, as follows:

H3   Other factors remaining constant, to the extent that a low-ranking participant has important expert knowledge not available to high-ranking participants, he is likely to have power over them.

Power stemming from expertise, however, is likely to be

15. Gresham M. Sykes, "The Corruption of Authority and Rehabilitation," in A. Etzioni, ed., *Complex Organizations* (New York, 1961), pp. 191–97.

16. As an example, it appears that six members of the cabinet, thirty important subcabinet officials, sixty-three senators, and two hundred thirty congressmen are lawyers (*New Yorker,* 14 April 1962, p. 62). Although one can cite many reasons for lawyers holding political posts, an important one appears to be their legal expertise.

limited unless it is difficult to replace the expert. This leads to two further hypotheses:

H4 Other factors remaining constant, a person difficult to replace will have greater power than a person easily replaceable.

H5 Other factors remaining constant, experts will be more difficult to replace than nonexperts.

While persons having expertise are likely to be fairly high-ranking participants in an organization, the same hypotheses that explain the power of lower participants are relevant in explaining the comparative power positions of intermediate- and high-ranking persons.

The application of our hypothesis about expertise is clearly relevant if we look at certain organizational issues. For example, the merits of medical versus lay hospital administrators are often debated. It should be clear, however, that all other factors remaining unchanged, the medical administrator has clear advantage over the lay administrator. Where lay administrators receive preference, there is an implicit assumption that the lay person is better at administrative duties. This may be empirically valid but is not necessarily so. The special expert knowledge of the medical administrator stems from his ability legitimately to oppose a physician who contests an administrative decision on the basis of medical necessity. Usually hospitals are viewed primarily as universalistic in orientation both by the general public and most of their participants. Thus medical necessity usually takes precedence over management policies, a factor contributing to the poor financial position of most hospitals. The lay administrator is not in a position to contest such claims independently, since he usually lacks the basis for evaluation of the medical problems involved and also lacks official recognition of his competence to make such decisions. If the lay administrator is to evaluate these claims adequately on the basis of professional necessity, he must have a group of medical consultants or a committee of medical men to serve as a buffer between medical staff and the lay administration.

As a result of growing specialization, expertise is increasingly important in organizations. As the complexity of organizational tasks increases, and as organizations grow in size, there is a limit to responsibility that can be efficiently exercised by one person. Delegation of responsibility occurs, experts and specialists are brought in to provide information and research, and the higher participants become dependent

340 Power and Manipulation

upon them. Experts have tremendous potentialities for power by withholding information, providing incorrect information, and so on, and to the extent that experts are dissatisfied, the probability of organizational sabotage increases.

Effort and Interest

The extent to which lower participants may exercise power depends in part on their willingness to exert effort in areas where higher-ranking participants are often reluctant to participate. Effort exerted is directly related to the degree of interest one has in an area.

> H6 Other factors remaining constant, there is a direct relationship between the amount of effort a person is willing to exert in an area and the power he can command.

For example, secretarial staffs in universities often have power to make decisions about the purchase and allocation of supplies, the allocation of their services, the scheduling of classes, and, at times, the disposition of student complaints. Such control may in some instances lead to sanctions against a professor by polite reluctance to furnish supplies, ignoring his preferences for the scheduling of classes, and giving others preference in the allocation of services. While the power to make such decisions may easily be removed from the jurisdiction of the lower participant, it can only be accomplished at a cost—the willingness to allocate time and effort to the decisions dealing with these matters. To the extent that responsibilities are delegated to lower participants, a certain degree of power is likely to accompany the responsibility. Also, should the lower participant see his perceived rights in jeopardy, he may sabotage the system in various ways.

Let us visualize a hypothetical situation where a department concludes that secretarial services are being allocated on a prejudicial basis as a result of complaints to the chairman of the department by several of the younger faculty. Let us also assume that, when the complaint is investigated, it is found to be substantially correct; that is, some of the younger faculty have difficulty obtaining secretarial services because of preferences among the secretarial staff. If in attempting to eliminate discretion by the secretarial staff, the chairman establishes a rule ordering the allocation of services on the basis of the order in which work appears, the rule can easily be made ineffective by complete conformity to it. Deadlines for papers, examinations, and the like will occur, and flexibility in the allocation of services is required if these deadlines are to be met. Thus the need for flexibility can be made to conflict with the rule by a staff usually not untalented in such operations.

When an organization gives discretion to lower participants, it is usually trading the power of discretion for needed flexibility. The cost of constant surveillance is too high, and the effort required too great; it is very often much easier for all concerned to allow the secretary discretion in return for cooperation and not too great an abuse of power.

> *H7*   Other factors remaining constant, the less effort and interest higher-ranking participants are willing to devote to a task, the more likely are lower participants to obtain power relevant to this task.

Attractiveness

Another personal attribute associated with the power of low-ranking persons in an organization is attractiveness or what some call "personality." People who are viewed as attractive are more likely to obtain access to persons, and, once such access is gained, they may be more likely to succeed in promoting a cause. But once again dependence is the key to the power of attractiveness, for whether a person is dependent upon another for a service he provides, or for approval or affection, what is most relevant is the relational bond which is highly valued.

> *H8*   Other factors remaining constant, the more attractive a person, the more likely he is to obtain access to persons and control over these persons.

Location and Position

In any organization the person's location in physical space and position in social space are important factors influencing access to persons, information, and instrumentalities.[17] Propinquity affects the opportunities for interaction, as well as one's position within a communication network. Although these are somewhat separate factors, we shall refer to their combined effect as centrality[18] within the organization.

17. There is considerable data showing the powerful effect of propinquity on communication. For summary, see Thibaut and Kelley, *The Social Psychology of Groups*, pp. 39–42.

18. The concept of centrality is generally used in a more technical sense in the work of Bavelas, Shaw, Gilchrist, and others. For example, Bavelas defines the central region of a structure as the class of all cells with the smallest distance between one cell and any other cell in the structure, with distance measured in link units. Thus the most central position in a pattern is the position closest to all others. Cf. Harold Leavitt, "Some Effects of Certain Communication Patterns on Group Performance," in E. Maccoby, T. N. Newcomb, and E. L. Hartley, eds., *Readings in Social Psychology* (New York, 1958), p. 559.

H9   Other factors remaining constant, the more central a person is in an organization, the greater is his access to persons, information, and instrumentalities.

Some low participants may have great centrality within an organization. An executive's or university president's secretary not only has access, but often controls access in making appointments and scheduling events. Although she may have no great formal authority, she may have considerable power.

Coalitions

It should be clear that the variables we are considering are at different levels of analysis; some of them define attributes of persons, while others define attributes of communication and organization. Power processes within organizations are particularly interesting in that there are many channels of power and ways of achieving it.

In complex organizations different occupational groups attend to different functions, each group often maintaining its own power structure within the organization. Thus hospitals have administrators, medical personnel, nursing personnel, attendants, maintenance personnel, laboratory personnel, and so on. Universities, similarly, have teaching personnel, research personnel, administrative personnel, maintenance personnel, and so on. Each of these functional tasks within organizations often becomes the sphere of a particular group that controls activities relating to the task. While these tasks usually are coordinated at the highest levels of the organization, they often are not coordinated at intermediate and lower levels. It is not unusual, however, for coalitions to form among lower participants in these multiple structures. A secretary may know the man who manages the supply of stores, or the person assigning parking stickers. Such acquaintances may give her the ability to handle informally certain needs that would be more time-consuming and difficult to handle formally. Her ability to provide services informally makes higher-ranking participants in some degree dependent upon her, thereby giving her power, which increases her ability to bargain on issues important to her.

Rules

In organizations with complex power structures lower participants can use their knowledge of the norms of the organization to thwart attempted change. In discussing the various functions of bureaucratic rules, Gouldner maintains that such rules serve as excellent substitutes for surveillance, since surveillance in addition to being expensive in time and effort arouses considerable hostility and antagonism.[19] Moreover, he argues, rules are a functional equivalent for direct, personally given orders, since they specify the obligations of workers to do things in specific ways. Standardized rules, in addition, allow simple screening of violations, facilitate remote control, and to some extent legitimize punishment when the rule is violated. The worker who violates a bureaucratic rule has little recourse to the excuse that he did not know what was expected, as he might claim for a direct order. Finally, Gouldner argues that rules are "the 'chips' to which the company staked the supervisors and which they could use to play the game";[20] that is, rules established a punishment which could be withheld, and this facilitated the supervisors' bargaining power with lower participants.

While Gouldner emphasizes the functional characteristics of rules within an organization, it should be clear that full compliance to all the rules at all times will probably be dysfunctional for the organization. Complete and apathetic compliance may do everything but facilitate achievement of organizational goals. Lower participants who are familiar with an organization and its rules can often find rules to support their contention that they not do what they have been asked to do, and rules are also often a rationalization for inaction on their part. The following of rules becomes especially complex when associations and unions become involved, for there are then two sets of rules to which the participant can appeal.

What is suggested is that rules may be chips for everyone concerned in the game. Rules become the "chips" through which the bargaining process is maintained. Scheff, as noted earlier, observed that attendants in mental hospitals often took on responsibilities assigned legally to the ward physician, and when attendants refused to share these responsibilities the physician's position became extremely difficult.[21]

The ward physician is legally responsible for the care and treatment of each ward patient. This responsibility requires attention to a host of details. Medicine, seclusion, sedation, and transfer orders, for example, require the doctor's signature. Tranquilizers are particularly troublesome in this regard since they require frequent adjustment of dosage in

19. Alvin W. Gouldner, *Patterns of Industrial Bureaucracy* (Glencoe, Ill., 1954).
20. Ibid., p. 173.
21. Scheff, "Control over Policy by Attendants."

order to get the desired effects. The physician's order is required to each change in dosage. With 150 patients under his care on tranquilizers, and several changes of dosages a week desirable, the physician could spend a major portion of his ward time in dealing with this single detail.

Given the time-consuming formal chores of the physician, and his many other duties, he usually worked out an arrangement with the ward personnel, particularly the charge (supervisory attendant), to handle these duties. On several wards, the charge called specific problems to the doctor's attention, and the two of them, in effect, would have a consultation. The charge actually made most of the decisions concerning dosage change in the back wards. Since the doctor delegated portions of his formal responsibilities to the charge, he was dependent on her good will toward him. If she withheld her cooperation, the physician had absolutely no recourse but to do all the work himself.[22]

In a sense such delegation of responsibility involves a consideration of reward and cost, whereby the decision to be made involves a question of what is more valuable—to retain control over an area, or to delegate one's work to lower participants.

There are occasions, of course, when rules are regarded as illegitimate by lower participants, and they may disregard them. Gouldner observed that, in the mine, men felt they could resist authority in a situation involving danger to themselves.[23] They did not feel that they could legitimately be ordered to do anything that would endanger their lives. It is probably significant that in extremely dangerous situations organizations are more likely to rely on commitment to work than on authority. Even within nonvoluntary groups dangerous tasks are regarded usually as requiring task commitment, and it is likely that commitment is a much more powerful organizational force than coercive authority.

Summary

The preceding remarks are general ones, and they are assumed to be in part true of all types of organizations. But power relationships in organizations are likely to be molded by the type of organization being considered, the nature of organizational goals, the ideology of organizational decision making, the kind of commitment participants have to the or-

22. Ibid., p. 97.
23. Gouldner, *Patterns of Industrial Bureaucracy.*

ganization, the formal structure of the organization, and so on. In short, we have attempted to discuss power processes within organizations in a manner somewhat divorced from other major organizational processes. We have emphasized variables affecting control of access to persons, information, and facilities within organizations. Normative definitions, perception of legitimacy, exchange, and coalitions have all been viewed in relation to power processes. Moreover, we have dealt with some attributes of persons related to power: commitment, effort, interest, willingness to use power, skills, attractiveness, and so on. And we have discussed some other variables: time, centrality, complexity of power structure, and replaceability of persons. It appears that these variables help to account in part for power exercised by lower participants in organizations.

Tactics of Lateral
Relationship
George Strauss

This is a study of the tactics used by one functional group in an organization—purchasing—to influence the behavior of other functional departments of relatively equal status. It deals in part with "office politics" and "bureaucratic gamesmanship."

Most studies of human relations in management have dealt with *vertical* relations between superiors and subordinates or between line and staff.[1] Yet the purchasing agent's[2] internal relationships (as opposed to his external relationships with salesmen) are almost entirely *lateral;* they are with other functional departments of about the same rank in the organizational hierarchy—departments such as production scheduling, quality control, engineering, and the like. Most agents receive relatively little attention from their superiors; they must sink or swim on their own, with support being given by higher management only in exceptional cases. They are given broad freedom to define their own roles and are "controlled" chiefly by the client departments with which they deal.

Although purchasing is technically a staff department, its relations with other departments can best be analyzed in terms of work flow rather than according to the typical staff-line concept. At the beginning of the typical work flow the sales department receives an order; on the basis of this the

Reprinted from *Administrative Science Quarterly* 7, no. 2 (September 1962): 161–86, by permission of the author and the publisher.

1. There have been many studies of lateral relations within or among primary work groups, but such studies have been concerned primarily with rank-and-file workers, not management. Three notable studies of horizontal relations within management are: Melville Dalton, *Men Who Manage* (New York, 1959); Elliot R. Chapple and Leonard Sayles, *The Measure of Management* (New York, 1961); and Henry A. Landsberger, "The Horizontal Dimension in a Bureaucracy," *Administrative Science Quarterly* 6 (1961): 298–332.

2. Henceforth, I shall refer to the purchasing agent as the "agent."

engineering department prepares a blueprint; next the production scheduling department initiates a work order for manufacturing and a requisition for purchasing; with this requisition the purchasing department buys the needed parts.

But this process does not always work smoothly. Each department has its specialized point of view which it seeks to impose on others, and each department is struggling for greater authority and status. The purpose of this exploratory study is to illustrate the range of tactics available in the inter-departmental conflict which almost inevitably results.

Research Method

The research methodology included a considerable number of informal contacts with agents, observation of them at work for periods of up to one week, twenty-five formal interviews, a written questionnaire, a review of purchasing journals, and an analysis of how agents, both individually and in groups, handled specially prepared case problems.[3] In the selection of firms to be studied there was a strong bias in favor of those with large engineering staffs, since agents in these firms face the most complex problems.

The discussion which follows will be largely impressionistic and will deal with broad aspects of tactics used by purchasing agents, since their problems vary greatly and various means are used to solve them. It should also be noted that the examples illustrate extreme cases, which, being extreme, illustrate some of the basic dilemmas which most agents face, though often in an attenuated form. This study is primarily concerned with the agent himself, the man who heads the purchasing office. It does not directy concern the buyers and expediters under him or the added complications that occur when divisions or plant agents have a staff relationship with a corporation-wide purchasing office.

Causes of Friction

The agent originally had two primary functions: (1) to nego-

3. I am indebted for assistance to the Buffalo and Northern California Association of Purchasing Agents and to the chairman of their respective Committees for Professional Development, Messrs. Roger Josslyn and M. J. MacMahon. Helpful criticism was provided by Professors Delbert Duncan, F. T. Malm, and Lyman Porter at the University of California, Berkeley; Professor John Gullahorn of Michigan State College; Professor Leonard Sayles at Columbia University; and Dean Arthur Butler and Professor Perry Bliss at the University of Buffalo. Part of the research was done while the author was a research associate at the Institute of Industrial Relations, University of California, Berkeley.

tiate and place orders at the best possible terms—but only in accordance with specifications set by others—and (2) to expedite orders, that is, to check with suppliers to make sure that deliveries are made on time. This arrangement gave the agent broad power in dealing with salesmen but made him little more than an order clerk in terms of power or status within the company.

The ambitious agent feels that placing orders and expediting deliveries are but the bare bones of his responsibilities. He looks upon his most important function as that of keeping management posted about market developments: new materials, new sources of supply, price trends, and so forth. And to make this information more useful, he seeks to be consulted before the requisition is drawn up, while the product is still in the planning stage. He feels that his technical knowledge of the market should be accorded recognition equal to the technical knowledge of the engineer and accountant.

Specifically, the ambitious agent would like to suggest (1) alternative materials or parts to use, (2) changes in specifications or redesign of components which will save money or result in higher quality or quicker delivery, and (3) more economical lot sizes, and to influence (4) "make or buy" decisions. The agent calls these functions "value analysis."

One way of looking at the agent's desire to expand his influence is in terms of interaction. Normally orders flow in one direction only, from engineering through scheduling to purchasing. But the agent is dissatisfied with being at the end of the line and seeks to reverse the flow. Value analysis permits him to initiate for others. Such behavior may, however, result in ill feeling on the part of other departments, particularly engineering and production scheduling.

Conflicts with Engineering

Engineers write up the *specifications* for the products which the agents buy. If the specifications are too tight or, what is worse, if they call for one brand only, agents have little or no freedom to choose among suppliers, thus reducing their social status internally and their economic bargaining power externally. Yet engineers find it much easier to write down a well-known brand name than to draw up a lengthy functional specification which lists all the characteristics of the desired item. Disagreements also arise because, by training and job function, engineers look first for quality and reliability and thus, agents charge, are indifferent to low cost and quick delivery, qualities of primary interest to purchasing.

All these problems are aggravated by the "completion barrier." Usually the agent seeks to change specifications only after the engineer has already committed his plans to blueprints and feels he has completed his work—in fact, he may be starting another project; the agent's interference inevitably threatens the engineer's feeling of accomplishment and completion. In any case, engineers are jealous of their professional status and often resent the efforts of the agent to suggest new techniques or materials. These are areas in which the engineer feels that he is uniquely competent. Finally, agents are particularly anxious to prevent "backdoor selling" which occurs when a salesman bypasses them and seeks to influence someone else in the organization (usually an engineer) to requisition the salesman's product by name or, more subtly, to list specifications which only this product can meet. Backdoor selling threatens the agent's status in two ways: (1) it encourages specification by brand and (2) it makes both salesmen and engineers less dependent on him.

Conflicts with Production Scheduling

The size of the order and the date on which it is to be delivered are typically determined by production scheduling. The agents's chief complaint against scheduling is that delivery is often requested on excessively short notice—that schedulers engage in sloppy planning or cry wolf by claiming they need orders earlier than they really do—and thus force the agent to choose from a limited number of suppliers, to pay premium prices, and to ask favors of salesmen (thus creating obligations which the agent must later repay). Schedulers, on the other hand, claim that "short lead times" are not their fault but the fault of departments farther up the line, such as engineering (which delays its blueprints) or sales (which accepts rush orders). In addition agents claim that schedulers order in uneconomic lot sizes and fail to consider inventory costs or the savings from quantity discounts. In some instances, as we shall see, the purchasing agent seeks to solve these problems through combining production scheduling, inventory control, and purchasing into one "materials handling" department, which he hopes he will head.

Techniques for Dealing with Other Departments

Normally the agent attempts to fill requisitions as instructed. The majority of interdepartmental contacts are handled routinely and without friction in accordance with standard operating procedures. Yet many difficult problems cannot be easily programmed. Other departments are constantly placing pressures on the agent, who must take countermeasures, if only to preserve the status quo. And if the purchasing agent wishes to expand his power aggressively, as many do, he will inevitably run into conflict.

Understandably, then, successful agents have developed an arsenal of techniques for dealing with other departments, particularly when they wish to influence the terms of the requisitions received. Suppose, for example, production scheduling submits a requisition with an unusually short delivery date. The agent might utilize one or more of the following tactics: (These tactics will first be summarized briefly under five general headings and then be discussed in greater detail.)

1. *Rule-oriented tactics*
   a. Appeal to some common authority to direct that the requisition be revised or withdrawn.
   b. Refer to some rule (assuming one exists) which provides for longer lead times.
   c. Require the scheduling department to state in writing why quick delivery is required.
   d. Require the requisitioning department to consent to having its budget charged with the extra cost (such as air freight) required to get quick delivery.

2. *Rule-evading tactics*
   a. Go through the motions of complying with the request but with no expectation of getting delivery on time.
   b. Exceed formal authority and ignore the requisitions altogether.

3. *Personal-political tactics*
   a. Rely on friendships to induce the scheduling department to modify the requisition.
   b. Rely on favors, past and future, to accomplish the same result.
   c. Work through political allies in other departments.

4. *Educational tactics*
   a. Use direct persuasion, that is, try to persuade scheduling that its requisition is unreasonable.
   b. Use what might be called indirect persuasion to help scheduling see the problem from the purchasing department's point of view (in this case it might ask the scheduler to sit in and observe the agent's difficulty in trying to get the vendor to agree to quick delivery).

5. *Organizational-interactional tactics*
   a. Seek to change the interaction pattern, for example,

have the scheduling department check with the purchasing department as to the possibility of getting quick delivery *before* it makes a requisition.

b. Seek to take over other departments, for example, to subordinate scheduling to purchasing in an integrated materials department.

Note that neither the overall categories nor the tactics listed under them are all-exclusive and that there is a great deal of overlapping. They are proposed not as comprehensive tools of analysis, but merely as fairly common examples of bureaucratic gamesmanship.

Each agent interviewed in the study was evaluated in terms of his reported success (in terms of specific accomplishments) in getting other departments to accept a wider role for purchasing. Although this measure was crude and subjective,[4] there seemed to be quite clear differences between the tactics used by those who looked upon their job description as a defensive bastion and those who sought to expand their power beyond it. (Note that success is measured here in terms of expansion of power rather than money saved for the company.)

Rule-oriented Tactics

The tactics listed below are rule-oriented in the sense that the agent's approach is perfectly legitimate under the formal rules of the organization. Agents who emphasize these tactics seem to fit into Melville Dalton's category of "systematizers."

Appealing to the Boss

According to traditional organizational theory, whenever two executives on about the same level cannot agree, they should take the problem to their common superior for solution. Yet, most agents looked upon this as a drastic step, to be taken only when other means failed.

Only five of the agents interviewed mentioned appealing to their superiors as a reasonably common means of dealing with interdepartmental problems. In three cases low status seemed to be largely responsible for their inability to handle problems on their own.

---

4. *Reported* success obviously involves a fair amount of wishful thinking—aspiration rather than accomplishment—but for the general character of this study this limitation was not too serious. It should be emphasized, however, that whether an agent was a successful expansionist depended not only on his own personality and his choice of techniques but also on the institutional characteristics of the organization in which he worked.

Two of these agents were new to the job. For example, one was a man in his early twenties, who had only a few months' experience and who commented that his chief problems were his age and his inability to understand what engineers were talking about. This man met daily to review his problems with his boss and commented that his boss ran interference for him, at least in big problems.

The purchasing agent of a large scientific laboratory was very successful in extending his authority. In dealing with research departments, however, he used the laboratory manager "as a buffer between me and the department heads." But in regard to equipment-maintenance departments, whose heads had much lower status than did the scientists, he commented that "if there were differences, I would discuss them with them. If we didn't agree the laboratory manager would have to arbitrate. But this has never happened here." Significantly, this agent did not have a college degree, while many of the scientists were Ph.Ds.

The other two agents who frequently worked through their superiors came from branch plants of nationwide firms, which placed strong emphasis on individual responsibility to live within rigid rules.

The more expansionist agents rarely relied on their superiors to help them in interdepartmental disputes (in part because they had little success in doing this). They often explained that they would take problems to a man's superior if necessary but that they rarely found it necessary. Many repeated versions of the following:

> We have a policy against engineers having lunch with salesmen. Since the engineer is on my level I couldn't *tell* him to stop it. But in a nice way I could talk to him. If this didn't work, I'd see the plant manager.
> Q: Have you ever done this [appealed to the boss]?
> A: No.

The general feeling, particularly among stronger agents, was that too frequent reference to the superior would weaken their relations both with the superior and with their fellow employees. ("After all you've got to live with them.") To bring in top management too often would, in effect, be an admission that the agent could not handle his own problems. Moreover, there is a myth in many corporations of being "one great big happy family," and, as a consequence, it is difficult to bring conflicts out in the open. Furthermore, since the agent is usually the aggressor, in the sense that he is seeking to expand his power beyond its formal limits, he is unlikely to go to the boss unless his case is unusually good.

On the other hand, the threat of going to the boss loses its effectiveness as a weapon if the threat is *never* carried out. The following quotation summarizes a common position:

> It depends on how much fuss you want to make. If it is really important, you can tell him you will discuss it with his boss. But, I don't want you to get the wrong impression. If you have to resort to this, you are probably falling down on the job. By and large, we have a good relationship with our engineers. However, there are times when you have to take a tough position. You aren't doing your job if you always go along with them in a wishy-washy fashion.

One agent explained how he "educated" engineers to accept substitute products instead of insisting on one brand:

> We prepared our evidence and we were all set to take it to the top—and then, at the last minute, we backed down and told them it was too late in the game. But we indicated that in the future we would take similar issues to the top and they knew we would. So there has been much more understanding. . . . You have to risk making a few enemies once in a while.

Use of Rules

A second traditional bureaucratic means of dealing with other departments is to cite applicable rules or to rely on a formal statement of authority (such as a job description). For instance, an agent may circumvent pressure to place an order with a given company by referring to company rules requiring competitive bidding on all purchases in excess of $10,000. Most agents agreed, in theory, that rules of this sort are useful weapons, but they varied greatly in the extent to which they relied upon them in practice.

Some agents went very much "by the book" day in and day out. In general, these were men without college training, and they worked for larger, rule-oriented companies that were not changing rapidly. In answer to questions, these men often said, "This matter is governed by corporate policy," or made references to manuals and procedures. They also had a tendency to draw the lines of responsibility quite tightly, so that there were few areas of joint decision making; for example, "Engineering has the final word as far as specs are concerned. But we decide from whom to buy, provided they meet the specs." On the other hand, many agents operated very effectively without any formal written statement of their authority; their authority was understood by everybody in the organization and there was no need to put it in writing.

The evidence suggests that the most successful expansionists preferred to operate informally until there was a showdown with another department. When this happened, they were very glad to refer to rules to bolster their position. Thus, paradoxically, we found strong agents who worked hard to introduce purchasing manuals and then paid relatively no attention to them in daily practice. In effect these agents take the position of "speak softly and carry a big stick." Indeed, the use of rules involves an implicit threat to appeal to higher management if the rules are not obeyed. ("When everyone in the organization knows what your responsibility is—and that you are backed up—then there is no need to mention it constantly.")

If flexibly used, procedure manuals provide the agent with an added bargaining weapon in dealing with other departments. Even though he may permit rules in the manual to be ignored most of the time, he can always do this as a favor in return for which he may ask favors. And the rules put a legal stamp on his efforts whenever he decides to ensnarl another department in a mass of red tape. But the expansionist agent must be careful not to become too rule-oriented. After all, his goal is to expand his influence beyond the areas over which the rules give him definite authority—not to retreat behind them.

Requiring Written Acceptance of Responsibility

Another bureaucratic technique used by many agents is to require others to justify their decisions in writing. For example, if a production scheduler orders a part for delivery with very short lead time, the agent can ask him to explain in writing why there is such a rush. He hopes the scheduler will be embarrassed unless he had a good excuse—and in any case, the effort will make him reluctant to make such last-minute requests in the future. Certainly this helps expose the scheduler who constantly cries wolf.

Agents may ask for written explanations to clear themselves. Just as often, however, this is done to make others hesitate or to have evidence against them later. In insisting that such reports be written, the purchasing agent can refer to company rules or to possible audits. Thus in asking for such a statement, agents often say, "I need it to document my records."

Again, it is the weaker, noncollege agent who makes the most persistent use of such tactics. Many seem to feel that an approach of this sort is cowardly and defeatist. As one put it, "If you are trying to get a man to say 'yes,' I don't see any value in forcing him to put his 'no' in writing. Then he will never move." And another said, "I suppose you do punish an engineer by forcing him to give you a long written explanation, but that's hardly the way to win friends or advance your point of view." Furthermore, "You can always ask an engineer to give you a formal test result, but, if he wishes, he can always make the test fail."

Financial Charges

Cost-accounting procedures may also be used as a lever. A number of agents made comments like this:

> Whenever I get a request for a rush delivery, I ask the department which wants it whether they are willing to authorize overtime[5] or air freight. Since this gets charged against their budget, they usually hesitate a bit. If they go along I know they really need it. And if they have too many extra charges the auditor starts asking questions.

This tactic resembles the one previously discussed, particularly when the agent enters a statement into his records that the product would have been cheaper had the requisition been received on time. (Some companies charge inbound freight to the budget of the purchasing or traffic department; in such cases purchasing's leverage is somewhat less effective.)

Some companies have what is often called efficiency (or profit) improvement plan. According to such a plan each department (and sometimes each executive) receives credit[6] for the cost savings which can be attributed to the department's activities. Agents in two companies reported that engineers showed little enthusiasm for value analysis because the purchasing department got all the credit, even though part of the work was done by the engineering department. The situation greatly improved in one of these companies

---

5. That is, the vendor is authorized to make an extra charge for having his men work overtime.

6. Though there is no direct payoff, performance under the plan is often taken into account in determining bonuses or promotions.

when "primary" credit was transferred to engineering, with purchasing retaining "participating" credit.

Rule-evading Tactics

Literal Compliance

In dealing with pressures from other departments the agent can always adopt a policy of passive resistance—that is, he can go through the motions in hopes of satisfying the demands. This tactic of feigned acceptance[7] is often used with production scheduling. For instance, after completing a lengthy phone call in which he half-heartedly tried to persuade a vendor to make a very quick delivery, an agent commented, "My buyer tried already and I knew that they just weren't going to be able to deliver that soon. Still production scheduling was screaming and they threatened to go to the plant manager. So I tried to handle it in such a way as not to hurt my relations with the vendor. They knew why I had to call."

This game of passive resistance can be skillfully played in such a way as to set a trap for the other department.

Example. One agent told how he dealt with an engineer who had placed a requisition for one company's products after having been lavishly entertained by its salesman. The agent wrote a long memo explaining why he felt this to be a poor choice and presented it to the engineer in a fashion which he knew the engineer would reject. The agent then placed the order. As he had predicted, the products arrived late and were totally inappropriate. The subsequent investigation led both to this engineer's transfer and demotion and to other engineers having greater respect for the agent's advice.[8]

It should be noted, however, that these tactics were reported by only a minority of agents. In almost every case the agent was "weak" (in terms of expansionism) or worked in large companies where there was considerable emphasis on following formal rule books. Instead of passively seeming to accept unreasonable requests, the stronger agents actively oppose them.

Exceeding Authority

Occasionally agents may revise the terms of requisitions on their own initiative, even though they have no formal authority to do so. For instance, an agent may extend a lead time if

---

7. Dalton, *Men Who Manage*, p. 232.
8. A tactic like this can always backfire. The agent himself may be blamed for the failure.

he knows the production scheduler has set the delivery date much earlier than is really required. Where a requisition calls for a given brand, he may purchase a substitute which he feels sure is an equivalent. Or, he may buy a larger quantity than requested in order to take advantage of quantity discounts.

When an agent revises requisitions in this manner, he may or may not tell the requisitioning department what he is doing. In either case he is exceeding his formal authority. In effect, he is daring the requisitioning department to make an issue of it. This requires considerable courage. No sensible agent will expose himself in this way unless (1) his overall political position is secure and (2) he feels the terms of the original requisition were clearly so unreasonable that the requisitioning department will hesitate to raise the issue and expose its mistake.

Most agents were reluctant to use this tactic. Even if they could safely change orders in a given case, continual flouting of the requisitioning department's desires would create too much antagonism in the long run.

Personal-Political Tactics

Friendships and exchange of favors are used in almost every organization to get things done and to grease the wheels of formal bureaucracy. The agent is no exception to this rule; yet the author found to his surprise that informal relations played a less important role than he had expected. Agents, on the whole, seemed oriented to doing things "through channels."

None of the tactics which follow are contemplated by the company's formal scheme; all involve the use of personal relations. It would seem that Dalton's "adapters" would make greatest use of these tactics.

Friendships

Most agents prefer to deal with friends. Friendships help reduce the kinds of tensions to which agents are commonly subject. Even where friendship is not involved, it is easier to deal with people when you know their idiosyncrasies and special interests. Not surprisingly, comments like this were common: "[In handling problems] friendships count a lot. Many of the people here started when I did, twenty-five years ago. We are all at about the same level and most of them are pretty good friends of mine. A lot is a matter of trust and confidence."

Agents seem to rely on friendship contacts as a means of

communication and of getting quick acceptances of proposals that could be justified or their merits in any case. Rarely do agents rely on friendship alone. As one put it, "You can accomplish some things on the basis of friendship, but you can't do too much or you will strain your friendship."

Exchange of Favors

To some extent agents operate on the principle of "reward your friends, punish your enemies" and are involved in a network of exchange of favors—and sometimes even reprisals. Favors of various sorts may be given. Most agents are under pressure to make personal purchases, for examples, to help someone in management buy a set of tires at wholesale rates. Since there are usually no formal rules as to such extracurricular purchasing, the agent has a strong incentive to help those who help him most. Similarly an agent is in a position to suggest to a salesman that it might be strategic to take a "cooperative" engineer to lunch. And there are always people in management who would like him to do a favor for a friend or relative who is a salesman or who owns a small business.

Other favors are more work-related. An agent may expedite delivery for a production scheduler who normally gives plenty of lead time for his orders but who now has a real emergency on his hands. Or he may rush parts for an engineer who is building a prototype model. "If a man is reasonable with me," one agent commented, "I'll kill myself to get him what he wants." The agent is less likely to exert himself for the man who has been uncooperative in the past. Yet, in general, agents seem to play down the exchange of favors, perhaps because they have relatively few favors to offer, other than trival ones such as personal purchases or lunches provided by salesmen.[9]

The use of reprisals can be seen most clearly in dealing with salesmen. As one agent put it, "I play ball with those who play ball with me. If a salesman operates behind my back, he's going to have a hell of a time getting me to give him an order." Reprisals are more risky in dealing with management.

Example. One assistant agent, for example, told how he "delayed" getting catalogues for "uncooperative" engineers

---

9. Reciprocity in the broader sense, as suggested by Gouldner and others, is, of course, inherent in the entire framework of relations discussed here. Cf. Alvin W. Gouldner, "The Norm of Reciprocity: A Preliminary Statement," *American Sociological Review* 25 (1960): 161–77.

and gave "slow service" to engineers who habitually cried wolf. But, both this man's supervisor and his personnel director expressed concern over his poor human relations and his tendency to antagonize others.

The typical agent, however, seemed to feel that if he used such techniques he ran the risk of permanently impairing his relations with others. Furthermore, these techniques might always backfire; for example, if production were delayed because components were delivered late, he would be blamed.

Interdepartmental Politics

In addition to their personal relations with people, agents inevitably get involved in interdepartmental power struggles. Indeed, as the following quotation suggests, the agent is often a man in the middle, subject to conflicting pressures from all sides:

> Production scheduling wants quick delivery, engineering wants quality, manufacturing wants something easy-to-make, accounting wants to save money, quality control has their own interests. And then you've got to deal with the supplier—and present the supplier's position back to your own organization (sometimes you think you are wearing two hats, you represent both the supplier and the company). Everybody has his own point of view and only the agent sees the overall picture.

Much of the agent's time is spent seeking informal resolution of such problems[10]—and in these meetings he often acts as a mediator. The following is a common situation:

Example. Production scheduling has been pushing hard to get early delivery of a particular component (perhaps because the sales department has been pressing for increased production). In response to this pressure the vendor puts new, inexperienced men on the job. But when the components are delivered, quality control declares the work is sloppy, rejects it in toto, and wants to disqualify the vendor from doing further work for the company. Production scheduling and the vendor are naturally upset; the vendor insists that the defects are trivial and can be easily remedied; and purchasing is placed in the difficult position of trying to mediate the issue.

---

10. Dalton (*Men Who Manage*, pp. 227–28) points out the function of meetings in short-circuiting formal means of handling problems.

If the agent is not careful in situations like this, he may become a scapegoat; everyone may turn on him and blame him for the unhappy turn of events. On the other hand, the successful agent is able to play one pressure off against another and free himself—or he may enlist the support of a powerful department to back him. If he is shrewd, he can get both sides to appeal to him to make the final decision and thus gain prestige as well as bestow favors which he may later ask returned.

Like it or not, agents of necessity engage in power politics. In doing this, they necessarily develop allies and opponents. Each department presents a special problem.

1. *Engineering.* Unless the relationship with engineering is handled with great tact, enginerring tends to become an opponent, since value analysis invades an area which engineers feel is exclusively their own. Purchasing is at a disadvantage here. Engineers have the prestige of being college-trained experts, and engineering is much more strongly represented than purchasing in the ranks of higher management.

2. *Manufacturing.* There is often a tug of war between purchasing and manufacturing over who should have the greatest influence with production scheduling. These struggles are particularly sharp where purchasing is trying to absorb either inventory control or all of production scheduling.

3. *Comptroller.* The comptroller is rarely involved in the day-to-day struggles over specifications or delivery dates. But when purchasing seeks to introduce an organizational change which will increase its power—for example, absorbing inventory control—then the comptroller can be a most effective ally. But the agent must present evidence that the proposed innovation will save money.

4. *Sales.* Sales normally has great political power, and purchasing is anxious to maintain good relations with it. Sales is interested above all in being able to make fast delivery and shows less concern with cost, quality, or manufacturing ease. In general, it supports or opposes purchasing in accordance with these criteria. But sales is also interested in reciprocity—in persuading purchasing "to buy from those firms which buy from us."

5. *Production scheduling.* Relations with production scheduling are often complex. Purchasing normally has closer relations with production scheduling than any other department, and conflicts are quite common. Yet these departments are jointly responsible for having parts available when

needed and, in several companies at least, they presented a common front to the outside world. Unfortunately, however, production scheduling has little political influence, particularly when it reports relatively low down in the administrative hierarchy.

The shrewd agent knows how to use departmental interests for his own ends. Two quotations illustrate this:

> Engineering says we can't use these parts. But I've asked manufacturing to test a sample under actual operating conditions—they are easy to use. Even if engineering won't accept manufacturing data, I can go to the boss with manufacturing backing me. On something like this, manufacturing is tremendously powerful.

> [To get acceptance of new products] I may use methods and standards. Or I might go to engineering first and then to methods and standards if engineering shows no interest. If I go to methods and standards I got to emphasize the cost-saving aspect [as contrasted to engineering's interest in quality].

Educational Tactics

Next we come to a set of tactics designed to persuade others to think in purchasing terms.

Direct Persuasion

Direct persuasion—the frank attempt to sell a point of view—is, of course, the agent's typical means of influencing others. Successful persuasion means "knowing your products backwards and forwards . . . building your case so that it can't be answered . . . knowing what you are talking about."

Most agents feel it essential that they have complete command of the facts, particularly if they are to bridge the status gap and meet engineers on equal terms. As one of them said, "The engineer thinks he is the expert; the only way you can impress him is to know more than he does." Thus many agents go to considerable lengths to acquire expertise; they spend a great deal of time learning production processes or reading technical journals.

Yet some of the stronger agents pointed out that too much expertise can be dangerous, that it threatens the other man's status. "Never put a man in a corner. Never prove that he is wrong. This is a fundamental in value analysis. It doesn't pay to be a know-it-all." Thus some agents look upon themselves primarily as catalysts who try to educate others to think in purchasing terms:

> Actually it is an asset not to be an engineer. Not having the [engineering] ability myself, I've had to work backwards. I can't tell them what to do but I can ask questions. They know that I'm not trying to design their instrument. . . . You have to give the engineer recognition. The less formal you are in dealing with them the better. It doesn't get their dander up.

Indirect Persuasion

Recognizing the danger of the frontal approach, agents often try forms of indirection—manipulation, if you like—which are designed to induce the other departments to arrive at conclusions similar to those of the agent but seemingly on their own. For example:

> We were paying $45.50 a unit, but I found a vendor who was producing a unit for $30 which I felt would meet our needs just as well. There was a lot of reluctance in engineering to accept it, but I knew the engineer in charge of the test was susceptible to flattery. So I wrote a letter for general distribution telling what a good job of investigating he was doing and how much money we'd save if his investigation was successful. . . . That gave him the motivation to figure out how it *could* work rather than how it *could not* work.

Indirect persuasion often involves presenting the facts and then letting the other person draw his own conclusions. The agent may ask the engineer to run a test on a product or even simply attach a sample of the product to an interoffice buck slip, asking, "Can we use this?" Similarly, choosing which salesmen may see engineers, he can indirectly influence the specification process. (In fact, once an agent decides that a product should be introduced, he and the salesman will often coordinate their strategies closely in order to get it accepted by others in management.)

Most agents feel engineers should have no part in negotiating prices; they feel this would be encroaching on purchasing's jurisdiction. But one successful agent encourages engineers to help out in the bargaining because "that's the best way I know to make these engineers cost conscious." Another arranges to have foremen and production schedulers sit in while he negotiates delivery dates with salesmen. "In that way they will know what I'm up against when they give me lead times which are too short for normal delivery."

Organizational-Interactional Techniques

Organizational factors play an important part in determining (1) whether the agent's relations with other departments will be formal or informal (for example, whether most contacts will be face-to-face, by phone, or in writing), (2) whether it will be easy or hard for other departments to initiate for purchasing, and (3) whether purchasing can make its point of view felt while decisions are being considered—or can intervene only after other departments have already taken a position. All these involve interaction patterns. We shall consider here only two types of organizational changes: informal measures which make it easier for other departments to initiate change in the usual flow of orders and formal changes involving grants of additional authority.

Inducing Others to Initiate Action

In most of the examples discussed here, the agent seeks to initiate change in the behavior of other departments. He is the one who is trying to change the engineer's specifications, the production scheduler's delivery schedules, and so forth. The other departments are always at the receiving (or resisting) end of these initiations. As might be expected, hard feelings are likely to develop if the initiations move only one way.[11]

Recognizing this, many of the stronger agents seem to be trying to rearrange their relations with other departments so that others might initiate changes in the usual work flow more often for them. Specifically they hope to induce the other departments to turn instinctively to purchasing for help whenever they have a problem—and at the earliest possible stage. Thus one agent explained that his chief reason for attending production planning meetings, where new products were laid out, was to make it easier for others to ask him questions. He hoped to encourage engineers, for example, to inquire about available components before they drew up their blueprints. Another agent commented, "I try to get

11. Actually, of course, initiations do occur in both directions. The production schedulers initiate for the agent when they file requisitions and the engineers initiate when they determine specifications. This normal form of programmed, routine initiation is felt to be quite different from the agent's abnormal attempts to introduce innovation. This distinction is quite important.

production scheduling to ask us what the lead times for the various products are. That's a lot easier than our telling them that their lead times are unreasonable after they have made commitments based on these."

Some purchasing departments send out what are, in effect, ambassadors to other departments. They may appoint purchase engineers, men with engineering background (perhaps from the company's own engineering group) who report administratively to purchasing but spend most of their time in the engineering department. Their job is to be instantly available to provide information to engineers whenever they need help in choosing components. They assist in writing specifications (thus making them more realistic and readable) and help expedite delivery of laboratory supplies and material for prototype models. Through making themselves useful, purchase engineers acquire influence and are able to introduce the purchasing point of view before the "completion barrier" makes this difficult. Similar approaches may be used for quality control.

Work assignments with purchasing are normally arranged so that each buyer can become an expert on one group of commodities bought. Under this arrangement the buyer deals with a relatively small number of salesmen, but with a relatively large number of "client" departments within the organization. A few agents have experimented with assigning men on the basis of the departments with which they work rather than on the basis of the products they buy. In one case work assignments in both purchasing and scheduling were so rearranged that each production scheduler had an exact counterpart in purchasing and dealt only with him. In this way closer personal relations developed than would have occurred if the scheduler had no specific individual in purchasing to contact.

Even the physical location of the agent's office makes a difference. It is much easier for the agent to have informal daily contacts with other departments if his office is conveniently located. Some companies place their agents away from the main office, to make it easier for salesmen to see them. Although this facilitates the agents' external communications, it makes their internal communications more difficult. Of course, those companies that have centralized purchasing offices and a widespread network of plants experience this problem in an exaggerated form. Centralized purchasing offers many economic advantages, but the agent must tour the plants if he is not to lose all contact with his client departments.

Value analysis techniques sharply highlight the agent's organizational philosophy. Some agents feel that value analysis should be handled as part of the buyer's everyday activities. If he comes across a new product which might be profitably substituted for one currently used, he should initiate engineering feasibility studies and promote the idea ("nag it" in one agent's words) until it is accepted. Presumably purchasing then gets the credit for the savings, but resistance from other departments may be high. Other agents, particularly those with college training, reject this approach as unnecessarily divisive; they prefer to operate through committees, usually consisting of engineers, purchasing men, and production men. Though committees are time-consuming, communications are facilitated, more people are involved, more ideas are forthcoming—and, in addition, the purchasing department no longer has the sole responsibility for value analysis.

To the extent that he allows others to take the initiative, the agent himself must take a passive role. Not all agents are emotionally prepared to do this.[12] Some feel that it smacks too much of the "order clerk." A number commented, in effect, "I don't want to be everyone's doormat." Many asked questions like, "How far do you go in cost estimating, in getting quotes for hypothetical orders? . . . What do you do if a man throws a label at you and says get me some of this? After all, our time is limited."

Formal Organizational Change

The final approach is for the agent to seek to expand the formal grant of authority given his department (which might mean a larger budget, too), as, for example, to place other functions such as traffic, stores, or even inventory control and production scheduling in one combined materials department. Agents who exert their energies in this direction generally reject the "human relations" or "participative" approach to management. They like to resolve problems through memoranda ("it helps keep emotions down") and are not particularly optimistic about the possibilities of converting other departments to think in purchasing terms ("after all every department has its own point of view—that's natural"). They spend considerable time developing statistical means of

12. After all, a certain type of active, initiating sort of personality is required if the agent is to bargain successfully with suppliers; it is hard for the same individual to adopt a passive role within the organization.

measuring their own efficiency and that of their subordinates, and they are more likely to be in companies that have similar philosophies. For example, one agent explained why value analysis in his organization was concentrated in the purchasing department, "[Our company] doesn't believe in joint assignments or committees. If a man isn't competent to do the job himself, then we find another man. We don't want weak sisters." And another argued, "The responsibility must be concentrated in one department or another. It can't fall between two stools."[13]

Choice of Techniques

The foregoing list of tactics are presented not as a formal typology but merely to illustrate the *range* of techniques available to the agent. Most agents use all of these techniques at one time or another, depending on the problem. A different technique might well be used in introducing a major policy change than in handling routine orders. In trying to push through changes, one agent observed:

> You have to choose your weapons. I vary them on purpose. . . . I ask myself, who has the final decision? How does the chief engineer operate? What does he delegate? What does he keep for himself? It all involves psychological warfare. Who are the people to be sold? Who will have the final say?

And even in dealing with one problem, a mixture of tactics will generally be used. Nevertheless, the overall strategies used by various agents seem to vary greatly in terms of which tactics receive the greatest emphasis.

1. Some agents seek formal grants of power (for example, to get inventory placed under purchasing); others merely seek influence (for example, to persuade inventory control to order in more economic lot sizes).

2. Some agents want to influence decisions *before* they are made (for example, through encouraging engineers to turn instinctively to purchasing for help whenever they are even considering the use of a new component); others *after* (for example, through having their decisions upheld often enough for engineering to hesitate to make an issue of a request whenever purchasing questions a specification).

3. Some agents think in terms of their long-run position

13. Yet it could be argued that the committee system does not itself divide responsibility; it merely recognizes the fact that responsibility for value analysis is of necessity divided among departments.

and thus seek to improve procedures; whereas others are interested chiefly in exerting their influence in each conflict as it comes along.

We have already noted a difference between successful expansionists and those content with their roles as they are. On the whole, expansionists seemed to be more likely to choose informal tactics such as indirect persuasion, inducing others to make changes in the work flow, and interdepartmental politics. They had long-run strategies and sought to influence decisions before they were made. Those who were successful in achieving more formal power were also well aware of the value of informal influence; those who merely *talked* about formal power seemed to be relatively unsuccessful in any area. In fact, one of the most noticeable characteristics of successful expansionists was their flexibility. Most were equally adept at using both formal and informal tactics and were not averse to turning the formal organization against itself.

Differences in success in expansionism seem to be due to a number of factors:

1. *Technology*. Obviously the agent cannot build up much of an empire in a service industry or one in which only raw materials are bought. He has his greatest chance for power in companies which make goods to order and in which there is a great deal of subcontracting.

2. *Management philosophy*. Where lines of authority are sharply drawn, the agent has little chance to extend his influence—except through direct seizure of another department's power, which is not easy. Note the comments of one agent in a highly rule-oriented company.

> We are a service department. . . . We must see that parts are here at the proper time. . . . I usually let engineering pretty much make its own decisions. I may try to persuade an engineer to accept a new product. But if he says "no," all I can do is wait till he gets transferred and try to persuade his successor.

Of the agents interviewed, the most successful was one in a company which had just introduced a new management and in which all relationships were in flux.

3. *Education*. Purchasing agents who were college graduates seemed to be more expansionist than those who were not. This may be due to their higher level of aspiration. Moreover, any company that appoints a college graduate may well expect to grant him greater influence. The college-

trained man may feel more the equal of the engineer and therefore be more willing to come into conflict with him.

Furthermore, the more educated men (and particularly those with a business-school background) seemed more prone to rely on techniques that were informal and not rule-oriented. Specifically, they were less likely to rely on formal statements of authority, to require others to take formal responsibilities for decisions, or to insist that an agent should "yell loudly whenever his rights are violated"; and they were more willing to work through committees.[14]

Conclusion

Traditional organization theory emphasizes authority and responsibility; it deals largely with two types of relationships: (1) those between superiors and subordinates, which it conceives as being primarily authoritarian (though perhaps modifiable by participation, general supervision, and the like) and (2) those of staff and line, which are nonauthoritarian. Though the purchasing department is traditionally classified as a staff department, my own feeling is that the staff-line dichotomy in this case (as perhaps for most other purposes) tends to obscure more problems than it illuminates. As we have seen, the purchasing department's relations with other departments cannot be explained by any one simple phrase, such as "areas of responsibility," "exchange of favors," "advice," "control," or the like. Instead the skillful agent blends all these approaches and makes use of authoritarian and persuasive tactics as the situation requires. His effectiveness is largely dependent on the political power he is able to develop.

Recent authors have suggested that the study of organization should begin first with "the work to be done and resources and techniques available to do it."[15] The emphasis is on the technology of the job ("technology" being defined

14. These conclusions are consistent with the findings of the questionnaire sample ($N = 142$). The results are in the direction indicated for both degree of education and business-school background (each taken separately) although only three out of eight relationships are significant at the .05 level. The questionnaire data are somewhat suspect, however, since the values which agents report are not always consistent with their observed behavior: in answering questionnaires many agents seem to place greater emphasis on formal techniques than they do in practice.

15. Wilfred Brown, *Explorations in Management* (London, 1960), p. 18. See Chapple and Sayles, *The Measure of Management;* William F. Whyte, *Men at Work* (Homewood, Ill., 1961).

broadly to include marketing problems and the like as well as external environment) and the relationships between people which this technology demands. "Organizations should be constructed from the *bottom up,* rather than from the *top down.* In establishing work-group boundaries and supervisory units, management should start with the actual work to be performed, an awareness of who must co-ordinate his job with whom, when, and where."[16]

Some of us who are interested in this area are groping toward a concept of *work flow,* meaning the communications or interactions required by the job and including the flow of raw materials and products on the assembly line, the flow of paper work when a requisition moves through engineering, scheduling, and purchasing, as well as the flow of instruction, which may move down the chain of command from president to janitor.

This has been an exploratory study of the interrelationship between power struggles and lateral work flow. Of particular interest in this study, are (1) the agent's strong desire for increased status, which upsets the stability of his relationship with other departments, (2) his attempts to raise his status through influencing the terms of the requisitions he receives and thus make interactions flow both ways, (3) the relatively limited interference on the part of higher management, which makes the lateral relationship especially important for the agent, (4) the "completion barrier," which requires the agent to contact an engineer before a blueprint is finished if the agent is to be successful in influencing the terms of the requisition, and (5) the differing vested interests or terms of reference of the various departments, which make agreement more difficult.

Finer mapping and more intensive research into interdepartmental relations is required; interactions should be precisely counted[17] and work should be done with specialties other than purchasing.

16. George Strauss and Leonard R. Sayles, *Personnel: The Human Problems of Management* (Englewood Cliffs, N.J., 1960), p. 392. The sentence is Sayle's.

17. Albert H. Rubenstein of Northwestern University has completed an unpublished quantitative study of communications within a purchasing department.

7

Leadership and Influence: Persuasion and Collaboration

Introduction

This chapter is about leadership. But it is about leadership which makes primary use of persuasion and collaboration to influence others, rather than formal authority or power tactics.

Leadership that relies on persuasion and collaboration has one big disadvantage. It takes longer. By contrast, the use of formal authority or power typically works much faster at getting other people to do what is wanted of them. But the continued use of power and authority often runs into two serious drawbacks. First, pressuring or ordering people to do what you want them to do (however subtly) is likely to result at best in only overt compliance, but not in internal commitment. Second, exclusive use of power and authority uses up the leader's inventory of good will, eventually leaving discontent and alienation in its wake. The papers in this chapter implicitly or explicitly argue for persuasive and collaborative styles of leadership for long-run success.

The first paper, by Bavelas, treats the concept of leadership rather abstractly. In doing so he lays the foundation for the other three papers. Bavelas's main point is that the qualities of a good leader are dependent in part on personality traits inherent in the man himself and in part on institutional factors. A particular man who is a good leader in one situation may be an ineffective leader in another. Some situations call for an extreme of aggressiveness; but in other cases, the best leadership strategy stresses compromise and accommodation.

The second paper, by the clinical and humanistic psychologist, Carl Rogers, argues that many of the attributes which make for a constructive relationship between therapist and client are also applicable to the relationship between teacher and student, boss and subordinate, or parent and child. Typically, Rogers argues, such relationships become *destruc-*

tive when they become *evaluative,* that is, when one person is in the unilateral position of judging the other, whether for good or ill. In this, his central theme is much like that already voiced in the paper by Jack Gibb in chapter 5. Rogers argues that one almost guaranteed way to make a person feel defensive is by appearing to treat him as an *object.* In this sense his analysis is much like that of Erich Fromm who characterized bureaucracy as being "objective," that is, dealing with persons as objects.

Like the paper by Hall and Whyte in chapter 5, Rogers argues that the most important messages in a relationship are communicated not by words but by a multitude of subliminal signals that convey the speaker's true attitudes. What seems to be important to the influencee is whether the influencer accepts him as a person, is engaging in a genuine relationship, and avoids engaging in what appear to be manipulative strategies. This highly personal view stands in sharp contrast to the bureaucratic view that people must be dealt with in a totally impartial way, a way governed by rules, not by personalities. But often in bureaucracies the result is not only impartial, but impersonal treatment. The message that the receiver actually gets is that the bureaucracy doesn't care about him as a human being, but only as a thing.

One other important point in Roger's analysis is his emphasis on the whole relationship, not just on short-run tactics of "human relations." Imagine (or remember), for example, your boss repeatedly asking for your opinion on important issues, but then always making decisions in opposition to your recommendation. At some point you begin to wonder whether his asking for your opinion is for real or just a human relations gambit intended to cool you out, while he does just what he wanted to do in the first place. This is just one example of what Rogers means when he talks about conveying *attitudes* about the relationship.

The reader should also consult the paper by Douglas McGregor in chapter 14. McGregor's paper, coupled with the one by Rogers, together lay the foundation for the theory of open, nonauthoritarian, participative management.

However, some recent authors have begun to question whether McGregor's "Theory Y" style of management is really best in all situations. The provocative paper, "Beyond Theory Y," by Morse and Lorsch, proposes a contingency view (as Bavelas does); the view that open, adaptive, nonauthoritarian styles of leadership work best when one is trying to cope with a highly uncertain environment. Their research suggests that when the environment is stable and predictable, "Theory X" leadership may work better than that espoused under Theory Y.

The last paper in this chapter, by Vroom and Yetton, represents a new departure in research on leadership, and may be the first genuine attempt to integrate social-psychological research on leadership with more analytic management science techniques. They present a computerlike flow chart or "decision tree" for choosing among alternative decision-making methods for different types of decision problems. Theirs, too, is thus a contingency scheme. They identify two authoritarian decision strategies, depending on whether the leader does or doesn't seek information from subordinates. They also identify two collective decision methods, depending on whether the leader brings his subordinates together as a group, or meets with them individually. Finally, they identify a group decision method in which the leader, together with his subordinates, analyze the problem, generate possible solutions, and attempt to reach consensus on the best solution. The essential point of their method is to choose the decision style which meets two "feasibility criteria" (group acceptance and decision quality) and which minimizes the time involved in making the decision.

Thus far in our introduction to this chapter we have put persuasive and collaborative styles of leadership in a pretty favorable, albeit contingent, light. But if those forms of leadership are so superior in so many situations, why then are the more authoritarian styles used so frequently in the organizations we all observe? Part of the reason has to do with the design of organizations. In many cases they are designed to reward short-run gains even at the expense of long-term difficulties. A second reason may be more cultural. We have grown up in a highly competitive society, which has generally been supportive of authoritarian and coercive means of advancing one's self-interest. Together with more subtle cultural messages emphasizing strength and force as desirable masculine traits, perhaps each of us has a propensity to mimic the stereotype of the successful organization man. Still another reason is that many organizational structures are old and outdated, built for other times, other people, and other tasks. But once built, such structures tend to persist and to constrain the behaviors that are feasible within them.

Leadership: Man and Function
Alex Bavelas

There is a useful distinction to be made between the idea of "leadership as a personal quality" and the idea of "leadership as an organizational function." The first refers to a special combination of personal characteristics; the second refers to the distribution throughout an organization of decision-making powers. The first leads us to look at the qualities and abilities of individuals; the second leads us to look at the patterns of power and authority in organizations. Both of these ideas or definitions of leadership are useful, but it is important to know which one is being talked about and to know under what conditions the two must be considered together in order to understand a specific organizational situation.

Early notions about leadership dealt with it almost entirely in terms of personal abilities. Leadership was explicitly associated with special powers. An outstanding leader was credited not only with extensions of the normal abilities possessed by most men but with extraordinary powers, such as the ability to read men's minds, to tell the future, to compel obedience hypnotically. These powers were often thought of as gifts from a god, as conditional loans from a devil, or as the result of some accidental supernatural circumstance attending conception, birth, or early childhood. Today, claims of supernatural powers are made more rarely, but they are not entirely unknown. Of course, milder claims—tirelessness, infallibility of intuition, lightning-quick powers of decision—are made in one form or another by many outstandingly successful men. And when they do not make them for themselves, such claims are made for them by others, who, for their own reasons, prefer such explanations of success to other more homely ones.

Outright supernatural explanations of leadership have, in

Reprinted from *Administrative Science Quarterly* 4, no. 4 (March 1960): 491–98, by permission of the author and the publisher.

recent times, given way to more rational explanations. Leadership is still generally thought of in terms of personal abilities, but now the assumption is made that the abilities in question are the same as those possessed by all normal persons: individuals who become leaders are merely presumed to have them to a greater degree.

For many years attempts to define these abilities and to measure them failed. This was not only because the early techniques of measurement were primitive and unreliable, but for a more important reason. The traits that were defined as important for leadership were often nothing more than purely verbal expressions of what the researcher felt leaders *ought* to be like. Few of the many lists of traits that were developed had very much in common. Typical of the items that frequently appeared on such lists were piety, honesty, courage, perseverance, intelligence, reliability, imagination, industriousness. This way of thinking about leadership is still very common. It persists, not because it is helpful in analyzing and understanding the phenomenon of leadership, but because it expresses a deep and popular wish about what leaders *should* be like.

Modern trait research proceeds in a very different way. Leadership traits are no longer selected arbitrarily. They are, instead, largely derived from the results of tests that are carefully designed, administered, and interpreted. And the techniques of measurement and analysis which are applied to the data that are gathered have been extensively developed and refined. Numerous trait studies have been made of the physical, intellectual, and social characteristics of leaders. On various tests, persons who are leaders tend to be brighter, tend to be better adjusted psychologically, and tend to display better judgment. Studies that have concentrated on the social behavior of leaders show that they "interact" more than nonleaders. They tend to give more information, to ask for more information, and to take the lead in summing up or interpreting a situation.

Despite these accomplishments, the trait approach has in recent years been subjected to increasing criticism. A common objection is that the results are obtained by a method that requires an initial separation of people into "leaders" and "nonleaders" or "good leaders" and "not-so-good leaders." The validity of the distinguishing traits that come out of such work, the argument goes, can only be as good as the validity of the preliminary grouping of the persons being studied. All of this leads to the question, "On what basis is the initial separation of subjects made, and how is it justified?"

At first glance, this may appear a trivial and carping question. In fact, however, it is one of the most serious obstacles in the way of all leadership research. It is obviously impossible to define "good leaders" without reference to a system of values. To say that a man is a "good leader" means that his behavior and its consequences are held to be of greater worth than other behaviors and results.

What system of values shall the researcher adopt that is both scientifically acceptable and socially useful in distinguishing good or successful leaders from others? Many attempts have been made to find a suitable criterion, but the results have been generally unsatisfactory—not that it is difficult to find standards which are desirable and inspiring, but that such standards tend to be based, just as the early lists of traits were, on qualities that are difficult or impossible to measure. And often they just do not seem to "work." For example, there have been attempts to distinguish leaders from nonleaders in terms that rest essentially on moral and ethical considerations. It may be a significant commentary on our society that there appears to be no particular correlation between a man's ethics and morals and his power to attract followers.

It has been suggested that many of the philosophical difficulties that attend the definition of "good leader" can be avoided if one accepts the more limited task of defining "good executive." In business and industry, one would like to think, there should be practical, quantitative ways of making the distinction. Many attempts have been made in this direction. Reputation, financial success, hierarchical position, influence, and many other criteria have been tried without much satisfaction. The inadequacies of such standards are obvious to any experienced executive.

There is a second and more interesting objection that has been made to the trait approach. It is based not on the question of the accuracy or the validity of the assumptions that are made but upon the nature of the "traits" themselves. Traits are, after all, statements about personal characteristics. The objection to this is that the degree to which an individual exhibits leadership depends not only on *his characteristics* but also on the *characteristics of the situation* in which he finds himself. For example, a man who shows all the signs of leadership when he acts as the officer of a well-structured authoritarian organization may give no indication of leadership ability in a less structured, democratic situation. A man may become influential in a situation requiring deliberation and planning but show little evidence of leadership if the situation demands immediate action with no opportunity for weighing alternatives or thinking things out. Or, to take still another instance, a man may function effectively and comfortably in a group whose climate is friendly and cooperative but retreat and become ineffective if he perceives the atmosphere as hostile.

The case for the situational approach to leadership derives its strength from this fact: while organizations in general may exhibit broad similarities of structure and function, they also, in particular, show strong elements of uniqueness.

It is a matter of common observation that within any normal industrial organization, providing there has been a sufficient past, there will be found patterns of relationships and interaction that are highly predictable and highly repetitive. Some of these reoccurring situations will be unique to that organization. It is this uniqueness that is referred to when one speaks of the "personality" of a company. This is what a management has in mind when it selects a new member with an eye to how he will "fit in." The argument of the researcher who stresses the situational aspects of leadership is that these unique characteristics of an organization are often crucial in determining which of two equally competent and gifted men will become a "leader," and further that in the very same organization these unique patterns may change significantly at different levels of the hierarchy. The very same "leadership abilities" that helped a man rise to the top may, once he is there, prove a positive detriment.

The status of trait and situational leadership research can be summed up in this way: (1) the broad similarities which hold for a great number of organizations make it possible to say useful things about the kind of person who is likely to become a leader in any of those organizations, and (2) the unique characteristics of a particular organization make it necessary to analyze the situational factors that determine who is likely to become a leader *in one particular organization.* To put it another way, when specific situational patterns are different from organization to organization, one cannot say what personal traits will lead to acknowledged leadership. Instead, one must try to define the leadership functions that must be performed in those situations and regard as leadership those acts which perform them. This point of view suggests that almost any member of a group may become its leader under circumstances that enable him to perform the required functions of leadership and that different persons may contribute in different ways to the leadership of the group.

In these terms we come close to the notion of leadership, not as a personal quality, but as an *organizational function.* Under this concept it is not sensible to ask of an organization, "Who is the leader?" Instead we ask, "How are the leadership functions distributed in this organization?" The distribution may be wide or narrow. It may be so narrow— so many of the leadership functions may be vested in a single person—that he is the leader in the popular sense. But in modern organizations this is becoming more and more rare.

What are these "leadership functions"? Many have been proposed: planning, giving information, evaluating, arbitrating, controlling, rewarding, punishing, and the like. All of these stem from the underlying idea that leadership acts are those which help the group achieve its objectives or, as it is also put, to satisfy its "needs." In most face-to-face groups, the emergence of a leader can well be accounted for on this basis. That person who can assist or facilitate the group most in reaching a satisfactory state is most likely to be regarded as the leader. If one looks closely at what constitutes assistance or facilitation in this sense, it turns out to be the making of choices or the helping of the group to make choices— "better" choices, of course.

But can the function of leadership be reduced simply to decision making or the facilitation of decision making? The objection can be raised that such a definition is much too wide to be useful. Every action, even every physical movement one makes, is after all "chosen" out of a number of possible alternatives. If when I am at my workbench I pick up a screwdriver in preference to a hammer, I am clearly making a choice; am I, by virtue of that choice, displaying leadership? Something is obviously wrong with a definition of leadership which imputes it to any act that can be shown to have involved a choice. Common sense would argue that customary, habitual, and "unconscious" actions, although they may logically contain elements of choice, should be separated from actions that are subjectively viewed by the person taking them as requiring a decision. Common sense would also argue that questions of choice that can be settled on the basis of complete information should be considered differently from questions of choice in which decisions must be taken in the face of uncertainty. And common sense would argue that some distinction should be made between decisions that, although made on equally uncertain grounds, involve very different orders of risk.

This is, of course, the implicit view of the practicing manager, and, although it may contain very knotty problems of logic, it is the view that will be taken here. Stated in general terms, the position that will be taken is that organizational leadership consists of *uncertainty reduction*. The actual behavior through which this reduction is accomplished is the making of choices.

We saw above that not all choices are equally difficult or equally important. Some choices are considered unimportant or irrelevant and are ignored, and, of course, whole areas may be seen as so peripheral to the interests of the organization that they are not perceived as areas of choice at all. Other choices that *must* be made are so well understood that they become habitual and automatic. Some of these are grouped into more or less coherent bundles and given a job name. The employee learns to make them correctly as he becomes skilled in the job. In most job-evaluation plans, additional credit is given if the job requires judgment. This is a way of saying that there are choices remaining in the job that cannot be completely taken care of by instructions but must be made by the employee as they come along.

There are other choices which, although they are equally clear and habitual, are of a more general nature and do not apply just to a specific job but apply to all. These are customarily embodied in rules and procedures. Rules and procedures are, in this sense, decisions made in advance of the events to which they are to be applied. Obviously, this is possible and practical only to the extent that the events to which the rules and procedures apply can be foreseen, and the practical limit of their completeness and specificity depends on how these future events can be predicted.

Following this line of analysis, it is theoretically possible to arrange all the logically inherent choices that must be made in operating an industrial organization along scales of increasing uncertainty and importance. At some level in this hierarchy of choices, it is customary for management to draw a line, reserving for itself from that point on the duty and the privilege of making the required decisions.

Precisely where a management draws this line defines its scope. The way in which a management distributes the responsibility for making the set of choices it has thus claimed to itself defines its structure. What organizational leadership *is* and what kinds of acts constitute it are questions that can be answered only within this framework of scope and structure. In these terms leadership consists of the continuous choice-making process that permits the organization as a whole to proceed toward its objectives despite all sorts of internal and external perturbations.

But as every practicing manager knows, problems occasionally arise that are not amenable to the available and customary methods of analysis and solution. Although uncertain about which choice to make, a management may nevertheless have to make a decision. It is in situations of this kind that many of the popular traits attributed to leaders find their justification: quickness of decision, the courage to take risks, coolness under stress, intuition, and, even, luck. There is no doubt that quick, effective, and daring decisions are a highly prized commodity in a crisis, but just as precious a commodity is the art of planning and organizing so that such crises do not occur. The trend of management has been to remove as many of its decisions as possible from the area of hunch and intuition to that of rational calculation. More and more, organizations are choosing to depend less on the peculiar abilities of rare individuals and to depend instead on the orderly processes of research and analysis. The occasions and opportunities for personal leadership in the old sense still exist, but they are becoming increasingly rare and circumscribed.

This new emphasis has not eliminated the role of personal leadership, but it has significantly redefined it. Under normal conditions of operation, leadership in the modern organization consists not so much in the making of decisions personally as it does of maintaining the operational effectiveness of the decision-making systems which comprise the management of the organization. The picture of the leader who keeps his own counsel and in the nick of time pulls the rabbit out of the hat is out of date. The popular stereotype now is the thoughtful executive discussing in committee the information supplied by a staff of experts. In fact, it may be that the brilliant innovator in the role of manager is rapidly becoming as much an organizational embarrassment as he is an asset.

This trend, reasonable though it may appear on the surface, conceals two serious dangers. First, we may be systematically giving up the opportunity of utilizing the highest expressions of personal leadership in favor of managerial arrangements which, although safer and more reliable, can yield at best only a high level of mediocrity. And second, having committed ourselves to a system that thrives on the ordinary, we may, in the interests of maintaining and improving its efficiency, tend to shun the extraordinary.

It is no accident that daring and innovation wane as an organization grows large and successful. On different levels this appears to have been the history of men, of industries, of nations, and even of societies and cultures. Success leads to "obligations"—not the least of which is the obligation to hold what has been won. Therefore, the energies of a man or administration may be absorbed in simply maintaining vested interests. Similarly, great size requires "system," and system, once established, may easily become an end in itself.

This is a gloomy picture, because it is a picture of decay. It has been claimed, usually with appeals to biological analogies, that this is an inevitable cycle, but this view is, very probably, incorrect. Human organizations are not biological organisms; they are social inventions.

The Characteristics of a Helping Relationship
Carl R. Rogers

My interest in psychotherapy has brought about in me an interest in every kind of helping relationship. By this term I mean a relationship in which at least one of the parties has the intent of promoting the growth, development, maturity, improved functioning, improved coping with life of the other. The other, in this sense, may be one individual or a group. To put it in another way, a helping relationship might be defined as one in which one of the participants intends that there should come about, in one or both parties, more appreciation of, more expression of, more functional use of the latent inner resources of the individual.

Now it is obvious that such a definition covers a wide range of relationships which usually are intended to facilitate growth. It would certainly include the relationship between mother and child, father and child. It would include the relationship between the physician and his patient. The relationship between teacher and pupil would often come under this definition, though some teachers would not have the promotion of growth as their intent. It includes almost all counselor-client relationships, whether we are speaking of educational counseling, vocational counseling, or personal counseling. In this last-mentioned area it would include the wide range of relationships between the psychotherapist and the hospitalized psychotic, the therapist and the troubled or neurotic individual, and the relationship between the therapist and the increasing number of so-called "normal" individuals who enter therapy to improve their own functioning or accelerate their personal growth.

These are largely one-to-one relationships. But we should also think of the large number of individual-group interactions which are intended as helping relationships. Some ad-

Reprinted by permission of the author and publisher from *Personnel and Guidance Journal* 37, no. 1 (1958): 6–16. Copyright 1958 by the American Personnel and Guidance Association, Inc.

ministrators intend that their relationship to their staff groups shall be of the sort which promotes growth, though other administrators would not have this purpose. The interaction between the group therapy leader and his group belongs here. So does the relationship of the community consultant to a community group. Increasingly the interaction between the industrial consultant and a management group is intended as a helping relationship. Perhaps this listing will point up the fact that a great many of the relationships in which we and others are involved fall within this category of interactions in which there is the purpose of promoting development and more mature and adequate functioning.

The Question

But what are the characteristics of those relationships which *do* help, which do facilitate growth? And at the other end of the scale is it possible to discern those characteristics which make a relationship unhelpful, even though it was the sincere intent to promote growth and development? It is to these questions, particularly the first, that I would like to take you with me over some of the paths I have explored, and to tell you where I am, as of now, in my thinking on these issues.

The Answers Given by Research

It is natural to ask first of all whether there is any empirical research which would give us an objective answer to these questions. There has not been a large amount of research in this area as yet, but what there is is stimulating and suggestive. I cannot report all of it but I would like to make a somewhat extensive sampling of the studies which have been done and state very briefly some of the findings. In so doing, oversimplification is necessary, and I am quite aware that I am not doing full justice to the researches I am mentioning, but it may give you the feeling that factual advances are being made and pique your curiosity enough to examine the studies themselves, if you have not already done so.

Studies of Attitudes

Most of the studies throw light on the attitudes on the part of the helping person which make a relationship growth-promoting or growth-inhibiting. Let us look at some of these.

A careful study of parent-child relationships made some years ago by Baldwin and others[1] at the Fels Institute con-

1. A. L. Baldwin, J. Kalhorn, and P. H. Breese, "Patterns of Parent Behavior," *Psychol. Monogr.* 58, no. 268 (1945): 1–75.

tains interesting evidence. Of the various clusters of parental attitudes toward children, the "acceptant-democratic" seemed most growth-facilitating. Children of these parents with their warm and equalitarian attitudes showed an accelerated intellectual development (an increasing IQ), more originality, more emotional security and control, less excitability than children from other types of homes. Though somewhat slow initially in social development, they were, by the time they reached school age, popular, friendly, nonaggressive leaders.

Where parents' attitudes are classed as "actively rejectant" the children show a slightly decelerated intellectual development, relatively poor use of the abilities they do possess, and some lack of originality. They are emotionally unstable, rebellious, aggressive, and quarrelsome. The children of parents with other attitude syndromes tend in various respects to fall in between these extremes.

I am sure that these findings do not surprise us as related to child development. I would like to suggest that they probably apply to other relationships as well, and that the counselor or physician or administrator who is warmly emotional and expressive, respectful of the individuality of himself and of the other, and who exhibits a nonpossessive caring, probably facilitates self-realization much as does a parent with these attitudes.

Let me turn to another careful study in a very different area. Whitehorn and Betz[2] investigated the degree of success achieved by young resident physicians in working with schizophrenic patients on a psychiatric ward. They chose for special study the seven who had been outstandingly helpful, and seven whose patients had shown the least degree of improvement. Each group had treated about fifty patients. The investigators examined all the available evidence to discover in what ways the A group (the successful group) differed from the B group. Several significant differences were found. The physicians in the A group tended to see the schizophrenic in terms of the personal meaning which various behaviors had to the patient, rather than seeing him as a case history or a descriptive diagnoisis. They also tended to work toward goals which were oriented to the personality of the

2. B. J. Betz and J. C. Whitehorn, "The Relationship of the Therapist to the Outcome of Therapy in Schizophrenia," *Psychiat. Research Reports* no. 5, *Research Techniques in Schizophrenia* (Washington, D.C.: American Psychiatric Association, 1956), pp. 89–117; J. C. Whitehorn and B. J. Betz, "A Study of Psychotherapeutic Relationships between Physicians and Schizophrenic Patients," *Amer. J. Psychiat.* 111 (1954): 321–31.

patient, rather than such goals as reducing the symptoms or curing the disease. It was found that the helpful physicians, in their day-by-day interaction, primarily made use of active personal participation—a person-to-person relationship. They made less use of procedures which could be classed as "passive permissive." They were even less likely to use such procedures as interpretation, instruction or advice, or emphasis upon the practical care of the patient. Finally, they were much more likely than the B group to develop a relationship in which the patient felt trust and confidence in the physician.

Although the authors cautiously emphasize that these findings relate only to the treatment of schizophrenics, I am inclined to disagree. I suspect that similar facts would be found in a research study of almost any class of helping relationship.

Another interesting study focuses upon the way in which the person being helped perceives the relationship. Heine[3] studied individuals who had gone for psychotherapeutic help to psychoanalytic, client-centered, and Adlerian therapists. Regardless of the type of therapy, these clients report similar changes in themselves. But it is their perception of the relationship which is of particular interest to us here. When asked what accounted for the changes which had occurred, they expressed some differing explanations, depending on the orientation of the therapist. But their agreement on the major elements they had found helpful was even more significant. They indicated that these attitudinal elements in the relationship accounted for the changes which had taken place in themselves: the trust they had felt in the therapist; being understood by the therapist; the feeling of independence they had had in making choices and decisions. The therapist procedure which they had found most helpful was that the therapist clarified and openly stated feelings which the client had been approaching hazily and hesitantly.

There was also a high degree of agreement among these clients, regardless of the orientation of their therapists, as to what elements had been unhelpful in the relationship. Such therapist attitudes as lack of interest, remoteness or distance, and an over-degree of sympathy, were perceived as unhelpful. As to procedures, they had found it unhelpful when therapists had given direct specific advice regarding decisions or had emphasized past history rather than present

3. R. W. Heine, "A Comparison of Patients' Reports on Psychotherapeutic Experience with Psychoanalytic, Nondirective, and Adlerian Therapists" (Doctoral dissertation, University of Chicago, 1950).

problems. Guiding suggestions mildly given were perceived in an intermediate range—neither clearly helpful nor unhelpful.

Fiedler, in a much quoted study,[4] found that expert therapists of differing orientations formed similar relationships with their clients. Less well known are the elements which characterized these relationships, differentiating them from the relationships formed by less expert therapists. These elements are: an ability to understand the client's meanings and feelings; a sensitivity to the client's attitudes; a warm interest without any emotional overinvolvement.

A study by Quinn[5] throws light on what is involved in understanding the client's meanings and feelings. His study is surprising in that it shows that "understanding" of the client's meanings is essentially an attitude of *desiring* to understand. Quinn presented his judges only with recorded therapist statements taken from interviews. The raters had no knowledge of what the therapist was responding to or how the client reacted to his response. Yet it was found that the degree of understanding could be judged about as well from this material as from listening to the response in context. This seems rather conclusive evidence that it is an attitude of wanting to understand which is communicated.

As to the emotional quality of the relationship, Seeman[6] found that success in psychotherapy is closely associated with a strong and growing mutual liking and respect between client and therapist.

An interesting study by Dittes[7] indicates how delicate this relationship is. Using a physiological measure, the psychogalvanic reflex, to measure the anxious or threatened or alerted reactions of the client, Dittes correlated the deviations on this measure with judge's ratings of the degree of warm acceptance and permissiveness on the part of the therapist. It was found that whenever the therapist's attitudes changed even slightly in the direction of a lesser degree of acceptance, the

4. F. E. Fiedler, "Quantitative Studies on the Role of Therapists' Feelings toward Their Patients," in O. H. Mowrer, ed., *Psychotherapy: Theory and Research* (New York: Ronald Press, 1953), chap. 12.

5. R. D. Quinn, "Psychotherapists' Expressions as an Index to the Quality of Early Therapeutic Relationships" (Doctoral dissertation, University of Chicago, 1950).

6. J. Seeman, "Counselor Judgments of Therapeutic Process and Outcome," in C. R. Rogers and R. F. Dymond, eds., *Psychotherapy and Personality Change* (Chicago: University of Chicago Press, 1954), chap. 7.

7. J. E. Dittes, "Galvanic Skin Response as a Measure of Patient's Reaction to Therapist's Permissiveness," *J. Abnorm. Soc. Psychol.* 55 (1957): 295–303.

number of abrupt GSR deviations significantly increased. Evidently when the relationship is experienced as less acceptant the organism organizes against threat, even at the physiological level.

Without trying fully to integrate the findings from these various studies, it can at least be noted that a few things stand out. One is the fact that it is the attitudes and feelings of the therapist, rather than his theoretical orientation, which are important. His procedures and techniques are less important than his attitudes. It is also worth noting that it is the way in which his attitudes and procedures are *perceived* which makes a difference to the client, and that it is this perception which is crucial.

"Manufactured" Relationships

Let me turn to research of a very different sort, some of which you may find rather abhorrent, but which nevertheless has a bearing upon the nature of a facilitating relationship. These studies have to do with what we might think of as manufactured relationships.

Verplanck,[8] Greenspoon,[9] and others have shown that operant conditioning of verbal behavior is possible in a relationship. Very briefly, if the experimenter says "Mhm," or "Good," or nods his head after certain types of works or statements, those classes of words tend to increase because of being reinforced. It has been shown that using such procedures one can bring about increases in such diverse verbal categories as plural nouns, hostile words, statements of opinion. The person is completely unaware that he is being influenced in any way by these reinforcers. The implication is that by such selective reinforcement we could bring it about that the other person in the relationship would be using whatever kinds of words and making whatever kinds of statements we had decided to reinforce.

Following still further the principles of operant conditioning as developed by Skinner and his group, Lindsley[10]

8. W. S. Verplanck, "The Control of the Content of Conversation: Reinforcement of Statements of Opinion," *J. Abnorm. Soc. Psychol.* 51 (1955): 668–76.

9. J. Greenspoon, "The Reinforcing Effect of Two Spoken Sounds on the Frequency of Two Responses," *Amer. J. Psychol.* 68 (1955): 409–16.

10. O. R. Lindsley, "Operant Conditioning Methods Applied to Research in Chronic Schizophrenia," *Psychiat. Research Reports* no. 5, *Research Techniques in Schizophrenia* (Washington, D.C.: American Psychiatric Association, 1956), pp. 118–53.

has shown that a chronic schizophrenic can be placed in a "helping relationship" with a machine. The machine, somewhat like a vending machine, can be set to reward a variety of types of behaviors. Initially it simply rewards—with candy, a cigarette, or the display of a picture—the lever-pressing behavior of the patient. But it is possible to set it so that many pulls on the lever may supply a hungry kitten—visible in a separate enclosure—with a drop of milk. In this case the satisfaction is an altruistic one. Plans are being developed to reward similar social or altruistic behavior directed toward another patient, placed in the next room. The only limit to the kinds of behavior which might be rewarded lies in the degree of mechanical ingenuity of the experimenter.

Lindsley reports that in some patients there has been marked clinical improvement. Personally I cannot help but be impressed by the description of one patient who had gone from a deteriorated chronic state to being given free grounds privileges, this change being quite clearly associated with his interaction with the machine. Then the experimenter decided to study experimental extinction, which, put in more personal terms, means that no matter how many thousands of times the lever was pressed, no reward of any kind was forthcoming. The patient gradually regressed, grew untidy, uncommunicative, and his grounds privilege had to be revoked. This (to me) pathetic incident would seem to indicate that even in a relationship to a machine, trustworthiness is important if the relationship is to be helpful.

Still another interesting study of a manufactured relationship is being carried on by Harlow and his associates,[11] this time with monkeys. Infant monkeys, removed from their mothers almost immediately after birth, are, in one phase of the experiment, presented with two objects. One might be termed the "hard mother," a sloping cylinder of wire netting with a nipple from which the baby may feed. The other is a "soft mother," a similar cylinder made of foam rubber and terry cloth. Even when an infant gets all his food from the "hard mother" he clearly and increasingly prefers the "soft mother." Motion pictures show that he definitely "relates" to this object, playing with it, enjoying it, finding security in clinging to it when strange objects are near, and using that security as a home base for venturing into the frightening

11. H. Harlow and associates, experiment in progress, as reported by Robert Zimmerman.

world. Of the many interesting and challenging implications of this study, one seems reasonably clear. It is that no amount of direct food reward can take the place of certain perceived qualities which the infant appears to need and desire.

Two Recent Studies

Let me close this wide-ranging—and perhaps perplexing—sampling of research studies with an account of two very recent investigations. The first is an experiment conducted by Ends and Page.[12] Working with hardened chronic hospitalized alcoholics who had been committed to a state hospital for sixty days, they tried three different methods of group psychotherapy. The method which they believed would be most effective was therapy based on a two-factor theory of learning; a client-centered approach was expected to be second; a psychoanalytically oriented approach was expected to be least efficient. Their results showed that the therapy based upon a learning theory approach was not only not helpful, but was somewhat deleterious. The outcomes were worse than those in the control group which had no therapy. The analytically oriented therapy produced some positive gain, and the client-centered group therapy was associated with the greatest amount of positive change. Follow-up data, extending over one and one-half years, confirmed the in-hospital findings, with the lasting improvement being greatest in the client-centered approach, next in the analytic, next the control group, and least in those handled by a learning theory approach.

As I have puzzled over this study, unusual in that the approach to which the authors were committed proved *least* effective, I find a clue, I believe, in the description of the therapy based on learning theory.[13] Essentially it consisted (1) of pointing out and labeling the behaviors which had proved unsatisfying, (2) of exploring objectively with the client the reasons behind these behaviors, and (3) of establishing through reeducation more effective problem-solving habits. But in all of this interaction the aim, as they formulated it, was to be impersonal. The therapist "permits

12. E. J. Ends and C. W. Page, "A Study of Three Types of Group Psychotherapy with Hospitalized Male Inebriates," *Quar. J. Stud. Alcohol.* 18 (1957): 263–77.
13. C. W. Page and E. J. Ends, "A Review and Synthesis of the Literature Suggesting a Psychotherapeutic Technique Based on Two-factor Learning Theory" (unpublished manuscript, loaned to the writer).

as little of his own personality to intrude as is humanly possible." The "therapist stresses personal anonymity in his activities, i.e., he must studiously avoid impressing the patient with his own (therapist's) individual personality characteristics." To me this seems the most likely clue to the failure of this approach, as I try to interpret the facts in the light of the other research studies. To withhold one's self as a person and to deal with the other person as an object does not have a high probability of being helpful.

The final study I wish to report is one just being completed by Halkides.[14] She started from a theoretical formulation of mine regarding the necessary and sufficient conditions for therapeutic change.[15] She hypothesized that there would be a significant relationship between the extent of constructive personality change in the client and four counselor variables: (1) the degree of empathic understanding of the client manifested by the counselor; (2) the degree of positive affective attitude (unconditional positive regard) manifested by the counselor toward the client; (3) the extent to which the counselor is genuine, his words matching his own internal feeling; and (4) the extent to which the counselor's response matches the client's expression in the intensity of affective expression.

To investigate these hypotheses she first selected, by multiple objective criteria, a group of ten cases which could be classed as "most successful" and a group of ten "least successful" cases. She then took an early and late recorded interview from each of these cases. On a random basis she picked nine client-counselor interaction units—a client statement and a counselor response—from each of these interviews. She thus had nine early interactions and nine late interactions from each case. This gave her several hundred units which were now placed in random order. The units from an early interview of an unsuccessful case might be followed by the units from a late interview of a successful case, etc.

Three judges, who did not know the cases or their degree of success, or the source of any given unit, now listened to this material four different times. They rated each unit on a seven point scale, first as to the degree of empathy, second as

14. G. Halkides, "An Experimental Study of Four Conditions Necessary for Therapeutic Change" (Doctoral dissertation, University of Chicago, 1958).

15. C. R. Rogers, "The Necessary and Sufficient Conditions of Psychotherapeutic Personality Change," *J. Consult. Psychol.* 21 (1957): 95–103.

to the counselor's positive attitude toward the client, third as to the counselor's congruence or genuineness, and fourth as to the degree to which the counselor's response matched the emotional intensity of the client's expression.

I think all of us who knew of the study regarded it as a very bold venture. Could judges listening to single units of interaction possibly make any reliable rating of such subtle qualities as I have mentioned? And even if suitable reliability could be obtained, could eighteen counselor-client interchanges from each case—a minute sampling of the hundreds or thousands of such interchanges which occurred in each case—possibly bear any relationship to the therapeutic outcome? The chance seemed slim.

The findings are surprising. It proved possible to achieve high reliability between the judges, most of the interjudge correlations being in the 0.80s or 0.90s, except on the last variable. It was found that a high degree of empathic understanding was significantly associated, at a 0.001 level, with the more successful cases. A high degree of unconditional positive regard was likewise associated with the more successful cases, at the 0.001 level. Even the rating of the counselor's genuineness or congruence—the extent to which his words matched his feelings—was associated with the successful outcome of the case, and again at the 0.001 level of significance. Only in the investigation of the matching intensity of affective expression were the results equivocal.

It is of interest too that high ratings of these variables were not associated more significantly with units from later interviews than with units from early interviews. This means that the counselor's attitudes were quite constant throughout the interviews. If he was highly empathic, he tended to be so from first to last. If he was lacking in genuineness, this tended to be true of both early and late interviews.

As with any study, this investigation has its limitations. It is concerned with a certain type of helping relationship, psychotherapy. It investigated only four variables thought to be significant. Perhaps there are many others. Nevertheless it represents a significant advance in the study of helping relationships. Let me try to state the findings in the simplest possible fashion. It seems to indicate that the quality of the counselor's interaction with a client can be satisfactorily judged on the basis of a very small sampling of his behavior. It also means that if the counselor is congruent or transparent, so that his words are in line with his feelings rather than the two being discrepant—if the counselor likes the client, unconditionally, and if the counselor understands the essential feelings of the client as they seem to the client—then there is a strong probability that this will be an effective helping relationship.

Some Comments

These then are some of the studies which throw at least a measure of light on the nature of the helping relationship. They have investigated different facets of the problem. They have approached it from very different theoretical contexts. They have used different methods. They are not directly comparable. Yet they seem to me to point to several statements which may be made with some assurance. It seems clear that relationships which are helpful have different characteristics from relationships which are unhelpful. These differential characteristics have to do primarily with the attitudes of the helping person on the one hand and with the perception of the relationship by the "helpee" on the other. It is equally clear that the studies thus far made do not give us any final answers as to what is a helping relationship, nor how it is to be formed.

How Can I Create a Helping Relationship?

I believe each of us working in the field of human relationships has a similar problem in knowing how to use such research knowledge. We cannot slavishly follow such findings in a mechanical way or we destroy the personal qualities which these very studies show to be valuable. It seems to me that we have to use these studies, testing them against our own experience and forming new and further personal hypotheses to use and test in our own further personal relationships.

So rather than try to tell you how you should use the findings I have presented I should like to tell you the kind of questions which these studies and my own clinical experience raise for me, and some of the tentative and changing hypotheses which guide my behavior as I enter into what I hope may be helping relationships, whether with students, staff, family, or clients. Let me list a number of these questions and considerations.

1. Can I *be* in some way which will be perceived by the other person as trustworthy, as dependable, or consistent in some deep sense? Both research and experience indicate that this is very important, and over the years I have found what I believe are deeper and better ways of answering this ques-

tion. I used to feel that if I fulfilled all the outer conditions of trustworthiness—keeping appointments, respecting the confidential nature of the interviews, and so on—and if I acted consistently the same during the interviews, then this condition would be fulfilled. But experience drove home the fact that to act consistently acceptant, for example, if in fact I was feeling annoyed or skeptical or some other nonacceptant feeling, was certain in the long run to be perceived as inconsistent or untrustworthy. I have come to recognize that being trustworthy does not demand that I be rigidly consistent but that I be dependably real. The term congruent is one I have used to describe the way I would like to be. By this I mean that whatever feeling or attitude I am experiencing would be matched by my awareness of that attitude. When this is true, then I am a unified or integrated person in that moment, and hence I can *be* whatever I deeply *am*. This is a reality which I find others experience as dependable.

2. A very closely related question is this: Can I be expressive enough as a person that what I am will be communicated unambiguously? I believe that most of my failures to achieve a helping relationship can be traced to unsatisfactory answers to these two questions. When I am experiencing an attitude of annoyance toward another person but am unaware of it, then my communication contains contradictory messages. My words are giving one message, but I am also in subtle ways communicating the annoyance I feel and this confuses the other person and makes him distrustful, though he too may be unaware of what is causing the difficulty. When as a parent or a therapist or a teacher or an administrator I fail to listen to what is going on in me, fail because of my own defensiveness to sense my own feelings, then this kind of failure seems to result. It has made it seem to me that the most basic learning for anyone who hopes to establish any kind of helping relationship is that it is safe to be transparently real. If in a given relationship I am reasonably congruent, if no feelings relevant to the relationship are hidden either to me or the other person, then I can be almost sure that the relationship will be a helpful one.

One way of putting this which may seem strange to you is that if I can form a helping relationship to myself—if I can be sensitively aware of and acceptant toward my own feelings —then the likelihood is great that I can form a helping relationship toward another.

Now, acceptantly to be what I am, in this sense, and to permit this to show through to the other person, is the most difficult task I know and one I never fully achieve. But to realize that this *is* my task has been most rewarding because it has helped me to find what has gone wrong with interpersonal relationships which have become snarled and to put them on a constructive track again. It has meant that if I am to facilitate the personal growth of others in relation to me, then I must grow, and while this is often painful it is also enriching.

3. A third question is: Can I let myself experience positive attitudes toward this other person—attitudes of warmth, caring, liking, interest, respect? It is not easy. I find in myself, and feel that I often see in others, a certain amount of fear of these feelings. We are afraid that if we let ourselves freely experience these positive feelings toward another we may be trapped by them. They may lead to demands on us or we may be disappointed in our trust, and these outcomes we fear. So as a reaction we tend to build up distance between ourselves and others—aloofness, a "professional" attitude, an impersonal relationship.

I feel quite strongly that one of the important reasons for the professionalization of every field is that it helps to keep this distance. In the clinical areas we develop elaborate diagnostic formulations, seeing the person as an object. In teaching and in administration we develop all kinds of evaluative procedures, so that again the person is perceived as an object. In these ways, I believe, we can keep ourselves from experiencing the caring which would exist if we recognized the relationship as one between two persons. It is a real achievement when we can learn, even in certain relationships or at certain times in those relationships, that it is safe to care, that it is safe to relate to the other as a person for whom we have positive feelings.

4. Another question the importance of which I have learned in my own experience is: Can I be strong enough as a person to be separate from the other? Can I be a sturdy respecter of my own feelings, my own needs, as well as his? Can I own and, if need be, express my own feelings as something belonging to me and separate from his feelings? Am I strong enough in my own separateness that I will not be downcast by his depression, frightened by his fear, nor engulfed by his dependency? Is my inner self hardy enough to realize that I am not destroyed by his anger, taken over by his need for dependence, nor enslaved by his love, but that I exist separate from him with feelings and rights of my own? When I can freely feel this strength of being a separate person, then I find that I can let myself go much more deeply

in understanding and accepting him because I am not fearful of losing myself.

5. The next question is closely related. Am I secure enough within myself to permit him his separateness? Can I permit him to be what he is—honest or deceitful, infantile or adult, despairing or overconfident? Can I give him the freedom to be? Or do I feel that he should follow my advice, or remain somewhat dependent on me, or mold himself after me? In this connection I think of the interesting small study by Farson[16] which found that the less well adjusted and less competent counselor tends to induce conformity to himself, to have clients who model themselves after him. On the other hand, the better adjusted and more competent counselor can interact with a client through many interviews without interfering with the freedom of the client to develop a personality quite separate from that of his therapist. I should prefer to be in this latter class, whether as parent or supervisor or counselor.

6. Another question I ask myself is: Can I let myself enter fully into the world of his feelings and personal meanings and see these as he does? Can I step into his private world so completely that I lose all desire to evaluate or judge it? Can I enter it so sensitively that I can move about in it freely, without tramping on meanings which are precious to him? Can I sense it so accurately that I can catch not only the meanings of his experience which are obvious to him, but those meanings which are only implicit, which he sees only dimly or as confusion? Can I extend this understanding without limit? I think of the client who said, "Whenever I find someone who understands a *part* of me at the time, then it never fails that a point is reached where I know they're *not* understanding me again. . . . What I've looked for so hard is for someone to understand."

For myself I find it easier to feel this kind of understanding, and to communicate it to individual clients than to students in a class or staff members in a group in which I am involved. There is a strong temptation to set students "straight," or to point out to a staff member the errors in his thinking. Yet when I can permit myself to understand in these situations, it is mutually rewarding. And with clients in therapy, I am often impressed with the fact that even a minimal amount of empathic understanding—a bumbling

16. R. E. Farson, "Introjection in the Psychotherapeutic Relationship" (Doctoral dissertation, University of Chicago, 1955).

and faulty attempt to catch the confused complexity of the client's meaning—is helpful, though there is no doubt that it is most helpful when I can see and formulate clearly the meanings in his experiencing which for him have been unclear and tangled.

7. Still another issue is whether I can be acceptant of each facet of this other person which he presents to me. Can I receive him as he is? Can I communicate this attitude? Or can I only receive him conditionally, acceptant of some aspects of his feelings and silently or openly disapproving of other aspects? It has been my experience that when my attitude is conditional, then he cannot change or grow in those respects in which I cannot fully receive him. And when—afterward and sometimes too late—I try to discover why I have been unable to accept him in every respect, I usually discover that it is because I have been frightened or threatened in myself by some aspect of his feelings. If I am to be more helpful, then I must myself grow and accept myself in these respects.

8. A very practical issue is raised by the question: Can I act with sufficient sensitivity in the relationship that my behavior will not be perceived as a threat? The work we are beginning to do in studying the physiological concomitants of psychotherapy confirms the research by Dittes in indicating how easily indivdivuals are threatened at a physiological level. The psychogalvanic reflex—the measure of skin conductance—takes a sharp dip when the therapist responds with some word which is just a little stronger than the client's feelings. And to a phrase such as, "My, you *do* look upset," the needle swings almost off the paper. My desire to avoid even such minor threats is not due to a hypersensitivity about my client. It is simply due to the conviction based on experience that if I can free him as completely as possible from external threat, then he can begin to experience and to deal with the internal feelings and conflicts which he finds threatening within himself.

9. A specific aspect of the preceding question but an important one is: Can I free him from the threat of external evaluation? In almost every phase of our lives—at home, at school, at work—we find ourselves under the rewards and punishments of external judgments. "That's good"; "that's naughty." "That's worth an A"; "that's a failure." "That's good counseling"; "that's poor counseling." Such judgments are a part of our lives from infancy to old age. I believe they have a certain social usefulness to institutions and organizations such as schools and professions. Like everyone else I

find myself all too often making such evaluations. But, in my experience, they do not make for personal growth and hence I do not believe that they are a part of a helping relationship. Curiously enough, a positive evaluation is as threatening in the long run as a negative one, since to inform someone that he is good implies that you also have the right to tell him he is bad. So I have come to feel that the more I can keep a relationship free of judgment and evaluation, the more this will permit the other person to reach the point where he recognizes that the locus of evaluation, the center of responsibility, lies within himself. The meaning and value of his experience is in the last analysis something which is up to him, and no amount of external judgment can alter this. So I should like to work toward a relationship in which I am not, even in my own feelings, evaluating him. This I believe can set him free to be a self-responsible person.

10. One last question: Can I meet this other individual as a person who is in process of *becoming,* or will I be bound by his past and by my past? If, in my encounter with him, I am dealing with him as an immature child, an ignorant student, a neurotic personality, or a psychopath, each of these concepts of mine limits what he can be in the relationship. Martin Buber, the existentialist philosopher of the University of Jerusalem, has a phrase, "confirming the other," which has had meaning for me. He says "Confirming means . . . accepting the whole potentiality of the other . . . I can recognize in him, know in him, the person he has been . . . *created* to become . . . I confirm him in myself, and then in him, in relation to this potentiality that . . . can now be developed, can evolve."[17] If I accept the other person as something fixed, already diagnosed and classified, already shaped by his past, then I am doing my part to confirm this limited hypothesis. If I accept him as a process of becoming, then I am doing what I can to confirm or make real his potentialities.

It is at this point that I see Verplanck, Lindsley, and Skinner, working in operant conditioning, coming together with Buber, the philosopher or mystic. At least they come together in principle, in an odd way. If I see a relationship as only an opportunity to reinforce certain types of words or opinions in the other, then I tend to confirm him as an object —a basically mechanical, manipulable object. And if I see this as his potentiality, he tends to act in ways which support

17. M. Buber and C. Rogers, transcription of dialogue held 18 April 1957, Ann Arbor, Mich. (unpublished manuscript).

this hypothesis. If, on the other hand, I see a relationship as an opportunity to "reinforce" *all* that he is, the person that he is with all his existent potentialities, then he tends to act in ways which support *this* hypothesis. I have then—to use Buber's term—confirmed him as a living person, capable of creative inner development. Personally I prefer this second type of hypothesis.

Conclusion

In the early portion of this paper I reviewed some of the contributions which research is making to our knowledge *about* relationships. Endeavoring to keep that knowledge in mind I then took up the kind of questions which arise from an inner and subjective point of view as I enter, as a person, into relationships. If I could, in myself, answer all the questions I have raised in the affirmative, then I believe that any relationships in which I was involved would be helping relationships, would involve growth. But I cannot give a positive answer to most of these questions. I can only work in the direction of a positive answer.

This has raised in my mind the strong suspicion that the optimal helping relationship is the kind of relationship created by a person who is psychologically mature. Or to put it in another way, the degree to which I can create relationships which facilitate the growth of others as separate persons is a measure of the growth I have achieved in myself. In some respects this is a disturbing thought, but it is also a promising or challenging one. It would indicate that if I am interested in creating helping relationships I have a fascinating lifetime job ahead of me, stretching and developing my potentialities in the direction of growth.

I am left with the uncomfortable thought that what I have been working out for myself in this paper may have little relationship to your interests and your work. If so, I regret it. But I am at least partially comforted by the fact that all of us who are working in the field of human relationships and trying to understand the basic orderliness of that field are engaged in the most crucial enterprise in today's world. If we are thoughtfully trying to understand our tasks as administrators, teachers, educational counselors, vocational counselors, therapists, then we are working on the problem which will determine the future of this planet. For it is not upon the physical sciences that the future will depend. It is upon us who are trying to understand and deal with the interactions between human beings—who are trying to create helping relationships. So I hope that the questions I ask of myself will be of some use to you in gaining understanding and perspective as you endeavor, in your way, to facilitate growth in your relationships.

Beyond Theory Y
John J. Morse and
Jay W. Lorsch

During the past thirty years, managers have been bombarded with two competing approaches to the problems of human administration and organization. The first, usually called the classical school of organization, emphasizes the need for well-established lines of authority, clearly defined jobs, and authority equal to responsibility. The second, often called the participative approach, focuses on the desirability of involving organization members in decision making so that they will be more highly motivated.

Douglas McGregor, through his well-known "Theory X and Theory Y," drew a distinction between the assumptions about human motivation which underlie these two approaches, to this effect:

1. Theory X assumes that people dislike work and must be coerced, controlled, and directed toward organizational goal. Furthermore, most people prefer to be treated this way, so they can avoid responsibility.

2. Theory Y—the integration of goals—emphasizes the average person's intrinsic interest in his work, his desire to be self-directing and to seek responsibility, and his capacity to be creative in solving business problems.

It is McGregor's conclusion, of course, that the latter approach to organization is the more desirable one for managers to follow.[1]

McGregor's position causes confusion for the managers who try to choose between these two conflicting approaches. The classical organizational approach that McGregor associated with Theory X does work well in some situations, although, as McGregor himself pointed out, there are also

Reprinted from the *Harvard Business Review*, May–June 1970, pp. 61–68, by permission of publisher. © 1970 by the President and Fellows of Harvard College; all rights reserved.

1. Douglas McGregor, *The Human Side of Enterprise* (New York: McGraw-Hill Book Company, Inc., 1960), pp. 34–35, 47–48.

some situations where it does not work effectively. At the same time, the approach based on Theory Y, while it has produced good results in some situations, does not always do so. That is, each approach is effective in some cases but not in others. Why is this? How can managers resolve the confusion?

A New Approach

Recent work by a number of students of management and organization may help to answer such questions.[2] These studies indicate that there is not one best organizational approach; rather, the best approach depends on the nature of the work to be done. Enterprises with highly predictable tasks perform better with organizations characterized by the highly formalized procedures and management hierarchies of the classical approach. With highly uncertain tasks that require more extensive problem solving, on the other hand, organizations that are less formalized and emphasize self-control and member participation in decision making are more effective. In essence, according to these newer studies, managers must design and develop organizations so that the organizational characteristics *fit* the nature of the task to be done.

While the conclusions of this newer approach will make sense to most experienced managers and can alleviate much of the confusion about which approach to choose, there are still two important questions unanswered:

1. How does the more formalized and controlling organization affect the motivation of organization members? (McGregor's most telling criticism of the classical approach was that it did not unleash the potential in an enterprise's human resources.)

2. Equally important, does a less formalized organization always provide a high level of motivation for its members? (This is the implication many managers have drawn from McGregor's work.)

We have recently been involved in a study that provides surprising answers to these questions and, when taken together with other recent work, suggests a new set of basic

2. See for example Paul R. Lawrence and Jay W. Lorsch, *Organization and Environment* (Boston: Harvard Business School, Division of Research, 1967); Joan Woodward, *Industrial Organization: Theory and Practice* (New York: Oxford University Press, Inc., 1965); Tom Burns and G. M. Stalker, *The Management of Innovation* (London: Tavistock Publications, 1961); Harold J. Leavitt, "Unhuman Organizations," *Harvard Business Review,* July–August 1962, p. 90.

assumptions which move beyond Theory Y into what we call "Contingency Theory: the fit between task, organization, and people." These theoretical assumptions emphasize that the appropriate pattern of organization is *contingent* on the nature of the work to be done and on the particular needs of the people involved. We should emphasize that we have labeled these assumptions as a step beyond Theory Y because of McGregor's own recognition that the Theory Y assumptions would probably be supplanted by new knowledge within a short time.[3]

The Study Design

Our study was conducted in four organizational units. Two of these performed the relatively certain task of manufacturing standardized containers on high-speed, automated production lines. The other two performed the relatively uncertain work of research and development in communications technology. Each pair of units performing the same kind of task were in the same large company, and each pair had previously been evaluated by that company's management as containing one highly effective unit and a less effective one. The study design is summarized in table 1.

Table 1

Study Design in "Fit" of Organizational Characteristics

Characteristics	Company 1 (predictable manufacturing task)	Company 2 (unpredictable R&D task)
Effective performer	Akron containers plant	Stockton research lab
Less effective performer	Hartford containers plant	Carmel research lab

The objective was to explore more fully how the fit between organization and task was related to successful performance. That is, does a good fit between organizational characteristics and task requirements increase the motivation of individuals and hence produce more effective individual and organizational performance?

An especially useful approach to answering this question is to recognize that an individual has a strong need to master the world around him, including the task that he faces as a

3. McGregor, *The Human Side of Enterprise.*

member of a work organization.[4] The accumulated feelings of satisfaction that come from successfully mastering one's environment can be called a "sense of competence." We saw this sense of competence in performing a particular task as helpful in understanding how a fit between task and organizational characteristics could motivate people toward successful performance.

Organizational Dimensions

Because the four study sites had already been evaluated by the respective corporate managers as high and low performers of tasks, we expected that such differences in performance would be a preliminary clue to differences in the "fit" of the organizational characteristics to the job to be done. But, first, we had to define what kinds of organizational characteristics would determine how appropriate the organization was to the particular task.

We grouped these organizational characteristics into two sets of factors:

1. Formal characteristics, which could be used to judge the fit between the kind of task being worked on and the formal practices of the organization.

2. Climate characteristics, or the subjective perceptions and orientations that had developed among the individuals about their organizational setting. (These too must fit the task to be performed if the organization is to be effective.)

We measured these attributes through questionnaires and interviews with about forty managers in each unit to determine the appropriateness of the organization to the kind of task being performed. We also measured the feelings of competence of the people in the organizations so that we could link the appropriateness of the organizational attributes with a sense of competence.

Major Findings

The principal findings of the survey are best highlighted by contrasting the highly successful Akron plant and the high-performing Stockton laboratory. Because each performed very different tasks (the former a relatively certain manufacturing task and the latter a relatively uncertain research task), we expected, as brought out earlier, that there would have to

4. See Robert W. White, "Ego and Reality in Psychoanalytic Theory," *Psychological Issues*, vol. 3, no. 3 (New York: International Universities Press, 1963).

be major differences between them in organizational characteristics if they were to perform effectively. And this is what we did find. But we also found that each of these effective units had a better fit with its particular task than did its less effective counterpart.

While our major purpose in this article is to explore how the fit between task and organizational characteristics is related to motivation, we first want to explore more fully the organizational characteristics of these units, so the reader will better understand what we mean by a fit between task and organization and how it can lead to more effective behavior. To do this, we shall place the major emphasis on the contrast between the high-performing units (the Akron plant and Stockton laboratory), but we shall also compare each of these with its less effective mate (the Hartford plant and Carmel laboratory respectively).

Formal Characteristics

Beginning with differences in formal characteristics, we found that both the Akron and Stockton organizations fit their respective tasks much better than did their less successful counterparts. In the predictable manufacturing task environment, Akron had a pattern of formal relationships and duties that was highly structured and precisely defined. Stockton, with its unpredictable research task, had a low degree of structure and much less precision of definition (see table 2).

Table 2
Differences in Formal Characteristics in High-performing Organizations

Characteristics	Akron	Stockton
1. Pattern of formal relationships and duties as signified by organization charts and job manuals	Highly structured, precisely defined	Low degree of structure, less well defined
2. Pattern of formal rules, procedures, control, and measurement systems	Pervasive, specific, uniform, comprehensive	Minimal, loose, flexible
3. Time dimensions incorporated in formal practices	Short-term	Long-term
4. Goal dimensions incorporated in formal practices	Manufacturing	Scientific

Akron's pattern of formal rules, procedures, and control systems was so specific and comprehensive that it prompted one manager to remark:

"We've got rules here for everything from how much powder to use in cleaning the toilet bowls to how to cart a dead body out of the plant."

In contrast, Stockton's formal rules were so minimal, loose, and flexible that one scientist, when asked whether he felt the rules ought to be tightened, said:

"If a man puts a nut on a screw all day long, you may need more rules and a job definition for him. But we're not novices here. We're professionals and not the kind who need close supervision. People around here *do* produce, and produce under relaxed conditions. Why tamper with success?"

These differences in formal organizational characteristics were well suited to the differences in tasks of the two organizations. Thus:

Akron's highly structured formal practices fit its predictable task because behavior had to be rigidly defined and controlled around the automated, high-speed production line. There was really only one way to accomplish the plant's very routine and programmable job; managers defined it precisely and insisted (through the plant's formal practices) that each man do what was expected of him.

On the other hand, Stockton's highly unstructured formal practices made just as much sense because the required activities in the laboratory simply could not be rigidly defined in advance. With such an unpredictable, fast-changing task as communications technology research, there were numerous approaches to getting the job done well. As a consequence, Stockton managers used a less structured pattern of formal practices that left the scientists in the lab free to respond to the changing task situation.

Akron's formal practices were very much geared to *short-term* and *manufacturing* concerns as its task demanded. For example, formal production reports and operating review sessions were daily occurrences, consistent with the fact that the through-put time for their products was typically only a few hours.

By contrast, Stockton's formal practices were geared to *long-term* and *scientific* concerns, as its task demanded. Formal reports and reviews were made only quarterly, reflecting the fact that research often does not come to fruition for three to five years.

At the two less effective sites (i.e., the Hartford plant and the Carmel laboratory), the formal organizational characteristics did not fit their respective tasks nearly as well. For example, Hartford's formal practices were much less structured and controlling than were Akron's, while Carmel's were more restraining and restricting than were Stockton's. A scientist in Carmel commented:

"There's something here that keeps you from being scientific. It's hard to put your finger on, but I guess I'd call it 'Mickey Mouse.' There are rules and things here that get in your way regarding doing your job as a researcher."

Climate Characteristics

As with formal practices, the climate in both high-performing Akron and Stockton suited the respective tasks much better than did the climates at the less successful Hartford and Carmel sites.

Perception of Structure. The people in the Akron plant perceived a great deal of structure, with their behavior tightly controlled and defined. One manager in the plant said:

"We can't let the lines run unattended. We lose money whenever they do. So we make sure each man knows his job, knows when he can take a break, knows how to handle a change in shifts, and so on. It's all spelled out clearly for him the day he comes to work here."

In contrast, the scientists in the Stockton laboratory perceived very little structure, with their behavior only minimally controlled. Such perceptions encouraged the individualistic and creative behavior that the uncertain, rapidly changing research task needed. Scientists in the less successful Carmel laboratory perceived much more structure in their organization and voiced the feeling that this was "getting in their way" and making it difficult to do effective research.

Distribution of Influence. The Akron plant and the Stockton laboratory also differed substantially in how influence was distributed and on the character of superior-subordinate and colleague relations. Akron personnel felt that they had much less influence over decisions in their plant than Stockton's scientists did in their laboratory. The task at Akron had already been clearly defined and that definition had, in a sense, been incorporated into the automated production flow itself. Therefore, there was less need for individuals to have a say in decisions concerning the work process.

Moreover, in Akron, influence was perceived to be concentrated in the upper levels of the formal structure (a hierarchical or "top-heavy" distribution), while in Stockton influence was perceived to be more evenly spread out among more levels of the formal structure (an egalitarian distribution).

Akron's members perceived themselves to have a low degree of freedom vis-à-vis superiors both in choosing the jobs they work on and in handling these jobs on their own. They also described the type of supervision in the plant as being relatively directive. Stockton's scientists, on the other hand, felt that they had a great deal of freedom vis-à-vis their superiors both in choosing the tasks and projects, and in handling them in the way that they wanted to. They described supervision in the laboratory as being very participatory.

It is interesting to note that the less successful Carmel laboratory had more of its decisions made at the top. Because of this, there was a definite feeling by the scientists that their particular expertise was not being effectively used in choosing projects.

Relations with Others. The people at Akron perceived a great deal of similarity among themselves in background, prior work experiences, and approaches for tackling job-related problems. They also perceived the degree of coordination of effort among colleagues to be very high. Because Akron's task was so precisely defined and the behavior of its members so rigidly controlled around the automated lines, it is easy to see that this pattern also made sense.

By contrast, Stockton's scientists perceived not only a great many differences among themselves, especially in education and background, but also that the coordination of effort among colleagues was relatively low. This was appropriate for a laboratory in which a great variety of disciplines and skills were present and individual projects were important to solve technological problems.

Time Orientation. As we would expect, Akron's individuals were highly oriented toward a relatively short time span and manufacturing goals. They responded to quick feedback concerning the quality and service that the plant was providing. This was essential, given the nature of their task.

Stockton's researchers were highly oriented toward a longer time span and scientific goals. These orientations meant that they were willing to wait for long-term feedback from a research project that might take years to complete. A scientist in Stockton said:

"We're not the kind of people here who need a pat on the

back every day. We can wait for months if necessary before we get feedback from colleagues and the profession. I've been working on one project now for three months and I'm still not sure where it's going to take me. I can live with that, though."

This is precisely the kind of behavior and attitude that spells success on this kind of task.

Managerial Style. Finally, the individuals in both Akron and Stockton perceived their chief executive to have a "managerial style" that expressed more of a concern for the task than for people or relationships, but this seemed to fit both tasks.

In Akron, the technology of the task was so dominant that top managerial behavior which was not focused primarily on the task might have reduced the effectiveness of performance. On the other hand, although Stockton's research task called for more individualistic problem-solving behavior, that sort of behavior could have become segmented and uncoordinated, unless the top executive in the lab focused the group's attention on the overall research task. Given the individualistic bent of the scientists, this was an important force in achieving unity of effort.

All these differences in climate characteristics in the two high performers are summarized in table 3.

As with formal attributes, the less effective Hartford and Carmel sites had organization climates that showed a perceptibly lower degree of fit with their respective tasks. For example, the Hartford plant had an egalitarian distribution of influence, perceptions of a low degree of structure, and a more participatory type of supervision. The Carmel laboratory had a somewhat top-heavy distribution of influence, perceptions of high structure, and a more directive type of supervision.

Competence Motivation

Because of the difference in organizational characteristics at Akron and Stockton, the two sites were strikingly different places in which to work. But these organizations had two very important things in common. First, each organization fit very well the requirements of its task. Second, although the behavior in the two organizations was different, the result in both cases was effective task performance.

Since, as we indicated earlier, our primary concern in this study was to link the fit between organization and task with individual motivation to perform effectively, we devised a

Table 3
Differences in "Climate" Characteristics in High-performing
Organizations

Characteristics	Akron	Stockton
1. Structural orientation	Perceptions of tightly controlled behavior and a high degree of structure	Perceptions of a low degree of structure
2. Distribution of influence	Perceptions of low total influence, concentrated at upper levels in the organization	Perceptions of high total influence, more evenly spread out among all levels
3. Character of superior-subordinate relations	Low freedom vis-à-vis superiors to choose and handle jobs, directive type of supervision	High freedom vis-à-vis superiors to choose and handle projects, participatory type of supervision
4. Character of colleague relations	Perceptions of many similarities among colleagues, high degree of coordination of colleague effort	Perceptions of many differences among colleagues, relatively low degree of coordination of colleague effort
5. Time orientation	Short-term	Long-term
6. Goal orientation	Manufacturing	Scientific
7. Top executive's "managerial style"	More concerned with task than people	More concerned with task than people

two-part test to measure the sense of competence motivation of the individuals at both sites. Thus:

The first part asked a participant to write creative and imaginative stories in response to six ambiguous pictures.

The second asked him to write a creative and imaginative story about what he would be doing, thinking, and feeling "tomorrow" on his job. This is called a "projective" test because it is assumed that the respondent projects into his stories his own attitudes, thoughts, feelings, needs, and wants, all of which can be measured from the stories.[5]

5. For a more detailed description of this survey, see John J. Morse, "Internal Organizational Patterning and Sense of Competence Motivation" (Doctoral dissertation, Harvard Business School, 1969).

The results indicated that the individuals in Akron and Stockton showed significantly more feelings of competence than did their counterparts in the lower-fit Hartford and Carmel organizations.[6] We found that the organization-task fit is simultaneously linked to and interdependent with both individual motivation and effective unit performance. (This interdependency is illustrated in figure 1.)

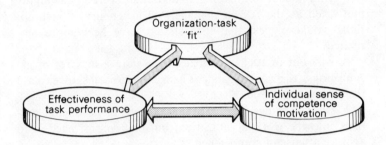

Fig. 1. Basic Contingent Relationships

Putting the conclusions in this form raises the question of cause and effect. Does effective unit performance result from the task-organization fit or from higher motivation, or perhaps from both? Does higher sense of competence motivation result from effective unit performance or from fit?

Our answer to these questions is that we do not think there are any single cause-and-effect relationships, but that these factors are mutually interrelated. This has important implications for management theory and practice.

Contingency Theory

Returning to McGregor's Theory X and Theory Y assumptions, we can now question the validity of some of his conclusions. While Theory Y might help to explain the findings in the two laboratories, we clearly need something other than Theory X or Y assumptions to explain the findings in the plants.

For example, the managers at Akron worked in a formalized organization setting with relatively little participation in decision making, and yet they were highly mo-

6. Differences between the two container plants are significant at .001 and between the research laboratories at .01 (one-tailed probability).

tivated. According to Theory X, people would work hard in such a setting only because they were coerced to do so. According to Theory Y, they should have been involved in decision making and been self-directed to feel so motivated. Nothing in our data indicates that either set of assumptions was valid at Akron.

Conversely, the managers at Hartford, the low-performing plant, were in a less formalized organization with more participation in decision making, and yet they were not as highly motivated as the Akron managers. The Theory Y assumptions would suggest that they should have been more motivated.

A way out of such paradoxes is to state a new set of assumptions, the Contingency Theory, that seems to explain the findings at all four sites:

1. Human beings bring varying patterns of needs and motives into the work organization, but one central need is to achieve a sense of competence.

2. The sense of competence motive, while it exists in all human beings, may be fulfilled in different ways by different people depending on how this need interacts with the strengths of the individuals' other needs—such as those for power, independence, structure, achievement, and affiliation.

3. Competence motivation is most likely to be fulfilled when there is a fit between task and organization.

4. Sense of competence continues to motivate even when a competence goal is achieved; once one goal is reached, a new, higher one is set.

While the central thrust of these points is clear from the preceding discussion of the study, some elaboration can be made. First, the idea that different people have different needs is well understood by psychologists. However, all too often, managers assume that all people have similar needs. Lest we be accused of the same error, we are saying only that all people have a need to feel competent; in this *one* way they are similar. But in many other dimensions of personality, individuals differ, and these differences will determine how a particular person achieves a sense of competence.

Thus, for example, the people in the Akron plant seemed to be very different from those in the Stockton laboratory in their underlying attitudes toward uncertainty, authority, and relationships with their peers. And because they had different need patterns along these dimensions, both groups were highly motivated by achieving competence from quite different activities and settings.

While there is a need to further investigate how people who work in different settings differ in their psychological makeup, one important implication of the Contingency Theory is that we must not only seek a fit between organization and task, but also between task and people and between people and organization.

A further point which requires elaboration is that one's sense of competence never really comes to rest. Rather, the real satisfaction of this need is in the successful performance itself, with no diminishing of the motivation as one goal is reached. Since feelings of competence are thus reinforced by successful performance, they can be a more consistent and reliable motivator than salary and benefits.

Implications for Managers

The major managerial implication of the Contingency Theory seems to rest in the task-organization-people fit. Although this interrelationship is complex, the best possibility for managerial action probably is in tailoring the organization to fit the task and the people. If such a fit is achieved, both effective unit performance and a higher sense of competence motivation seem to result.

Managers can start this process by considering how certain the task is, how frequently feedback about task performance is available, and what goals are implicit in the task. The answers to these questions will guide their decisions about the design of the management hierarchy, the specificity of job assignments, and the utilization of rewards and control procedures. Selective use of training programs and a general emphasis on appropriate management styles will move them toward a task-organization fit.

The problem of achieving a fit among task, organization, and people is something we know less about. As we have already suggested, we need further investigation of what personality characteristics fit various tasks and organizations. Even with our limited knowledge, however, there are indications that people will gradually gravitate into organizations that fit their particular personalities. Managers can help this process by becoming more aware of what psychological needs seem to best fit the tasks available and the organizational setting, and by trying to shape personnel selection criteria to take account of these needs.

In arguing for an approach which emphasizes the fit among task, organization, and people, we are putting to rest the question of which organizational approach—the classical or the participative—is best. In its place we are raising a new question: What organizational approach is most appropriate given the task and the people involved?

For many enterprises, given the new needs of younger employees for more autonomy, and the rapid rates of social and technological change, it may well be that the more participative approach is the most appropriate. But there will still be many situations in which the more controlled and formalized organization is desirable. Such an organization need not be coercive or punitive. If it makes sense to the individuals involved, given their needs and their jobs, they will find it rewarding and motivating.

Concluding Note

The reader will recognize that the complexity we have described is not of our own making. The basic deficiency with earlier approaches is that they did not recognize the variability in tasks and people which produces this complexity. The strength of the contingency approach we have outlined is that it begins to provide a way of thinking about this complexity, rather than ignoring it. While our knowledge in this area is still growing, we are certain that any adequate theory of motivation and organization will have to take account of the contingent relationship between task, organization, and people.

A Normative Model of Leadership Style
Victor H. Vroom and Philip Yetton

Introduction

One of the most persistent and controversial issues in the study of management concerns the issue of participation in decision making by subordinates. Traditional models of the managerial process have been autocratic in nature. The manager makes decisions on matters within his area of freedom, issues orders or directives to his subordinates, and monitors their performance to ensure conformity with these directives. Scientific Management, from its early developments in time and motion study to its contemporary manifestations in linear and heuristic programming, has contributed to this centralization of decision making in organizations by focusing on the development of methods by which managers can make more rational decisions, substituting objective measurements and empirically validated methods for casual judgments.

Most social psychologists and other behavioral scientists who have turned their attention toward the implications of psychological and social processes for the practice of management have called for greater participation by subordinates in the problem-solving and decision-making process. Pointing to evidence of restriction of output and lack of involvement under traditional managerial systems, they have argued for greater influence in decision making on the part of those who are held responsible for decision execution.

The empirical evidence provides some, but not overwhelming, support for beliefs in the efficacy of participative management. Field experiments on rank-and-file workers by Coch and French,[1] Bavelas,[2] and Strauss[3] indicate that

Abridged from Victor H. Vroom and Philip Yetton, *Leadership and Decision Making* (Pittsburgh: University of Pittsburgh Press, 1973), by permission of the publisher and authors. © 1973 by the University of Pittsburgh Press.

1. L. Coch and J. R. P. French, Jr., "Overcoming Resistance to Change," *Human Relations* 1 (1948): 512–32.

2. Reported in J. R. P. French, Jr., "Field Experiments: Changing Group Productivity," in J. G. Miller, ed., *Experiments in Social Process: A Symposium on Social Psychology* (New York: McGraw-Hill, 1950), pp. 79–96.

3. Reported in W. F. Whyte, *Money and Motivation* (New York: Harper, 1955).

impressive increases in productivity can be brought about by giving workers an opportunity to participate in decision making and goal setting. In addition, several correlational field studies[4] indicate positive relationships between the amount of influence which supervisors afford their subordinates in decisions which affect them and individual or group performance. On the other hand, in an experiment conducted in a Norwegian factory, French, Israel, and As[5] found no significant differences in production between workers who did and workers who did not participate in decisions regarding introduction of changes in work methods; and in a recent laboratory experiment, Sales and Rosen[6] found no significant differences between groups exposed to democratic and autocratic supervision. To complicate the picture further, Morse and Reimer[7] compared the effects of two programs of change, each of which was introduced in two divisions of the clerical operations of a large insurance company. One of the programs involved increased participation in decision making by rank-and-file workers, while the other involved increased hierarchical control. The results show a significant increase in productivity under both programs, with the hierarchically controlled program producing the greater increase.

Reconciliation of these discrepant findings is not an easy task. It is made complex by different empirical interpretations of the term "participation"[8] and by great differences in the situations in which it is applied. It appears highly likely that an increase in participation of subordinates in decision making may increase productivity under some circumstances but decrease productivity under other circumstances. Identification of the situational conditions which determine the efficacy of participative management requires the specification of the decision-making processes which it entails

4. D. Katz, N. Maccoby, and Nancy C. Morse, *Productivity, Supervision and Morale in an Office Situation* (Ann Arbor: University of Michigan, Institute for Social Research, 1950); V. H. Vroom, *Some Personality Determinants of the Effects of Participation* (Englewood Cliffs, N. J.: Prentice-Hall, 1960).

5. J. R. P. French, Jr., J. Israel, and D. As, "An Experiment on Participation in a Norwegian Factory," *Human Relations* 13 (1960): 3–9.

6. S. M. Sales and N. A. Rosen, "A Laboratory Investigation of the Effectiveness of Two Industrial Supervisory Patterns" (unpublished manuscript, Cornell University, 1965).

7. Nancy C. Morse and E. Reimer, "The Experimental Change of a Major Organizational Variable," *Journal of Abnormal Social Psychology* 52 (1956): 120–29.

8. G. Strauss, "Some Notes on Power Equalization," in H. J. Leavitt, ed., *The Social Science of Organizations* (Englewood Cliffs, N. J.: Prentice-Hall, 1963), pp. 39–84.

and of the various mechanisms by which it may influence the extent to which the formal objectives of the organization are attained.

The conclusion appears inescapable that participation in decision making has consequences which vary from one situation to another. Given the potential importance of this conclusion for the study of leadership and its significance to the process of management, it appears to be critical for social scientists to begin to develop some definitions of the circumstances under which participation in decision making may contribute to or hinder organizational effectiveness. These could then be translated into guidelines of potential value to managers in choosing the leadership styles to fit the demands of the situations which they encounter.

In this chapter, one approach to dealing with this important problem will be described. A normative model is developed which is consistent with existing empirical evidence concerning the consequences of participation and which purports to specify a set of rules which should be used in determining the form and amount of participation in decision making by subordinates to be used in different classes of situations.

Basic Assumptions

1. The normative model should be constructed in such a way as to be of potential value to managers or leaders in determining which leadership styles they should employ in each of the various situations that they encounter in carrying out their formal leadership roles. Consequently, it should deal with behaviors which are within their repertoire and their control.

2. There are a number of discrete social processes by which organizational problems can be translated into solutions and these processes vary in terms of the potential amount of participation by subordinates in the problem-solving process.

The term participation has been used in a number of different ways. Perhaps the most influential definitions have been those of French, Israel, and As[9] and Vroom,[10] who define participation as a process of joint decision making by two or more parties. The amount of participation of any individual is the amount of influence he has on the decisions and

9. French, Israel, and As, "An Experiment on Participation."
10. Vroom, *Some Personality Determinants.*

plans agreed upon. Given the existence of a property such as participation which varies from high to low, it should be possible to define leadership styles or behaviors which represent clear alternative processes for making decisions which can be related to the amount of participation each process affords the managers' subordinates.

A taxonomy of leadership style created for normative purposes should distinguish among methods which are likely to have different outcomes but should not be so elaborate that leaders are unable to determine which style they are employing in any given instance. The taxonomy to be used in the normative model is shown in table 1.

Table 1
Decision Methods for Group and Individual Problems

Group Problems	*Individual Problems*
AI You solve the problem or make the decision yourself, using information available to you at that time.	AI You solve the problem or make the decision yourself, using information available to you at that time.
AII You obtain the necessary information from subordinates, then decide on the solution to the problem yourself. You may or may not tell subordinates what the problem is in getting the information from them. The role played by your subordinates in making the decision is clearly one of providing the necessary information to you, rather than generating or evaluating alternative solutions.	AII You obtain necessary information from the subordinate, then decide on solution to problem yourself. You may or may not tell the subordinate what the problem is in getting the information from him. The role played by the subordinate in making the decision is clearly one of providing the necessary information to you, rather than generating or evaluating alternative solutions.
CI You share the problem with relevant subordinates individually, getting their ideas and suggestions without bringing them together as a group. Then you make the decision which may or may not reflect your subordinates' influence.	CI You share the problem with the subordinate, getting his ideas and suggestions, then you make the decision which may or may not reflect your subordinate's influence.

CII You share the problem with your subordinates as a group, collectively obtaining their ideas and suggestions. Then, you make the decision which may or may not reflect your subordinates' influence.

GII You share the problem with your subordinates as a group. Together you generate and evaluate alternatives and attempt to reach agreement (consensus) on a solution.

GI You share the problem with your subordinate and together you analyze the problem and arrive at a mutually agreeable solution.

DI You delegate the problem to your subordinate, providing him with any relevant information that you possess, but giving him responsibility for solving the problem by himself. You may or may not request him to tell you what solution he has reached.

It should be noted that the styles are arranged in two columns corresponding to their applicability to problems which involve the entire group or some subset of it (hereafter called group problems) or a single subordinate (hereafter called individual problems). If a problem or decision clearly affects only one subordinate, the leader would choose among the methods shown in the right-hand column; if it had potential effects on the entire group (or subset of it), he would choose among the methods shown in the left-hand column. The styles in both columns are arranged from top to bottom in terms of the opportunity for subordinates to influence the solution to the problem. (The principle behind the numbering system is as follows: The letters A, C, G, and D stand for autocratic, consultative, group, and delegation. The numerals I and II denote variations on the basic decision processes.)

3. No single leadership style is applicable to all situations; the function of a normative model should be to provide a framework for the analysis of situational requirements which can be translated into prescriptions of leadership styles.

The fact that the most effective leadership method or style is dependent on the situation is becoming widely recognized by behavioral scientists interested in problems of leadership and administration. A decision-making process which is optimal for a quarterback on a football team making decisions under severe time constraints is likely to be far from optimal when used by a dean introducing a new curriculum to be implemented by his faculty. Even the advocates of participative management have noted this "situational relativity" of leadership styles. Thus, Argyris writes:

> No one leadership style is the most effective. Each is probably effective under a given set of conditions. Consequently, I suggest that effective leaders are those who are capable of behaving in many different leadership styles, depending on the requirements of reality as they and others perceive it. I call this "reality-centered" leadership.[11]

It is necessary to go beyond noting the importance of situational factors and begin to move toward a road map or normative model which attempts to prescribe the most appropriate leadership style for different kinds of situations. The most comprehensive treatment of situational factors as determinants of the effectiveness and efficiency of participation in decision making is found in the work of Tannenbaum and Schmidt.[12] They list and discuss a large number of variables including attributes of the manager, his subordinates, and the situation, which ought to enter into the manager's decision about the degree to which he should share his power with his subordinates. But they do not go beyond this inventory of variables to show how these might be combined and translated into different forms of actions.

4. The most appropriate unit for the analysis of the situation is the particular problem to be solved and the context in which the problem occurs.

While it is becoming widely recognized that different situations require different leadership methods, there is less agreement concerning the appropriate units for the analysis of the situation. One approach is to assume that the situations which interact with or condition the choice and effectiveness of different leadership styles correspond to the environment of the system. Alternatively, one

11. C. Argyris, *Interpersonal Competence and Organizational Effectiveness* (Homewood, Ill.: Irwin-Dorsey, 1962), p. 81.

12. R. Tannenbaum and W. H. Schmidt, "How to Choose a Leadership Pattern," *Harvard Business Review* 36 (1958): 95–101.

might assume that the critical features of the situation concern the role of the leader, including his relations with his subordinates.

The approach taken here is to utilize the properties of the problem to be solved as the most critical situational dimensions for determining the appropriate form or amount of participation. Different prescriptions would be made for a given leader for different problems within a given role. It should be noted that constructing a normative model with the problem rather than the role or any organizational differences as the unit of analysis does not rule out the possibility that different roles and organizations may involve different distributions of problem types and which in aggregate may require different modal styles or levels of participation.

5. The leadership method used in response to one situation should not constrain the method or style used in other situations.

This assumption is necessary to make possible the construction of a normative model founded on problem differences. It may seem inconsistent with the view, first proposed by McGregor,[13] that consistency in leadership style is desirable because it enables subordinates to predict or anticipate their superiors' behavior and to adapt to it. However, predictability does not preclude variability. There are many variable phenomena which can be predicted quite well because the rules or processes which govern them are understood. The antithesis of predictability is randomness and, if McGregor is correct, a normative model to regulate choices among alternative leadership styles should be deterministic rather than stochastic. The model developed here is deterministic; the normatively prescribed style for a given problem type is a constant.

Conceptual and Empirical Basis of the Model

A model designed to regulate, in some rational way, choices among the leadership styles shown in table 1 should be based on sound empirical evidence concerning the likely consequences of the styles. The more complete the empirical base of knowledge, the greater the certainty with which one can develop the model and the greater will be its usefulness. In this section we will restrict ourselves to the development of a model concerned only with group problems and, hence,

13. D. McGregor, "Getting Effective Leadership in the Industrial Organization," *Advanced Management* 9 (1944): 148–53.

will use only the methods shown at the left-hand column of table 1. To aid in this analysis, it is important to distinguish three classes of outcomes which bear on the ultimate effectiveness of decisions. These are:

1. The quality or rationality of the decision.
2. The acceptance of commitment on the part of subordinates to execute the decision effectively.
3. The amount of time required to make the decision.

The evidence regarding the effects of participation on each of these outcomes or consequences has been reviewed elsewhere. He concluded that

> The results suggest that allocating problem solving and decision-making tasks to entire groups as compared with the leader or manager in charge of the groups, requires a greater investment of man hours but produces higher acceptance of decisions and a higher probability that the decisions will be executed efficiently. Differences between these two methods in quality of decisions and in elapsed time are inconclusive and probably highly variable. . . . It would be naïve to think that group decision-making is always more "effective" than autocratic decision-making, or vice versa; the relative effectiveness of these two extreme methods depends both on the weights attached to quality, acceptance and time variables and on differences in amounts of these outcomes resulting from these methods, neither of which is invariant from one situation to another. The critics and proponents of participative management would do well to direct their efforts toward identifying the properties of situations in which different decision-making approaches are effective rather than wholesale condemnation or deification of one approach.[14]

Stemming from this review, an attempt has been made to identify these properties of the situation or problem which will be the basic elements in the model. These problem attributes are of two types: (1) Those which specify the importance of quality and acceptance for a particular problem (see A and D below) and (2) those which, on the basis of available evidence, have a high probability of moderating the effects of participation on each of these outcomes (see B, C, E,

14. V. H. Vroom, "Industrial Social Psychology," in G. Lindsey and E. Aronson, eds., *Handbook of Social Psychology* (Reading, Mass.: Addison-Wesley, 1970), chap. 5, pp. 239–40.

G, and H below). The following are the problem attributes used in the present form of the model.

A. The importance of the quality of the decision.
B. The extent to which the leader possesses sufficient information/expertise to make a high quality decision by himself.
C. The extent to which subordinates, taken collectively, have the necessary information to generate a high quality decision.
D. The extent to which the problem is structured.
E. The extent to which acceptance or commitment on the part of subordinates is critical to the effective implementation of the decision.
F. The prior probability that the leader's autocratic decision will receive acceptance by subordinates.
G. The extent to which subordinates are motivated to attain the organizational goals as represented in the objectives explicit in the statement of the problem.
H. The extent to which subordinates are likely to be in disagreement over preferred solutions.

Table 2 shows the same eight problem attributes expressed in the form of questions which might be used by a leader in diagnosing a particular problem before choosing his leadership style. In phrasing the questions, technical language has been held to a minimum. Furthermore, the questions have been phrased in Yes-No form, translating the continuous variables defined above into dichotomous variables. For example, instead of attempting to determine how important the decision quality is to the effectiveness of the decision (attribute A), the leader is asked in the first question to judge whether there is any quality component to the problem. Similarly, the difficult task of specifying exactly how much information the leader possesses that is relevant to the decision (attribute B) is reduced to a simple judgment by the leader concerning whether he has sufficient information to make a high quality decision.

Expressing what are obviously continuous variables in dichotomous form greatly simplifies the problem of developing a model incorporating these attributes which can be used by leaders. It sidesteps the problem of scaling each problem attribute and reduces the complexities of the judgments required of leaders.

It has been found that managers can diagnose a situation quite quickly and accurately by answering this set of eight questions concerning it. But how can such responses generate a prescription concerning the most effective leadership style or decision process? What kind of normative model of participation in decision making can be built from this set of problem attributes?

Table 2
Problem Attributes

A. If decision were accepted, would it make a difference?
B. Do I have sufficient information to make a high quality decision?
C. Do subordinates have sufficient additional information to result in a high quality decision?
D. Do I know exactly what information is needed, who possesses it, and how to collect it?
E. Is acceptance of decision by subordinates critical to effective implementation?
F. If you were to make the decision by yourself, is it certain that it would be accepted by your subordinates?
G. Can subordinates be trusted to base solutions on organizational considerations?
H. Is conflict among subordinates likely in preferred solutions?

A Normative Model of Leadership Styles

Let us assume that you are a manager faced with a concrete problem to be solved. We will also assume that you have judged that this problem could potentially affect more than one of your subordinates. Hence, it is what we have defined as a group problem, and you have to choose among the five decision processes (AI, AII, CI, CII GII) shown at the left side of table 1.

On a priori grounds any one of these five decision processes could be called for. The judgments you have made concerning the status of each of the problem's attributes can be used to define a set of feasible alternatives. This occurs through a set of rules which eliminate decision processes from the feasible set under certain specifiable conditions.

The rules are intended to protect both the quality and acceptance of the decision. In the present form of the model, there are three rules which protect decision quality and four which protect acceptance. The seven rules are presented here both as verbal statements and the more formal language of set theory. In the set theoretic formulation, the letters refer to the problem attributes as stated in question form in table 2. A signifies that the answer to question A for a particular problem is *yes*; $\bar{A}$ signifies that the answer to that question is no; $\cap$ signifies intersection; $\Rightarrow$ signifies "implies"; and $\overline{AI}$ signifies not AI. Thus $A \cap \bar{B} \Rightarrow \overline{AI}$ may be read as follows; when both the answer to question A is yes and the answer to question B is no, AI is eliminated from the feasible set.

1. *The Information Rule.* If the leader does not possess enough information or expertise to solve the problem by himself, AI is eliminated from the feasible set. (Its use risks a low quality decision.) ($A \cap \bar{B} \Rightarrow \overline{AI}$)

2. *The Trust Rule.* If the subordinates cannot be trusted to base their efforts to solve the problems on organizational goals, GII is eliminated from the feasible set. (Alternatives which eliminate the leader's final control over the decision reached may jeopardize the quality of the decision.) ($A \cap \bar{G} \Rightarrow \overline{GII}$)

3. *The Structured Problem Rule.* If the leader lacks the necessary information or expertise to solve the problem by himself, and if the problem is unstructured, i.e., he does not know exactly what information is needed and where it is located, the method used must provide not only for him to collect the information but to do so in an efficient and effective manner. Methods which involve interaction among all subordinates with full knowledge of the problem are likely to be both more efficient and more likely to generate a high quality solution to the problem. Under these conditions, AI, AII, and CI are eliminated from the feasible set. (AI does not provide for him to collect the necessary information, and AII and CI represent more cumbersome, less effective and less efficient means of bringing the necessary information to bear on the solution of the problem than methods which do permit those with the necessary information to interact.) ($A \cap \bar{B} \cap \bar{D} \Rightarrow \overline{AI}, \overline{AII}, \overline{CI}$)

4. *The Acceptance Rule.* If the acceptance of the decision by subordinates is critical to effective implementation and if it is not certain that an autocratic decision made by the leader would receive that acceptance, AI and AII are eliminated from the feasible set. (Neither provides an opportunity for subordinates to participate in the decision and both risk the necessary acceptance.) ($E \cap \bar{F} \Rightarrow \overline{AI}, \overline{AII}$)

5. *The Conflict Rule.* If the acceptance of the decision is critical, and an autocratic decision is not certain to be accepted, and subordinates are likely to be in conflict or disagreement over the appropriate solution, AI, AII, and CI are eliminated from the feasible set. (The method used in solving

the problem should enable those in disagreement to resolve their differences with full knowledge of the problem. Accordingly, under these conditions, AI, AII, and CI, which involve no interaction or only "one-on-one" relationships and therefore provide no opportunity for those in conflict to resolve their differences, are eliminated from the feasible set. Their use runs the risk of leaving some of the subordinates with less than the necessary commitment to the final decision.) ($E \cap \bar{F} \cap H \Rightarrow \overline{AI}, \overline{AII}, \overline{CI}$)

6. *The Fairness Rule.* If the quality of decision is unimportant, and if acceptance is critical and not certain to result from an autocratic decision, AI, AII, CI, and CII are eliminated from the feasible set. (The method used should maximize the probability of acceptance as this is the only relevant consideration in determining the effectiveness of the decision. Under these circumstances AI, AII, CI, and CII which create less acceptance or commitment than GII are eliminated from the feasible set. To use them is to run the risk of getting less than the needed acceptance of the decision.) ($\bar{A} \cap E \cap \bar{F} \Rightarrow \overline{AI}, \overline{AII}, \overline{CI}, \overline{CII}$)

7. *The Acceptance Priority Rule.* If acceptance is critical, not assured by an autocratic decision and if subordinates can be trusted, AI, AII, CI, and CII are eliminated from the feasible set. (Methods which provide equal partnership in the decision-making process can provide greater acceptance without risking decision quality. Use of any method other than GII results in an unnecessary risk that the decision will not be fully accepted or receive the necessary commitment on the part of subordinates.) ($A \cap E \cap \bar{F} \cap G \Rightarrow \overline{AI}, \overline{AII}, \overline{CI}, \overline{CII}$)

Application of these rules to a problem is aided by their pictorial representation in the form of a decision tree. Figure 1 shows a simple decision tree which serves this purpose.

The problem attributes are arranged along the top of the figure. To apply the rules to a particular problem one starts at the left-hand side and works toward the right, asking oneself the question immediately above any box that is encountered. When a terminal node is reached, the number designates the problem type which in turn designates a set of methods which remains feasible after the rules have been applied.[15] It can be seen that this method of representing the decision tree generates fourteen problem types. Problem type

15. Rule 2 has not been applied to problem types 4, 9, 10, 11, and 14. This rule eliminates GII from the feasible set when the answer to question G is No. Thus, we can distinguish two variants of each of these types.

is a nominal variable designating classes of problems generated by the paths which lead to the terminal nodes. Thus, all problems which have no quality requirements and in which acceptance is not critical are defined as type 1; all problems which have no quality requirement in which acceptance is critical but the prior probability of acceptance of the leader's decision is high are defined as type 2 and so on.

The feasible set for each of the fourteen problem types is shown in table 3. It can be seen that there are some problem types for which only one method remains in the feasible set, others for which two methods remain feasible and still others for which five methods remain feasible. It should be recalled that the feasible set is defined as the set of methods which remains after all those which violate rules designated to protect the quality and acceptance of the decision have been excluded.

Choosing among Alternatives in the Feasible Set

When more than one method remains in the feasible set, there are a number of alternative decision rules which might dictate the choice among them. One, which will be examined in greatest depth, utilizes the number of man-hours used in solving the problem as the basis for choice. Given a set of methods with equal likelihood of meeting both quality and acceptance requirements for the decision, it chooses that method which requires the least investment in man-hours. This is deemed to be the method furthest to the left within the feasible set. Thus, if AI, AII, CI, CII, and GII are all feasible as in problem types 1 and 2, AI would be the method chosen. This decision rule acts to minimize man-hours subject to quality and acceptance constraints.

This decision rule for choosing among alternatives in the feasible set results in the prescription of each of the five decision processes in some situations. AI is prescribed for four problem types (1, 2, 4, and 5); AII is prescribed for two problem types (9 and 10); CI is prescribed for only one problem type (8); CII is prescribed for four problem types (7, 11, 13, and 14); and GII is prescribed for three problem types (3, 6, and 12). The relative frequency with which the five decision processes would be prescribed for any leader would, of course, be dependent on the distribution of problem types in his role.

Application of the Model

To illustrate how the model might be applied in actual administrative situations, a set of four cases will be presented

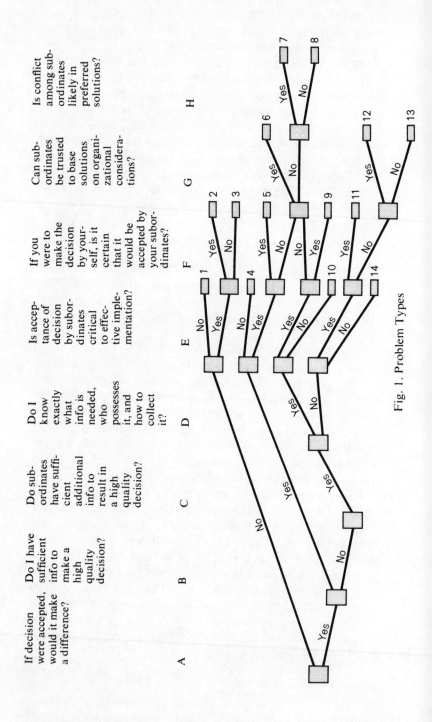

Fig. 1. Problem Types

Table 3
Problem Types and the Feasible Set of Leadership Styles

Problem Type	Acceptable Methods
1	AI, AII, CI, CII, GII
2	AI, AII, CI, CII, GII
3	GII
4	AI, AII, CI, CII, GII*
5	AI, AII, CI, CII, GII*
6	GII
7	CII
8	CI, CII
9	AII, CI, CII, GII*
10	AII, CI, CII, GII*
11	CII, GII*
12	GII
13	CII
14	CII, GII*

*Within the feasible set only when the answer to question G is Yes

and analyzed with the use of the model. Following the description of the case, the authors' analysis will be given including a specification of problem type, feasible set, and solution indicated by the model. While an attempt has been made to describe these cases as completely as is necessary to permit the reader to make the judgments required by the model, there may remain some room for subjectivity. The reader may wish after reading the case to analyze it himself using the model and then to compare his analysis with that of the authors.

Case 1

You are general foreman in charge of a large gang laying an oil pipeline. It is now necessary to estimate your expected rate of progress in order to schedule material deliveries to the next field site.

You know the nature of the terrain you will be traveling and have the historical data needed to compute the mean and variance in the rate of speed over that type of terrain. Given these two variables it is a simple matter to calculate the earliest and latest times at which materials and support facilities will be needed at the next site. It is important that your estimate be reasonably accurate. Underestimates result in idle foremen and workers, and an overestimate results in tying up materials for a period of time before they are to be used.

Progress has been good and your five foremen and other members of the gang stand to receive substantial bonuses if the project is completed ahead of schedule.

Analysis
Questions: A (Quality?) = Yes
            B (Manager's information?) = Yes
            E (Acceptance?) = No
Problem type: 4
Feasible set: AI, AII, CI, CII, GII
Minimum man-hours solution: AI
Rule violations: None

Case 2

You are supervising the work of twelve engineers. Their formal training and work experience are very similar, permitting you to use them interchangeably on projects. Yesterday, your manager informed you that a request had been received from an overseas affiliate for four engineers to go abroad on extended loan for a period of six to eight months. For a number of reasons, he argued and you agreed that this request should be met from your group.

All your engineers are capable of handling this assignment and, from the standpoint of present and future projects, there is no particular reason why any one should be retained over any other. The problem is somewhat complicated by the fact that the overseas assignment is in what is generally regarded in the company as an undesirable location.

Analysis
Questions: A (Quality?) = No
            E (Acceptance?) = Yes
            F (Prior probability of acceptance?) = No
Problem type: 3
Feasible set: GII
Minimum man-hours solution: GII

Rule violations: AI and AII violate rules 4, 5, and 6
CI violates rules 5 and 6
CII violates rule 6

Case 3

You are the head of a staff unit reporting to the vice-president of finance. He has asked you to provide a report on the firm's current portfolio to include recommendations for changes in the selection criteria currently employed. Doubts have been raised about the efficiency of the existing system in the current market conditions, and there is considerable dissatisfaction with prevailing rates of return.

You plan to write the report, but at the moment you are quite perplexed about the approach to take. Your own specialty is the bond market and it is clear to you that a detailed knowledge of the equity market, which you lack, would greatly enhance the value of the report. Fortunately, four members of your staff are specialists in different segments of the equity market. Together, they possess a vast amount of knowledge about the intricacies of investment. However, they seldom agree on the best way to achieve anything when it comes to the stock market. While they are obviously conscientious as well as knowledgeable, they have major differences when it comes to investment philosophy and strategy.

You have six weeks before the report is due. You have already begun to familiarize yourself with the firm's current portfolio and have been provided by management with a specific set of constraints that any portfolio must satisfy. Your immediate problem is to come up with some alternatives to the firm's present practices and select the most promising for detailed analysis in your report.

Analysis
Questions: A (Quality?) = Yes
B (Manager's information?) = No
C (Subordinates' information?) = Yes
D (Structured?) = No
E (Acceptance?) = No
Problem type: 14
Feasible set: CII, GII
Minimum man-hours solution: GII
Rule violations: AI violates rules 1 and 3
AII violates rule 3
CI violates rule 3

Case 4

You are on the division manager's staff and work on a wide variety of problems of both an administration and technical nature. You have been given the assignment of developing a universal method to be used in each of the five plants in the division for manually reading equipment registers, recording the readings, and transmitting the scorings to a centralized information system. All plants are located in a relatively small geographical region.

Until now there has been a high error rate in the reading and/or transmittal of the data. Some locations have considerably higher error rates than others, and the methods used to record and transmit the data vary between plants. It is probable, therefore, that part of the error variance is a function of specific local conditions rather than anything else, and this will complicate the establishment of any system common to all plants. You have the information on error rates but no information on the local practices which generate these errors or on the local conditions which necessitate the different practices.

Everyone would benefit from an improvement in the quality of the data as it is used in a number of important decisions. Your contracts with the plants are through the quality-control supervisors who are responsible for collecting the data. They are a conscientious group committed to doing their jobs well, but are highly sensitive to interference on the part of higher management in their own operations. Any solution which does not receive the active support of the various plant supervisors is unlikely to reduce the error rate significantly.

Analysis

Questions: A (Quality?) = Yes

B (Manager's information?) = No

C (Subordinates' information?) = Yes

D (Structured?) = No

E (Acceptance?) = Yes

F (Prior probability of acceptance?) = No

G (Trust?) = Yes

Problem type: 12

Feasible set: GII

Minimum man-hours solution: GII

Rule violations: AI violates rules 1, 3, 4 and 7

AII violates rules 3, 4, and 7

CI violates rules 3 and 7

CII violates rule 7

Short- versus Long-Term Models

The model described above seeks to protect, if relevant, the quality of the decision, to create any necessary acceptance of the decision, and to expend the least number of man-hours in the process. In view of its attention to conditions surrounding the making and implementation of a particular decision rather than any long-term considerations, it could be termed a short-term model.

It seems likely, however, that the leadership methods which may be optimal for short-term results may be different from those which would be optimal when executed over a longer period of time. Consider a leader who has been uniformly pursuing an autocratic style (AI or AII) and, perhaps as a consequence, has subordinates who cannot be trusted to pursue organizational goals (attribute G) and who have have little additional knowledge or experience to bring to bear on the decisions to be made (attribute C). An examination of the structure of the time-minimizing model reveals that with few exceptions, the leader would be instructed by the model to continue his present autocratic style.

It appears likely, however, that the use of more participative methods would, in time, change the status of these problem attributes (i.e., increase the extent to which subordinates would have information relevant to the solution of problems in the future and increase the extent to which their goals are congruent with those of the organization) so as to develop ultimately a more effective problem-solving system. In the example given above, an autocratic approach would be indicated to maximize short-run benefits but a higher degree of participation might maximize performance aggregated over a longer period.

A promising approach to the development of a long-term model is one which places less weight on man-hours as the basis for choice of method within the feasible set. Given a long-term orientation one would be interested in the trade-off between man-hours in problem solving and team development, both of which increase with participation. Viewed in these terms, the time-minimizing model places maximum relative weight on man-hours and no weight on development and hence chooses the style furthest to the left within the feasible set. A model which places less weight on man-hours and more weight on development would, if these assumptions are correct, choose a style further to the right within the feasible set.

Summary

In this chapter, a normative model of leadership style was developed. The model attempts to deal with the complexities of the processes involved in leadership by specifying (1) a set of alternatives among which a choice is to be made, (2) the general nature of the processes which they affect, (3) the principal variables governing the effects of the alternatives on each process and (4) explicit rules for decision making based on estimates of the outcome of each process.

Some might argue that it is premature for social scientists to attempt to be prescriptive. Our knowledge is too little and the issues too complex to warrant explicit normative models dealing with matters such as leadership style. It it also true, however, that leaders are facing daily the task of selecting decision-making processes which in turn reflect their leadership style. Is it likely that a model which requires them to deal analytically with the forces impinging upon them and which is consistent with admittedly imperfect research base would produce less rational choices that those which they do make? The criterion for social ability is not perfection but improvement over present practice.

Furthermore, social scientists are increasingly having an influence not only on people's leadership style but also on such matters as job design, training methods, and compensation systems. Too frequently, in the view of the present authors, their prescriptions for action, whether it be job enrichment, sensitivity training, or group decision making, are not based on a systematic analysis of the situation in a manner which would point to the costs and benefits of available alternatives.

Perhaps the most convincing argument for the development of normative models is the fact that in developing and using them their weaknesses can be identified. Insofar as these weaknesses stem from lack of basic knowledge, this deficiency can be remedied through further research. A strong case can be made for the continued interplay between the worlds of practice and social science on the basis of their mutual contributions to one another.

3

Collections of Individuals: Group Processes

**Individuals and
Groups:
Three Points
of View**

Introduction

In the last several chapters, we have been concerned with the flow of influence between two people. When we add a third person to this relationship, and a fourth and a fifth, new kinds of issues begin to arise. These unique "emergent properties" of the human group are our subject matter in these next chapters. Just as we were concerned in the first seven chapters with the conditions that make for individual and two-person effectiveness, our next three chapters consider the effectiveness of the human group.

Shepherd's paper, the first one in this chapter, defines a successful group as one which is both highly cohesive and highly productive. Productivity, of course, implies some group objective, either a goal imposed from outside, like an output quota for an industrial work group, or else determined by the group members themselves. The difference may be crucial.

Shepherd goes on to argue that a group will become successful, by his definition, only if all of several characteristics are present. Some of these criteria (shared values and norms; clear conditions for membership) are designed to minimize interpersonal differences. Other criteria (clear group objectives; well-defined roles including leadership roles) are designed to direct and focus the efforts of individual group members. Shepherd's final criterion, open and full communication among members, may serve two functions: to maintain and build consensus among group members on goals and expectations, but also to make the group members aware of differences of opinion as soon as they become apparent and while they are still manageable.

Implicit in Shepherd's analysis is the notion that conformity of group members to a common set of beliefs, expectations, and procedures is necessary to prevent the group from flying apart. Cohesion and productivity therefore exact their price: forced conformity to the group's standards of behavior. While such pressures to conform may seem unattractive to the free spirit, it should be fairly obvious that *some* degree of conformity is essential to any successful collective action. We all conform in our everyday lives by speaking the same language, by recognizing the same currency, by following the same customs. When conformity to some broad set of values begins to break down, the cohesion and viability of the group is immediately threatened. Witness the social turmoil in the wake of the civil rights movement. This is not at all to suggest that change toward a new set of customs is somehow bad. On the contrary, it's frequently necessary, and often useful. But as the old conformity begins to break down and the group moves toward a new equilibrium, we must expect it to pass through an "unfrozen" period.

The paper by Mancur Olson presents a different point of view. Olson is an economist, and like most economists starts out by assuming that individuals will attempt to pursue their own self-interest, and will regard all actions, including group membership, only as means to the ultimate end of satisfying their own individual preferences. In contrast, Shepherd, like most social psychologists, seems to be saying that if only the members of a group could have perfect consensus on all important issues, they would automatically be motivated to be productive on behalf of the group.

Olson uses some terms which we should define before going on with our own argument. He uses the terms "public goods" or "collective goods" to refer to products, services, or conditions which cannot be denied to any member of the group. We all benefit from national defense. We all benefit from clean air, and there is no effective way to deny anyone in the society access either to national defense or clean air. Members of labor unions all benefit from increased wage rates that result from collective bargaining.

But now suppose you're a member of the group, and will benefit from whatever the group does, whether or not you contribute your share. If everyone thinks that way, it's conceivable that no single individual would be willing to work toward the public good himself, despite the fact that all members would be in agreement that the public good is worth the effort of all members. So Olson argues that consensus on goals is not enough. Furthermore, the failure to provide collective goods becomes more serious as the group grows larger. What is needed, he argues, is individual incentives which will harness each individual's self-interest in the pursuit of the group goal.

Very small groups, in which individual action on the group's behalf springs forth spontaneously, Olson calls "privileged groups." And groups which are of medium size where *some* collective action emerges spontaneously he calls "intermediate groups." The problem of how to get group action in what Olson terms a "large latent" group is more problematic. His solution is to break the large group into a federation of smaller groups so that each small group is cohesive and the large "group-of-groups" is also cohesive. Later, in chapter 12, Simon's paper on "The Architecture of Complexity" presents a similar idea. Simon argues that large systems can be stable only if they are organized hierarchically—not in the sense of a status or authority hierarchy, but in the sense that the large system is composed of stable subsystems, which in turn are composed of stable sub-subsystems.

The final piece in this chapter, by Maxine Bucklow, contains an excellent history of the development of the theory of industrial groups. Although she focuses primarily on the rank-and-file worker, her comments apply with only minor modifications to groups within managerial echelons as well. Her concern is less with the group as a unit than with the group's impact on the motivation of the individual worker.

As she points out, early studies of industrial work groups argued that the group provided only marginal motivation to the worker to be more productive. She presents evidence suggesting that using work groups in that old way does indeed have little impact on individual productivity. If the group is to be a truly effective force in motivating the individual worker to be productive, she points out, it (the group) must be given "responsible autonomy" to make decisions about important aspects of the group's work assignments, and so forth, and not just responsibility for marginal decisions like whether the ten-minute coffee break shall start at 9:30 or 10:00.

As she quite correctly observes, management personnel are apt to be quite anxious and resistant about relaxing traditional management controls over the primary work group. There are two possible reasons for this anxiety. One is that management may fear that the workers will set output quotas too low, and use their power to satisfy their own personal needs. A second source of anxiety is that even though the group may wind up being highly productive, they may do so in a way which imposes substantial external costs on the rest of the organization. This is the coordination problem. We suspect that delegation of responsible autonomy would work best under technological conditions which permitted the decomposition of the whole job into relatively independent subjobs big enough for small work groups. Consider a long assembly line on which perhaps hundreds of workers are employed. Simply breaking up the workers into primary groups of adjacent workers and assigning them "responsible autonomy" might well be disastrous, unless the whole work process were redesigned too.

There is one disturbing note to Bucklow's analysis. She seems to be assuming that transferring power to a group of workers will cause those workers to adhere more closely to management objectives of high productivity. Unless one is willing to assume the existence of a Veblenesque "instinct of workmanship," it is not clear that transferring power will necessarily lead to higher productivity.

Features of the
Successful Group
Clovis R. Shepherd

The following portrait of a successful group is provided in order to give the reader a model against which to assess his personal experiences and to indicate what the author feels is consistent with small-group theory and research. It is a descriptive (as opposed to analytic) model and embodies discussion of some of the problems which confront groups.

The model includes five features of groups. These five features do not exhaust all descriptive categories but they do serve the purpose here reasonably well. These features are objectives, role differentiation, values and norms, membership, and communication. The meaning of these terms will become clearer as they are discussed.

Objectives refers to the goals of a group, its purposes, its reasons for existence, the ends it seeks, or whatever other term one may wish to use. Generally a successful group has clear objectives, not vague ones, and the members of the group have personal objectives which are identical or compatible with the group's objectives. If the group's objectives are vague the members will probably be working at cross purposes since they are unlikely to have the same or compatible personal objectives. Consequently, the more time a group spends in developing agreement on clear objectives the less time it need spend in achieving them and the more likely the members' contributions will converge toward a solution.

Role differentiation refers to the clarity of the roles played by and expected of the members of the group, including whatever leadership roles exist. A successful group is one in which each member's role is clear and known to himself and to others in the group. It is also important that the official and unofficial leaders be known and that they function in ways to facilitate communication so that no member hesitates

Reprinted from *Small Groups: Some Sociological Perspectives* (San Francisco: Chandler Publishing Co., 1964) by permission of the publisher and author.

to contribute his ideas and feelings, and so that some degree of shared influence is present. The confusion when roles are unknown or unclear is obvious, but it is less obvious that the successful group is one in which role differentiation is clear and graded in terms of status and prestige. The popular notion that the democratic ideal is a group in which all members exert an equal amount of leadership may be a desirable ideology, but it has little support in research.

Values and norms deal, respectively, with the desirable and with the expected. A value is something desired or wanted by a person, something believed in. In everyday life a value is usually signified by one or more of the following verbs: *believe, desire, wish, want, value,* or *prefer*. A norm is a rule governing behavior, established and enforced by a group (or by some collectivity). Some of the verbs used in everyday life to denote a norm are: *ought, should, must,* or *had better*.

Values, although an individual phenomenon and, hence, apt to differ among any collection of persons, are similar in at least some ways in a successful group. Having similar values may not (and probably does not) stem from members influencing each other, but from members discovering that they already hold some values in common. A group in which members do not share at least some relevant values is likely to be successful only for limited and short-run objectives. Though some differences in values may be present in a successful group, very little difference in norms can be tolerated. To be sure, some variation in general social norms is possible (people have different backgrounds and group affiliations), but the norms that develop in the group to govern the behavior of its members must be agreed upon. These group norms refer to procedure, including how decisions are to be made and implemented, as well as to the roles of the members. In a successful group these norms of various types are clear and agreed upon, and the group takes action through consensus, not through majority vote or minority railroading. Values and norms, though different, shade into each other at some point, especially when people try to justify a norm, since their justification often turns out to be that the norm is consistent with or contributes to some shared value.

Membership in a successful group is clearcut and members are heterogeneous. Clarity in membership criteria helps ensure continuity, commitment, and the development of group structure and process. Membership criteria, when made explicit, also involve attention to other features of the group, since at least some membership criteria will be relevant to the nature of the group's objectives, its values and norms, and its role differentiation. Heterogeneity in the group refers to diverse skills, experience, and interest, factors which will encourage role differentiation and flexibility in functioning. Few things destroy or incapacitate a group more than discontinuity or homogeneity in membership. Too much heterogeneity, however, may make it impossible to agree on shared values, much less accepted norms. Of course, a successful group can absorb some discontinuity—it will likely have to weather the loss of a member or two and the admittance of a newcomer or two.

Communication in a successful group is open and full. No one withholds relevant information, whether it be ideas or feelings, and each member provides that information when appropriate. In addition, at least some biographical information becomes shared, since open and full communication includes nonverbal as well as verbal responses. It is possible, of course, that some relevant information will be withheld, especially when disruptive consequences may occur. No husband tells his wife everything, nor do members of a successful group act solely on impulse. On the other hand, in a successful group no member withholds information because he is frightened, anxious, disgusted, or curious to see what will happen when he finally drops his bomb or quietly provides crucial information after the rest of the group has gone down some divergent path.

These five features, of course, do not exhaust relevant characteristics of groups. No mention has been made of cohesion, an admittedly important feature, nor of productivity, equally important. Cohesion and productivity are, in a sense, outcomes of a group. Cohesion is an internal product which, in a successful group, is likely to be high. Productivity is partly an external product, the contribution or output of a group, which is also likely to be high in a successful group. So, in effect, the above five features of a successful group are features of a group with high cohesion and high productivity. Or, to put it another way, the definition of a successful group is a group with high cohesion and high productivity, in which objectives, role differentiation, values and norms, and membership criteria are clear and agreed upon, and in which communication is open and full.

Finally, some mention must be made of another feature of groups, their autonomy—their degree of freedom from control or influence by other groups or persons. A group of high autonomy is apt to be a fairly successful group since there are few if any external forces maintaining it. If members do not have to be in the group, or the group need not exist, its very existence is some testimony to the presence of shared objectives and shared values and norms. Also, since no forces external to the group have organized it, whatever organization exists is likely to be a spontaneous, evolved product. This kind of origin means that the developing character of the group is considered desirable by the members if it continues to exist. On the other hand, a group of low autonomy is confronted at first with an organization—with objectives, roles, values and norms, membership criteria, and communication styles already established. But merely because they are established does not mean that they are understood or accepted by the group. Having them, a group of low autonomy can appear to be successful when, in fact, it is not.

Group Size and
Group Behavior
Mancur Olson

A. The Coherence and Effectiveness of Small Groups

The greater effectiveness of relatively small groups—the "privileged" and "intermediate" groups—is evident from observation and experience as well as from theory. Consider, for example, meetings that involve too many people, and accordingly cannot make decisions promptly or carefully. Everyone would like to have the meeting end quickly, but few if any will be willing to let their pet concern be dropped to make this possible. And though all of those participating presumably have an interest in reaching sound decisions, this all too often fails to happen. When the number of participants is large, the typical participant will know that his own efforts will probably not make much difference to the outcome, and that he will be affected by the meeting's decision in much the same way no matter how much or how little effort he puts into studying the issues. Accordingly, the typical participant may not take the trouble to study the issues as carefully as he would have if he had been able to make the decision by himself. The decisions of the meeting are thus public goods to the participants (and perhaps others), and the contribution that each participant will make toward achieving or improving these public goods will become smaller as the meeting becomes larger. It is for these reasons, among others, that organizations so often turn to the small group; committees, subcommittees, and small leadership groups are created, and once created they tend to play a crucial role.

This observation is corroborated by some interesting research results. John James, among others, has done empirical work on this subject, with results that support the theory offered in this study, though his work was not done to prove any such theory. Professor James found that in a variety of institutions, public and private, national and local, "action

Reprinted by the permission of the publishers from Mancur Olson, *The Logic of Collective Action: Public Goods and the Theory of Groups* (Cambridge, Mass.: Harvard University Press, 1965). Copyright 1965, 1971 by the President and Fellows of Harvard College.

taking" groups and subgroups tended to be much smaller than "non–action taking" groups and subgroups. In one sample he studied, the average size of the "action taking" subgroups was 6.5 members, whereas the average size of the "non–action taking" subgroups was 14 members. These subgroups were in a large banking concern, whose secretary spontaneously offered the following opinion: "We have found," he wrote, "that committees should be small when you expect action and relatively large when you are looking for points of view, reactions, etc."[1] This is apparently not a situation restricted to banking. It is widely known that in the United States Congress and in the state legislatures, power resides to a remarkable, and what is to many an alarming degree, in the committees and subcommittees.[2] James found that U.S. Senate subcommittees at the time of his investigation had 5.4 members on the average, House subcommittees had 7.8, the Oregon state government, 4.7, and the Eugene, Oregon, municipal government, 5.3.[3] In short, the groups that actually do the work are quite small. A different study corroborates James's findings; Professor A. Paul Hare, in controlled experiments with groups of five and twelve boys, found that the performance of the groups of five was generally superior.[4] The sociologist Georg Simmel explicitly stated that smaller groups could act more decisively and use their resources more effectively than large groups: "Small, centripetally organized groups usually call on and use all their energies, while in large groups, forces remain much oftener potential."[5]

The fact that the partnership can be workable institutional form when the number of partners is quite small, but is generally unsuccessful when the number of partners is very large, may provide another illustration of the advantages of

1. John James, "A Preliminary Study of the Size Determinant in Small Group Interaction," *American Sociological Review* 16 (August 1951): 474–77.

2. Bertram M. Gross, *The Legislative Struggle* (New York: McGraw-Hill, 1953), pp. 265–337; see also Ernest S. Griffith, *Congress* (New York: New York University Press, 1951).

3. For a lighthearted and humorous, but nonetheless helpful, argument that the ideal committee or cabinet has only five members, see C. Northcote Parkinson, *Parkinson's Law* (Boston: Houghton Mifflin, 1957), pp. 33–34.

4. A. Paul Hare, "A Study of Interaction and Consensus in Different Sized Groups," *American Sociological Review* 17 (June 1952): 261–68.

5. Georg Simmel, *The Sociology of George Simmel,* trans. Kurt H. Wolff (Glencoe, Ill.: Free Press [1950]), p. 92. In another place Simmel says that socialist societies, by which he appears to mean voluntary groups that share their incomes according to some principle of equity, must necessarily be small. "Up to this day, at least, socialistic or nearly socialistic societies have been possible only in very small groups and have always failed in larger ones" (p. 88).

smaller groups. When a partnership has many members, the individual partner observes that his own effort or contribution will not greatly affect the performance of the enterprise, and expects that he will get his prearranged share of the earnings whether or not he contributes as much as he could have done. The earnings of a partnership, in which each partner gets a prearranged percentage of the return, are a collective good to the partners, and when the number of partners increases, the incentive for each partner to work for the welfare of the enterprise lessens. This is to be sure only one of a number of reasons why partnerships tend to persist only when the number of partners is fairly small, but it is one that could be decisive in a really large partnership.[6]

The autonomy of management in the large modern corporation, with thousands of stockholders, and the subordination of management in the corporation owned by a small number of stockholders, may also illustrate the special difficulties of the large group. The fact that management tends to control the large corporation and is able, on occasion, to further its own interest at the expense of the stockholders, is surprising, since the common stockholders have the legal power to discharge the management at their pleasure, and since they have, as a group, also an incentive to do so, if the management is running the corporation partly or wholly in the interest of the managers. Why, then, do not the stockholders exercise their power? They do not because, in a large corporation, with thousands of stockholders, any effort the typical stockholder makes to oust the management will probably be unsuccessful; and even if the stockholder should be successful, most of the returns in the form of higher dividends and stock prices will go to the rest of the stockholders, since the typical stockholder owns only a trifling percentage of the outstanding stock. The income of the corporation is a collective good to the stockholders, and the stockholder who holds only a minute percentage of the total stock, like any member of a latent group, has no incentive to work in the group interest. Specifically, he has no incentive to challenge the management of the company, however inept or corrupt it might be. (This argument does not, however, entirely apply to the stockholder who wants the manager's position and pelf for himself, for he is not working for a collective good; it is significant that most attempts to overthrow corporate management are started by those who want to take over the man-

6. The foregoing argument need not apply to partners that are *supposed* to be "sleeping partners," i.e., provide only capital. Nor does it take account of the fact that in many cases each partner is liable for the losses of the whole partnership.

agement themselves.) Corporations with a small number of stockholders, by contrast, are not only de jure, but also de facto, controlled by the stockholders, for in such cases the concepts of privileged or intermediate groups apply.[7]

There is also historical evidence for the theory presented here. George C. Homans, in one of the best-known books in American social science,[8] has pointed out that the small group has shown much more durability throughout history than the large group:

> At the level of . . . the small group, at the level, that is, of a social unit (no matter by what name we call it) each of whose members can have some firsthand knowledge of each of the others, human society, for many millennia longer than written history, has been able to cohere. . . . They have tended to produce a surplus of the goods that make organization successful.
>
> [A]ncient Egypt and Mesopotamia were civilizations. So were classical India and China; so was Greco-Roman civilization, and so is our own Western civilization that grew out of medieval Christendom. . . .
>
> The appalling fact is that, after flourishing for a span of time, every civilization but one has collapsed . . . formal organizations that articulated the whole have fallen to pieces . . . much of the technology has even been forgotten for lack of the large scale cooperation that could put it in effect . . . the civilization has slowly sunk to a Dark Age, a situation, much like the one from which it started on its upward path, in which the mutual hostility of small groups is the condition of the internal cohesion of each one . . . Society can fall thus far, but apparently no farther . . . One can read the dismal story, eloquently told, in the historians of civilization from Spengler to Toynbee. The one civilization that has not entirely gone to pieces is our Western Civilization, and we are desperately anxious about it.
>
> [But] At the level of the tribe or group, society has always found itself able to cohere.[9]

7. See Adolph A. Berle, Jr., and Gardiner C. Means, *The Modern Corporation and Private Property* (New York: Macmillan, 1932); J. A. Livingston, *The American Stockholder,* rev. ed. (New York: Collier Books, 1963); P. Sargent Florence, *Ownership, Control and Success of Large Companies* (London: Sweet & Maxwell, 1961); William Mennell, *Takeover* (London: Lawrence & Wishart, 1962).

8. George C. Homans, *The Human Group* (New York: Harcourt, Brace, 1950).

9. Ibid, pp. 454–56. See also Neil W. Chamberlain, *General Theory of Economic Process* (New York: Harper, 1955), esp. pp. 347–48, and Sherman Krupp, *Pattern in Organization Analysis* (Philadelphia: Chilton, 1961), pp. 118–39 and 171–76.

Homans's claim that the smallest groups are the most durable is quite persuasive and certainly supports the theory offered here. But his deduction from these historical facts is not wholly consistent with the approach in this study. His book focuses on the following idea: "Let us put our case for the last time: At the level of the small group, society has always been able to cohere. We infer, therefore, that if civilization is to stand, it must retain . . . some of the features of the small group itself."[10] Homans's conclusion depends on the assumption that the techniques or methods of the small group are more effective. But this is not necessarily true; the small, or "privileged," group is in a more advantageous position from the beginning, for some or all of its members will have an incentive to see that it does not fail. This is not true of the large group; the large group does not automatically find that the incentives that face the group also face the individuals in the group. Therefore, it does not follow that, because the small group has historically been more effective, the very large group can prevent failure by copying its methods. The "privileged" group, and for that matter the "intermediate" group, are simply in a more advantageous position.[11]

B. Problems of the Traditional Theories

Homans's belief that the lessons of the small group should be applied to large groups has much in common with the assumption upon which much small-group research is based. There has been a vast amount of research into the small group in recent years, much of it based on the idea that the results of (experimentally convenient) research on small groups can be made directly applicable to larger groups merely by multiplying these results by a scale factor.[12] Some social psychologists, sociologists, and political scientists assume that the small group is so much like the large group, in matters other than size, that it must behave according to somewhat similar laws. But if the distinctions drawn here among the "privileged" group, the "intermediate" group, and the "latent" group have any meaning, this assumption is un-

10. Homans, *The Human Group,* p. 468.

11. The difference between latent groups and privileged or intermediate groups is only one of several factors accounting for the instability of many ancient empires and civilizations. I have pointed to another such factor myself in a forthcoming book.

12. Kurt Lewin, *Field Theory in Social Change* (New York: Harper, 1951), pp. 163–64; Harold H. Kelley and John W. Thibaut, *The Social Psychology of Groups* (New York: John Wiley, 1959), pp. 6, 191–92; Hare, "Study of Interaction and Consensus," pp. 261–68; Sidney Verba, *Small Groups and Political Behavior* (Princeton, N.J.: Princeton University Press, 1961), pp. 4, 14, 99–109, 245–48.

warranted, at least so long as the groups have a common, collective interest. For the small, privileged group can expect that its collective needs will probably be met one way or another, and the fairly small (or intermediate) group has a fair chance that voluntary action will solve its collective problems, but the large, latent group cannot act in accordance with its common interests so long as the members of the group are free to further their individual interests.

The distinctions developed in this study also suggest that the traditional explanation of voluntary associations needs amendment. The traditional theory emphasizes the (alleged) universality of participation in voluntary associations in modern societies and explains small groups and large organizations in terms of the same causes. In its most sophisticated form, the traditional theory argues that the prevalence of participation in the modern voluntary association is due to the "structural differentiation" of developing societies; that is, to the fact that as the small, primary groups of primitive society have declined or become more specialized, the functions that multitudes of these small groups used to perform are being taken over by large voluntary associations. But, if the meaningless notion of a universal "joiner instinct" is to be rejected, how is the membership in these new, large voluntary associations recruited? There are admittedly functions for large associations to perform, as small, primary groups become more specialized and decline. And the performance of these functions no doubt would bring benefits to large numbers of people. But will these benefits provide an incentive for any of the individuals affected to join, much less create, a large voluntary association to perform the function in question? The answer is that, however beneficial the functions large voluntary associations are expected to perform, there is no incentive for any individual in a latent group to join such as association.[13] However important a function may be, there is no presumption that a latent group will be able to organize and act to perform this function. Small primary groups by contrast presumably can act to perform functions that are beneficial to them. The traditional theory of voluntary associations is therefore mistaken to the extent that it implicitly assumes that latent groups will act to perform functional purposes the same way small groups will. The existence of such large organizations as do exist must moreover be explained by different factors from those that explain the

13. There is no suggestion here, of course, that all groups are necessarily explained in terms of monetary or material interests. The argument does not require that individuals have only monetary or material wants. See note 17 below.

existence of smaller groups. This suggests that the traditional theory is incomplete, and needs to be modified in the light of the logical relationships explained in this study. This contention is strengthened by the fact that the traditional theory of voluntary associations is not at all in harmony with the empirical evidence, which indicates that participation in large voluntary organizations is very much less than that theory would suggest.[14]

There is still another respect in which the analysis developed here can be used to modify the traditional analysis. This involves the question of group consensus. It is often assumed (though usually implicitly) in discussions of organizational or group cohesion that the crucial matter is the degree of consensus; if there are many serious disagreements, there will be no coordinated, voluntary effort, but if there is a high degree of agreement on what is wanted and how to get it there will almost certainly be effective group action.[15] The degree of consensus is sometimes discussed as though it were the *only* important determinant of group action or group cohesion. There is, of course, no question that a lack of consensus is inimical to the prospects for group action and group cohesion. But it does not follow that perfect consensus, both about the desire for the collective good and the most efficient means of getting it, will always bring about the achievement of the group goal. In a large, latent group there will be no tendency for the group to organize to achieve its goals through the voluntary, rational action of the members of the group, even if there is perfect consensus. Indeed, the assumption made in this work is that there is perfect consensus. This is, to be sure, an unrealistic assumption, for perfection of consensus, as of other things, is at best very rare. But the results obtained under this assumption are, for that reason,

14. Mirra Komaravsky, "The Voluntary Associations of Urban Dwellers," *American Sociological Review* 11 (December 1946): 686–98; Floyd Dotson, "Patterns of Voluntary Membership among Working Class Families," *American Sociological Review* 16 (October 1951): 687; John C. Scott, Jr., "Membership and Participation in Voluntary Associations," *American Sociological Review* 22 (June 1957): 315; and Murray Hausknecht, *The Joiners—A Sociological Description of Voluntary Association Membership in the United States* (New York: Bedminster Press, 1962).

15. See Hare, "Study of Interaction and Consensus"; Raymond Cattell, "Concepts and Methods in the Measurement of Group Syntality," in *Small Groups,* ed. A. Paul Hare, Edward F. Borgatta, and Robert F. Bales (New York: Alfred A. Knopf, 1955); Leon Festinger, *A Theory of Cognitive Dissonance* (Evanston, Ill.: Row, Peterson, 1957); Leon Festinger, Stanley Schachter, and Kurt Back, "The Operation of Group Standards," in *Group Dynamics,* ed. Dorwin Cartwright and Alvin Zander (Evanston, Ill.: Row, Peterson, 1953); David B. Truman, *The Governmental Process* (New York: Alfred A. Knopf, 1958).

all the stronger, for if voluntary, rational action cannot enable a large, latent group to organize for action to achieve its collective goals, even with perfect consensus, then a fortiori this conclusion should hold in the real world, where consensus is usually incomplete and often altogether absent. It is thus very important to distinguish between the obstacles to group-oriented action that are due to a lack of group consensus and those that are due to a lack of individual incentives.

C. Social Incentives and Rational Behavior

Economic incentives are not, to be sure, the only incentives; people are sometimes also motivated by a desire to win prestige, respect, friendship, and other social and psychological objectives. Though the phrase "socioeconomic status" often used in discussions of status suggests that there may be a correlation between economic position and social position, there is no doubt that the two are sometimes different. The possibility that, in a case where there was no economic incentive for an individual to contribute to the achievement of a group interest, there might nonetheless be a social incentive for him to make such a contribution, must therefore be considered. And it is obvious that this is a possibility. If a small group of people who had an interest in a collective good happened also to be personal friends, or belonged to the same social club, and some of the group left the burden of providing that collective good on others, they might, even if they gained economically by this course of action, lose socially by it, and the social loss might outweigh the economic gain. Their friends might use "social pressure" to encourage them to do their part toward achieving the group goal, or the social club might exclude them, and such steps might be effective, for everyday observation reveals that most people value the fellowship of their friends and associates, and value social status, personal prestige, and self-esteem.

The existence of these social incentives to group-oriented action does not, however, contradict or weaken the analysis of this study. If anything, it strengthens it, for social status and social acceptance are individual, noncollective goods. Social sanctions and social rewards are "selective incentives"; that is, they are among the kinds of incentives that may be used to mobilize a latent group. It is in the nature of social incentives that they can distinguish among individuals: the recalcitrant individual can be ostracized, and the cooperative individual can be invited into the center of the charmed circle. Some students of organizational theory have rightly emphasized that social incentives must be analyzed in much the same way as monetary incentives.[16] Still other types of incentives can be analyzed in much the same way.[17]

16. See especially Chester I. Barnard, *The Functions of the Executive* (Cambridge, Mass.: Harvard University Press, 1938), chap. 11, "The Economy of Incentives," pp. 139–60, and the same author's *Organization and Management* (Cambridge, Mass.: Harvard University Press, 1948), chap. 9, "Functions and Pathology of Status Systems in Formal Organizations," pp. 207–44; Peter B. Clark and James Q. Wilson, "Incentive Systems: A Theory of Organizations," *Administrative Science Quarterly* 6 (September 1961): 129–66; and Herbert A. Simon, *Administrative Behavior* (New York: Macmillan, 1957), esp. pp. 115–17. I am indebted to Edward C. Banfield for helpful suggestions on social incentives and organization theory.

17. In addition to monetary and social incentives, there are also erotic incentives, psychological incentives, moral incentives, and so on. To the extent that any of these types of incentives leads a latent group to obtain a collective good, it could again only be because they are or can be used as "selective incentives," i.e., because they distinguish between those individuals who support action in the common interest and those who do not. Even in the case where moral attitudes determine whether or not a person will act in a group-oriented way, the crucial factor is that the moral reaction serves as a "selective incentive." If the sense of guilt, or the destruction of self-esteem, that occurs when a person feels he has forsaken his moral code, affected those who had contributed toward the achievement of a group good, as well as those who had not, the moral code could not help to mobilize a latent group. To repeat: the point is that moral attitudes could mobilize a latent group only to the extent they provided selective incentives. The adherence to a moral code that demands the sacrifices needed to obtain a collective good therefore need *not* contradict any of the analysis in this study; indeed, this analysis shows the need for such a moral code or for some other selective incentive.

At no point in this study, however, will any such moral force or incentive be used to explain any of the examples of group action that will be studied. There are three reasons for this. First, it is not possible to get empirical proof of the motivation behind any person's action; it is not possible definitely to say whether a given individual acted for moral reasons or for other reasons in some particular case. A reliance on moral explanatons could thus make the theory untestable. Second, no such explanation is needed, since there will be sufficient explanations on other grounds for all the group action that will be considered. Third, most organized pressure groups are explicitly working for gains for themselves, not gains for other groups, and in such cases it is hardly plausible to ascribe group action to any moral code. Moral motives or incentives for group action have therefore been discussed, not to explain any given example of group action, but rather to show that their existence need not contradict the theory offered here, and could if anything tend to support it.

The erotic and psychological incentives that must be important in family and friendship groups could logically be analyzed within the framework of the theory. On the other hand, "affective" groups such as family and friendship groups could normally be studied much more usefully with entirely different sorts of theories, since the analysis used in this study does not shed much light on these groups. On the special features of "affective" groups, see Verba (note 12, above), p. 6 and pp. 142–84.

In general, social pressure and social incentives operate only in groups of smaller size, in the groups so small that the members can have face-to-face contact with one another. Though in an oligopolistic industry with only a handful of firms there may be strong resentment against the "chiseler" who cuts prices to increase his own sales at the expense of the group, in a perfectly competitive industry there is usually no such resentment; indeed, the man who succeeds in increasing his sales and output in a perfectly competitive industry is usually admired and set up as a good example by his competitors. Anyone who has observed a farming community, for instance, knows that the most productive farmer, who sells the most and thus does the most to lower the price, is usually the one with the highest status. There are perhaps two reasons for this difference in the attitudes of large and small groups. First, in the large, latent group, each member, by definition, is so small in relation to the total that his actions will not matter much one way or another; so it would seem pointless for one perfect competitor, or a member of some other latent group, to snub or abuse another for a selfish, antigroup action, because the recalcitrant's action would not be decisive in any event. Second, in any large group everyone cannot possibly know everyone else, and the group will ipso facto not be a friendship group; so a person will ordinarily not be affected socially if he fails to make sacrifices on behalf of his group's goals. To return to the case of the farmer, it is clear that one farmer cannot possibly know all the other farmers who sell the same commodity; he would not feel that the social group within which he measured his status had much to do with the group with which he shared the interest in the collective good. Accordingly, there is no presumption that social incentives will lead individuals in the latent group to obtain a collective good.

There is, however, one case in which social incentives may well be able to bring about group-oriented action in a latent group. This is the case of a "federal" group—a group divided into a number of small groups, each of which has a reason to join with the others to form a federation representing the large group as a whole. If the central or federated organization provides some service to the small constituent organizations, they may be induced to use their social incentives to get the individuals belonging to each small group to contribute toward the achievement of the collective goals of the whole group. Thus, organizations that use selective social incentives to mobilize a latent group interested in a collective good must be federations of smaller groups. The more important point, however, is that social incentives are important mainly only in the small group, and play a role in the large group only when the large group is a federation of smaller groups.

The groups small enough to be classified here as "privileged" and "intermediate" groups are thus twice blessed in that they have not only economic incentives, but also perhaps social incentives, that lead their members to work toward the achievement of the collective goods. The large, "latent" group, on the other hand, always contains more people than could possibly know each other, and is not likely (except when composed of federated small groups) to develop social pressures that would help it satisfy its interest in a collective good. There is, of course, much evidence for this skepticism about social pressures in a large group in the history of perfectly competitive industries in the United States. Now, if the conclusion that the strength of social pressures varies greatly between small and large groups has validity, it further weakens the traditional theory of voluntary organizations.[18]

Some critics may protest that even if social pressure does not exist in the large or latent group, it does not follow that the completely selfish or profit-maximizing behavior, which the concept of latent groups apparently assumes, is necessarily significant either; people might even in the absence of social pressure act in a selfless way. But this criticism of the

18. There is, however, another kind of social pressure that may occasionally be operative. That is the social pressure that is generated, not primarily through person-to-person friendships, but through mass media. If the members of a latent group are somehow continuously bombarded with propaganda about the worthiness of the attempt to satisfy the common interest in question, they may perhaps in time develop social pressures not entirely unlike those that can be generated in a face-to-face group, and these social pressures may help the latent group to obtain the collective good. A group cannot finance such propaganda unless it is already organized, and it may not be able to organize until it has already been subjected to the propaganda; so this form of social pressure is probably not ordinarily sufficient by itself to enable a group to achieve its collective goals. It would, for example, seem unlikely that there would be much prospect of success in a program to persuade farmers through propaganda to further their interests by voluntarily restricting output, unless there were some captive source of funds to finance the effort. So this form of social pressure generated by mass media does not seem likely to be an important independent source of coordinated effort to bring about the satisfaction of a common interest. Moreover, as was emphasized earlier, the nation-state, with all the emotional loyalty it commands, cannot support itself without compulsion. Therefore it does not seem likely that many large private groups could support themselves solely through social pressure.

concept of the latent group is not relevant, for that concept does *not* necessarily assume the selfish, profit-maximizing behavior that economists usually find in the marketplace. The concept of the large or latent group offered here holds true whether behavior is selfish or unselfish, so long as it is strictly speaking "rational." Even if the member of a large group were to neglect his own interests entirely, he still would not rationally contribute toward the provision of any collective or public good, since his own contribution would not be perceptible. A farmer who placed the interests of other farmers above his own would not necessarily restrict his production to raise farm prices, since he would know that his sacrifice would not bring a noticeable benefit to anyone. Such a rational farmer, however unselfish, would not make such a futile and pointless sacrifice, but he would allocate his philanthropy in order to have a perceptible effect on someone. Selfless behavior that has no perceptible effect is sometimes not even considered praiseworthy. A man who tried to hold back a flood with a pail would probably be considered more of a crank than a saint, even by those he was trying to help. It is no doubt possible infinitesimally to lower the level of a river in flood with a pail, just as it is possible for a single farmer infinitesimally to raise prices by limiting his production, but in both cases the effect is imperceptible, and those who sacrifice themselves in the interest of imperceptible improvements may not even receive the praise normally due selfless behavior.

The argument about large, latent groups, then, does not necessarily imply self-interested behavior, though such behavior would be completely consistent with it.[19] The only requirement is that the behavior of individuals in large groups or organizations of the kind considered should generally be rational, in the sense that their objectives, whether

19. Organizations with primarily economic purposes, like labor unions, farm organizations, and other types of pressure groups, normally claim that they are serving the interests of the groups they represent, and do not contend that they are mainly philanthropic organizations out to help other groups. Thus it would be surprising if most of the members of these "interest groups" should always neglect their own, individual interests. An essentially selfish group interest would not normally attract members who were completely selfless. Thus self-interested behavior may in fact be common in organizations of the kind under study. For intelligent arguments contending that self-interested behavior is general in politics, see James M. Buchanan and Gordon Tullock, *The Calculus of Consent* (Ann Arbor; University of Michigan Press, 1962), pp. 3–39. See also the interesting book by Anthony Downs, *An Economic Theory of Democracy* (New York: Harper, 1957), pp. 3–35.

selfish or unselfish, should be pursued by means that are efficient and effective for achieving these objectives.

The foregoing arguments, theoretical and factual, in this and the previous chapter should at the least justify the separate treatment that large and small groups are given in this study. These arguments are not meant as attacks on any previous interpretations of group behavior, though it seems that some of the usual explanations of large voluntary associations may need elaboration because of the theories offered here. All that need be granted, to accept the main argument of this study, is that large or latent groups will *not* organize for coordinated action merely because, as a group, they have a reason for doing so, though this could be true of smaller groups.

A New Role for the
Work Group
Maxine Bucklow

This article discusses the role assigned to the work group to
bring about desired changes in employee motivation, and
suggests that the role proposed by the Tavistock Institute of
Human Relations in London has been more successful than
earlier approaches which derived largely from the Hawthorne
studies.[1] The Hawthorne work directed attention to the existence of small informal face-to-face groups within larger
work groups. Members of the informal groups shared in a variety of activities and beliefs common to the group, which
were a source of satisfaction, strength, and security, and
provided a buffer against the demands of the larger world of
department and factory. Elton Mayo extrapolated from these
studies to a general social theory centered on the assumption
of a basic human need to be gregarious. His influence was
largely responsible for the widely held belief that employees
were motivated by membership in small primary groups.[2]

The Influence of Lewin

This interest in small groups was greatly reinforced in the immediate postwar years by the research associated with Kurt
Lewin. He defined the group as a dynamic system of interaction between at least two people, and group life as involving
a continuous process of adaptation of individuals to one
another and to their mutual needs and problems. In this

Reprinted from *Administrative Science Quarterly* 11, no. 1 (June
1966): 59–78, by permission of the author and the publisher.

1. F. J. Roethlisberger and W. J. Dickson, *Management and the
Worker* (Cambridge, Mass.: Harvard University Press, 1949).
2. Elton Mayo, *The Human Problems of an Industrial Civilization*
(New York: Macmillan, 1933); idem, *The Social Problems of an Industrial Civilization* (Cambridge, Mass.: Harvard University Press, 1946);
and idem, *The Political Problems of an Industrial Civilization*
(Cambridge, Mass.: Harvard University Press, 1947).

process a structure emerged, which became more stable and organized as the group continued to function. Lewin initiated an era of rigorous laboratory studies into the dynamics of group functioning, designed to reveal fundamental laws of group life. Although much was learned about communication networks, leadership, group cohesion, norms, and so on, empirical results were often conflicting and progress toward basic laws disappointing.

Participation in Group Decision Making

Lewin's influence on industrial practice came largely from the three field studies he directed with children's play groups, housewives, and young-girl pajama machinists at the Harwood Manufacturing Company. The results suggested that involvement in group decision and democratic methods of leadership increased output and member satisfaction. This evidence gave rise to a long period of uncritical adherence to participation and democratic management as means of increasing employee motivation.[3]

In industry, research did not reproduce results as marked as those of the original Lewin studies, and, in general, democratic practices were more successful in achieving satisfaction than efficiency. Research workers such as Maier, Likert, and McGregor realized that their techniques had to be linked to the organizational framework. Likert used overlapping group families and linking-pin functions to tie his participation groups to all levels of the organization.[4] Similarly, Maier's new look at organization envisaged participation in problem-solving conferences at all levels through overlapping membership.[5] Katz and Argyris criticized these proposals because they only softened organizational impact, and made no basic change in the distribution of rewards, and of power and authority. It would also be difficult for the rank-and-file worker to take part in such proposals.[6]

The results achieved at Harwood were consistently interpreted in terms of the motivating power of involvement in

3. K. Lewin, *Resolving Social Conflict* (New York; Harper and Row, 1948); and K. Lewin, R. Lippitt, and R. K. White, "Patterns of Aggressive Behavior in Experimentally Created Social Climates," *Journal of Social Psychology* 10(1939):271–99.

4. R. Likert, *New Patterns of Management* (New York: McGraw-Hill, 1961).

5. N. R. F. Maier and J. J. Hayes, *Creative Management* (New York: John Wiley, 1962).

6. D. Katz, "The Motivational Basis of Organizational Behavior," *Behavioral Science* 9(1964): 131–46; and C. Argyris, *Integrating the Individual and the Organization* (New York: John Wiley, 1964).

group decision making, irrespective of the kind of decision or the extent of participation. Maier saw unanimous group decision as the critical motivating device. He considered the type of problems involved as unimportant, and restricted decisions largely to human relations problems.[7] He has more recently been concerned to demonstrate that the quality of decisions need not be lowered by the use of group methods.[8] Likert saw the central role of the face-to-face work group almost through Mayo's eyes. The group motivated members through their need for approval and support and maintained a sense of personal worth. For Likert an important device in building effective groups of this kind was group participation in a limited area of decisions, although decisions did not have to be unanimous. This approach of Likert's is widely held by managers and researchers at the present time.[9]

There has been persistent criticism of the original Lewin studies. Neal Miller and Edith Bennett both criticized the uncontrolled variables in the experiment with housewives. Lawrence and Smith, in an experiment similar to that at the Harwood Company, found involvement in goal setting to be a necessary condition for an increase in output.[10] Argyris criticized the use of decisions of only peripheral interest to workers, and suggested that the experimental conditions created at Harwood by Coch and French were atypical. Normal factory routine had been temporarily set aside and replaced by one in which the employees had vastly increased responsibility for and control over their jobs and work environment.[11] Changes of this kind were omitted in most attempts to reproduce the Harwood results. In French's replication in a Norwegian factory, the original total participation conditions could not be obtained, and problems of only intermediate importance to the workers were used. This limited participation led to improvements in satisfactions and labor-management relations but not in production, and inter-

7. N. R. F. Maier, *Principles of Human Relations* (New York: John Wiley, 1952).

8. N. R. F. Maier, *Problem-Solving Discussions and Conferences* (New York: McGraw-Hill, 1963).

9. R. Likert, *New Patterns of Management*.

10. N. Miller, "Learnable Drives and Rewards," in S. S. Stevens, ed., *Handbook of Experimental Psychology* (New York: John Wiley, 1951); E. B. Bennett, "Discussion, Decision, Commitment and Consensus in Group Decision," *Human Relations* 8(1955):251–74; and L. C. Lawrence and P. C. Smith, "Group Decision and Employee Participation," *Journal of Applied Psychology* 39(1955):334–37.

11. C. Argyris, *Personality and Organization* (New York: Harper and Row, 1957).

views showed that the output had been restricted to standards felt to be safe from rate-cutting.[12]

Gomberg attacked the general human relations movement for its neglect of trade unions and conflict, since their techniques did not change the basic power relationships, nor challenge management's right to control.[13]

Involvement in T-Groups

Lewin's second major influence was in the development of the training laboratory by those working at the National Training Laboratory at Bethel from 1947 onwards. New psychological knowledge about groups was used to facilitate group and individual learning, largely through the development of the T-group. In the beginning participants came from all kinds of backgrounds, including business and industry. More recently, Bethel and the universities in which laboratories have been set up, such as Texas, California, and Boston, provided training for executive groups and special programs for individual firms. The assumption was that increased self-knowledge and capacity to understand group interrelationships would carry over from the laboratory to the work situation and would be reflected in changed behavior there, but empirical evidence for this was difficult to find. Dubin criticized T-group supporters for overestimating the contribution made by interpersonal relations to organizational effectiveness, which he considered to be largely determined by technology.[14]

Bennis pointed to the shift in emphasis from personal change to organizational development among those anxious to demonstrate impact by the laboratory.[15] In 1957 and 1958, a new training program for staff and action leaders was conducted at Bethel, and special programs were developed and used in firms. The most important was that conducted by

12. J. R. French, J. Israel, and D. As, "An Experiment in Participation in a Norwegian Factory," *Human Relations* 13(1960):3–19.

13. W. Gomberg, "The Use of Psychology in Industry: A Trade Union Point of View," *Management Science* 3(1956–57):348–70.

14. L. P. Bradford, J. R. Gibb, and K. P. Benne, *T-Group Theory and the Laboratory Method* (New York: John Wiley, 1964); C. Argyris, *Interpersonal Competence and Organizational Effectiveness* (New York: Dorsey, 1962); R. Tannenbaum, I. R. Wechsler, and P. Massarik, *Leadership and Organization* (New York: McGraw-Hill, 1961); and R. Dubin, "Psyche, Sensitivity and Social Structure," in R. Tannenbaum et al., *Leadership and Organization*.

15. W. G. Bennis, "A New Role for the Behavioral Sciences: Effecting Organizational Change," *Administrative Science Quarterly* 8(1963):125–65.

the Employee Relations Department of the Esso Company under the leadership of R. R. Blake, J. S. Mouton, and H. A. Shepard from the Southwest Human Relations Laboratory of the University of Texas.[16]

Their long-term program was directed at changing individual cognitive maps through the instrumented T-group, which involved virtual self-direction by participants. This modification was intended to strengthen motivation to transfer learning from the laboratory. For this reason the program was also tied to the organization through the use in laboratories of members from diagonal slices of levels and horizontal units, and superior-subordinate pairs. Special problem-solving groups were also set up within the organization to diagnose needs, clarify goals, and plan for organizational change.

Shepard's evaluation showed that this long-term program had no greater impact than the typical short laboratory. Personal change was widespread through many levels and groups, but this had little impact on organizational practices.[17] As Blake and his associates were more concerned with organizational than individual development, their latest program excluded the T-group and used a more structured seminar approach. This was built around the managerial grid, a device to help participants assess their managerial styles and attitudes, using concepts from Blake's integrated theory of management. The program was tied to the organization through problem-solving groups, which used simulated organizational problems and later real problems of increasingly more critical and long-term significance. An evaluation within a firm showed that managers could learn these new styles and apply them with some effectiveness for the organization.[18]

The evidence suggests that the use of T-group training in industry leads to increased self-knowledge, but that other

16. R. R. Blake and J. S. Mouton, "The Developing Revolution in Management Practices," *American Society of Training Directors' Journal* 16 (1962): 29–52; also *Group Dynamics—Key to Decision Making* (Houston: Gulf Publishing Co., 1961); and H. R. Shepard and R. R. Blake, "Changing Behavior through Cognitive Maps," *Human Organization* 21(1962): 88–96.

17. H. A. Shepard, "An Action Research Model," in *An Action Research Program for Organization Improvement* (Ann Arbor, Mich.: Foundation for Research on Human Behavior, 1960).

18. R. R. Blake, J. S. Mouton, L. R. Barnes, and L. E. Greiner, "Breakthrough in Organization Development," *Harvard Business Review* 42(1964): 133–55; and R. R. Blake and J. S. Mouton, *The Managerial Grid* (Houston: Gulf Publishing Co., 1964).

approaches are needed if organizational development is desired. Blake's ambitious program concentrated on changing managerial behavior and tying the learning process to the organization by considering organizational needs and problems. He failed to consider the limitations imposed by technology and organization structure, and to see that basic changes in these might be necessary.

Argyris has been the only T-group exponent to understand these limitations and to suggest ways to overcome them. He recommends that laboratory training should be used only with management groups, as behavior at the top is considerably influenced by skill in interpersonal relationships. Behavior at lower levels is determined largely by technology and control systems, and can be changed only by new thinking about job design, controls, and the authority system.[19]

The Concept of Group Autonomy

It is difficult to accept the concept of the motivating power of the primary work group in the face of research results. Herbert Thelen in 1954 drew attention to the limitations imposed by technology on the use of T-groups, and suggested the development of small, autonomous work groups. This would involve responsibility for the organization of work, goal setting, and training.[20] This proposal was neglected by the T-group adherents, but taken up by Argyris in *Personality and Organization* in 1957. At the time there were few studies on such groups. George Strauss reported a study in which a group of girls in a paint room was given control over the speed of the conveyor, which resulted in marked increases in output and satisfaction. More recently, Non-Linear Systems Inc. in California carried the implementation of McGregor's Theory Y down to the level of the rank-and-file worker. The assembly line was abolished and workers reorganized into small, self-paced groups of seven members responsible for building complete instruments. The result was an increase of 30 percent in productivity. Motivation was believed to come partly from gregariousness, but largely from the opportunity to use skills, learn and teach, and to take responsibility.[21]

19. C. Argyris, *Integrating the Individual and the Organization.*

20. Herbert Thelen, *The Dynamics of Groups at Work* (Chicago: University of Chicago Press, 1954).

21. G. Strauss, "An Experiment in Worker Control over Pacing," in W. F. Whyte, *Money and Motivation* (New York: Harper and Row, 1955); and A. H. Kuriloff, "An Experiment in Management—Putting Theory Y to the Test," *Personnel* 40 (1963): 8–17.

In 1954, Katz cautioned against "the glorification of the primary group as a source of work satisfaction," and suggested the importance of group autonomy. This led to the well-known study by Morse and Reimer in which autonomous groups were compared with hierarchically controlled ones.[22] The autonomy of these groups however, was, largely restricted to decisions about work assignments, length of recess, lunch periods, and so on. It was in no way comparable to the self-direction envisaged by Thelen and Argyris. Workers tried to expand the scope of their decisions, but management refused to delegate more authority, and "the curve of worker decisions soon reached a peak and began to decline." Morse and Reimer concluded that "the granting of 'safe' areas of decision making and the withholding of 'hot' ones is not likely to work for long."[23]

Disappointment with small groups and employee participation focused attention on the concepts of power and control and on power equalization.[24] Michigan studies of organizational control structures suggested that there was no basis for management's fears that the granting of more control to groups at the bottom would lessen their own authority. Organizational efficiency was found to be related to increased control at all levels, and control was not considered undesirable by low-level workers, when it was a source of involvement for them.[25] Research into communication networks by Guetzkow and Simon, by Trow, and by Mulder has made it

22. D. Katz, "Satisfactions and Deprivations in Industrial Life," in A. Kornhauser, R. Dubin, and A. Ross, eds., *Industrial Conflict* (New York: McGraw-Hill, 1954), Chap. 6; N. Morse and E. Reimer, "Experimental Change of a Major Organizational Variable," *Journal of Abnormal and Social Psychology* 52 (1956): 120–29.

23. H. L. Wilensky, "Human Relations in the Work Place: An Appraisal of Some Recent Research," in C. M. Arensberg et al., eds., *Research in Industrial Human Relations* (New York: Harper and Row, 1957), p. 42; and Morse and Reimer, "Experimental Change," p. 219.

24. George Strauss, "Some Notes on Power Equalization," in H. J. Leavitt, ed., *The Social Science of Organizations* (Englewood Cliffs, N.J.: Prentice-Hall, 1963); H. J. Leavitt, "Applied Organizational Change in Industry: Structural, Technical, and Human Approaches," in W. W. Cooper et al., eds., *New Perspectives in Organization Research* (New York: John Wiley, 1964); H. J. Leavitt and B. M. Bass, "Organizational Psychology," in P. R. Farnsworth, O. McNemar, and Q. McNemar, eds., *Annual Review of Psychology, vol. 15, 1964* (Palo Alto, California, 1964); and B. M. Bass, *Organizational Psychology* (Pittsburgh: Allyn and Bacon, 1965).

25. C. G. Smith and A. S. Tannenbaum, "Organizational Control Structure: A Comparative Analysis," *Human Relations* 16 (1963): 299–317; and A. S. Tannenbaum, "Control in Organization, Individual Adjustment, and Organizational Performance," *Administrative Science Quarterly* 7(1962): 236–57.

doubtful that group performance is related to the degree of centrality in networks, but decision centrality, freedom to exert power, responsibility for the completion of one's task, and position autonomy have been found important.[26]

Research at I.B.M. has shown that engineer control of work standards from outside the department was not thought to be legitimate by employees, and correlated negatively with output and satisfactions.[27] Leavitt points out that despite general agreement that power equalization is a key step in organizational change, there is no movement for its achievement at present.[28] In America the problems of the nature and degree of control to be given to employees, including the rank-and-file worker, are little understood, and recent significant English research has either been overlooked or misinterpreted by research workers.[29]

The Influence of Bion

W. R. Bion, a psychoanalyst of the Melanie Klein school at the Tavistock Clinic in London, used his wartime experiences with group selection methods and small therapy groups to make an important reformulation of psychoanalytic concepts to explain group as well as individual behavior.[30] He thought that the emotional life of the group could best be understood by the use of psychotic mechanisms, particularly regression. He proposed the concept of work as necessary to keep the group related to reality and to the external environment, in much the same way as the ego functioned to maintain personality and its links with reality.

He assumed a basic capacity for cooperation within the group to achieve its task. He further assumed that the group

26. H. Guetzkow and H. A. Simon, "The Impact of Certain Communication Nets upon Organization and Performance in Task-oriented Groups," *Management Science* 1(1955):233–50; D. B. Trow, "Autonomy and Job Satisfaction in Task-oriented Groups," *Journal of Abnormal and Social Psychology* 54 (1954): 204–9; and M. Mulder, "Power and Satisfaction in Task-oriented Groups," *ACTA Psychologica* 16 (1959): 178–225.

27. D. Sirota, "A Study of Work Measurement," and S. M. Klein, "Two Systems of Management," both in *Proceedings of the Sixteenth Annual Meeting of the Industrial Relations Research Association,* Publication no. 32 (Madison: Industrial Relations Research Association, 1963).

28. H. J. Leavitt, "Applied Organizational Change," in Cooper et al., eds., *New Perspectives in Organization Research.*

29. B. M. Bass, *Organizational Psychology.*

30. W. R. Bion, *Experiences in Groups and Other Papers* (London: Tavistock, 1961); also "Group Dynamics: A Review," in M. Klein, P. Heimann, and R. E. Money-Kyrle, eds., *New Directions in Psycho-Analysis* (London: Tavistock, 1955).

functioned always at two levels, at the conscious level toward its work task and at the unconscious level toward satisfaction of powerful emotional drives. Bion believed that the group acted as if it had certain basic assumptions about its aims. He termed these assumptions: dependence, fight-flight, and pairing, and felt that they would hinder task achievement. These were the source of emotional drives toward aims far different from the tasks of the group, deriving from a very primitive level and having the characteristics of defensive reactions to psychotic anxiety.

Use of Small Interpretive Groups

Bion had two major influences on the work of the Tavistock Institute of Human Relations in their role of independent consultants in industry. They assumed that the consultant's task was to work with the appropriate small groups within the organization, so that members became aware of the hidden emotional life which hindered the group's work task. This type of group discussion to facilitate change was first used extensively at the Glacier Metal Co. from 1948 onwards. The research team was headed by Elliott Jaques, and included Eric Trist and A. K. Rice.[31] They showed how unconscious mechanisms operated to prevent the effective functioning of the group, and how social institutions were used by members to reinforce individual mechanisms of defense against anxiety, particularly against the recurrence of early paranoid and depressive anxieties first described by Klein.[32]

Research was carried out as a collaborative venture between consultant and client firm. Many of the problems for which assistance was sought arose from difficulties with the system of worker-managment consultation. This led to extensive use of small groups to work through the problems and to systematic rethinking and reformulation of the functions of worker-management consultation. As a result, according to agreed-upon policy, regular consultative machinery was set up, and employees were involved in a considerable degree of consultation and in making contributions to company policy. The reorganization had also been aimed at the "split at the bottom of the executive chain," the apparently unbridgeable gap between first-line supervisor and rank-and-file worker.

31. Elliott Jaques, *The Changing Culture of a Factory* (London: Tavistock, 1951).

32. Elliott Jaques, "Social Systems as a Defense against Persecutory and Depressive Anxiety," in Klein, Heimann, and Money-Kyrle, eds., *New Directions in Psycho-Analysis*.

Wilfred Brown, the managing director, reported regretfully, in 1960, that this gap continued to exist. Eric Trist commented that "the alienation of the worker in contemporary industrial society is a problem which has not yielded to more than a limited extent to any remedy that has been tried, whether political, economic, or sociological."[33]

In a reassessement of his techniques, Jaques discussed his early reliance on group discussion methods, which arose from his belief that an organization consisted primarily of groups and group relations. Gradually, however, he realized that "work is done by individuals occupying executive roles and not by groups of individuals." Since 1952, he has seen people in their organizational roles using the technique of private discussion between individual and consultant, in which the individual could think aloud and the consultant interpret and feed back.[34]

Autonomous Work Groups

Although interpretive groups did not facilitate change at the level of the rank-and-file worker, Bion's second influence was more successful. In their early studies in coal mining, the Tavistock workers used his assumptions as a guide to the nature of the work group. These related to size, whole task, a basic capacity for cooperation to achieve the primary task, and satisfactions deriving from its effective accomplishment. Their first comparison of the earliest hand methods with those of the conventional longwall production system focused attention on the responsible autonomy of the multiskilled individual miner, and on the organization of the small, underground work group. Responsibility for the work and for supervision rested with the men themselves, requiring a high level of interdependence between members, rotation of roles and tasks, and sharing in a common paynote. This work organization was productive and did not place undue stress on the men and suggested that industrial production systems were essentially sociotechnical systems, in which the social and technical aspects could be causes of stress.[35]

Rice developed the first detailed formulation of the Tavistock's view of the work group in his research in an Indian

33. Wilfred Brown, *Exploration in Management* (London: Heinemann, 1960); see especially Foreword by E. L. Trist, p. xxi.

34. Elliott Jaques, "Social Analysis and the Glacier Project," *Human Relations* 17(1964): 361–76.

35. E. L. Trist and K. W. Bamforth, "Some Social and Psychological Consequences of the Longwall Method of Coal Getting," *Human Relations* 4(1951):3–38.

textile mill.[36] He began with more detailed assumptions about the way in which groups should be organized as to size, skills, status, roles, member control of tasks, opportunity to complete a whole task, and the location of tasks within definite physical boundaries. These were used to develop a theoretical work group organization for an experimental reorganization of the automatic weaving department, in which there had been problems of output and damage following the introduction of automatic looms.

The workers' acceptance of the idea of internally led small groups and their determination to make the new system work, were felt to be some indication of its goodness of fit. After many difficulties and setbacks, quality and quantity were established at higher levels than before the reorganization, so that Rice felt that his assumptions about task organization had some validity. Similar reorganization into small internally structured groups was later introduced into a nonautomatic shed with similar results. Recent evidence from India indicated that the increase in efficiency and decrease in damage had been maintained in both sheds, and that the group system had been extended.[37]

Autonomous Groups in Coal Mining

Rice's Indian study was limited by subjectivity and language difficulties. These were not problems, however, in the Tavistock's rigorous research into problems arising from mechanization in the British coal industry, a study undertaken at the request of the National Coal Board. Comparative studies were made of different stages of technological development, from the early hand methods through the longwall, to more advanced mechanization. The introduction of the longwall had replaced the many different short coal faces throughout the seam with a continuous longwall of coal up to two hundred yards long. In its early stage there were no machines and the face was still worked by pairs of men. Later, however, a moving mechanical conveyor belt was introduced to take the coal away from the face. This transformed the whole underground operation. The belt moved along the whole face, so that it had to be treated as a single unit requiring forty to fifty men.

The operation underground was now rather like a small

36. A. K. Rice, *Productivity and Social Organization: The Ahmedabad Experiment* (London: Tavistock, 1958).
37. A. K. Rice, *The Enterprise and Its Environment* (London: Tavistock, 1963).

factory, and managers and engineers drew on factory practice to organize the production of coal under these new conditions. The whole coal-getting cycle was broken down into a standard series of operations, each requiring a minimum of skill, and the cycle was finished every twenty-four hours instead of each shift as before. Men were no longer multiskilled but spent their lives in one job and on one shift. Instead of one rate of payment, there were now five different ones, which brought new differences in pay and status among the men. To keep the cycle running smoothly, close cooperation was needed between the various categories of workers and between the shifts. Responsibility for this now rested with management, not with the men. The men did little to help, so great strains were placed on the managers.

There were many problems in this production system. Coal output was below standard and shifts rarely finished their part of the cycle, as the men tended to do only those tasks for which they were paid. Absence rates were high and men were leaving the industry. There was friction between the shifts and many miners were suffering from neurotic illnesses. The research team believed that the factory type of work organization was not well suited to the demands of the longwall situation, judged either by output or by the men's reactions. It went against all the long-standing traditions of British coal mining by eliminating the complete self-supervising miner, taking responsibility for the allocation, coordination, and supervision of the cycle away from the work team, and destroying the small interdependent group.

The research team devised a new composite work organization for the longwall. This was based on their theoretical assumptions, and on changes already introduced by miners dissatisfied with the conventional longwall. In the composite organization, a small group of men shared a common paynote and carried out all the production operations in each shift. It was successfully tried out in short faces where six to eight men were responsible for the planning of the total cycle in one shift. There was, however, some doubt that the composite would work with much larger coal faces where forty to fifty men would be needed to produce coal.

In a face where the conventional system was in use, management, miners, and the union agreed to try the new system. Forty men worked out a new shift pattern, reorganized production operations, and agreed to share equally in a paynote. The men also accepted responsibility for a wider range of jobs, and jobs were rotated. Responsibility for the whole cycle rested largely with the men, and management provided supporting services rather than direct supervision.

A careful comparison was made over one year of a conventional and a composite work organization under very similar underground conditions. The composite work organization rated better in measures of output, turnover, absence, accidents, and stress illnesses. This was important confirmation that the composite, which relied on the characteristics of traditional methods, was a more satisfactory form of work organization. Its strength lay in altering the basis of the task and shift systems, so that miners were again multiskilled, and had responsibility for the cycle. It was later found that with still higher levels of mechanization, the work organization that best fitted the new technology again had much in common with the earlier unmechanized system.

A New Role for the Work Group

In the most recent reporting of their work, Trist and his colleagues have reformulated their theoretical position.[38] The concept that integrates the technological, economic, and sociopsychological aspects of a production system is the primary task: the work it has to perform. Work is the key transaction which relates an operating group to its environment and allows it to maintain a steady state. The concept of organizational choice is introduced so as to direct attention to the existence of a range of possible production systems. The task of management is to choose that which best fits the technical and the human requirements.

Major theoretical importance is now given to the concept of responsible autonomy. The organization of small autonomous work groups has been demonstrated in mining and textile situations. Success with composite longwall groups of forty men would widen the practical implications of the concept.

Responsible autonomy is seen as crucial for the satisfactory design of production systems. It gives the work group a central role in the production system, not the peripheral supporting role envisaged by Mayo and Likert, and has successfully motivated rank-and-file workers to greater cooperative effort than other methods. It also makes more basic changes in the distribution of control and power, by transferring some of the traditional authority of management for the control and coordination of jobs, i.e., the part appropriate to the

38. E. L. Trist, G. W. Higgin, H. Murray, and A. B. Pollock, *Organizational Choice* (London: Tavistock, 1963).

primary group's task, to the men who actually perform the task. Trist criticizes the proposals of McGregor and Likert to achieve these ends, for failing to understand the difficulties involved, particularly the initial anxiety at relaxing traditional management controls over the primary group.

This real transferring of power and control to the group for the operation of the primary task has other advantages. The coal study supports other evidence that increasing control at lower levels does not decrease control at higher levels nor adversely affect efficiency. As Trist suggests, it exerts an upwards pressure in the managing system which affects all roles, so that all levels have more, rather than less, opportunity to carry out their managerial roles in a broader way. Trist now believes that the transfer of some control to autonomous work groups is the only means of overcoming the split at the bottom of the executive system at Glacier Metal Co.

Emery has recently reassessed the Tavistock work at Glacier, and criticizes the early concern with the working through of problems and with the formal aspects of industrial democracy, without making any basic change in the role of the rank-and-file worker. He now sees the development of autonomous work groups as "the democratisation of the work place" and suggests that industrail democracy, while making decisions more democratic, has not altered the content of a worker's relation to his job.[39]

Herbst, who made the first detailed day-to-day study of the interactions of a composite group of miners, criticized the Morse and Reimer study for changing only the locus of decision making and not the activities about which decisions were made. He suggested that joint participation in the task may be a necessary prerequisite for joint decision making to be maintained.[40]

It has been argued that the Tavistock concept of the autonomous work group goes far towards solving some of the problems of worker motivation, participation, and power equalization, with which American researchers are preoccupied. The Tavistock concept also provides a new role for the work group different from that advocated by Mayo, Lewin, and Likert. The reorganized groups at Non-Linear Systems, which were virtually autonomous, give further sup-

39. F. E. Emery, "Technology and Social Organization," *Scientific Business* 1(1963):132–36.
40. P. G. Herbst, *Autonomous Group Functioning* (London: Tavistock, 1962).

port to the Tavistock concept. King's reorganizations and re-
training of women in a Norwegian clothing factory can also
be cited as supporting evidence. They were given responsibility for control over their work and work organization, and
the result was an increase in output and satisfaction and a
broadening of the functions of the unit manager.[41]

Implications

The success of autonomous work groups where other group
techniques have failed highlights the failure of research
workers and managers to make basic changes in organizational structure, and in the nature and the organization of
work. This failure has its roots in unquestioned acceptance of
the methods and assumptions of scientific management and
the traditional management theorists.

Louis Davis's survey of management practices and assumptions about job design showed the strong influence of
scientific management. Adverse effects of greatly reduced job
content were thought to be adequately controlled by selection, training, incentives, and working conditions.[42] Miles
demonstrated that long exposure to the ideas of democratic
management had not changed managers' perceptions and attitudes; these were closer to those of Taylor than to
McGregor's Theory Y.[43]

Taylor and the early management theorists believed that
their proposals would eliminate the problems of restriction of
output, lack of cooperation, apathy, and worker-management
conflict.[44] The persistence of these problems over the years
led to a succession of new approaches. Human relations and
group techniques were part of this pattern, and had only
limited success.

There is very little awareness that new thinking about
structure and the design of work is a necessary condition for
the elimination of apathy, restriction of output, and similar
problems. For this reason the Tavistock research and the
transformation of Non-Linear Systems are of major
significance. They both involve basic organizational changes
and suggest that the motivation of rank-and-file workers can
be achieved by increasing job content and giving men control

41. D. King, *Training within the Organization* (London: Tavistock,
1964).
42. L. E. Davis, R. R. Canter, and J. F. Hoffman, "Current Job
Design Criteria," *Journal of Industrial Engineering,* vol. 61 (1955).
43. R. E. Miles, "Conflicting Elements in Managerial Ideologies," *Industrial Relations* 4(1964): 77–91.
44. F. W. Taylor, *Scientific Management* (New York: Harper and
Row, 1947).

of their work environment. Louis Davis has worked toward a new theory of job design which avoids the limitations of scientific management. He has successfully redesigned assembly-line jobs so that the individual carries out a whole task and is responsible for control of quality. The assumptions on which he enlarges individual jobs are similar to those of the Tavistock group.[45]

Also most proposals for joint consultation and worker participation in management do not involve any radical rethinking about organizational design and technology. In Britain, joint consultation has been dominated by concern with the organization and functions of joint committees. The evidence shows preoccupation with welfare problems and little measurable impact on output and satisfaction.[46] American experience with labor-management cooperation has been very similar, showing increases in satisfaction rather than in output.[47]

The Scanlon plan is of special interest, because it has raised productivity. Although Scanlon stressed the importance of the incentive aspects of his plan, its success could well come from the role played by the production committees. These operated continuously, were easily accessible to workers, and had a minimum of red tape and machinery associated with them. They also had power to make production decisions appropriate to their level, and this gave some control over production problems. Workers also had direct access to staff men through the committees, which served to break down the traditional barriers and resentments of outside control, particularly engineer control, which has always been a source of restriction of output. Scanlon saw that the machinery for consultation and participation had to provide some control over production decisions.[48]

Milton Derber's report on Israeli industries run by the Histadrut, the trade union federation, provides an excellent example of misunderstanding about worker behavior.[49] The Histadrut expected worker-management relations to be

45. Louis E. Davis, "Job Design and Productivity: A New Approach," *Personnel* 33(1957): 418–30.
46. W. H. Scott, *Industrial Leadership and Joint Consultation* (Liverpool: Liverpool University Press, 1952); The National Institute of Industrial Psychology, London, *Joint Consultation in British Industry* (London: Staples Press, 1952).
47. Ernest Dale, *Greater Producitivity through Labor-Management Co-operation,* Research Report 14 (New York: American Management Association, 1949).
48. F. Lesieur, ed., *The Scanlon Plan* (New York: John Wiley, 1958).
49. Milton Derber, "Worker Participation in Israeli Management," *Industrial Relations* 3(1963): 51–72.

changed by the fact of trade union ownership, by worker representation on boards, and by widespread participation of workers through joint production committees. The familiar problems of restriction of output and apathy remained, however. Labor-management relations were characterized by complaints and misunderstandings and by two-sided bargaining rather than the harmonious family relations expected.

Perceptions of Histadrut managers about industrial relations and their roles as managers were also very similar to those of other managers. Their relations with their subordinates were still based on the dependency built into the organization structure. Trade union ownership had done nothing to soften the impact of the organization.

Extensive training of foremen and workers in the plant and classroom failed to arouse interest in participation, and Histadrut plans to develop plant councils and joint management came to nothing. Derber concluded that we must not expect too much of worker participation in management, but must see that it adds a new dimension to management.

> While workers are capable of making some useful technical contributions out of their work experience, this is most likely to occur at the department or shop level (as illustrated by suggestion schemes), and least likely at the overall plant level. In other words, worker participation in management is not a useful means of tapping the same kinds of talents and ideas which are supplied by managers, but rather is a way to utilize different values and experiences. Worker representatives are most valuable playing a criticizing, modifying role rather than an initiating one.

In Yogoslavia Kolaja found lack of interest among workers in the councils' affairs. There was also resistance to time study, and worker attitudes were generally similar to those found in British and American studies.[50] Blumenthal, studying codetermination in the German steel industry, found that the labor directors who were key figures in the operation of codetermination plans had made few changes in the procedures and practices they had inherited.[51] They accepted existing industrial organization as a fixed and unchanging framework within which to operate.

50. J. Kolaja, *Workers' Councils: The Yugoslav Experience* (London: Tavistock, 1965).

51. W. M. Blumenthal, *Codetermination in the German Steel Industry* (Princeton: Princeton University Press, 1956).

Interest in ways of training workers to partake more broadly in management functions and to overcome their resistance to involvement in management continues in many countries. Swedish experience has been unsuccessful, and this led Eric Rhenman to suggest that an important aspect of industrial democracy for the future is to consider the possibility of giving employees a constructive influence over rationalization programs. This kind of insight is rare.[52]

Considerable understanding has also been shown by Hugh Clegg in his plea for a clarification of the aims of industrial democracy. These should relate only to the protection of the rights and the interests of workers. Modern management is now far too complex for workers to share directly in it. There is, however, urgent need to devise ways of providing workers with opportunities for self-government at the work level.[53]

Conclusion

It has been argued that the Tavistock concept of the autonomous work group has more explanatory power than those concepts deriving from traditional group-dynamic thinking. Their coal and textile studies could well supplement the classical studies of Mayo and Lewin as the mainsprings of thinking and action.

52. Eric Rhenman, *Industrial Democracy and Industrial Organization* (Stockholm: P. A. Norstedt and Soners Forlag, 1964).

53. Hugh Clegg, *A New Approach to Industrial Democracy* (Oxford: Basil Blackwell, 1960).

Groups as Managerial Tools: Pros and Cons

Introduction

This chapter, like chapter 8, is also about groups; but it is about groups as influences on managerial attitudes and behavior. The first paper, by Edgar Schein, presents a general theory of influence and attitude change. Schein compares the process of management development to processes of "coercive persuasion," like the brainwashing techniques used by the Chinese Communists on American prisoners during the Korean War. Because of the intense pressures they can bring to bear on individuals, groups are powerful changers of attitudes. By depriving the individual of the support of his familiar, comfortable groups, "unfreezing" his old attitudes becomes much easier. And on the other end, by providing new "models" for the individual to follow and social support for new attitudes, a new group can help to "refreeze" the individual into a new set of beliefs.

Underlying this general theory of influence is the notion that superficial knowledge and skills are relatively easy to change in bits and pieces, but attitudes must be changed in large chunks or not at all. As we suggested in chapter 3, attitudes tend to hang together in large interlocking systems. In attempting to change only one attitude, one tends to create "cognitive dissonance," and the person may restore consistency to his attitudes more easily by rejecting one new attitude than by changing all the rest.

One specific approach to attitude change revolves around the use of T- (for Training) groups, or sensitivity training. In the second paper in this chapter, Argyris discusses both the techniques of sensitivity training and some of the things it can and can't do. T-group methods are often used to implant and support a very specific set of attitudes—typically, attitudes of interpersonal trust and openness.

One key element in the T-group process is increasing the participants' awareness of himself and how he affects others. For the purpose of increasing such self-awareness, Argyris

476

considers whether members of a T-group should all come from the same organization, or be drawn from different organizations. If group members are drawn from different organizations, it is usually easier for them to be open with one another. Groups of strangers tend to be more successful in "unfreezing" and "changing" their members' attitudes about themselves and their interpersonal relations. But the one disadvantage of such "stranger" groups is that, when each member returns to his parent organization, he is unlikely to find the group support necessary to maintain his newfound attitudes. "Refreezing" isn't very effective for the individual who goes back to his own organization all alone. Behaving openly and trustingly in an organization where others behave politically and strategically puts one, to say the least, at a disadvantage. Sensitivity training is thus likely to be more successful in changing the way a person (and an organization) functions only if a number of key organization members have been influenced by the T-group experience.

For an excellent summary of research on the effectiveness of T-groups, the reader can profitably consult the thorough review by Campbell and Dunnette.[1]

Because sensitivity training may in some cases be seen as an invasion of individual privacy, we have included one paper in this chapter that deals directly with the ethical issues. The piece by Martin Lakin is good reading for anyone contemplating involvement in T-groups, either for himself or for his organization. In growing up, each of us has built up an elaborate set of psychological defenses for protecting himself from external threat. T-groups often partially strip away these defenses, leaving the person's attitude structure vulnerable to change. For a person with insufficient ego strength, such an experience, if not backed up by appropriate rebuilding experiences, might be psychologically more stressful to the individual than it is worth. That is, "incomplete" sensitivity training may make the person extremely sensitive to his environment, without giving him the necessary skills for coping with that greater sensitivity. Because the T-group trainer or leader plays such a crucial role in these processes, and because many persons have acted as trainers without the necessary competence for the job, one of Lakin's central concerns is the inadequate preparation and certification of T-group trainers.

1. John P. Campbell and Marvin D. Dunnette, "Effectiveness of T-Group Experiences in Managerial Training and Development," *Psychological Bulletin* 70, no. 2 (August 1968): 73–103.

Another dilemma may emerge from sensitivity training. The gap between actual behavior in organizations and the ideals of trust and openness advocated in sensitivity training may be difficult for the individual to reconcile back in the real world. If the T-group participant takes those ideals seriously, having to return to life in one of our "normal" bureaucratic, authoritarian organizations may be frustrating or even alienating. The effort to develop open organizations in which mature, confident people can function comfortably, can in the short run generate considerable pain for those caught in the middle.

Management Development as a Process of Influence
Edgar H. Schein

The continuing rash of articles on the subject of developing better managers suggests, on the one hand, a continuing concern that existing methods are not providing the talent which is needed at the higher level of industry and, on the other hand, that we continue to lack clear-cut formulations about the process by which such development occurs. We need more and better managers, and we need more and better theories of how to get them.

In the present paper[1] I would like to cast management development as the problem of how an organization can influence the beliefs, attitudes, and values (hereafter simply called attitudes) of an individual for the purpose of "developing" him, i.e., changing him in a direction which the organization regards to be in his own and the organization's best interests. Most of the existing conceptions of the development of human resources are built upon assumptions of how people learn and grow, and some of the more strikingly contrasting theories of management development derive from disagreements about such assumptions.[2] I will attempt to build on a different base: instead of starting with assumptions about learning and growth, I will start with some assumptions from the social psychology of influence and attitude change.

Building on this base can be justified quite readily if we consider that adequate managerial performance at the higher levels is at least as much a matter of attitudes as it is a matter

Reprinted from the *Industrial Management Review,* vol. 2, no. 2 (May 1961), by permission of the author and the publisher. © 1961 by the Industrial Management Review Association; all rights reserved.

1. I am greatly indebted to Warren Bennis and Douglas McGregor, whose helpful comments on the first draft of this paper have helped me to refine many of the ideas in it.

2. An excellent discussion of two contrasting approaches—the engineering vs. the agricultural—deriving from contrasting assumptions about human behavior can be found in D. McGregor, *The Human Side of Enterprise* (New York: McGraw-Hill, 1960), chap. 14.

of knowledge and specific skills, and that the acquisition of such knowledge and skills is itself in part a function of attitudes. Yet we have given far more attention to the psychology which underlies change in the area of knowledge and abilities than we have to the psychology which underlies change in attitudes. We have surprisingly few studies of how a person develops loyalty to a company, commitment to a job, or a professional attitude toward the managerial role; how he comes to have the motives and attitudes which make possible the rendering of decisions concerning large quantities of money, materials, and human resources; how he develops attitudes toward himself, his coworkers, his employees, his customers, and society in general which give us confidence that he has a sense of responsibility and a set of ethics consistent with his responsible position or at least which permits us to understand his behavior.

It is clear that management is becoming increasingly professionalized, as evidenced by increasing emphasis on undergraduate and graduate education in the field of management. But professionalization is not only a matter of teaching candidates increasing amounts about a set of relevant subjects and disciplines; it is equally a problem of preparing the candidate for a role which requires a certain set of attitudes. Studies of the medical profession (Merton, Reader, and Kendall,[3] for example), have turned their attention increasingly to the unraveling of the difficult problem of how the medical student acquires those attitudes and values which enable him to make responsible decisions involving the lives of other people. Similar studies in other professions are sorely needed. When these are undertaken, it is likely to be discovered that much of the training of such attitudes is carried out implicitly and without a clearly formulated rationale. Law schools and medical schools provide various kinds of experiences which insure that the graduate is prepared to fulfill his professional role. Similarly, existing approaches to the development of managers probably provide ample opportunities for the manager to learn the attitudes he will need to fulfill high level jobs. But in this field, particularly, one gets the impression that such opportunities are more the result of intuition or chance than of clearly formulated policies. This is partly because the essential or pivotal aspects of the managerial role have not as yet been clearly delineated, leaving ambiguous

3. R. K. Merton, G. G. Reader, and Patricia L. Kendall, *The Student-Physician* (Cambridge, Mass.: Harvard University Press, 1957).

both the area of knowledge to be mastered and the attitude to be acquired.

Existing practice in the field of management development involves activities such as: indoctrination and training programs conducted at various points in the manager's career; systematic job rotation involving changes both in the nature of the functions performed (e.g., moving from production into sales), in physical location, and in the individual's superiors; performance appraisal programs including various amounts of testing, general personality assessment, and counseling both within the organization and through the use of outside consultants: apprenticeships, systematic coaching, junior management boards, and special projects to facilitate practice by the young manager in functions he will have to perform later in his career; sponsorship and other comparable activities in which a select group of young managers is groomed systematically for high level jobs (i.e., made into "crown princes"); participation in special conferences and training programs, including professional association meetings, human relations workshops, advanced management programs conducted in business schools or by professional associations like the American Management Association, regular academic courses like the Sloan programs offered at Stanford and MIT, or liberal arts courses like those offered at the University of Pennsylvania, Dartmouth, Northwestern, and so on. These and many other specific educational devices, along with elaborate schemes of selection, appraisal, and placement, form the basic paraphernalia of management development.

Most of the methods mentioned above stem from the basic conception that it is the responsibility of the business enterprise, as an institution, to define what kind of behavior and attitude change is to take place and to construct mechanisms by which such change is to occur. Decisions about the kind of activity which might be appropriate for a given manager are usually made by others above him or by specialists hired to make such decisions. Where he is to be rotated, how long he is to remain on a given assignment, or what kind of new training he should undertake, is masterminded by others whose concern is "career development." In a sense, the individual stands alone against the institution where his own career is concerned, because the basic assumption is that the institution knows better than the individual what kind of man it needs or wants in its higher levels of management. The kind of influence model which is relevant, then, is one which considers the whole range of resources available to an organization.

In the remainder of this paper I will attempt to spell out these general themes by first presenting a conceptual model for analyzing influence, then providing some illustrations from a variety of organizational influence situations, and then testing its applicability to the management development situation.

A Model of Influence and Change

Most theories of influence or change accept the premise that change does not occur unless the individual is *motivated* and *ready* to change. This statement implies that the individual must perceive some need for change in himself, must be able to change, and must perceive the influencing agent as one who can facilitate such change in a direction acceptable to the individual. A model of the influence process, then, must account for the development of the motivation to change as well as the actual mechanisms by which the change occurs.

It is usually assumed that pointing out to a person some of his areas of deficiency or some failure on his part in these areas, is sufficient to induce in him a readiness to change and to accept the influencing agent's guidance or recommendations. This assumption may be tenable if one is dealing with deficiencies in intellectual skills or technical knowledge. The young manager can see, with some help from his superiors, that he needs a greater knowledge of economics or marketing or production methods and can accept the suggestion that spending a year in another department or six weeks at an advanced management course will give him the missing knowledge and/or skills.

When we are dealing with attitudes, however, the suggestion of deficiency or the need for change is much more likely to be perceived as a basic threat to the individual's sense of identity and to his status position vis-à-vis others in the organization. Attitudes are generally organized and integrated around the person's image of himself, and they result in stabilized, characteristic ways of dealing with others. The suggestion of the need for change not only implies some criticism of the person's image of himself but also threatens the stability of his working relationships because change at this level implies that the expectations which others have about him will be upset, thus requiring the development of new relationships. It is not at all uncommon for training programs in human relations to arouse resistance or to produce, at best, temporary change because the expectations of coworkers operate to keep the individual in his "normal" mold. Management development programs which ignore these psychological resistances to change are likely to be self-defeating, no matter how much attention is given to the actual presentation of the new desired attitudes.

Given these general assumptions about the integration of attitudes in the person, it is appropriate to consider influence as a process which occurs over time and which includes three phases:

1. *Unfreezing:*[4] an alteration of the forces acting on the individual, such that his stable equilibrium is disturbed sufficiently to motivate him and to make him ready to change; this can be accomplished either by increasing the pressure to change or by reducing some of the threats of resistances to change.

2. *Changing:* the presentation of a direction of change and the actual process of learning new attitudes. This process occurs basically by one of two mechanisms: *(a) identification*[5]—the person learns new attitudes by identifying with and emulating some other person who holds those attitudes or *(b) internalization*—the person learns new attitudes by being placed in a situation in which new attitudes are demanded of him as a way of solving problems which confront him and which he cannot avoid; he discovers the new attitudes essentially for himself, though the situation may guide him or make it probable that he will discover only those attitudes which the influencing agent wishes him to discover.

3. *Refreezing:* the integration of the changed attitudes into the rest of the personality and/or into ongoing significant emotional relationships.

In proposing this kind of model of influence we are leaving out two important cases—the individual who changes because he is *forced* to change by the agent's direct manipulation of rewards and punishments (what Kelman calls "compliance") and the individual whose strong motivation to rise in the organizational hierarchy makes him eager to accept the attitudes and acquire the skills which he perceives to be nec-

4. These phases of influence are a derivation of the change model developed by K. Lewin, "Frontiers in Group Dynamics: Concept, Method, and Reality in Social Science." *Human Relations* 1 (1957): 5–42.

5. These mechanisms of attitude change are taken from H. C. Kelman, "Compliance, Identification, and Internalization: Three Processes of Attitude Change," *Conflict Resolution* 2 (1958): 51–60.

essary for advancement. I will ignore both of these cases for the same reason—they usually do not involve genuine, stable change but merely involve the adoption of overt behaviors which imply to others that attitudes have changed, even if they have not. In the case of compliance, the individual drops the overt behavior as soon as surveillance by the influence agent is removed. Among the upwardly mobile individuals, there are those who are willing to be unfrozen and to undergo genuine attitude change (whose case fits the model to be presented below) and those whose overt behavior change is dictated by their changing perception of what the environment will reward but whose underlying attitudes are never really changed or refrozen.

I do not wish to imply that a general reward-punishment model is incorrect or inappropriate for the analysis of attitude change. My purpose, rather, is to provide a more refined model in terms of which it becomes possible to specify the differential effects of various kinds of rewards and punishments, some of which have far more significance and impact than others. For example, as I will try to show, the rewarding effect of approval from an admired person is very different in its ultimate consequences from the rewarding effect of developing a personal solution to a difficult situation.

The processes of unfreezing, changing, and refreezing can be identified in a variety of different institutions in which they are manifested in varying degrees of intensity. The content of what may be taught in the influence process may vary widely from the values of communism to the religious doctrines of a nun, and the process of influence may vary drastically in its intensity. Nevertheless, there is value in taking as our frame of reference a model like that proposed and testing its utility in a variety of different organizational contexts, ranging from Communist "thought reform" centers to business enterprises' management development programs. Because the value system of the business enterprise and its role conception of the manager are not as clear-cut as the values and role prescriptions in various other institutions, one may expect the processes of unfreezing, changing, and refreezing to occur with less intensity and to be less consciously rationalized in the business enterprise. But they are structurally the same as in other organizations. One of the main purposes of this paper, then, will be to try to make salient some features of the influence of the organization on the attitudes of the individual manager by attempting to compare institutions in which the influence process is more drastic and explicit with the more implicit and less drastic methods of the business enterprise.

Illustrations of Organizational Influence

Unfreezing

The concept of unfreezing and the variety of methods by which influence targets can be unfrozen can best be illustrated by considering examples drawn from a broad range of situations. The Chinese Communists in their attempt to inculcate Communist attitudes into their youth or into their prisoners serve as a good prototype of one extreme. First and most important was the removal of the target person from those situations and social relationships which tended to confirm and reinforce the validity of the old attitudes. Thus the targets, be they political prisoners, prisoners of war, university professors, or young students, were isolated from their friends, families, and accustomed work groups and cut off from all media of communication to which they were accustomed. In addition, they were subjected to continuous exhortations (backed by threats of severe punishment) to confess their crimes and adopt new attitudes and were constantly humiliated in order to discredit their old sense of identity.

The isolation of the target from his normal social and ideological supports reached its height in the case of Western civilians who were placed into group cells with a number of Chinese prisoners who had already confessed and were committed to reforming themselves and their lone Western cell mate. In the prisoner of war camps such extreme social isolation could not be produced, but its counterpart was created by the fomenting of mutual mistrust among the prisoners, by cutting off any supportive mail from home, and by systematically disorganizing the formal and informal social structure of the POW camp (by segregation of officers and noncommissioned officers from the remainder of the group, by the systematic removal of informal leaders or key personalities, and by the prohibition of any group activity not in line with the indoctrination program).[6]

The Chinese did not hesitate to use physical brutality and threats of death and/or permanent nonrepatriation to enforce the view that only by collaboration and attitude change could the prisoner hope to survive physically and psychologically.

6. E. H. Schein, *Brainwashing* (Cambridge, Mass.: Center for International Studies, M.I.T., 1961); and E. H. Schein, "Interpersonal Communication, Group Solidarity, and Social Influence," *Sociometry* 23: 148–61.

In the case of the civilians in group cells, an additional and greater stress was represented by the social pressure of the cell mates who would harangue, insult, revile, humiliate, and plead with the resistant Westerner twenty-four hours a day for weeks or months on end, exhorting him to admit his guilt, confess his crimes, reform, and adopt Communist values. This combination of physical and social pressures is perhaps a prototype of the use of coercion in the service of unfreezing a target individual in attitude areas to which he is strongly committed.

A somewhat milder, though structurally similar, process can be observed in the training of a nun.[7] The novice enters the convent voluntarily and is presumably ready to change, but the kind of change which must be accomplished encounters strong psychological resistances because, again, it involves deeply held attitudes and habits. Thus the novice must learn to be completely unselfish and, in fact, selfless; she must adapt to a completely communal life; she must give up any source of authority except the absolute authority of God and of those senior to her in the convent; and she must learn to curb her sexual and aggressive impulses. How does the routine of the convent facilitate unfreezing? Again a key element is the removal of the novice from her accustomed routines, sources of confirmation, social supports, and old relationships. She is physically isolated from the outside world, surrounded by others who are undergoing the same training as she, subjected to a highly demanding and fatiguing physical regimen, constantly exhorted toward her new role and punished for any evidence of old behaviors and attitudes, and subjected to a whole range of social pressures ranging from mild disapproval to total humiliation for any failure.

Not only is the novice cut off from her old social identity, but her entry into the convent separates her from many aspects of her physical identity. She is deprived of all means of being beautiful or even feminine; her hair is cut off and she is given institutional garb which emphasizes formlessness and sameness; she loses her old name and chronological age in favor of a new name and age corresponding to length of time in the convent; her living quarters and daily routine emphasize an absolute minimum of physical comfort and signify a total devaluation of anything related to the body. At the same time the threat associated with change is minimized

7. K. Hulme, *The Nun's Story* (Boston: Little, Brown, 1957).

by the tremendous support which the convent offers for change and by the fact that everyone else either already exhibits the appropriate attitudes or is in the process of learning them.

If we look at the process by which a pledge comes to be a full-fledged member of a fraternity, we find in this situation also a set of pressures to give up old associations and habits, a devaluation of the old self by humiliations ranging from menial, senseless jobs to paddling and hazing, a removal of threat through sharing of training, and support for good performance in the pledge role. The evangelist seeking to convert those who come to hear him attempts to unfreeze his audience by stimulating guilt and by devaluating their former selves as sinful and unworthy. The teacher wishing to induce motivation to learn sometimes points out deficiencies in the student's knowledge and hopes at the same time to induce some guilt for having those deficiencies.

Some of the elements which all unfreezing situations have in common are the following: (1) the physical removal of the influence target from his accustomed routines, sources of information, and social relationships; (2) the undermining and destruction of all social supports; (3) demeaning and humiliating experience to help the target see his old self as unworthy and thus to become motivated to change; and (4) the consistent linking of reward with willingness to change and of punishment with unwillingness to change.

Changing

Once the target has become motivated to change, the actual influence is most likely to occur by one of two processes. The target finds one or more models in his social environment and learns new attitudes by identifying with them and trying to become like them; or the target confronts new situations with an experimental attitude and develops for himself attitudes which are appropriate to the situation and which remove whatever problem he faces. These two processes—*identification* and *internalization*—probably tend to occur together in most concrete situations, but it is worthwhile, for analytical purposes, to keep them separate.[8]

The student or prisoner of the Chinese Communists took his basic step toward acquiring Communist attitudes when he began to identify with his more advanced fellow student or

---

8. Both are facilitated greatly if the influence agent saturates the environment with the new message or attitude to be learned.

prisoner. In the group cell it was the discovery by the Western prisoner that his Chinese cell mates were humans like
himself, were rational, and yet completely believed in their
own and his guilt, which forced him to reexamine his own
premises and bases of judgment and led him the first step
down the path of acquiring the Communist point of view. In
other words, he began to identify with his cell mates and to
acquire their point of view as the only solution to getting out
of prison and reducing the pressure on him. The environment
was, of course, saturated with the Communist point of view,
but it is significant that such saturation by itself was not
sufficient to induce genuine attitude change. The prisoner
kept in isolation and bombarded with propaganda was less
likely to acquire Communist attitudes than the one placed
into a group cell with more reformed prisoners. Having a
personal model was apparently crucial.

In the convent the situation is essentially comparable except that the novice is initially much more disposed toward
identifying with older nuns and has a model of appropriate
behavior around her all the time in the actions of the others.
It is interesting to note also that some nuns are singled out as
particularly qualified models and given the appropriate name
of "the living rule." It is also a common institution in initiation or indoctrination procedures to attach to the target individual someone who is labeled a "buddy" or "big brother,"
whose responsibility it is to teach the novice "the ropes" and
to communicate the kinds of attitudes expected of him.

In most kinds of training and teaching situations, and even
in the sales relationship, it is an acknowledged fact that the
process is facilitated greatly if the target can identify with the
influence agent. Such identification is facilitated if the social
distance and rank difference between agent and target are not
too great. The influence agent has to be close enough to the
target to be seen as similar to the target, yet must be himself
committed to the attitudes he is trying to inculcate. Thus, in
the case of the Chinese Communist group cell, the cell mates
could be perceived as sharing a common situation with the
Western prisoner and this perception facilitated his
identification with them. In most buddy systems, the buddy is
someone who has himself gone through the training program
in the recent past. If the target is likely to mistrust the
influence attempts of the organization, as might be the case in
a management-sponsored training program for labor or in a
therapy program for delinquents in a reformatory, it is even
more important that the influence agent be perceived as simi-

lar to the target. Otherwise he is dismissed as a "company man" or one who has already sold out, and hence is seen as someone whose message or example is not to be taken seriously.

Internalization, the discovery of attitudes which are the target's own solutions to his perceived dilemmas, can occur at the same time as identification. The individual can use the example of others to guide him in solving his own problems without necessarily identifying with them to the point of complete imitation. His choice of attitude remains ultimately his own in terms of what works for him, given the situation in which he finds himself. Internalization is only possible in an organizational context in which, from the organization's point of view, a number of different kinds of attitudes will be tolerated. If there is a "party line," a company philosophy, or a given way in which people have to feel about things in order to get along, it is hardly an efficient procedure to let trainees discover their own solutions. Manipulating the situation in such a way as to make the official solution the only one which is acceptable can, of course, be attempted, but the hazards of creating real resentment and alienation on the part of the individual when he discovers he really had no choice may outweigh the presumed advantages of letting him think he had a choice.

In the case of the Chinese Communists, the convent, the revival meeting, the fraternity, or the institutional training program, we are dealing with situations in which the attitudes to be learned are clearly specified. In this kind of situation, internalization will not occur unless the attitudes to be learned happen to fit uniquely the kind of personal problem the individual has in the situation. For example, a few prisoners of the Communists reacted to the tremendous unfreezing pressures with genuine guilt when they discovered they held certain prejudices and attitudes (e.g., when they realized that they had looked down on lower class Chinese in spite of their manifest acceptance of them). These prisoners were then able to internalize certain portions of the total complex of Communist attitudes, particularly those dealing with unselfishness and working for the greater good of others. The attitudes which the institution demanded of them also solved a personal problem of long standing for them. In the case of the nun, one might hypothesize that internalization of the convent's attitudes will occur to the extent that asceticism offers a genuine solution to the incumbent's personal conflicts.

Internalization is a more common outcome in those influence settings where the direction of change is left more to the individual. The influence which occurs in programs like Alcoholics Anonymous, in psychotherapy or counseling for hospitalized or incarcerated populations, in religious retreats, in human relations training of the kind pursued by the National Training Laboratories,[9] and in certain kinds of progressive education programs is more likely to occur through internalization or, at least, to lead ultimately to more internalization.

Refreezing

Refreezing refers to the process by which the newly acquired attitude comes to be integrated into the target's personality and ongoing relationships. If the new attitude has been internalized while being learned, this has automatically facilitated refreezing because it has been fitted naturally into the individual's personality. If it has been learned through identification, it will persist only so long as the target's relationship with the original influence model persists unless new surrogate models are found or social support and reinforcement is obtained for expressions of the new attitude.[10]

In the case of the convent such support comes from a whole set of expectations which others have of how the nun should behave, from clearly specified role prescriptions, and from rituals. In the case of individuals influenced by the Chinese Communists, if they remained in Communist China they received constant support for their new attitudes from superiors and peers; if they returned to the West, the permanence of their attitude change depended on the degree of support they actually received from friends and relations back home or from groups which they sought out in an attempt to get support. If their friends and relatives did not support Communist attitudes, the repatriates were influenced once again toward their original attitudes or toward some new integration of both sets.

The importance of social support for new attitudes was demonstrated dramatically in the recent Billy Graham

9. National Training Laboratory in Group Development, *Explorations in Human Relations Training: An Assessment of Experience, 1947–53* (Washington, D.C.: National Education Association, 1953).

10. In either case the change may be essentially permanent, in that a relationship to a model or surrogate can last indefinitely. It is important to distinguish the two processes, however, because if one were to try to change the attitude, different strategies would be used depending upon how the attitude had been learned.

crusade in New York City. An informal survey of individuals who came forward when Graham called for converts indicated that only those individuals who were subsequently integrated into local churches maintained their faith. Similar kinds of findings have been repeatedly noted with respect to human relations training in industry. Changes which may occur during the training program do not last unless there is some social support for the new attitudes in the "back home" situation.

The kind of model which has been discussed above might best be described by the term "coercive persuasion." The influence of an organization on an individual is coercive in the sense that he is usually forced into situations which are likely to unfreeze him, in which there are many overt and covert pressures to recognize in himself a need for change, and in which the supports for his old attitudes are in varying degrees coercively removed. It is coercive also to the degree that the new attitudes to be learned are relatively rigidly prescribed. The individual either learns them or leaves the organization (if he can). At the same time, the actual process by which new attitudes are learned can best be described as persuasion. In effect, the individual is forced into a situation in which he is likely to be influenced. The organization can be highly coercive in unfreezing its potential influence targets, yet be quite open about the direction of attitude change it will tolerate. In those cases where the direction of change is itself coerced (as contrasted with letting it occur through identification or internalization), it is highly unlikely that anything is accomplished other than surface behavioral change in the target. And such surface change will be abandoned the moment the coercive force of the change agent is lessened. If behavioral changes are coerced at the same time as other unfreezing operations are undertaken, actual influence can be facilitated if the individual finds himself having to learn attitudes to justify the kinds of behavior he has been forced to exhibit. The salesman may not have an attitude of cyncism toward his customers initially. If, however, he is forced by his boss to behave as if he felt cynical, he might develop real cynicism as a way of justifying his actual behavior.

Management Development: Is It Coercive Persuasion?

Do the notions of coercive persuasion developed above fit the management development situation? Does the extent to which they do or do not fit such a model illuminate for us some of the implications of specific management development practices?

Unfreezing

It is reasonable to assume that the majority of managers who are being "developed" are not ready or able to change in the manner in which their organization might desire and therefore must be unfrozen before they can be influenced. They may be eager to change at a conscious motivation level, yet still be psychologically unprepared to give up certain attitudes and values in favor of untried, threatening new ones. I cannot support this assumption empirically, but the likelihood of its being valid is high because of a related fact which is empirically supportable. Most managers do not participate heavily in decisions which affect their careers, nor do they have a large voice in the kind of self-development in which they wish to participate. It is the manager's superior or a staff specialist in career development who makes the key decisions concerning his career.[11] If the individual manager is not trained from the outset to take responsibility for his own career and given a heavy voice in diagnosing his own needs for a change, it is unlikely that he will readily be able to appreciate someone else's diagnosis. It may be unclear to him what basically is wanted of him or, worse, the ambiguity of the demands put upon him combined with his own inability to control his career development is likely to arouse anxiety and insecurity which would cause even greater resistance to genuine self-assessment and attitude change.[12] He becomes preoccupied with promotion in the abstract and attempts to acquire at a surface level the traits which he thinks are necessary for advancement.

If the decisions made by the organization do not seem valid to the manager or, if the unfreezing process turns out to be quite painful to him, to what extent can he leave the situation? His future career, his financial security, and his social status within the business community all stand to suffer if he resists the decisions made for him. Perhaps the most coercive feature is simply the psychological pressure that what he is being asked to do is "for his own ultimate welfare." Elementary loyalty to his organization and to his managerial role

11. T. M. Alfred, personal communication, 1960.
12. An even greater hazard, of course, is that the organization communicates to the manager that he is not expected to take responsibility for his own career at the same time that it is trying to teach him how to be able to take responsibility for important decisions!

demands that he accept with good grace whatever happens to him in the name of his own career development. In this sense, then, I believe that the business organization has coercive forces at its disposal which are used by it in a manner comparable to the uses made by other organizations.

Given the assumption that the manager who is to be developed needs to be unfrozen and given that the organization has available coercive power to accomplish such unfreezing, what mechanisms does it actually use to unfreeze potential influence targets?

The elements essential to unfreezing are the removal of supports for the old attitudes, the saturation of the environment with the new attitudes to be acquired, a minimizing of threat, and a maximizing of support for any change in the right direction. In terms of this model it becomes immediately apparent that training programs or other activities which are conducted in the organization at the place of work for a certain number of hours per day or week are far less likely to unfreeze and subsequently influence the participant than those programs which remove him for varying lengths of time from his regular work situation and normal social relationships.

Are appraisal interviews, used periodically to communicate to the manager his strengths, weaknesses, and areas for improvement, likely to unfreeze him? Probably not, because as long as the individual is caught up in his regular routine and is responding, probably quite unconsciously, to a whole set of expectations which others have about his behavior and attitudes, it is virtually impossible for him to hear, at a psychological level, what his deficiencies or areas needing change are. Even if he can appreciate what is being communicated to him at an intellectual level, it is unlikely that he can emotionally accept the need for change, and even if he can accept it emotionally, it is unlikely that he can produce change in himself in an environment which supports all of his old ways of functioning. This statement does not mean that the man's coworkers necessarily approve of the way he is operating or like the attitudes which he is exhibiting. They may want to see him change, but their very expectations concerning how he normally behaves operate as a constraint on him which makes attitude change difficult in that setting.

On the other hand, there are a variety of training activities which are used in management development which approximate more closely the conditions necessary for effective unfreezing. These would include programs offered at special training centers such as those maintained by IBM on Long Island and General Electric at Crotonville, New York; university-sponsored courses in management, liberal arts, and/or the social sciences; and, especially, workshops or laboratories in human relations such as those conducted at Arden House, New York, by the National Training Laboratories. Programs such as these remove the participant for some length of time from his normal routine, his regular job, and his social relationships (including his family in most cases), thus providing a kind of moratorium during which he can take stock of himself and determine where he is going and where he wants to go.

The almost total isolation from the pressures of daily life in the business world which a mountain chateau such as Arden House provides for a two-week period is supplemented by other unfreezing forces. The de-emphasis on the kind of job or title the participant holds in his company and the informal dress remove some of the symbolic or status supports upon which we all rely. Sharing a room and bath facilities with a roommate requires more than the accustomed exposure of private spheres of life to others. The total involvement of the participant in the laboratory program leaves little room for reflection about the back home situation. The climate of the laboratory communicates tremendous support for any efforts at self-examination and attempts as much as possible to reduce the threats inherent in change by emphasizing the value of experimentation, the low cost and risk of trying a new response in the protected environment of the lab, and the high gains to be derived from finding new behavior patterns and attitudes which might improve back home performance. The content of the material presented in lectures and the kind of learning model which is used in the workshop facilitate self-examination, self-diagnosis based on usable feedback from other participants, and rational planning for change.[13]

The practice of rotating a manager from one kind of assignment to another over a period of years can have some of the same unfreezing effects and thus facilitate attitude change. Certainly his physical move from one setting to another removes many of the supports to his old attitudes, and in his new job the manager will have an opportunity to try new behaviors and become exposed to new attitudes. The

13. Although, as I will point out later, such effective unfreezing may lead to change which is not supported or considered desirable by the "back home" organization.

practice of providing a moratorium in the form of a training program prior to assuming a new job would appear to maximize the gains from each approach, in that unfreezing would be maximally facilitated and change would most probably be lasting if the person did not go back to a situation in which his coworkers, superiors, and subordinates had stable expectations of how he should behave.

Another example of how unfreezing can be facilitated in the organizational context is the practice of temporarily reducing the formal rank and responsibilities of the manager by making him a trainee in a special program, or an apprentice on a special project, or an assistant to a high-ranking member of the company. Such temporary lowering of formal rank can reduce the anxiety associated with changing and at the same time serves officially to destroy the old status and identity of the individual because he could not ordinarily return to his old position once he had accepted the path offered by the training program. He would have to move either up or out of the organization to maintain his sense of self-esteem. Of course, if such a training program is perceived by the trainee as an indication of his failing rather than a step toward a higher position, his anxiety about himself would be too high to facilitate effective change on his part. In all of the illustrations of organizational influence we have presented above, change was defined as being a means of gaining status —acceptance into Communist society, status as a nun or a fraternity brother, salvation, and so on. If participants come to training programs believing they are being punished, they typically do not learn much.

The above discussion is intended to highlight the fact that some management development practices do facilitate the unfreezing of the influence target but that such unfreezing is by no means automatic. Where programs fail, therefore, one of the first questions we must ask is whether they failed because they did not provide adequate conditions for unfreezing.

Changing

Turning now to the problem of the mechanisms by which changes actually occur, we must confront the question of whether the organization has relatively rigid prescribed goals concerning the direction of attitude change it expects of the young manager or whether it is concerned with growth in the sense of providing increasing opportunities for the young manager to learn the attitudes appropriate to ever more challenging situations. It is undoubtedly true that most programs would claim growth as their goal, but the degree to which they accomplish it can only be assessed from an examination of their actual practice.

Basically the question is whether the organization influences attitudes primarily through the mechanism of identification or the mechanism of internalization. If the development programs stimulate psychological relationships between the influence target and a member of the organization who has the desired attitudes, they are thereby facilitating influence by identification but, at the same time, are limiting the alternatives available to the target and possibly the permanence of the change achieved. If they emphasize that the target must develop his own solutions to ever more demanding problems, they are risking that the attitudes learned will be incompatible with other parts of the organization's value system but are producing more permanent change because the solutions found are internalized. From the organization's point of view, therefore, it is crucial to know what kind of influence it is exerting and to assess the results of such influence in terms of the basic goals which the organization may have. If new approaches and new attitudes toward management problems are desired, for example, it is crucial that the conditions for internalization be created. If rapid learning of a given set of attitudes is desired, it is equally crucial that the conditions for identification with the right kind of models be created.

One obvious implication of this distinction is that programs conducted within the organization's orbit by its own influence agents are much more likely to facilitate identification and thereby the transmission of the "party line" or organization philosophy. On the other hand, programs like those conducted at universities or by the National Training Laboratories place much more emphasis on the finding of solutions by participants which fit their own particular needs and problems. The emphasis in the human relations courses is on "learning how to learn" from the participant's own interpersonal experiences and how to harness his emotional life and intellectual capacities to the accomplishment of his goals rather than on specific principles of human relations. The nearest thing to an attitude which the laboratory staff, acting as influence agents, does care to communicate is an attitude of inquiry and experimentation, and to this end the learning of skills of observation, analysis, and diagnosis of interpersonal situations is given strong emphasis. The training group, which is the acknowledged core of the laboratory approach, provides its own unfreezing forces by being unstructured as to the content of discussion. But it is strongly committed to a method of learning by analysis of the member's own experiences in the group, which facilitates the discovery of the value of an attitude of inquiry and experimentation.

Mutual identification of the members of the group with each other and member identifications with the staff play some role in the acquisition of this attitude, but the basic power of the method is that the attitude of inquiry and experimentation *works* in the sense of providing for people valuable new insights about themselves, groups, and organizations. To the extent that it works and solves key problems for the participants, it is internalized and carried back into the home situation. To the extent that it is learned because participants wish to emulate a respected fellow member or staff member, it lasts only so long as the relationship with the model itself, or a surrogate of it, lasts (which may, of course, be a very long time).

The university program in management or liberal arts is more difficult to categorize in terms of an influence model, because within the program there are usually opportunities both for identification (e.g., with inspiring teachers) and internalization. It is a safe guess in either case, however, that the attitudes learned are likely to be in varying degrees out of phase with any given company's philosophy unless the company has learned from previous experience with a given course that the students are taught a point of view consistent with its own philosophy. Of course, universities, as much as laboratories, emphasize the value of a spirit of inquiry and, to the extent that they are successful in teaching this attitude, will be creating potential dissidents or innovators, depending on how the home company views the result.

Apprenticeships, special jobs in the role of "assistant to" somebody, job rotation, junior management boards, and so on stand in sharp contrast to the above methods in the degree to which they facilitate, indeed almost demand, that the young manager learn by watching those who are senior or more competent. It is probably not prescribed that in the process of acquiring knowledge and skills through the example of others he should also acquire their attitudes, but the probability that this will happen is very high, if the trainee develops any degree of respect and liking for his teacher and/or supervisor. It makes little difference whether the teacher, coach, or supervisor intends to influence the attitudes of his trainee or not. If a good emotional relationship develops between them, it will facilitate the learning of knowledge and skills, and will, at the same time, result in some degree of attitude change. Consequently, such methods do not maximize the probability of new approaches being invented to management problems, nor do they really by themselves facilitate the growth of the manager in the sense of providing opportunities for him to develop solutions which fit his own needs best.

Job rotation, on the other hand, can facilitate growth and innovation provided it is managed in such a way as to insure the exposure of the trainee to a broad range of points of view as he moves from assignment to assignment. The practice of shifting the developing manager geographically as well as functionally both facilitates unfreezing and increases the likelihood of his being exposed to new attitudes. This same practice can, of course, be merely a convenient way of indoctrinating the individual by sending him on an assignment, for example, "in order to acquire the sales point of view from Jim down in New York," where higher management knows perfectly well what sort of a view Jim will communicate to his subordinates.

Refreezing

Finally, a few words are in order about the problem of refreezing. Under what conditions will changed attitudes remain stable, and how do existing practices aid or hinder such stabilization? Our illustrations from the nonindustrial setting highlighted the importance of social support for any attitudes which were learned through identification. Even the kind of training emphasized in the National Training Laboratories programs, which tends to be more internalized, does not produce stable attitude change unless others in the organization, especially superiors, peers, and subordinates, have undergone similar changes and give each other stimulation and support, because lack of support acts as a new unfreezing force producing new influence (possibly in the direction of the original attitudes).

If the young manager has been influenced primarily in the direction of what is already the company philosophy, he will, of course, obtain strong support and will have little difficulty maintaining his new attitudes. If, on the other hand, management development is supposed to lead to personal growth and organizational innovation, the organization must recognize the reality that new attitudes cannot be carried by isolated individuals. The lament that we no longer have strong individualists who are willing to try something new is a fallacy based on an incorrect diagnosis. Strong individuals have always gained a certain amount of their strength from the support of others, hence the organizational problem is how to create conditions which make possible the nurturing of new ideas, attitudes, and approaches. If organizations seem to lack innovators, it may be that the climate of the organization and its methods of management development do not foster innovation, not that its human resources are inadequate.

An organizational climate in which new attitudes which differ from company philosophy can nevertheless be maintained cannot be achieved merely by an intellectual or even emotional commitment on the part of higher-ranking managers to tolerance of new ideas and attitudes. Genuine support can come only from others who have themselves been influenced, which argues strongly that at least several members of a given department must be given the same training before such training can be expected to have effect. If the superior of the people involved can participate in it as well, this strengthens the group that much more, but it would not follow from my line of reasoning that this is a necessary condition. Only some support is needed, and this support can come as well from peers and subordinates.

From this point of view, the practice of sending more than one manager to any given program at a university or human relations workshop is very sound. The National Training Laboratories have emphasized from the beginning the desirability of having organizations send teams. Some organizations like Esso Standard have created their own laboratories for the training of the entire management complement of a given refinery, and all indications are that such a practice maximizes the possibility not only of the personal growth of the managers, but of the creative growth of the organization as a whole.

Conclusion

In the above discussion I have deliberately focused on a model of influence which emphasizes procedure rather than content, interpersonal relations rather than mass media, and attitudes and values rather than knowledge and skills. By placing management development into a context of institutional influence procedures which also include Chinese Communist thought reform, the training of a nun, and other more drastic forms of coercive persuasion, I have tried to highlight aspects of management development which have remained implicit yet which need to be understood. I believe that some aspects of management development are a mild form of coercive persuasion, but I do not believe that coercive persuasion is either morally bad in any a priori sense nor inefficient. If we are to develop a sound theory of career development which is capable of including not only many of the formal procedures discussed in this paper but the multitudes of informal practices, some of which are more and some of which are less coercive than those discussed, we need to suspend moral judgments for the time being and evaluate influence models solely in terms of their capacity to make sense of the data and to make meaningful predictions.

T-Groups for Organizational Effectiveness
Chris Argyris

What causes dynamic, flexible, and enthusiastically committed executive teams to become sluggish and inflexible as time goes by? Why do they no longer enjoy the intrinsic challenge of their work, but become motivated largely by wages and executive bonus plans?

Why do executives become conformists as a company becomes older and bigger? Why do they resist saying what they truly believe—even when it is in the best interests of the company?

How is it possible to develop a top-management team that is constantly innovating and taking risks?

Is it inevitable that we get things done only when we create crises, check details, arouse fears, and penalize and reward in ways that inadvertently create "heroes" and "bums" among our executive group?

Ask managers why such problems as these exist and their answers typically will be abstract and fatalistic:

"It's inevitable in a big business."

"Because of human nature."

"I'll be damned if I know, but every firm has these problems."

"They are part of the bone and fabric of the company."

Statements like these *are* true. Such problems *are* ingrained into corporate life. But in recent years there has evolved a new way of helping executives develop new inner resources which enable them to mitigate these organizational ills. I am referring to *laboratory education*—or "sensitivity training" as it is sometimes called. Particularly in the form of "T-groups," it has rapidly become one of the most controversial educational experiences now available to management. Yet, as I will advocate in this article, if laboratory education

Reprinted from *Harvard Business Review,* March–April 1964, pp. 60–74, by permission of the author and the publisher. © 1964 by the President and Fellows of Harvard College; all rights reserved.

is conducted competently, and if the right people attend, it can be a very powerful educational experience.

How does laboratory education remedy the problems I have mentioned? By striving to expose and modify certain values held by typical executives, values which, unless modified and added to, serve to impair interpersonal effectiveness. As exhibit 1 explains, these values are ingrained in the pyramidal structure of the business enterprise. The exhibit summarizes several basic causes of management ineffectiveness as isolated by three studies: (1) in a large corporate division—30,000 employees, grossing $500 million per year; (2) a medium-size company—5,000 employees, grossing in excess of $50 million per year; and (3) a small company—300 employees. The results of these studies are reported in detail elsewhere.[1]

Exhibit 1

The Pyramidal Values

There are certain values about effective human relationships that are inherent in the pyramidal structure of the business organization and which successful executives (understandably) seem to hold. Values are learned commands which, once internalized, coerce human behavior in specific directions. This is why an appreciation of these values is basic in understanding behavior.

What are these "pyramidal" values? I would explain them this way.

1. The important human relationships—the crucial ones—are those which are related to achieving the organization's objective, i.e., getting the job done, as, for example: "We are here to manufacture shoes, that is our business, those are the important human relationships; if you have anything that can influence those human relationships, fine."

2. Effectiveness in human relationships increases as behavior becomes more rational, logical, and clearly communicated; but effectiveness decreases as behavior becomes more emotional. Let me illustrate by citing a typical conversation:

> "Have you ever been in a meeting where there is a lot of disagreement?"
> "All the time."
> "Have you ever been in a meeting when the disagreement got quite personal?"
> "Well, yes I have, but not very often."

1. Chris Argyris, *Interpersonal Competence and Organizational Effectiveness* (Homewood, Ill.: Richard D. Irwin, Inc., 1962); idem, *Understanding Organizational Behavior* (Homewood, Ill.: The Dorsey Press, Inc., 1960); and idem, *Explorations in Human Competence* (manuscript, Department of Industrial Administration, Yale University, New Haven, 1964).

"What would you do if you were the leader of this group?"
"I would say, 'Gentlemen, let's get back to the fact,' or I would say, 'Gentlemen, let's keep personalities out of this.' If it really got bad, I would wish it were five o'clock so I could call it off, and then I would talk to the men individually."

3. Human relationships are most effectively motivated by carefully defined direction, authority, and control, as well as appropriate rewards and penalties that emphasize rational behavior and achievement of the objective.

If these are the values held by most executives, what are the consequences? To the extent that executives believe in these organizational values, the following changes have been found to happen.

1. There is a *decrease* in receiving and giving information about executives' interpersonal impact on each other. Their interpersonal difficulties tend to be either suppressed or disguised and brought up as rational, technical, intellectual problems. As a result, they may find it difficult to develop competence in dealing with feelings and interpersonal relations. There is a corresponding decrease in their ability to own up to or be responsible for their ideas, feelings, and values. Similarly there is a dropping off of experimentation and risk-taking with new ideas and values.

2. Along with the decrease in owning,* openness, risk-taking, there is an *increase* in the denial of feelings, in closeness to new ideas, and in need for stability (i.e., "don't rock the boat"). As a result, executives tend to find themselves in situations where they are not adequately aware of the human problems, where they do not solve them in such a way that they remain solved without deteriorating the problem-solving process. Thus, if we define interpersonal competence as (a) being aware of human problems, (b) solving them in such a way that they remain solved without deteriorating the problem-solving process, these values serve to decrease interpersonal competence.

3. As the executives' interpersonal competence decreases, conformity, mistrust, and dependence, especially on those who are in power, increase. Decision making becomes *less effective,* because people withhold many of their ideas, especially those that are innovative and risky, and organizational defenses (such as management by crisis, management by detail, and through fear) *increase.* So do such "protective" activities as "JIC" files (just in case the president asks), "information" meetings (to find out what the opposition is planning), and executive politicking.

If this analysis is valid, then we must alter executives' values if we are to make the system more effective. The question arises as to what changes can and *should* be made in these values.

But since executives are far from unknowledgeable, why have they clung to these pyramidal values? First, because they are *not necessarily wrong.* Indeed, they are a necessary part of effective human relationships. The difficulty is that alone they are not enough. By themselves they tend to lead to the above consequence. What is needed is an additional set of values for the executives to hold. Specifically there are three.

* Defined in text.

1. The important human relationships are not only those related to achieving the organization's objectives but those related to maintaining the organization's internal system and adapting to the environment, as well.

2. Human relationships increase in effectiveness as *all* the relevant behavior (rational and interpersonal) becomes conscious, discussable, and controllable. (The rationality of feelings is as crucial as that of the mind.)

3. In addition to direction, controls, and rewards and penalties, human relationships are most effectively influenced through authentic relationships, internal commitment, psychological success, and the process of confirmation. (These terms are clarified in the body of the article.)

Change through Education

But how does one change an executive's values? One way is by a process of reeducation. First there is an unfreezing of the old values, next the development of the new values, and finally a freezing of the new ones.

In order to begin the unfreezing process, the executives must experience the true ineffectiveness of the old values. This means they must have a "gut" experience of how incomplete the old values are. One way to achieve this is to give them a task to accomplish in situations where their power, control, and organizational influences are minimized. The ineffectiveness of the old values, if our analysis is correct, should then become apparent.

A second requirement of reeducation arises from the fact that the overwhelming number of educational processes available (e.g., lecture, group discussion, and the like) are based on the pyramidal values. Each lecture or seminar at a university has clearly defined objectives and is hopefully staffed by a rational, articulate teacher who is capable of controlling, directing, and appropriately rewarding and penalizing the students. But, as I have just suggested, these represent some of the basic causes of the problems under study. The educator is in a bind. If he teaches by the traditional methods, he is utilizing the very values that he is holding up to be incomplete and ineffective.

To make matters more difficult, if the reeducational process is to be effective, it is necessary to create a *culture* in which the new values can be learned, practiced, and protected until the executives feel confident in using them. Such a culture would be one which is composed of people striving to develop authentic relationships and psychological success. Briefly, *authentic relationships* exist when an individual can behave in such a way as to increase his self-awareness and esteem and, at the same time, provide an opportunity for others to do the same. *Psychological success* is the experience of realistically challenging situations that tax one's capacities. Both are key components of executive competence.

The creation of a reeducational process where the unfreezing of the old values, relearning of the new values, and refreezing of the new values under primary control of the students, embedded in a culture that is rarely found in our society, is an extremely difficult task. Yet an approach to fulfilling these requirements is offered by laboratory education.

Probably because of its novelty, laboratory education has become one of the most talked about, experimented with, lauded, and questioned educational experiences for top executives. The interest of top executives has been so great that the National Training Laboratories (a nonprofit educational organization which administers most of the laboratories) has had to increase the programs manyfold in the past ten years.

Any educational experience that is as novel as laboratory education is destined to be controversial. And this is good because reasoned controversy can be the basis for corrections, refinements, and expansions of the process. Research (unfortunately not enough) is being conducted under the auspices of the National Training Laboratories and at various universities such as the University of California, Case Institute of Technology, Columbia, George Washington, Harvard, M.I.T., Michigan, Texas, and Yale, to name a few.

Aims of Program

The first step in a laboratory program is to help the executives teach themselves as much about their behavior as possible. To do so they create their own laboratory in which to experiment. This is why the educational process has been called "laboratory education." The strategy of an experiment begins with a dilemma. A dilemma occurs when, for a given situation, there is no sound basis for selecting among alternatives, or there is no satisfactory alternative to select, or when habitual actions are no longer effective.

What do people do when confronted with a dilemma? Their immediate reaction is to try out older methods of behaving with which they are secure, or else to seek guidance from an "expert." In this way, the anxiety so invariably associated with not knowing what to do can be avoided. In the laboratory, then, the anticipated first reactions by participants to a dilemma are to try traditional ways of responding.

Only when conventional or traditional ways of dealing with a dilemma have been tried—unsuccessfully—are conditions ripe for inventive action. Now people are ready to think, to shed old notions because they have not worked, to experiment, and to explore new ways of reacting to see if they will work. The period when old behavior is being abandoned and when new behavior has yet to be invented to replace it is an "unfrozen" period, at times having some of the aspects of a crisis. It is surrounded by uncertainty and confusion.[2]

Fullest learning from the dilemma-invention situation occurs when two additional types of action are taken:

One is feedback, the process by which members acquaint one another with their own characteristic ways of feeling and reacting in a dilemma-invention situation. Feedback aids in evaluating the consequences of actions that have been taken as a result of the dilemma situation. By "effective" feedback I mean the kind of feedback which minimizes the probability of the receiver or sender becoming defensive and maximizes his opportunity to "own" values, feelings, and attitudes. By "own" I mean being aware of and accepting responsibility for one's behavior.

The final step in the dilemma-invention cycle is generalizing about the total sequence to get a comprehensive picture of the "common case." When this is done, people are searching to see to what extent behavior observed under laboratory conditions fits outside situations. If generalization is not attempted, the richness of dilemma-invention learning is "lost."

T for Training

The core of most laboratories is the T (for training) group.[3] This is most difficult to describe in a few words. Basically it is a group experience designed to provide maximum possible opportunity for the individuals to expose their behavior, give and receive feedback, experiment with new behavior, and develop everlasting awareness and acceptance of self and others. The T-group, when effective, also provides individuals with the opportunity to learn the nature of effective group functioning. They are able to learn how to develop a group

2. See Robert K. Blake and Jane S. Mouton, *The Managerial Grid* (Houston, Tex.: Gulf Publishing Co., 1963).

3. For a detailed summary of research related to laboratory education, see Dorothy Stock, "A Summary of Research on Training Groups," in *T-Group Theory and Laboratory Method: Innovation in Education*, ed. Leland Bradford, Kenneth Benne, and Jack Gibb (New York: John Wiley & Sons, Inc., 1964).

that achieves specific goals with minimum possible human cost.

The T-group becomes a learning experience that most closely approximates the values of the laboratory regarding the use of leadership, rewards, penalties, and information in the development of effective groups. It is in the T-group that one learns how to diagnose his own behavior, to develop effective leadership behavior and norms for decision making that truly protect the "wild duck."

Role of Educator

In these groups, some of the learning comes from the educator, but most of it from the members interacting with each other. The "ground rules" the group establishes for feedback are important. With the help of the educator, the group usually comes to see the difference between providing help and attempting to control or punish a member; between analyzing and interpreting a member's adjustment (which is not helpful) and informing him of the impact it has on others. Typically, certain features of everyday group activity are blurred or removed. The educator, for example, does not provide the leadership which a group of "students" would normally expect. This produces a kind of "power vacuum" and a great deal of behavior which, in time, becomes the basis of learning.

There is no agenda, except as the group provides it. There are no norms of group operation (such as *Robert's Rules of Order*) except as the group decides to adopt them. For some time the experience is confusing, tension-laden, frustrating for most participants. But these conditions have been found to be conducive to learning. Naturally, some individuals learn a great deal, while others resist the whole process. It is rare, however, for an individual to end a two-week experience feeling that he has learned nothing.

Usually the T-group begins with the educator making explicit that it is designed to help human beings to (1) explore their values and their impact on others, (2) determine if they wish to modify their old values and develop new ones, and (3) develop awareness of how groups can inhibit as well as facilitate human growth and decision making.

Thus a T-group does not begin without an objective, as far as the educator is concerned. It has a purpose, and this purpose, for the educator, is emotionally and intellectually clear.

However, the educator realizes that the purpose is, at the moment, only intellectually clear to the members. Thus, to begin, the educator will probably state that he has no specific goals in mind for the group. Moreover, he offers no specific agenda, no regulations, no rules, and so on. The group is created so its members can determine their own leadership, goals, and rules.

There is very little that is nondirective about a T-group educator's role. He is highly concerned with growth, and he acts in ways that he hopes will enhance development. He is nondirective, however, in the sense that he does not require others to accept these conditions. As one member of the T-group, he will strive sincerely and openly to help establish a culture that can lead to increased authentic relationships and interpersonal competence.

However, he realizes that he can push those in the group just so far. If he goes too far, he will fall into the trap of masterminding their education. This is a trap into which group members might like to see him fall, since it would decrease their uncomfortableness and place him in a social system similar (in values) to their own. In other words, his silence, the lack of predefined objectives, leadership, agenda, rules, and so on, are not designed to be malicious or hurt people. True, these experiences may hurt somewhat, but the hypothesis is that the pain is "in the service of growth."

At this point, let me assume that you are a member of such a T-group, so that I can tell you what you are likely to experience.

Action and Reaction

At the outset you are likely to expect that the educator will lead you. This expectation is understandable for several reasons:

1. An educator in our culture tends to do precisely this.

2. Because of the newness of the situation, the members may also fear that they are not competent to deal with it effectively. They naturally turn to the educator for assistance. It is common in our culture that when one member of a group has more information than the others as to how to cope with the new, difficult situation, he is expected by the others, *if he cares for them,* to help them cope with the new situation. For example, if I am in a cave with ten other people who are lost and I know how to get out, it would be from their viewpoint the height of noncaring for me to fail to help them get out.

3. Finally, the members may turn to the educator because they have not as yet developed much trust for each other.

The educator may believe it is helpful, during the early

stages of a T-group, to tell you that he understands why you feel dependent on him. But he will also add that he believes that learning can take place more effectively if you first develop an increasing sense of trust of one another and a feeling that you can learn from one another.

In my case, when I act as the educator for a T-group, I freely admit that silence is not typical of me and that I need to talk, to be active, to participate. In fact, I may even feel a mild hostility if I am in a situation in which I cannot participate in the way that I desire. Thus, anything you (members) can do to help me "unfreeze" by decreasing your dependence on me would be deeply appreciated. I add that I realize that this is not easy and that I will do my share.

Typically, the members begin to realize that the educator supports those individuals who show early signs of attempting to learn. This is especially true for those who show signs of being open, experimentally minded, and willing to take risks by exposing their behavior. How are these qualities recognized?

There are several cues that are helpful. First, there is the individual who is not highly upset by the initial ambiguity of the situation and who is ready to begin to learn. One sign of such an individual is one who can be open about the confusion that he is experiencing. He is able to own up to his feelings of being confused, without becoming hostile toward the educator or the others. Such an individual is willing to look at his and others' behavior under stress, diagnose it, and attempt to learn from it. Some of these individuals even raise questions about other members' insistence that the educator should get them out of the ambiguous situation.

Some members, on the other hand, react by insisting that the educator has created the ambiguity just to be hostile. You will find that the educator will encourage them to express their concern and hostility as well as help them to see the impact that this behavior (i.e., hostility) is having on him. There are two reasons for the educator's intervention: (1) to reinforce (with feelings) the fact that he is not callous about their feelings and that he is not consciously attempting to be hostile; and (2) to unfreeze others to explore their hostility toward him or toward each other. Such explorations can provide rich data for the group to diagnose and from which to learn.

Problem of Mimicking

As the group continues, some members begin to realize that

the educator's behavior now may serve for what it is. That is, it may be as valid a model as the educator can manifest of how he would attempt (a) to help create an effective group, and (b) to integrate himself into that group so that he becomes as fully functioning a member as possible. The model is his; he admits owning it, but he is *not* attempting to "sell" it to others or in any way to coerce them to own it.

You may wonder if viewing the educator as a source of "model behavior" would not lead you simply to *mimic* him. (In the technical literature this is discussed as "identification with the leader," or "leader modeling behavior.") Although this may be the case, we should not forget that as you begin to "unfreeze" your previous values and behavior, you will find yourself in the situation of throwing away the old and having nothing new that is concrete and workable. This tends to create states of vacillation, confusion, anxiety, ambivalence, and so on.[4] These states in turn may induce you to "hang on" to the old with even greater tenacity. To begin to substitute the new behavior for the old, you will feel a need to see (1) that you can carry out the new behavior effectively and (2) that the new behavior leads to the desired results.[5]

Under these conditions the members usually try out any bit of behavior that represents the "new." Experimentation not only is sanctioned; it is rewarded. One relatively safe way to experiment is to "try out the educator's behavior." It is at this point that the individual is mimicking. And he should feel free to mimic and *to talk about the mimicking and explore it openly*. Mimicking is helpful if you are aware of and accept the fact that you do not *own* the behavior, for the behavior with which you are experimenting is the educator's. If the educator is not anxious about the mimicking, the member may begin safely to explore the limits of the new behavior. He may also begin to see whether or not the educator's behavior is, for him, realistic.

Individual vs. Group

At the outset the educator tends to provide that assistance which is designed to help the members to (1) become aware of their present (usually) low potential for establishing authentic relationships, (2) become more skillful in providing

4. Roger Barker, Beatrice A. Wright, and Mollie R. Gonick, "Adjustment to Physical Handicap and Illness," *Social Science Research Council Bulletin* 55(1946): 19–54.

5. Ronald Lippitt, Jeanne Watson, and Bruce Westley, *The Dynamics of Planned Change* (New York: Harcourt, Brace & World, Inc., 1958).

and receiving nonevaluative descriptive feedback, (3) minimize their own and others' defensiveness, and (4) become increasingly able to experience and own up to their feelings.

Although interpersonal assistance is crucial, it is also important that the T-group not be limited to such interventions. After the members receive adequate feedback from one another as to their inability to create authentic relationships, they will tend to want to become more effective in their interpersonal relationships. It is at this point that they will need to learn that group structure and dynamics deeply influence the probability of increasing the authenticity of their interpersonal relations. For example:

As soon as the members realize that they must become more open with those feelings that typically they have learned to hide, they will need to establish group norms to sanction the expression of these feelings. Also, if members find it difficult in the group to express their important feelings, this difficulty will tend to be compounded if they feel they must "rush" their contribution and "say something quick," lest someone else take over the communication channels. Ways must be developed by which members are able to use their share of the communication channels. Also, group norms are required that sanction silence and thought, so that members do not feel coerced to say something, before they have thought it through, out of fear that they will not have an opportunity to say anything later.

An example of the interrelationship between interpersonal and group factors may be seen in the problems of developing leadership in a group. One of the recurring problems in the early stages of a T-group is the apparent need on the part of members to appoint a leader or a chairman. Typically, this need is rationalized as a group need because "without an appointed leader a group cannot be effective." For example, one member said, "Look, I think the first thing we need is to elect a leader. Without a leader we are going to get nowhere fast." Another added, "Brother, you are right. Without leadership, there is chaos. People hate to take responsibility and without a leader they will goof off."

There are several ways that your group might consider for coping with this problem, each of which provides important but different kinds of learning:

One approach is to see this as a group problem. How does leadership arise and remain helpful in a group? This level of learning is important and needs to be achieved.

Another possibility is for the group members to explore

the underlying assumptions expressed by those individuals who want to appoint leaders. For example, in the case illustrated above, both men began to realize that they were assuming that people "need" appointed leadership because, if left alone, they will not tend to accept responsibility. This implies a lack of confidence in and trust of people. It also implies mistrust of the people around the table. These men were suggesting that without an appointed leader the group will flounder and become chaotic. Someone then took the initiative and suggested that their comments implied a lack of trust of the people around the table. Another individual suggested that another dimension of mistrust might also be operating. He was concerned how he would decide if he could trust the man who might be appointed as the leader. The discussion that followed illustrated to the group the double direction of the problem of trust. Not only do superiors have feelings of mistrust of subordinates, but the latter may also mistrust the former.

One of the defendants of the need for leadership then said, "Look, Mr. B. over there has been trying to say something for half an hour, and hasn't succeeded. If we had a leader, or if he himself were appointed leader temporarily, then he might get his point of view across." Several agreed with the observation. However, two added some further insightful comments. One said, "If we give Mr. B. authority, he will never have to develop his internal strength so that he can get his point across without power behind him." "Moreover," the other added, "if he does get appointed leader, the group will never have to face the problem of how it can help to create the conditions for Mr. B. to express his point of view." Thus we see that attempting to cope with the basic problems of group membership can lead to an exploration of problems of group membership as well as requirements of effectively functioning groups.

The question of trust, therefore, is a central problem in a T-group, indeed, as it is in any group organization. If this can be resolved, then the group has taken an important step in developing authentic relationships. As the degree of trust increases, "functional leadership" will tend to arise spontaneously because individuals in a climate of mutual trust will tend to delegate leadership to those who are most competent for the subject being discussed. In doing so, they also learn an important lesson about effective leadership.

Another kind of learning that usually develops clearly is that the group will not tend to become an effective task-oriented unit without having established effective means to diagnose problems, make decisions, and so on. It is as the group becomes a decision-making unit that the members can "test" the strength and depth of their learning. The pressure and stress of decision making can help to show the degree to which authenticity is apparent rather than real. It can also provide opportunity for further learning, because the members will tend to experience new aspects of themselves as they attempt to solve problems and make decisions.

Further Components

Laboratory education has other components. I have focused in detail on T-groups because of their central role. This by no means describes the total laboratory experience. For example, laboratory education is helpful in diagnosing one's organizational problems.

Diagnosing Problems. When a laboratory program is composed of a group of executives who work in the same firm, the organizational diagnostic experiences are very important. Each executive is asked to come to the laboratory with any agenda or topic that is important to him and to the organization. During the laboratory, he is asked to lead the group in a discussion of the topic. The discussion is taped and observed by the staff (with the knowledge of the members).

Once the discussion is completed, the group members listen to themselves on the tape. They analyze the interpersonal and group dynamics that occurred in the making of the decision and study how these factors influenced their decision making. Usually, they hear how they cut each other off, did not listen, manipulated, pressured, created win-lose alternatives, and so on.

Such an analysis typically leads the executives to ask such questions as: Why do we do this to each other? What do we wish to do about it, if anything?

On the basis of my experience, executives become highly involved in answering these questions. Few hold back from citing interpersonal and organizational reasons why they feel they have to behave as they do. Most deplore the fact that time must be wasted and much energy utilized in this "windmilling" behavior. It is quite frequent for someone to ask, "But if we don't like this, why don't we do something about it?"

Under these conditions, the things learned in the laboratory are intimately interrelated with the everyday "real" problems of the organization. Where this has occurred, the members do not return to the organization with the same degree of bewilderment that executives show who have gone to laboratories full of strangers. In the latter case, it is quite common for the executive to be puzzled as to how he will use what he has learned about human competence when he returns home.[6]

Consultation Groups. Another learning experience frequently used is to break down the participants into groups of four. Sessions are held where each individual has the opportunity both to act as a consultant giving help and as an individual receiving help. The nature of help is usually related to increasing self-awareness and self-acceptance with the view of enhancing interpersonal competence.

Lectures. As I pointed out above, research information and theories designed to help organizational learning are presented in lectures—typically at a time when it is most clearly related to the learnings that the participants are experiencing in a laboratory.

Role-Playing of "Real" Situations. As a result of the discussions at the laboratory program, many data are collected illustrating situations in which poor communications exist, objectives are not being achieved as intended, and so on. It is possible in a laboratory to role-play many of these situations, to diagnose them, to obtain new insights regarding the difficulties, as well as to develop more effective action possibilities. These can be role-played by asking the executives to play their back-home role. For other problems, however, important learnings are gained by asking the superiors to take the subordinates' role.

Developing and Testing Recommendations. In most organizations, executives acknowledge that there are long-range problems that plague an organization, but that they do not have time to analyze them thoroughly in the back-home situation (for example, effectiveness of decentralization). In a laboratory, however, time is available for them to discuss these problems thoroughly. More important, as a result of their laboratory learnings and with the assistance of the educators, they could develop new action recommendations. They could diagnose their effectiveness as a group in developing these recommendations—have they really changed; have they really enhanced their effectiveness?

Intergroup Problems. One of the central problems of organizations is the intergroup rivalries that exist among depart-

6. For an example, see Argyris, *Interpersonal Competence and Organizational Effectiveness,* chap. 9.

ments. If there is time in a laboratory, this topic should be dealt with. Again, it is best introduced by creating the situation where the executives compete against one another in groups under "win-lose" conditions (i.e., where only one can win and someone must lose).

Correcting Misunderstandings

Any educational activity that is as new and controversial as laboratory education is bound to have misconceptions and misunderstandings built around it. Therefore, I should like to attempt briefly to correct a few of the more commonly heard misunderstandings about laboratory education.

1. Laboratory methods in general, and T-groups in particular, are not a set of hidden, manipulative processes by which individuals can be "brainwashed" into thinking, believing, and feeling the way someone might want them to without realizing what is happening to them.

Central to a laboratory is openness and flexibility in the educational process. It is open in that it is continually described and discussed with the participants as well as constantly open to modification by them.

Along with the de-emphasis of rigidity and emphasis on flexibility, the emphasis is on teaching that kind of knowledge and helping the participants develop those kinds of skills which increase the strength and competence to question, to examine, and to modify. The objectives of a laboratory are to help an individual learn to be able to reject that which he deeply believes is inimical to his self-esteem and to his growth—and this would include, if necessary, the rejection of the laboratory experience.

2. A laboratory is not an educational process guided by a staff leader who is covertly in control and by some magic hides this fact from the participants.

A laboratory means that people come together and create a setting where (as is the case in any laboratory) they generate their own data for learning. This means that they are in control and that any behavior in the laboratory, including the staff member's, is fair game for analysis.

I should like to suggest the hypothesis that if anything is a threat to the participants, it is not the so-called covert control. The experience becomes painful when the participants begin to realize the scope and depth to which the staff is ready "to turn things over to them." Initially this is seen by many participants as the staff abdicating leadership. Those who truly learn come to realize that in doing this the staff is expressing, in a most genuine way, their faith in the potentiality of the participants to develop increasing competence in controlling more of their learning. As this awareness increases, the participants usually begin to see that their cry of "abdication of leadership" is more of a camouflage that hides from them how little they trusted each other and themselves and how overprotected they were in the past from being made to assume some responsibility for their learning.

3. The objective of laboratory education is not to suppress conflict and to get everyone to like one another.

The idea that this is the objective is so patently untrue that I am beginning to wonder if those who use it do not betray their own anxiety more than they describe what goes on in a laboratory. There is no other educational process that I am aware of in which conflict is generated, respected, and cherished. Here conflict, hostility, and frustration become motivations for growth as well as food for learning. It is with these kinds of experiences that participants learn to take risks —the kinds of risks that can lead to an increase in self-esteem. As these experiences are "worked through" and the learnings internalized, participants soon begin to experience a deeper sense of self-awareness and acceptance. These, in turn, lead to an increased awareness and acceptance of others.

And this does *not* necessarily mean liking people. Self-acceptance means that individuals are aware of themselves and care so much about themselves that they open themselves to receiving and giving information (sometimes painful) about their impact on others and others' impact on them, so that they can grow and become more competent.

4. Laboratory education does not attempt to teach people to be callous, disrespectful of society, and to dislike those who live a less open life.

If one truly begins to accept himself, he will be less inclined to condemn nongenuineness in others, but to see it for what it is, a way of coping with a nongenuine world by a person who is (understandably) a nongenuine individual.

5. Laboratory education is neither psychoanalysis nor intensive group therapy.

During the past several years I have been meeting with a group of psychiatrists and clinical psychologists who are trying to differentiate between group therapy and everything else. One problem we discovered is that therapists define therapy as any change. The difficulty with this definition is that it means any change is therapy.

We have concluded that it may be best to conceive of a continuum of "more" or "less" therapy. The more the group deals with unconscious motivations, uses clinical constructs, focuses on "personal past history," and is guided in these activities by the leader, the more it is therapy. Therapy is usually characterized by high proportions of these activities because the individuals who are participating are so conflicted or defensive that they are not able to learn from these activities.

In my view, a T-group is—or should be—a group that contains individuals whose internal conflicts are low enough to learn by:

Dealing with "here and now" behavior (what is going on in the room).

Using relatively nonclinical concepts and nonclinical theory.

Focusing on relatively conscious (or at most preconscious) material.

Being guided increasingly less by the leader and increasingly more by each other.

Accomplishing this in a relatively (to therapy) short time (at the moment, no more than three weeks).

This does not mean that T-groups do not, at times, get into deeper and less conscious problems. They do; and, again, they vary primarily with the staff member's biases. Usually most educators warn the group members against striving to become "two-bit" psychologists.

6. Laboratory education does not have to be dangerous, but it must focus on feelings.

Interpersonal problems and personal feelings exist at all levels of the organization, serving to inhibit and decrease the effectiveness of the system. Does it seem to be logical (in fact, moral) for a company to say that it is not going to focus on something that people are already experiencing and feeling? The truth is that people *do* focus on interpersonal problems every hour of the day. They simply do not do it openly.

Now for the argument that the laboratory program can hurt people and is, therefore, dangerous. The facts of life are that people are being hurt every day. I do not know of any laboratory program that did, or could, create for people as much tension as they are experiencing in their everyday work relationships.

It is true that laboratory education does require people to take risks. But does anyone know of any learning that truly leads to growth which does not involve some pain and cost? The value of laboratory education is that it keeps out the people who want to learn "cheaply" and it provides the others with control over how much they wish to learn and what they want to pay for it.

7. The objective of laboratory education is to develop effective reality-centered leaders.

Some people have expressed concern that if an executive goes through such a learning experience, he might somehow become a weak leader. Much depends on how one defines strong leadership. If strong leadership means unilateral domination and directiveness, then the individual will tend to become "weaker." But why is such leadership strong? Indeed, as I have suggested, it may be weak. Also it tends to develop subordinates who conform, fear to take risks, and are not open, and an organization that becomes increasingly rigid and has less vitality.[7]

Nor can one use the argument that directive leadership has worked and that is why it should remain. There are data to suggest that directive leadership can help an organization under certain conditions (e.g., for routine decisions and under extreme emergencies). But these conditions are limited. If directive leadership is effective beyond these relatively narrow conditions, it may be because of a self-fulfilling prophecy. Directive leadership creates dependence, submissiveness, and conformity. Under these conditions subordinates will tend to be afraid to use their initiative. Consequently, the superior will tend to fill in the vacuum with directive leadership. We now have a closed cycle.

The fact is that directive leaders who learn at a laboratory do not tend to throw away their directive skills. Rather, they seem to use directive leadership where and when it is appropriate. It cannot be emphasized too strongly that there is nothing in laboratory education which requires an individual to throw away a particular leadership pattern. The most laboratory education can do is help the individual see certain unintended consequences and costs of his leadership, and help him to develop other leadership styles *if* he wishes.

8. Change is not guaranteed as a result of attendance.

Sometimes I hear it said that laboratory education is not worthwhile, because some individuals who have attended do not change, or if they do change, it is only for a relatively short period of time.

Let me acknowledge that there is an immense gap in our

7. Ibid.

knowledge about the effectiveness of a laboratory. Much research needs to be done before we know exactly what the payoff is in laboratory education. However, there are a few statements that can be made partially on the basis of research and experience and partially on the basis of theory.

One of the crucial learnings of a laboratory is related to the development of openness and trust in human relationships. These factors are not generated easily in a group. It takes much effort and risk. Those who develop trust in a group learn something very important about it. Trust cannot be issued, inspired, delegated, and transferred. It is an interpersonal factor which has to be *earned* in each relationship. This is what makes trust difficult to develop and precious to have.

Thus, it does not make very much sense to expect that suddenly an individual will act as if he can trust and can be trusted in a setting where this was never true. One executive was needled by the corporate president, who observed that he had not seen any change in the former's behavior. The executive responded: "What makes you think I feel free to change my behavior in front of you?"

This remark points up the possibility that if there is not any observable change, it could mean that the individual has not learned much. But it could also mean that he has learned a great deal, *including* the fact that he ought not to behave differently when he returns. For, it must be emphasized, laboratory education is only a partial attack on the problem of organizational effectiveness. If the changes are to become permanent, one must also change the nature of the organizational structure, managerial controls, incentive systems, reward and penalty systems, and job designs.[8]

Impact on Organization

The impact of laboratory education on the effectiveness of an organization is extremely difficult to isolate and measure.[9] Organizations are so complex, and their activities influenced by so many factors, that it is difficult to be precise in specifying the causes of the impact.

8. For a more theoretical discussion of this matter, see Chris Argyris, *Integrating the Individual and the Organization* (New York: John Wiley & Sons, Inc., 1964).

9. Robert K. Blake and Jane S. Mouton, "Toward Achieving Organization Excellence," in *Organizational Change,* ed. Warren Bennis (New York: John Wiley & Sons, Inc., 1964). As this article went to press, I read an excellent manuscript of a speech evaluating the effectiveness of laboratory education, "The Effect of Laboratory Education upon Individual Behavior," given by Douglas R. Bunker before the Industrial Relations Research Association in Boston on 28 December 1963.

In one study that I conducted of the twenty top executives of a large corporate division, I did find a significant shift on the part of the experimental group toward a set of values that encouraged the executives to handle feelings and emotions, deal with problems of group maintenance, and develop greater feelings of responsibility on the part of their subordinates for the effectiveness of the organization. This shift is quantified in table 1.

As the table shows, the impact of laboratory education

Table 1

Before and After Values of 11 Executives Who Experienced Laboratory Education

In an administrative situation, whenever possible . . .	*Before T-group*	*Six months after*
1a. The leader should translate interpersonal problems into rational intellective ones	100%	10%
1b. The leader should deal with the interpersonal problems	0	81
2a. The leader should stop emotional disagreement by redefining the rational purpose of the meeting	90	10
2b. The leader should bring out emotional disagreements and help them to be understood and resolved	6	81
3a. When strong emotions erupt, the leader should require himself and others to leave them alone and not deal with them	100	18
3b. When strong emotions erupt, the leader should require himself and offer others the opportunity to deal with them	0	82
4a. If it becomes necessary to deal with feelings, the leader should do it even if he feels he is not the best qualified	100	9
4b. The leader should encourage the most competent members	0	90
5a. The leader is completely responsible for keeping the group "on the track" during a meeting	100	0
5b. The group members as well as the leader are responsible for keeping the group "on the track"	0	100

continued at a high level for a period in excess of six months. However, during the tenth month a fade-out began to appear. This was studied and data were obtained to suggest that the executives had not lost their capacity to behave in a more open and trustful manner, but they had to suppress some of this learning because the corporate president and the other divisional presidents, who were not participants in the laboratory, did not understand them.

This finding points up two important problems. Change is not going to be effective and permanent *until the total organization* accepts the new values. Also, effective change does *not* mean that the executives must lose their capacity to behave according to the pyramidal values. They do so whenever it is necessary. However, now they have an additional way to behave, and they use it whenever possible. They report that irrespective of the problem of acceptance by others, they find the pyramidal values are effective when they are dealing primarily with *routine, programed* decisions. The new values and manner of leadership seem to be best suited for decisions that are *unprogramed, innovative,* and require high commitment.

It is important to emphasize that laboratory education does *not* tell anyone what type of leadership to select. It does not urge him always to be more "democratic" or "collaborative." A successful laboratory helps the executives realize the unintended costs of the "old," develop "new" leadership behavior and philosophies, and become competent in utilizing whatever leadership style is appropriate in a given situation. A laboratory helps an individual increase his repertory of leadership skills and his freedom to choose how he will behave. If it coerces the executive, it is for him to become more *reality-centered.*

Another way of describing the impact of a laboratory program on an organization is for me to offer you excerpts from a tape of a meeting where the executives discussed the difficulties as well as successes that they were having thirty days after the program. The first part of the tape contains a discussion of examples of concrete changes which the members felt were a result of the laboratory. Here is a sample of the changes reported:

1. Executives reported the development of a new program for certain pricing policies that could not be agreed upon before, and laid part of the success to their new ability to sense feelings.

2. One executive stated, "We are consciously trying to

change our memos. For example, we found a way to decrease the 'win-lose' feelings and 'rivalries.' "

3. The personnel director reported a distinct improvement in the sensitivity of the line managers to the importance of personnel problems, which before the laboratory seemed to have a second-class status. He said he was especially pleased with the line executives' new awareness of the complexity of personnel problems and their willingness to spend more time on solving them.

The rest of the tape is excerpted and presented in exhibit 2.

Exhibit 2

Discussion of Attitude Changes by T-Group Members

The excerpt presented here mirrors the tone of the entire meeting. I have not purposely selected only that section in which the men praised the laboratory. If the men had criticized the laboratory, such criticism would have been included. As you may see, the researcher actually pushed the group for more negative comments.

Except for minor editing, these are direct quotes:

No. 4 [after reporting that his superior, a member of the experimental group, had made a decision which should have been left to him]: I was really fuming. I was angry as hell. I walked into his office and I said to myself, "No matter what the hell happens, I'm going to tell him that he cannot do that any more." Well, I told him so, I was quite emotional. You know it floored me. He looked at me and said, "You're right; I made a mistake, and I won't do that again." Well I just don't think he would have done that before.

No. 7: The most important factor in motivating people is not what you say or do; it's giving a person the opportunity to express his views and the feeling that one is seriously interested in his views. I do much less selling but it sure takes longer.

No. 2: I've had a problem. I now have a greater need for feedback than before, and I find it difficult to get. The discussion on internal commitment made much sense to me, and I try to see if I can create conditions for it.

The thing that bothers me is that I try to handle it correctly, but I don't get feedback or cues as to how well I'm doing, as I used to at the lab. The meeting is over, and you don't know whether you've scored or not. So after each meeting I've got ten question marks. The things that before were never questions are now question marks.

You don't get feedback. You ask for something and they respond, "I know what you're trying to do." They think I've something up my sleeve. All I want is to get feedback. It was obvious to me they were all waiting for me to make the decision. But I wanted them to make it. This was their baby, and I wanted them to make it. Two days later they made it. Fine, in this case I got feedback. The point was that their decision was a severe reversal, and I realize it was difficult for them to make. But they made it. Before, I simply would have pointed out the facts, and they would have "agreed" with the reversal, but down deep inside they would have felt that they could have continued on. As it is now, it's their decision. I think they now have a greater sense of internal commitment. People are now freer to disagree.

No. 11: My list of decisions to be made is longer. I am hoping that they will make some decisions. I now know how much they wait for me.

No. 11 [after telling how he wrote a note which in effect damned No. 2 and maintained his own correctness, then reread it and realized how defensive he was]: Before I wouldn't have even seen this.

No. 2: One of our most difficult jobs will be to write our feelings and to write in such a way that others can express their feelings.

No. 3: I have some difficulties in evaluating this program. What have we gotten out of this? What are we able to verbalize about what we got out of this? Do others of you have difficulty in verbalizing it?

No. 2: I have the same difficulty. I have been totally ineffective describing the experience.

No. 8: Each time I try I give a different answer.

No. 1: I don't have too much difficulty. One thing that I am certain of is that I see people more as total human beings. I see aspects of them that I had never seen before.

No. 9: I'm frustrated because I now realize the importance of face-to-face communication. I'm so far from the general managers that it is not so hot. Has anyone tried to write memos that really get feelings brought out?

I find myself questioning much more than I ever did before. I have a more questioning attitude. I take into account more factors.

No. 4: We've been talking about things as if we've slowed down a bit. We haven't. For example, remember you [No. 1] and I had a problem? I'm sure Arden House was very helpful. If I hadn't been there, my reaction to you would have been different. I would have fought you for hours.

No. 1: I know we can talk to each other more clearly. It's not a conscious way. It's spontaneous.

No. 3: I have to agree we can make some decisions much faster. For example, with No. 2 I simply used to shut up. But now I can be more open. Before the laboratory, if I had an intuitive feeling that something was wrong, but I wasn't sure, I'd keep quiet until things got so bad that then I'd have a case to go to the boss. Now I feel freer to talk about it sooner and with No. 2.

I now feel that we are going to say exactly how we feel to anyone. You [the president], for example, don't have to worry, and, therefore, question, probe, and draw us out.

President: Yes, and today I found No. 1, who told me that he simply would not agree with me. And I said to myself, "God bless you. He really is open now."

No. 1: I agree. I would not have expressed this feeling before being in this group. It's obvious that one should but I didn't.

[No. 2 and No. 1 show real insight into how they are being manipulated by people outside and above the group. They are much more aware of the manipulative process. "This kind of manipulation is dynamite. It burns me up."]

No. 1: Yes, it's really horrible to see it and not be able to do anything about it.

No. 7: In this case it seems to me you've got to really hit hard, because you're dealing with an untrained man [laughter].... I think I now have a new understanding of decision making. I am now more keenly aware of the importance of getting a consensus so that the *implementation* is effective. I am not trying to say that I do this in every meeting. But I do strive more to give opportunity for consensus.

No. 1: One of the problems that I feel is that the "initiated" get confused so they don't play the game correctly. Sometimes I feel walked upon, so I get sore. This is difficult. [Many others expressed agreement.]

No. 6: Does it help to say, "I trust you?" I think it does.

No. 11: For example, No. 2, you went to a meeting where you admitted you had made a mistake. Boy, you should have heard the reaction. Boy, Mr. —— admitted a mistake. Well, wonderful; it helped to get these guys to really feel motivated to get the job done.

No. 9: Yes, I heard that many took on a deeper feeling of responsibility to get the program on the right track.

No. 7: I'd like to come back to what No. 6 said. I used to say to people that I trusted them, that I was honest, and so on. But now I wonder if people really believe me, or if they don't begin to think if I'm not covering that I'm not honest.

No. 3: Another example which I am now aware of is the typical way we write memos. We start off: "I have confidence in your judgment to handle this question," and so on. Few more paragraphs. Then fifth paragraph reads: "Please confirm by return mail exactly what you have done and what controls have been set up."

No. 2: I agree. We do an awful lot to control people. Although I think that we're trying.

[No. 7 gave examples of how he stopped making a few phone calls to exert pressure. Others agreed.]

The researcher: Aren't there negative comments?

No. 11: We have one man who has chosen not to be here. I wonder why?

No. 3: Well, really, to me that is a sign of health in the group. He feels he would still be accepted even if he didn't come. It certainly would be easy for him to come and just sit here.

No. 1: Yes, he wouldn't go to the trouble of avoiding a meeting that you didn't think was important.

No. 3: The only negative that I can think is: "What can you tell me that actually increases effectiveness?" I am not sure, but I must agree that there is a whale of a different climate.

No. 7: Well, I'd like to develop a list of things that we feel we have gotten out of this program so far. How do others of you feel? [All agreed, "Let's try."]

[All group members reporting they reached the following conclusions]:

a. All of us begin to see ourselves as others see us . . . a real plus.

b. A degree of greater confidence in oneself in meetings and in interviews. Beginning to be more comfortable with self.

c. Greater confidence in associates. We feel more secure that you're telling what you think. . . . Greater feeling of freedom of expression to say what you really think.

d. Individuals have a greater understanding and appreciation of viewpoint of associates.

e. Greater appreciation of the opposite viewpoint.

f. An awareness of what we do and others do that inhibits discussion.

g. More effective use of our resources . . . getting more from them, and they feel this . . . patient to listen more.

h. Meetings do not take longer and implementation is more effective. Internal commitment is greater.

i. We have had a great realization that being only task-oriented, we will not get the best results. We must not forget worrying about the organization and the people.

j. We get more irritated to infringement of our jobs and unique contributions.

k. Fewer homemade crises.

No. 6: One of the difficult things about the list is that when you look at it, you wake up to the fact that you haven't really been using these principles. When you tell someone else who doesn't realize the gap between knowing something and actually doing it, he doesn't realize.

No. 7: But I think I really did learn and do care. Now when I think what I used to do, because that was the way. Today I realize that I could have had three times as much if I had known what I know now."

Conclusion

While I do not hold up laboratory education as a panacea to remedy all organizational problems, I do feel that six conclusions can fairly be drawn:

1. Laboratory education is a very promising educational process. Experience to date suggests that it can help some organizations to *begin* to overcome some of their problems.

2. Laboratory education is *not* a panacea, nor is it a process that can help every organization. Furthermore, it must be followed by changes in the organization, its policies, managerial controls, and even technology. Not all organizations can profit from it; nor do all organizations need similar

amounts of it. All these factors should be carefully explored before becoming involved.

3. Not all laboratory programs are alike. Some focus more on interpersonal learning, some on intellectual problem solving, some on small groups, some on intergroups, and some on varying combinations of all of these. Again a careful diagnosis can help one to choose the right combination for the organization, as well as the appropriate educators. Nor are all laboratory programs equally effective. The competence of the educators can vary tremendously, as well as the receptivity of those who attend. The best thing to do is to attempt to attend a laboratory program conducted by competent professionals.

4. Openness, trust, commitment, and risk-taking grow only where the climate is supportive. A one-shot program, even at its best, can only begin the process of unfreezing the executive system. For optimum results, repeat or "booster" programs will be necessary.

5. Although I personally believe that a laboratory program with the "natural" or actual working groups has the greatest probable payoff, it also has the greatest risk. However, one does not have to begin the process this way. There are many different ways to "seed" an organization, hoping to develop increasing trust and risk-taking. The way that will be most effective can best be ascertained by appropriate study of the executive system.

6. Finally, if you ever talk to an individual who has had a successful experience in a laboratory, you may wonder why he seems to have difficulty in describing the experience. I know I still have difficulty describing this type of education to a person who is a stranger to it.

I am beginning to realize that one reason for the difficulty in communication is that the meaningfulness of a laboratory experience varies enormously with each person. Some learn much; some learn little. I find that my learning has varied with the success of the laboratory. Some can hardly wait until it is over; others wish that it would never end. Anyone who understands a laboratory realizes that all these feelings can be real and valid. Consequently, to attempt to describe a laboratory (especially a T-group) to an individual who has never experienced one is difficult because he may be one of those persons who would not have enjoyed the process at all. Therefore, an enthusiastic description may sound hollow.

Another reason why it is difficult to communicate is that the same words can have different meanings to different people. Thus one of the learnings consistently reported by people who have completed a laboratory is that the trust, openness, leveling, risk-taking (and others) take on a new meaning—a meaning that they had not appreciated before the laboratory. This makes it difficult for a person who found laboratory education meaningful to describe it to another. He may want very much to communicate the new meanings of trust, risk-taking, and so on, but he knows, from his own skepticism before the laboratory, that this is a difficult undertaking and that it is not likely to succeed.

The point to all this is that the results of laboratory education are always individualistic; they reflect the individual and the organization. The best way to learn about it is to experience it for one's self.

Some Ethical Issues in Sensitivity Training
Martin Lakin

Sensitivity training, in its various forms, has evolved over the past two decades. It is a powerful form of experiential learning that includes self, interactional, and organizational understanding. It has its origins in the study of change and conflict resolution through attention to underlying as well as overt interactional processes. It has been widely used to reexamine managerial, pedagogic, and "helping relationships" from the factory to the classroom, from the community to the home. Typically, small groups of participants under the guidance of a "trainer" use the data of their own spontaneous interactions and reactions to one another. The trainer functions to facilitate communication, to indicate underlying problems of relating, and to model constructive feedback. He keeps the group moving and productively learning about the processes and persons and helps to avoid counterproductive conflict or unnecessary damage to participants. With the evolution of mutant forms of training, particularly over the past few years, and their growing popularity, examination of latent ethical questions has become urgent. This article is presented not to censure an obviously significant and often helpful growth in American psychology, but rather to open for discussion and scrutiny elements of it that affect public welfare and reflect on professional standards.

The number of persons who have experienced some form of training is rapidly growing. However named (training, encounter, human relations), the experience invariably involves emotional confrontations and even an implicit injunction to reconsider if not actually to change personal behavior patterns. Since participants are not self-avowed psychotherapy patients but "normal" persons, and because the trainers are presumably not concerned with reparative but with learning

Reprinted from *American Psychologist* 24, no. 10 (October 1969): 923–28. Copyright 1969 by the American Psychological Association, and reproduced by permission.

or personal enhancement, it is difficult to draw a firm line between it and other psychotherapeutic forms. Indeed, comparison inevitably forces itself upon us and suggests strongly what many of us realize so well, that a distinction between "normal" and "pathological" behavior is hazy at best. However, the comparison also compels one to consider ethical implications of the differences between the contractual relationships between participant and trainer, on the one hand, and those between patient and therapist, on the other. Concerns about the contractual implications have been only partially met by statements of differences in the goals of training from those of therapy and by the difference in self-definition of a participant from that of a patient, as well as by the avowed educational objectives of trainers. Also, formerly it could be argued that the trainer had little therapeutic responsibility because he initiated little; that interactions of the group were the resultant of collective interchange and give-and-take, and did not occur at his instance; that is, a participant "discloses" intimate details of his life or "changes" behavior patterns as a result of a personal commitment or a collective experience rather than because a trainer directs him to do so. Training groups evolved from a tradition of concern with *democratic* processes and *democratic* change. The generally accepted hypothesis was that the best psychological protection against unwarranted influence was individual and collective awareness that could forestall insidious manipulation by dominant leaders or conformist tyranny by a group.

Many people currently involved in the various forms of training are not as psychologically sophisticated or able to evaluate its processes as were the mainly professional participants of some years ago. The motivation of many present participants is cathartic rather than intellectual (e.g., seeking an emotional experience rather than an understanding). Particularly because training is increasingly used as a vehicle for achieving social change, it is necessary to explore its ethical implications—notwithstanding our as yet incomplete understanding of its special processes. There are ethically relevant problems in setting up a group experience, in conducting the group, and following its termination.

Pregroup Concerns

A psychotherapeutic intention is clear by contrast with the training intention. Sophisticated therapists know that this clarity is not absolute; complex issues of values and commitment to specific procedures cannot really be shared with patients, despite the best intentions of a therapist to be candid. Nevertheless, the therapist's mandate is relatively clear—to provide a corrective experience for someone who presents himself as psychologically impaired. By contrast, participant expectancies and fantasies about training vary much more widely. By comparison with the therapist, the trainer's mandate is relatively ambiguous. For example, some trainers view the group experience primarily as a vehicle to produce increased awareness of interactional processes to be employed in social or organizational settings. However, currently, some others dismiss this goal as trivial in favor of an expressive or "existential" experience. Both approaches are similar in that they require a participant-observer role for the trainee. Yet, the emphasis upon rational and emotional elements differs in these approaches, and this difference makes for divergent experiences. The problem is that there is no way for a participant to know in advance, much less to appraise, intentions of trainers, processes of groups, or their consequences for him. It is not feasible to explain these because training, like psychotherapy, depends upon events that counter the participant's accustomed expectations in order to have maximum impacts. Since it is inimical to training to preprogram participant or process, the nature of the training experience depends more than anything upon the particular translations, intentions, and interventions the trainer makes. This makes it imperative for the trainer to be first of all clear about his own intentions and goals.

Training has begun to attract the participation of more psychologically disturbed persons in recent years—a higher proportion of more frustrated individuals seeking personal release or solutions. Correspondingly, there is a larger supply of inadequately prepared persons who do training. To my knowledge, only the National Training Laboratories—Institute of Applied Behavioral Science has given systematic consideration to the training of leaders, but even its accredited trainers are not all prepared to deal with the range of expectations and pathologies currently exhibited by some participants. Some people who are inadequately prepared are suggesting to other people what they feel, how to express their feelings, and interpreting how others respond to them. Some, equally poorly prepared persons, are engaged in applying training to social action and to institutions. Recently, it has come to my attention that there are inadequately prepared trainers who lead student groups on college campuses without supervision. Several eyewitness accounts of these groups suggest that highest value is placed upon intensity of emotionality and on dramatic confrontations. Screening of participants is virtually unknown and follow-up investigation of the effects of these groups is unheard of. Their leaders are usually individuals who have participated in only one or two experiences themselves. Most disturbing of all, there is no sign that these leaders are aware of or concerned about their professional limitations. I think it must be recognized that it will be difficult to restrain poorly prepared individuals from practicing training in the absence of a clear statement of standards of training, trainer preparation, and the publication of a code of training ethics. (An antiprofessional bias is very popular just now, as we all know, and training fits nicely the image of "participative decision making.") Unfortunately, accredited and competent trainers have done little to deter the belief that training requires little preparation and is universally applicable. I do not exempt the National Training Laboratories from responsibility in this regard.

"Adequate preparation" should be spelled out. One would wish to avoid jurisdictional protectionism, although a degree in a recognized educative or therapeutic discipline is certainly one index of responsible preparation. For work with the public, trainers should have had, in addition to a recognized advanced degree in one of the "helping professions," background preparation in personality dynamics, a. knowledge of psychopathology as well as preparation in group dynamics, social psychology, and sociology. They should also have had an internship and extensive supervised experience.

It should be recognized that it is difficult, if not impossible, to do effective screening in order to prevent the participation of persons for whom training is inappropriate. One reason is that it is almost impossible to prevent false assertions about one's mental status on application forms. It is also true that it is difficult to assess the precise effects of training upon a particular individual. It could be argued that short-range discomfort might be followed by long-range benefits. Probably the most important step that could be taken immediately would be the elimination of promotional literature that suggests by implication that training is, indeed, "psychotherapy," and that it can promise immediate results. Why has such a step not been taken until now? I suggest that one reason is that currently many trainers do indeed view training as a form of therapy even though they do not explicitly invite psychologically troubled applicants. They do not wish to screen out those who do seek psychotherapy. But this reluctance to exclude such persons makes it almost certain that psychologically impaired individuals will be attracted in large numbers to training as a therapy.

More serious is the fact that there is little evidence on which to base a therapeutic effectiveness claim. To me it seems indefensible that advertising for training should be as seductive as it is in offering hope for in-depth changes of personality or solutions to marital problems in the light of present inadequate evidence that such changes or solutions do occur. Greater candor is necessary about the needs that are being addressed by the newer training forms. A legitimate case could perhaps be made for the temporary alleviation of loneliness that is unfortunately so widespread in contemporary urban and industrial life, but the training experience as a palliative is neither learning about group processes nor is it profound personal change. Such candor is obviously a first requisite in face of the fact that some training brochures used in promotion literallly trumpet claims of various enduring benefits. I suggest that immediate steps need to be taken to investigate these claims, to reconsider the implementation of screening procedures, set up and publicize accreditation standards, and monitor promotional methods in order to safeguard the public's interest and professional integrity.

Ethical Questions Related to the Processes of Training Groups

Being a trainer is an exciting role and function. Being looked to for leadership of one kind or another and being depended upon for guidance is a very "heady" thing as every psychotherapist knows. On the other hand, training, in its beginnings, was based on the idea that participation and involvement on the part of all the members of the group would lead to the development of a democratic society in which personal autonomy and group responsibility were important goals. The trainer had only to facilitate this evolution. Personal exertion of power and influence, overt or covert, was naturally a significant issue for study and learning in group after group. Evaluation of the trainer's influence attempts was crucial for learning about one's responses to authority. The trainer was indeed an influence, but the generally accepted commitment to objectification of his function made his behavior accessible to inquiry and even to modification. Correspondingly, experienced trainers have almost always been aware that the degree of influence they wield is disproportionately large; therefore they, themselves, tried to help the group understand the need for continual assessment of this factor. Awareness of this "transference" element has stimulated trainers in the past to emphasize group processes that would reveal its operations and effects.

However, with the advent of a more active and directing training function that includes trainer-based pressures upon participants to behave in specific ways, but without provision for monitoring of trainer practices, the "democratic" nature of the group interaction is subverted. More important is the fact that there is less possibility for participants to overtly evaluate the influences exerted upon them by the trainer. In some groups that emphasize emotional expressiveness, some trainers purposefully elicit aggressive and/or affectionate behaviors by modeling them and then by inviting imitation. Some even insist that members engage one another in physically aggressive or affectionate acts. Still others provide music to create an emotional experience. Such leadership intends to create certain emotional effects. It does so, however, without sufficient opportunity to work them through. Moreover, analytic or critical evaluation of such experiences would almost certainly be viewed as subversive of their aims.

It will be argued that participants willingly agree to these practices. The fact that the consumer seeks or agrees to these experiences does not justify them as ethically defensible or psychologically sound. It should be remembered that "the contract" is not between persons who have an equal understanding of the processes involved. It cannot be assumed that the participant really knows what he is letting himself in for. At the request of the trainer, and under pressure of group approval, some aggressive displays (e.g., slappings) or affectional displays (e.g., hugging) have occurred that some participants later came to view as indignities.

The question of group acquiescence involves a related point. A crucial element in the history of training was its stress upon genuine consensus. This emphasis was a deterrent to the domination of any single power figure or to the establishment of arbitrary group norms. Action and "decision" were painstakingly arrived at out of group interaction, consisting of increasingly candid exchanges. Influence could be exerted only under continuing group scrutiny and evaluation. Some trainers who are impelled to elicit expressiveness as a primary goal are also committed to democratic values; however, owing to their primary commitment to the significance of emotional expressiveness, they may employ their sensitivities and skills to achieving it in ways that are relatively subtle or even covert. When the participant is encouraged to experience and express strong emotions, the trainer's function in promoting these is often obscured. What is often *his* decision or initiative is presented as *group* initiative. In his recent book, Kelman[1] has suggested that a group leader has the responsibility of making group members aware of his own operations and values. I find no fault with that suggestion; however, it is very difficult to accomplish this. It is made even more difficult, if I am correct, because some trainers may even have an interest in the group remaining *unaware* of their particular manipulations because they wish to sustain the illusion that it is the group's rather than their own personal decision that results in a particular emotional process. The intention may not be to deceive consciously. It is difficult for trainers to practice complete candor with their participants and yet to facilitate the processes of training for reasons I suggested above. Nevertheless, in the light of these questions, trainers should reexamine their own activities. It might be that aroused concern will lead established trainers to take the necessary steps to educate aspirants for professional status to a new sensitivity to these issues.

Learning and Experiential Focuses

There are genuine differences in point of view and in emphasis between trainers. Some regard the emotional-experiential as the primary value in training. Others uphold a more cognitive emphasis, while recognizing that a high degree of emotional engagement is a vital part of training. For their part, participants are, more often than not, so emotionally involved as to be confused about just what it is that they are doing, feeling, or thinking at a given point in time. We know that participants slide back and forth between cognitive and affective experiencing of training. The participant must partially depend upon external sources for confirmation or disconfirmation. He looks to other members, but most of all to the trainer himself, for clarification. Surely, dependency plays a huge role, but it will not be destroyed by fiat. It is the responsibility of the trainer to make as clear as he can his own activities, his own view of what is significant, and to encourage exchanges of views among participants so that all can have the possibility of differential self-definition and ori-

1. H. C. Kelman, *A Time to Speak—On Human Values and Social Research?* (San Francisco: Jossey-Bass, 1968).

entation during the training process. This would help prevent a situation where inchoate and inarticulated pressures push individual participants beyond their comprehension.

In training, as in any other society, there are pressures of majority upon minority, of the many upon the one. Scapegoating, where recognized, would be objected to as demeaning whether it occurs as a means of inducing conformity or to build self-esteem. When the focus is upon group processes, it is often brought into the open, discussed, and countered. Where, however, the emphasis is purely on personal expressiveness, the same phenomenon may be used as a pressure rather than exposed. The implicit demand for emotionality and emphasis upon nonverbal communication even makes it more difficult to identify scapegoating when it occurs in such groups.

Ethical Issues and Evaluations

Participants sometimes come to training under "threat" of evaluation. The implications of a refusal to participate by an employee, a subordinate, or a student have not been sufficiently studied. I recall one instance where an employee of a highly sensitive security agency was sent for training. His anxious, conflicted, and disturbed response to training norms of "trust" and "openness" were not only understandable but, in retrospect, predictable. True, the commitment to maintain confidentiality was honored; nevertheless, should his participation have been solicited or even permitted? Evaluation as a participant concern is unavoidable, despite protestations and reassurances to the contrary. Training of trainers should emphasize the professional's ethical responsibility in these matters, but it will not obviate these concerns. The increase in unaccredited and marginally prepared trainers must increase them. It is difficult for most people to monitor their own tendencies to gossip or inform. Especially if the trainer is also an evaluator of participants, he cannot really compartmentalize the impressions he gets of behavior in training, from other data that he has about the participants. Perhaps it would help to make everyone aware of this fact. At least the "risk" then becomes explicit from everyone's point of view.

A diminution of risk was thought to be one of the major advantages of "stranger" groups where time-limited contact was thought to encourage a degree of candor and interpersonal experiment that was nominally proscribed. Obviously, this cannot be the case in groups where participants are related, classmates, or involved in the same company or

agency. It should be recognized that it is almost impossible to assure confidentiality under such circumstances or to prevent "out of school" reports. Trainers need to be especially sensitive to this in preparing other trainers. For example, where graduate students are involved in training groups and have social or other connections with one another, or with those they observe, numerous possibilities
. for teaching the importance of professional detachment present themselves. Trainees should learn how important it is to avoid irresponsible behavior in order to maintain the confidence of participants, how vital it is to inhibit a desire for personal contact when they have a professional role to play. Essentially, they have the same problem that faces the fledgling psychotherapist in inhibiting his own curiosity and social impulse in order to fulfill a professional function. The necessary detachment emphasized here is yet another significant and ethically relevant area that emotional expressiveness as an end in itself does not articulate. Responsibility is taught and modeled. It should be as consciously done in training as in any other helping relationship.

Posttraining Ethical Issues

A strongly positive reaction to training more frequently than not impels the gratified participant to seek further training experiences. Unfortunately, almost as frequently he seeks to do training himself. After all, it appears relatively easy. The apparent power and emotional gratifications of the trainer seem very attractive. If steps in professional preparation in becoming a trainer are not better articulated, and closely wedded to the traditional helping professions, we shall soon have vast numbers of inadequate trainers who practice their newly discovered insights on others, in the naïve conviction that they have all but mastered the skills involved in group processes and application to personal and social problems.

A final issue to which I wish to call your attention is that of posttraining contact with the participant. Participants are often dramatically affected by training. In some cases, trainer and group are mutually reluctant to end the group. In a recent case that came to my attention, my view is that the trainer was seduced, as it were, by the group's responsiveness to him. In turn, the participants were delighted by the trainer's continuing interest. Trainers must be aware of the powerful desire to sustain a relationship with them. Therefore, they must be clear at the outset what limits they propose for training. It is as important to be determinate about the termination point of training as about any other aspect of its conduct. Under the conditions of ambiguity and ambivalence of an "indeterminate" relationship, participants appear to be caught, as it were, midstream, uncertain as to the definition or possibilities of a relationship with this presumed expert upon whom they naturally depend for guidance and limit setting.

The questions that I have raised do not admit of a quick solution. They are ethical dilemmas. Steps to eliminate or ameliorate the grossest of them can be taken through awareness and self-monitoring. One practical step that I propose is the immediate creation of a commission by our professional organization to investigate training practices, standards of training preparation, and to recommend a code of ethics for accredited trainers. Research may help, but I doubt that it can come quickly enough to affect the increasing danger of the current and potentially still greater excesses in this area.

Sensitivity training is one of the most compelling and significant psychological experiences and vehicles for learning as well as a promising laboratory for the study of human relationships, dyadic, and group. It may be a superior device for personal and social change, even for amelioration or resolution of social conflict. However, it may also be abused or subverted into an instrument of unwarranted influence and ill-considered, even harmful, practices. The immediate attention of the profession is necessary to maintain its positive potential and correspondingly respectable standards of practice.

10   **Conflict within and between Groups**

Introduction

This chapter is about conflict within and between groups. The key ideas we shall be discussing are these:

1. People in organizations have both personal and role preferences about the organization's actions and policies. In his role, the marketing manager may prefer a broad product line to a narrow one; the production manager longer production runs to shorter ones.

Invariably each person's personal preferences or role preferences are different from other people's. But a difference in preferences does not necessarily imply incompatibility. Only when people are interdependent in some relevant way is a difference likely to lead to incompatibility. Thus, the marketing manager and the production manager are likely to be interdependent because the production manager depends on the marketing manager to make accurate sales forecasts, while the marketing manager depends upon the production manager to maintain adequate inventories of all goods. The same propositions about preferences and interdependence tend to be true for groups as well as individuals (although we must exercise some care when saying that a *group* has preferences.)

2. Sometimes the incompatibility between two persons or two roles or groups is only apparent. In such cases efforts at *joint* problem solving may help to uncover new alternative actions satisfactory to all. Thus the presence of conflict is not necessarily a sign of trouble. It may be "functional" for the organization, as well as for the individuals involved, if conflict leads to a more intensive search for better ways of doing things. The best (i.e., most efficient, most creative) organization is not necessarily the one that is conflict-free; it is more likely to be the one which is characterized by some "optimal" level of conflict.

3. But sometimes the incompatibility between parties *is* real enough so that new ways of doing things cannot be found which allow all parties to reach their most desired positions. What then? Frequently the results in such cases are dysfunctional for the organization. The parties to the conflict, in attempting to pursue their own self-interests, are likely to adopt competitive postures and enact their organizational roles as if they were players in a game of strategy. In chapter 6, we described in detail some tactics of such competitive, often political, behavior. But, as in the familiar "prisoner's dilemma," all parties may be made worse off by the competition, when they all could have been better off by cooperating.

4. There are several constructive ways of resolving incompatible conflicts. One of them is direct head-to-head bargaining between the parties, in which each party makes concessions. Bargaining differs from joint problem solving in that all pretense at agreement on fundamental preferences is dropped. A second familiar procedure is the appeal to third parties. Although such third-party arbitration or mediation is used frequently in labor-management conflict, it is by no means limited to that particular arena, as Assael's paper in this chapter makes clear. When the conflict occurs between the top management of an organization and some rebellious subgroup, still another strategy is frequently followed—the strategy of "protest absorption," in which the organization tries to harness the energies of the rebellious subgroup by legitimating them.

5. Since many incompatibilities between persons and groups are often recurrent and more or less unavoidable, it is possible and often useful to set up formal machinery for recognizing and for resolving them. The legal system of our courts reflects one such way of institutionalizing conflict resolution.

6. Sometimes the source of incompatibility in a conflict is the boss-subordinate relationship itself. This type of incompatibility is one of the most difficult of all to resolve. As the paper by Mechanic made clear in chapter 6, lower participants in an organization develop means for protecting and advancing their self-interests. But such short-run tactics do not really solve the problem. Competition for dominance is a zero-sum game. A long-run strategy for resolving authority conflicts may be for our organizations to modify their structures to de-emphasize the importance of authority. That is the idea at the heart of the proposals of several papers in

chapter 7 dealing with more collaborative strategies of influence.

The first paper in this chapter, Henry Assael's "Constructive Role of Interorganizational Conflict," illustrates several of the ideas discussed above. In addition, he introduces an important new concept, that of power balance. Assael argues that incompatibility of goals is most likely to lead to violence when the exploited party has no nonviolent means of pressuring the high power party without damaging itself in the process. Groups in positions of substantial power are prone to ignore the grievances and complaints of low power groups. Thus, the Automobile Dealers Association described by Assael secured concessions from the automobile manufacturers only when they appealed to Congress for a congressional investigation of the automobile industry. Minor conflicts are less likely to develop into explosive situations if the parties to the relationship, whether individuals or groups, are roughly balanced in their power to reward and deprive one another. We would emphasize the importance of a rough balance of power as a prerequisite to the other four conditions that Assael argues facilitate constructive conflict: (1) a critical review of past actions, (2) effective communication among the groups, (3) equitable resource allocation, and (4) the standardization of procedures for resolving conflict.

The second paper in this chapter, Love's "The Absorption of Protest," presents a penetrating sociological analysis of the strategies by which organizations deal with nonconforming subgroups within themselves. In particular, she contrasts protest absorption with other strategies for dealing with internal conflict, such as condemnation, avoidance, or expulsion of the nonconforming subgroup. The beauty of the protest absorption strategy (from the organization's perspective) is that it both encapsulates the nonconforming subgroup (and thereby prevents the spread of its rebellious ideas) and also harnesses the innovative energies of the nonconforming subgroup. Appended to her original paper, which was written in 1962, is a postscript written in 1972 especially for this revised version of *Readings in Managerial Psychology*. The postscript attempts to apply the theory of protest absorption to the prominent forms of social conflict that characterized American society during the middle and late 1960s. In the process Professor Love also makes some minor modifications and extensions of her central theory. Since her original paper on protest absorption first appeared in the early 1960s, the reader will see that it was a prescient piece of work.

The third paper in this chapter, by William Mitchell, discusses bargaining as a means of resolving conflicts. Mitchell also presents several brief case studies illustrating the role of bargaining tactics in a variety of political settings, including the American Presidency, the Supreme Court, and the processes of government budgeting.

Finally, Pondy's paper also focuses on the budgeting process, but this time in an industrial setting. Intergroup conflict about the allocation of resources, Pondy feels, can be ascribed primarily to the existence of subloyalties within the firm. Like Mitchell, Assael, and Love, he emphasizes the need for formal mechanisms for resolving such recurrent conflicts, so that they do not become dysfunctional by causing blockage or distortion of communication channels.

Constructive Role
of Interorganizational
Conflict
Henry Assael

Conflict between organizations is an inevitable outgrowth of functional interdependence and the scarcity of resources. Managers and organizational theorists have more frequently been concerned with resolving conflict within the organization rather than conflict between organizations that are part of a system. Pressures for internal organizational stability and adaptation have outweighed the equally important requirements for management of the system of organizations; therefore studies of the consequences of conflict on business systems have been rare.

The potential for conflict is high in systems of selective and exclusive distribution, since they are characterized by a high level of functional interdependence between manufacturers and dealers.[1] During periods of short demand, manufacturers typically accuse dealers of poor performance and failure to comply with their directives about retail management, promotion, and price policies; and dealers accuse manufacturers' representatives of unwarranted pressures in ensuring compliance, particularly in the maintenance of inventories.

Effective management of such systems requires evaluation and control of the effects of interorganizational conflict on the performance and stability of the system. Criteria must be established to distinguish between constructive and destructive conflict. Such criteria should help management to identify potential conflict situations and to avoid undesirable effects on dealer profits and performance.

Reprinted from *Administrative Science Quarterly* 14, no. 4 (December 1969): 573–83, by permission of the author and the publisher.

1. Valentine F. Ridgway, "Administration of Manufacturer-Dealer Systems," *Administrative Science Quarterly* 1 (1957): 464–83; Thomas L. Berg, "Designing the Distribution System," in Stuart H. Britt and Harper W. Boyd, Jr., eds., *Marketing Management and Administrative Action* (New York: McGraw-Hill, 1963), pp. 400–408; Henry Assael, "The Political Role of Trade Associations in Distributive Conflict Resolution," *Journal of Marketing* 32 (1968): 21–28.

This article attempts to establish a set of criteria for identifying constructive conflict in such systems. The criteria are based on premises about intergroup conflict derived from the sociological literature. They are applied to a specific system, automobile distribution, to test their validity in distinguishing between constructive and destructive conflict.

The conceptual framework for this distinction may be found in the writings of large-system sociologists—those who study conflict between organized groups. They regard conflict as potentially beneficial to the system when it brings about a more equitable allocation of political power and economic resources by the formation of new countervailing forces, and greater balance and stability within the system. Conflict is destructive when a lack of recognition of mutual objectives results. Continued coercion by the more powerful economic forces drive less powerful, yet functionally essential, members from the system.[2]

This view of conflict contrasts with the more traditional view developed by managerial theorists—those who have concentrated on the study of conflict within rather than between organizations. They refer to conflict primarily in intraorganizational terms as a breakdown in the decision-making apparatus resulting in difficulty in selecting alternative courses of action.[3]

Setting and Method

Automobile distribution is characterized by an exclusive franchise system requiring close interaction between manufacturers and dealers. The manufacturer relies on his dealers as the primary sales contact with the consumer; the dealer relies on the manufacturer to create adequate sales potential through product development, advertising, and pricing strategies. This high level of interdependence has led to persistent economic conflicts between manufacturers and dealers, particularly in periods of short demand.

2. George Simmel, *Conflict* (Glencoe, Ill.: Free Press, 1949); Lewis A. Coser, *The Functions of Social Conflict* (Glencoe, Ill.: Free Press, 1956); Robert Dubin, "Industrial Conflict and Social Welfare," *Journal of Conflict Resolution* 1 (1957): 179–99; Ralf Dahrendorf, *Class and Class Conflict in Industrial Society* (Stanford: Stanford University Press, 1959); Robert Presthus, *The Organizational Society* (New York: Knopf, 1962).

3. Chris Argyris, *Personality and Organization* (New York: Harper, 1957); James G. March and Herbert A. Simon, *Organizations* (New York: Wiley, 1958); Reinhard Bendix and Lloyd H. Fisher, "The Perspectives of Elton Mayo," in Amitai Etzioni, ed., *Complex Organizations* (New York: Holt, Rinehart and Winston, 1962), pp. 113–26.

The industry was a good subject for analysis because of the predominance of a well-defined set of policy issues and the existence of conditions typical of other industries using exclusive and selective forms of distribution. Conflicts in the automobile distribution system are similar to those between manufacturers and dealers in the petroleum, farm implements, and television industries.[4] In addition, conflict has occurred on the local level between "cut-rate" and "traditional" dealers over price and promotional policies. Similar conflicts between retailers have occurred in the drug, food, and liquor industries.

Distribution in the automobile industry was studied on an exploratory basis over a two-year period. Extensive open-ended interviews were conducted in the greater New York area from 1963 to 1964 with eighty-one franchised dealers representing the four domestic manufacturers and Studebaker, and with nine field representatives of the manufacturers. Dealers were selected on a quota basis by controlling for number of years in the industry and type of franchise.

The questionnaire attempted to determine dealer reactions to manufacturers' policies at the time of the interviews (1963-64) and during the mid-1950s. The mid-1950s provided a good basis for comparison since the level of conflict was significantly more intense than in the mid-1960s. Published sources described the mid-1950s as a period of strong pressure from the manufacturers because of the buyers' market and excessive factory inventories after the Korean War. The early 1960s were marked by increasing sales and few incidents of pressure from manufacturers to take new cars.

Dealers were asked to evaluate manufacturers' actions in general and in eleven specific policies such as cooperative advertising, warranty, manufacturer-owned branches, new car distribution, and so on. They were asked to describe past and present policies, evaluate the importance of each policy, and then describe their personal reactions to these policies. In this way, the intensity and direction of dealer attitudes was determined.

Questions about reactions to current and past policies permitted an estimate of changes in perception about both the content and effect of manufacturers' policies. A classification of dealers into those favorably and unfavorably disposed toward the manufacturers was obtained by assessing

4. Henry Assael, *The Political Role of Trade Associations* (Hempstead, N. Y.: Hofstra University Press, 1967).

responses to the policy areas and to more general questions on manufacturers' control. No added recall was used beyond reference to specific components of policy. For instance, in the distribution of new cars, reference was made to sales quotas, scheduling, dealer financing, and minimum inventories.

Key issues of concern to the dealers at the time of the interviews included:

1. Factory involvement in retail operations through dealerships owned and financed by manufacturers.

2. Too many dealers in a given area.

3. Leasing by the manufacturers and direct sales of fleets to large accounts.

4. Service and warranty policies, particularly lack of acceptance by manufacturers of dealer warranty claims.

5. Cooperative advertising policies, largely managed by the manufacturers.

6. Alleged interference by manufacturers' personnel in dealer store management.

Issues which had resulted in conflict in the past, but were not of great concern at the time of the study, included:

7. Threats of franchise cancellation.

8. Manufacturers forcing new cars.

9. Pressures to increase investment in the dealership.

10. Pressures to stock manufacturer-owned parts and accessories.

Economic Basis for Conflict

The economic basis for most of these conflicts lies in the differing cost structures of automobile manufacturers and dealers. Because of plant facilities and retooling costs, the manufacturer has a much higher proportion of fixed to total costs compared to the average dealer. The need to spread out the overhead tends to create substantial pressures to operate at sufficiently high volume levels, particularly in periods of short demand when the market has not absorbed a quantity permitting production near the lowest average cost level. Shrinking revenues then cause economic interdependence to become a source of friction.

Fixed costs are less of a problem to the dealer, who is often protected by revenue from sources other than new cars, such as used cars and parts and accessories. To increase volume when demand is low may require increased allowances on used cars and result in shrinking profit margins. Dealers may be unwilling to carry the number of cars the manufacturer wishes to produce. As a result, there are sharp differences of opinion between dealers and manufacturers on definitions of reasonable price and sales potential.

The importance of economic position in causing conflict is clear when dealer and manufacturer profits are compared to past and present dealer attitudes towards the factory. Figure 1 presents net profits as a percentage of sales for all automobile dealers and for General Motors, Ford, and Chrysler. Profits for 1953 and 1954 are revealing, since this

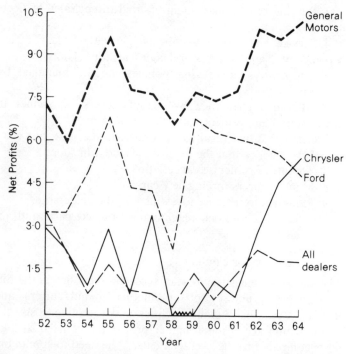

Fig. 1. Automobile Dealers' and Manufacturers' Net Profits as Percentages of Sales
Sources: Standard and Poor, *Industry Surveys, Basic Analysis* (Autos), section 2, 1966; *Automotive News Almanac* (Detroit: Slocum, 1965).

period marked the beginning of the buyers' market following the Korean War. Faced with lagging demand, manufacturers maintained production levels and prevailing list prices, and pressured dealers to promote sales. Partly as a consequence, dealer profits decreased by almost 75 percent from 1953 to

1954, while profits of General Motors and Ford increased by over 25 percent.

Attitudes of dealers mirrored the shift in their economic position. When asked to evaluate manufacturers' policies since the mid-1950s, 56 percent of all dealers (table 1) and

Table 1
Dealers' Responses to Changes in Manufacturers' Policies from 1954 to 1963

Dealer response	Ford		General Motors		Chrysler		American Motors		Studebaker	
	N	%	N	%	N	%	N	%	N	%
No change: liberal policies	1	6	4	18	3	16	6	55	2	67
No change: intermediate view	3	17	—		4	21	1	9	—	
No change: poor policies	—		—		8	42	1	9	—	
Change for the better	14	78	21	82	4	21	3	27	1	33
New dealer (last 5 yrs)	—		—		—		1		4	

81 percent of the Ford and General Motors dealers saw an improvement over time. Significantly, no dealer described a worsening of relations, although several maintained a consistently poor view of the actions of the manufacturers. In addition, dealers with a favorable attitude towards the manufacturers sold more than twice as many cars on the average in 1963 compared to dealers with an unfavorable view of manufacturers. Clearly, economic position conditions dealers' views of manufacturers, so that policies of manufacturers that are acceptable during prosperity may cause conflict in periods of lagging sales.

Conditions for Constructive Conflict

A review of the writings of large-system sociologists suggests five basic requirements for constructive conflict:

1. A critical review of past actions.

2. More frequent and effective communications between disputants, and the establishment of outlets to express grievances.

3. A more equitable distribution of system resources.

4. Standardization of modes of conflict resolution.

5. Creation of a balance of power within the system.

These premises were selected from among many developed in studies of intergroup relations, because they referred specifically to the resolution of group conflict.[5] In addition, they were applicable to organized systems since they were concerned with adjustments in power and resources between interdependent groups.

This section deals with how these premises distinguish between constructive and destructive conflict in automobile distribution.

Critical Review of Past Actions

Constructive conflict promotes a critical inquiry of organizational policies.[6] Interorganizational conflict, by leading management to review the organizational policies in dispute, may lead to a general review of related areas and foster a recognition of the interdependence of the parties in conflict.

This was the case in the automobile industry. Almost all of the General Motors dealers and field representatives agreed that dealer complaints in the mid-1950s were instrumental in leading General Motors to search for more dealer-oriented policies. The dealers attributed initial change to pressures from congressional hearings. Later changes in policy were attributed to the influence of a new and more dealer-oriented management team after 1957.

Senate hearings into manufacturer-dealer relations began in 1955 as an outgrowth of hearings designed to determine the monopoly power of General Motors and lasted for two years.[7] General Motors reacted to the publicity by liberalizing franchise provisions. Threats of contract cancellation made in 1955 were withdrawn, the length of the franchise was extended, dealer equity was assured in case of cancellation, allowances for model changes were increased, warranty rebates to dealers were liberalized, and dealer councils were democratized to provide more dealer representation and better communication with the manufacturer. Most important, the open-ended provision in the franchise,

5. Coser, *The Functions of Social Conflict*; Dahrendorf, *Class and Class Conflict*; Dubin, "Industrial Conflict"; O. Kahn-Freund, "Intergroup Conflicts and Their Settlement," *British Journal of Sociology* 5 (1954): 192–97; Presthus, *The Organizational Society*.

6. Presthus, *The Organizational Society*, p. 291.

7. U.S., Congress, Senate, Committee on the Judiciary, *A Study of the Antitrust Laws, General Motors*, 84th Cong., 1st sess.; idem, Subcommittee of the Committee on Interstate and Foreign Commerce, *Automobile Marketing Practices*, 84th Cong., 2d sess.

specifying that dealers had to develop the sale of motor vehicles to the satisfaction of the manufacturer, was eliminated; sales expectations were to be made explicit. Ford and Chrysler duplicated many of these provisions within two years.

The question arises whether these changes were due to change in management philosophy toward the dealers or to an attempt to reduce the threat of governmental intervention by placating the dealers. Initial policy adjustments were made under the stress of governmental pressures. Yet policy changes continued after governmental pressure abated, possibly due to General Motors' concern with dealer demoralization. Policy review was broadened beyond the dealers' immediate complaints and focused on methods to strengthen the economic position of the dealer. The outcome was a series of actions designed to reduce the number of dealers, increase the market potential of the remaining dealers, and encourage additional dealer investment in facilities. This policy reflected the stated desire of General Motors to "increase profit opportunities by keeping the right number of quality dealers at the right location."[8] The General Motors dealer population was reduced by over 20 percent after 1957, largely as a result of buying dealers out, relocation, and natural business closures. Contract cancellations were rare. Pressures by field representatives to order more cars and invest in facilities were no longer sanctioned by manufacturers. Both General Motors dealers and field representatives frequently described this reorientation as a change from "a tell to a sell approach."

Moreover, recessions in 1957–58 and in 1960 saw no attempt by General Motors to increase pressure for sales, as had the buyers market following the Korean War. Had change in policy been a short-term expedient, such pressure could have been expected. Apparently, General Motors extended the so-called marketing concept to dealers—that is, greater sensitivity and adjustment of marketing policies to exogenous market forces, particularly consumer needs.

General Motors' policy changes may have reduced the potential for future conflicts in two respects: First, a remarkable change in dealers' attitudes resulted in a more favorable view of the manufacturer (table 1). Second, the economic basis for conflict may have been limited. As dealers become fewer and investment in facilities increases, overhead at the retail level

8. General Motors, *How General Motors and Its Dealers Build for the Future* (Detroit: General Motors, 1957), p. 10.

becomes a larger proportion of total costs. The dealer must thus spread overhead over a larger volume of sales. He is willing to exert a greater sales effort and comes closer to reflecting the sales and promotional policies of the manufacturer.

But there are several limitations to the potential benefits derived from policy adjustment. First, dealers with greater investment and larger trading areas are likely to experience more severe sales pressures in a recession compared to that experienced in the mid-1950s. Past sales pressure came from the manufacturer, whereas future pressure would result from the dealer's drive to meet overhead as reflected in local price competition. Conflict would thus swing from manufacturer-dealer conflict over inventory and sales effort to local dealer competition over price and promotion.

Second, a reorientation of policy, no matter how equitable in redistributing resources, is likely to be disadvantageous to certain members of the system. A 20 percent reduction in General Motors' dealers must have forced some dealers to sell or relocate their business. The interviewed General Motors' dealers were a poor sample to determine the stress of readjustment, since they represented the survivors in the process.

Finally, a critical review of organizational policies does not ensure a resolution of existing conflicts. Organizations with overcentralized decision making and structural rigidity may merely foster new conflict areas through policy review. Ford and Chrysler created additional conflicts by instituting a process of comprehensive policy search in the late 1950s and early 1960s. Ford acted positively from the dealer's standpoint by reducing the number of dealers and liberalizing managerial controls. Yet it created friction by increasing the emphasis on dealerships owned and financed by the manufacturer.

Chrysler instituted policies which, in the view of many dealers, increased selling pressure. Greater emphasis was placed on retail branches owned and financed by the manufacturer and on leasing operations by the manufacturer. The number of dealerships increased, despite a lower ratio of sales per dealer compared to General Motors and Ford. Some dealers interpreted these changes as direct manufacturer competition at the retail level. Frequent reference was made to inflexibilities in organization, lack of policy direction, and shortcomings in communication with the manufacturer. Overcentralization and lack of policy direction were implied by a Chrysler field representative in referring to a "frantic period" of policy search at a time of low profits in the late 1950s and early 1960s: "When management fully recognized a declining position, all decision making had to be centralized because they were sure the problem lay at the lower level, and then things got tight. This used to be a frantic place."

Thus, policy search can be a two-edged sword from the dealer's standpoint. It is a necessary, but by no means sufficient, condition for constructive interorganizational conflict, since it must be combined with appropriate system communication.

System Communication and Outlets for Grievances

Constructive conflict results in improved communications between organizations, allowing for legitimate differences of interests and beliefs to emerge. Formal means of communication may act as outlets to relieve accumulated hostility and redress grievances.[9]

Effective system management requires establishment of channels of communication without blocks or distortion. Such communication permits a clear statement of policy and a free flow of reactions to policy from the interdependent organizations. This avoids accumulation of conflict by providing a formalized outlet for expressing grievances. Interorganizational communication is particularly difficult, since organizations within business systems are often ignorant of each other's attitudes and economic policies. Conflict external to the organization is required to demonstrate the need for better communications between the organizations in the system, a necessary prerequisite to the equitable resolution of conflict.

General Motors' management was genuinely surprised by the intensity and pervasiveness of dealer complaints in the mid-1950s. One outcome of governmental pressure and the subsequent policy review was generally improved communications within the General Motors distribution system. General Motors strengthened its existing network of dealer-elected councils, giving the dealer greater representation and opportunity for review. Ford dealers also described improved communications; Ford developed a semiformal method of review through a dealer review board after 1956. Field representatives then became a means of transmitting dealer reactions to management as well as a means of transmitting the manufacturer's directives to dealers.

9. Coser, *The Functions of Social Conflict*, pp. 39, 48, 122.

In contrast, Chrysler dealers reported no formalized means of communication and adjudication. When asked, "Is it helpful to go up the chain of command in case of disagreement?" 58 percent of the Chrysler dealers replied negatively, compared to only 13 percent of the other dealers. Disaffection by Chrysler dealers at the time of the study could be attributed, in part, to this lack of communication. A number of the aggrieved Chrysler dealers may have reflected accumulated hostility resulting from a lack of any outlets to express grievances.

Resource Allocation

Constructive conflict results in a more equitable allocation of system power and resources.[10] One of the basic problems of system management is the allocation of resources and functions to participating organizations. Manufacturers allocate such resources by establishing pricing policies and awarding dealers franchises stipulating the performance of marketing functions. Conflict between interdependent business organizations may be viewed as an attempt to achieve a reallocation of system resources. In any equitable resolution, organizational responsibilities must be redefined for the benefit of the total system.

The conflict period of the mid-1950s resulted in such a reallocation of responsibility. General Motors redefined dealer responsibilities by allocating to the dealer marketing functions it had previously performed: administration of local advertising was left entirely to the dealers; service and warranty policies were liberalized to provide dealers with greater independence in allowances and administration of claims; dealers were given greater latitude in ordering new cars, parts, and accessories, and in determining additional investment; and they were allotted greater sales responsibilities to enhance profit potentials. The uniformly positive assessment of these policies by General Motors dealers is an illustration of constructive conflict.

Destructive conflict is likely to arise when the most powerful member of the system denies the legitimacy of any reallocation of its power. In maintaining participation in retail operations, Chrysler, and to a lesser extent Ford, ignored an extremely sensitive issue. Three-fourths of the Chrysler dealers and over one-half of the Ford dealers (table 2) reacted sharply against manufacturer involvement in retail branches and financed dealerships, considering this a viola-

10. Ibid., pp. 48–54.

Table 2
Dealers' Negative Reactions to Manufacturers' Policies

Policy of manufacturer	Ford %	General Motors %	Chrys- ler %	Ameri- can Motors %	Stude- baker %
Manufacturers' branches	72	*	77	0	*
Dealerships financed by manufacturers	44	4	74	17	*
Leasing by manufacturers	*	*	47	13	*
Fleet sales by manufacturers	50	*	30	14	*
Cooperative advertising	22	*	41	25	0
Number of dealers	17	4	48	17	0
Service and warranty	11	12	21	17	0
Cancellation and the franchise	11	0	32	17	14
Distribution of new cars	6	0	32	0	0
Investment requirements	20	0	17	0	0
Distribution of parts	11	0	0	0	0

*Manufacturer is not involved in this area.

tion of the traditional delegation of responsibilities within the distribution system. The local market was regarded as the dealer's legitimate province and interference by the supplier was considered a threat.

Ford dealers restricted their grievances to this particular issue; yet one-third of the Chrysler dealers reacted negatively to most manufacturers' policies, even where a positive consensus existed among the other dealers; for example, distribution of new cars, service and warranty requirements, franchise agreements, and sales of fleets to large accounts. It is possible that factory policies are being rejected outright, regardless of content by the six or seven anti-Chrysler dealers based on previous disenchantment with the manufacturer. Eventually, the dealer no longer cares about the franchise, and the economic interdependence necessary for the maintenance of a well-integrated system is lost. One anti-Chrysler dealer stated simply, "This business isn't for me. I want out. Chrysler doesn't meet my standards." Given these conditions, why did the six or seven aggrieved Chrysler dealers stay in the system? Their average performance of 375 cars sold is significantly lower than the other Chrysler dealers' average of 525, but perhaps not sufficiently low to warrant selling out.

Standardization of Conflict Resolution

Constructive conflict results in a standardization of procedures for conflict resolution. Such routinized interaction will facilitate resolution of future conflicts.[11] A system cannot bear continuous conflict among its components unless such conflict is consistently regulated and resolved. If commonly accepted procedures for conflict resolution can be developed, then the system can establish a degree of stability, despite the competing self-interests of its members.

Conflict over industry-wide issues invariably moves to the national level through spokesmen for dealers and manufacturers. On this level, conflict resolution may become routinized by standard appeals through trade associations to either industry members or third-party regulatory forces. In the automobile distribution system, actions by dealer associations have come close to routinizing the resolution of conflict through a combination of self-regulation and appeals to government. Between 1954 and 1957, definite steps were undertaken by dealer spokesmen to resolve conflict. Appeals were first made by the National Automobile Dealers Association (NADA) to the Automobile Manufacturers Association and to individual manufacturers, encouraging self-resolution. When this did not bring results, state associations became more militant and looked to state legislatures for relief. From there, conflict shifted back to the NADA and demands for support were made to regulatory agencies and finally to Congress. The application of political power by dealer associations was more effective in causing manufacturers to reexamine policy than in producing legislation.[12] At times, in the final phase, conflict moved from governmental power sources back to the industry, leading to a more permanent and acceptable mode of internal resolution.

This procedure of moving in stages from internal resolution to appeals to external power sources was followed in limiting pressures on dealers to take new cars, in restricting franchise cancellations, and in unsuccessful attempts to eliminate sales of new cars to unauthorized dealers.

The weakness of conflict resolution in the mid-1950s was the necessity to appeal to powers external to the industry for support. With the acceptance by certain manufacturers of system management, it became possible to develop internal mechanisms for conflict resolution by improving channels of communication and developing system-oriented policies of distribution. Internal resolution has provided more generally

11. Dubin, "Industrial Conflict," pp. 187–90.
12. Assael, "The Political Role of Trade Associations in Distributive Conflict Resolution."

accepted procedures for dealing with conflict and greater promise of stability.

Balance of Power

Constructive conflict creates countervailing power. "Dominance by one end of the distributive chain often promotes grouping at the other end, for those subordinated to economic power will naturally tend to organize in an attempt to create and use economic or political power."[13] The establishment of countervailing power is beneficial to the distribution system in restraining the indiscriminate use of power, assuring greater equity in resource allocation, and counteracting the complacency of the managing organization.

The conflict of the mid-1950s did reflect a mobilization of political and economic power by the dealers through national and state associations; yet countervailing power did not result, in the sense of a capture and balancing of power comparable to that captured by labor from management. The manufacturer could still exert unilateral control over an individual dealer with little recourse on the dealer's part to group action.

The reallocation of economic power resulted as much from the willingness of some manufacturers to exercise self-restraint in the application of power as it did from action by dealer groups. Constructive conflict led General Motors in particular to move from exerting pressure in the mid-1950s to allowing greater freedom. The General Motors dealers also won greater economic power through a redefinition of market responsibilities, a reduction in the number of dealers, and an increase in their profit potential.

Conclusion

The automobile distribution system must be characterized by flexibility in adjusting to the conflicting demands of its member organizations. An analysis of manufacturer-dealer relations within the system has suggested five conditions for constructive conflict. First, organizations should encourage a continuous reappraisal of policies to maintain flexibility in defining and fulfilling the economic and organizational requirements of the system.

Second, organizations within the system must be willing to

13. Joseph C. Palamountain, Jr., *The Politics of Distribution* (Cambridge, Mass: Harvard University Press, 1955), p. 56; also see John Kenneth Galbraith, *American Capitalism* (Boston: Houghton Mifflin, 1962).

communicate objectives and ensure constant feedback. Insufficient communication could produce misunderstanding and a denial of the legitimacy of organizational objectives.

Third, member organizations must be willing to redefine allocation of resources and division of labor in light of long-term system benefits rather than short-term organizational goals.

Fourth, the disputants should promote systematic resolution of conflict, relying on self-regulatory procedures rather than appeals to government. Greater advances have been made in attempts to manage conflict by exchanges of views— most notably through dealer relations committees and policy readjustments.

Fifth, interaction among organizations that encourages self-restraint in the use of power by the dominant organization facilitates conflict resolution. Arbitrary use of power would seem to preclude constructive conflict, since the subordinated elements may eventually reject the legitimacy of management directives.

Should these conditions fail to prevail, there is the danger that a substantial segment of the dealer population may no longer feel economically motivated to remain in the system. High dealer turnover and lack of representation in certain areas would mean a weakening of the manufacturer's basic link to the consumer. Such destructive consequences must be avoided through conflict management requiring the establishment of economic and organizational conditions to insure constructive channels for conflict.

The Absorption of Protest
Ruth Leeds Love

Introduction—The Nonconformist and the Enclave

The usual fate of the nonconformist who occupies a position of some responsibility in a complex organization has been established: the cleric who wavers from the true path goes on retreat; the maverick army officer is appointed to an innocuous position; the recalcitrant political party deputy is temporarily suspended.[1] If temporary suspension or relegation to an insignificant position does not suffice to curb the nonconformist, he is gradually eased out of the organization. But what happens when an organization is faced with not just a single nonconformist but with several who form a cohesive enclave in its midst? The organization—specifically incumbents of positions superordinate to the nonconformists—must now check not just one individual but many who could potentially divert organization resources from their current commitments, undermine organizational effectiveness, or form a front capable of capturing control of the organization.

To control a nonconforming enclave, the organization has to employ techniques other than those typically used to check a single nonconformist. An individual's nonconformity often as not stems primarily from personality factors, although structural determinants do contribute to it. The nonconform-

Reprinted (except for postscript) from *New Perspectives in Organization Research,* ed. W. W. Cooper, H. J. Leavitt, and M. W. Shelly (New York: John Wiley & Sons, 1964), by permission of the publisher. The postscript was added in 1972.

This paper is the theoretic part of a project initiated and directed by Amitai Etzioni. I very much appreciate his devotion to the project, and the many ideas he contributed to it in our discussions. I am grateful to John C. Pock for reading critically several drafts of this paper, and for offering suggestions on debatable points. The work on this paper was supported in part by a fellowship (MF–13,085) from the National Institute of Mental Health, U.S. Public Health Service.

1. Amitai Etzioni, *A Comparative Analysis of Complex Organizations* (Glencoe, Ill.: The Free Press, 1961), pp. 241–44. This paper represents an expansion of an idea briefly discussed by Etzioni, pp. 245–48.

ity of an enclave, which is shared by all its members, stems primarily from structural determinants rather than personality factors. Hence, different techniques are called for to check nonconforming enclaves.

There is one organizational technique—the subject of this chapter—that is particularly suited for controlling wayward groups. It consists of integrating the protest of the nonconforming enclave into the organization by converting it into a new legitimate subunit. Through conversion, the nonconforming enclave obtains a legitimate outlet for its nonconformity, and thereby contributes to the attainment of legitimate goals of the organization. The conversion from nonconforming enclave to legitimate subunit will be called the protest-absorbing process. Protest absorption might take as little as a year or as long as a generation. Regardless, by the end of the process, the nonconforming enclave and the top authorities of the organization reach an accommodation such that the enclave is given some autonomy to pursue a specific activity (usually the activity which was the focus of the nonconformity), but, at the same time, it is expected to abide by the regulations and restrictions to which all legitimate subunits adhere.

Protest absorption is a structural "weapon" available to the organization. It is a weapon insofar as it is used to control nonconforming groups. It is a structural weapon insofar as its effectiveness rests on formal changes in the organizational structure, that is, on the formal positions of subunits vis-à-vis each other. As will be seen, the weapon is unleashed through the exercise of *authority,* although *power* is a variable in the protest-absorption process. Protest absorption should not be confused with cooptation which comes about through power differentials between the coopters and the coopted regardless of the authority structure.[2] Although reductionist concepts like power and charisma are variables in the protest-absorption process, they are not the major explanatory concepts. Structure and authority are the key concepts to an understanding of protest absorption, although these terms will be used only rarely to avoid awkward phrasing.

Organizational analyses which generate theories about the organization as if all structures were cut from the same cloth must be qualified when applied to specific organizations, e.g., a prison, an army, or a factory. The development of a comparative approach permits the enrichment of organizational

2. Philip Selznick, *TVA and the Grass Roots* (Berkeley: University of California Press, 1949).

theories by adding statements of regularities within one type of organization to statements of universal uniformities. Given this consideration, the first step is to delineate the type of organization in which protest absorption is expected to be an effective weapon. Then we can characterize the nonconforming enclave and the process by which it is converted into a legitimate and quiescent unit. The appendix presents an outline of cases which *illustrate* the protest-absorption model. Since this paper represents both an exploratory study and a preliminary report, we are not concerned here with the frequency with which the model is approximated.

Normative Organizations and the Distribution of Charisma[3]

Organizations can be characterized by the nature of the primary power that is used to control its lowest ranking participants. *Coercive* organizations, e.g., prisons, keep order through the use of physical force (or the threat of it); *utilitarian* organizations, e.g., factories, keep order primarily through monetary rewards; *normative* organizations, e.g., churches, elicit compliance through the allocation and manipulation of symbolic rewards. For reasons to be evident shortly, protest absorption is expected to occur most frequently in normative organizations.

Two other major characteristics distinguish the normative from the coercive and utilitarian organizations. First, a normative organization tends to demand a high degree of commitment and loyalty from its members, often to the point that members are expected to give their primary allegiance to the organization. The priest is symbolically wedded to the Church; in those organizations where secular marriage is permitted, the wife is drawn into the structure and is known by its name, e.g., a navy wife.[4] Voluntary exiting from the organization is perceived as a sign of insufficient loyalty; for example, resignation from academic departments tends to precipitate feelings of resentment and rejection among the professors who remain.[5] Criticism of the organization's institutionalized norms and methods is also taken as a sign of insufficient loyalty.

Second, most offices in normative organizations have charisma ascribed to them. The performances associated with

3. Based on Etzioni, *A Comparative Analysis.*

4. Arthur K. Davis, "Bureaucratic Patterns in the Navy Officers Corps," in R. K. Merton et al., eds., *Reader in Bureaucracy* (Glencoe, Ill.: The Free Press, 1952).

5. Theodore Caplow and R. J. McGee, *The Academic Marketplace* (New York: Basic Books, 1958), p. 66.

the position of priest or military officer are charismatic and are symbolized by such devices as special dress, badges of office, and ritual courtesies. The charismatic elements of a particular office enrich the organization's symbols and rituals with additional meaning, and increase their reward value for the loyalty and discipline which lowest ranking members exhibit. Moreover, personal contact with an incumbent of a charismatic office is itself perceived as a reward by members. Thus charismatic power in its routinized form reenforces the normative power of the organization.

At the same time that charisma helps to generate loyalty and discipline among the personnel, it also is a potential disrupter of discipline and loyalty to the organization itself. The problem is present in latent form when the lower participants of the organization attribute the functionally specific charisma of office to a *particular* incumbent, and, in so doing, generalize the charisma so that it takes on diffuse characteristics. Where this occurs, the participants make personal commitments to the particular individual who occupies a charismatic office rather than to the office itself. If the charismatic officer uses these particularistic commitments for purposes that are functional to the organization as a whole (or for purposes that do not generate dysfunctions), then the problem remains latent. The case might be, however, that the charismatic employs these commitments to challenge organizational hegemony and integration, and to compete against regular subunits (sometimes laterally related) for resources, thereby undermining the organization's allocation and reward system. (That such a situation might occur indicates both the desirability and the apparent impossibility of routinizing charisma.)

The potential strain between charisma and discipline is greatest in those organizations where the gift of grace parallels the formal organizational chart, being characteristic of many offices as well as the top ones, and yet where formal authority is centralized. The Catholic Church and wartime military organizations are the major examples of organizations that have charisma distributed throughout their lines combined with a strong, centralized authority structure. Protest absorption is more likely to be used in these organizations to control nonconforming enclaves than in normative structures which have the potential for strain between charisma and discipline but lack a strong central authority (e.g., Protestant denominations and the early Catholic Church).

The Process of Protest Absorption

The potential strain between charisma and discipline erupts into a tempest in a tepid teapot with the formation of a nonconforming enclave. More often than not, the enclave is led by a charismatic who is concerned with devising new ways for carrying out his responsibilities more effectively. The leadership of the enclave is strengthened by able lieutenants. The enclave itself is endowed with a militant spirit; its members are eager to undertake large-scale tasks and to execute them with novel strategies. The organization, grown weak internally in one or several respects, either cannot or prefers not to initiate change (although from some objective perspective change might be functionally required if the organization is to continue being effective). Protest absorption has two major consequences for the organization: it checks the nonconforming enclave by turning it into a legitimate subunit which remains loyal to the organization and it permits the introduction of change. The descriptive model of protest absorption contains three parts: (1) The characteristics of the nonconforming enclave; (2) the state of the organization; and (3) the process of absorbing protest.

The Nonconforming Enclave

Two conditions are basic to the emergence of a nonconforming enclave. First, some members of a normative organization must attribute personal charisma to an official. This provides the official with an opportunity to lead a loyal following over which diffuse influence and control can be exercised. Second, the official must have tendencies toward nonconformity and unorthodoxy, and must disregard at least some traditional norms and strategies. Once the official has proved his capacity to acquire a personal following, he may be referred to as the enclave leader; once he leads in unorthodox directions, the enclave becomes a nonconforming group.

The leader's nonconformity stems in large measure from his position in the organization. Assume that the leader is in unit C_4 (fig. 1). Assume further that C_4 is not functioning effectively with regard to its subunit goals. Lack of effectiveness could stem from one or several factors. For example, the unit is functionally peripheral and so does not receive the optimum quantity and quality of inputs; or the unit is a long-established one which has become more concerned with self-maintenance than with attainment of goals; or changes in the unit's environment have occurred which make present

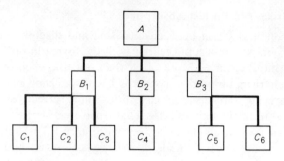

Fig. 1. Boxes Denote Units in Organization

methods and procedures obsolete; or contingencies have emerged for which there is no formal provision. In short, the unit's responsibility for goals far exceeds its capacity for attainment of goals, thereby making it relatively ineffective.[6] One response to lack of effectiveness is to exercise trained incapacity, that is, to continue conforming to rules and procedures which have become inappropriate.[7] A second response is to search for new rules and procedures which would permit increased unit effectiveness. The first response is symptomatic of functional rationality and the second of substantive rationality.[8] The leader, either in his capacity as head of C_4 or as a member of it, exercises some degree of substantive rationality and assumes responsibility for devising methods which will make the unit more effective. Increased unit effectiveness would permit him to fulfill his own particular position more adequately.

In large measure, one's position determines whether one perceives the discrepancy between responsibility and control, and whether one chooses to respond functionally or substantively to it. The greater the responsibility for goal attainment or the greater the environmental contact associated with a given position, the more likely is the incumbent to respond substantively rather than functionally. In our simplified organization chart, the A level has overall responsibility for organization goals; the C level is responsible for subunit goals. Moreover, both A and C levels have some contact with the environment. The B level serves internal coordination and communication functions. On a probability basis, then, the

6. See Etzioni, *A Comparative Analysis*, pp. 77–79 for a discussion of effectiveness.
7. R. K. Merton, *Social Theory and Social Structure*, rev. ed. (Glencoe, Ill.: The Free Press, 1957), p. 198.
8. Karl Mannheim, *Ideology and Utopia* (New York: Harcourt, Brace and Co., 1936), pp. 112–17.

enclave leader is more likely to occupy a position in A or C rather than in B. To simplify presentation of our model, we assume that the enclave leader is located in C.

The leader's nonconformity is not to be confused with deviancy. Unlike a deviant, a nonconformist does not hide his dissent from the prevailing norms. He publicly challenges the efficacy of the existing norms and their applicability to specific situations in the hope of changing them without destroying the organization. The nonconformist justifies his challenge of the status quo by appealing to what the organization recognizes as its highest morality or its ultimate set of values.[9] The official who emerges as a leader of a nonconforming enclave is justified in saying, in the area of his specific responsibility, "It is written . . . but I say unto you . . ." on two counts. First, because he has charisma attributed to him, and second, because as a nonconformist he is oriented to existing rules only in a negative sense——to challenge them.[10]

Concomitant with his personal charisma and tendency toward nonconformity, the leader also has a flair for originality which permits him to create new strategies, ideologies, and symbols to counter those of the organization.[11] The de-

---

9. If the leader appeals to a morality or values not recognized by the organization, the likelihood of protest absorption is reduced and the organization will resort to other means to check him. Orde Wingate was able to organize and arm Jews to quell Arab raids on the British pipelines in Palestine in the late 1930s, despite British policy not to give arms to Jews. Wingate also hoped that his Special Night Squad would form the basis for a Jewish army which would help to pave the way for Palestine's independence. Wingate's advocacy of a cause which extended beyond military purlieus led to his recall from Palestine, and probably helps to account for the rapid deJudification of the Special Night Squad. See Christopher Sykes, *Orde Wingate* (London: Collins, 1959).

10. R. K. Merton, "Social Problems and Sociological Theory," in R. K. Merton and R. A. Nisbet, eds., *Contemporary Social Problems* (New York: Harcourt, Brace and World, 1961), pp. 725–26; and Max Weber, *The Theory of Social and Economic Organization*, trans. A. M. Henderson and T. Parsons (New York: Oxford University Press; Glencoe, Ill.: The Free Press, 1947), p. 361.

11. Dorothy Emmet, *Function, Purpose and Powers* (London: Macmillan, 1958), p. 258. The problem of what an administrator should do with the single nonconformist, the "creative genius," the person with a flair who is "beyond good and evil," receives excellent treatment by Professor Emmet. She feels that a solution might develop if the administrator has the capacity to comprehend different roles; with such understanding the administrator might create a special role in the organization for the nonconformist. In the present context, protest absorption would require the administrator to have some understanding of structure. Emmet does not deal with the problems presented by a group of nonconformists.

velopment and implementation of new strategies come to represent the goal of the enclave. The new ideology and symbols serve as extensions to the leader's charisma in welding the enclave into a cohesive, dynamic group.

The charismatic rarely leads the enclave by himself.[12] He is usually assisted by lieutenants who support his unorthodox tactics and innovations, and spearhead the enclave with their own missionary fire and ability to influence others. The leader, by granting his lieutenants some autonomy in a specialized area like procuring supplies, insures that they will remain subservient to him. Since the lieutenants are likely to promulgate their own ideas, a limited amount of autonomy may prevent rival ideas and methods from disrupting the unity of the enclave.

The energy and zeal of the nonconforming enclave are focused on innovations, which often assume the form of techniques intended to facilitate attainment of organizational goals. New techniques might be more effective in attaining existing goals by permitting higher output or they might revitalize goals which have grown fallow. (Later we shall have more to say about the enclave's objectives and their bearing on the protest absorption process). In essence, the enclave maintains a high commitment to the basic goals of the organization, and desires to display this commitment through recognition of its innovations. The commitment inspiring the nonconformists is frequently viewed as higher than that possessed by others in the organization. The perceived or alleged discrepancy between the extremely high degree of loyalty to basic organizational values exhibited by the nonconforming enclave and the moderate degree of loyalty exhibited by other organization participants is likely to provoke conflict. Other participants have little tolerance for the enthusiasm of the enclave, for, by comparison, they appear less diligent and less loyal to the organization.

The nonconforming enclave is further distinguished by an unorthodox atmosphere which permeates many aspects of its life. This atmosphere varies from extreme austerity and asceticism to romance, adventure, and heroic sacrifice. The unorthodox behavior of the enclave, whether reflected in the wearing of special clothing or in reckless courage, not only sets the enclave apart from the rest of the organization but also contributes to its cohesiveness and strength. A member

12. See Weber, *The Theory of Social and Economic Organization,* p. 360.

can readily identify with a group symbolized by noticeable objects or mannerisms. If the group merits esteem from outsiders, it can be bestowed on easily recognized members. The symbols of unorthodoxy also facilitate recruitment in that they help publicize the group to potential members who share similar values and similar tendencies toward nonconformity.

In summary, the nonconforming enclave is characterized by a leader whose charisma of office has become personal. He pursues a course of action or cause which is perceived as unorthodox, and for which he creates symbols and an ideology. His immediate lieutenants are nonconformers in their own right, although less influential and original than the leader. The cause served is usually a means to revive allegedly neglected organizational goals or to achieve present organizational goals more effectively. Lastly, a peculiar aura, either of asceticism or of romance, envelops the enclave, contributing to its integration and highlighting its dedication to its cause.

The State of the Organization

Although nonconformity can erupt at all times, a cohesive nonconforming enclave is likely to emerge in a context in which one or a combination of the following variations of organizational weakness is prevalent. If, over time, the legitimacy of the organization procedures decreases generally or within any subunit, charisma tends to shift from office to person among those dedicated to the ultimate purposes of the organization. If an organization is insensitive to potential nonconformity (due to such factors as inadequacies of communication networks), control mechanisms might not be activated in time to forestall a nonconforming official before he gains a personal following.[13] If an organization's internal authority is weak, owing to the corruption of officers responsible for enforcing conformity or owing to the lack of (or limited) control over enforcement facilities, then whatever control mechanisms the organization might employ are ineffectual. Finally, resources diverted outside the organization

13. In some instances the "following" emerges first and then casts about for a leader. According to Erle Wilson's less romantic account of the Bounty mutiny, the potential mutineers were ship's sailors, who, on becoming cognizant of each other's discontents, recruited Fletcher Christian to be their leader. Subsequent events indicated that the choice was not entirely fortunate, for Christian lacked the capacity to live up to the charisma which his followers attributed to him. See Erle Wilson, *Adams of the Bounty* (New York: Popular Library, 1959).

to meet an external challenge, or stoppage of inputs, limit the availability of the means needed to combat nonconformity.

Once the enclave emerges, mild checks to contain the non-conformity are no longer adequate. If the organizational elite ousts the leader, his immediate lieutenants could assume control of the enclave, or members of the enclave might follow their leader and form the beginnings of a competing structure. Such a possibility is particularly threatening when the organization enjoys a monopoly or duopoly position. If the organization is one of several of its kind, then one more similar structure in the environment makes little difference. Finally, if both the leader and the members of the enclave are dispersed throughout the organization, in an effort to disband the group, nonconformity might be spread rather than eliminated.

Given the inadequacy of control techniques which are typically applied to single nonconformists, the organizational elite must choose between several alternatives: condemnation, avoidance, expulsion, or protest absorption. The first three alternatives are not effective in containing the nonconformity unless the enclave itself is quite weak to begin with. Condemnation contains the danger of widening the rift between the enclave and the rest of the organization by forcing a polarization of issues.[11] Avoidance, which means consciously taking little account of the existence of the enclave, sidesteps the danger of polarization.[15] During the period that the organization elite ostensibly ignores the enclave, however, the enclave might grow in size and strength instead of dying out. Expulsion of the enclave represents a costly loss of resources which might yet be channeled to serve organizational goals.[16] Also, expulsion could lead to the emergence of a rival structure (albeit it does permit tightening of organizational ranks). The negative consequences which might result from attempting to control the enclave through condemnation, avoidance, or explusion are particularly dysfunctional to the organization when it displays one or more signs of weakness. Although protest absorption also entails some

14. Z. Brzezinski, "Deviation Control: A Study in the Dynamics of Doctrinal Conflict," *American Political Science Review* 56 (1962): 9–10.

15. Ibid., pp. 11–12.

16. A recent report of the AFL-CIO council stated: "It is obvious that expulsion as such does not cure the offending practices. And, what is more important, once outside the federation the membership of such an organization is no longer accessible to corrective influences from the parent body through education and persuasion." (Quoted in the *Reporter*, 26 October 1961, p. 18.)

dangers, it is a more promising way of checking nonconformity on several counts.

If protest absorption is successful, it not only eliminates the pocket of nonconformity but also strengthens the organization by providing it with the services of an energetic, devoted group. Moreover, the process permits the legitimation of innovation which better equips the organization to face external challenges or to attain its own goals more effectively. Protest absorption can also lead to the elimination of nonconformity without the emergence of a devoted group or the introduction of innovation. This form results when the organization provides the enclave with an "opportunity to fail." When the enclave protests about matters beyond its ken or original bailiwick, and it is accorded legitimacy in the area of protest, it is likely to fail because it lacks the skills and knowledge to carry out the now legitimate activity. Any nonconformity which survives outright failure is expected to be sufficiently weakened so as to be eliminated easily. Should the enclave succeed despite its opportunity to fail, then the organization can reap the benefits. The risk accompanying protest absorption is that the nonconforming enclave may during the time that the organization attempts to check it, gain access to the key power positions and, subsequently, assume control of the total structure.

The Process of Protest Absorption

Once the nonconforming enclave has been converted into a new legitimate subunit, the organization is strengthened. During the protest-absorption process, however, the organization, especially that sector of it in which the enclave has erupted, faces a series of internal battles involving several levels of its hierarchy. The charismatic leader and his followers oppose those persons who formally are their immediate superiors. These shall be called the middle hierarchy and represent the enemy in the battles. Insofar as the organization has a centralized top hierarchy which can exercise authority over the middle hierarchy, these battles tend not to be fought to the death of one or the other set of combatants. Instead, the top hierarchy intercedes and more or less arbitrarily terminates the conflict. Protest absorption essentially is a process whereby the top hierarchy attempts to balance the two opposing forces—members of the nonconforming enclave against members of the middle hierarchy who are the immediate superiors of the former.

In some instances, units which are laterally related to the

nonconforming enclave will also be aligned with the middle hierarchy in opposing the enclave. In other cases, the opposition will be made up only of heads of laterally related units and an opposing middle hierarchy will be absent. The varying composition of the "enemy" depends upon the location of the enclave in the organizational structure. The general pattern, however, might be diagramed as shown in fig. 2.

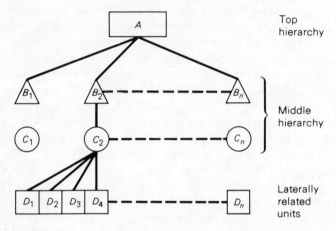

Fig. 2

Assume that the enclave erupts in D_4. If the leader is the head of D_4, the enclave will encompass the entire unit. If the leader is only a member, the enclave will set itself up as D_4'. In either case, the enclave will have to contend with C_2 who is responsible for D_1–D_4. Directly, or indirectly, the enclave will also have to contend with the other D units. The emergence of the nonconforming enclave creates increased competition for resources among the D units. In addition, they perceive themselves as being cast in an unfavorable light by the enthusiasm and heightened activity of the enclave. Hence, the D units will pressure C_2 to suppress the enclave. The D units do not always form part of the opposition to the enclave; another variation is that C_2 might also be directly in charge of one D unit as well as having general responsibility for the entire D section. Such structural variations in the formation of the opposition to the nonconforming enclave do not affect the general pattern of protest absorption, although they help to explain slight variations from case to case. Hence, for simplicity's sake, in describing the process we shall limit the opposition to the middle hierarchy, although the reader should bear in mind that the opposition can vary in its composition.

Incumbents of positions constituting the middle hierarchy are more likely to exhibit "trained incapacity" than incumbents of other levels. Hence, they are usually incapable of comprehending the significance of the enclave's protest. Furthermore, their positions are threatened by the enclave, both because it reveals that their loyalty to basic values of the organization is not as strong as it could be and because it indicates that they cannot make use of the authority vested in them to maintain order in their own bailiwicks. Their response to the enclave is to attempt to suppress it through such means as closing the communication links between the charismatic leader and the top hierarchy, restricting the enclave members' freedom of movement, and reducing the resources available to them. From the perspective of the middle hierarchy, the use of such techniques represents the full exercise of their rights of office.[17] From the perspective of the nonconforming enclave, such techniques are obstructions which indicate that the organization is against it, and hence, to carry out its cause, the enclave must try to be even more dynamic and more cohesive.

If the charismatic leader is to demonstrate his basic loyalty to organizational values and if he is to gain recognition and legitimation for his cause, he must have access to the top hierarchy. When such access via regular channels is barred, the leader develops his own routes to the top. Frequently this is done through an intermediary who is outside the organization but has legitimate access to the top echelon. Insofar as the charismatic leader is able to establish a particularistic relationship with such an intermediary which is beyond organizational control, he has relatively easy access to the top.

The particularistic communication line gives the nonconforming enclave some leverage in an attempt to have its cause recognized and legitimized. That the intermediary is willing to use his power over the top hierarchy in behalf of the enclave is regarded by its members as a significant step forward and as a sign of incipient legitimation.

At the same time that a particularistic communication line gives the enclave hope that its cause will be successful, it also produces potential instability and unreliability. First, the communication line is maintained at the will—or the whim—of the intermediary, which means that it can be opened and

17. When legitimate techniques fail to quell the enclave, the middle hierarchy might resort to illegitimate or nonlegitimate ones. Paradoxically, it is at such times that the middle hierarchy overcomes its "trained incapacity."

closed arbitrarily. Second, a particularistic request to the top hierarchy in behalf of the nonconforming enclave might elicit informal instructions to the middle hierarchy which it can easily overlook in its continued attempts to obstruct the enclave.

In some instances the charismatic leader need not resort to particularistic communication channels for he might be able to go to the top directly;[18] or the attention of the top hierarchy might be drawn to the nonconforming enclave as a result of the conflict between it and the middle hierarchy, especially if the conflict has affected task performance adversely.

Regardless of the means by which the attention of the top hierarchy is directed to the enclave, the leader who has gained this attention can demonstrate his basic loyalty to organizational values and communicate his ideas for their more effective realization in the hope of gaining official approval. Concerned with blocking such approval, the middle hierarchy urges the top to suppress the enclave. The top hierarchy is interested in enhancing general organizational effectiveness, and, by extension, is concerned with maintaining internal order. With its broader, more substantive, perspective, the top is more amenable to innovation than the middle hierarchy, especially when faced with internal weakness or external challenge. Hence, the top is more likely to accede to some demands of the nonconforming enclave, especially if its leader is backed by a powerful intermediary, than to the insistence of the middle hierarchy that the enclave be thoroughly curbed or eliminated.

The first round in the protest-absorption process is completed when the top hierarchy recognizes the nonconforming enclave and gives it a modicum of autonomy to pursue its advocated innovation. This is followed by several more rounds of obstruction by the middle hierarchy, unorthodox communication to the top by the nonconforming enclave, and a gradually increasing grant of resources, autonomy, and legitimacy to the enclave by the top hierarchy. With each round the enclave comes closer to approximating a new legitimate subunit.

In exchange for autonomy and legitimacy from the top hierarchy, the enclave must agree to accept certain stabilizers. The stabilizers are mechanisms to insure the loyalty of the new unit to the organization and its conformity to organiza-

18. The leader's ability to communicate with the top hierarchy directly is determined in large part by other capacities, roles, and statuses which he might have within or outside of the organization.

tion regulations. First, the protest-absorbing unit is expected to develop rules, subject to approval by the top echelon, to guide its conduct; any changes in these rules are also subject to approval by the top. Second, the unit must accept a regular source of finance through which it will acquire all or most of its inputs. In this way, unauthorized appropriations of resources and competition with existing units for available resources are minimized, and the frustrations of an irregular source of income, typical of a group during its nonconformist period, are avoided. Third, and most important, the unit's activity is limited to a particular sphere of operation, usually that for which the leader and his followers advocated their innovation.[19]

With the introduction of stabilizers, the leader's personal charisma becomes attenuated. The personal charisma is reconverted to charisma of office as the leader (or his successor) assumes legitimate control of the protest-absorber unit. Furthermore, the most radical members of the former enclave perceive the leader as bowing to the dictates of the top hierarchy, thereby betraying the cause; they cease to accept the leader as a charismatic figure, leave the unit, and, where possible, even the organization. The more visible to his followers are the leader's negotiations with the top hierarchy, the more likely is this to be the case. In fact, the top hierarchy could reduce the leader's personal charisma considerably by sending a representative directly to the members of the enclave to grant it legitimacy. By circumventing the leader, the top hierarchy gives the impression that it has been wise enough to recognize the value of the enclave's cause of its own accord and so no credit need be given to the leader who has spearheaded the cause. Circumvention of the leader does present certain dangers, however. Such a procedure is most likely to be successful only if the representative has instructions to grant all or the most important of the enclave's demands. Otherwise, enclave members are likely to perceive the visitation of the representative as an attempt by the top hierarchy to sabotage the cause. Since, in most cases, the top is unlikely to grant major concessions in one fell swoop, this

19. The nature of the task limitation imposed on the protest-absorber unit is in part determined by the form of the organization's division of labor, i.e., whether it is structured along geographic lines such that each unit engages in the same task but in a different locality, or around functionally specific lines where each unit engages in its own speciality, or is a combination of geography and functional specificity. See C. I. Barnard, *The Functions of the Executive* (Cambridge, Mass.: Harvard University Press, 1938), p. 129ff.

danger is almost always present and serves to strengthen the enclave. A second danger is that the representative himself might be affected by the leader's charisma and join the enclave rather than fulfill his orders.

Occasionally other stabilizers are also introduced, e.g., limiting the size of the protest-absorber unit, appointing a special supervisor to watch for and check any excessive enthusiasm which the unit might display, and restricting the use it may make of its particularistic communication channel. Generally, these particular stabilizers are instituted if the newly legitimized unit still remains somewhat recalcitrant in its adherence to organization rules.

The conformity of the unit is further enhanced through pressures arising within it to replace the instability of its charismatic nature with the stabilizing characteristics which accompany routinization. The nonconforming enclave, like the large-scale charismatic movement, faces "everyday" problems of economic and administrative organization. For example, the unit at some point must provide for the selection of a successor to replace its charismatic leader. (The criteria for selection may be established either by the enclave or by the organization.)

The external pressures toward protest absorption and the internal pressures toward routinization eventually tame the nonconforming enclave and convert it into a quiescent unit concerned with maintaining order in its own bailiwick.[20] The unit may show signs of quiescence simultaneously with its legitimation through protest absorption, or after a period of dynamism during which it expands and gives devoted service to the organization. Its concern with expansion and innovation is replaced by one of self-maintenance. The zeal and energy of the unit are dissipated in legitimized action without being replenished. Once the original members of the unit are gone, or have become concerned with preserving their newly legitimized positions within the organization, the verve that sparked the unit when it was a nonconforming enclave cannot be sustained. Successors to key positions in the unit most likely have been socialized by the organization, and tend to resemble the middle hierarchy more than the original members of the enclave.

The unit's agreement to restrict itself to a specialized sphere of operation is itself another contributing factor to the emerging quiescent period. The agreement helps to preclude

20. Robert Michels, *Political Parties* (New York: Dover Publications, 1959), pp. 174–75.

the possibility that the unit will attempt innovation beyond its allotted sphere; and whatever success the unit has in its speciality also drains it of further nonconformity. Success is its own detriment when the question of new risks arises: members of the unit prefer to maintain rather than gamble their resources and status on a new venture.

Another factor in the elimination of nonconformity from the unit is time itself. Norms which the enclave had revitalized once again become eroded through increasing lack of strict adherence to them. Members of the unit remain committed to their once-new methods even though they have become outmoded and ineffectual. The unit as a whole is no longer dedicated to the ultimate values of the organization but rests content with the sinecure provided it through protest absorption.

The factors that contribute to quiescence—cessation of innovation, dissipation of zeal and energy, emergent conservative tendencies, modification of norms, and the obsolescence of methods—also set the stage for new protest and new forms of nonconformity, which are likely to erupt because the unit legitimized through protest absorption is more vulnerable to the strains between charisma and discipline than are other units. Its history of nonconformity remains unforgotten and lends it an aura of prestige, thereby distinguishing the former enclave from ordinary units. It is further distinguished by having institutionalized a more arduous socialization period for its recruits. Finally, its standards tend to be more strict and demanding than those of the organization as a whole, even with the corroding effects of time. These factors not only militate against the complete integration of the unit into the organization but also make it extremely attractive to recruits, particularly to those who tend to be strongly or rigidly committed to its original values. In short, the unit, limited to its own sphere of action, tamed by stabilizers, concerned with its own well-being, and yet, endowed with the aura of its unorthodox past which facilitates recruitment of potential nonconformers, nurtures a fertile field for the regeneration of a nonconforming enclave and another cycle of protest absorption.

In summary, the process of protest absorption follows several steps. A nonconforming enclave is able to gain some power within the organization because the latter is internally weak or faced with an external crisis. To check the internal threat without further weakening itself, the organization forms a new administrative unit to absorb the enclave, based on the institutionalization of new norms. The emergence of the unit represents a *Sturm und Drang* period: the enclave demands more autonomy and resources so that it can pursue its course of action while the organization reluctantly grants some autonomy and resources, and permits some innovation, in order to maintain peace and overcome the crisis confronting it. The *Sturm und Drang* begins to subside when the enclave achieves the status of a more or less legitimate unit within the organization, and is virtually quelled as the unit loses its initial élan, no longer taking on new ventures and becoming concerned with its own maintenance. From the perspective of the top hierarchy of the organization, protest absorption is a process of encapsulation. The nonconforming enclave becomes encased in a network of stabilizers which limits its freedom of action.

Implications of Protest Absorption for the Organization

In large measure, the significance of protest absorption for the organization as a whole depends upon the bearing which the enclave's cause has on the core policies and practices of the organization. From the standpoint of its proponents, the cause usually has a greater degree of significance for core policies than the top hierarchy is willing to acknowledge.

It is convenient to formalize what is generally involved here by means of a continuum in which the cause advocated by an enclave is scaled relative to the degree with which it is likely to affect core policies and practices. Then, as in fig. 3, the enclave can be characterized as to where it *aspires to be* on the continuum, and where it is *willing to be placed*. The organization can be characterized as to where it would *like* to locate the enclave, and where it is *willing to place it*. The shaded area indicates the range of acceptability for an enclave and its organization; in this instance there is an overlap, although this is not necessarily always the case. Moreover, the ranges of acceptability can shift in the course of the protest-absorption process.

Once these ranges are known, further statements can be made about protest absorption. Where there is an overlap in ranges, protest absorption should prove more successful in controlling the enclave's nonconformity than where such an overlap does not exist. In the case where an overlap is absent (or in the case where the organization makes strong attempts to place the enclave below its minimum acceptable position —in fig. 3 this would be below 4), the enclave will retain its zeal and unorthodoxy in order to attempt to achieve its cause in the face of control measures. For as the enclave is forced

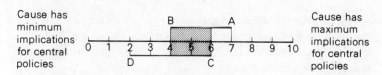

Fig. 3. *A*. Enclave desires cause to have value of 7. *B*. Enclave willing to accept value of 4. *C*. Organization willing to permit value of 6. *D*. Organization prefers value of 2.

toward the lower end of the continuum, its cause becomes more attenuated, and its chances are lessened for realizing the goals which sparked it in the first place.

Furthermore, by locating the ranges of acceptability, we can predict approximately the number of rounds the protest-absorption process is likely to undergo. More rounds can be anticipated as the overlap between the two ranges is lessened. For the organization will usually try to check the enclave by locating it as low on the continuum as it can, while the enclave will continue its nonconformist activity until it is located as high on the continuum as it can be.

The more that protest absorption takes place at the higher end of the continuum, the more likely it is that an organization's central policies and practices will undergo a change. This is likely, if only for the reason that the more central the protest-absorber unit is to the organization, the more probable it is that its members will be promoted upward in the hierarchy until they reach the top.[21] The variables which determine where, on the continuum, the enclave will ultimately be absorbed, are those involved in the protest-absorption process itself: the degree of weakness of the organization, the strength of the nonconforming enclave, the power of the intermediary, the nature of the stabilizers, and so on. Thus the protest-absorption process can lead to a long-term chain reaction of major changes in the organization, as well as check nonconformity and introduce a particular innovation.

Finally, protest absorption can have implications for organizational policy for dealing with nonconformity. An organization which has had long experience with nonconformity, e.g., the Catholic Church, might institutionalize the rounds of protest absorption. This means that, as a nonconforming enclave emerges, it "automatically" will be converted into a new subunit over several stages, as it is able to meet criteria specified by the top hierarchy. If the adoption of protest ab-

21. The most cogent illustration of this process can probably be found in the history of the United States Air Force and of the submarine and aircraft carrier units in the United States Navy.

sorption as a conscious organization policy is carried out effectively, an organization will strengthen its ability to cope with nonconformity and to implement changes flowing upward from the bottom.

Appendix

Some Historical Examples

Following a presentation of a middle-range theory model, ideally, one should develop indicators for the variables that make up the model, and then collect a sample of cases to test the model. Traditional limitations of time and space prevent the realization of the ideal. To facilitate comprehension of the protest-absorption model, however, the history of two nonconforming enclaves is presented in table 1. One enclave emerged within the Carmel Order in sixteenth-century Spain under the leadership of St. Teresa. The second enclave began when Claire Chennault was faced with the problem of developing a Chinese Air Force in the late 1930s.

Space does not permit even a skeleton consideration of other enclaves. Examples abound however. To name a few: Orde Wingate's Special Night Squad, his Gideon Force which fought in Ethiopia, and his long-range penetration unit known as the Chindits; the Cistercian Order which began as an enclave within the Benedictine Order, and the Trappist Order which emerged from the Cistercian Order, and so on. Our examples have been limited to military groups and to the cenobitic structures of the Catholic Church, not only because these are normative organizations with strong centralized authorities but also because of availability of data. The reader should bear in mind, however, that nonconforming enclaves and their containment through protest absorption can occur in other normative organizations. An example is the Fund for the Republic which has been described as "Paul Hoffman's severance pay." In his unofficial biography of the Ford Foundation, Dwight MacDonald writes:[22]

> The Foundation's trustees decided that (the program) should be implemented by a new agency, which finally emerged in December, 1952 as the Fund for the Republic. . . . Hoffman originally supported Hutchins in proposing it, and its establishment coincided with Hoffman's extrusion from the Foundation. . . . The Fund's elephantine gestation is perhaps explained by the dilemma of the Ford trustees . . . who found them-

22. Dwight MacDonald, *The Ford Foundation* (New York: Reynal & Co., 1956), p. 71.

selves being chivied by Hoffman and Hutchins into
doing something that was as "controversial" as it was
logical on the basis of the program they themselves had
adopted.

Postscript 1972

After this working paper was completed in 1962, no systematic effort was undertaken to test the hypotheses implicit in
the description of the protest absorption process. But other
research endeavors, and the militant, and at times violent,
protest that has permeated many American institutions in
recent years have stimulated some additional thoughts about
protest absorption. I shall describe these briefly here.

Protest Absorption in Competitive Organizations

Protest absorption is almost always shrouded with uncertainty, because it depends on the charismatic strength of the
leader as he pursues his cause, among other reasons. His
charisma might only be adequate through one round of absorption. But there is one structural characteristic that might
compensate for the leader's deficiency and assure the establishment of a new legitimate subunit, and that is competition.

Among a set of organizations competing within the same
market, either for resources or for clientele, the process of
absorbing protest in one unit may have implications for
structural change within a competing unit. Let us assume that
organization A has, after much strife, converted a nonconforming enclave into a new legitimate subunit, with a
delimited amount of autonomy to pursue its innovative ideas.
Further, assume that the new subunit is visible to competing
organizations. It may be the case that competing organization
B is already faced with a similar nonconforming enclave. In
this instance, B might convert the enclave into a legitimate
subunit without as much conflict as occurred in A, to assure
the maintenance of its competitive position. And this might
occur regardless of the energies that the leader of the enclave
brings to his cause, a particularistic link to the top leader of
B, or the presence of other conditions that contribute to the
protest absorption process.[23]

23. This hypothesis about the effects of competition on protest ab-
sorption emerged from a review of the histories of the news units
within CBS and NBC. See Mitchell V. Charnley, *News by Radio* (New
York: Macmillan, 1948); A. A. Schechter, *I Live on Air* (New York:
Frederick A. Stokes, 1941); Francis Chase, Jr., *Sound and Fury* (New
York: Harper & Bros., 1942); Eric Sevareid, *Not So Wild a Dream*
(New York: Alfred Knopf, 1946), and other memoirs by broadcasters.

Table 1
History of Two Nonconforming Enclaves

	Discalced Carmelites, 1562–93	Flying Tigers, 1941–60
Organization Leader Lieutenants	Catholic Church St. Teresa St. John of the Cross	United States Army General C. L. Chennault Colonel C. V. Haynes Colonel R. L. Scott
Cause	Greater concern with salvation. Revive asceticism of early Carmelites. Concern with action as well as contemplation, e.g., praying for the souls of others. This was to lead to emphasis on missionary work.	Develop and put into action fighter pilot tactics. Train American pilots in the use of fighter planes. Furnish air support for Chinese land forces and fight delaying action against Japanese.
Symbols	Alpargatas (hemp and rope sandals). Rough material for clothing.	Flying Tiger sharks painted on planes. Cowboy boots instead of regulation military boots.
State of Organization	Carmel Order had its strict Rule modified in 1432. By the sixteenth century, adherence to the modified rule had become lax. Nuns spent time in gossip rather than in prayer. Spanish Church beginning to seethe with reform to meet challenge of Reformation.	Tactics for use of planes not developed at pace commensurate with technological progress. Tendency by military to view planes as auxiliary to infantry and artillery. Lack of preparation to deal with onset of World War II.
Middle hierarchy Top hierarchy Intermediary	Officials of Carmel Order in Spain and Italy The Pope Philip II of Spain	Generals Bissell and Stilwell President Roosevelt Madame Chiang Kai-shek
Obstruction techniques	Teresa assigned for three-year period to head of a Carmel convent to halt her activities. Excommunication of nuns who voted for Teresa when her three-year term was concluded. Assigning Calced confessors to Discalced houses. Kidnapping an imprisoning friars loyal to Teresa.	Limiting allocation of supplies and personnel. Detaining Flying Tiger recruits in India, enroute to China, to indoctrinate them against Chennault. Attempting to select Chennault's chief of staff for him.
Stabilizers	Constitution for Discalced providing for a centralized government.	Induction of Flying Tigers into U.S. Army which meant that group would have to adhere to military regulations.

Origin of enclave and rounds of protest absorption

Within convent at Avila, Teresa gained small following. Permission granted to start her own house.

1. Discalced established as separate province, 1579. Free to establish religious houses. Subject to General of Order of Spain.
2. Established as separate congregation, 1587. Subject to General of entire Carmel order but elected its own Vicar-General.
3. Established by papal bull as separate order, 1593, subject only to Pope.
4. In succeeding centuries Discalced Order engaged in missionary work and spread beyond the boundaries of Spain.

Chennault invited to China by Madame Chiang Kai-shek to develop Chinese Air Force. From 1936 to 1940, Chennault fought Japanese with whatever pilots and equipment drifted to China. From 1940 to 1941, American Volunteer Group organized; group commanded by Chennault and paid by Chinese government.

1. AVG transformed into China Air Task Force and inducted into USAAF, July 1942, subject to Bissell as head of parent 10th Air Force.
2. CATF converted into 14th Air Force, March 1943, subject to Stilwell's command as head of China-Burma-India theatre.
3. No further rounds of protest absorption occurred, for General Marshall felt that Chennault should continue under Stilwell's command, but Stilwell was instructed to give Chennault all that he asked for.
4. 14th Air Force deactivated in 1960.

Note: For references pertaining to table 1, see the following:

Discalced Carmelites:
Nigg, Walter, *Warriors of God*, New York: Alfred A. Knopf, 1959.
Peers, E. A., *Handbook to the Life and Times of St. Teresa and St. John of the Cross*, Westminster, Maryland: Newman Press, 1954.
———, *Spirit of Flame*, New York: Morehouse-Gorham, 1945.
St. Teresa, *Life of St. Teresa* (trans. by Rev. John Dalton), New York: P. J. Kennedy & Sons, N.D.
Zimmerman, B., *Carmel in England*, London: Burns & Oates, 1899.

Flying Tigers:
Romanus, C. F. and Sunderland, R., *Stilwell's Mission to China*, Washington, D.C.: Office of the Chief of Military History, Dept. of the Army, 1953.
Scott, R. L., *God is my Co-Pilot*, New York: Ballantine, 1959.
———, *Flying Tiger: Chennault of China*, New York: Doubleday, 1959.
Wedemeyer, A. C., *Wedemeyer Reports*, New York: Henry Holt, 1958.

Finally, organization C may not have a nonconforming enclave, but in response to protest absorption in A, it may introduce a new unit in order to maintain its competitive position. In this way protest absorption within one organization may have implications for structural change, if not protest absorption, for other organizations that compete in the same environment.

Protest and Organizational Learning

What has just been hypothesized about competing organizations implies that they learn from each other. The question that might be asked now is to what extent organizations which are functionally similar, such as universities, but are not competitive in the usual market sense, learn from each other in controlling nonconformity. Specifically, to what extent did the demand for and the institutionalization of such innovations as Black Studies programs or coed dormitories in one university, affect the institutionalization process in other universities? The question is pertinent insofar as on some campuses such innovations emerged from the efforts of university officials to control nonconforming student enclaves. Probably a key explanatory variable for answering the question is the degree to which institutions of higher learning see themselves as similar to the university that is absorbing student protest by developing a new specialized curriculum.

The same types of questions about protest absorption could be raised vis-à-vis public school systems. Within the last five years some of the larger urban systems have been experimenting with innovative learning centers which replace the traditional public school for some students. Did these centers emerge from the efforts of school officials to control nonconforming enclaves or through other avenues?

Separation as an Alternative to Absorption

Certainly not all nonconforming enclaves are absorbed by their parent organizations. The history of Protestantism is, in large measure, the history of nonconforming sects that separated from their parent religions. The history of western political parties details the rise of splinter groups that either died out or established themselves as separate parties. Voluntary organizations also tend to produce splinter groups. A recent example is the Friends of the Earth, a conservation organization that arose soon after the more radical leaders of the Sierra Club refused to be checked by the board of directors, and resigned. A full account of the conditions leading to separation rather than absorption cannot be undertaken here, but a brief listing of them may serve to highlight the protest absorption process.

These conditions will be presented in the form of separate hypotheses. First, separation of the enclave, rather than its absorption, is more likely to occur when the parent organization lacks a long span of control. Where the middle hierarchy is short or absent the enclave is likely to pose a direct threat to the authority of the top leadership. Second, separation is more likely to occur when the enclave's cause directly challenges the premises underlying the organization's central policies. In both of these instances there is little room for arriving at solutions that would be acceptable both to the enclave and the top leadership. Third, separation is more likely when the organization feels it is sufficiently strong that it can afford to lose its protesting members, and face them as a part of its environment. (A small liberal arts college let the dissident members of its faculty go, to form a new type of college, at a time when Ph.Ds were beginning to be a glut on the market. The rift in the Sierra Club became complete as its membership was expanding rapidly.) Fourth, separation is more likely when an individual can easily obtain and shed member status in the organization. Fifth, separation rather than absorption is more likely to occur when the organization does not have a monopoly or partial monopoly on means and rewards. These last two conditions tend to be interrelated, and when they obtain, the enclave is more likely to believe that it can survive on its own.

Absorption and the Content of Protest

In view of the varieties of protest that institutions have sustained in recent years, the phrase of "protest absorption," which refers to the process by which a nonconforming enclave is checked through conversion into a new legitimate subunit, may be unfortunate. Even though the phrase is broader than the process it denotes, it shall be retained.

At least two types of protest within organizations have been evident in recent years, where protest absorption would not be feasible. The first type occurs when the protestors are advocating something for another party rather than for themselves. A case in point would be student objection to university actions such as research contracts with the Department of Defense. A university might create a new college that would have no defense contracts, for protesting students to attend. But since these students are not likely to be involved in activities relating to such contracts in the first place, it is unclear how a new subcampus would dampen their protest.

The second type occurs when the protestors are advocating a change in the organization's central policies. Pertinent examples are the pressures within the Catholic Church to change its position on the rule of clerical celibacy and on the use of contraceptives. Logically, protests on both matters could be handled through the creation of new subunits. For the former there could be a cenobitic order whose members would be permitted to marry. For the latter, subparishes could be established whose members would be permitted to use contraceptives. But the creation of such subunits would mean institutionalizing actions that contravene central beliefs (see figure 3 in the main text of the article).

All this suggests that the incidence of protest absorption within organizations broadly bears some kind of curvilinear relationship to societal change in general. When a society is extremely stable some of the conditions that produce a nonconforming enclave are probably absent, so the incidence of protest absorption would be very low. When a society has been accumulating extensive changes, noncomforming enclaves within organizations abound, but their protests are not always amenable to absorption through the creation of new subunits. Consequently, the incidence of protest absorption would be much smaller than the incidence of nonconforming enclaves. Between these extremes of stability and change, when conditions are present to produce nonconforming enclaves but the types of change that generate extreme pressures on an organization's central policies are absent, one might anticipate a much higher incidence of protest absorption.

Bargaining and Public Choice
William C. Mitchell

Why Is Bargaining Necessary?

Although bargaining is approved of in the private and business life of Americans, many entertain a deep and abiding distrust of bargaining as a means of settling public disputes and reaching political agreements. Certainly a part of our ambivalence toward politicians is based on this view of bargaining since the politician is the chief bargainer. While bargaining has its defects we must recognize that it is a fact of life and cannot be readily eliminated. Bargaining is practiced because men (1) have different policy preferences; (2) are sufficiently powerful not to be ignored; and (3) regard some solution to differences as better than none. Bargaining could only be eliminated if all men agreed on every course of action: then there would be no need for it. But since differences do exist each must be prepared to give and take. In fact, for one to take requires that another give. If we cherish the individual's right to pursue his choices in the polity, bargaining cannot be avoided. In addition, each group's control of resources enables it to demand that it be permitted to bargain. Only those groups whose political resources are minimal are excluded from bargaining circles, and these circles have been narrowing of late.

Types of Bargaining

Bargaining is a type of interaction in which two or more persons attempt to attain better positions by offering rewards to others in exchange for their rewards or concessions. To understand how bargaining operates in political choice, we must consider two factors: what types of payoffs (rewards) are sought and how do people set out to acquire them. These

Reprinted by permission of the author and the publisher from William C. Mitchell, *Public Choice in America: An Introduction to American Government* (Chicago: Markham Publishing Company, 1971), pp. 125–31, 135–42.

two factors alone will allow us to make some useful discriminations among types of bargaining situations.

Payoffs are either fixed in quantity or unlimited. When they are fixed, the situation is called "zero-sum" or "constant-sum" because the gains of one bargainer must be achieved at the expense of another. When one man's gains are not at another's expense the situation is termed "positive" or "non-zero-sum." There are examples of each in political life, but perhaps the most prevalent and difficult to analyze combine the two properties—situations in which some payoffs are fixed or zero-sum and others are positive.

The other factor—how bargains are arrived at—is not only fascinating but crucial to an understanding of the payoffs and the generation of difficulties for the participants. Bargaining can be *implicit* or *explicit*. In the latter methods, bargainers make explicit trades; that is, they knowingly discuss exact terms and make concrete offers without embarrassment. Lawyers do this in labor negotiations.

Senator Kerr of Oklahoma, a rich and powerful oil man turned U.S. senator, is reputed to have bargained explicitly on most matters. According to a lobbyist who knew him well and dealt with him face to face in negotiating terms for a government contract for North American Aviation, Senator Kerr said, "If you get it (the contract), what can North American do for Oklahoma?"[1] Mr. Black, the lobbyist for North American, replied that he would put plants in Oklahoma to build parts for Apollo or to provide other types of work and relieve unemployment. Senator Kerr may have been more explicit and more selfish than other senators for he once said "I represent myself first, the State of Oklahoma second, and the people of the United States third, and don't you forget it."[2]

In implicit bargaining, agreements are arrived at without direct reference to the issues or the terms. Instead, somewhat ambiguous cues are issued by each bargainer in the hope that other bargainers will understand and respond in such a manner that agreement can be reached. Politicians, especially in international politics, must negotiate in this slow, costly, and burdensome way. Lovers frequently do the same. Terms that are seemingly clear to one of the bargainers may not be for the other, and discrepancy causes much misunderstanding and belated efforts at clarification and apology.

But there is an even worse case than implicit bargaining—

1. Hugo Young, Bryan Silcock, and Peter Dunn, "Why We Went to the Moon," *Washington Monthly* 2 (April 1970): 45.
2. Ibid., p. 43.

that of *conjectural* bargaining, in which neither partner is even clear about the terms of settlement. Perhaps this type best characterizes relationships between voters and their representatives. Voters may have only a very general notion of a presidential candidate's policy commitments. They do not know how he will treat specific issues as they arise. Further, the candidate does not know his supporters' preferences; neither the candidates nor the voters sign contracts stating their expectations.

All these considerations involving processes and payoffs of bargaining are set forth in diagrammatic form in figure 1. Readers are encouraged to offer illustrations of some bargaining situations for each of the nine cells. Compare the following: a presidential nominating convention; a vote on a bill establishing a new tax; an appropriation for a new public building; negotiation with the North Vietnamese over ending

Nature of payoffs

	Fixed	Positive sum	Mixed
Explicit			
Implicit			
Conjectural			

Means of bargaining

Fig. 1. Types of Bargaining Situations

the Vietnam war; President Nixon's decision to invade Cambodia; racial desegregation in a local school system; dress regulations in a local high school. Are these bargaining issues easily typed? When and how can a single issue be converted into another type of bargaining situation? Why should different voters and politicians want to treat the same events in different ways; for example, why might one politician wish racial integration to be accorded a zero-sum status while another would like it to be converted into a positive situation?

Explicit Bargains: Some Illustrations

Explicit bargaining is less prevalent in politics than in the economic system but it is not unknown. Professional politicians have left some rather clear records of bargaining outcomes if not always of the actual bargaining sessions. Our Constitution is a first-rate example of a fundamental set of rules that were bargained over by highly rational men. Many of its major provisions are the compromises of the founding fathers making mutually beneficial exchanges. The Bill of Rights, for example, was appended to the Constitution in exchange for support on its passage.

The federal structure of our government was itself a product of negotiation and compromise. The bicameral nature of our legislative bodies was another bargained agreements. Two of the most famous bargains in American history—the Missouri Compromise of 1820 and the Compromise of 1877—are now remembered chiefly because they were achieved at the expense of a third party, the Negro.

In the former, the issue of slavery was temporarily "resolved" by an agreement between the North and the South that permitted slavery south of the line 36°30′ across the Louisiana Territory but not north of that line. The compromise was intended to maintain equal power between northern and southern states and thus give each a veto power over the other. This bargain governed regional relationships until 1850, when new territories gained after the Mexican War posed a problem for which the old compromise did not have an answer. As the Missouri Compromise became outmoded, the possibilities for conflict increased and tensions culminated in the Civil War.

The Compromise of 1877 ended reconstruction and its hard-line policies. Whites in the South were allowed to reestablish white supremacy in exchange for their support of the reestablished Union and the Republican party. Whites gained control of any possible claims of labor, western agrarians, and reformers who might have posed a threat to the capitalists and the Republican party. The Republican party and Southern Democrats have managed to maintain a fairly effective coalition on the basis of that bargain to this day.

The Etiquette of Bargaining

Bargainers chiefly aim to advance their own interests, but if they do not use means that others feel are legitimate and appropriate, the outcome itself will be viewed as illegitimate. This is especially true in state legislatures and the Congress. Etiquette or norms of fair play are honored among politicians far more often than they are ignored or violated. Honoring rules is itself a resource in bargaining; the bargainer who acquires a reputation for being fair and upholding rules even when they may reduce his payoffs is viewed as highly honorable and dependable.

What are these rules? First, they are informal. The rules are rarely written down and certainly are not enacted into laws; rather they are the gradual accumulation of customary ways of bargaining. Politicians learn them as one learns the rules of etiquette in private life. Since they are informal they may be misunderstood; amateurs, especially, will be prone to inadvertent violations. Some of the more general rules among politicians include:

1. A politician does not threaten the use of violence.
2. A politician keeps his word.
3. A politician shows a willingness to compromise.
4. A politician shares in the workload.
5. A politician respects his elders.
6. A politician honors his office.

More specialized etiquette develops around each type of office and particularly around legislatures. Because legislators engage in collective choice they must have means of regulating and minimizing public acrimony and personal hostilities that are likely to arise on a continuing basis. Most legislators are fully aware of the norms of good political behavior. In addition to the above, which seem to apply to all politicians, the following norms have great significance among legislators:

1. Respect the rights of other members.
2. Remain impersonal in debate.
3. Retain self-restraint in debate.
4. Observe common courtesies.
5. Keep aims open and explicit.
6. Give advance notice of a changed stand.
7. Never campaign against a colleague in his district.
8. Be graceful in defeat.
9. Serve one's apprenticeship.

These legislative norms were found by scholars in at least four state legislatures along with about thirty other norms of good behavior.[3] Not all are equally important nor as important in one legislature as another.

Still more specialized obligations can arise around the committees of Congress, for example. Richard Fenno has

---

3. John C. Wahlke, Heinz Eulau, William Buchanan, and LeRoy C. Ferguson, *The Legislative System* (New York: John Wiley & Sons, Inc., 1962), chap. 7.

written about some norms observed by members of the House Appropriations Committee.[4] According to Fenno some four obligations are viewed as paramount by the membership:

1. Protect the "Power of the Purse" (Congressional control over appropriations).
2. Guard the federal Treasury.
3. Reduce budget estimates.
4. Serve member constituency interests.

Committeemen who violate these norms have their bargaining power reduced commensurate to the extent to which they violate expectations. A beginner may be permitted a few lapses as he learns; one is forgiven lapses when he is put into an especially difficult position of survival as a politician; but in all other cases one is expected to conform. This pattern should not be too surprising; almost all people comply in organizations they belong to. Conformity is one of the costs we pay for civilization.

Four Phases of Bargaining

Once an issue arises, politicians and other leaders begin the long and tiring process of trying to achieve a mutually acceptable agreement or settlement. That settlement may only be a phase or episode in a longer and wider range of bargaining over many issues. Within its own confines, however, we can detect a variety of quite different activities taking place through time. This bargaining process has four distinct phases: discovering the bargainable, finding areas of agreement, critical bargaining, and presenting results to the public.

Discovering the Bargainable

In the first phase the parties discover the bargainable issues. At the outset, neither party really knows what the other wants or is fully prepared to trade or exchange. Much of this stage is public ritual, but another, more private, aspect is establishment of actual bargainable objects and definition of the range of disagreement and possible avenues of agreement. Bargainers express hopes for successful negotiations but also issue dramatic claims and counterclaims. A tough stance is an integral element of the ritual.

4. Richard Fenno, *The Power of the Purse* (Boston: Little, Brown & Co., 1966), pp. 95–112.

Finding Areas of Agreement

This second phase comes into being when politicians get down to the "nitty gritty" and hard bargaining begins. These bargaining probes are made easier whenever the objects of bargaining are quantifiable and do not involve basic moral or ethical commitments. It is easier to arrange acceptable compromises when men contend over the number of miles of highways to be built, the rate of an income tax, or the number of persons to be included under social security than it is to set conditions for interracial relationships or loyalty to the nation. Bargainers will attempt a great variety of tactics to ferret out hard and soft positions on both symbolic and material payoffs. They may test sincerity by threatening to walk out or make secret proposals. (President-Elect Nixon used this tactic with the North Vietnamese in 1968.) A bargainer may send somewhat concealed messages to the other side through third parties. A bargainer may even leave a conference in order to test the other side. Depending on the situation, use of these probing tactics may make conditions worse, but since that isn't known at the outset, they are always tried. That is the nature of bargaining, and only experience can teach men these skills.

Critical Bargaining

When this third phase begins, bargaining can break down or proceed to a successful conclusion. In the critical phase, actual proposals and counterproposals are offered. By judging reactions, each side learns whether the other (s) will continue to offer concessions. Each side must be careful to offer enough, but not too much. Mutual concessions must be made. Once a concession is offered it can rarely be retracted; each negotiator must live with his proposals. This is the critical period because actual concessions are offered and considered. If an agreement is reached a fourth phase begins in which a wider public is informed.

Public Presentation of Results

Not all political bargaining situations entail public presentation of the results, but in a nation that values publicity, many do. Woodrow Wilson expressed the nation's feelings when he said he favored "open covenants openly arrived at." While some bargaining is done publicly, usually only the final agreements are made public. Congressional committees frequently meet in "executive session," at which only the members may be present along with whomever they invite—usually an Administration witness. The news media are barred.

When results are final the followings of the bargainers must be convinced that a good bargain was struck—a difficult task since the inevitable compromises and concessions may disappoint the followings on one or both sides.

The bargainer must satisfy his more vehement and vocal supporters that he did well in the bargaining. Our foreign emissaries, especially, are expected to get the best of all bargains. President Eisenhower had to convince the Rightists of his party that he did not lose or sell out in ending the Korean conflict. President Nixon had, has, or will have the same dilemma in ending the Vietnam war. Local politicians, to a lesser extent, must also show how much they benefited the local community. Public presentation of results is an important phase because it may contain the seeds for future breakdown or success of the bargain.

Strategic Considerations in Bargaining

In a previous section we stressed the cooperative aspect of bargaining by describing the etiquette of participation. While bargaining is cooperative in the sense that an agreement is sought, we cannot ignore the equally strong desire on the part of each bargainer to get as large a share of the payoff as possible. This is the competitive element, the strategic nexus. Emphasis is on how to gain larger shares. In this section a variety of actual bargaining situations in recent history are described. The first two cases concern two presidents; a third deals with Supreme Court justices; a fourth with the strategies of budget officers in Illinois. In addition, examples show national and international compromises. The illustrations may seem offensive because they smack of self-interest and are not in accord with civics book ideals for our leaders.

A President Bargains

Because our presidents are not dictators, they too must bargain with other politicians in order to accomplish their programs and honor pledges made during campaigns. President Nixon found himself in a somewhat weak bargaining position when he first came into office in 1968 without a majority vote and confronted by a Democratic Congress. He played his role with considerable care and caution until he had a stronger base among the American people. He bargained with skill, as this example indicates.[5]

In 1970 Senator Jackson (Washington Democrat and "hawk" on defense), preparing for reelection, found himself opposed by the peace wing of the Democratic party. Because Jackson feared a major primary election challenge he felt he had to blunt the attack as much as possible. So he requested President Nixon to hold back the expansion of the ABM system as much as possible and especially to delay the construction of an ABM site in his own state.

This request was unusual since Jackson was a strong supporter of military demands and of Nixon's defense policies. Jackson was attempting to develop a middle-of-the-road position to cut the ground out from under his peace opponents. Nixon readily agreed to accommodate Jackson's request, although defense measures would be temporarily set back. He agreed to delay construction activities on the ABM because he feared that if Jackson were defeated it would be a major defeat for a powerful Democratic supporter on defense. It might also, he feared, he interpreted as a weakness of the Administration and would encourage other peace candidates. Jackson was able to unify and stimulate his supporters to greater efforts by employing the threat of opposition.

A President Sometimes Miscalculates

In our previous case the success of the calculation of strategic advantage was not known at the time of writing. In the present case, the outcomes are history. This case involves a series of presidential miscalculations rather than astute maneuvering. Although the president eventually achieved his goal, it took far more time, and required far more bargaining costs than it would have had he made better calculations. Even worse, the year-long delay in achieving his ends led to bad economic consequences for the American people. Because many discussions of political bargaining leave an impression of continuously clever strategic reasoning and invariable success, it is essential that the possibilities of failure, costliness, and miscalculation be emphasized.

President Johnson, in 1968, pressed for a "surtax"; that is, a 10 percent tax on regular income tax liabilities.[6] He

5. The case is based on A. Robert Smith, "Jackson Modifies ABM Stand to Mollify Fellow Democrats," *Oregonian*, 4 March 1970, p. 24.

6. This case is based on an account provided in "Lobbying by Business Leaders Key to Passage," *Congressional Quarterly Almanac* 24 (Washington, D.C.: Congressional Quarterly Service, 1968): 275.

defended his tax proposal with a series of complicated economic arguments intended to show how it could halt inflation. The public could not understand the complicated economic theory of inflation. To compound his error he simultaneously campaigned for additional "Great Society" measures that would entail much greater federal expenditures. For ten months the president resisted efforts to cut his federal spending proposals or to strategically tie them to his surtax.

Some commentators have argued that he should have termed the tax a "war tax" and defended it as providing necessary revenue to conduct the Vietnam war. Congressman Wilbur Mills, chairman of the Ways and Means Committee, who held up the surtax measure for almost a year, hinted at a press conference that if Johnson would label the bill a "war tax" it could go through Congress easily.

Still another miscalculation of the president was labeling the bill a "ten percent surtax" instead of a one percent tax on income. Although the dollar amounts would be the same for each taxpayer, the ten percent figure sounded ten times as bad as the one percent figure. Once this mistake was made there was no way of rectifying it.

President Johnson was finally able to get his bill through Congress by promising a $6 billion reduction in expenditures. This promise required him to mobilize a vast lobbying effort on the part of big business. At the same time Johnson lost substantial political gains. Not only did he have to give up $6 billion of his Great Society programs but the antiinflationary effect of the surtax had been substantially vitiated because of the delay. Why President Johnson made these miscalculations may never be entirely clear, but the case does suggest that even astute and experienced politicians make stupendous errors.

Bargaining among Supreme Court Justices

Some readers may be shocked to learn that Supreme Court justices bargain with one another over some of the most important public policies. How they bargain is something of a mystery because their sessions are private, but their public papers often reveal important insights. In any case, bargaining among such a small, exclusive, high-status, highly trained, and intelligent group of men over highly contentious issues must provide some fascinating material for study. Walter Murphy, a distinguished student of the Supreme

Court, has made our task considerably easier with his book on judicial strategy.[7] We make liberal use of it.

Justices behave in a rarefied and demanding legal and political universe; their traditions are long and powerful, public opinion is ever present, and their work is endlessly scrutinized by legal demons—the lawyers. To add pressure, the problems they deal with are often highly emotional and important to the litigants and others affected by their decisions. Supreme Court justices apparently do not bargain in the more exposed and sometimes crass manner of elected officials and bureaucrats. Most of their bargaining takes place not only in private quarters, but through the indirect means of writing legal opinions, briefs, memos, and the like. Since longevity on the court can be considerable, a justice is likely to get to know his colleagues very well. This familiarity has advantages but also poses some severe constraints on negotiation.

Apparently the justices do not bargain explicitly, in the sense of congressional logrolling over their votes and positions, but they do attempt to influence the choice of cases to be considered, the language to be employed in decisions, allocation of workloads, and decisions. Leadership is vital in all these matters because nine men cannot resolve disputes in an anarchic manner. In some instances some of the justices actually have intense personal dislikes for certain colleagues, and these must be moderated. Normally the chief justice plays a powerful leadership role in the activities of the court; he tends to be the chief bargainer in arranging the ultimate outcomes of the most significant cases.

Unlike the Supreme Court, most bargaining in the criminal and civil courts is a highly explicit and very pervasive activity. Lawyers, judges, prosecutors, and litigants engage in a great deal of pretrial negotiation over the charges to be levied, timing of the trial if there is to be one, members of the jury, and actual terms of the settlement whether in or out of court. Of course, an accused person may bargain to turn state's witness in exchange for a shorter sentence; such agreements are commonplace. In most civil cases the objective is to settle the suit out of court. In divorce cases, for example, estranged husbands and wives bargain through their lawyers over the disposition of property, children, visiting rights, and alimony payments.

7. *Elements of Judicial Strategy* (Chicago: University of Chicago Press, 1964).

Strategies in a State Budgetary Process

In a unique and illuminating study of public expenditure in the state of Illinois, Thomas J. Anton detected and elaborated upon a set of "rules" or strategies wise budget officers follow in dealing with the state legislature.[8] We cannot know how legislators would respond to public knowledge of these rules, but experienced politicians presumably are fully aware of them and play complementary roles. These are the rules Anton has identified for the strategy-minded budget official:

1. Spend the entire appropriation and, if possible, a little bit more.

2. Avoid any sudden increase or decrease in expenditure.

3. Avoid requests for sums smaller than the current appropriations.

4. Put as much as possible of a new request into the basic budget.

5. When increases are desired, make them appear as small as possible, and show that they grow out of existing operations.

6. Give the Budgetary Commission something to cut.

These rules suggest that the budget officer has a good understanding of voter demands on the legislators. Accordingly, budget men attempt to protect their own budgets by enabling legislators (the Budgetary Commission) to achieve some of their ends. In addition, careful rationalizations of proposed expenditures serve to convince not only the politician, but also his supporters, of the need for the expenditures.

8. *The Politics of State Expenditure in Illinois* (Urbana: University of Illinois Press, 1966). The strategy presented above is on pp. 49–53.

Budgeting and Intergroup Conflict in Organizations
Louis R. Pondy

This paper was stimulated by field studies made by the author of capital budgeting practices in large manufacturing corporations. Capital budgeting is the process by which funds for plant and equipment are allocated to the various investment projects proposed by operating divisions or by functional departments (e.g., marketing, engineering). Budgeting is necessary because demands for capital funds invariably outrun the resources available. The budget provides a way of choosing among these competing claims for resources.

The engineering economics literature and the accounting literature usually treat the budgeting and resource allocation problem solely as a problem in economics, e.g., to choose those projects which will maximize the present value of invested capital. To understand and explain the practices observed during the field studies, however, it became necessary to use additional concepts from the behavioral sciences. In brief, it proved helpful to interpret capital budgeting for resource allocation as a process of resolving intergroup conflict.

The Organization as a Conflict System

The classical bureaucratic way of describing an organization is as a hierarchy with each person responsible to the person directly above him in the authority structure. Through the pyramiding of this authority structure, each participant in the organization has eventual responsibility and loyalty to the organization's prime goal (presumably profit in the case of a business organization).

Development of Subgroup Loyalties

But each participant is a member not only of "the corpora-

Reprinted by permission from the *Pittsburgh Business Review*, April 1964.

tion," but also of the Marketing Department or of Division X, as well as of various professional organizations. In fact, because the Marketing Department is smaller and more congenial than "the corporation," there is a good chance that he has a closer identification with its immediate goals than with the long range goals of "the corporation."[1] This insight into the multiple membership and subgroup identifications of each organizational participant suggests the following alternative to the classical description: The organization is a collection of interest groups who have goals which may be only partially consistent with those of other interest groups and with the superordinate goal of the organization.[2]

Subgroup loyalties develop not only because of a common professional background of the subgroup members, not only because of a selective exposure of the business environment, not only because in-group communication supports and reinforces subgroup goals, but also because each subgroup engages in competition with every other subgroup for an adequate share of the available resources.[3]

Effect of Subgroup Loyalties

The existence of subgroup loyalties has an important effect on the budgeting process. Characteristically each functional department either originates or participates actively in the organization and development of investment projects. It is natural that the production department will be most energetic in the development of projects which improve production facilities, the marketing department in projects which improve product quality or customer service, and so on. Thus each functional department has a vested interest in each of its projects considered for the budget, and will find it very hard

1. There are both motivational and cognitive processes producing subgroup identification. Examples of motivational factors are conformity of group goals and the self-image and affective ties with other group members. Examples of cognitive factors are the selective exposure to environmental cues (marketing personnel talk most to customers and therefore are most sensitive to marketing and commercial goals), reinforcement of group attitudes by ingroup communication, and uniform professional training and its effects on perception. See J. G. March and H. A. Simon, *Organizations* (New York: Wiley, 1958), pp. 93–106, 150–54.

2. See. J. G. March, "The Business Firm as a Political Coalition," *Journal of Politics,* December 1962.

3. See Muzafer Sherif et al., *Intergroup Cooperation and Conflict: The Robbers Cave Experiment* (Norman, Okla.: Institute of Intergroup Relations, University of Oklahoma, 1961) for a description of the effect of intergroup competition on in-group loyalties in a boys' summer camp.

to be objective in judging the entire set of projects or in genuinely accepting the budgeting decisions of an impartial budget committee.[4]

Not only do subgroup loyalties distort the perceptions of the investment projects, but they lead subgroups to adopt "political strategies" for more nearly assuring approval of its projects. What strategies are adopted depend on the particular loopholes available in the budgeting system of the parent company.[5] For example, in companies which have long-range facilities plans, it is advantageous for an operating division or functional department to place a project in the long-range plan on a presumably tentative basis, only to have it gradually assume a more certain status. Or, if the budget committee requests the division to *rank* all of its proposed projects, the division will rank last those projects the budget committee is known to favor and is likely to approve regardless of the ranking, and rank first those projects the division favors most but which have the least chance of approval otherwise. Or again, if the budget committee sets up a minimum acceptable rate of return, the division is likely to "doctor" the economic analysis of marginal projects so that the target rate is met. In one case the division accounting department had been blocking a project for several years because the division manager could not prove rigorously that anticipated savings from a renovation would be assured. Eventually the division manager overrode the accounting department and made a rough guess of the savings so that the target rate of return would be exceeded by about three percentage points. The assistant to the division manager was quite candid in reporting the handling of this project.

The Budget Committee and Conflict Resolution

In order to mediate this intense intergroup competition for funds most companies have set up budget committees, composed of functional representatives, to review the proposals

4. See Jane S. Morton and Robert R. Blake, "The Influence of Competitively Vested Interests on Judgment," *Journal of Conflict Resolution* 6, no. 2 (June 1962): 149–53, for experimental documentation of the effects of subgroup loyalties on perception and satisfaction in a judgment situation.

5. Aaron Wildavsky has studied the use of subgroup strategies in the formation of the federal budget. In particular these include the cultivation of the "confidence" of the Budget Bureau and congressional committees, where confidence refers to affective ties and mutual rapport between the agency and the official group (private communication). See also his "Political Implications of Budgetary Reform," *Public Administration Review* 21, no. 4 (Autumn 1961): 183–90.

made by the operating divisions or by the central staff. Representatives of the operating divisions are not usually members of the committee. That there is considerable conflict among the committee members is almost certain. To demonstrate the divergence of judgments and evaluations of projects in a large primary metal processing firm, the author asked two comparable members of the marketing and engineering-planning departments to make independent rankings from project summaries of nine projects from the company's previous budget. Though each man was familiar with all nine projects, the degree of agreement between their rankings was not statistically significant. These differences of course provide the basis for interfunctional conflict on the budget committee. Though no direct evidence is available on how these conflicts of project preference are settled, it is likely that bargaining and compromise take precedence over analytical efforts. This is true partially because group loyalties affect evaluation criteria as well as specific project preferences.

Project Classifications as Bargaining Residues

The loyalties to evaluation criteria are reflected in the project classification system. Characteristically the accounting and finance representatives on the budget committee insist that all projects satisfy economic criteria, such as rate of return or payback. The legal representative of course will insist that compliance with government regulations (e.g., regarding smoke control or stream pollution) obviously is consistent with the firm's financial well-being and needs no economic justification. Similarly the marketing representative will insist that market share is really a more appropriate measure of the worth of a project than is rate of return. The production representative will push for operating efficiency criteria to supplement the financial criteria, all the time arguing of course that his criteria, while superficially different, are really related to the financial criteria and, in fact, are more operational.[6] To avoid resurrecting the criterion conflict anew each time, the committee legitimizes the use of different criteria by defining different investment categories. A typical classification system comprises cost reduction, replacement, com-

6. March and Simon (*Organizations*, pp. 156–57) assert that bargaining behavior will take precedence over analytic behavior in the absence of shared, operational goals. My own observations suggest that long-run profit maximization is *not* an operational goal when it comes to ranking complex capital investment projects.

mercial, legal, and employee welfare categories. I choose to interpret these investment categories as "residues" from past conflict and bargaining among the functional departments over the issue of appropriate investment criteria.

Once formed, these investment categories provide an institutional framework for resolving the interfunctional conflict since each category requires a different set of criteria, so that the criterion conflict is repressed.[7] The project preference conflict is alleviated as follows: A rough, and more or less unintentional, balance is maintained among the various categories. There is no conscious attempt to allocate X percent of the budget to cost reduction projects, for example, but it does appear that, by unwritten rule, the share of the budget spent on cost reduction projects may legitimately range *only* between certain percentages of the total budget or between certain dollar amounts.

Other Devices for Conflict Resolution

Two other miscellaneous devices for resolving conflict may be more accurately described as defense mechanisms for the budget committee. A complete ranking of the projects is not attempted, so that some unresolved conflict remains latent. A practice adopted by one company is to break the budget up into four priority increments to be authorized for expenditures in increments (if at all) by the board of directors.

The use of long-range plans is in some sense a defense mechanism. Suppose that only $10 million can be spent in each of the next three years, and each of these divisions has a prime project which will require the entire $10 million. Engineering economics or financial analysis may indicate which of the three projects to approve, but will provide no answer on how to handle the disappointment of the other two divisions. It is small consolation to the "losers" to know that they came out a close second. On the other hand, if the division knows that its project has been placed in a long-range plan for the next year hence, its feelings will at least be partially mollified, and the budget committee will experience less pressure from the divisional management.

Conclusion

We have argued that two factors are sufficient for intergroup

---

7. One of the other strategies commonly employed by subgroups is to classify, with appropriate justifications, a marginal project in a category which is currently favored by the central staff of the firm. Once a project is placed in a certain category, it tends to be compared only with the other projects in that category.

conflict to exist: subgroup loyalties and intergroup competition. Both these factors were shown to be present in the budgeting-resource allocation process in the modern, large corporation. Budgeting can therefore be viewed as a process of resolving intergroup conflicts. This finding has crucial implications for the design of budgeting systems. Not only must the system provide procedures for the rational, economic analysis of budget proposals, but it must also provide procedures for the resolution of intergroup conflict over scarce resources that will inevitably arise.

4

People in Complex Systems: Formal Organizations

11

Environment and Organization

Introduction

In part 4 we move again to a higher level of complexity, this time from groups to large formal organizations. Our strategy in these four chapters will be to work from the outside in. The papers in chapter 11 were selected to describe the variety of organizational environments, and the different strategies that organizations use to deal with different types of environment. The papers in the next chapter examine organization structure, how structure evolves to mesh with environment, and how structure influences the creativity of organizations. Then chapter 13 looks at decision making in organizations and at the impact of computer technology on organizational decision making—that is, at both the software and hardware of information technology. Finally, in chapter 14, we come full circle back to the role of human values in organization and the relationship between the organization and the individual, a topic that we raised back in the very first chapter of the book.

But to get on with the issues of this particular chapter: In the last five or six years, no problem in organization theory has attracted more attention than the relation between an organization and its environment. By "environment" we mean all those factors that are relevant to the organization, yet outside of its immediate control. Thus customers, suppliers, government, developments in science and technology, and broad and sweeping social and cultural changes are all environmental factors. One reason for the great increase in concern about all these is that the environment seems to be moving and changing faster than it used to. Hence the old search for "one best organization" has given way to a more contingent view in which the right organization is seen as dependent on the state of environment.

Thus bureaucracies, with fixed, well-defined jobs and rigid rules, may function very efficiently in stable, predictable environments, but may tend to be unresponsive and unadaptive in environments which change both rapidly and often unpredictably. On the other hand, more loosely structured organizations may be adaptive to environmental volatility, but function quite inefficiently in a stable, predictable environment. For an organization to prosper it must match the texture—often the changing texture—of its social, political, economic, and technological environments. The Lawrence and Lorsch paper, the first in this chapter, presents several cogent examples of *mismatches* between specific organizations and their respective environments. This selection is only a small part of a larger, more systematic study by Lawrence and Lorsch of environmental influences on organization.

The second paper, by Emery and Trist, classifies organizational environments into four types, ranging from the "placid, randomized environment" through what they call "turbulent fields." Increased uncertainty in the environment—that is, movement toward turbulence—Emery and Trist argue, pushes the organization to elaborate its standard operating procedures into more contingent tactics and longer-run strategies, and to decentralize some control so that local environmental variations can be sensed and handled more rapidly and more selectively.

But, decentralizing control *inside* the organization in order to cope with uncertainty on the *outside* may generate new uncertainty *within* the organization. Thus, top management may be faced with the unenviable choice of *centralizing* to maintain internal control (thereby losing some control of the external environment) or *decentralizing* for greater control over the environment (thereby risking loss of control over its own membership).

An organization can cope with extremely turbulent environments in either of two ways: it can try to become so big that it can dominate its environment; or it can break up into smaller, less permanent organizations designed to deal flexibly with local and temporary problems. We shall return to this latter alternative in chapter 14 when we discuss the paper by Warren Bennis.

The third and last paper in this chapter, March's "The Technology of Foolishness," reaches a somewhat startling conclusion about the relationship between an organization and its environment. For long-run survival, he argues, an organization (or a person, group, or any social system) cannot be completely rational. Survival in uncertain environments requires the organization to be able to act nonrationally, playfully, even foolishly—some of the time. This conclusion has some of its roots in a mathematical theorem of enormous importance proved by the German mathematician Kurt Goedel in 1931. Goedel's theorem says that no system of logic which is consistent can also be complete. No consistent system of logic can be used to derive all true propositions; there must be what cyberneticians (e.g., Stafford Beer) have called "completion from without."

What all this may mean for organizational behavior runs something like this: Any rational organization is a consistent system of logic. Goedel's theorem says that there must be at least some environmental contingencies for which the organization has no response. The organization may therefore on occasion need to suspend rationality and to engage in what March has called "playfulness." March argues that play is "an instrument of intelligence," not merely idle or misdirected behavior.

We spoke in earlier chapters of differences in cognitive styles and of the impact—often unconscious—that cultural values have on our behavior. One of the strongest of these cultural values is the bias toward a rational style of cognition, with a corresponding bias against thinking that is not orderly or clearly directed toward some well-defined goal. While rationality may be an achievable and desirable mode of behavior in stable, well-defined environments, this line of argument suggests that in unstable environments strict adherence to a norm of rationality may actually be detrimental to the organization.

Organization-Environment Interface
Paul R. Lawrence and
Jay W. Lorsch

It is no mystery that organizations must carry on transactions with their environment simply to survive, and, even more importantly, to grow. In the first chapter, we identified the quality of these transactions as posing one of the fundamental developmental problems of any organization. Other analysts of organizational affairs have consistently mentioned transactions with the environment as a crucial if not the most crucial issue. It is an issue that has been dealt with extensively by economists and by specialists in business policy and strategy. They have dealt primarily with the content of these relationships—the actual kind and amount of goods, services, and funds that are part of these transactions. But the issue has not been extensively studied by specialists in the application of behavioral sciences, and attention has not been focused on such human aspects affecting the quality of these transactions as: What is the quality of the information exchanged across the organizational boundaries? What are the major determinants of the quality? What are its consequences?[1] Such questions have been asked many times of the relations between individuals and groups within the organization, but the boundary-spanning relations have simply not been subjected to comparable scrutiny. It is not surprising therefore, that systematic efforts to diagnose and improve the quality of these organization-environment relations have also lagged behind the effort applied to improving internal relations.

Problems at the environment-organization interface are likely to manifest themselves eventually through economic results. For example, at the sales-customer interface, it is in a

Abridged with permission from chapter 3 of Paul R. Lawrence and Jay W. Lorsch, *Developing Organizations: Diagnosis and Action* (Reading, Mass.: Addison-Wesley, 1969).

1. One notable exception has been the work on boundary transactions reported in Kahn et al., *Organizational Stress* (New York: John Wiley and Sons, 1964).

loss of sales volume; in research and development, it is in a drop in the flow of new products, and so on. However, these indicators of interface trouble are fairly slow to show up, and managers learn to be sensitive to earlier clues of difficulty. These often take the form of complaints from the outside— letters from customers, a private word dropped at lunch by a banker, an important move by a competitor that caught everyone flatfooted. The customer may be saying that your organization is unresponsive, that you cannot seem to tailor your products to his needs, that he is getting tired of fighting his way through your red tape. In other cases, the concern will develop because a competitor seems too frequently to be first with a new-product introduction, or a new marketing technique. Perhaps in the production area it is a failure to realize economies through process innovation or falling behind in the race with rising wages and salaries. Another clue might be that the best specialists are not staying in the company— there is a worrisome amount of turnover among the more promising professionals in the physical or managerial sciences. These are the clues that might well be traced back to human problems at the environment-organization interface.

Examples of Organization-Environment Mismatches

Our first case of an organizational development problem at this interface was initially identified by worrisome symptoms of an economic nature. During our research activity in an organization developing, marketing, and manufacturing plastics products, we heard numerous complaints that the basic research laboratory was not turning out new process and product ideas. An analysis of the data we had collected on organizational practices in this laboratory revealed that the laboratory had a highly peaked management hierarchy, with most of the decisions being made exclusively by higher management. This was clearly inconsistent with the uncertainty and complexity of the information with which these scientists were expected to deal. The scientists complained that they did not have enough autonomy to follow research leads which seemed highly important to them. As one lower-level research administrator put it:

> When one project gets killed, we get another one. This is a sore point with me because we aren't given a chance to look around ourselves for new projects. We are given a project and told to work on it. My objection is that we don't give the group leader and the bench chemist the

time to investigate different problems before they are
being thrust into a [management-defined] program.

This high degree of formalized decision making made it
difficult for these scientists to carry on meaningful transactions with the dynamic environment confronting them. It was
difficult for them to freely respond to new information from
the scientific environment. In addition, they had neither the
authority to make decisions about research activities nor
direct access to persons with market information, which
could have enabled them to make effective decisions. In addition to constraining and confusing the flow of environmental information into this unit, this inappropriate structure
undoubtedly also affected the motivation of these scientists.

The remedy for this sort of problem is not hard to see.
Find ways of getting lower-level scientists and managers
more involved in decision making, and in general loosen up
the structure. While we were involved only as researchers,
and thus were not expected to propose such actions, it is interesting to note that individual laboratory members were already finding ways out of these constraints. As one research
manager put it:

> The individual chemist can initiate a program to a
> greater degree than the research manager would like to
> believe. It isn't always possible to get the control [the
> managers want] because what's going on in a certain
> project is always linked somewhat to the influence of the
> man who is working on it.

This kind of sub rosa response probably improves matters to
some extent, but it is suboptimal as compared with forthright
mutual decision making between junior and senior people.

A more complicated problem at the organization-environment interface is illustrated by a situation which one of the
authors encountered in his consulting activities. The organization in question was a unit of a major chemical company
which had as its assigned mission the development, manufacture, and marketing of entirely new and unique products
which did not fall within the realm of existing product
divisions. Once this division, which we shall label the New
Products Division (NPD), had demonstrated that a product
was commercially successful, the product was transferred to
an existing division, or a new division was established for it.
The NPD thus dealt with products for only a limited time
and during the most uncertain phase of their existence, when
both markets and technology were ill-defined. In sum, the

parts of the environment confronting this organization were highly uncertain.

The NPD had sales, development, and research units and drew upon various manufacturing facilities within the company, depending upon the nature of the particular product. The division general manager was aware of what he considered to be an unhealthy amount of conflict among all of these functional units, but particularly between sales and development. As a result, he asked that we help him define the nature and causes of these conflicts and then help him develop solutions to these problems. Accordingly, a diagnostic study was undertaken.

The study confirmed that the organization was achieving relatively poor integration between the functional units, and that certain conflict-management practices were not as effective as they might be. But, central to the issues we are considering here, the diagnosis also revealed that the differentiation within the organization was not in tune with its environmental demands. While the research and the development units both had structure and member orientations that were consistent with their task requirements, the sales unit did not. Whereas members of the sales unit needed to have a relatively short-term time orientation and a strong marketing-goal orientation, they actually had a long-term time horizon and were oriented toward a balance of technical and market goals. In fact, along these two dimensions, the sales unit was almost identical to the development unit. What seemed to be happening was that the two units were trying to perform the same task, and, in essence, were competing with each other for control of this task. This competition was one important source of the poor integration and unresolved conflict about which the general manager was concerned.

The reason that the sales unit had drifted into the sphere of the development group was not difficult to explain. At the time of our involvement, the NPD had not yet brought many products to the stage where an active test marketing program was required. As a result, the kind of information with which the managers in the sales unit were accustomed to dealing just did not exist. However, these managers wanted something to do so they began taking a longer-range look at potential markets. As a consequence, they were dealing with information which was the legitimate concern of developmental personnel. This threatened the position of the latter group and hostility developed between the groups, making it difficult for them to cooperate.

With these data and this explanation in hand, we made a feedback presentation to the general manager and his chief subordinates. The data and their implications were accepted without too much difficulty by the general manager, the research manager, and even the development manager. The sales manager, however, showed a great deal of resistance to this interpretation. The chief reason for this was that accepting this interpretation brought into serious question the role of his unit in the organization for the immediate future. He had brought together a group of five experienced sales managers, and had gotten them involved in identifying market opportunities, since there was very little to be done in marketing with the few new products already available. Accepting our interpretation meant either finding a more appropriate activity for these managers, which was not possible without something to sell, or having them reassigned to another division. The latter obviously would involve a loss of face for the sales manager.

Because of this resistance from the sales manager, several sessions of this management group were held with and without the consultant present. Ultimately, even though some limited progress was made in working through this problem, the general manager concluded that the most viable solution, given the bind in which the sales manager was caught, was to have him reassigned to another job of equal status and responsibility. This was accomplished and his replacement reduced the size of the sales unit and limited its activity to dealing with more immediate market issues. As a result, much of the tension between the marketing and development groups was relieved. With each unit having orientations fitting the information requirements of its task, the organization seemed to function more effectively.

As a final brief example of a rather unusual form of mismatching at the environment-organization interface, we cite a particular unit of a large electronics manufacturing firm which was charged with doing research, development, and manufacturing of some esoteric types of semiconductors. It put a heavy emphasis on participatory management, with an extensive use of product teams for decision purposes. There was also careful planning of physical arrangements so as to facilitate necessary interactions between groups. Management officials hoped to secure high involvement from all levels and a working climate that induced creative work. In many ways their experiment succeeded, but they were troubled by serious complaints from many of the specialized engineering and technical people who held critical positions. The comments below from some of these people indicate the nature of their concerns:

> In a way, the [unit] is not a satisfying place for the [technical] professional. You seem to have to go through a lot of red tape and coordination to get something technical done.

> The technical guy is principally interested in technical things and the business team in economic problems. There's a certain type of research-oriented person who would be completely frustrated in the team. He's not interested in business or human relations unless they have a direct bearing on what he's doing.

> I'm basically a scientist. Scientists are individualists and you appreciate freedom in your thoughts and action. And this basically goes across the grain of the business team.

The complaints stand in sharp contrast to the highly favorable responses of almost all of the nontechnical personnel. This contrast became apparent to one of the authors in the course of research in preparing a teaching case. The senior officials of the unit, upon seeing the pattern, concluded that the heavy emphasis being placed on securing integration through the use of group methods had not allowed the technical people enough of an opportunity to differentiate their role and orientation. A careful internal study was made of the issue, and a modification of the group procedures was adopted. This seemed to correct the situation. In essence, the engineering personnel were freed from involvement in business activity, and an integrator was provided to link them to these activities. Thus technical personnel were freer to develop orientations related to their major task.

Identification of the Problem

A main problem in the study of organizational change is that the environmental contexts in which organizations exist are themselves changing, at an increasing rate, and towards increasing complexity. This point, in itself, scarcely needs laboring. Nevertheless, the characteristics of organizational environments demand consideration for their own sake, if there is to be an advancement of understanding in the behavioral sciences of a great deal that is taking place under the impact of technological change, especially at the present time. This paper is offered as a brief attempt to open up some of the problems, and stems from a belief that progress will be quicker if a certain extension can be made to current thinking about systems.

In a general way it may be said that to think in terms of systems seems the most appropriate conceptual response so far available when the phenomena under study—at any level and in any domain—display the character of being organized, and when understanding the nature of the interdependencies constitutes the research task. In the behavioral sciences, the first steps in building a systems theory were taken in connection with the analysis of internal processes in organisms, or organizations, when the parts had to be related to the whole. Examples include the organismic biology of Jennings, Cannon, and Henderson; early Gestalt theory and its later derivatives such as balance theory; and the classical theories of social structure. Many of these problems could be represented in closed-system models. The next steps were taken when wholes had to be related to their environments. This led to open-system models.

A great deal of the thinking here has been influenced by

Reprinted from *Human Relations* 18 (1965): 21–32, by permission of the author and of the original publisher, The Plenum Publishing Company, Ltd.

cybernetics and information theory, though this has been used as much to extend the scope of closed-system as to improve the sophistication of open-system formulations. It was von Bertalanffy[1] who, in terms of the general transport equation which he introduced, first fully disclosed the importance of openness or closedness to the environment as a means of distinguishing living organisms from inanimate objects. In contradistinction to physical objects, any living entity survives by importing into itself certain types of material from its environment, transforming these in accordance with its own system characteristics, and exporting other types back into the environment. By this process the organism obtains the additional energy that renders it "negentropic"; it becomes capable of attaining stability in a time-independent steady state—a necessary condition of adaptability to environmental variance.

Such steady states are very different affairs from the equilibrium states described in classical physics, which have far too often been taken as models for representing biological and social transactions. Equilibrium states follow the second law of thermodynamics, so that no work can be done when equilibrium is reached, whereas the openness to the environment of a steady state maintains the capacity of the organism for work, without which adaptability, and hence survival, would be impossible.

Many corollaries follow as regards the properties of open systems, such as equifinality, growth through internal elaboration, self-regulation, constancy of direction with change of position, and so on—and by no means all of these have yet been worked out. But though von Bertalanffy's formulation enables exchange processes between the organism, or organization, and elements in its environment to be dealt with in a new perspective, it does not deal at all with those processes in the environment itself which are among the determining conditions of the exchanges. To analyze these an additional concept is needed—*the causal texture of the environment*—if we may reintroduce, at a social level of analysis, a term suggested by Tolman and Brunswik[2] and drawn from S. C. Pepper.[3]

With this addition, we may now state the following general

1. L. von Bertalanffy, "The Theory of Open Systems in Physics and Biology," *Science* 111 (1950): 23–29.

2. E. C. Tolman and E. Brunswik, "The Organism and the Causal Texture of the Environment," *Psychol. Rev.* 42 (1935): 43–47.

3. S. C. Pepper, "The Conceptual Framework of Tolman's Purposive Behaviorism," *Psychol. Rev.* 41 (1934): 108–33.

proposition: that a comprehensive understanding or organizational behavior requires some knowledge of each member of the following set, where L indicates some potentially lawful connection, and the suffix 1 refers to the organization and the suffix 2 to the environment:

$$L_{11}, L_{12}$$
$$L_{21}, L_{22}$$

L_{11} here refers to processes within the organization—the area of internal interdependencies; L_{12} and L_{21} to exchanges between the organization and its environment—the area of transactional interdependencies, from either direction; and L_{22} to processes through which parts of the environment become related to each other—i.e. its causal texture—the area of interdependencies that belong within the environment itself.

In considering environmental interdependencies, the first point to which we wish to draw attention is that the laws connecting parts of the environment to each other are often incommensurate with those connecting parts of the organization to each other, or even with those which govern the exchanges. It is not possible, for example, always to reduce organization-environment relations to the form of "being included in"; boundaries are also "break" points. As Barker and Wright,[4] following Lewin,[5] have pointed out in their analysis of this problem as it affects psychological ecology, we may lawfully connect the actions of a javelin thrower in sighting and throwing his weapon; but we cannot describe in the same concepts the course of the javelin as this is affected by variables lawfully linked by meteorological and other systems.

The Development of Environmental Connectedness (Case 1)

A case history, taken from the industrial field, may serve to illustrate what is meant by the environment becoming organized at the social level. It will show how a greater degree of system-connectedness, of crucial relevance to the organization, may develop in the environment, which is yet not directly a function either of the organization's own characteristics or of its immediate relations. Both of these, of course, once again become crucial when the response of the organization to what has been happening is considered.

4. R. G. Barker and H. F. Wright, "Psychological Ecology and the Problem of Psychosocial Development," *Child Development* 20 (1949): 131–43.
5. K. Lewin, *Principles of Topological Psychology* (New York: McGraw-Hill, 1936).

The company concerned was the foremost in its particular market in the foodcanning industry in the U.K. and belonged to a large parent group. Its main product—a canned vegetable—had some 65 percent of this market, a situation which had been relatively stable since before the war. Believing it would continue to hold this position, the company persuaded the group board to invest several million pounds sterling in erecting a new, automated factory, which, however, based its economies on an inbuilt rigidity—it was set up exclusively for the long runs expected from the traditional market.

The character of the environment, however, began to change while the factory was being built. A number of small canning firms appeared, not dealing with this product nor indeed with others in the company's range, but with imported fruits. These firms arose because the last of the postwar controls had been removed from steel strip and tin, and cheaper cans could now be obtained in any numbers—while at the same time a larger market was developing in imported fruits. This trade being seasonal, the firms were anxious to find a way of using their machinery and retaining their labor in winter. They became able to do so through a curious side effect of the development of quick-frozen foods, when the company's staple was produced by others in this form. The quick-freezing process demanded great constancy at the growing end. It was not possible to control this beyond a certain point, so that quite large crops unsuitable for quick freezing but suitable for canning became available—originally from another country (the United States) where a large market for quick-frozen foods had been established. These surplus crops had been sold at a very low price for animal feed. They were now imported by the small canners—at a better but still comparatively low price, and additional cheap supplies soon began to be procurable from underdeveloped countries.

Before the introduction of the quick-freezing form, the company's own canned product—whose raw material had been specially grown at additional cost—had been the premier brand, superior to other varieties and charged at a higher price. But its position in the product spectrum now changed. With the increasing affluence of the society, more people were able to afford the quick-frozen form. Moreover, there was competition from a great many other vegetable products which could substitute for the staple, and people preferred this greater variety. The advantage of being the premier line among canned forms diminished, and demand increased both for the not-so-expensive varieties among them and for the quick-frozen forms. At the same time, major changes were taking place in retailing; supermarkets were developing, and more and more large grocery chains were coming into existence. These establishments wanted to sell certain types of goods under their own house names, and began to place bulk orders with the small canners for their own varieties of the company's staple that fell within this class. As the small canners provided an extremely cheap article (having no marketing expenses and a cheaper raw material), they could undercut the manufacturers' branded product, and within three years they captured over 50 percent of the market. Previously, retailers' varieties had accounted for less than 1 percent.

The new automatic factory could not be adapted to the new situation until alternative products with a big sales volume could be developed, and the scale of research and development, based on the type of market analysis required to identify these, was beyond the scope of the existing resources of the company either in people or in funds.

The changed texture of the environment was not recognized by an able but traditional management until it was too late. They failed entirely to appreciate that a number of outside events were becoming connected with each other in a way that was leading up to irreversible general change. Their first reaction was to make a herculean effort to defend the traditional product, then the board split on whether or not to make entry into the cheaper unbranded market in a supplier role. Group H.Q. now felt they had no option but to step in, and many upheavals and changes in management took place until a "redefinition of mission" was agreed, and slowly and painfully the company reemerged with a very much altered product mix and something of a new identity.

Four Types of Causal Texture

It was this experience, and a number of others not dissimilar, by no means all of them industrial (and including studies of change problems in hospitals, in prisons, and in educational and political organizations), that gradually led us to feel a need for redirecting conceptual attention to the causal texture of the environment, considered as a quasi-independent domain. We have now isolated four "ideal types" of causal texture, approximations to which may be thought of as existing simultaneously in the "real world" of most organizations—though, of course, their weighting will vary enormously from case to case.

The first three of these types have already, and indeed

repeatedly, been described—in a large variety of terms and with the emphasis on an equally bewildering variety of special aspects—in the literature of a number of disciplines, ranging from biology to economics and including military theory as well as psychology and sociology. The fourth type, however, is new, at least to us, and is the one that for some time we have been endeavoring to identify. About the first three, therefore, we can be brief, but the fourth is scarcely understandable without reference to them. Together, the four types may be said to form a series in which the degree of causal texturing is increased, in a new and significant way, as each step is taken. We leave as an open question the need for further steps.

Step One

The simplest type of environmental texture is that in which goals and noxiants ("goods" and "bads") are relatively unchanging in themselves and randomly distributed. This may be called the *placid, randomized environment*. It corresponds to Simon's idea of a surface over which an organism can locomote: most of this is bare, but at isolated, widely scattered points there are little heaps of food.[6] It also corresponds to Ashby's limiting case of no connection between the environmental parts;[7] and to Schutzenberger's random field.[8] The economist's classical market also corresponds to this type.

A critical property of organizational response under random conditions has been stated by Schutzenberger: that there is no distinction between tactics and strategy, "the optimal strategy is just the simple tactic of attempting to do one's best on a purely local basis."[9] The best tactic, moreover, can be learned only by trial and error and only for a particular class of local environmental variances.[10] While organizations under these conditions can exist adaptively as single and indeed quite small units, this becomes progressively more difficult under the other types.

Step Two

More complicated, but still a placid environment, is that which can be characterized in terms of clustering: goals and

6. H. A. Simon, *Models of Man* (New York: Wiley, 1957), p. 137.
7. W. Ross Ashby, *Design for a Brain* (London: Chapman & Hall, 1960), chap. 15, sec. 4.
8. M. P. Schutzenberger, "A Tentative Classification of Goal-seeking Behaviours," *J. Ment. Sci.* 100 (1954): 100.
9. Ibid., p. 101.
10. Ashby, *Design for a Brain*, p. 197.

noxiants are not randomly distributed but hang together in certain ways. This may be called the *placid, clustered environment,* and is the case with which Tolman and Brunswik were concerned; it corresponds to Ashby's "serial system" and to the economist's "imperfect competition." The clustering enables some parts to take on roles as signs of other parts or become means-objects with respect to approaching or avoiding. Survival, however, becomes precarious if an organization attempts to deal tactically with each environmental variance as it occurs.

The new feature of organizational response to this kind of environment is the emergence of strategy as distinct from tactics. Survival becomes critically linked with what an organization knows of its environment. To pursue a goal under its nose may lead it into parts of the field fraught with danger, while avoidance of an immediately difficult issue may lead it away from potentially rewarding areas. In the clustered environment the relevant objective is that of "optimal location," some positions being discernible as potentially richer than others.

To reach these requires concentration of resources, subordination to the main plan, and the development of a "distinctive competence," to use Selznick's[11] term, in reaching the strategic objective. Organizations under these conditions, therefore, tend to grow in size and also to become hierarchical, with a tendency towards centralized control and coordination.

Step Three

The next level of causal texturing we have called the *disturbed-reactive environment.* It may be compared with Ashby's ultrastable system or the economist's oligopolic market. It is a type 2 environment in which there is more than one organization of the same kind; indeed, the existence of a number of similar organizations now becomes the dominant characteristic of the environmental field. Each organization does not simply have to take account of the others when they meet at random, but has also to consider that what it knows can also be known by the others. The part of the environment to which it wishes to move itself in the long run is also the part to which the others seek to move. Knowing this, each will wish to improve its own chances by hindering the others, and each will know that the others must not only wish

11. P. Selznick, *Leadership in Administration* (Evanston, Ill: Row, Peterson, 1957).

to do likewise, but also know that each knows this. The presence of similar others creates an imbrication, to use a term of Chein's,[12] of some of the causal strands in the environment.

If strategy is a matter of selecting the "strategic objective" —where one wishes to be at a future time—and tactics a matter of selecting an immediate action from one's available repertoire, then there appears in type 3 environments to be an intermediate level of organizational response—that of the *operation*—to use the term adopted by German and Soviet military theorists, who formally distinguish tactics, operations, and strategy. One has now not only to make sequential choices, but to choose actions that will draw off the other organizations. The new element is that of deciding which of someone else's possible tactics one wishes to take place, while ensuring that others of them do not. An operation consists of a campaign involving a planned series of tactical initiatives, calculated reactions by others, and counteractions. The flexibility required encourages a certain decentralization and also puts a premium on quality and speed of decision at various peripheral points.[13]

It now becomes necessary to define the organizational objective in terms not so much of location as of capacity or power to move more or less at will, i.e., to be able to make and meet competitive challenge. This gives particular relevance to strategies of absorption and parasitism. It can also give rise to situations in which stability can be obtained only by a certain coming-to-terms between competitors, whether enterprises, interest groups, or governments. One has to know when not to fight to the death.

Step Four

Yet more complex are the environments we have called *turbulent fields*. In these, dynamic processes, which create significant variances for the component organizations, arise from the field itself. Like type 3 and unlike the static types 1 and 2, they are dynamic. Unlike type 3, the dynamic properties arise not simply from the interaction of the component organizations, but also from the field itself. The "ground" is in motion.

Three trends contribute to the emergence of these dynamic field forces:

12. I. Chein, "Personality and Typology," *J. Soc. Psychol.* 18 (1943): 89–101.

13. Lord Heyworth, *The Organization of Unilever* (London: Unilever Limited, 1955).

i. The growth to meet type 3 conditions of organizations, and linked sets of organizations, so large that their actions are both persistent and strong enough to induce autochthonous processes in the environment. An analogous effect would be that of a company of soldiers marching in step over a bridge.

ii. The deepening interdependence between the economic and the other facets of the society. This means that economic organizations are increasingly enmeshed in legislation and public regulation.

iii. The increasing reliance on research and development to achieve the capacity to meet competitive challenge. This leads to a situation in which a change gradient is continuously present in the environmental field.

For organizations, these trends mean a gross increase in their area of *relevant uncertainty*. The consequences which flow from their actions lead off in ways that become increasingly unpredictable: they do not necessarily fall off with distance, but may at any point be amplified beyond all expectation; similarly, lines of action that are strongly pursued may find themselves attenuated by emergent field forces.

The Salience of Type 4 Characteristics (Case 2)

Some of these effects are apparent in what happened to the canning company of case 1, whose situation represents a transition from an environment largely composed of type 2 and type 3 characteristics to one where those of type 4 began to gain in salience. The case now to be presented illustrates the combined operation of the three trends described above in an altogether larger environmental field involving a total industry and its relations with the wider society.

The organization concerned is the National Farmers Union of Great Britain to which more than 200,000 of the 250,000 farmers of England and Wales belong. The presenting problem brought to use for investigation was that of communications. Headquarters felt, and was deemed to be, out of touch with county branches, and these with local branches. The farmer had looked to the N.F.U. very largely to protect him against market fluctuations by negotiating a comprehensive deal with the government at annual reviews concerned with the level of price support. These reviews had enabled home agriculture to maintain a steady state during two decades when the threat, or existence, of war in relation to the type of military technology then in being had made it imperative to maintain a high level of food without increasing prices to the consumer. This policy, however, was becoming obsolete as the conditions of thermonuclear stalemate established themselves. A level of support could no longer be counted upon which would keep in existence small and inefficient farmers—often on marginal land and dependent on family labor—compared with efficient medium-size farms, to say nothing of large and highly mechanized undertakings.

Yet it was the former situation which had produced N.F.U. cohesion. As this situation receded, not only were farmers becoming exposed to more competition from each other, as well as from Commonwealth and European farmers, but the effects were being felt of very great changes which had been taking place on both the supply and marketing sides of the industry. On the supply side, a small number of giant firms now supplied almost all the requirements in fertilizer, machinery, seeds, veterinary products, and so on. As efficient farming depended upon ever greater utilization of these resources, their controllers exerted correspondingly greater power over the farmers. Even more dramatic were the changes in the marketing of farm produce. Highly organized food processing and distributing industries had grown up dominated again by a few large firms, on contracts from which (fashioned to suit their rather than his interests) the farmer was becoming increasingly dependent. From both sides deep inroads were being made on his autonomy.

It became clear that the source of the felt difficulty about communications lay in radical environmental changes which were confronting the organization with problems it was ill-adapted to meet. Communications about these changes were being interpreted or acted upon as if they referred to the "traditional" situation. Only through a parallel analysis of the environment and the N.F.U. was progress made towards developing understanding on the basis of which attempts to devise adaptive organizational policies and forms could be made. Not least among the problems was that of creating a bureaucratic elite that could cope with the highly technical long-range planning now required and yet remain loyal to the democratic values of the N.F.U. Equally difficult was that of developing mediating institutions—agencies that would effectively mediate the relations between agriculture and other economic sectors without triggering off massive competitive processes.

These environmental changes and the organizational crisis they induced were fully apparent two or three years before

the question of Britain's possible entry into the Common
Market first appeared on the political agenda—which, of
course, further complicated every issue.

A workable solution needed to preserve reasonable autonomy for the farmers as an occupational group, while meeting the interests of other sections of the community. Any
such possibility depended on securing the consent of the large
majority of farmers to placing under some degree of N.F.U.
control matters that hitherto had remained within their own
power of decision. These included what they produced, how
and to what standard, and how most of it should be
marketed. Such thoughts were anathema, for however dependent the farmer had grown on the N.F.U. he also remained
intensely individualistic. He was being asked, he now felt, to
redefine his identity, reverse his basic values, and refashion
his organization—all at the same time. It is scarcely
surprising that progress has been, and remains, both fitful
and slow, and ridden with conflict.

Values and Relevant Uncertainty

What becomes precarious under type 4 conditions is how organizational stability can be achieved. In these environments
individual organizations, however large, cannot expect to
adapt successfully simply through their own direct actions—
as is evident in the case of the N.F.U Nevertheless, there are
some indications of a solution that may have the same general significance for these environments as have strategy and
operations for types 2 and 3. This is the emergence of *values
that have overriding significance for all members of the field.*
Social values are here regarded as coping mechanisms that
make it possible to deal with persisting areas of relevant uncertainty. Unable to trace out the consequences of their actions as these are amplified and resonated through their extended social fields, men in all societies have sought rules,
sometimes categorical, such as the ten commandments, to
provide them with a guide and ready calculus. Values are not
strategies or tactics; as Lewin[14] has pointed out, they have
the conceptual character of "power fields" and act as injunctions.

So far as effective values emerge, the character of richly
joined, turbulent fields changes in a most striking fashion.
The relevance of large classes of events no longer has to be
sought in an intricate mesh of diverging casual strands, but is

14. Lewin, *Principles of Topological Psychology.*

given directly in the ethical code. By this transformation a field is created which is no longer richly joined and turbulent but simplified and relatively static. Such a transformation will be regressive, or constructively adaptative, according to how far the emergent values adequately represent the new environmental requirements.

Ashby, as a biologist, has stated his view, on the one hand, that examples of environments that are both large and richly connected are not common, for our terrestrial environment is widely characterized by being highly subdivided;[15] and, on the other, that, so far as they are encountered, they may well be beyond the limits of human adaptation, the brain being an ultrastable system. By contrast the role here attributed to social values suggests that this sort of environment may in fact be not only one to which adaptation is possible, however difficult, but one that has been increasingly characteristic of the human condition since the beginning of settled communities. Also, let us not forget that values can be rational as well as irrational and that the rationality of their rationale is likely to become more powerful as the scientific ethos takes greater hold in a society.

Matrix Organization and Institutional Success

Nevertheless, turbulent fields demand some overall form of organization that is essentially different from the hierarchically structured forms to which we are accustomed. Whereas type 3 environments require one or another form of accommodation between like, but competitive, organizations whose fates are to a degree negatively correlated, turbulent environments require some relationship between dissimilar organizations whose fates are, basically, positively correlated. This means relationships that will maximize cooperation and which recognize that no one organization can take over the role of "the other" and become paramount. We are inclined to speak of this type of relationship as an *organizational matrix*. Such a matrix acts in the first place by delimiting on value criteria the character of what may be included in the field specified—and therefore who. This selectivity then enables some definable shape to be worked out without recourse to much in the way of formal hierarchy among members. Professional associations provide one model of which there has been long experience.

We do not suggest that in other fields than the professional

15. Ashby, *Design for A Brain*, p. 205.

the requisite sanctioning can be provided only by state-controlled bodies. Indeed, the reverse is far more likely. Nor do we suggest that organizational matrices will function so as to eliminate the need for other measures to achieve stability. As with values, matrix organizations, even if successful, will only help to transform turbulent environments into the kinds of environment we have discussed as "clustered" and "disturbed-reactive." Though, with these transformations, an organization could hope to achieve a degree of stability through its strategies, operation, and tactics, the transformations would not provide environments identical with the originals. The strategic objective in the transformed cases could no longer be stated simply in terms of optimal location (as in type 2) or capabilities (as in type 3). It must now rather be formulated in terms of *institutionalization*. According to Selznick organizations become institutions through the embodiment of organizational values which relate them to the wider society. As Selznick has stated in his analysis of leadership in the modern American corporation, "the default of leadership shows itself in an acute form when *organizational* achievement or survival is confounded with *institutional* success"; "the executive becomes a statesman as he makes the transition from administrative management to institutional leadership."[16]

The processes of strategic planning now also become modified. Insofar as institutionalization becomes a prerequisite for stability, the determination of policy will necessitate not only a bias towards goals that are congruent with the organization's own character, but also a selection of goal-paths that offer maximum convergence as regards the interests of other parties. This became a central issue for the N.F.U. and is becoming one now for an organization such as the National Economic Development Council, which has the task of creating a matrix in which the British economy can function at something better than the stop-go level.

Such organizations arise from the need to meet problems

16. Selznick, *Leadership in Administration*, pp. 27, 154. Since the present paper was presented, this line of thought has been further developed by Churchman and Emery in their discussion of the relation of the statistical aggregate of individuals to structured role sets: "Like other values, organizational values emerge to cope with relevant uncertainties and gain their authority from their reference to the requirements of larger systems within which people's interests are largely concordant" (C. W. Churchman and F. E. Emery, *Operational Research and the Social Sciences* [London: Tavistock Publications, 1965]).

emanating from type 4 environments. Unless this is recognized, they will only too easily be construed in type 3 terms, and attempts will be made to secure for them a degree of monolithic power that will be resisted overtly in democratic societies and covertly in others. In the one case they may be prevented from ever undertaking their missions; in the other one may wonder how long they can succeed in maintaining them.

An organizational matrix implies what McGregor[17] has called Theory Y. This in turn implies a new set of values. But values are psychosocial commodities that come into existence only rather slowly. Very little systematic work has yet been done on the establishment of new systems of values, or on the type of criteria that might be adduced to allow their effectiveness to be empirically tested. A pioneer attempt is that of Churchman and Ackoff.[18] Likert[19] has suggested that, in the large corporation or government establishment, it may well take some ten to fifteen years before the new type of group values with which he is concerned could permeate the total organization. For a new set to permeate a whole modern society the time required must be much longer—at least a generation, according to the common saying—and this, indeed, must be a minimum. One may ask if this is fast enough, given the rate at which type 4 environments are becoming salient. A compelling task for social scientists is to direct more research onto these problems.

Summary

a. A main problem in the study of organizational change is that the environmental contexts in which organizations exist are themselves changing—at an increasing rate, under the impact of technological change. This means that they demand consideration for their own sake. Towards this end a redefinition is offered, at a social level of analysis, of the causal texture of the environment, a concept introduced in 1935 by Tolman and Brunswik.

b. This requires an extension of systems theory. The first steps in systems theory were taken in connection with the analysis of internal processes in organisms, or organizations,

17. D. McGregor, *The Human Side of Enterprise* (New York, Toronto, London: McGraw-Hill, 1960).

18. C. W. Churchman and R. L. Ackoff, *Methods of Inquiry* (St. Louis: Educational Publishers, 1950).

19. R. Likert, *New Patterns of Management* (New York, Toronto, London: McGraw-Hill, 1961).

which involved relating parts to the whole. Most of these problems could be dealt with through closed-system models. The next steps were taken when wholes had to be related to their environments. This led to open-system models, such as that introduced by Bertalanffy, involving a general transport equation. Though this enables exchange processes between the organism, or organization, and elements in its environment to be dealt with, it does not deal with those processes in the environment itself which are the determining conditions of the exchanges. To analyze these an additional concept— the causal texture of the environment—is needed.

c. The laws connecting parts of the environment to each other are often incommensurate with those connecting parts of the organization to each other, or even those which govern exchanges. Case history 1 illustrates this and shows the dangers and difficulties that arise when there is a rapid and gross increase in the area of relevant uncertainty, a characteristic feature of many contemporary environments.

d. Organizational environments differ in their causal texture, both as regards degree of uncertainty and in many other important respects. A typology is suggested which identifies four "ideal types," approximations to which exist simultaneously in the "real world" of most organizations, though the weighting varies enormously:

1. In the simplest type, goals and noxiants are relatively unchanging in themselves and randomly distributed. This may be called the placid, randomized environment. A critical property from the organization's viewpoint is that there is no difference between tactics and strategy, and organizations can exist adaptively as single, and indeed quite small, units.

2. The next type is also static, but goals and noxiants are not randomly distributed; they hang together in certain ways. This may be called the placid, clustered environment. Now the need arises for strategy as distinct from tactics. Under these conditions organizations grow in size, becoming multiple and tending towards centralized control and coordination.

3. The third type is dynamic rather than static. We call it the disturbed-reactive environment. It consists of a clustered environment in which there is more than one system of the same kind, i.e., the objects of one organization are the same as, or relevant to, others like it. Such competitors seek to improve their own chances by hindering each other, each knowing the others are playing the same

game. Between strategy and tactics there emerges an intermediate type of organizational response—what military theorists refer to as operations. Control becomes more decentralized to allow these to be conducted. On the other hand, stability may require a certain coming-to-terms between competitors.

4. The fourth type is dynamic in a second respect, the dynamic properties arising not simply from the interaction of identifiable component systems but from the field itself (the "ground"). We call these environments turbulent fields. The turbulence results from the complexity and multiple character of the causal interconnections. Individual organizations, however large, cannot adapt successfully simply through their direct interactions. An examination is made of the enhanced importance of values, regarded as a basic response to persisting areas of relevant uncertainty, as providing a control mechanism, when commonly held by all members in a field. This raises the question of organizational forms based on the characteristics of a matrix.

e. Case history 2 is presented to illustrate problems of the transition from type 3 to type 4. The perspective of the four environmental types is used to clarify the role of Theory X and Theory Y as representing a trend in value change. The establishment of a new set of values is a slow social process requiring something like a generation—unless new means can be developed.

The Technology of Foolishness
James G. March

I

The concept of choice as a focus for interpreting human behavior has rarely had an easy time in the realm of ideas. It is beset by theological disputations over free will, by the dilemmas of absurdism, by the doubts of psychological behaviorism, by the claims of historical, economic, social, and demographic determinism. Nevertheless, the idea that humans make choices has proven robust enough to become a major matter of faith in important segments of contemporary western civilization.

The major tenets of this faith run something like this: Human beings make choices. They do this by evaluating their alternatives in terms of their goals on the basis of information available to them. They choose the alternative that is most attractive in terms of the goals. The process of making choices can be improved by using the technology of choice. Through the paraphernalia of modern techniques, we can

Previously published in *Civiløkonomen* (Copenhagen) 18, no. 4 (May 1971): 7–12. Reprinted with permission of the author.

This essay is one part of a general examination of the problems of choice in worlds in which goals are unclear. It reviews some ideas that have been the basis for conversations with a number of friends. Although they may not recognize the present form, I want to acknowledge the help particularly of Lance Bennett, Patricia Nelson Bennett, Michael Butler, Søren Christensen, Michael D. Cohen, James R. Glenn, Jr., John Miller, Johan Olsen, Gail Whitacre Raffel, and Richard C. Snyder. In the late summer of 1970 I was invited to attend a conference on organizations of the future held in the Netherlands, and exploited that opportunity to solicit help from the group there, particularly Warren G. Bennis, Michel Crozier, Claude Faucheux, Misha Jezernik, Harold J. Leavitt, Andre Massart, Lawrence T. Pinfield, Alexander Szalai, and Eugene J. Webb.

If with all this pedigree the remarks are still curious, I can only plead that the coincidence of an invitation to summarize my musings from the conference and the desire to understand the problems of university leadership overcame the probity of cautious laziness. The Carnegie Commission on Higher Education and the Ford Foundation are financially responsible.

improve the quality of the search for alternatives, the quality of information, and the quality of the analysis used to evaluate alternatives. Although actual human choice may fall short of this ideal in various ways, it is an attractive model of how choices should be made by individuals and organizations.

Whatever the merits of such a faith within the academic worlds of philosophy, psychology, economics, history, and sociology, it is, I believe, a dominant view among businessmen, politicians, engineers, educators, scientists, and bureaucrats. It qualifies as a key part of the current conception of intelligence. It affirms the efficacy and possibility of intelligent human action.

These articles of faith have been built upon, and have stimulated, some scripture. It is the scripture of theories of individual and organizational decision making. The scripture is partly a codification of received doctrine and partly a source for that doctrine. As a result, our cultural ideas of intelligence and our theories of choice bear some substantial resemblance. In particular, they share three conspicuous interrelated ideas:

The first idea is the *preexistence of purpose*. We find it natural to base an interpretation of human choice behavior on a presumption of human purpose. We have, in fact, invented one of the most elaborate terminologies in the professional literature: "values," "needs," "wants," "goods," "preferences," "utility," "objectives," "goals," "aspirations," "drives." All of these reflect a strong tendency to believe that a useful interpretation of human behavior involves defining a set of objectives that (a) are prior attributes of the system, and (b) make the observed behavior in some sense intelligent vis-à-vis those objectives.

Whether we are talking about individuals or about organizations, purpose is an obvious presumption of the discussion. An organization is often defined in terms of its purpose. It is seen by some as the largest collectivity directed by a purpose. Action within an organization is justified (or criticized) in terms of the purpose. Individuals explain their own behavior, as well as the behavior of others, in terms of a set of value premises that are presumed to be antecedent to the behavior. Normative theories of choice begin with an assumption of a preexistent preference ordering defined over the possible outcomes of a choice.

The second idea is the *necessity of consistency*. We have come to recognize consistency both as an important property of human behavior and as a prerequisite for normative models of choice. Dissonance theory, balance theory, theories of congruency in attitudes, statuses, and performances have all served to remind us of the possibilities for interpreting human behavior in terms of the consistency requirements of a limited capacity information-processing system.

At the same time, consistency is a cultural and theoretical virtue. Action should be made consistent with belief. Beliefs should be consistent with each other, and stable over time. Actions taken by different parts of an organization should be consistent with each other. Individual and organizational activities are seen as connected with each other in terms of their consequences for some consistent set of purposes. In an organization, the structural manifestation of the dictum of consistency is the hierarchy with its obligations of coordination and control. In the individual, the structural manifestation is a set of values that generates a consistent preference ordering.

The third idea is the *primacy of rationality*. By rationality I mean a procedure for deciding what is correct behavior by relating consequences systematically to objectives. By placing primary emphasis on rational techniques, we implicitly have rejected—or seriously impaired—two other procedures for choice: (a) The processes of intuition, by means of which people may do things without fully understanding why. (b) The processes of tradition and faith, through which people do things because that is the way they are done.

Both within the theory and within the culture we insist on the ethic of rationality. We justify individual and organizational action in terms of an analysis of means and ends. Impulse, intuition, faith, and tradition are outside that system and viewed as antithetical to it. Faith may be seen as a possible source of values. Intuition may be seen as a possible source of ideas about alternatives. But the analysis and justification of action lies within the context of reason.

These ideas are obviously deeply embedded in the culture. Their roots extend into ideas that have conditioned much of modern western history and interpretations of that history. Their general acceptance is probably highly correlated with the permeation of rationalism and individualism into the style of thinking within the culture. The ideas are even more obviously embedded in modern theories of choice. It is fundamental to those theories that thinking should precede action; that action should serve a purpose; that purpose should be defined in terms of a consistent set of preexistent goals; and that choice should be based on a consistent theory of the relation between action and its consequences.

Every tool of management decision that is currently a part of management science, operations research, or decision theory assumes the prior existence of a set of consistent goals. Almost the entire structure of microeconomic theory builds on the assumption that there exists a well-defined, stable, and consistent preference ordering. Most theories of individual or organizational choice behavior accept the idea that goals exist and that (in some sense) an individual or organization acts on those goals, choosing from among some alternatives on the basis of available information.

From the perspective of all of man's history, the ideas of purpose, consistency, and rationality are relatively new. Much of the technology currently available to implement them is extremely new. Over the past few centuries, and conspicuously over the past few decades, we have substantially improved man's capability for acting purposively, consistently, and rationally. We have substantially increased his propensity to think of himself as doing so. It is an impressive victory, won—where it has been won—by a happy combination of timing, performance, ideology, and persistence. It is a battle yet to be concluded, or even engaged, in many cultures of the world; but within most of the western world, individuals and organizations see themselves as making choices.

II

The tools of intelligence as they are fashioned in modern theories of choice are necessary to any reasonable behavior in contemporary society. It is difficult to see how we could, and inconceivable that we would, fail to continue their development, refinement, and extension. As might be expected, however, a theory and ideology of choice built on the ideas outlined above is deficient in some obvious, elementary ways, most conspicuously in the treatment of human goals.

Goals are thrust upon the intelligent man. We ask that he act in the name of goals. We ask that he keep his goals consistent. We ask that his actions be oriented to his goals. But we do not concern ourselves with the origin of goals. Theories of individual and organizational choice assume actors with preexistent value systems.

Since it is obvious that goals change over time and that the character of those changes affects both the richness of personal and organizational development and the outcome of choice behavior, a theory of choice must somehow justify ignoring the phenomena. Although it is unreasonable to ask a theory of choice to solve all of the problems of man and his development, it is reasonable to ask how something as conspicuous as the fluidity of objectives can plausibly be ignored in a theory that is offered as a guide to human choice behavior.

There are three classic justifications. The first is that goal development and choice are independent processes, conceptually and behaviorally. The second is that the model of choice is never satisfied in fact and that deviations from the model accommodate the problems of introducing change. The third is that the idea of changing goals is so intractable in a normative theory of choice that nothing can be said about it. Since I am unpersuaded of the first and second justifications, my optimism with respect to the third is somewhat greater than most of my fellows.

The argument that goal development and choice are independent behaviorally seems clearly false. It seems to me perfectly obvious that a description that assumes goals come first and action comes later is frequently radically wrong. Human choice behavior is at least as much a process for discovering goals as for acting on them. Although it is true enough that goals and decisions are "conceptually" distinct, that is simply a statement of the theory. It is not a defense of it. They are conceptually distinct if we choose to make them so.

The argument that the model is incomplete is more persuasive. There do appear to be some critical "holes" in the system of intelligence as described by standard theories of choice. There is incomplete information, incomplete goal consistency, and a variety of external processes impinging on goal development—including intuition and tradition. What is somewhat disconcerting about the argument, however, is that it makes the efficacy of the concepts of intelligent choice dependent on their inadequacy. As we become more competent in the techniques of the model, and more committed to it, the "holes" become smaller. As the model becomes more accepted, our obligation to modify it increases.

The final argument seems to me sensible as a general principle, but misleading here. Why are we more reluctant to ask how human beings might find "good" goals than we are to ask how they might make "good" decisions? The second question appears to be a relatively technical problem. The first seems more pretentious. It claims to say something about alternative virtues. The appearance of pretense, however, stems directly from the theory and the ideology associated with it.

In fact, the conscious introduction of goal discovery as a

consideration in theories of human choice is not unknown to modern man. We have two kinds of theories of choice behavior in human beings. One is a theory of children. The other is a theory of adults. In the theory of childhood, we emphasize choices as leading to experiences that develop the child's scope, his complexity, his awareness of the world. As parents, or psychologists, we try to lead the child to do things that are inconsistent with his present goals because we know (or believe) that he can only develop into an interesting person by coming to appreciate aspects of experience that he initially rejects.

In the theory of adulthood, we emphasize choices as a consequence of our intentions. As adults, or economists, we try to take actions that (within the limits of scarce resources) come as close as possible to achieving our goals. We try to find improved ways of making decisions consistent with our perceptions of what is valuable in the world.

The asymmetry in these models is conspicuous. Adults have constructed a model world in which adults know what is good for themselves, but children do not know what is good for themselves. It is hard to react positively to the conceit. Reaction to the asymmetry has, in fact, stimulated a rather large number of ideologies and reforms designed to allow children the same moral prerogative granted to adults—the right to imagine that they know what they want. The efforts have cut deeply into traditional child-rearing, traditional educational policies, traditional politics, and traditional consumer economics.

In my judgment, the asymmetry between models of choice for adults and models of choice for children is awkward; but the solution we have adopted is precisely wrong-headed. Instead of trying to adapt the model of adults to children, we might better adapt the model of children to adults. For many purposes, our model of children is better. Of course, children know what they want. Everyone does. The critical question is whether they are encouraged to develop more interesting "wants." Values change. People become more interesting as those values and the interconnections made among them change.

One of the most obvious things in the world turns out to be hard for us to accommodate in our theory of choice: A child of two will almost always have a less interesting set of values (yes, indeed, a *worse* set of values) than a child of twelve. The same is true of adults. Although one of the main natural arenas for the modification of human values is the arena of choice, our theories of adult and organizational decision making ignore the phenomenon entirely.

Introducing ambiguity and fluidity to the interpretation of individual and organizational goals obviously has implications for behavioral theories of decision making. The main point here, however, is not to consider how we might describe the behavior of individuals and organizations that are discovering goals as they act. Rather it is to examine, how we might improve the quality of that behavior, how we might aid the development of interesting goals.

We know how to advise an organization or an individual if we are first given a consistent set of preferences. Under some conditions, we can suggest how to make decisions if the preferences are only consistent up to the point of specifying a series of independent constraints on the choice. But what about a normative theory of goal-finding behavior? What do we say when our client tells us that he is not sure his present set of values is the set of values in terms of which he wants to act?

It is a question familiar to many aspects of ordinary life. It is a question that friends, associates, students, college presidents, business managers, voters, and children ask at least as frequently as they ask how they should act within a set of consistent and stable values.

Within the context of the normative theory of choice as it exists, the answer we give is: First determine the values, then act. The advice is frequently useful. Moreover, we have developed ways in which we can use conventional techniques for decision analysis to help discover what our value premises are and to expose value inconsistencies for resolution. These techniques involve testing the decision implications of some successive approximations to a set of preferences. The object is to find a consistent set of preferences with implications that are acceptable to the person or organization making the decisions. Variations on such techniques are used routinely in operations research, as well as in personal counseling and analysis.

The utility of such techniques, however, apparently depends on the assumption that a primary problem is the excavation of preexistent values. The metaphors—"finding oneself," "goal clarification," "self-discovery"—are metaphors of search. If our value premises are to be "constructed" rather than "discovered," our standard procedures may be useful; but we have no a priori reason for assuming they will.

Perhaps we should explore a somewhat different approach

to the normative question of how we ought to behave when our value premises are not yet (and never will be) full determined. Suppose we treat actions as a way of creating interesting goals at the same time as we treat goals as a way of justifying action. It is an intuitively plausible and simple idea, but one that is not immediately within the domain of standard normative theories of intelligent choice.

Interesting people and interesting organizations construct complicated theories of themselves. In order to do this, they need to supplement the technology of reason with a technology of foolishness. Individuals and organizations need ways of doing things for which they have no good reason. Not always. Not usually. But sometimes. They need to act before they think.

III

In order to use the act of intelligent choice as a planned occasion for discovering new goals, we apparently require some idea of sensible foolishness. Which of the many foolish things that we might do now will lead to attractive value consequences? The question is almost inconceivable. Not only does it ask us to predict the value consequences of action, it asks us to evaluate them. In what terms can we talk about "good" changes in goals?

In effect, we are asked either to specify a set of supergoals in terms of which alternative goals are evaluated, or to choose among alternatives now in terms of the unknown set of values we will have at some future time (or the distribution over time of that unknown set of future values). The former alternative moves us back to the original situation of a fixed set of values—now called "supergoals"—and hardly seems an important step in the direction of inventing procedures for discovering new goals. The latter alternative seems fundamental enough, but it violates severely our sense of temporal order. To say that we make decisions now in terms of goals that will only be knowable later is nonsensical —as long as we accept the basic framework of the theory of choice and its presumptions of preexistent goals.

I do not know in detail what is required, but I think it will be substantial. As we challenge the dogma of preexistent goals, we will be forced to reexamine some of our most precious prejudices: the strictures against imitation, coercion, and rationalization. Each of those honorable prohibitions depends on the view of man and human choice imposed on us by conventional theories of choice.

Imitation is not necessarily a sign of weak blood. It is a prediction. It is a prediction that if we duplicate the behavior or attitudes of someone else, the chances of our discovering attractive new goals for ourselves are relatively high. In order for imitation to be normatively attractive we need a better theory of who should be imitated. Such a theory seems to be eminently feasible. For example, what are the conditions for effectiveness of a rule that you should imitate another person whose values are in a close neighborhood of yours? How do the chances of discovering interesting goals through imitation change as the number of other people exhibiting the behavior to be imitated increases?

Coercion is not necessarily an assault on individual autonomy. It can be a device for stimulating individuality. We recognize this when we talk about parents and children (at least sometimes). What has always been difficult with coercion is the possibility for perversion that it involves, not its obvious capability for stimulating change. What we require is a theory of the circumstances under which entry into a coercive system produces behavior that leads to the discovery of interesting goals. We are all familiar with the tactic. We use it in imposing deadlines, entering contracts, making commitments. What are the conditions for its effective use?

Rationalization is not necessarily a tricky way of evading morality. It can be a test for the feasibility of a goal change. When deciding among alternative actions for which we have no good reason, it may be sensible to develop some definition of how "near" to intelligence alternative "unintelligent" actions lie. Effective rationalization permits this kind of incremental approach to changes in values. To use it effectively, however, we require a better idea of the kinds of metrics that might be possible in measuring value distances. At the same time, rationalization is the major procedure for integrating newly discovered goals into an existing structure of values. It provides the organization of complexity without which complexity itself becomes indistinguishable from randomness.

There are dangers in imitation, coercion, and rationalization. The risks are too familiar to elaborate. We should, indeed, be able to develop better techniques. Whatever those techniques may be, however, they will almost certainly stress the superstructure of biases erected on purpose, consistency, and rationality. They will involve some way of thinking about action now as occurring in terms of a set of unknown future values.

IV

A second requirement for a technology of foolishness is some strategy for suspending rational imperatives toward consistency. Even if we know which of several foolish things we want to do, we still need a mechanism for allowing us to do it. How do we escape the logic of our reason?

Here, I think, we are closer to understanding what we need. It is playfulness. Playfulness is the deliberate, temporary relaxation of rules in order to explore the possibilities of alternative rules. When we are playful, we challenge the necessity of consistency. In effect, we announce—in advance—our rejection of the usual objections to behavior that does not fit the standard model of intelligence.

Playfulness allows experimentation. At the same time, it acknowledges reason. It accepts an obligation that at some point either the playful behavior will be stopped or it will be integrated into the structure of intelligence in some way that makes sense. The suspension of the rules is temporary.

The idea of play may suggest three things that are, in my mind, quite erroneous in the present context. First, play may be seen as a kind of Mardi Gras for reason, a release of the emotional tensions of virtue. Although it is possible that play performs some such function, that is not the function with which I am concerned. Second, play may be seen as part of some mystical balance of spiritual principles: Fire and water, hot and cold, weak and strong. The intention here is much narrower than a general mystique of balance. Third, play may be seen as an antithesis of intelligence, so that the emphasis on the importance of play becomes a support for simple self-indulgence. Without prejudicing the case for self-indulgent behavior, my present intent is to propose play as an instrument of intelligence, not a substitute.

Playfulness is a natural outgrowth of our standard view of reason. A strict insistence on purpose, consistency, and rationality limits our ability to find new purposes. Play relaxes that insistence to allow us to act "unintelligently" or "irrationally," or "foolishly" to explore alternative ideas of possible purposes and alternative concepts of behavioral consistency. And it does this while maintaining our basic commitment to the necessity of intelligence.

Although play and reason are in this way functional complements, they are often behavioral competitors. They are alternative styles and alternative orientations to the same situation. There is no guarantee that the styles will be equally well-developed. There is no guarantee that all individuals or all organizations will be equally adept in both styles. There is no guarantee that all cultures will be equally encouraging to both.

Our design problem is either to specify the best mix of styles or, failing that, to assure that most people and most organizations most of the time use an alternation of strategies rather than perseverate in either one. It is a difficult problem. The optimization problem looks extremely difficult on the face of it, and the learning situations that will produce alternation in behavior appear to be somewhat less common than those that produce perseveration.

Consider, for example, the difficulty of sustaining playfulness as a style within contemporary American society. Individuals who are good at consistent rationality are rewarded early and heavily. We define it as intelligence, and the educational rewards of society are associated strongly with it. Much of the press from social norms is in the same direction, particularly for men. Many of the demands of modern organizational life reinforce the same abilities and style preferences.

The result is that many of the most influential, best educated, and best placed citizens have experienced a powerful overlearning with respect to rationality. They are exceptionally good at maintaining consistent pictures of themselves, of relating action to purposes. They are exceptionally poor at a playful attitude toward their own beliefs, toward the logic of consistency, or toward the way they see things as being connected in the world. The dictates of manliness, forcefulness, independence, and intelligence are intolerant of playful urges if they arise. The playful urges that arise are weak ones.

The picture is probably overdrawn, but not, I believe, the implications. Both for organizations and for individuals reason and intelligence have had the unnecessary consequence of inhibiting the development of purpose into more complicated forms of consistency. In order to move away from that position, we need to find some ways of helping individuals and organizations to experiment with doing things for which they have no good reason, to be playful with their conception of themselves. It is a facility that requires more careful attention than I can give it, but I would suggest five things as a small beginning:

First, we can treat *goals as hypotheses*. Conventional decision theory allows us to entertain doubts about almost everything except the thing about which we frequently have the greatest doubt—our objectives. Suppose we define the decision process as a time for the sequential testing of hypotheses about goals. If we can experiment with alternative goals, we stand some chance of discovering complicated and interesting combinations of good values that none of us previously imagined.

Second, we can treat *intuition as real*. I do not know what intuition is, or even if it is any one thing. Perhaps it is simply an excuse for doing something we cannot justify in terms of present values or for refusing to follow the logic of our own beliefs. Perhaps it is an inexplicable way of consulting that part of our intelligence that is not organized in a way anticipated by standard theories of choice. In either case, intuition permits us to see some possible actions that are outside our present scheme for justifying behavior.

Third, we can treat *hypocrisy as a transition*. Hyprocrisy is an inconsistency between expressed values and behavior. Negative attitudes about hypocrisy stem from two major things. The first is a general onus against inconsistency. The second is a sentiment against combining the pleasures of vice with the appearance of virtue. Apparently, that is an unfair way of allowing evil to escape temporal punishment. Whatever the merits of such a position as ethics, it seems to me distinctly inhibiting toward change. A bad man with good intentions may be a man experimenting with the possibility of becoming good. Somehow it seems to me more sensible to encourage the experimentation than to insult it.

Fourth, we can treat *memory as an enemy*. The rules of consistency and rationality require a technology of memory. For most purposes, good memories make good choices. But the ability to forget, or overlook, is also useful. If I do not know what I did yesterday or what other people in the organization are doing today, I can act within the system of reason and still do things that are foolish.

Fifth, we can treat *experience as a theory*. Learning can be viewed as a series of conclusions based on concepts of action and consequences that we have invented. Experience can be changed retrospectively. By changing our interpretive concepts now, we modify what we learned earlier. Thus, we expose the possibility of experimenting with alternative childhoods. The usual strictures against "self-deception" in experience need occasionally to be tempered with an awareness of the extent to which all experience is an interpretation subject to conscious revision. Personal histories, like national histories, need to be rewritten rather continuously as a base for the retrospective learning of new self-conceptions.

12

Organization Structure: The Tension between Too Little and Too Much

Introduction

This chapter is about the formal structure of complex organizations. Formal structure usually means the more or less permanently specified set of roles in the organization and their official relationship to one another. People may come and go and times can change, but the structure can go on and on. Norbert Wiener once observed that a whirlpool is still the same whirlpool though billions of water molecules enter and leave it every second. And Lewis Carroll defined a grin to be what was left when you erased the rest of the Cheshire cat. In the same spirit, formal structure is what an organization has left when you "erase" the temporary and transient, the particular people and the particular activities of any period.

When most people think of formal structure, they think of the formal authority hierarchy, of who reports to whom. That is part of the structural story, but only part. There are several other important parts: How the organization is divided up into parts, for example, like the refining division part of an oil company, or the English department part of a university, or the obstetrics department part of a hospital. How the parts of the organization are hooked together is another element of structure—not only the chain of authority, but also the hooking together provided by the pattern of work flow and the communication network. We can also describe an organization structure along a scale of "differentiation," depending on whether it is divided into a small number of large departments at one extreme versus a large number of small departments at the other. How tightly the parts of an organization hang together can also be described along a rough continuum, depending on whether the parts are richly interconnected or only loosely coupled. The terms in this brief paragraph form the core of vocabulary that may help us think about organization structure in a useful way.

There are only two papers in this chapter, one by Herbert

Simon and one by Gary Steiner. But there are several papers in other chapters that could just as easily have been placed here. For example, much of the paper by Lawrence and Lorsch in chapter 11 is about structure; so is Bennis's piece in chapter 14; and so is March's paper in chapter 11. Several others throughout this book also refer less directly either to the causes of formal structure, or the effects of formal structure on behavior, or both.

In considering the problem of designing an organizational structure, most traditional textbooks seem to focus on problems like these: "Should the corporation be organized by process or by product?" That is, should you group together those activities that have a common fund of knowledge and technology but cut across different products, or should you put together all of the diverse skills and functions that go into the design, production, financing, and marketing of a single class of products? We feel that such issues are *not* the main issue in structural design. Instead of worrying just about what *kind* of departmentalization an organization ought to have, a more central issue is *how much* formal structure one should impose on the organization. As the title to this chapter suggests, there is a natural tension between having too much formal structure and not enough. The two papers in this chapter have been selected to illustrate and investigate this dilemma.

The central point of Simon's paper is that systems of all kinds—physical, biological, social, psychological, political, and even artistic—are most likely to have hierarchical structures if they are to survive over long periods of time. Simon takes great care to point out that his use of the word "hierarchical" does not refer to a hierarchy of authority, but rather to the progressive "nesting" of small parts within larger parts. He argues that a complex system can survive the interference of environmental influences only if it is made up of a hierarchical structure of stable subsystems; that the survival pressures of evolution have favored systems with stable, functional parts that are connected into the whole. Consider, for example, the human body. It is made up of distinct organs, like the stomach, which are in turn part of stable subsystems like the digestive system. Or consider that successful nations are in turn composed of successful states, containing viable counties, which in turn are broken up into precincts, wards, neighborhoods, and eventually the family as a governing unit. Or consider highly complex formal organizations that are built up progressively of groups, sections, departments, and divisions. Although Simon does not do so in this particular paper, one can also study the human personality itself from this hierarchical point of view.

Simon's second important point is that our ability to deal with complex systems (to describe, analyze, and control them) depends on our ability to find orderly ways of describing them. The very structure of this book was designed with these notions in mind. The reader has probably already noticed our attempt to use hierarchical principles in the design of this book: papers within chapters, chapters within four main parts, and the four main parts arranged in what is hoped to be a meaningful order of ascending complexity from the individual through the pair-wise relationship and the small group to the large, complex organization.

We have argued so far that an orderly, hierarchical structure is necessary for the long-run survival of any complex system including large organizations. But can formal structure be carried too far? There is a very real danger that the concept of hierarchy as used by Simon will be transformed and distorted solely into a hierarchy of authority for possible use in tightly controlling every action of organization members. An organization can also be overstructured in other ways—by the use of elaborate checking procedures, by the promulgation of pervasive sets of rules, and by the enforcement of detailed operating procedures. Although such an organization in certain environments (see chapter 11) might be efficient in the short run, it is unlikely to provide fertile ground for creative ideas. That is the key point of the paper by Gary Steiner on "the creative organization."

The first part of Steiner's paper deals with individual creativity and in this sense it might well have been better placed in chapter 2 dealing with the thinking parts of man. But the latter part of his paper deals directly with the ways in which organization can and cannot create conditions that nourish creativity. Like many of the other papers in this book, Steiner argues for a more open, less structured organizational environment. But he goes on to describe some of the costs of fostering creativity that the organization must be prepared to bear, costs like decreased predictability.

As the pluses and minuses enumerated by Steiner make clear, the decision of how much structure to build into your organization is far from an easy one. Since we seem to be living in an age of uncertainty, perhaps the best strategy is to adopt a provisional and experimental attitude toward the design of organization structures. You will probably recognize that this represents a direct extension of some of the ideas developed by March in "The Technology of Foolishness" in chapter 11. The best we can hope to do at this stage is at least to highlight the issues and outline some of the alternatives available to you.

The Architecture of Complexity
Herbert A. Simon

A number of proposals have been advanced in recent years for the development of "general systems theory" that, abstracting from properties peculiar to physical, biological, or social systems, would be applicable to all of them.[1] We might well feel that, while the goal is laudable, systems of such diverse kinds could hardly be expected to have any nontrivial properties in common. Metaphor and analogy can be helpful, or they can be misleading. All depends on whether the similarities the metaphor captures are significant or superficial.

It may not be entirely vain, however, to search for common properties among diverse kinds of complex systems. The ideas that go by the name of cybernetics constitute, if not a theory, at least a point of view that has been proving fruitful over a wide range of applications.[2] It has been useful to look at the behavior of adaptive systems in terms of the concepts of feedback and homeostasis, and to analyze adaptiveness in terms of the theory of selective information.[3] The ideas of feedback and information provide a frame of reference for viewing a wide range of situations, just as do the ideas of evolution, relativism, of axiomatic method, and of operationalism.

In this essay I should like to report on some things we have

Reprinted with permission from *Proceedings of the American Philosophical Society* 106 (December 1962): 467–82.

1. See especially the yearbooks of the Society for General Systems Research. Prominent among the exponents of general systems theory are L. von Bertalanffy, K. Boulding, R. W. Gerard, and J. G. Miller. For a more skeptical view—perhaps too skeptical in the light of the present discussion—see H. A. Simon and A. Newell, "Models: Their Uses and Limitations," in L. D. White, ed., *The State of the Social Sciences* (Chicago: University of Chicago Press, 1956), pp. 66–83.

2. N. Wiener, *Cybernetics* (New York: Wiley, 1948), For an imaginative forerunner, see A. J. Lotka, *Elements of Mathematical Biology* (New York: Dover Publications, 1951), first published in 1924 as *Elements of Physical Biology*.

3. C. Shannon and W. Weaver, *The Mathematical Theory of Communication* (Urbana: University of Illinois Press, 1949); W. R. Ashby, *Design for a Brain* (New York: Wiley, 1952).

been learning about particular kinds of complex systems encountered in the behavioral sciences. The developments I shall discuss arose in the context of specific phenomena, but the theoretical formulations themselves make little reference to details of structure. Instead they refer primarily to the complexity of the systems under view without specifying the exact content of that complexity. Because of their abstractness, the theories may have relevance—application would be too strong a term—to other kinds of complex systems that are observed in the social, biological, and physical sciences.

In recounting these developments, I shall avoid technical detail, which can generally be found elsewhere. I shall describe each theory in the particular context in which it arose. Then, I shall cite some examples of complex systems, from areas of science other than the initial application, to which the theoretical framework appears relevant. In doing so, I shall make reference to areas of knowledge where I am not expert—perhaps not even literate. The reader will have little difficulty, I am sure, in distinguishing instances based on idle fancy or sheer ignorance from instances that cast some light on the ways in which complexity exhibits itself whereever it is found in nature.

I shall not undertake a formal definition of "complex systems."[4] Roughly, by a complex system I mean one made up of a large number of parts that interact in a nonsimple way. In such systems, the whole is more than the sum of the parts, not in an ultimate, metaphysical sense, but in the important pragmatic sense that, given the properties of the parts and the laws of their interaction, it is not a trivial matter to infer the properties of the whole. In the face of complexity, an in-principle reductionist may be at the same time a pragmatic holist.[5]

The four sections that follow discuss four aspects of

4. W. Weaver, in "Science and Complexity," *American Scientist* 36 (1948): 536, has distinguished two kinds of complexity, disorganized and organized. We shall be concerned primarily with organized complexity.

5. See also John R. Platt, "Properties of Large Molecules That Go beyond the Properties of Their Chemical Sub-groups," *Journal of Theoretical Biology* 1 (1961): 342–58. Since the reductionism-holism issue is a major *cause de guerre* between scientists and humanists, perhaps we might even hope that peace could be negotiated between the two cultures along the lines of the compromise just suggested. As I go along, I shall have a little to say about complexity in the arts as well as in the natural sciences. I must emphasize the pragmatism of my holism to distinguish it sharply from the position taken by W. M. Elsasser in *The Physical Foundation of Biology* (New York: Pergamon Press, 1958).

complexity. The first offers some comments on the frequency with which complexity takes the form of hierarchy—the complex system being composed of subsystems that, in turn, have their own subsystems, and so on. The second section theorizes about the relation between the structure of a complex system and the time required for it to emerge through evolutionary processes; specifically, it argues that hierarchic systems will evolve far more quickly than non-hierarchic systems of comparable size. The third section explores the dynamic properties of hierarchically organized systems and shows how they can be decomposed into subsystems in order to analyze their behavior. The fourth section examines the relation between complex systems and their descriptions.

Thus, my central theme is that complexity frequently takes the form of hierarchy and that hierarchic systems have some common properties and are independent of their specific content. Hierarchy, I shall argue, is one of the central structural schemes that the architect of complexity uses.

Hierarchic Systems

By a *hierarchic system,* or hierarchy, I mean a system that is composed of interrelated subsystems, each of the latter being, in turn, hierarchic in structure until we reach some lowest level of elementary subsystem. In most systems in nature, it is somewhat arbitrary as to where we leave off the partitioning and what subsystems we take as elementary. Physics makes much use of the concept of "elementary particle," although particles have a disconcerting tendency not to remain elementary very long. Only a couple of generations ago, the atoms themselves were elementary particles; today, to the nuclear physicist they are complex systems. For certain purposes of astronomy, whole stars, or even galaxies, can be regarded as elementary subsystems. In one kind of biological research, a cell may be treated as an elementary subsystem; in another, a protein molecule; in still another, an amino acid residue.

Just why a scientist has a right to treat as elementary a subsystem that is in fact exceedingly complex is one of the questions we shall take up. For the moment, we shall accept the fact that scientists do this all the time and that, if they are careful scientists, they usually get away with it.

Etymologically, the word "hierarchy" has had a narrower meaning than I am giving it here. The term has generally been used to refer to a complex system in which each of the subsystems is subordinated by an authority relation to the system it belongs to. More exactly, in a hierarchic formal organization, each system consists of a "boss" and a set of subordinate subsystems. Each of the subsystems has a "boss" who is the immediate subordinate of the boss of the system. We shall want to consider systems in which the relations among subsystems are more complex than in the formal organizational hierarchy just described. We shall want to include systems in which there is no relation of subordination among subsystems. (In fact, even in human organizations, the formal hierarchy exists only on paper; the real flesh-and-blood organization has many interpart relations other than the lines of formal authority.) For lack of a better term, I shall use "hierarchy" in the broader sense introduced in the previous paragraphs, to refer to all complex systems analyzable into successive sets of subsystems, and speak of "formal hierarchy" when I want to refer to the more specialized concept.[6]

Social Systems

I have already given an example of one kind of hierarchy that is frequently encountered in the social sciences: a formal organization. Business firms, governments, and universities all have a clearly visible parts-within-parts structure. But formal organizations are not the only, or even the most common, kind of social hierarchy. Almost all societies have elementary units called families, which may be grouped into villages or tribes, and these into larger groupings, and so on. If we make a chart of social interactions, of who talks to whom, the clusters of dense interaction in the chart will identify a rather well-defined hierarchic structure. The groupings in this structure may be defined operationally by some measure of frequency of interaction in this sociometric matrix.

Biological and Physical Systems

The hierarchical structure of biological systems is a familiar fact. Taking the cell as the building block, we find cells organized into tissues, tissues into organs, organs into systems. Moving downward from the cell, well-defined subsystems—for example, nucleus, cell membrane, microsomes, mitochondria, and so on—have been identified in animal cells.

The hierarchic structure of many physical systems is equally clear-cut. I have already mentioned the two main series. At the microscopic level we have elementary particles,

6. The mathematical term "partitioning" will not do for what I call here a hierarchy; for the set of subsystems, and the successive subsets in each of these defines the partitioning, independently of any systems of relations among the subsets. By "hierarchy" I mean the partitioning in conjunction with the relations that hold among its parts.

atoms, molecules, and macromolecules. At the macroscopic level we have satellite systems, planetary systems, galaxies. Matter is distributed throughout space in a strikingly nonuniform fashion. The most nearly random distributions we find, gases, are not random distributions of elementary particles but random distributions of complex systems, that is, molecules.

A considerable range of structural types is subsumed under the term "hierarchy" as I have defined it. By this definition, a diamond is hierarchic, for it is a crystal structure of carbon atoms that can be further decomposed into protons, neutrons, and electrons. However, it is a very "flat" hierarchy, in which the number of first-order subsystems belonging to the crystal can be indefinitely large. A volume of molecular gas is a flat hierarchy in the same sense. In ordinary usage, we tend to reserve the word "hierarchy" for a system that is divided into a *small or moderate number* of subsystems, each of which may be further subdivided. Hence, we do not ordinarily think of or refer to a diamond or a gas as a hierarchic structure. Similarly, a linear polymer is simply a chain, which may be very long, of identical subparts, the monomers. At the molecular level it is a very flat hierarchy.

In discussing formal organizations, the number of subordinates who report directly to a single boss is called his *span of control*. I shall speak analogously of the *span* of a system, by which I shall mean the number of subsystems into which it is partitioned. Thus, a hierarchic system is flat at a given level if it has a wide span at that level. A diamond has a wide span at the crystal level, but not at the next level down, the molecular level.

In most of our theory construction in the following sections we shall focus our attention on hierarchies of moderate span, but from time to time I shall comment on the extent to which the theories might or might not be expected to apply to very flat hierarchies.

There is one important difference between the physical and biological hierarchies, on the one hand, and social hierarchies, on the other. Most physical and biological hierarchies are described in spatial terms. We detect the organelles in a cell in the way we detect the raisins in a cake—they are "visibly" differentiated substructures localized spatially in the larger structure. On the other hand, we propose to identify social hierarchies not by observing who lives close to whom but by observing who interacts with whom. These two points of view can be reconciled by defining hierarchy in terms of intensity of interaction, but observing that in most biological and physical systems relatively intense interaction implies relative spatial propinquity. One of the interesting characteristics of nerve cells and telephone wires is that they permit very specific strong interactions at great distances. To the extent that interactions are channeled through specialized communications and transportation systems, spatial propinquity becomes less determinative of structure.

Symbolic Systems

One very important class of systems has been omitted from my examples thus far: systems of human symbolic production. A book is a hierarchy in the sense in which I am using that term. It is generally divided into chapters, the chapters into sections, the sections into paragraphs, the paragraphs into sentences, the sentences into clauses and phrases, the clauses and phrases into words. We may take the words as our elementary units, or further subdivide them, as the linguist often does, into smaller units. If the book is narrative in character, it may divide into "episodes" instead of sections, but divisions there will be.

The hierarchic structure of music, based on such units as movements, parts, themes, phrases, is well known. The hierarchic structure of products of the pictorial arts is more difficult to characterize, but I shall have something to say about it later.

The Evolution of Complex Systems

Let me introduce the topic of evolution with a parable. There once were two watchmakers, named Hora and Tempus, who manufactured very fine watches. Both of them were highly regarded, and the phones in their workshops rang frequently —new customers were constantly calling them. However, Hora prospered, while Tempus became poorer and poorer and finally lost his shop. What was the reason?

The watches the men made consisted of about 1,000 parts each. Tempus had so constructed his that if he had one partly assembled and had to put it down—to answer the phone, say —it immediately fell to pieces and had to be reassembled from the elements. The better the customers liked his watches, the more they phoned him and the more difficult it became for him to find enough uninterrupted time to finish a watch.

The watches that Hora made were no less complex than those of Tempus. But he had designed them so that he could put together subassemblies of about ten elements each. Ten of these subassemblies, again, could be put together into a larger subassembly; and a system of ten of the latter subassemblies constituted the whole watch. Hence, when Hora had to put down a partly assembled watch in order to answer the phone, he lost only a small part of his work, and he assembled his watches in only a fraction of the man-hours it took Tempus.

It is rather easy to make a quantitative analysis of the relative difficulty of the tasks of Tempus and Hora: Suppose the probability that an interruption will occur while a part is being added to an incomplete assembly is p. Then the probability that Tempus can complete a watch he has started without interruption is $(1 - p)^{1000}$—a very small number unless p is 0.001 or less. Each interruption will cost, on the average, the time to assemble $1/p$ parts (the expected number assembled before interruption). On the other hand, Hora has to complete 111 subassemblies of ten parts each. The probability that he will not be interrupted while completing any one of these is $(1 - p)^{10}$, and each interruption will cost only about the time required to assemble five parts.[7]

Now if p is about 0.01—that is, there is one chance in a hundred that either watchmaker will be interrupted while adding any one part to an assembly—then a straightforward calculation shows that it will take Tempus, on the average, about four thousand times as long to assemble a watch as Hora.

We arrive at the estimate as follows:
1. Hora must make 111 times as many complete assemblies per watch as Tempus; but

7. The speculations on speed of evolution were first suggested by H. Jacobson's application of information theory to estimating the time required for biological evolution. See his paper "Information, Reproduction, and the Origin of Life," in *American Scientist* 43 (January 1955): 119–27. From thermodynamic considerations it is possible to estimate the amount of increase in entropy that occurs when a complex system decomposes into its elements. (See, for example, R. B. Setlow and E. C. Pollard, *Molecular Biophysics* (Reading, Mass.: Addison-Wesley, 1962), pp. 63–65, and references cited there.) But entropy is the logarithm of a probability, hence information, the negative of entropy, can be interpreted as the logarithm of the reciprocal of the probability—the "improbability," so to speak. The essential idea in Jacobson's model is that the expected time required for the system to reach a particular state is inversely proportional to the probability of the state—hence it increases exponentially with the amount of information (negentropy) of the state.

Following this line of argument, but not introducing the notion of levels and stable subassemblies, Jacobson arrived at estimates of the time required for evolution so large as to make the event rather improbable. Our analysis, carried through in the same way, but with attention to the stable intermediate forms, produces very much smaller estimates.

2. Tempus will lose on the average 20 times as much work for each interrupted assembly as Hora (100 parts, on the average, as against 5); and

3. Tempus will complete an assembly only 44 times per million attempts ($0.99^{1000} = 44 \times 10^{-6}$), while Hora will complete nine out of ten ($0.99^{10} = 9 \times 10^{-1}$). Hence Tempus will have to make 20,000 as many attempts per completed assembly as Hora. $(9 \times 10^{-1})/(44 \times 10^{-6}) = 2 \times 10^4$. Multiplying these three ratios, we get

$$1/111 \times 100/5 \times 0.99^{10}/0.99^{1000}$$
$$= 1/111 \times 20 \times 20,000 \sim 4,000.$$

Biological Evolution

What lessons can we draw from our parable for biological evolution? Let us interpret a partially completed subassembly of k elementary parts as the coexistence of k parts in a small volume—ignoring their relative orientations. The model assumes that parts are entering the volume at a constant rate, but that there is a constant probability, p, that the part will be dispersed before another is added, unless the assembly reaches a stable state. These assumptions are not particularly realistic. They undoubtedly underestimate the decrease in probability of achieving the assembly with increase in the size of the assembly. Hence the assumptions understate—probably by a large factor—the relative advantage of a hierarchic structure.

Although we cannot, therefore, take the numerical estimate seriously, the lesson for biological evolution is quite clear and direct. The time required for the evolution of a complex form from simple elements depends critically on the numbers and distribution of potential intermediate stable forms. In particular, if there exists a hierarchy of potential stable "subassemblies," with about the same span, $s,$ at each level of the hierarchy, then the time required for a subassembly can be expected to be about the same at each level—that is, proportional to $1/(1 - p)^{s}$. The time required for the assembly of a system of n elements will be proportional to $\log_s n,$ that is, to the number of levels in the system. One would say—with more illustrative than literal intent—that the time required for the evolution of multicelled organisms from single-celled organisms might be of the same order of magnitude as the time required for the evolution of single-celled organisms from macromolecules. The same argument could be applied to the evolution of proteins from amino acids, of molecules from atoms, of atoms from elementary particles.

A whole host of objections to this oversimplified scheme will occur, I am sure, to every working biologist, chemist, and physicist. Before turning to matters I know more about, I shall mention three of these problems, leaving the rest to the attention of the specialists.

First, in spite of the overtones of the watchmaker parable, the theory assumes no teleological mechanism. The complex forms can arise from the simple ones by purely random processes. (I shall propose another model in a moment that shows this clearly.) Direction is provided to the scheme by the stability of the complex forms, once these come into existence. But this is nothing more than survival of the fittest—that is, of the stable.

Second, not all large systems appear hierarchical. For example, most polymers—such as nylon—are simply linear chains of large numbers of identical components, the monomers. However, for present purposes we can simply regard such a structure as a hierarchy with a span of one—the limiting case. For a chain of any length represents a state of relative equilibrium.[8]

Third, the evolution of complex systems from simple elements implies nothing, one way or the other, about the change in entropy of the entire system. If the process absorbs free energy, the complex system will have a smaller entropy than the elements; if it releases free energy, the opposite will be true. The former alternative is the one that holds for most biological systems, and the net inflow of free energy has to be supplied from the sun or some other source if the second law of thermodynamics is not to be violated. For the evolutionary process we are describing, the equilibria of the intermediate states need have only local and not global stability, and they may be stable only in the steady state—that is, as long as there is an external source of free energy that may be drawn upon.[9]

Because organisms are not energetically closed systems,

8. There is a well-developed theory of polymer size, based on models of random assembly. See, for example, P. J. Flory, *Principles of Polymer Chemistry* (Ithaca, N.Y.: Cornell University Press, 1953), chap. 8. Since *all* subassemblies in the polymerization theory are stable, limitation of molecular growth depends on "poisoning" of terminal groups by impurities or formation of cycles rather than upon disruption of partially formed chains.

9. This point has been made many times before, but it cannot be emphasized too strongly. For further discussion, see Setlow and Pollard, *Molecular Biophysics*, pp. 49–64; E. Schrödinger, *What Is Life?* (Cambridge: Cambridge University Press, 1945); and H. Linschitz, "The Information Content of a Bacterial Cell," in H. Quastler, ed., *Information Theory in Biology* (Urbana: University of Illinois Press, 1953), pp. 251–62.

there is no way to deduce the direction, much less the rate, of evolution from classical thermodynamic considerations. All estimates indicate that the amount of entropy, measured in physical units, involved in the formation of a one-celled biological organism is trivially small—about -10^{-11} cal/degree.[10] The "improbability" of evolution has nothing to do with this quantity of entropy, which is produced by every bacterial cell every generation. The irrelevance of quantity of information, in this sense, to speed of evolution can also be seen from the fact that exactly as much information is required to "copy" a cell through the reproductive process as to produce the first cell through evolution.

The effect of the existence of stable intermediate forms exercises a powerful effect on the evolution of complex forms that may be likened to the dramatic effect of catalysts upon reaction rates and steady-state distribution of reaction products in open systems.[11] In neither case does the entropy change provide us with a guide to system behavior.

Problem Solving as Natural Selection

Let us turn now to some phenomena that have no obvious connection with biological evolution: human problem-solving processes. Consider, for example, the task of discovering the proof for a difficult theorem. The process can be—and often has been—described as a search through a maze. Starting with the axioms and previously proved theorems, various transformations allowed by the rules of the mathematical systems are attempted, to obtain new expressions. These are modified in turn until, with persistence and good fortune, a sequence or path of transformations is discovered that leads to the goal.

The process ordinarily involves much trial and error. Various paths are tried; some are abandoned, others are pushed further. Before a solution is found, many paths of the maze may be explored. The more difficult and novel the problem, the greater is likely to be the amount of trial and error required to find a solution. At the same time, the trial and error is not completely random or blind; it is, in fact, rather highly selective. The new expressions that are obtained by transforming given ones are examined to see whether they represent progress toward the goal. Indications of progress spur further search in the same direction; lack of

10. See Linschitz, "The Information Content." This quantity, 10^{-11} cal/degree, corresponds to about 10^{13} bits of information.

11. See H. Kacser, "Some Physico-chemical Aspects of Biological Organization," in C. H. Waddington, *The Strategy of the Genes* (London: George Allen & Unwin, 1957), pp. 191–249.

progress signals the abandonment of a line of search. Problem solving requires *selective* trial and error.[12]

A little reflection reveals that cues signaling progress play the same role in the problem-solving process that stable intermediate forms play in the biological evolutionary process. In fact, we can take over the watchmaker parable and apply it also to problem solving. In problem solving, a partial result that represents recognizable progress toward the goal plays the role of a stable subassembly.

Suppose that the task is to open a safe whose lock has 10 dials, each with 100 possible settings, numbered from 0 to 99. How long will it take to open the safe by a blind trial-and-error search for the correct setting? Since there are 100^{10} possible settings, we may expect to examine about one-half of these, on the average, before finding the correct one—that is, 50 billion billion settings. Suppose, however, that the safe is defective, so that a click can be heard when any one dial is turned to the correct setting. Now each dial can be adjusted independently and does not need to be touched again while the others are being set. The total number of settings that have to be tried is only 10 x 50, or 500. The task of opening the safe has been altered, by the cues the clicks provide, from a practically impossible one to a trivial one.[13]

A considerable amount has been learned in the past five years about the nature of the mazes that represent common human problem-solving tasks—proving theorems, solving puzzles, playing chess, making investments, balancing assembly lines, to mention a few. All that we have learned

12. See A. Newell, J. C. Shaw, and H. A. Simon, "Empirical Explorations of the Logic Theory Machine," *Proceedings of the 1957 Western Joint Computer Conference* (New York: Institute of Radio Engineers, February 1957); "Chess-Playing Programs and the Problem of Complexity," *IBM Journal of Research and Development* 2 (October 1958): 320–35; and for a similar view of problem solving, W. R. Ashby, "Design for an Intelligence Amplifier, in C. E. Shannon and J. McCarthy, *Automata Studies* (Princeton: Princton University Press, 1956), pp. 215–33.

13. The clicking safe example was supplied by D. P. Simon. Ashby, "Design for an Intelligence Amplifier," p. 230, has called the selectivity involved in situations of this kind "selection by components." The even greater reduction in time produced by hierarchization in the clicking safe example, as compared with the watchmaker's metaphor, is due to the fact that a random *search* for the correct combination is involved in the former case, while in the latter the parts come together in the right order. It is not clear which of these metaphors provides the better model for biological evolution, but we may be sure that the watchmaker's metaphor gives an exceedingly conservative estimate of the savings due to hierarchization. The safe may give an excessively high estimate because it assumes all possible arrangements of the elements to be equally probable.

about these mazes points to the same conclusion: that human problem solving, from the most blundering to the most insightful, involves nothing more than varying mixtures of trial and error and selectivity. The selectivity derives from various rules of thumb, or heuristics, that suggest which paths should be tried first and which leads are promising. We do not need to postulate processes more sophisticated than those involved in organic evolution to explain how enormous problem mazes are cut down to quite reasonable size.[14]

The Sources of Selectivity

When we examine the sources from which the problem-solving system, or the evolving system, as the case may be, derives its selectivity, we discover that selectivity can always be equated with some kind of feedback of information from the environment.

Let us consider the case of problem solving first. There are two basic kinds of selectivity. One we have already noted: various paths are tried out, the consequences of following them are noted, and this information is used to guide further search. In the same way, in organic evolution, various complexes come into being, at least evanescently, and those that are stable provide new building blocks for further construction. It is this information about stable configurations, and not free energy or negentropy from the sun, that guides the process of evolution and provides the selectivity that is essential to account for its rapidity.

The second source of selectivity in problem solving is previous experience. We see this particularly clearly when the problem to be solved is similar to one that has been solved before. Then, by simply trying again the paths that led to the earlier solution, or their analogues, trial-and-error search is greatly reduced or altogether eliminated.

What corresponds to this latter kind of information in organic evoluton? The closest analogue is reproduction. Once we reach the level of self-reproducing systems, a complex system, when it has once been achieved, can be multiplied indefinitely. Reproduction, in fact, allows the inheritance of acquired characteristics, but at the level of genetic material, of course; that is, only characteristics acquired by the genes can be inherited. We shall return to the topic of reproduction in the final section of this essay.

14. A. Newell and H. A. Simon, "Computer Simulation of Human Thinking," *Science* 134 (22 December 1961): 2011–17.

On Empires and Empire Building

We have not exhausted the categories of complex systems to which the watchmaker argument can reasonably be applied. Philip assembled his Macedonian empire and gave it to his son, to be later combined with the Persian subassembly and others into Alexander's greater system. On Alexander's death, his empire did not crumble to dust but fragmented into some of the major subsystems that had composed it.

The watchmaker argument implies that if one would be Alexander, one should be born into a world where large stable political systems already exist. Where this condition was not fulfilled, as on the Scythian and Indian frontiers, Alexander found empire building a slippery business. So too, T. E. Lawrence's organizing of the Arabian revolt against stable building blocks, the separate, suspicious desert tribes.

The profession of history places a greater value upon the validated particular fact than upon tendentious generalization. I shall not elaborate upon my fancy, therefore, but shall leave it to historians to decide whether anything can be learned for the interpretation of history from an abstract theory of hierarchic complex systems.

Conclusion: The Evolutionary Explanation of Hierarchy

We have shown thus far that complex systems will evolve from simple systems much more rapidly if there are stable intermediate forms than if there are not. The resulting complex forms in the former case will be hierarchic. We have only to turn the argument around to explain the observed predominance of hierarchies among the complex systems nature presents to us. Among possible complex forms, hierarchies are the ones that have the time to evolve. The hypothesis that complexity will be hierarchic makes no distinction among very flat hierarchies, like crystals and tissues and polymers, and the intermediate forms. Indeed, in the complex systems we encounter in nature, examples of both forms are prominent. A more complete theory than the one we have developed here would presumably have something to say about the determinants of width of span in these systems.

Nearly Decomposable Systems

In hierarchic systems, we can distinguish between the interactions *among* subsystems, on the one hand, and the interactions *within* subsystems—that is, among the parts of those subsystems—on the other. The interactions at the different levels may be, and often will be, of different orders of magnitude. In a formal organization there will generally be more interaction, on the average, between two employees who are members of the same department than between two employees from different departments. In organic substances, intermolecular forces will generally be weaker than molecular forces, and molecular forces weaker than nuclear forces.

In a rare gas, the intermolecular forces will be negligible compared to those binding the molecules—we can treat the individual particles, for many purposes, as if they were independent of each other. We can describe such a system as *decomposable* into the subsystems comprised of the individual particles. As the gas becomes denser, molecular interactions become more significant. But over some range, we can treat the decomposable case as a limit and as a first approximation. We can use a theory of perfect gases, for example, to describe approximately the behavior of actual gases if they are not too dense. As a second approximation, we may move to a theory of *nearly decomposable* systems, in which the interactions among the subsystems are weak but not negligible.

At least some kinds of hierarchic systems can be approximated successfully as nearly decomposable systems. The main theoretical findings from the approach can be summed up in two propositions: *(a)* in a nearly decomposable system, the short-run behavior of each of the component subsystems is approximately independent of the short-run behavior of the other components; *(b)* in the long run, the behavior of any one of the components depends in only an aggregate way on the behavior of the other components.

Let me provide a very concrete simple example of a nearly decomposable system.[15] Consider a building whose outside walls provide perfect thermal insulation from the environment. We shall take these walls as the boundary of our system. The building is divided into a large number of rooms, the walls between them being good, but not perfect, insulators. The walls between rooms are the boundaries of our major subsystems. Each room is divided by partitions into a number of cubicles, but the partitions are poor

15. This discussion of near decomposability is based upon H. A. Simon and A. Ando, "Aggregation of Variables in Dynamic Systems," *Econometrica* 29 (April 1961): 111–38. The example is drawn from the same source, pp. 117–18. The theory has been further developed and applied to a variety of economic and political phenomena by Ando and F. M. Fisher. See F. M. Fisher, "On the Cost of Approximate Specification in Simultaneous Equation Estimation," *Econometrica* 29 (April 1961): 139–70, and F. M. Fisher and A. Ando, "Two Theorems on *Ceteris Paribus* in the Analysis of Dynamic Systems," *American Political Science Review* 61 (March 1962): 103–13.

insulators. A thermometer hangs in each cubicle. Suppose that at the time of our first observation of the system there is a wide variation in temperature from cubicle to cubicle and from room to room—the various cubicles within the building are in a state of thermal disequilibrium. When we take new temperature readings several hours later, what shall we find? There will be very little variation in temperature among the cubicles within each single room, but there may still be large temperature variations *among* rooms. When we take readings again several days later, we find an almost uniform temperature throughout the building; the temperature differences among rooms have virtually disappeared.

We can describe the process of equilibration formally by setting up the usual equations of heat flow. The equations can be represented by the matrix of their coefficients, r_{ij}, where r_{ij} is the rate at which heat flows from the ith cubicle to the jth cubicle per degree difference in their temperatures. If cubicles i and j do not have a common wall, r_{ij} will be zero. If cubicles i and j have a common wall and are in the same room, r_{ij} will be large. If cubicles i and j are separated by the wall of a room, r_{ij} will be nonzero but small. Hence, by grouping together all the cubicles that are in the same room, we can arrange the matrix of coefficients so that all its large elements lie inside a string of square submatrices along the main diagonal. All the elements outside these diagonal squares will be either zero or small (see figure 1). We may take some small number, ϵ, as the upper bond of the extradiagonal elements. We shall call a matrix having these properties a *nearly decomposable matrix*.

Now it has been proved that a dynamic system that can be described by a nearly decomposable matrix has the properties, stated earlier, of a nearly decomposable system. In our simple example of heat flow this means that in the short run each room will reach an equilibrium temperature (an average of the initial temperatures of its offices) nearly independently of the others; and that each room will remain approximately in a state of equilibrium over the longer period during which an overall temperature equilibrium is being established throughout the building. After the intraroom short-run equilibria have been reached, a single thermometer in each room will be adequate to describe the dynamic behavior of the entire system—separate thermometers in each cubicle will be superfluous.

Near Decomposability of Social Systems

As a glance at figure 1 shows, near decomposability is a

	A1	A2	A3	B1	B2	C1	C2	C3
A1	–	100	–	2	–	–	–	–
A2	100	–	100	1	1	–	–	–
A3	–	100	–	–	2	–	–	–
B1	2	1	–	–	100	2	1	–
B2	–	1	2	100	–	–	1	2
C1	–	–	–	2	–	–	100	–
C2	–	–	–	1	1	100	–	100
C3	–	–	–	–	2	–	100	–

Fig. 1. A Hypothetical Nearly Decomposable System
In terms of the heat-exchange example of the text, A1, A2, and A3 may be interpreted as cubicles in one room, B1 and B2 as cubicles in a second room, and C1, C2, and C3 as cubicles in a third. The matrix entries then are the heat diffusion coefficients between cubicles.

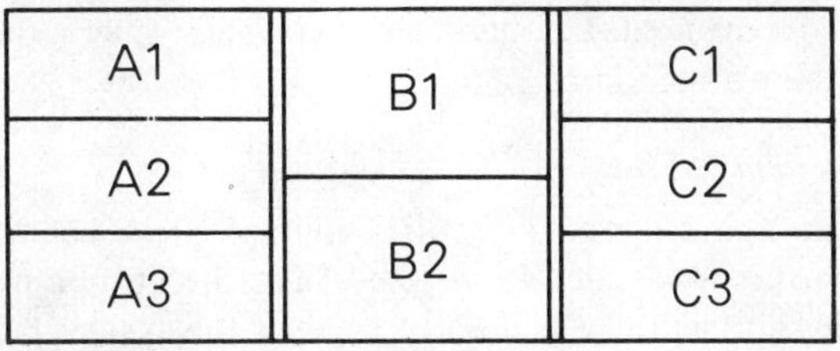

rather strong property for a matrix to possess, and the matrices that have this property will describe very special dynamic systems—vanishingly few systems out of all those that are thinkable. How few they will be depends, of course, on how good an approximation we insist upon. If we demand that epsilon be very small, correspondingly few dynamic systems will fit the definition. But we have already seen that in the natural world nearly decomposable systems are far from rare. On the contrary, systems in which each variable is linked with most equal strength with almost all other parts of the system are far rarer and less typical.

In economic dynamics, the main variables are the prices and quantities of commodities. It is empirically true that the price of any given commodity and the rate at which it is exchanged depend to a significant extent only on the prices and quantities of a few other commodities, together with a few other aggregate magnitudes, like the average price level or some overall measure of economic activity. The large linkage coefficients are associated, in general, with the main flows of raw materials and semifinished products within and between industries. An input-output matrix of the economy, giving the magnitudes of these flows, reveals the nearly decomposable structure of the system—with one qualification. There is a consumption subsystem of the economy that is linked strongly to variables in most of the other subsystems. Hence, we have to modify our notions of decomposability slightly to accommodate the special role of the consumption subsystem in our analysis of the dynamic behavior of the economy.

In the dynamics of social systems, where members of a system communicate with and influence other members, near decomposability is generally very prominent. This is most obvious in formal organizations, where the formal authority relation connects each member of the organization with one immediate superior and with a small number of subordinates. Of course, many communications in organizations follow other channels than the lines of formal authority. But most of these channels lead from any particular individual to a very limited number of his superiors, subordinates, and associates. Hence, departmental boundaries play very much the same role as the walls in our heat example.

Physicochemical Systems

In the complex systems familiar in biological chemistry, a similar structure is clearly visible. Take the atomic nuclei in such a system as the elementary parts of the system, and construct a matrix of bond strengths between elements. There will be matrix elements of quite different orders of magnitude. The largest will generally correspond to the covalent bonds, the next to the ionic bonds, the third group to hydrogen bonds, still smaller linkages to van der Waals forces.[16] If we select an epsilon just a little smaller than the magnitude of a covalent bond, the system will decompose into subsystems—the constituent molecules. The smaller linkages will correspond to the intermolecular bonds.

It is well known that high-energy, high-frequency vibrations are associated with the smaller physical subsystems,

16. For a survey of the several classes of molecular and intermolecular forces, and their dissociation energies, see Setlow and Pollard, *Molecular Biophysics,* chap. 6. The energies of typical covalent bonds are of the order of 80–100 k cal/mole, of the hydrogen bonds, 10 K cal/mole. Ionic bonds generally lie between these two levels; the bonds due to van der Waals forces are lower in energy.

low-frequency vibrations with the larger systems into which the subsystems are assembled. For example, the radiation frequencies associated with molecular vibrations are much lower than those associated with the vibrations of the planetary electrons of the atoms; the latter, in turn, are lower than those associated with nuclear processes.[17] Molecular systems are nearly decomposable systems, the short-run dynamics relating to the internal structures of the subsystems, the long-run dynamics to the interactions of these subsystems.

A number of the important approximations employed in physics depend for their validity on the near decomposability of the systems studied. The theory of the thermodynamics of irreversible processes, for example, requires the assumption of macroscopic disequilibrium but microscopic equilibrium,[18] exactly the situation described in our heat-exchange example. Similarly, computations in quantum mechanics are often handled by treating weak interactions as producing perturbations on a system of strong interactions.

Some Observations on Hierarchic Span

To understand why the span of hierarchies is sometimes very broad—as in crystals—and sometimes narrow, we need to examine more detail of the interactions. In general, the critical consideration is the extent to which interaction between two (or a few) subsystems excludes interaction of these subsystems with the others. Let us examine first some physical examples.

Consider a gas of identical molecules, each of which can form covalent bonds, in certain ways, with others. Let us suppose that we can associate with each atom a specific number of bonds that it is capable of maintaining simultaneously. (This number is obviously related to the number we usually call its valence.) Now suppose that two atoms join and that we can also associate with the combination a specific number of external bonds it is capable of maintaining. If this number is the same as the number associated with the individual

17. Typical wave numbers for vibrations associated with various systems (the wave number is the reciprocal of wave length hence proportional to frequency):

steel wire under tension—10^{-10} to 10^{-9} cm^{-1}
molecular rotations—10^{0} to 10^{2} cm^{-1}
molecular vibrations—10^{2} to 10^{3} cm^{-1}
planetary electrons—10^{4} to 10^{5} cm^{-1}
nuclear rotations—10^{9} to 10^{10} cm^{-1}
nuclear surface vibrations—10^{11} to 10^{12} cm^{-1}

18. S. R. de Groot, *Thermodynamics of Irreversible Processes* (New York: Interscience Publishers, 1951), pp. 11–12.

atoms, the bonding process can go on indefinitely—the atoms can form crystals or polymers of indefinite extent. If the number of bonds of which the composite is capable is less than the number associated with each of the parts, then the process of agglomeration must come to a halt.

We need only mention some elementary examples. Ordinary gases show no tendency to agglomerate, because the multiple bonding of atoms "uses up" their capacity to interact. While each oxygen atom has a valence of two, the O_2 molecules have a zero valence. Contrariwise, indefinite chains of single-bonded carbon atoms can be built up, because a chain of any number of such atoms, each with two side groups, has a valence of exactly two.

Now what happens if we have a system of elements that possess both strong and weak interaction capacities and whose strong bonds are exhaustible through combination? Subsystems will form, until all the capacity for strong interaction is utilized in their construction. Then these subsystems will be linked by the weaker second-order bonds into larger systems. For example, a water molecule has essentially a valence of zero—all the potential covalent bonds are fully occupied by the interaction of hydrogen and oxygen molecules. But the geometry of the molecule creates an electric dipole that permits weak interaction between the water and salts dissolved in it—whence such phenomena as its electrolytic conductivity.[19]

Similarly, it has been observed that, although electrical forces are much stronger than gravitational forces, the latter are far more important than the former for systems on an astronomical scale. The explanation, of course, is that the electrical forces, being bipolar, are all "used up" in the linkages of the smaller subsystems, and that significant net balances of positive or negative charges are not generally found in regions of macroscopic size.

In social as in physical systems there are generally limits on the simultaneous interaction of large numbers of subsystems. In the social case, these limits are related to the fact that a human being is more nearly a serial than a parallel information-processing system. He can carry on only one conversation at a time, and although this does not limit the size of the audience to which a mass communication can be addressed, it does limit the number of people simultaneously involved in most other forms of social interaction. Apart from requirements of direct interactions, most roles impose

19. See, for example, L. Pauling, *General Chemistry*, 2d ed. (San Francisco: W. H. Freeman, 1953), chap. 15.

tasks and responsibilities that are time consuming. One cannot, for example, enact the role of "friend" with large numbers of other people.

It is probably true that in social as in physical systems, the higher-frequency dynamics are associated with the sub-systems, the lower-frequency dynamics with the larger systems. It is generally believed, for example, that the relevant planning horizon of executives is longer, the higher their location in the organizational hierarchy. It is probably also true that both the average duration of an interaction between executives and the average interval between interactions are greater at higher than at lower levels.

Summary: Near Decomposability

We have seen that hierarchies have the property of near decomposability. Intracomponent linkages are generally stronger than intercomponent linkages. This fact has the effect of separating the high-frequency dynamics of a hierarchy —involving the internal structure of the components—from the low-frequency dynamics—involving interaction among components. We shall turn next to some important consequences of this separation for the description and comprehension of complex systems.

The Description of Complexity

If you ask a person to draw a complex object—such as a human face—he will almost always proceed in a hierarchic fashion.[20] First he will outline the face. Then he will add or insert features: eyes, nose, mouth, ears, hair. If asked to elaborate, he will begin to develop details for each of the features —pupils, eyelids, lashes for the eyes, and so on—until he reaches the limits of his anatomical knowledge. His information about the object is arranged hierarchically in memory, like a topical outline.

When information is put in outline form, it is easy to include information about the relations among the major parts and information about the internal relations of parts in each of the suboutlines. Detailed information about the relations of subparts belonging to different parts has no place in the outline and is likely to be lost. The loss of such information and the preservation mainly of information about hierarchic order is a salient characteristic that distinguishes the

20. George A. Miller has collected protocols from subjects who were given the task of drawing faces and finds that they behave in the manner described here (private communication). See also E. H. Gombrich, *Art and Illusion* (New York: Pantheon Books, 1960), pp. 291–96.

drawings of a child or someone untrained in representation from the drawing of a trained artist. (I am speaking of an artist who is striving for representation.)

Near Decomposability and Comprehensibility

From our discussion of the dynamic properties of nearly decomposable systems, we have seen that comparatively little information is lost by representing them as hierarchies. Subparts belonging to different parts only interact in an aggregative fashion—the detail of their interaction can be ignored. In studying the interaction of two large molecules, generally we do not need to consider in detail the interactions of nuclei of the atoms belonging to the one molecule with the nuclei of the atoms belonging to the other. In studying the interaction of two nations, we do not need to study in detail the interactions of each citizen of the first with each citizen of the second.

The fact, then, that many complex systems have a nearly decomposable, hierarchic structure is a major facilitating factor enabling us to understand, to describe, and even to "see" such systems and their parts. Or perhaps the proposition should be put the other way round. If there are important systems in the world that are complex without being hierarchic, they may to a considerable extent escape our observation and our understanding. Analysis of their behavior would involve such detailed knowledge and calculation of the interactions of their elementary parts that it would be beyond our capacities of memory or computation.[21]

21. I believe the fallacy in the central thesis of W. M. Elsasser's *The Physical Foundation of Biology*, memtioned earlier, lies in his ignoring the simplification in description of complex systems that derives from their hierarchic structure. Thus (p. 155):

"If we now apply similar arguments to the coupling of enzymatic reactions with the substratum of protein molecules, we see that over a sufficient period of time, the information corresponding to the structural details of these molecules will be communicated to the dynamics of the cell, to higher levels of organization as it were, and may influence such dynamics. While this reasoning is only qualitative, it lends credence to the assumption that in the living organism, unlike the inorganic crystal, the effects of microscopic structure cannot be simply averaged out; as time goes on this influence will pervade the behavior of the cell 'at all levels.' "

But from our discussion of near decomposability, it would appear that those aspects of microstructure that control the slow developmental aspects of organismic dynamics can be separated out from the aspects that control the more rapid cellular metabolic processes. For this reason we should not despair of unraveling the web of causes. See also J. R. Platt's review of Elsasser's book in *Perspectives in Biology and Medicine* 2 (1959): 243–45.

I shall not try to settle which is chicken and which is egg: whether we are able to understand the world because it is hierarchic or whether it appears hierarchic because those aspects of it which are not hierarchic elude our understanding and observation. I have already given some reasons for supposing that the former is at least half the truth—that evolving complexity would tend to be hierarchic—but it may not be the whole truth.

Simple Descriptions of Complex Systems

One might suppose that the description of a complex system would itself be a complex structure of symbols—and indeed, it may be just that. But there is no conservation law that requires that the description be as cumbersome as the object described. A trivial example will show how a system can be described economically. Suppose the system is a two-dimensional array like this:

$$A\ B\ M\ N\ R\ S\ H\ I$$
$$C\ D\ O\ P\ T\ U\ J\ K$$
$$M\ N\ A\ B\ H\ I\ R\ S$$
$$O\ P\ C\ D\ J\ K\ T\ U$$
$$R\ S\ H\ I\ A\ B\ M\ N$$
$$T\ U\ J\ K\ C\ D\ O\ P$$
$$H\ I\ R\ S\ M\ N\ A\ B$$
$$J\ K\ T\ U\ O\ P\ C\ D$$

Let us call the array $\begin{vmatrix} AB \\ CD \end{vmatrix}$ a, the array $\begin{vmatrix} MN \\ O\ P \end{vmatrix}$ m, the array $\begin{vmatrix} RS \\ TU \end{vmatrix}$ r, and the array $\begin{vmatrix} HI \\ JK \end{vmatrix}$ h. Let us call the array $\begin{vmatrix} am \\ ma \end{vmatrix}$ w, and the array $\begin{vmatrix} rh \\ hr \end{vmatrix}$ x. Then the entire array is simply $\begin{vmatrix} wx \\ xw \end{vmatrix}$. While the original structure consisted of sixty-four symbols, it requires only thirty-five to write down its description:

$$S = \frac{wx}{xw}$$

$$w = \frac{am}{ma} \qquad\qquad x = \frac{rh}{hr}$$

$$a = \frac{AB}{CD} \qquad m = \frac{MN}{OP} \qquad\qquad r = \frac{RS}{TU} \qquad h = \frac{HI}{JK}$$

We achieve the abbreviation by making use of the redundancy in the original structure. Since the pattern $\frac{AB}{CD}$, for example, occurs four times in the total pattern, it is economical to represent it by the single symbol, a.

If a complex structure is completely unredundant—if no aspect of its structure can be inferred from any other—then it is its own simplest description. We can exhibit it, but we cannot describe it by a simpler structure. The hierarchic structures we have been discussing have a high degree of redundancy, hence can often be described in economical terms. The redundancy takes a number of forms, of which I shall mention three:

1. Hierarchic systems are usually composed of only a few different kinds of subsystems, in various combinations and arrangements. A familiar example is the proteins, their multitudinous variety arising from arrangements of only twenty different amino acids. Similarly, the ninety-odd elements provide all the kinds of building blocks needed for an infinite variety of molecules. Hence, we can construct our description from a restricted alphabet of elementary terms corresponding to the basic set of elementary subsystems from which the complex system is generated.

2. Hierarchic systems are, as we have seen, often nearly decomposable. Hence only aggregative properties of their parts enter into the description of the interactions of those parts. A generalization of the notion of near decomposability might be called the "empty world hypothesis"—most things are only weakly connected with most other things; for a tolerable description of reality only a tiny fraction of all possible interactions needs to be taken into account. By adopting a descriptive language that allows the absence of something to go unmentioned, a nearly empty world can be described quite concisely. Mother Hubbard did not have to check off the list of possible contents to say that her cupboard was bare.

3. By appropriate "recoding," the redundancy that is present but unobvious in the structure of a complex system can often be made patent. The commonest recoding of descriptions of dynamic systems consists in replacing a description of the time path with a description of a differential law that generates that path. The simplicity, that is, resides in a constant relation between the state of the system at any given time and the state of the system a short time later. Thus, the structure of the sequence 1 3 5 7 9 11 . . . is

most simply expressed by observing that each member is obtained by adding 2 to the previous one. But this is the sequence that Galileo found to describe the velocity at the end of successive time intervals of a ball rolling down an inclined plane.

It is a familiar proposition that the task of science is to make use of the world's redundancy to describe that world simply. I shall not pursue the general methodological point here, but I shall instead take a closer look at two main types of description that seem to be available to us in seeking an understanding of complex systems. I shall call these *state description* and *process description,* respectively.

State Descriptions and Process Descriptions

"A circle is the locus of all points equidistant from a given point." "To construct a circle, rotate a compass with one arm fixed until the other arm has returned to its starting point." It is implicit in Euclid that if you carry out the process specified in the second sentence, you will produce an object that satisfies the definition of the first. The first sentence is a state description of a circle, the second a process description.

These two modes of apprehending structures are the warp and weft of our experience. Pictures, blueprints, most diagrams, and chemical structural formulas are state descriptions. Recipes, differential equations, and equations for chemical reactions are process descriptions. The former characterize the world as sensed; they provide the criteria for identifying objects, often by modeling the objects themselves. The latter characterize the world as acted upon; they provide the means for producing or generating objects having the desired characteristics.

The distinction between the world as sensed and the world as acted upon defines the basic condition for the survival of adaptive organisms. The organism must develop correlations between goals in the sensed world and actions in the world of process. When they are made conscious and verbalized, these correlations correspond to what we usually call means-end analysis. Given a desired state of affairs and an existing state of affairs, the task of an adaptive organism is to find the difference between these two states and then to find the correlating process that will erase the difference.[22]

Thus, problem solving requires continual translation be-

22. See H. A. Simon and A. Newell, "Simulation of Human Thinking," in M. Greenberger, ed., *Management and the Computer of the Future* (New York: Wiley, 1962), pp. 95–114, esp. pp. 110 ff.

tween the state and process descriptions of the same complex reality. Plato, in the *Meno*, argued that all learning is remembering. He could not otherwise explain how we can discover or recognize the answer to a problem unless we already know the answer.[23] Our dual relation to the world is the source and solution of the paradox. We pose a problem by giving the state description of the solution. The task is to discover a sequence of processes that will produce the goal state from an initial state. Translation from the process description to the state description enables us to recognize when we have succeeded. The solution is genuinely new to us—and we do not need Plato's theory of remembering to explain how we recognize it.

There is now a growing body of evidence that the activity called human problem solving is basically a form of means-end analysis that aims at discovering a process description of the path that leads to a desired goal. The general paradigm is: given a blueprint, to find the corresponding recipe. Much of the activity of science is an application of that paradigm: given the description of some natural phenomena, to find the differential equations for processes that will produce the phenomena.

The Description of Complexity in Self-Reproducing Systems

The problem of finding relatively simple descriptions for complex systems is of interest not only for an understanding of human knowledge of the world but also for an explanation of how a complex system can reproduce itself. In my discussion of the evolution of complex systems, I touched only briefly on the role of self-reproduction.

Atoms of high atomic weight and complex inorganic molecules are witnesses to the fact that the evolution of complexity does not imply self-reproduction. If evolution of complexity from simplicity is sufficiently probable, it will occur repeatedly; the statistical equilibrium of the system will find a large fraction of the elementary particles participating in complex systems.

If, however, the existence of a particular complex form increased the probability of the creation of another form just like it, the equilibrium between complexes and components could be greatly altered in favor of the former. If we have a description of an object that is sufficiently clear and complete, we can reproduce the object from the description.

23. *The Works of Plato*, trans. B. Jowett, vol. 3 (New York: Dial Press, 1936), pp. 26–35.

Whatever the exact mechanism of reproduction, the description provides us with the necessary information.

Now we have seen that the descriptions of complex systems can take many forms. In particular, we can have state descriptions, or we can have process descriptions—blueprints or recipes. Reproductive processes could be built around either of these sources of information. Perhaps the simplest possibility is for the complex system to serve as a description of itself—a template on which a copy can be formed. One of the most plausible current theories, for example, of the reproduction of deoxyribonucleic acid (DNA) proposes that a DNA molecule, in the form of a double helix of matching parts (each essentially a "negative" of the other), unwinds to allow each half of the helix to serve as a template on which a new matching half can form.

On the other hand, our current knowledge of how DNA controls the metabolism of the organism suggests that reproduction by template is only one of the processes involved. According to the prevailing theory, DNA serves as a template both for itself and for the related substance ribonucleic acid (RNA). RNA, in turn, serves as a template for protein. But proteins—according to current knowledge—guide the organism's metabolism not by the template method but by serving as catalysts to govern reaction rates in the cell. While RNA is a blueprint for protein, protein is a recipe for metabolism.[24]

Ontogeny Recapitulates Phylogeny

The DNA in the chromosomes of an organism contains some, and perhaps most, of the information that is needed to determine its development and activity. We have seen that, if current theories are even approximately correct, the information is recorded not as a state description of the organism but as a series of "instructions" for the construction and maintenance of the organism from nutrient materials. I have already used the metaphor of a recipe; I could equally well compare it with a computer program, which is also a sequence of instructions, governing the construction of symbolic structures. Let me spin out some of the consequences of the latter comparison.

24. C. B. Anfinsen, *The Molecular Basis of Evolution* (New York: Wiley, 1959), chaps. 3 and 10, will qualify this sketchy, oversimplified account. For an imaginative discussion of some mechanisms of process description that could govern molecular structure, see H. H. Pattee, "On the Origin of Macromolecular Sequences," *Biophysical Journal* 1(1961):683–710.

If genetic material is a program—viewed in its relation to the organism—it is a program with special and peculiar properties. First, it is a self-reproducing program; we have already considered its possible copying mechanism. Second, it is a program that has developed by Darwinian evolution. On the basis of our watchmaker's argument, we may assert that many of its ancestors were also viable programs—programs for the subassemblies.

Are there any other conjectures we can make about the structure of this program? There is a well-known generalization in biology that is verbally so neat that we would be reluctant to give it up even if the facts did not support it: ontogeny recapitulates phylogeny. The individual organism, in its development, goes through stages that resemble some of its ancestral forms. The fact that the human embryo develops gill bars and then modifies them for other purposes is a familiar particular belonging to the generalization. Biologists today like to emphasize the qualifications of the principle—that ontogeny recapitulates only the grossest aspects of phylogeny, and these only crudely. These qualifications should not make us lose sight of the fact that the generalization does hold in rough approximation—it does summarize a very significant set of facts about the organism's development. How can we interpret these facts?

One way to solve a complex problem is to reduce it to a problem previously solved—to show what steps lead from the earlier solution to a solution of the new problem. If, around the turn of the century, we wanted to instruct a workman to make an automobile, perhaps the simplest way would have been to tell him how to modify a wagon by removing the singletree and adding a motor and transmission. Similarly, a genetic program could be altered in the course of evolution by adding new processes that would modify a simpler form into a more complex one—to construct a gastrula, take a blastula and alter it!

The genetic description of a single cell may, therefore, take a quite different form from the genetic description that assembles cells into a multicelled organism. Multiplication by cell division would require, as a minimum, a state description (the DNA, say), and a simple "interpretive process"—to use the term from computer language—that copies this description as a part of the larger copying process of cell division. But such a mechanism clearly would not suffice for the differentiation of cells in development. It appears more natural to conceptualize that mechanism as based on a process description, and a somewhat more complex interpretive process that produces the adult organism in a sequence of stages, each new stage in development representing the effect of an operator upon the previous one.

It is harder to conceptualize the interrelation of these two descriptions. Interrelated they must be, for enough has been learned of gene-enzyme mechanisms to show that these play a major role in development, as in cell metabolism. The single clue we obtain from our earlier discussion is that the description may itself be hierarchical, or nearly decomposable, in structure, the lower levels governing the fast, "high-frequency" dynamics of the individual cell, the higher-level interactions governing the slow, "low-frequency" dynamics of the developing multicellular organism.

There are only bits of evidence, apart from the facts of recapitulation, that the genetic program is organized in this way, but such evidence as exists is compatible with this notion.[25] To the extent that we can differentiate the genetic information that governs cell metabolism from the genetic information that governs the development of differentiated cells in the multicellular organization, we simplify enormously—as we have already seen—our task of theoretical description. But I have perhaps pressed this speculation far enough.

The generalization that, in evolving systems whose descriptions are stored in a process language, we might expect ontogeny partially to recapitulate phylogeny has applications outside the realm of biology. It can be applied as readily, for example, to the transmission of knowledge in the educational process. In most subjects, particularly in the rapidly

25. There is considerable evidence that successive genes along a chromosome often determine enzymes controlling successive stages of protein syntheses. For a review of some of this evidence, see P. E. Hartman, "Transduction: A Comparative Review," in W. D. McElroy and B. Glass, eds., *The Chemical Basis of Heredity* (Baltimore: Johns Hopkins Press, 1957), at pp. 442–54. Evidence for differential activity of genes in different tissues and at different stages of development is discussed by J. G. Gall, "Chromosomal Differentiation," in W. D. McElroy and B. Glass, eds., *The Chemical Basis of Development* (Baltimore: Johns Hopkins Press, 1958), at pp. 103–35. Finally, a model very like that proposed here has been independently, and far more fully, outlined by J. R. Platt, "A 'Book Model' of Genetic Information Transfer in Cells and Tissues," in M. Kasha and B. Pullman, eds., *Horizons in Biochemistry* (New York: Academic Press, 1962). Of course, this kind of mechanism is not the only one in which development could be controlled by a process description. Induction, in the form envisaged in Spemann's organizer theory, is based on process description, in which metabolites in already formed tissue control the next stages of development.

advancing sciences, the progress from elementary to advanced courses is to a considerable extent a progress through the conceptual history of the science itself. Fortunately, the recapitulation is seldom literal—any more than it is in the biological case. We do not teach the phlogiston theory in chemistry in order later to correct it. (I am not sure I could not cite examples in other subjects where we do exactly that.) But curriculum revisions that rid us of the accumulations of the past are infrequent and painful. Nor are they always desirable—partial recapitulation may, in many instances, provide the most expeditious route to advanced knowledge.

Summary: The Description of Complexity

How complex or simple a structure is depends critically upon the way in which we describe it. Most of the complex structures found in the world are enormously redundant, and we can use this redundancy to simplify their description. But to use it, to achieve the simplification, we must find the right representation.

The notion of substituting a process description for a state description of nature has played a central role in the development of modern science. Dynamic laws, expressed in the form of systems of differential or difference equations, have in a large number of cases provided the clue for the simple description of the complex. In the preceding paragraphs I have tried to show that this characteristic of scientific inquiry is not accidental or superficial. The correlation between state description and process description is basic to the functioning of any adaptive organism, to its capacity for acting purposefully upon its environment. Our present-day understanding of genetic mechanisms suggests that even in describing itself the multicellular organism finds a process description—a genetically encoded program—to be the parsimonious and useful representation.

Conclusion

Our speculations have carried us over a rather alarming array of topics, but that is the price we must pay if we wish to seek properties common to many sorts of complex systems. My thesis has been that one path to the construction of a nontrivial theory of complex systems is by way of a theory of hierarchy. Empirically, a large proportion of the complex systems we observe in nature exhibit hierarchic structure. On theoretical grounds we could expect complex systems to be hierarchies in a world in which complexity had to evolve from simplicity. In their dynamics, hierarchies have a property, near decomposability, that greatly simplifies their behavior. Near decomposability also simplifies the description of a complex system and makes it easier to understand how the information needed for the development of reproduction of the system can be stored in reasonable compass.

In both science and engineering, the study of "systems" is an increasingly popular activity. Its popularity is more a response to a pressing need for synthesizing and analyzing complexity than it is to any large development of a body of knowledge and technique for dealing with complexity. If this popularity is to be more than a fad, necessity will have to mother invention and provide substance to go with the name. The explorations reviewed here represent one particular direction of search for such substance.

The Creative
Organization
Gary A. Steiner

Definitions

First, a few words about what the key terms in this summary mean: "Creativity" has been defined in a number of ways in the psychological literature, in business discussion, in the arts and sciences generally. Within the transcript of this seminar there appear many explicit, and many more implicit, definitions of varying degrees of generality. We make no attempt to frame a master definition at this point. But for purposes of this overview, it is necessary and hopefully sufficient to make this general distinction: *Creativity* has to do with the development, proposal, and implementation of *new* and *better* solutions; *productivity,* with the efficient application of *current* "solutions."

What "better" means, and who is to say, is one of the sticky methodological issues in the field. What it most often means in these pages is better according to professional colleagues or superiors. The meaning of "solution" obviously varies by field; in the following, solutions range from practical answers to specific problems through new concepts in art, music, or architecture to the most general and abstract conceptualizations that characterize a breakthrough in, say, theoretical physics.

Many of the studies we will cite distinguish "high-creative" from "low-" or "average-creative" groups. It should be clear that "high" and "low" are relative, and not absolute, designations. In most of the samples under investigation, both "high" and "low groups would qualify as highly creative within the population at large and often even within the profession. It would therefore not have been euphemistic—just too clumsy—to use the designations "more highly" and "less

Reprinted in somewhat abridged form from Gary A. Steiner, *The Creative Organization* (Chicago: University of Chicago Press, 1965), Introduction, by permission of the publisher. © 1965 by The University of Chicago.

highly" creative. Bear in mind, though, that this is what the shorthand distinction between "high" and "low" means.

1. The Raw Material: Individual Creativity

Do individual differences in creativity exist? Does it make sense to speak of more and less creative people in some such way as we speak of more and less intelligent, more or less co-ordinated, or more or less musical people? Or is personal creativity, like fathering twins, mostly a matter of being in the right place at the right time?

As important as circumstances are in determining who will create what and when, it seems that there are consistent and persistent differences in individual creativity. Holding conditions constant, some people are likely to be more creative than others; and these differences are likely to show up in other situations and at other times. In fact, in most fields, the distribution of creative contributions is something like the distribution of personal income in the United States: a small percentage of people accounts for a large share of the total.

Are these differences in personal creativity specific to particular areas of endeavor, or is there such a thing as general creativity?

That issue involves the distinction between *capacity* and *performance*. Except for a few outstanding historical examples, the most creative people in one field are not likely at the same time to be the most creative in another. But this may be largely a matter of specialization in training and effort. Is an unusually creative architect likely to be highly creative in chemistry also, assuming equal training and opportunity? And are highly creative architects, or chemists, distinguished only by greater creativity in their respective professions, or can they be distinguished from their less creative colleagues in personal capacities and characteristics beyond differential performance on the job?

The results of various testing programs suggest that the qualities and capacities that distinguish more from less creative practitioners of given fields *do* extend beyond the specific area of professional competence. Creative architects, for instance, differ not only in the way they approach architecture but also in the way they approach any number of situations and tasks, some far removed and apparently unrelated to the specific demands of their profession.

What is more, there seem to be at least some differences that hold across diverse fields; for example, some of the same personality characteristics that distinguish between architects of high and average creativity have been observed in studies of creativity not only in industrial research chemists, but even among high school children differing in general creativity.

Granted that people differ in "creativity," are we really talking about anything more than general intelligence?

Yes. General intelligence seems to bear about the same relationship to on-the-job creativity at the professional level as weight does to ability in football. You have to have a lot of it to be in the game at all; but among those on the team— all of whom have a great deal of weight to begin with—differences in performance are only slightly, if at all, related to weight. In short, in the total population, creativity in most fields is associated with high intelligence, probably more so in some (e.g., physics) than in others (art). But within a given group of practitioners, operating at roughly the same professional level, differences in general intelligence provide no significant prediction of differences in creative performance.

What, then, are the characteristics of the creative individual, especially those that might be subject to measurement before the fact so as to make prediction possible?

Although many characteristics of the creative individual, perhaps some of the most important, undoubtedly vary according to the area of creativity, studies of "highs" and "lows" in various fields are beginning to yield some common denominators. The following list concentrates on those differences that are probably more general. In some cases, this assumption of generality stems only from the fact that it seems reasonable on analysis of the characteristics involved vis-à-vis the general demands of the creative process. In others, the generality of the finding is actually supported by research from independent studies in diverse areas.

Intellectual Characteristics

Although measures of general intelligence fail to predict creativity, highs, as a group, typically outscore lows in tests of the following mental abilities:

Conceptual Fluency. The ability to generate a large number of ideas rapidly: List tools beginning with the letter "t"; novel uses for a brick; possible consequences of a situation; categories into which the names of a thousand great men can be sorted—to name just a few of the tasks that have actually been used.

Conceptual Flexibility. The ability to shift gears, to discard one frame of reference for another; the tendency to change approaches spontaneously.

Originality. The ability and/or tendency to give unusual, atypical (therefore more probably new) answers to questions, responses to situations, interpretations of events.

Highs, for instance, are more apt to give rare—as well as more—uses of bricks; they give fewer "popular" interpretations of what an inkblot looks like; in high school, uncommon vs. common career aspirations (e.g., explorer rather than lawyer).

Preference for Complexity. Highs often exhibit a preference for the complex, and to them intriguing, as against the simple and easily understood.

When confronted with complex inkblots, for instance, they tend to seek a more difficult "whole" interpretation that takes the entire blot into account, rather than to identify detailed aspects that clearly resemble certain things.

The usual interpretation is that highs take complexity as a challenge, that they enjoy the attempt to integrate and resolve it.

Personality

Several closely related personality characteristics distinguish highs and lows in a number of studies:

Independence of Judgment. Highs are more apt to stick to their guns when they find themselves in disagreement with others.

In a situation where an artificially induced group consensus contradicts the evidence of their own senses, lows more often yield in their expressed judgment. The same is true when the issue at stake is not a factual one but involves voicing an opinion on an aesthetic, social, or political matter.

Deviance. Highs see themselves as more different from their peers and, in fact, they appear to *be* more different in any number of significant as well as trivial characteristics.

At the extreme, highs sometimes feel lonely and apart, with a sense of mission that isolates them, in their own minds, from average men with average concerns.

Attitudes toward Authority. A related distinction with far-reaching implications for organizations has to do with the way authority is viewed. The difference between highs and lows is a matter of degree, but to make the point we describe the extremes.

Lows are more apt to view authority as final and absolute; to offer unquestioning obedience, allegiance, or belief (as the case may be), with respect approaching deference; to accept present authority as "given" and more or less permanent.

Highs are more likely to think of authority as conventional or arbitrary, contingent on continued and demonstrable superiority; to accept dependence on authority as a matter of expedience rather than personal allegiance or moral obligation; to view present authority as temporary.

Attitudes toward subordinates are related in the appropriate direction; those who pay unquestioned allegiance tend to expect it, and vice versa.

Similarly, and in general, highs are more apt to separate source from content in their evaluation of communications; to judge and reach conclusions to the basis of the information itself. Lows are more prone to accept or reject, believe or disbelieve messages on the basis of their attitudes toward the sender.

"Impulse Acceptance." Highs are more willing to entertain and express personal whims and impulses; lows stick closer to "realistic" expected behavior. Highs pay more heed to inner voices, while lows suppress them in favor of external demands.

So, for example, highs may introduce humor into situations where it is not called for and bring a better sense of humor to situations where it is. And, in general, highs exhibit a richer and more diverse "fantasy life" on any number of clinical tests.

Does the more creative man have more inner impulses or fewer inhibitions, or both, and to what degree? The answer is unknown, but there is at least one intriguing finding that suggests a strange combination of two normally opposing traits:

In the genius and near-genius, a widely used personality test shows "schizoid" tendencies (bizarre, unusual, unrealistic thoughts and urges) coupled with great "ego strength" (ability to control, channel, and manipulate reality effectively). This line of inquiry begins to speak the cliché that the dividing line between madman and genius is a fine one. According to this finding, the line is fine, but firm.

In sum, highly creative people are more likely than others to view authority as conventional rather than absolute; to make fewer black-and-white distinctions; to have a less dogmatic and more relativistic view of life; to show more independence of judgment and less conventionality and conformity, both intellectual and social; to be more willing to entertain, and sometimes express, their own "irrational" impulses; to place a greater value on humor and in fact to have a better sense of humor; in short, to be somewhat freer and less rigidly—but not less effectively—controlled.

Approach to Problems

The more detailed aspects of the creative process are taken up in the next section, where we see highs at work. We briefly note three distinctions as personal characteristics of creative problem solvers; all are especially significant in the management of creativity and are elaborated upon later.

Motivation. Highs are more perceptive to, and more motivated by, the interest inherent in the problem and its solution. Accordingly, they get more involved in the task, work harder and longer in the absence of external pressures or incentive, and generally place *relatively* greater value on "job interest" versus such extrinsic rewards as salary or status. There is no evidence, however, that the *absolute* importance of external incentives is any less for highs than for lows.

Orientation. Along somewhat the same lines:

Lows are more likely to see their future largely within the boundaries of one organization, to be concerned chiefly with its problems and with their own rise within it, and to develop extensive ties and associations within the community; in short, to be "local" in their loyalties and aspirations.

Highs are more apt to think in terms of a larger community, both residential and professional; to view themselves more as members of the profession (whether management, chemistry, or teaching) than as members of Company X; to take their cues from the larger professional community and attempt to rise within it; to be more mobile, hence less "loyal" to any specific organization; in short, to be cosmopolitan in orientation and aspiration.

Hence, the local is more willing to change assignments, even professions (for example, from chemistry or engineering to administration), in the interest of the organization and his own career within it. The cosmopolitan is more likely to change organizations to pursue *his* interests and career within the larger profession. In short, highs change jobs to pursue their interests, not their interests to pursue their jobs.

Pace. Highs often spend more time in the initial stages of problem formulation, in broad scanning of alternatives. Lows are more apt to "get on with it."

For example, in problems divisible into analytic and synthetic stages, highs spend more time on the former, in absolute as well as relative terms. As a result, they often leave lows behind in the later stages of the solution process, having disposed of more blind alleys and being able to make more comprehensive integrations as a result of more thorough analysis.

One interpretation is that highs have less anxiety to produce, that they are confident enough of their eventual success to be able to step back and take a broad look before making commitments.

Can such differences be measured reliably enough to be of use in selection programs?

Many of these qualities can be measured, at least in part, by simple paper-and-pencil tests or other controlled observations. But the instruments are far from perfect and, perhaps more seriously, the correlation between each of these distinguishing characteristics and on-the-job creativity is limited. The characteristics "distinguish" highs from lows only in the sense that highs, on the average, have more of, or more often exhibit, the particular quality. And that is far from saying that all highs have more of each than all lows.[1]

As a result, as with all actuarial predictions of this sort, the procedure becomes more useful as the number of cases to be predicted increases. If many people are to be selected and it is important that some of them will turn out to be highs, a testing program can improve the odds. This would apply, for instance, in the selection of college or graduate students, Air Force Research and Development Officers, or chemists in a major industrial laboratory.

But if a few people are being selected and it is important that almost all of them turn out to be highly creative (the chiefs of staff; the top management team; or the scientists to head a project), it is doubtful that, at present, a testing program will improve the odds beyond those of careful personal appraisal and judgment.

In this connection, there is the interesting suggestion (not documented) that highs may themselves be better judges of creativity in others; that it "takes one to tell one."

As the examples suggest, testing to predict creativity is perhaps least effective where needed most: where the importance of the individual cases is the greatest.

What are the observable characteristics of the creative process; how does it look to an outsider while it is going on?

The appearance of the creative process, especially in its early stages, poses a problem to administrators. Up to a point, it may be hard to distinguish from totally nonproductive behavior; undisciplined disorder, aimless rambling, even total inactivity.

---

1. In general, validity coefficients for specific tests at best attain values around .60, which means that they predict about 36 percent of the variation in observed creativity.

Irregular Progress. Creativity is rarely a matter of gradual, step-by-step progress; it is more often a pattern of large and largely unpredictable leaps after relatively long periods of no apparent progress.

The extreme example is the sudden insight that occurs after a difficult problem is put aside, and at a time of no conscious concern with the matter. Many anecdotes support the film cliché where the great man cries "Eureka!" in the middle of the night or while shaving—or, as in this famous case, while getting on a bus:

> Just at this time I left Caen, where I was then living, to go on a geological excursion under the auspices of the school of mines. The changes of travel made me forget my mathematical work. Having reached Coutances, we entered an omnibus to some place or other. At the moment when I put my foot on the step the idea came to me, without anything in my former thoughts seeming to have paved the way for it, that the transformations I had used to define the Fuchsian functions were identical with those of non-Euclidean geometry. I did not verify the idea; I should not have had the time, as, upon taking my seat in the omnibus, I went on with a conversation already commenced, but I felt a perfect certainty. On my return to Caen, for conscience' sake I verified the result at my leisure.—Poincaré.

At a level of more immediate concern to most administrators, since few have the problem or the prowess of a Poincaré, the same sort of progress pattern distinguishes creative from merely productive work, and more from less creative activity, in the kind of problem solving that characterizes the day-to-day activities of the organization.

Suspended Judgment. The creative process often requires and exhibits suspended judgment. The dangers of early commitment—sometimes to "incorrigible strategies"—are apparent at various levels. In the perceptual laboratory, for example, people who make an early, incorrect interpretation of a picture in an "ambiguitor" (a device that gradually brings a blurred picture into focus), will tend to retain the wrong perception—actually fail to "see"—even when the picture has been fully and clearly exposed.

Similarly, in the type of small-group problem solving or decision making so typical of the modern organization, people will "stick to their guns" to support a position they have taken publicly, beyond its apparent validity and usefulness.

Finally, at the level of the organization itself, financial, technical, or corporate commitments to products, techniques, physical facilities, affiliations, and the like, often stand in the way of change even when it is recognized as necessary and inevitable.

"Undisciplined" Exploration. Again, many creators stress the importance of undisciplined thinking, especially in the initial stages, probably because it serves to expand the range of consideration and raw material from which the new solution will emerge.

In this connection, we hear of the use of artificial disorganizers and "boundary expanders," such as alcohol, brainstorming sessions, sometimes even narcotics; and, frequently, the observation that inspiration cannot be willed or worked on, that pressure and preoccupation with the problem are least likely to produce insight—though they may indeed sustain effort in other phases of the process.

The administrative enigma, then, is to distinguish, before the fact, incubation from laziness; suspended judgment from indecision; "boundary expansion" from simple drinking; undisciplined thinking as a deliberate exploratory step from undisciplined thinking as a permanent characteristic; brainstorming from gibberish by committee. In short, how can one tell the temporarily fallow mind—open and receptive, working subconsciously, and just on the threshold of the brilliant flash—from the permanently idle one? There may, of course, not be an answer. In time, outward predictors and distinguishing characteristics (beyond the individual's past history) may emerge. But for the moment, tolerance for high-risk gambles on creativity is probably one of the prerequisites or costs of playing for the higher stakes creativity provides when it does pay off.

What are the characteristics of the psychological state optimal for creative production?

Motivation. How much should be at stake; how hard should a man be trying, in order to maximize his chances of being creative? There is an apparent paradox:

First, we often hear that the creative process is characterized by a tremendous sense of commitment, a feeling of urgency, even of mission, that results in enormous preoccupation with the problem and perseverance.

On the other hand, there is evidence that extremely high motivation narrows the focus and produces rigidity, perseveration rather than perseverance, which not only precludes creativity but reduces productivity (freezing up in the clutch). Some go so far as to say that the absence of pressure is a common denominator in situations conducive to creativity.

There are two suggested resolutions: One is that the relationship is curvilinear; that creativity first rises, then falls, with motivation—you need enough to maintain effort at high levels but not so much as to produce panic attempts at immediate solution (jumping out of the window instead of looking for the fire escape). And there is, in fact, good evidence of such a relationship in laboratory studies of human and even animal problem solving.

The other possible resolution involves a distinction in quality of motivation—between "inner" and "outer," "involvement" and "pressure," "drive" and "stress"—related to the earlier observation that highs are more driven by interest and involvement in the task itself than by external incentives. Perhaps external pressure impedes creativity, while inner drive and task-involvement are prerequisites.

In short, it may very well be that "Genius is 90 percent hard work" but that inducing hard work is unlikely to produce genius.

The two resolutions are not mutually exclusive. Motivation of both kinds may have a breaking point, a level where they do more harm than good; although it seems reasonable to suppose that higher levels of "intrinsic" than of "extrinsic" motivation are compatible with creativity.

At any rate, other things being equal, interest in, and commitment to, the problem for its own sake should point to a creative outcome more often than sustained effort purchased by some externally attached reward, simply because the former is more apt to channel energy in the relevant directions.

Open-Mindedness versus Conviction. What intellectual attitude toward one's ideas and suggestions is optimal: how much conviction versus continual reappraisal; self-involvement versus objective detachment? Again, both tendencies appear, and in the extreme.

On the one hand, creativity is characterized by a willingness to seek and accept relevant information from any and all sources, to suspend judgment, defer commitment, remain aloof in the face of pressures to take a stand. On the other hand, creators in the process of creating are often described as having conviction approaching zeal.

There may in fact be a sort of simultaneous "antinomy" or interaction between "passion and decorum," "commitment and detachment," domination *by* a problem and yet a view of it as objective and external. The process may involve the continual and conflicting presence of both components. Or it may be a matter of stages. Perhaps the creative process is characterized by open-mindedness in the early, idea-getting phases; then by a bullheaded conviction at the point of dissemination and execution.

There could be at least two reasons. A more open mind, that initially examines more alternatives, is more likely to be convinced of the one it finally selects. An early commitment to a less carefully analyzed approach may be more vulnerable in the face of attack; beliefs developed through more painful and agonizing appraisal are more apt to stand the test of time.

In addition, creators almost always find themselves on the defensive in the period after the idea has been developed but before it has been "sold." There is an inevitable stepping on toes, effrontery to the status quo and those responsible for it, that usually leads to some rejection of the maverick, especially if the innovation is not immediately, demonstrably superior. And people on the defensive are apt to overstate their case. In short, open-minded probers may become fervent proselytizers.

As a working summary hypothesis:

In the exploratory, idea-getting stages, there is great interest in the problem; perhaps commitment to its eventual solution but certainly not to any particular approach; an open-minded willingness to pursue leads in any direction; a relaxed and perhaps playful attitude that allows a disorganized, undisciplined approach, to the point of putting the problem aside entirely. But at the point of development and execution, where the selected alternative is pursued, tested, and applied, there is great conviction, dogged perseverance, perhaps strong personal involvement, and dogmatic support of the new way.

II. The Organization Itself

What does all this have to do with organization? What are the characteristics of the creative organization; and what are the implications of individual creativity, if any?

There are various ways to approach this question.

One is to reason, deductively, *from* the characteristics of creators and the creative process *to* the kind of environment that ought to be congenial to them and conducive to creative activity. What does the nature of individual creativity imply about the environmental factors that foster or impede it? For the most part, this is the way we proceed in what follows.

Another approach is to treat the organization, as a whole, as the creative unit. Perhaps some of the characteristics that distinguish "high" and "low" individuals also apply to high and low organizations as such.

The characteristics of creative individuals suggest a number of rather direct translations or counterparts at the organizational level; and many of the characteristics independently attributed to creative organizations seem to match items in our description of individual highs.

Here is a brief summary:

The Creative Individual	*The Creative Organization*
Conceptual fluency . . . is able to produce a large number of ideas quickly	Has idea men
	Open channels of communication
	Ad hoc devices: Suggestion systems, Brainstorming, Idea units absolved of other responsibilities
	Encourages contact with outside sources
Originality . . . generates unusual ideas	Heterogenous personnel policy
	Includes marginal, unusual types
	Assigns nonspecialists to problems
	Allows eccentricity
Separates source from content in evaluating information . . . is motivated by interest in problem . . . follows wherever it leads	Has an objective, fact-founded approach
	Ideas evaluated on their merits, not status of originator
	Ad hoc approaches: anonymous communications, blind votes
	Selects and promotes on merit only
Suspends judgment . . . avoids early commitment . . . spends more time in analysis, exploration	Lack of financial, material commitment to products, policies
	Invests in basic research; flexible, long-range planning

	Experiments with new ideas rather than prejudging on "rational" grounds; everything gets a chance
Less authoritarian . . . has relativistic view of life	More decentralized; diversified
	Administrative slack; time and resources to absorb errors
	Risk-taking ethos . . . tolerates and expects taking chances
Accepts own impulses . . . playful, undisciplined exploration	Not run as "tight ship"
	Employees have fun
	Allows freedom to choose and pursue problems
	Freedom to discuss ideas
Independence of judgment, less conformity	Organizationally autonomous
Deviant, sees self as different	Original and different objectives, not trying to be another "X"
Rich, "bizarre" fantasy life *and* superior reality orientation; controls	Security of routine . . . *allows* innovation . . . "philistines" provide stable, secure environment that allows "creators" to roam
	Has separate units or occasions for generating vs. evaluating ideas . . . separates creative from productive functions

This analogizing has serious limitations and it may be misleading. But the table does serve as an organized index to some of the major characteristics attributed to creative organizations, and it is interesting that so many of them sound like the distinguishing characteristics of individual highs.

Finally, there is direct, empirical study of actual creative organizations. This may well turn out to be the most fruitful approach, but it was not the major focus of the seminar. In part, this reflects the state of knowledge; systematic studies of creative organizations, as such, simply do not exist as yet. In part, the composition of the symposium is responsible. A meeting with six psychologists and one psychoanalyst, against three sociologists, inevitably speaks mostly in psychological terms.

At any rate, we make no attempt to represent, let alone do justice to, the sociological investigation and analysis of organizational factors that relate to creativity. In what follows, we reason and abstract mostly from the nature of individual creativity, partly from rather informal observations of actual organizations.

What, specifically, can management do—beyond selecting creative participants—to foster creativity within and on the part of the organization?

Values and Rewards. What explicit and implicit goals and values characterize the creative organization? What system of rewards and incentives maximizes creativity?

First, the creative organization in fact prizes and rewards creativity. A management philosophy that stresses creativity as an organizational goal, that encourages and expects it at all levels, will increase the chances of its occurrence.

But it is one thing to call for creativity, another to mean it, and still another to reward it adequately and consistently when it occurs. More specifically, creativity as a value should find expression in the following:

Compensation. In most areas of day-to-day functioning, productivity rather than creativity is and should be the principal objective; thus, general reward policies tend to measure and stress regular output. But even where creativity is truly desired and encouraged in good faith, activities that are potentially more creative may be subordinated to those more visibly and closely tied to reward policies. (A familiar academic illustration is the "pressure to publish," which may lead to a plethora of relatively insignificant formula-projects that minimize chances of failure—nonpublication—but also of creativity.)

In the business enterprise, a similar grievance centers on discrepancies in reward between the sowing and reaping aspects of the operation; with the greater rewards for work that shows immediate, measurable results (e.g., sales) as against that which may pay off in the longer run (such as basic research).

It may be inevitable that work closer to the balance sheet will be more swiftly and fully compensated than efforts that have tenuous, uncertain, and in any case long-range effects on corporate profits. But creativity and guaranteed, immediate results do not go together; not between, nor within, assignments. If creativity is to be fostered, not impeded, by material incentives, they will have to be applied by a different yardstick.

It is probably this simple: Where creativity and not productivity is in fact the goal, then creativity and not productivity should in fact be measured and rewarded. And if creativity is harder to measure and takes longer periods to assess, then this probably requires some speculative investment on the part of the firm that wants to keep and nurture the few men and the few activities that will eventually be worth it.[2]

Channels for Advancement. Where concern is with creativity in a professional unit or other specialized function operating within the larger organization, there is this related implication: To the extent possible, there should be formal channels for advancement and status within the area of creativity.

Where it is impossible to promote a creative chemist without taking him out of chemistry, he faces a choice between money and position on the one hand, and chemistry on the other. The company is likely to lose his services as chemist in either case: to administration within its own walls or to another organization where a chemist as such can get ahead. (This is one of the chief organizational advantages and attractions of the major university for the research scientist or scholar: parallel channels for advancement, of at least equal status, exist outside of administration.)

To some extent this is a matter of size; it is hard to provide for advancement within a department of one or two persons. But size alone is not enough. The nature and number of status levels established, their labels, and especially their actual value within the firm and the larger community, will determine their worth to individuals who hold them.

"Freedom." Within rather broad limits, creativity is increased by giving creators freedom in choice of problem and method of pursuit. In line with the high's greater interest and involvement in his work, greater freedom is necessary to maximize those satisfactions that are important to him and that channel his efforts into avenues most likely to prove creative. Whether and where there is an upper limit is a point of much contention and no evidence.

But such freedom often puts the appropriate objectives of the organization at odds with the demands of maximum creativity. The symposium itself produced two striking examples.

In one instance, a participant "distracted" himself and the group by working out and presenting an elegant general solution to a mathematical problem that had been mentioned

2. High potential payoff and low risk are, unfortunately, incompatible—just as they are in the stock market and at the gambling tables.

only in passing, as a task assigned to subjects in a creativity experiment. From the point of view of the seminar, he was out of bounds. By following his own interest, he was creative. (Would he have arrived at an equally elegant psychological insight had he been constrained to the issue as externally defined?)

More dramatically, after the first few hours of the meeting had been spent in rather academic and abstract discussion, one participant reminded us that the purpose of the meeting was to develop useful and understandable guidelines for management and that we had better get on with it. This precipitated a short but heartfelt donnybrook between the advocates of "No nonsense! Keep your eye on the target," and "Take it easy; it's interesting; let's see where it leads"; between "What good is it if you can't tell us what it means for management?" and "Our job is to create, yours to apply."

Both approaches are valid but as means to different ends. Those responsible for a meeting are rightfully concerned with maximizing its output. By the same token, creative individuals who attend it are not so concerned with the product of the particular conference as with the pursuit of interesting lines of inquiry, whether or not they happen to reach fruition during the session. And curtailing and channeling discussion into areas known to be productive obviously limits the chances of coming up with something outside the range of the ordinary.

This, then, is probably one of the principal costs in the nurture of creativity: Except in the rare and fortunate case where a creative individual's interests exactly match the day-to-day operating objectives of his organization, and continue to do so over time, the organization pays a price, at least in the short run, for giving him his head. What he returns to the organization may or may not compensate it manyfold.

Communication. Many observations point to the importance of free and open channels of communication, both vertical and horizontal.

On the one hand, potential creators need and seek relevant information whatever its source, within or without the organization; on the other hand, they are stimulated by diverse and complex input.

Equally important, ideas wither for lack of a grapevine. A possible approach, a feasible but half-baked notion, or even a well worked-out solution must be communicated to those with the power to evaluate, authorize, and implement.

The presence of formal channels is not enough. People

must feel free to use them, and channels must not be clogged by routine paperflow that ties up time with "programmed trivia," and creates an air of apathy and neglect toward incoming messages because it is so unlikely that they will contain anything of value.

Since highs tend toward cosmopolitan, professional orientation, the organization must at least provide for and perhaps encourage contact and communication with colleagues and associations on the outside.

As a special case, there is the matter of scientific and professional publication in the appropriate journals, which is often of great personal importance to creators.

There may be problems of security and the natural jealousy of corporate secrets and employee lo.alties. But in many cases, these are unrealistic or exaggerated, given the high rate of horizontal mobility, the discretion of the professional, and the fact that most "secrets" are not. At any rate, there may be no reason to think that the balance of payments will be "out"; there should be at least as much information gained as given away in most external contacts. And in many cases, and within broad limits, the net gain in satisfaction, creativity, and perhaps tenure of highs will probably offset the time and trade secrets lost to the outside.

What, specifically, are the costs of creativity? What must an organization be prepared to give up or tolerate if it wants to increase its creativity?

Answers were scattered throughout the preceding, but it may help to pull them together.

First, creativity, by definition, is a high-risk enterprise, not for society or industry at large, but for any given unit that attempts it. The greater the departure from present practice, the less likelihood that the innovation will work; the greater the potential payoff, the less the odds of its occurring. Conversely, the larger the number of workers or units independently pursuing any problem, the better the chances that one or more of them will succeed.

In the abstract, then, decisions as to whether and where to attempt creativity, and how much to try for, are much like decisions concerning what to insure, and for how much— although the hopes and fears are reversed.

Second, within the unit under consideration, fostering creativity assesses costs in assured productivity. To the extent that energy is consumed in investigation and exploration, it does not go into work known to be productive.

Finally, depending on the personal tastes and preferences

of management, there may or may not be costs in "security," "comfort," and "congeniality" of the environment: (a) Highs are not as deferent, obedient, flattering, easy to control, flexible to *external* demands and changes, conventional, predictable, and so on, through a long list of desiderata in "good" employees. (b) In addition, highs are more mobile, less "loyal"—harder to hold by ordinary extrinsic rewards—but easier to acquire by the offer of interesting opportunities. At any rate, they make for a less stable and secure, more challenging but perhaps more disturbing environment. (c) A creative organization itself is more committed to change; operates on a faster track; has a less certain or predictable future than the efficient, me-too operation.

In short, maximizing creativity is not the principal objective of any organization at all times, or even of all organizations at some times. When it is, there are some rough guidelines to how it may be fostered—but not, it is suggested, at no cost.

Consider the organization as a whole, operating within a larger social and economic environment. What type of situation is most likely to produce a creative organization?

The seminar produced little agreement, let alone evidence, on this matter. There was some discussion about the effects of competitive position, size, age, and general success of an organization as they affect its need and chances for creativity. But nothing approaching a conclusion is visible.

One of the more interesting recurrent debates centered on the relative merits of firmly led, "one-man" organizations versus decentralized corporate entities; on charismatic, inspired leadership by a "great man" versus the greater democracy of the professionally managed organization. This debate was not resolved, but it does call attention to some distinctions that may be important.

Some Final Distinctions. Last, we take note of some distinctions that may be helpful, suggested simply by the experience of trying to discuss "the creative organization." For instance, the preceding debate may reflect a failure to distinguish between a creative organization and one that produces for a creator.

An organization can be an efficient instrument for the execution of externally created ideas and yet not be in itself creative: for instance, a smooth military unit under a great strategist, a top-notch symphony orchestra, or, in the same terms, a business that hums to the tune of a creative president. These may all implement creativity or yield a product appropriately called creative, but they are not, *ipso facto,* creative organizations. And the characteristics that make for creativity within and on the part of an organization as a whole may in fact be quite different from those that make it the efficient tool of a creative master.

Along the same lines, it may be helpful to distinguish between getting people to be more creative and getting creative people to be more productive. The conditions that induce a Frank Lloyd Wright, an Ogilvy, or a Shockley to turn out more of the same—to repeat or elaborate earlier innovations—may be quite different from those that produce the original and subsequent departures.

In short, organizations, like people, may increase their net yield of creative *products* either by the terms that go into their conception or those that enter into their output. And while the net effects may often be the same, the means are probably not.

For the eventual understanding of "the creative organization," it may be important to learn the difference between creating productivity and producing creativity.

Decision Making: Software and Hardware

Introduction

This chapter is about decision making in complex organizations. Many of the ideas in this chapter are a direct extension of those developed in chapter 2, which dealt with individual thinking and problem solving. One important difference between decision making in organizations and problem solving by an isolated individual is that the organizational process tends to be more formalized; that is, decisions are more likely to be written down as standard operating procedures. Another difference is that each decision in the organization is only part of a "decision system," with the outputs of one decision process providing the inputs to another.

We have subtitled this chapter "Software and Hardware" because organizational decisions these days are influenced both by physical equipment (hardware) like the computer and the telephone; and also by the logical procedures that describe how decisions are to be made (software).

The first paper in this chapter, Churchman's "The X of X," raises the disturbing philosophical question, "Can we successfully understand human decision making even if we try?" More fundamentally, is it possible for us to be self-reflective? If you wish to decide how to make good decisions, you *already* need to be practiced at good decision making. But suppose you try decision strategies randomly until you find one that is good; that avoids the self-reflective problem. Or does it? How do you decide what "good" is? Trying to decide about decision making is very much like trying to lift yourself by your own bootstraps.

In order to think about thinking or to decide about deciding (that is, to be self-reflective or self-referencing), our logical propositions must at the very least be consistent with themselves. But Churchman asks us to consider the man who claims, "I am now lying." The truth of this statement implies its falsity and vice versa. What this means, Churchman points

693

out, is that we must either sacrifice consistency or avoid certain types of statements. If we sacrifice consistency, our whole system of logic breaks down; if we prohibit some self-referencing statements, it is impossible to know ourselves completely.

In an attempt to resolve this dilemma, Churchman invokes the "principle of the maximum loop": that "self-reflection is possible only if one returns to the self after the longest possible journey." That is, you can know yourself only by experiencing everything that you influence and that influences you. In a sense, although we did not realize it until we wrote this chapter introduction, the organization of this book incorporates that same principle. We started from the individual and progressed through pairs, groups, and formal organizations, and in the next chapter we come full circle back to the individual.

In contrast with Churchman's wide-ranging philosophical approach to decision making, Dill's paper may seem almost prosaic. Nevertheless, it represents an important and realistic description of the nature of decision making in formal organizations. As with most modern approaches, Dill stresses the fact that decision making is not limited to choosing among alternatives but also includes agenda building (defining goals and finding problems), search (for alternative solutions and for information about their consequences), commitment (to one of the proposed solutions), implementation (by elaborating the solution and selling it to the members of the organization), and finally evaluation (or testing how well the solution worked out and finding new problems for the organization to solve). In a sense, each of these phases of the decision process is itself a decision. Each can range from highly programmed or routinized to highly unprogrammed. ·For example, agenda building may proceed intuitively, by the seat-of-the-pants, or in a very orderly and routinized way whereby the same set of problems is taken up on a regular periodic schedule.

Dill also emphasizes the role of division of decision-making labor within the management sector of the organization. That is, different decision phases are typically assigned to different people. One part of the organization may have responsibility for agenda building, while another may have responsibility for generating solution to problems already identified, while a third may have responsibility for gathering information (e.g., marketing research) about the consequences of various alternatives. But once the responsibility for making decisions has thus been disaggregated, it must subsequently be reintegrated. The design of management decision systems thus must typically deal with these twin problems of dividing up the decision task and then putting it back together.

In the latter part of his paper, Dill also goes on to describe other dimensions along which decisions can be classified. He distinguishes between "critical" and "routine" decisions. By critical decisions, Dill means those involving the organization's basic values. A railroad company faces the critical decision of deciding whether it is in the railroad business or the transportation business. Or an oil company may choose to treat itself as being in the energy business as opposed to the petroleum business. A university must decide whether it will place major emphasis on undergraduate or graduate education. In a sense, critical decisions are to an organization what an identity crisis is to an individual.

Routine decisions on the other hand are all those which do not strike at the heart of the organization's identity. Dill suggests that there is no evidence that "critical" decisions necessarily require patterns of organization or processes of analysis different from "routine" decisions. While we can offer no hard data to refute Dill's contention, our own practical organizational experiences leads us to question that belief. Critical decisions, those that have a major influence on the organization's future survival, seem to us to require much broader participation by the organization members and a much more thoroughgoing analysis of the ramifications of possible alternatives. Organizations often get into trouble by making critical decisions as casually as their routine ones.

One such critical decision which many organizations have recently faced is whether or not to follow a policy of wholesale computerization of their information and decision systems. A number of studies in the late 1950s and early 1960s made predictions about the impact of computers on the structure and behavior of organizations. Until recently there have been no systematic studies of the actual impact of computers on organizations. One major exception is represented by the third paper in this chapter excerpted from a recent book by Thomas L. Whisler. Whisler carried out a comprehensive study of the impact of computers on (a) the structure, (b) job content, (c) patterns of authority and control, and (d) decision making within a number of insurance companies. Following computerization he found structural changes like these: clerical employment decreased significantly; the span of control at lower levels in the organization decreased; and there was a tendency for a change from parallel (or product) to functional modes of departmentalization. In regard to job content, the clerical functions tended to become routinized, and supervisory functions tended to be enlarged in authority and responsibility. But he found no clear effects on the job content of middle management. The general impact of the computer on authority patterns was toward a general tightening of control and discipline at lower levels of the organizations. His findings about the impact on decision making are presented in the excerpt from his book that we have included here. In general, they point to a more rigid, centralized decision structure, but one within which a more flexible use of information, paradoxically, is possible.

The reader may wish, after reading this chapter, to ask himself whether the computerization of decision-making processes will make it easier or harder to answer Churchman's question about the possibility of "real" self-reflection.

The X of X
C. West Churchman

The world of decision making seems to be ever expanding—
in scope and in complexity. Each major decision appears to
have endless ramifications in the lives of men of today and tomorrow's days.

We would love ever so dearly to understand our own
decision making. We sense all too well that it is a phenomenon far more mysterious than the phenomena of matter, or of
life, or of space.

The peculiar thing is that we humans created decision
making and the many different edifices of decisions: the company, the university, the government. We conceive ourselves
to be the creators of these wonders of Nature, but we don't
understand them. Our creations have become complicated
and uncertain. Even our most astute mathematical analysis
uncovers only a very small bit of the true structure of man-
made organizations.

It is almost as though because we build these things, we
don't want to know what they are like. Men turn their in-
tellecual attention in the main to phenomena they did not
create—the physical and the organic world. It may be that
we suspect the dangers of investigating our own creations in
depth. The investigation may well be at the cost of revealing
the basic evil of man's ways.

The suspicion is a sound one, as all the wise men of history
have told us. He who seeks to understand himself seeks the
devil in himself as well as his God. The view that his understanding will open up may be too much for his contempla-
tion, for it may display to him what he really is: perhaps the
agent of all that is decadent in Nature.

Almost a decade ago a courageous designer of constitu-
tions wrote that he hoped a new Institute of Management
Science would strive for a "unified science of management." I

do not know whether this man was waggish or wise. He may have felt that there was something of the subtle joke in suggesting that science could ever become astute enough to understand how men manage. Or he may have felt that the time had come at last for men to understand their own decision making, even at the risk of thereby discovering their own ineptitude.

To understand oneself is the problem of reflection. It is the fundamental problem of philosophy. We call it the self-reflective, or self-referencing problem. It keeps reappearing in all the ages of history—in all its intellectual pursuits. It is exciting to explore, it is frustrating to try to solve, it is deadly serious in its import.

Consider, if you will, that most fascinating discipline called logic. Logic is the caretaker of man's reason. Without logic we are all insane. The hallmark of reason is consistency. The hallmark of consistency is redundancy. If I say "p is true" then this implies "p is true." To give up such a straightforward principle of reasoning is to give up all grounds for thinking. A proposition must imply itself—at least—and above all.

What's wrong with this? It merely says that a proposition reflects its own truth, a beautiful way to say the most prosaic thing we know. What can disturb the equanimity of logical perfection? Why, a Cretan can. This Cretan—call him Epimenedes—says that all Cretans are liars. More specifically, he says, "I am now lying." If he is truly referring to his own veracity, he must be truly telling us that he lies, in which case he truly tells us that he is untruthful. If he is falsely referring to his own veracity, he must be falsely telling us that he lies, in which case he untruthfully tells us that he is truthful. Seemingly, we must forbid Epimenedes to speak about his own lying. But we will permit him to say that a true proposition implies itself. Can we forbid the one and permit the other? Anyone who has studied the problem knows the tortuous pathways that must be constructed to keep our logic sane: the theory of types, the fundamental inability of arithmetic to prove its own consistency. To some it comes as a distinct shock to realize that even in today's enlightened world, we still do not fully understand what it means to be consistent: We may not understand the consistency of consistency, or the sanity of being sane.

Turn now to another example. A careful man is measuring a length. Curious, we ask him how he knows that the figures he reports are reliable. He replies by describing to us the process by which he has calibrated his instruments. As he takes us, step by step, back to the standard meter rod, we cannot help but suspect that he has assumed that which he wants to prove. His calibration methods involve measuring temperature. But the normal methods of measuring temperatures involve comparisons of the length of a rod of mercury, for example. Hence to measure length accurately one must assume that he can measure length accurately.

How can a system, or measurement or any other kind of production, tell itself that it is performing adequately? The question is certainly a subtle one, no matter how often one repeats the negligent answer, "because it works." Actually, those who say "because it works" don't want to consider the issue. If they did, they would have to ask, "how do I know it works?" They might then answer, "because no one complains." If they did, they would have to understand why people complain. And *that* problem would be beyond their patience.

We are all familiar with one answer to the problem of a system's telling itself that it is performing adequately. This answer consists of modeling the system using an input, an output, and a feedback device. In very general and somewhat vague terms, the feedback tells the system how it is performing. It normally does this by means of an analysis of the output, based on imposed criteria of statistical stability.

Everyone recognizes that such systems are only partially self-reflective. If the input is regarded to be part of the system, it is safe to say that the system does not fully understand itself; it does not understand its own input. If the criteria of stability are imposed from outside, the system does not understand its own criteria.

These remarks are merely challenges to the system designer. If the inputs might turn out to be unsatisfactory, then design the system so it can scan the quality of the input. Thus, if the human programmer of computers makes many mistakes, then get the computer to query the programmer. Better still, get the computer to program itself. And if the computer can't tell whether an output has any value, get the computer to understand its goals and to query the user whether the problem is a sensible or useful one. Better still, get the computer to create its own problems.

How far will this design process go? Will the computer become a self-conscious scientist—even more self-conscious than present-day scientists (which is really not very self-conscious at that)?

This question, of course, suggests the next example of the self-reflective problem: the understanding of "adaptive systems." Adaptive systems are systems that can react to their own performance, that is, can judge the effectiveness of their choices, and learn to do better next time. The crucial points in the life of an adaptive system are the moments when it says, "I like it" or "I don't like it." The system lives by making exploratory tries, and evaluating the outcomes. If it doesn't like the outcome, and yet survives, it will try another pathway. Eventually, it may find some pathway that is satisfactory. If so, it sticks to it, the "it" being one course of action or perhaps a mixed strategy of actions.

The adaptive system is not a reflective system. It only becomes so when it first whispers to itself, "*Why* don't I like it?" Sometimes the answer that is forthcoming is very simple and direct; for example, "I don't like it because I lost," or "I don't like it because it hurts." In the first case, the system recognizes externally imposed conditions of winning and losing. It doesn't understand *why* it wins or loses, or even what winning or losing means. In the second case, the system has an inbuilt pain and pleasure response. If there is pain, "it" isn't all right. If there is pleasure, "it" is all right. This is the childish adaptive system, beautiful in design, highly effective in its limited environment. Nature's gift is pain, a resource of infinite value in a world of complicated dangers. As the child becomes an adolescent, he typically will ask, "What's wrong with pain?" He will be asking the next question of reflection, and he may well explore, or be forced to explore, the possibilities of adapting to pain. It is the initiation to manhood—this simple doubting of a dearly held principle of adaptation. So the young man substitutes honor, courage, fame, wealth, and now and then love, for the absence of pain and the presence of pleasure. Or now and then he substitutes evil—sadism, cruelty, criminality. In such an event we say that his adaptation went wrong. But how do we tell ourselves that a principle of adaptation is wrong?

In the literature of decision making today, it has become popular to talk of "levels of aspiration." The point is that a man does not always seek the best; instead, he seeks that which satisfies him, which meets his level of aspiration. But how shall a man know that his aspiration level is correct? What lessons does experience—or reason—teach him about his decision-making framework?

Perhaps the question so posed is the question of how a man can come to understand himself. Both the tragedy and the comedy of man lie in his self-deception: He can really believe fully and honestly that he understands his own psyche, and yet be as fooled as can the most imbecile fool. A man's misunderstanding of himself can be at least as deep as a manager's misunderstanding of his organization. The trouble is that we are often at a loss to find any guidance in our effort to find ourselves. Some seek religion, some psycho-analysis, some a friend, some quiet, some noise—and some, society.

The philosophical tradition of social sanctions cannot be ignored. It is the one great answer to the problem of self-reflection. Society will tell us whether our criteria of satisfaction are really satisfactory. The man bent on evil may feel satisfied with his choices, but society will not. If society cannot recondition him, it will eliminate him. It's that simple. "Law and order" must prevail, mustn't they?

The problem of self-reflection is too persistent—that's its trouble. If society is the answer for the individual, then what's the answer for society?

Who controls the controller? Who guards the custodian? Who imposes law on the law maker?

A worker receives his criteria of satisfactory work from his superior, and his superior from his superior, and so on to the top. And what of the "top?" The board of directors. And they? The stockholders. And they? The law makers. And they? The "people." And they?

The central problem of management today is internal control, in the broadest sense of the word, because internal control means instituting procedures to assure a satisfactory performance of the company. But what are the controls of internal control?

The founders of our nation were geniuses of organization. They saw that the only adequate answer to the problem of a free society was a system of "checks and balances": The people elect the law makers and executives, who freely appoint the courts, who control the people, the law makers, and the executives.

But how self-reflective is the U.S.A. today? Who tells the people that the national goals are satisfactory? Who tells the people that they no longer truly elect their representatives? Or that the courts are honest? Or that the executive has failed to be merely an executive?

How can man ever come to be self-reflective about his own goals? This seems to be the very deepest problem of the self-reflective mind. To gain some hint as to its nature, suppose we retrace our steps by means of a question that naturally occurs to a scientific mind. It is the question that demands of all questions that they be precisely put. Have we really been pursuing the same problem throughout this book?

Perhaps not. The problem of logic is a very direct one: How can a proposition talk about itself? The other problems —of measurement, of adaptive systems, of self, of society— seem to be different. They ask how a system can control itself. But each of these questions may entail quite different meanings, because the proper control of measurement may be describable in terms of statistical stability, whereas the proper control of society may not.

Nonetheless, there may be a hint in the distinction. The problem of logic is very direct. It arises because a proposition seemingly implies itself and yet implies its contradictory. It must therefore be false. But its negation does the same thing: It implies itself and its contradictory. The original proposition must therefore be true. Without trying at the present time to be any more precise, suppose we say that the logical paradox involves a *minimum loop*.

By the same score, we might then say that the successful outcome of the problem of self-reflection is to find a minimum loop that leads from x to x. This seems to have been the spirit that guided the intellectual efforts of Descartes and Spinoza in the seventeenth century. For Descartes, the problem was to find a proposition that leads directly to its own validity. No creation of the intellectual mind has ever been so direct as his "I think, therefore I am." The one thing that no thinking mind can ever do is to obliterate its own thinking. I cannot doubt that I think without thinking about it. In the same way, Spinoza posits a human faculty of mind which he calls "intuition"; it is the faculty that guarantees knowledge. It has the supremely elegant ability to know— directly—that it knows.

It is the judgment of history that these great minds of the seventeenth century failed. The philosophical skeptics have pointed out that Descartes's class of undeniable propositions is empty, and that Spinoza's faculty of intuition—if it exists —is inoperative.

The opposite of the minimum loop is the maximum loop. The principle is fantastic. It says that self-reflection is possible only if one returns to the self after the longest possible journey. It is exemplified in the great myths of the heroes: Ulysses must go through every deep experience of human life before he can come to his resting point. In the great dramas of music: The simple Freude of the Ninth is only possible after the gigantic explorations of the first three movements.

The principle of the maximum loop was well expressed by the nineteenth-century scientists: The need to sweep into the model of Nature "all" that is relevant. No matter how small the disturber nor how minuscule his disturbance, he must eventually become a part of the scheme of Nature as we push on to the next decimal place. He, like the giants, will take his place in the scheme of things—or, as we say today, in the model.

The maximum-loop principle is based on a monistic philosophy: There is one world of interconnected entities, not many. The most distant galaxies and the most menial worker somehow have a connection.

The principle is also teleological. For the mind to know itself, it must also know the destiny of all minds as well as all matters. Indeed, the principle comes straight down to us from Plato, who taught its formulation in a clearly teleological style.

Perhaps I can capture both the obscurity and the spirit of the maximum loop by referring to three historical incidents, two quite ancient, one very recent. The last is a development made possible by the advent of the high-speed computer. Computers can be used to "simulate" various aspects and processes of reality. They can behave like people, or business firms, or fire-fighting equipment, or an air force. Could they simulate a scientific experimenter? Presumably, little ingenuity would be required to create a simulator that would develop hypotheses, make observations, run appropriate statistical tests of significance, write a paper, submit it to a journal, reply to the referee, and even read galleys. The number of accepted papers of such a simulator might easily qualify it for a tenure position within a very few years. But we would want to say that a simulator that generates hypotheses in so facile a manner is not an experimenter at all, because the next result an experimenter demands is as complete an understanding of the data as can be obtained: The loop that begins with one test and ends in the next must be maximal. To simulate an experimenter must require all that a discipline can offer.

The second incident is that point in history when Euclid was trying to prove a very important theorem of his *Elements,* and, failing to find the proof, postulated instead. At that point in time a minimum-loop logician would have said that Euclid's Parallel Postulate "implies itself." Afterward were two millennia of intellectual struggle to prove the postulate. Only by the time of Gauss, a century and a half ago, could it be said that the implications of the Parallel Postulate were getting clearer. Would it be perverting language to say that only then could we truly say that men understood what "implies itself" really means—only when all the fundamental implications and implicators had been laid before us by the historical struggle? A proposition can only be shown to imply itself when one can demonstrate all the fundamental implication links of the formal system that lead to it and away from it.

The last incident, already referred to, is all too well known. It occurs when Plato, simulating Socrates, suggests that the proper way to understand justice for the individual is via the route of political science, that is, justice for the state. He merely voiced the common sense of the ages: A man comes last of all to understanding himself—after he has come to understand all there is for him to understand.

These three illustrations capture so well the feeling of frustration that many systems scientists experience when they try to study the fundamental problems of sectors of our society. I can well remember my attempts to advise railroad managers. These were men who had come up through the ranks and clearly knew far more than I could ever hope to about the intricacies of railroad operations. They were correct in saying that what I could contribute would be naïve. They were wrong, however, in saying that a naïve system-science approach to railroads was useless. The approach provided another way of looking at a railroad—as a system, not as a physical instance of transportation. Since then, I have had the same experience with managers in health, law, education, defense, and production. They all want to know how an operations researcher in six months, or a year, or ten years, could ever hope to "solve" their problems. Of course, he can't, for he is no more of an expert than they are about the really fundamental problems. But he can provide a link of the maximum loop, a way to reflect, that no profession by itself can ever hope to provide.

"For a mind to understand itself, it must understand everything." But neither Plato, nor Leibniz, nor any subsequent philosopher has yet succeeded in giving the principle a precise and satisfactory form.

In the first place, can one take it seriously? Or ought one to do so? We cannot understand precisely even the smallest of organisms or organizations. How could we ever obtain a model of everything?

The intellectual opposition becomes clear. On the one side are those who are satisfied with being satisfied. They are the scientists who appeal to agreement, to precision, to esteem of one's peers. They wish to keep the problem small enough so it can be worked on. What comes after, or over and above, is a matter of common faith.

On the other side are those who are dissatisfied with satisfaction. They are the scientists who wonder why men study the problems they do, why they reach intellectual agreement, why esteem is a desirable outcome of research. They wish to make the problem large enough so the next problem that emerges will be a better one. They are faithless at heart. Or rather, they put their faith in the nonobvious rather than the obvious. In a way, their faith is deeply obscure.

A *unified science of management*—is it a matter of faith or of enterprise? A unified science of management conceals the self-reflective paradox. Science is an organized activity. Hence it operates according to some managerial principles. A unified science of management implies a management of science: a science of science, a self-reflective science.

The intellectually curious can at least go so far as to try to define the concept of a loop, and indeed have already started to do so. They may even begin to talk about the length of a loop. In this way they may begin to make clear what this part is talking about. But they will not thereby display the dangers of a self-reflective science. The danger is clear: If men begin to understand what they are trying to do, they may understand the worse as well as the better about themselves. Can they stand to understand?

Varieties of Administrative Decisions
William R. Dill

What sorts of activity are encompassed in the phrase "administrative decision making"? At the simplest level, a decision is a choice among alternatives. We present a board of directors with studies of three possible plant sites; they decide which one to buy. We make a wage offer to a group of striking employees; they vote whether to accept it or whether to continue on strike. We interview candidates for a job vacancy; a manager reviews our reports and decides which of the men—if any—is to be offered the job.

An administrative decision usually involves something more complicated than a single choice among a set of alternatives.[1] We make some of our most important "decisions," in effect, by doing nothing. Sometimes we simply do not recognize that we have alternatives from which to choose and opportunities to act. One purpose of advertising, for example, is to make people aware of decision opportunities that they did not previously know about. Other times we may deliberately avoid making decisions because a commitment or action on our part would be to our eventual disadvantage. Unintentionally or deliberately, we ignore many of the alternatives that the world presents to us. An understanding of when "not to decide," according to Barnard, is an essential mark of the good manager.

When we do make decisions, we are often unaware that a choice or commitment has been made. As Barnard points

Abridged from "Administrative Decision-Making" by William R. Dill, in Sidney Mailick and Edward H. Van Ness, *Concepts and Issues in Administrative Behavior,* © 1962 by Prentice-Hall, Inc., Englewood Cliffs, N.J., by permission of the author and the publisher.

1. As examples of how complicated such decisions can look, see R. M. Cyert, H. A. Simon, and D. B. Trow, "Observation of a Business Decision," *Journal of Business* 29 (1956): 237–48; R. M. Cyert, W. R. Dill, and J. G. March, "The Role of Expectations in Business Decision Making," *Administrative Science Quarterly* 3 (1958): 307–40; and R. C. Snyder and G. D. Paige, "The United States' Decision to Resist Aggression in Korea: The Application of an Analytical Scheme," *Administrative Science Quarterly* 3 (1958): 341–78.

out, "Most executive decisions produce no direct evidence of themselves and . . . knowledge of them can only be derived from the cumulation of indirect evidence."[2] Policy discussions at top management levels sometimes end in a vote or in an explicitly stated choice, but more often they do not. Yet from the discussion and from their prior experiences about what such discussion means, individual managers can carry away clear impressions of what "has been decided" and can work within the organization to carry the "decisions" out.

It is easy to pass from discussions to commitments, because we are "programmed" to respond in certain ways to the things that we see or hear. The programs which govern our behavior are based on what we have previously experienced, but they may also be shaped in anticipation of things that we expect to experience in the future. Managers have programs, for example, which tell them where to go to get supplementary information if an accident occurs in the plant, if a customer sends in an order for a product, or if a new law on minimum wage levels is passed. A call from Dr. Smith that one of his patients is being sent to the hospital for an emergency appendectomy is enough to set in motion a complex series of programs for decision and action within the hospital organization. His patient's chances for survival, in fact, may depend on the extent to which programs for quick and efficient action are available and on the smoothness with which they take effect.

It is surprising how highly programmed most of our behavior is. Programs generally govern the time an executive starts work in the morning, the order in which he tackles such jobs as answering correspondence, the time he allocates to different persons or tasks, the "decision" whether to read— or to ignore—certain incoming reports on company operations, and the manner in which he trains or controls his subordinates. To the extent that such programs for action are appropriate for the environment in which an organization is operating, they lend simplicity and stability to the organization's operations. To the extent that they lead managers to overlook important information or to limit the time and energy that can be devoted to important new tasks, programs for decision making can handicap an organization's chances for survival and growth.

Administrative decisions are usually hard to interpret as a single choice among alternatives. Most such decisions really

2. C. I. Barnard, *The Functions of the Executive* (Cambridge, Mass.: Harvard University Press, 1938), p. 193.

consist of a series of choices and commitments that have been made in sequence. Imagine a department head setting a price for a new product. His decision rests on how he expects customers to react and on what he expects competitors to do. But the choice he finally makes depends as well on earlier decisions about how to predict the behavior of customers and competitors, about how soon the new product must start showing a profit, and about how much can be spent to publicize and promote the new product in the market place.

A board of directors meeting to decide whether or not to buy a computer does not review all the relevant information before it decides. It commits the company on the basis of recommendations which others have prepared. Concealed in these recommendations are important decisions that staff subordinates or outside consultants have made about what information the board "needs" to see. What the board learns depends on who made the preliminary studies, on how much time and money was set aside to explore alternatives, and on how influential members of the organization feel about the project. The board's decision may be little more than a confirmation of choices and commitments that have already been made. The computer decision, broadly viewed, includes all the work that preceded the directors' meeting, as well as the meeting itself.

Phases of Decision-making Activity

Any major decision can be viewed in phases, each of which contributes toward the final commitment and its action consequences. These phases, which involve commitments and choices themselves, are concerned with

1. Agenda building—defining goals and tasks for the organization and assigning priorities for their completion.

2. Search—looking for alternative courses of action and for information that can be used to evaluate them.

3. Commitment—testing proposed "solutions" to choose one for adoption by the organization.

4. Implementation—elaborating and clarifying decisions so that they can be put into effect; motivating members of the organization to help translate decisions into action.

5. Evaluation—testing the results of previous choices and actions to suggest new tasks for the organizational agenda or to facilitate organizational learning.

In studying managerial decisions, we find that action does not move smoothly from phase to phase in the order suggested here. A sample of the kinds of shifts that occur is given in this summary of an actual decision sequence from a small clothing manufacturer:

Agenda: President asks sales manager to design a program to promote the sale of a new line of men's underwear.

Search: The sales manager gets the management committee to suggest and discuss various kinds of promotional campaigns. He talks the problem over with the company salesman. He gets cost accounting data on the new product so that he can estimate how much the company can spend for the campaign.

New Agenda: The sales manager discovers, in analyzing the cost data, that the underwear costs considerably more to produce than the price he can expect it to sell for. Questions: Are the cost estimates accurate? Can costs be reduced? Should the product be taken off the market?

Commitment: Implicitly, everyone behaves as if he would prefer to check cost data and to find ways of cutting costs or raising prices before taking the product off the market.

Search: The office manager and chief accountant undertake a check of the cost data. The production supervisors make new estimates of manufacturing costs and explore ways of reducing the costs. The sales manager consults with the president and the salesmen about the conditions under which prices could be increased.

Commitment: The sales manager and office manager agree that the company's cost accounting procedures are badly out-of-date and that certain revisions are necessary.

Implementation: The chief accountant is assigned to design new cost accounting procedures for all products in the company line.

Commitment: Several actions are approved to reduce manufacturing costs for the line of underwear; the selling price is increased; and plans for special advertising and promotion (except for development of a counter-top display) are dropped.

Evaluation: The chief accountant is judged by the president and sales manager to be incapable of improving the costs records system by himself.

Implementation and New Agenda: The sales manager is given authority to take over the revision of the cost records system. He and the president make the job a top-priority one for the organization.

Search: Production supervisors meet with the sales manager and the office manager to analyze the existing system and to suggest needed changes.

Commitment: Ways of collecting, storing, communicating, and testing cost information are agreed upon and are approved by the president.

Implementation: Production supervisors assign their assistants to collect up-to-date materials cost estimates for the new system. The chief industrial engineer and his assistant work with the production supervisors to bring estimates of labor costs up to date. The chief accountant works with clerks in the office to put the estimates together and to add appropriate allowances for overhead, selling expenses, and profit margin. The management committee discusses questions of measuring or classifying special kinds of costs. The sales manager tries to coordinate the efforts of different groups.

New Agenda: The requirements of the coming selling season and the signing of a new labor contract create pressures for early completion of the cost review. Some subordinate personnel within the organization feel threatened by the review and are reluctant to cooperate in the project.

Several things should be noted in this example. First, the problem that the organization is working on changes as new information reveals new problems to work on. In some cases, the shift is to an alternative definition of the agenda; for example, the change from the task of designing a promotional campaign to the task of improving cost accounting procedures. In other cases, the shift is to a subproblem that must be solved as part of the task of completing the original agenda; for example, the change from the task of improving cost accounting procedures to the task of getting better estimates of labor cost.

Labeling the phases depends on interpretation of the organization's agenda. The original agenda-setting phase in the example above, for instance, can be viewed as an implementation phase if the agenda is thought of as the more general goal of earning profits within the organization. The labels used in our example are only illustrative ones; other sets of labels would be possible, given a different view of the decision sequence.

It should also be clear that the course of a decision sequence within an organization is seldom clear at the outset. It develops and changes as the various phases are carried through and as different groups, with new information and new points of view, become involved in the decision process.

Patterns of Participation in Decision Making

Few administrative decisions are the work of a single person or group within an organization. Generally a number of people will be involved, working together or in sequence. Many variables affect the division of activities among members of an organization.

The simplest set of assumptions about how the work should be divided is in "classical" notions about the advantages of pyramidal forms of organization; that is, organizations which can be represented by the sort of chart shown in figure 1.

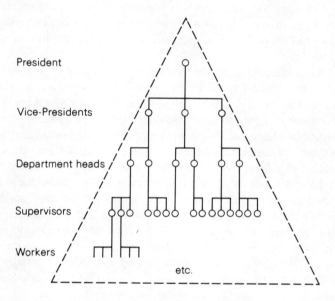

Fig. 1

The essential argument of classical theory is that as work on a decision becomes more complicated, more comprehensive in scope, and more significant to the organization, responsibility for that work should be shifted upward to higher-level personnel. A secondary argument is that disagreements between men or groups at the same organizational level should be resolved by a common superior at the next higher level. As one author puts it:

> Decisions at the various levels, however, differ as to scope and time element. At the lower levels, the area is limited and definitely delineated for questions of imme-

diacy. Proceeding up the levels of authority, the area is less limited and may include succeeding or sequential events. Finally, at the topmost levels, decisions are very broad and, in the main, involve questions having to do with the future. . . . Lower-level decisions are always subject to upper-level approval or veto, but lower-level decision-making reduces the labor of upper-level executives.

Two major types of decisions are to be found: (1) occasional, superior, or formal; (2) routine or habitual. Although both kinds are found at every level, the occasional are characteristic of the superior aspects; the routine, of the inferior.[3]

Evidence on the degree to which such procedures are followed in the day-to-day functioning of real organizations has been presented in a few studies,[4] but more research needs to be done.

Assignment of decision-making responsibility on this basis presumes several conditions not easily met in real organizations. The first of these is that roles in decision-making activity are *assigned to* individuals and groups in some uniform manner and are not simply *assumed by* them as opportunities present themselves. A second condition is that there are effective organizational means for recognizing the complexity and significance of decision problems and for routing them to the appropriate level within the organization. A third condition is that, moving up in an organization, the men are superior to men at lower levels in access to information, in analytic skills for diagnosing problems, and in competence to render decisions and get them carried out. A final condition is that the men at the top of the pyramid have time to deal with the problems that are shifted up to them.

The manager's job description tells him in general terms the limits to his authority and responsibility, but it leaves more to his imagination than the "classical" theorist likes to admit. To perform effectively, men at subordinate levels must assume roles where none have been assigned. To maintain status and to get ahead, they often feel compelled to try to expand their influence in the organization. Both

3. R. T. Livingston, *The Engineering of Organization and Management* (New York: McGraw-Hill, 1949), p. 97.
4. See E. Jacques, *Measurement of Responsibility* (London: Tavistock, 1956); N. H. Martin, "Differential Decisions in the Management of an Industrial Plant," *Journal of Business* 29 (1956): 249–60; and W. R. Dill, "Environment as an Influence on Managerial Autonomy," in J. D. Thompson et al., *Comparative Studies in Administration* (Pittsburgh: University of Pittsburgh Press, 1959), pp. 131–61.

improvisation and aggrandizement, for example, are shown in the behavior of the sales manager for the clothing manufacturer. When others in the organization could not verify the accuracy of the cost estimates on the new line of men's underwear, the sales manager undertook to check these himself, because he needed to have a basis for planning his promotional campaign. His later activities in making the primary decisions about redesigning the cost accounting system were seen both by himself and by others in management as an effort to consolidate his position as the "number two" man in the firm. To assume the leadership role, he was taking advantage of the absence of the president for contract negotiations with the union, of the indifference of the office manager and the chief accountant to the problems that had been discovered, and of his own previous experience with the design of accounting systems in another firm.

The man or the group who recognizes that a problem exists for an organization has an important voice in the way in which the problem is formulated and in the extent to which it is communicated to others in the organization. The outside environment provides information from which an organization can construct an agenda, but it rarely presents an organization with a clearly defined set of "decisions to be made." Even in small organizations, information enters through a variety of channels; and to understand how decision-making activities are divided—or should be divided —among an organization's members, one must understand the routes by which various kinds of information come to their attention.

Consider the decisions an organization must make about the steps that are taken to insure acceptable levels of product quality in the manufacturng process. According to the classical model, these decisions are the responsibility of the production executives, who work within the general quality control objectives defined by top management. Much of the information that the production men need to define their quality problems comes from their own inspection and control personnel who are stationed along the production line. Other very important information, though, comes from customers who use the product. This information is not available directly to the production executives in many instances but must be relayed to them by company salesmen. If the salesmen transmit relevant data about customers' experiences to the production executives, the production executives assume the job of deciding how to do a better job of satisfying customers. If, however, the salesmen interpret the information in other ways, it may be handed to the marketing executives as a problem in devising an advertising campaign to overcome customers' resistance to the product.

Even in cases where inputs from the environment define the organization's tasks clearly, the scope and significance of the task is often still obscure. Research indicates that administrators have difficulty estimating the significance of many of the problems they work on.[5] Under conditions in which the dimensions of a problem's potential impact on the organization are not clear or are estimated inaccurately, the pattern of participation in dealing with the problem will differ from the pattern predicted by classical theory. The pattern may rest on estimates of the problem's scope and significance, but the estimates will be erroneous. Or, in the absence of any estimates, the pattern will depend on who formulates the task, who has time to work on it, and who feels interested or obligated enough to make the necessary decisions.

For different kinds of decisions, different amounts of time and different sorts of skills are required of the organization. The importance of a decision and the kinds of strategies that will lead to the selection of a good alternative often pull in different directions, as far as the assignment of responsibility for the decision within the organization is concerned. Decisions about the allocation of capital to various projects, for example, can be improved by the use of sophisticated mathematical and statistical techniques which most senior executives know little or nothing about. If the techniques are to be applied, they frequently have to be applied by young men, fresh from college courses in applied mathematics and advanced financial analysis, to whom the company would not ordinarily entrust investment decisions. Yet in a real sense, by their knowledge of the new methods by which decisions can be made, these younger men can gain a substantial influence on the outcomes which will later govern company operations.

In addtion, because of the scarcity of certain skills (knowledge of engineering or economic techniques, for instance) or

5. Dill, "Environment as an Influence," p. 154. See also papers by R. M. Cyert and J. G. March in which they set forth the concept of "organizational slack"—in essence, the notion that the attention of organizations tends to focus on tasks identified as "critical" by the environment rather than on tasks of equal but less obvious significance. (See "Organizational Factors in the Theory of Oligopoly," *Quarterly Journal of Economics* 70 [1956]: 44–64.)

equipment (such as computers) that are demanded for making many kinds of decisions, traditional departmental boundaries break down. A company which has a group using statistical methods within the production department to make inventory control decisions will often not be in a position to set up a duplicate group (with duplicate computer equipment) for the sales department to make market forecasts or for the personnel department to set up a wage and salary evaluation system. In many organizations, the statistically-oriented group, originally associated with production, will begin to perform similar services for the other departments. We begin, then, to get groups in the organization identified by the kinds of analysis they do rather than by the level of importance or the functional characteristics of the decisions they are working on.

Finally, within most organizations there are informal patterns of influence and authority which often do not square with the pyramidal organization chart. When management anticipates difficulties in getting a decision accepted, considerations of how "important" the decision is or of who is "best able" to develop a satisfactory solution may be overruled by questions of who needs to be involved in the decision to facilitate its implementation. Depending on the decision which is to be made, on the situation of the company at the time of the decision, and on the governing philosophy of management about employee participation in decision making, one of two shifts from the classical model may occur. In some instances, to give added authority and force to a decision that would normally be left to a lower level in the organization, top management may make the choice. This enhances the legitimacy and the urgency of the decision for the people who will have to carry it out. In other cases, people from subordinate levels in the organization participate in decisions which top management would ordinarily make alone. A great deal of research with laboratory groups and real organizations indicates that this step makes the subordinates feel more closely identified with management and with the course of action that is finally chosen, and thus, more willing to carry it out.

The characteristics of decision problems that determine who works on them, then, include more than dimensions of importance, comprehensiveness, and complexity. We have highlighted four others: (1) the initiative of subordinate groups in planning their own job activities; (2) the information from which problems are formulated and the routes by which this information enters the organization; (3) the specialized training, experience, or equipment used to obtain improved decisions and the ways in which such resources are distributed in the organization; and (4) the kinds of people who will be called on to implement decisions once they are made and their expectations regarding participation in making decisions.

The Role of Computers in Decision Making

The question of who makes decisions becomes more complicated as electronic data-processing units begin to make choices for organizations as well as to perform calculations for them. There is no longer any doubt that computers will be able to assume many of the decision-making functions that administrators now perform. The discussion now centers around how soon this will happen and where computers will have the strongest initial impact.[6]

As electronic data-processing systems multiply in number and influence, our theories of administrative decision making will have to be modified to consider the following developments:

1. An increase in the influence of men who know how to use the new equipment and to fit it into company operations. At least temporarily, pending further development of both managers and computers, an organization must have men who can translate managers' instructions into a language the computer understands and who can define for management the limits to what the computer will do.

2. The already well-developed applications of computers to aid human decision makers, particularly in recording, storing, finding, and interpreting information and in preparing analyses for use in reaching decisions.

3. The use of computers to replace human decision makers, at levels ranging from routine production scheduling or inventory management to such complex decisions as the scheduling of nonrepetitive operations, the long-range allocation of capital funds, or the planning of sales campaigns for new products.

6. For a summary of what has been accomplished in the few years that organizations have had access to large-scale computers, and for some predictions of what lies ahead, see H. A. Simon, *The New Science of Management Decision* (New York: Harper Bros., 1960); *Management, Organization, and the Computer*, ed. G. P. Schultz and T. Whisler (Glencoe, Illinois: Free Press, 1960); and H. A. Simon, "The Corporation: Will It Be Managed by Men or Machines," in *Management and Corporation: 1985*, ed. M. Anshen and G. L. Bach (New York: McGraw-Hill, 1960).

4. The ability of computers to learn from the outcomes of their decisions and to improve the programs which govern their operations without intervention by human operators. A theory of decision making will have to cover not only the programs initially given to computers but the rules by which programs modify and improve themselves.

Some Issues in the Analysis of Administrative Decisions

What are the important varieties of administrative decision? The answer to this question depends on our purpose in asking it, for there are as many ways of categorizing and labeling decisions as there are reasons for doing so. In this final section, we shall summarize a few of the many dimensions of administrative decision making and discuss our reasons for interest in them.

One set of dimensions describes the place of a decision or of a decision sequence in the life history of an organization. Relative to an organization's chances for survival and growth or for attaining more specific objectives, some decisions are clearly more important than others. A major point of many discussions of decision making, especially in public administration, is that administrators must know what decisions to make as well as how to make them well.[7] The distinction lies, in Selznick's terms, between "routine" decisions, which can be made without changing the character of the organization and "critical" decisions, which raise questions about the basic values to which the organization subscribes.

There is no evidence that, other things being equal, "critical" decisions require patterns of organization or modes of analysis and choice different from "routine" decisions. Often the two kinds of decisions cannot be told apart before their outcomes are known. The difference between what is routine and what is critical, in fact, may rest in the circumstances of the organization vis-à-vis its environment at a particular point in time rather than on the intrinsic characteristics of the decision problem. The importance of the distinction lies in its use by real organizations and in the effects of this use on the order in which they approach different tasks.

Roughly speaking, what Selznick identifies as critical decisions, March and Simon identify as planning decisions. As March and Simon point out, there seems to exist a "Gresham's Law" of decision making; that is, routine activity

7. H. A. Kissinger, "The Policymaker and the Intellectual," *The Reporter* 20 (5, March 1959): 30–35; P. Selznick, *Leadership in Administration* (Evanston, Ill.: Row, Peterson, 1957), chap. 2.

drives out innovative, planning activity.[8] In their eyes, this results from the tendency for routine decision-making activities to carry more immediate and more explicit time deadlines and for them to be associated with more clearly defined goals and more explicit rewards and penalties. Selznick and Kissinger would add another explanation: the tendency for administrators in our culture to avoid any decisions which threaten to disrupt the customary workings of the organization.

The placement of decisions in the history of an organization also requires some labels for linking decisions with one another. Several dimensions become relevant here. One we have already discussed—the separation of agenda-building, search, commitment, implementation, and evaluation phases in a decision sequence. This corresponds closely to the fourfold breakdown of decision theory which Cyert and March set forth. They name "four basic subtheories required for a behavioral theory of organizational decision-making: first, the theory of organizational objectives; second, the theory of organizational expectations; third, the theory of organizational choice; fourth, the theory of organizational implementation."[9]

A second link between decisions is hierarchical in nature. An administrator decides to put greater emphasis on reducing accidents within his organization. He diverts resources from other kinds of programs, such as those for methods improvement or cost reduction, to the safety campaign. This choice, and the organization's response to it, sets up a series of additional decision problems; decisons on these generate still more problems; and so on. All the problems can be traced back to the original choice which the administrator made.

A particular decision problem in such a hierarchy is located by identifying the prior decisions that give rise to it and by tracing out the subsequent problems that it, in turn, raises.

A third type of sequential link is the one which Thompson and Tuden suggest.[10] They define three essential kinds of issues which can confront decision makers and which, taken

8. J. G. March and H. A. Simon, *Organization* (New York: John Wiley & Sons, 1958), p. 185; J. G. March, "Business Decision Making," *Industrial Research*, vol. 1 (Spring 1959).

9. From "Introduction to a Behavioral Theory of Organizational Decision Making: Organizational Objectives," in M. Haire, *Modern Organization Theory* (New York: John Wiley & Sons, 1959), p. 78.

10. J. D. Thompson and A. Tuden, "Strategies, Structures, and Processes of Organizational Decision," in Thompson et al., *Comparative Studies in Administration*, pp. 195–216.

together, make up a total decision problem: issues of choice among alternative courses of action, issues of choice among possible consequences of the different alternatives (in their terms, the question of *causation*), and issues of choice about the desirability of different possible outcomes (the question of *preferences*).

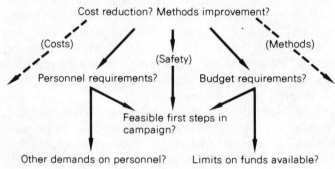

Fig. 2

All of these classifications are similar in their emphasis. They assume initial questions of goals, agenda, or preferences in the organization; a move from these considerations toward the discovery of alternatives and the estimation of what will happen if various alternatives are chosen; the choice of a course of action, including in many instances a review of the basis on which the choice was originally supposed to be made; and subsequent steps throughout the organization to realize the administrative commitment.

A weakness of all these schemes is that, although they describe the phases of a closely integrated sequence (such as the decisions involved in a computer feasibility study), they do not describe the relations between sequences (e.g., the interaction within a firm between action to find a site for a new plant and action to reorganize the headquarters staff functions).

Describing these relationships may mean considering the contribution of both decision sequences to a more general goal (in the example of the last paragraph, the contribution, say, to a decision to double the size of the firm's operations within five years). More often, though, the overriding relation between such decision sequences lies in their competition for the time and attention of groups within the organization. Choosing the new plant site may take precedence over reorganizing staff functions, not for logical or strategic reasons, but because it is being pushed by the president, because it can be carried through without hiring an outside consultant, because a group of subordinate executives have decided it is a more interesting project to work on, or because the men who must supply the basic data for the staff reorganization are already overcommitted to other projects.

The fate of a decision sequence depends, then, on the support and interest that the problems it poses generate within the organization; on the degree to which it runs afoul of organizational "bottlenecks" where men, equipment, or monetary resources are tied down to other assignments; and on the programs which exist in the organization for making procedural transfer of activity on the decision sequence from one part of the organization to another.

Closely related to the placement of decisions in the overall history of the organization are questions about the origins of decision problems. In analyzing and categorizing administrative decisions it is useful to know the route by which information relating to a decision problem enters the organizaton. As we have already seen, this has an impact both on the way in which the problem is formulated and on the manner in which it is handled by the organization. It is also useful to distinguish those problems which come to the administrative decision makers preformulated, as clearly defined tasks, from those which come as a series of information inputs, from which the decision makers must formulate tasks for themselves. In the case of the former, there is less danger that the decision makers will overlook the problem or will misstate it. There is probably a greater danger, though, that they will react against it, trying either to redefine it or to curtail action on it.

Other ways of classifying administrative decisions relate to the processes used in making the decisions. There are many process categories—from those relating to the cognitive aspects of decision making to those relating to the interpersonal organizational aspects.

Statistical decision theory, for example, classifies decisions according to the amount of knowledge available about the alternatives, about the consequences that can follow a particular choice, and about the probabilities of given consequences. Most administrative decisions, however, have to be made on the basis of less knowledge than the statistical decision theorists require to apply their decision models.

Simon has drawn a meaningful distinction between

programed and unprogramed decisions; that is, between decisions which can be made according to rules, strategies, precedents, or instructions that members of the organization know and can follow and decisions for which appropriate rules and precedents do not exist. Distinctions are also possible between "well-structured" decisions (for which a rule of choice guaranteeing an optimal solution can be found) and "ill-structured" decisions (for which the best we can do is to look for a satisfactory solution).

In addition to the kinds of analysis that they require, various administrative decisions seem to generate different patterns of organizational action. Thompson and Tuden, for example, define four sorts of decision situations, according to whether there is agreement or disagreement among the prospective decision makers on their beliefs about causation in the environment or on their preferences about possible outcomes. Agreement on both causation and preferences makes it possible to reach a decision by straightforward analysis or common sense. Agreement on preferences but disagreement on causation leads to judgments by majority rule, often through some sort of voting procedure. Agreement on causation but disagreement on preferences requires compromise among the preferences which have been expressed. Disagreement about both causation and preferences, if it does not produce disintegration of the decision-making group or withdrawal from the problem, may result in recourse to "Divine Guidance" or to a charismatic leader (Thompson and Tuden use the example of de Gaulle's 1958 election in France).[11]

Another set of constraints which decision problems impose on organizations applies to the flow of information through the organization before a solution can be reached. Many experiments have explored how organizations with restricted communications among their members manage to handle different kinds of decision problems.[12] If the information relevant to a decision is not easily coded, it it must be relayed to

11. Thompson and Tuden, "Strategies, Structures, and Processes," especially pp. 198–204.

12. See H. J. Leavitt, "Effects of Certain Communication Patterns on Group Performance," *Journal of Abnormal and Social Psychology* 46 (1951): 38–50; L. S. Christie, "Organization and Information-handling in Task Groups," *Operations Research* 2 (1954): 186–96; H. Guetzkow and W. R. Dill, "Factors in the Organizational Development of Task-oriented Groups," *Sociometry* 20 (1957): 175–204; M. Glanzer and R. Glaser, "Techniques for the Study of Group Structure and Behavior: 2. Empirical Studies of the Effects of Structure in Small Groups," *Psychological Bulletin* 58 (1961): 1–27.

be used, if it must be rewritten or restated as it is relayed, or if a great deal of information has to be processed in a short period of time, the facilities within the organization for transmitting information from one person or group to another become critical factors in organizational performance.

A final set of dimensions pertinent to the analysis of administrative decisions looks ahead to the problems an organization faces in implementing its choices. Two aspects are particularly important here: the degree to which the decision can be stated in operational terms, so that it can be understood and elaborated effectively within the organization; and the degree to which the decision implies disturbance of existing organizational patterns.

Operational or clearly defined, formulations of a decision are useful when the objective is to obtain specific responses from the organization. A clear formulation tells the implementers what to do; and it reduces any friction that might be caused by a vague, uncertain decision statement. On the other hand, nonoperational statements of decisions are often useful too. In a situation where the consequences of a decision can be serious, but the possibilities of changing it easily or of reversing it are small, the first response to uncertainty is to delay making a decision. The second, when a commitment becomes necessary, is often to frame the decision in such terms that it can be interpreted by the organization differently at different times. Political party platforms are sometimes regarded as the example, par excellence, of nonoperational decisions.

Decisions that imply disturbance of existing patterns of behavior in the organization are important to identify because they are the ones that require most careful planning of the procedures by which a choice is made and carried out. It may be strategic, for example, to conceal much of the preliminary search effort and discussion of alternatives from some members of the organization so that they do not become upset about steps not likely to be carried through. It may be important to give some of those who will have to live with the decision's outcomes a voice in exploring the problem and making the choice. It may be important to compare and evaluate alternatives more carefully and thoroughly so that the choice can be explained and defended for those whom it affects.

A Final Observation

Much ambiguity remains in our conception of what an administrative decision is and of how it can be described. Further work is needed to enable us to characterize the dimensions of decision problems, the circumstances that we recognize as choice or commitment, and the relationships that link decisions together in the life history of an organization. It would be premature at this point to try to specify a rigid typology of administrative decisions. Most useful in the short run, while we proliferate hypotheses about organizational behavior and models for making decisions, will be studies (like those of Snyder and Paige, Thompson and Tuden, and Cyert and March) which begin from an empirical base to spell out theories that apply to particular classes of decisions and inquiries (like those of Simon and his colleagues) into basic aspects of human problem-solving and decision-making behavior.

The Impact of Computers on Decision Making
Thomas L. Whisler

Decision Making in Organizations

Although the concept of decision making is discussed a great deal by managers, and perhaps even more by people who do research on organizations, there are many different definitions of decision making. Some of the current controversy over the effects of the computer on managerial decision making probably stems from these differences.

Most businessmen are inclined to think of a decision as the act of choosing between doing this or doing that, between taking action or not taking action. People who are believed to have made the choices are considered the decision makers. Decision making, in other words, is thought of as an individual act.

However, the elements of decision making are frequently carried out by a number of different people in an organization. Decision making involves more than just the act of making a choice; it involves establishment of a goal, definition of the problems related to attaining that goal, collection and consideration of information, drawing up possible alternative courses of action, estimation of the probable outcomes of the various alternatives, and, finally, actual commitment to some course of action. Seldom do all these responsibilities lie with a single individual. In an organization, any decision usually involves a number of people—people at different levels and with different sorts of jobs.

Although it may be possible to diagram in a logical sequence the activities of the various individuals involved in making a decision, these activities clearly feed back upon one another and are interdependent. The interdependence seems

Abridged from Thomas L. Whisler, *The Impact of Computers on Organizations* (New York: Praeger Publishing Co., 1970), chap. 4, by permission of the author and publisher.

to grow as companies get larger and jobs become more specialized.

A phrase used throughout this chapter is "decision system." Systems consist of interrelated parts. Decision making, as a process, is broken down into a number of components, and these components are performed in the organization by different people in different places at different times. Thus, we have parts and interrelationships, and, thus, a system.

We can think of a decision system as covering an "area." This area has boundaries, and these boundaries represent, simultaneously, the *limits of authority and responsibility* of a particular department and its head (or some subunit of a department and its head) and the *limits of search and analytical consideration* when a decision is made. That is, beyond these limits the manager does not concern himself about the effects of the decision he "makes," and he treats the areas outside these limits as having certain relatively fixed characteristics that he takes into account when he manages the activities within his own authority and responsibility. If he did not set such limits and regard them as real, he would be tied up in an almost endless problem of search for information and analysis of the external effects of his decisions on other parts of the organization.

Some people have referred to the activities of a typical manager as "suboptimization." That is, the manager does what he can to bring about the best possible result for the unit over which he has jurisdiction and leaves to someone else (a higher authority) the task of coordinating his decisions with those made by others elsewhere in the organization.

Anyone who has ever managed is aware of the existence of these decision systems and subsystems, and, even though he treats matters outside "his" system as not his concern, he is usually aware that, in fact, what he does will affect others just as what they do in the way of decision making affects him. These secondary effects frequently give him problems, as they do his colleagues, and these problems generate conferences and committee meetings and phone calls to the boss.

In summary, a decision system is typically defined by the boundaries of authority and responsibility of the decision maker and represents, for practical purposes, the limits of search for information, the range of variables and factors considered in choosing a course of action, and the area of subsequent problems of coordination and control over the subordinates reporting to the particular manager.

Computers and Decision Making: Findings

Integration and Consolidation of Decision Making

Without exception, the companies in this study reported that computer applications have consolidated or will soon consolidate decision-making areas that were previously separate. In no case has the reverse effect occurred, they say.

The examples given by the companies in the study range over various functions. One example cited frequently was the consolidation of the premium billing and premium accounting areas. Another was policy administration or policy service; subdecision areas formerly scattered through as many as five different departments have been pulled together into one unit. Other examples cited are consolidation of the investment accounting, actuarial, and accounting areas; consolidation of personnel and payroll; and consolidation of policy development, actuarial studies, and underwriting research.

The tying together of these subdecision areas, whatever they may be, is usually paralleled by an organizational consolidation of the units responsible for each of the parts. As one company put it:

> The integration of many functions through EDP has demanded the tying together of decision areas that were heretofore separated. . . . A prime example is the entire sphere of policy-servicing operations subsequent to issue, where all related functions have been centralized, with the bulk of the decisions made at levels above the division or section level.

However, at least one company indicated that tying decision systems together need not result in the consolidation of formal units in the organization. Where a computer application joins separate units together procedurally, this company respondent said, the result may simply be informal group decision making, with the structural units remaining separate. As he put it:

> Here again, a distinction has to be made between "decisions" relating to the performance of work and "decisions" relating to the policy and control aspect of the work.
>
> As pointed out previously, the organization for the performance of work in the manual and punched-card area generally had a direct relationship to the control and maintenance of a major record file, i.e., actuarial, investment, general ledger, premium and policy loan

records (often further divided by lines of business, methods of premium collection, etc.).

In the earlier stages of computer processing, most of the organizational consolidation was directly related to the consolidation of subfunctions within a major area of responsibility because of the consolidation of related file information.

However, with the newer concepts of "total information systems," in due · course, probably *all* records requiring maintenance updating will be consolidated in a central service and communications organization. It is obviously impractical to assume that a company's organizational structure could be similarly consolidated at a level much lower than the office of the president. Accordingly, it now seems logical to assume that a company's organizational structure will be more related to its intercommunication with its various "publics," i.e., agents, policyholders, employees, stockholders, insurance departments, taxing units, etc.

Thus, various sections of the company's organization become specialists in keeping current with the changing attitudes and desires of their particular "publics." Computer automation certainly can, and should, greatly support the function of trying to determine current attitudes and needs of these "publics," but it is not likely to replace intuitive decision making at this level.

On the other hand, one of the greatest benefits of computer automation, in my opinion, has been the development of group decision making as a staff function rather than hierarchical decision making through line relationships. The unifying relationship in these varying groups assembled for decision making usually is either a consolidated record file (i.e., personnel and payroll functions *joined procedurally* through a common master record but *separate organizationally*) or a series of separate record files that are joined together procedurally in a *continuous computer operation* with input and output cutting across existing organizational lines.

The trend toward group decision making has evolved largely on a voluntary basis, I believe. What probably began as a "getting together" for the purpose of coordination and communication has subtly evolved into something more like "consensus decision making." Generally, however, the person upon whom the responsibility for a decision would be expected to fall, from an organizational standpoint, would be considered by the group as having actually made the final decision. This, again, points up the increasingly complex line-and-staff relationships now involved in decision making in highly computer-oriented organizations.

Clearly, this description of "consensus decision making" refers to decisions at a high level—decisions concerned with corporate objectives and policy or procedural changes. Participating executives are situated at key input-output points in the information network. The relationship described in this statement may well be the pattern of executive relationships in the long run.

But, meanwhile, as consolidation of decision systems occurs at operating levels within the traditional hierarchy, an organization "trace" is left in the form of counterpart consolidation of departments and sections. The before-and-after organization charts (furnished by one of the companies in the study) of computer-affected areas illustrate this consolidation effect.

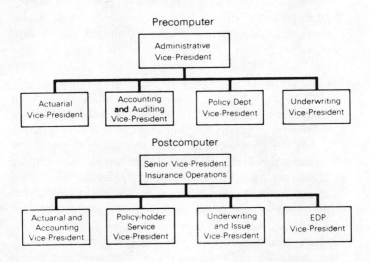

Fig. 1

This example also illustrates how functions shift from old departments to new ones as computer systems develop. For example, the functions of individual-policyholder accounting, due for early mechanizaton, were separated from the overall company accounting function and moved to the new policyholder service department. The remaining accounting and auditing functions were combined with acturial in an area unaffected by the early development of the computer operation. Similarly, the issue function (monthly debit ordinary and industrial), due for later mechanization, was moved from the policy department to a new department called underwriting and issue. And, finally, electronic data-processing was created as a separate department to serve the data-processing needs of the entire company. These shifts reflect the emergence of new computer-defined information and decision systems. The new organization chart is, in effect, a photograph of new systems built around natural work flows.

Changes in the Location of Decision Making

With a small number of exceptions, companies reported that the effect of using computers is to push decisions (choice making) to a higher level in the organization. Various explanations were given by participants for this effect: (1) The consolidation of formerly separate systems makes the potential impact of any change in method or policy much greater than before. Therefore, a manager with broader responsibility (and higher rank) must make the decision to accept or reject a change. (2) Consolidation of formerly separate systems is accompanied by a more pervasive development of decision rules, which are built into computer systems themselves (see the section on rationalization). Therefore, exceptions are more important, because it is likely that they have not been anticipated, even though the most thorough consideration and planning of which managers and analysts are capable may have gone into developing the systems. These exceptions are truly novel events. In most companies, coping with novel situations is a function of higher-level rather than lower-level management.

Respondents in several companies indicated that, in their judgment, certain decisions have been downgraded or moved to a lower level, since they have essentially been built into a computer system. If the machine makes a decision, it is on a lower level than if a human being had made it. This response is in line with the popular belief that a completely determined decision—one in which no judgment need be exercised after all computations have been made—is not really a decision. Thus, computer programs turn decision making into automatic rules. Recognizing that a great deal of this sort of rationalization of decisions has gone on in the process of developing systems, some feel that the effect of the computer is to pull much decision making down to a lower level—its own.

Although all the companies with one exception could cite examples of decision making having been moved to a higher level, a third of them could think of no examples of its having been moved to a lower level. One respondent (the exception) stated: "The level of decision making has not changed. The need for decision making has been reduced, as many of the rules are incorporated in the programs."

Most respondents were inclined to hedge their statements that decision making has moved to a higher level, and a careful reading of their answers makes it clear that their caution stems, to a great extent, from the complexity of the concept of decision making. Nevertheless, the tie between consolidation of formerly separate systems and the pressure to place decision making or decision review on a higher level seemed apparent to almost all respondents. The following three statements from different companies illustrate the point:

> It is agreed that the development and installation of our consolidated master policy record system has had the effect of centralizing decision making, authority, and, to some extent, control at the division-officer level. This has occurred due to the need for more coordination between work units (sections) and a greater need for awareness of the overall impact of the decisions made.

> In all areas where EDP has been applied, decisions bearing on exceptions to standard company policy or practice are being made at higher levels than before. Because divisions are not aware of the impact that deviation will have on other areas affected by their actions, staff personnel and upper middle management must rule on such conditions on a continuing basis.

> In practically all functions, decisions are made on a higher level. The use of a "consolidated system" has forced us to a centralized control over additions, deletions, or changes to the system. The department managers initiate action through the "planning memo system." This system has had the effect of involving higher levels in decisions that were previously resolved at a lower level (usually in one department).

Respondents were asked to indicate on a checklist the functions in which, in their judgment, decisions are now made on a higher level and those in which they are made on a lower level. The total number of checks in the higher-level column was ninety-three; in the lower-level column it was twenty-two.

Despite the fact that twenty-two checks were made in the lower-level column, indicating movement of decisions downward, only one respondent attempted to furnish an example of such downward movement (other than those who indicated that absorption of decisions by the computer constituted a downgrading):

> There were only a few isolated situations where it was felt that *decisions* were made on a lower level. These involved simple procedures where the clerk would decide on the transaction to be submitted to the system. The computer, through its editing and monitoring, would usually reject any transaction not approved by the management of the department. In other areas where the computer is monitoring the work of the individual, decisions are being made at a lower level (clerical) to accomplish a more flexible and convenient operational work flow.

Another expectation was that decision making would tend to move laterally and that this movement would be toward the department responsible for systems applications and data processing. This study does not provide a clear yes-or-no answer, partly because the question was not directly posed to respondents. Nevertheless, a number of companies spelled out the growing role of the computer group in solving problems, making decisions on changes, and setting up future plans and objectives. Consider these six statements:

> On the surface, greater cooperation is required among managers, but, underneath, the forward-planning function of almost all department managers has been transferred to the EDP manager. The line and staff relationship has not changed appreciably, except that within the EDP area there is a greater amount of planning for the company as a whole.

> The installation of large-scale EDP systems has increased the staff role of planning and defining objectives in cooperation with line operating personnel.

> The managers feel that the line divisions are much more dependent upon the systems analysts and programmers than ever before. This is due to the fact

that many "secrets" are buried in the programs and the EDP staff is responsible for revising systems to accommodate new products and practices.

Formerly, two people at the same level may have been able to work out a satisfactory solution between themselves to a problem which affected their respective areas. When the computer is involved, however, frequently they are not able to work out the problem between themselves. They must first consult with EDP personnel. In other words, a third party (party C) has been injected into the picture, thus affecting the working relationships between party A and party B.

With the introduction of EDP, line executives were still responsible for the control elements of their work but (in effect) delegated much of the work performance to the computer. In order to maintain a continuing control relationship with EDP, the line executive must rely much more heavily on the staff support of EDP technicians for systems design, computer programming, and computer processing. Furthermore, work previously performed entirely within the area of one line executive might now, with EDP, involve several other line areas; for example, input controlled by one line area might be part of the output controlled by other line areas. Such a complex relationship of line and staff responsibility is inherently frustrating to a strong administrator. The only satisfactory answer seems to be to develop a group relationship in which the individuals are able to work as a team and still not lose their personal enthusiasm and initiative.

We believe there has been a definite change in the relationship between line and staff operations where EDP has been introduced. In many instances, a complete knowledge of the operating system is actually found only in the EDP staff function. As a result of this, line departments have in many instances become dependent upon close coordination with the staff function in any diviation from normal day-to-day operations which have previously been documented for handling by the staff function.

Thus, one can see evidence of a pattern of increasing dependence on computer personnel in dealing with problems and making decisions of various kinds, largely because of the interdependence and closely knit operations generated by computer systems. Wherever the computer manager may sit, in the finance or control function, in the actuarial function, or in a separate administrative-services function, he possesses the "authority of knowledge" and has acquired the power that comes from being in the mainstream of information flow. An increasing number of changes must have his approval, and he also takes the initiative for planning and developing interfunctional systems and changes to these systems.

Perhaps it is accurate to say that decision making is becoming more group-oriented. A new and powerful member of the decision team is present. This is a change, and, as is true of many changes, it may not necessarily generate universal enthusiasm among those accustomed to earlier and more familiar patterns of managerial behavior.

Rationalization and Quantification of Decision Making

As expected, all the companies in the study perceived the computer and computer-related systems as having induced a substantial degree of quantification in decision areas that had previously been regarded as unquantifiable for one reason or another. The reasons why such decisions were previously unquantifiable were perceived differently by different respondents.

Some see quantification as a concession to the computer, in that they believe that computers cannot function, at least in terms of making choices, unless precise and quantified rules are built into them. Others see quantification as a matter of cost. Previously, it was prohibitively expensive to secure sufficient current data, and, hence, it was not worth while to attempt to base decisions on live data. The computer has made this economically feasible. Still others see the computer as having forced quantification where people had previously been simply uninterested in thinking through completely and logically the rules that they were following in making choices. Finally, some see the new emphasis on quantification and rationalization as a consequence of the integrating effect of the computer: It become necessary to establish rules of priority and queueing in order to properly coordinate the various activities assigned to the computer.

Not all see quantification as a blessing: "The pressure exists due to the idiocy of current computers. Quantification occurs many times at the expense of the product. This is the lazy system."

The following functions were cited by respondents as ones

in which quantified decision making is playing a greater role as a consequence of computer development:

Actuarial analysis (four companies)
Mortality studies (two companies)
Agency simulation models (two companies)
Corporate financial simulation model
Underwriting research (two companies)
Investment analysis
Establishment of priority rules for information-processing
Queueing model for an IBM 360 system with remote input-output terminals

The last two items are examples of the pressure for quantification that is associated directly with computer systems. The other examples represent the enlargement of quantitative decision making in traditional management decision areas.

Respondents pointed out that, although there is clear evidence of pressure for rationalization and quantification, important decisions still have intuitive or judgmental elements in them. But judgmental residue continues to get smaller, and traditional reliance on rule of thumb is being challenged.

Middle Management and the Computer

Responses from the companies in this study leave little doubt that the primary impact of computer systems on decision making has generally been at the middle-management level. There is not complete unanimity on this point, however, nor is there complete agreement on the nature of the impact. Furthermore, companies differ in the degree of present and estimated future top-management involvement in computer systems.

Each company was asked to indicate which level of management had been most affected, in terms of decision making, by computer activities. Seventeen gave direct answers:

	Number of companies
Middle management	9
Middle and lower management	2
Middle and top management	3
Supervisors	1
Top management	1
All levels	1

If the primary impact has been at the middle-management level, what has been its nature? Consider the following different opinions.

1. *The role of middle management has been circumscribed:*

> All department heads who have been involved at all with the application of EDP feel that the middle manager is most affected because he no longer controls forward planning and does not understand a good deal of the system and procedures that subordinates must use.

2. *The role of middle management has grown at the expense of lower-level management:*

> Middle management (division assistant managers and managers) are making decisions formerly made in many cases by first-line management. This . . . refers to scheduling, work flow, and systems problems. . . . The complexity and cost of these decisions has pushed them up to this level.

3. *The role of middle management has been enlarged somewhat at the expense of top management:*

> It is very clear that top management today is more dependent upon our middle-management group for utilization and interpretation of EDP activities. This is resulting in a significant role for the officers in middle management who have direct computer responsibility. Before many top decisions are made, they must be cleared with middle management in the computer area in order to determine the practicality of the idea or plan before it is put into effect.

4. *The role of middle management has increased at the expense of both top and lower management:*

> Because of its direct involvement in the dynamic changes that have taken place over the last decade, middle management has, of necessity, had to usurp some of the decision-making authority that was formerly reserved for top management in order to get the job done. At the same time, it has had to assimilate many of the duties of lower management in order to protect and solidify the gains realized in this radically different period.

5. *The process of transition to computer decision systems has increased the decision load on middle management:*

> The main impact of EDP upon middle management was in the elimination of clerical personnel. Line middle management was thus relieved of much of its decision

making with respect to personnel administration and routine work-scheduling. On the other hand, the middle-management staff (though fewer in number) have either retained most of their decision-making responsibilities with respect to nonroutine work situations or have had their responsibilities considerably increased in this respect.

Since the decision-making function appears to be evolving in the direction of computer-made decisions, lower and middle management appear to be making more decisions than formerly. Since many decisions are made to enable processes to be computerized, those lower- and middle-management areas which are directly concerned with installing computer applications appear to be making more and more decisions.

At first glance, these opinions seem to contradict one another. One might shrug off the contradiction by the easy assumption that every company is different from other companies in terms of the way it uses the computer; but this really is not true. The summary data [not included here] about the functional applications of the computer make it clear that there is a great commonality in terms of areas of application and that the nature of the applications is quite similar from company to company.

Perhaps a better interpretation of the apparent contradictions lies in the distinction between transitional effects and ultimate effects. Respondents are saying that, during the development of new systems, a great number of choices must be made with respect to objectives, goals, and the nature of the systems themselves. These choices fall upon the shoulders of the people in middle management, whose former decision responsibilities are being knit together and changed by the application of the systems. Top management entrusts them with responsibility for making the choices in the areas of their expert knowledge. At the same time, the span of the systems is broad enough to substantially transcend the responsibility areas of lower-level management. Thus, middle management winds up with a highly active and powerful role during the transition period.

When the transition period is over and stabilization has been achieved, it may turn out that many people in the middle-management area have somewhat reduced responsibilities for making decisions. These responsibilities will have been incorporated into decision rules built into the computer systems. Dealing with exceptions and dealing with changes in the systems are still middle-management responsibilities in most life insurance companies at this time, but there has been a specialization effect. The "staff" at this level now carries the basic responsibility for the more creative aspects of decision making. Those with line responsibility may have lost, or feel they have lost, the authority to deal with problems of exception and change. Meanwhile, supervisory personnel have definitely experienced a reduction in the scope of their decision-making authority in most companies.

Thus, one can see an interesting situation in which, during a period of change and upheaval, some members of the organization (middle management) acquire a degree of authority, at least temporarily, that raises their status in the organization. Others, at all levels, become more dependent on them during this transition period. But, once the change has been made, this group may find that it has effectively reduced its own role. If this view is correct, it gives us some insight into the different assumptions and experiences that have produced the considerable controversy that exists among the experts about the impact of the computer on middle management. Some are talking about long-range effects; others are speaking on the basis of the experience of transitional effects. Opposite conclusions are reached, and the argument is joined.

But what of top management? Has it made direct use of computer systems in decision making? Will it in the future? In some companies, at least, top managers are already using computer-based systems as aids in making decisions:

> Members of top management at the vice-president level (in both line and staff functions) have been very greatly affected by EDP. Their ability to continuously stay "on top of the situation," detect developing trends, and rapidly change their orientation within established policy or recommended newly directed policy is so much more effective with EDP (as compared to previous recordkeeping techniques) that their day-to-day work has *completely* changed, even though their overall responsibility may not have changed.
>
> The very top echelon of executives at our company do not normally make direct use of EDP systems themselves but deal with vice-presidents *who do deal directly* with EDP systems.

But not all companies have such a glowing statement to make about top management's response to computers:

It is disappointing to record that top management, for the most part, has not taken advantage of EDP systems to any noticeable extent. As has often been cited, top management takes one of two opposing views of EDP and therefore shies away from it:

1. Computers are large-scale adding or bookkeeping machines and, therefore, not worthly of my attention, or

2. Computers are miracle machines requiring technological awareness beyond my capabilities; therefore, leave EDP to the "experts."

While it is apparent that none are opposed to EDP, it is not apparent, at this time, that they see future payoffs for themselves. Exceptions to this are the top-management members who have been directly involved in the acquisition of EDP equipment and the installation of major projects.

Top-management computer involvement seems to be an inverse function of corporate size. Reports of strong top-management interest and involvement came from the smallest companies; the largest companies said just the opposite. Perhaps this is to be expected. The magnitude of the task of systems development in a large company is far greater than in a small one. Top management is only periodically involved. Furthermore, even the largest contemporary computers have limitations in their capacities. These computers can "hold" small companies, not the largest ones. Finally, the largest companies are almost always the oldest ones. Changing the procedures and philosophy of a hundred-year-old company probably is more difficult than revising the methods and approaches of a company that is ten or twenty years old.

Companies that report some top-management computer involvement indicate that it is in the areas of actuarial analysis, budgeting and sales analysis, underwriting research, and making decisions on the scope and nature of EDP systems. Companies that see top-management involvement in the near or distant future expect it in areas of agency development, investment analysis, financial forecasting, marketing analysis, and dividend analysis.

In their comments on the subject of present and future areas of top-management involvement, respondents made frequent mention of the development of "models." These abstract representations of decision problems are usually developed by operations-research specialists. When models are used for decision purposes, a large data base and a rapid transformation of data through the model by the computer are usually required.

It seems reasonable to conclude that increasing involvement of top management is to be expected, even in the largest companies. Current involvement has apparently not changed the responsibilities of executives or the formal organization of their divisions or departments. But one insurance company president sees the possibility that substantial organizational change may be in the cards at even the highest levels:

> The growing importance of the role occupied by the vice president in charge of electronics is certain to raise many other organizational questions. As more and more information flows directly from source to computer, more and more functional areas may become part of his responsibility.
>
> The increasing capacity of computers generally tends to bring together the internal administration of our various product lines, particularly in those life insurance companies that cannot be considered to be among the giants. It so happens that at the same time there is in most companies an increasing emphasis on the integration and unification of the marketing of separate product lines. The distinction between group and individual sales has tended to become blurred. The movement toward an integrated marketing organization and the coincidental push to a total information system seem to point the way to a life insurance company structure which, if the investment function is eliminated, falls neatly into two large areas, marketing and administration. Traditionally, we have organized with divisions based on product lines. It is doubtful if we will long remain that way.[1]

Problems of Rigidity and Inflexibility

The majority of insurance-company respondents believe that computer-based systems tend to introduce inflexibility. It is more difficult to change computerized decision systems, because it is more expensive. Also, change is less likely to occur, because fewer people have a real grasp of the logic involved in these systems. The authority and impetus for change has shifted to a higher level in the organization and has tended to move into the hands of technical experts. Often

1. David G. Scott, "Great Expectations as Seen from a President's Desk," *Toward Total Systems for Total Service,* Proceedings of the Life Office Management Association Automation Forum (New York, 1965), pp. 7–8.

the former agents of change—lower-level line managers—
have lost, or feel they have lost, their ability to institute
changes that they believe to be important. A tabulation of
the instances of increased or decreased flexibility in decision
making mentioned by respondents shows the following:

	Number of instances mentioned
Decision making is more flexible	
Where flexibility was built into the system	7
Because more information is available for decision making	7
For those who know the system	1
In the design of new products	1
Total	16
Decision making is less flexible	
Because design changes or exceptions are more difficult to execute in the operating programs (unless flexibility was built into the program)	13
Because of the high costs and time needed to reprogram large, interdependent systems (in contrast to easy rearrangement of manual systems)	9
Because of restrictions in scheduling	8
For introduction of new policies and new features	2
For people not familiar with the complexities of the system	1
Total	33

A careful analysis of the answers indicates that it is important to differentiate the problems of flexibility and change according to the kind of computer system used. The problems
connected with *complex* decision systems are different from
those connected with *simple* decision systems.

Simple decision systems are systems that involve a single
function and are relatively self-contained and highly determined (requiring little judgment or intuition). A good example would be a payroll system. In simple systems, environmental factors such as laws or customer and supplier behavior would tend to be stable over long periods of time.

Complex systems are those that are multifunctional, tied
directly into other systems, and only partially determined
(still requiring some judgment and intuition). These systems
confront dynamic elements of the environment. Often, they
are still in the process of development toward a state
regarded as still achieveable.

In simple systems, the stimulus for review and change is

relatively infrequent. Since the costs of change (to systems analysis and programming) are high, the system is left alone as long as it performs reasonably well. One respondent made an interesting observation concerning the resistance of such systems to "deterioration." Deterioration, he says, comes about through human error and human deviation from the initial system design. In noncomputer systems, it is common for individuals to take shortcuts, make deviations, and fail to perform in detail as planners had initially expected them to. In time, the accumulation of these deviations can so modify performance (either for better or for worse) as to produce all sorts of unintended results and, possibly, substandard performance. But the computer is inexorable, refusing to cooperate or to operate unless the human component conforms in every detail. Thus, the system is rigid and reliable. As long as it works well, no one bothers it.

In complex systems, there is constant stimulus for change. The size of the system is larger, there is a wider variety of users, and the number and variety of "loose ends" (parts of the system still to be quantified and rationalized) is large. As a result, there is frequent stimulus for review of the system, with the possibility of change. The scope of the review can be quite broad. That is, the proposed change in one subsystem of a complex system must be traced in terms of its effects on all other subsystems. Respondents indicate that this is a characteristic peculiar to computer systems. Before the advent of the computer, a change in any subsystem was instituted usually without intensive scrutiny of its effects on other subsystems.

But, if the frequency of review for possible changes is greater in complex systems than in simple systems, potential costs of change are also much higher. Because of the interdependency of the parts of complex systems and the awareness of the widespread effects of any given change, motivation to change is inhibited. Thus, as systems evolve toward a more integrated, more complex state, the stimulus for change becomes more frequent but the costs of change rise. The net effect on flexibility and change is likely to vary from company to company, although the judgment of the majority of those included in the study was that change is less frequent and that inflexibility is a characteristic of computer-based decision systems.

A tabulation of the frequency of review and of actual change in decision systems mentioned by respondents reveals the following:

	More frequent after *the computer*	*Less frequent after* *the computer*
Review is	20	11
Actual change is	11	19

The perception of the effects of the computer seems to depend on whom you ask. A number of respondents report that line managers see the opportunity for change as having been reduced because of the high costs of change and because their own role in initiating change has been reduced. In contrast, staff managers, especially those in the computer area, see the probable frequency of change as having been increased by introduction of the computer. This disagreement is not surprising. If authority for initiating change is indeed shifted to those who develop and maintain the computer systems, these people will be acutely aware of the pressures for change and the frequency and costs of change. On the other hand, those who see themselves as having lost authority for making changes in the area for which they are responsible will surely feel that decision systems have become more rigid, more inflexible, and more difficult to change.

For the present and for the immediate future, perceived gain in flexibility seems to be in the areas in which models have been developed and in which simulations can be utilized. Underwriting research, actuarial analysis, financial analysis, and so on can use models. The computer can simulate various choices in speedy fashion. There is a perceived net gain in flexibility. And, even in some operating areas in which procedures have not changed basically and in which estimates of future changes are not involved, some increase in flexibility has, in fact, been achieved by permitting a more sophisticated range of choices or combinations of benefits or the like.

Looking to the future and keeping in mind the opinions expressed by respondents, it seems reasonable to expect increasing versatility and flexibility in managerial decision making as a consequence of the development of computer systems. As men learn, adapt, and change their behavior and attitudes, and as technology becomes more sophisticated and powerful, present problems of rigidity and inflexibility should diminish.

Summary

We may conclude that the introduction of computer systems in an organization affects decision making in the following ways: Decision systems or areas are consolidated; decision making moves to a higher level in the organization; decision making is increasingly quantified and rationalized. Also, the study indicates that the primary impact on decision making is at the middle-management level, that top-management decision making is little affected by the technology, and that substantial new problems of inflexibility in decision making have resulted from computer use. Finally, the effect on decision flexibility has been self-contradictory: Use of computers in decision making stimulates ideas for change but greatly increases the costs of adopting these changes.

14

**Full Circle:
The Individual in
the Organization**

Introduction

This is the last chapter in this collection of readings, but in
one sense it is also the first. This book started with a chapter
about the nature of individual people, and it finishes on the
same note. But there are two differences. In the first four
chapters of part 1 we explored the nature of the individual—how he feels, thinks, forms his attitudes and values. But
in this concluding chapter we try to explore the relationship
between the individual and the organization in which he
spends much of his time; particularly the way the organization affects the psychological well-being of the individuals
that make it up. And we also consider how the larger environment affects the organization and, thereby, the individuals
in it.

It seems characteristic of modern societies that individuals
in organizations are treated primarily as instruments of the
institution's will, as means to other ends. Not only do many
people regard such treatment as inconsistent with our society's professed values but some think it is not even good
business. One of the most clearly written and widely
reprinted papers espousing this viewpoint is the classic paper
by Douglas McGregor, reprinted again here. Although
subsequent empirical research has somewhat modified the validity of McGregor's early position (see the paper by Morse
and Lorsch in chapter 7), McGregor's analysis of the human
side of enterprise still stands as a strong and effective statement.

But McGregor's paper leaves at least one crucial question
unanswered. How do we go about achieving the ideal of democratic, humanitarian (and perhaps even effective) organizations? The move toward more open organizations would, of
course, require that persons in power give up some of their
power. It seems to us unlikely that persons in authority will

give up very much of their power voluntarily. It is more likely that pressures on the organization from out there in the environment will force such release of power. The paper by Warren Bennis, "A Funny Thing Happened on the Way to the Future," offers one view of how this change toward more equal distribution of organizational power may come about.

The core of Bennis's argument is that authoritarian bureaucracies are no longer adaptive to modern environments. The prime cause of the breakdown of authoritarian bureaucracy is the increased uncertainty of the environment. As chapter 11 tried to show, environments which are complex and uncertain demand more open, organic, flexible forms of organization. But these are precisely the kinds of systems in which individual persons, according to people like McGregor, can thrive and prosper—a happy coincidence. Bennis argues that the pressure for more adaptive forms of organization will be particularly great in public organizations such as universities, hospitals, and governments. Those organizations do not have an economic market to rationalize their decision making and are therefore much more susceptible to pressures from their various clienteles. Bennis also considers other forces which contribute to the decline of authoritarian bureaucracy, including a generally growing denial of the legitimacy of organizational authority, perhaps because existing authorities have failed to cope successfully with the manifold problems facing large organizations: a new population of younger, more mobile, and better educated employees; people less likely to accept authority without question; and a general shift in the attitudes of organizational designers toward greater respect for individual integrity.

But if bureaucracy declines, what form of organization is likely to replace it? Because of the changeability of the organization's environment and because of accelerating technological change, Bennis argues that organizations will tend to shift to more temporary forms. Instead of belonging to just one organization at a time, and perhaps to only one for his entire working life, a person may belong to several different organizations simultaneously and shift more frequently and rapidly from one organization to another. And organizations themselves may come and go and combine and procreate more quickly. One great benefit that may emerge from temporary and multiple membership is that one will never need to feel the frustration—so common now—of being trapped inside one organization's walls. Almost anything seems tolerable if it is temporary. It is appropriate that Bennis ends his paper on an open note, since it is oriented primarily toward the future. And since it has been our intention to open issues rather than to close them, it also seems appropriate to end this book with an open-ended paper.

The Human Side of Enterprise
Douglas M. McGregor

It has become trite to say that the most significant developments of the next quarter-century will take place not in the
physical but in the social sciences, that industry—the economic organ of society—has the fundamental know-how to
utilize physical science and technology for the material
benefit of mankind, and that we must now learn how to
utilize the social sciences to make our human organizations
truly effective.

Many people agree in principle with such statements; but
so far they represent a pious hope—and little else. Consider
with me, if you will, something of what may be involved
when we attempt to transform the hope into reality.

Problems and Opportunities Facing Management

Let me begin with an analogy. A quarter-century ago basic
conceptions of the nature of matter and energy had changed
profoundly from what they had been since Newton's time.
The physical scientists were persuaded that under proper
conditions new and hitherto unimagined sources of energy
could be made available to mankind.

We know what has happened since then. First came the
bomb. Then, during the past decade, have come many other
attempts to exploit these scientific discoveries—some successful, some not.

The point of my analogy, however, is that the application
of theory in this field is a slow and costly matter. We expect it
always to be thus. No one is impatient with the scientist
because he cannot tell industry how to build a simple, cheap,
all-purpose source of atomic energy today. That it will take
at least another decade and the investment of billions of
dollars to achieve results which are economically competitive

with present sources of power is understood and accepted.

It is transparently pretentious to suggest any *direct* similarity between the developments in the physical sciences leading to the harnessing of atomic energy and potential developments in the social sciences. Nevertheless, the analogy is not as absurd as it might appear to be at first glance.

To a lesser degree, and in a much more tentative fashion, we are in a position in the social sciences today like that of the physical sciences with respect to atomic energy in the thirties. We know that past conceptions of the nature of man are inadequate and in many ways incorrect. We are becoming quite certain that, under proper conditions, unimagined resources of creative human energy could become available within the organizational setting.

We cannot tell industrial management how to apply this new knowledge in simple, economic ways. We know it will require years of exploration, much costly development research, and a substantial amount of creative imagination on the part of management to discover how to apply this growing knowledge to the organization of human effort in industry.

May I ask that you keep this analogy in mind—overdrawn and pretentious though it may be—as a framework for what I have to say.

Management's Task: Conventional View

The conventional conception of management's task in harnessing human energy to organizational requirements can be stated broadly in terms of three propositions. In order to avoid the complications introduced by a label, I shall call this set of propositions "Theory X":

1. Management is responsible for organizing the elements of productive enterprise—money, materials, equipment, people—in the interest of economic ends.

2. With respect to people, this is a process of directing their efforts, motivating them, controlling their actions, modifying their behavior to fit the needs of the organization.

3. Without this active intervention by management, people would be passive—even resistant—to organizational needs. They must therefore be persuaded, rewarded, punished, controlled—their activities must be directed. This is management's task—in managing subordinate managers or workers. We often sum it up by saying that management consists of getting things done through other people.

Behind this conventional theory there are several additional beliefs—less explicit, but widespread:

4. The average man is by nature indolent—he works as little as possible.

5. He lacks ambition, dislikes responsibility, prefers to be led.

6. He is inherently self-centered, indifferent to organizational needs.

7. He is by nature resistant to change.

8. He is gullible, not very bright, the ready dupe of the charlatan and the demagogue.

The human side of economic enterprise today is fashioned from propositions and beliefs such as these. Conventional organization structures, managerial policies, practices, and programs reflect these assumptions.

In accomplishing its task—with these assumptions as guides—management has conceived of a range of possibilities between two extremes.

The Hard or the Soft Approach?

At one extreme, management can be "hard" or "strong." The methods for directing behavior involve coercion and threat (usually disguised), close supervision, tight controls over behavior. At the other extreme, management can be "soft" or "weak." The methods for directing behavior involve being permissive, satisfying people's demands, achieving harmony. Then they will be tractable, accept direction.

This range has been fairly completely explored during the past half century, and management has learned some things from the exploration. There are difficulties in the "hard" approach. Force breeds counterforces: restriction of output, antagonism, militant unionism, subtle but effective sabotage of management objectives. This approach is especially difficult during times of full employment.

There are also difficulties in the "soft" approach. It leads frequently to the abdication of management—to harmony, perhaps, but to indifferent performance. People take advantage of the soft approach. They continually expect more, but they give less and less.

Currently, the popular theme is "firm but fair." This is an attempt to gain the advantages of both the hard and the soft approaches. It is reminiscent of Teddy Roosevelt's "speak softly and carry a big stick."

Is the Conventional View Correct?

The findings which are beginning to emerge from the social sciences challenge this whole set of beliefs about man and human nature and about the task of management. The evidence is far from conclusive, certainly, but it is suggestive. It comes from the laboratory, the clinic, the schoolroom, the home, and even to a limited extent from industry itself.

The social scientist does not deny that human behavior in industrial organization today is approximately what management perceives it to be. He has, in fact, observed it and studied it fairly extensively. But he is pretty sure that this behavior is *not* a consequence of man's inherent nature. It is a consequence rather of the nature of industrial organizations, of management philosophy, policy, and practice. The conventional approach of Theory X is based on mistaken notions of what is cause and what is effect.

"Well," you ask, "what then is the *true* nature of man? What evidence leads the social scientist to deny what is obvious?" And, if I am not mistaken, you are also thinking, "Tell me—simply, and without a lot of scientific verbiage—what you think you know that is so unusual. Give me—without a lot of intellectual claptrap and theoretical nonsense—some practical ideas which will enable me to improve the situation in my organization. And remember, I'm faced with increasing costs and narrowing profit margins. I want proof that such ideas won't result simply in new and costly human relations frills. I want practical results, and I want them now."

If these are your wishes, you are going to be disappointed. Such requests can no more be met by the social scientist today than could comparable ones with respect to atomic energy be met by the physicist fifteen years ago. I can, however, indicate a few of the reasons for asserting that conventional assumptions about the human side of enterprise are inadequate. And I can suggest—tentatively—some of the propositions that will comprise a more adequate theory of the management of people. The magnitude of the task that confronts us will then, I think, be apparent.

Man as a Wanting Animal

Perhaps the best way to indicate why the conventional approach of management is inadequate is to consider the subject of motivation. In discussing this subject I will draw heavily on the work of my colleague, Abraham Maslow of Brandeis University. His is the most fruitful approach I know. Naturally, what I have to say will be overgeneralized and will ignore important qualifications. In the time at our disposal, this is inevitable.

Physiological and Safety Needs

Man is a wanting animal—as soon as one of his needs is satisfied, another appears in its place. This process is unending. It continues from birth to death.

Man's needs are organized in a series of levels—a hierarchy of importance. At the lowest level, but preeminent in importance when they are thwarted, are his physiological needs. Man lives by bread alone, when there is no bread. Unless the circumstances are unusual, his needs for love, for status, for recognition are inoperative when his stomach has been empty for a while. But when he eats regularly and adequately, hunger ceases to be an important need. The sated man has hunger only in the sense that a full bottle has emptiness. The same is true of the other physiological needs of man—for rest, exercise, shelter, protection from the elements.

A satisfied need is not a motivator of behavior! This is a fact of profound significance. It is a fact which is regularly ignored in the conventional approach to the management of people. I shall return to it later. For the moment, one example will make my point. Consider your own need for air. Except as you are deprived of it, it has no appreciable motivating effect upon your behavior.

When the physiological needs are reasonably satisfied, needs at the next higher level begin to dominate man's behavior—to motivate him. These are called safety needs. They are needs for protection against danger, threat, deprivation. Some people mistakenly refer to these as needs for security. However, unless man is in a dependent relationship where he fears arbitrary deprivation, he does not demand security. The need is for the "fairest possible break." When he is confident of this, he is more than willing to take risks. But when he feels threatened or dependent, his greatest need is for guarantees, for protection, for security.

The fact needs little emphasis that since every industrial employee is in a dependent relationship, safety needs may assume considerable importance. Arbitrary management actions, behavior which arouses uncertainty with respect to continued employment or which reflects favoritism or discrimination, unpredictable administration of policy—these can be powerful motivators of the safety needs in the employment relationship *at every level* from worker to vice-president.

Social Needs

When man's physiological needs are satisfied and he is no longer fearful about his physical welfare, his social needs become important motivators of his behavior—for belonging, for association, for acceptance by his fellows, for giving and receiving friendship and love.

Management knows today of the existence of these needs, but it often assumes quite wrongly that they represent a threat to the organization. Many studies have demonstrated that the tightly knit, cohesive work group may, under proper conditions, be far more effective than an equal number of separate individuals in achieving organizational goals.

Yet management, fearing group hostility to its own objectives, often goes to considerable lengths to control and direct human efforts in ways that are inimical to the natural "groupiness" of human beings. When man's social needs— and perhaps his safety needs, too—are thus thwarted, he behaves in ways which tend to defeat organizational objectives. He becomes resistant, antagonistic, uncooperative. But this behavior is a consequence, not a cause.

Ego Needs

Above the social needs—in the sense that they do not become motivators until lower needs are reasonably satisfied —are the needs of greatest significance to management and to man himself. They are the egoistic needs, and they are of two kinds:

1. Those needs that relate to one's self-esteem—needs for self-confidence, for independence, for achievement, for competence, for knowledge.

2. Those needs that relate to one's reputation—needs for status, for recognition, for appreciation, for the deserved respect of one's fellows.

Unlike the lower needs, these are rarely satisfied; man seeks indefinitely for more satisfaction of these needs once they have become important to him. But they do not appear in any significant way until physiological, safety, and social needs are all reasonably satisfied.

The typical industrial organization offers few opportunities for the satisfaction of these egoistic needs to people at lower levels in the hierarchy. The conventional methods of organizing work, particularly in mass production industries, give little heed to these aspects of human motivation. If the practices of scientific management were deliberately calculated to thwart these needs—which, of course, they are not—they could hardly accomplish this purpose better than they do.

Self-Fulfillment Needs

Finally—a capstone, as it were, on the hierarchy of man's

needs—there are what we may call the needs for self-fulfill-ment. These are the needs for realizing one's own potenti-alities, for continued self-development, for being creative in the broadest sense of that term.

It is clear that the conditions of modern life give only limited opportunity for these relatively weak needs to obtain expression. The deprivation most people experience with respect to other lower-level needs diverts their energies into the struggle to satisfy *those* needs, and the needs for self-ful-fillment remain dormant.

The Dynamics of Motivation

Now, briefly, a few general comments about motivation:

We recognize readily enough that a man suffering from a severe dietary deficiency is sick. The deprivation of physiolo-gical needs has behavioral consequences. The same is true—although less well recognized—of deprivation of higher-level needs. The man whose needs for safety, association, indepen-dence, or status are thwarted is sick just as surely as is he who has rickets. And his sickness will have behavioral consequences. We will be mistaken if we attribute his result-ant passivity, his hostility, his refusal to accept responsibility to his inherent "human nature." These forms of behavior are *symptoms* of illness—of deprivation of his social and egoistic needs.

The man whose lower-level needs are satisfied is not mo-tivated to satisfy those needs any longer. For practical pur-poses they exist no longer. (Remember my point about your need for air.) Management often asks, "Why aren't people more productive? We pay good wages, provide good working conditions, have excellent fringe benefits and steady employment. Yet people do not seem to be willing to put forth more than minimum effort."

The fact that management has provided for these physio-logical and safety needs has shifted the motivational empha-sis to the social and perhaps to the egoistic needs. Unless there are opportunities *at work* to satisfy these higher-level needs, people will be deprived; and their behavior will reflect this deprivation. Under such conditions, if management con-tinues to focus its attention on physiological needs, its efforts are bound to be ineffective.

People *will* make insistent demands for more money under these conditions. It becomes more important than ever to buy the material goods and services which can provide limited satisfaction of the thwarted needs. Although money has only limited value in satisfying many higher-level needs, it can become the focus of interest it if is ths *only* means available.

The Carrot and Stick Approach

The carrot and stick theory of motivation (like Newtonian physical theory) works reasonably well under certain circumstances. The *means* for satisfying man's physiological and (within limits) his safety needs can be provided or withheld by management. Employment itself is such a means, and so are wages, working conditions, and benefits. By these means the individual can be controlled so long as he is struggling for subsistence. Man lives for bread alone when there is no bread.

But the carrot and stick theory does not work at all once man has reached an adequate subsistence level and is motivated primarily by higher needs. Management cannot provide a man with self-respect, or with the respect of his fellows, or with the satisfaction of needs for self-fulfillment. It can create conditions such that he is encouraged and enabled to seek such satisfactions *for himself,* or it can thwart him by failing to create those conditions.

But this creation of conditions is not "control." It is not a good device for directing behavior. And so management finds itself in an odd position. The high standard of living created by our modern technological know-how provides quite adequately for the satisfaction of physiological and safety needs. The only significant exception is where management practices have not created confidence in a "fair break"—and thus where safety needs are thwarted. But by making possible the satisfaction of low-level needs, management has deprived itself of the ability to use as motivators the devices on which conventional theory has taught it to rely—rewards, promises, incentives, or threats and other coercive devices.

Neither Hard nor Soft

The philosophy of management by direction and control—*regardless of whether it is hard or soft*—is inadequate to motivate because the human needs on which this approach relies are today unimportant motivators of behavior. Direction and control are essentially useless in motivating people whose important needs are social and egoistic. Both the hard and the soft approach fail today because they are simply irrelevant to the situation.

People, deprived of opportunities to satisfy at work the needs which are now important to them, behave exactly as we might predict—with indolence, passivity, resistance to change, lack of responsibility, willingness to follow the demagogue, unreasonable demands for economic benefits. It would seem that we are caught in a web of our own weaving.

In summary, then, of these comments about motivation: Management by direction and control—whether implemented with the hard, the soft, or the firm but fair approach —fails under today's conditions to provide effective motivation of human effort toward organizational objectives. It fails because direction and control are useless methods of motivating people whose physiological and safety needs are reasonably satisfied and whose social, egoistic, and self-fulfillment needs are predominant.

A New Perspective

For these and many other reasons, we require a different theory of the task of managing people based on more adequate assumptions about human nature and human motivation. I am going to be so bold as to suggest the broad dimensions of such a theory. Call it "Theory Y," if you will:

1. Management is responsible for organizing the elements of productive enterprise—money, materials, equipment, people—in the interest of economic ends.

2. People are *not* by nature passive or resistant to organizational needs. They have become so as a result of experience in organizations.

3. The motivation, the potential for development, the capacity for assuming responsibility, the readiness to direct behavior toward organizational goals are all present in people. Management does not put them there. It is a responsibility of management to make it possible for people to recognize and develop these human characteristics for themselves.

4. The essential task of management is to arrange organizational conditions and methods of operation so that people can achieve their own goals *best* by directing *their own* efforts toward organizational objectives.

This is a process primarily of creating opportunities, releasing potential, removing obstacles, encouraging growth, providing guidance. It is what Peter Drucker has called "management by objectives" in contrast to "management by control."

And I hasten to add that it does *not* involve the abdication of management, the absence of leadership, the lowering of standards, or the other characteristics usually associated with the "soft" approach under Theory X. Much to the contrary. It is no more possible to create an organization today which will be a fully effective application of this theory than it was to build an atomic power plant in 1945. There are many formidable obstacles to overcome.

Some Difficulties

The conditions imposed by conventional organization theory and by the approach of scientific management for the past half century have tied men to limited jobs which do not utilize their capabilities, have discouraged the acceptance of responsibility, have encouraged passivity, have eliminated meaning from work. Man's habits, attitudes, expectations—his whole conception of membership in an industrial organization—have been conditioned by his experience under these circumstances. Change in the direction of Theory Y will be slow, and it will require extensive modification of the attitudes of management and workers alike.

People today are accustomed to being directed, manipulated, controlled in industrial organizations and to finding satisfaction for their social, egoistic, and self-fulfillment needs away from the job. This is true of much of management as well as of workers. Genuine "industrial citizenship"—to borrow again a term from Drucker—is a remote and unrealistic idea, the meaning of which has not even been considered by most members of industrial organizations.

Another way of saying this is that Theory X places exclusive reliance upon external control of human behavior, while Theory Y relies heavily on self-control and self-direction. It is worth noting that this difference is the difference between treating people as children and treating them as mature adults. After generations of the former, we cannot expect to shift to the latter overnight.

Applications of the Theory

Before we are overwhelmed by the obstacles, let us remember that the application of theory is always slow. Progress is usually achieved in small steps.

Consider with me a few innovative ideas which are entirely consistent with Theory Y and which are today being applied with some success:

Decentralization and Delegation

These are ways of freeing people from the too-close control of conventional organization, giving them a degree of freedom to direct their own activities, to assume responsibility, and, importantly, to satisfy their egoistic needs. In this connection, the flat organization of Sears, Roebuck and Company provides an interesting example. It forces "management by objectives" since it enlarges the number of people reporting to a manager until he cannot direct and control them in the conventional manner.

Job Enlargement

This concept, pioneered by I.B.M. and Detroit Edison, is quite consistent with Theory Y. It encourages the acceptance of responsibility at the bottom of the organization; it provides opportunities for satisfying social and egoistic needs. In fact, the reorganization of work at the factory level offers one of the more challenging opportunities for innovation consistent with Theory Y. The studies by A.T.M. Wilson and his associates of British coal mining and Indian textile manufacture have added appreciably to our undersstanding of work organization. Moreover, the economic and psychological results achieved by this work have been substantial.

Participation and Consultative Management

Under proper conditions these results provide encouragement to people to direct their creative energies toward organizational objectives, give them some voice in decisions that affect them, provide significant opportunities for the satisfaction of social and egoistic needs. I need only mention the Scanlon Plan as the outstanding embodiment of these ideas in practice.

The not infrequent failure of such ideas as these to work as well as expected is often attributable to the fact that a management has "bought the idea" but applied it within the framework of Theory X and its assumptions.

Delegation is not an effective way of exercising management by control. Participation becomes a farce when it is applied as a sales gimmick or a device for kidding people into thinking they are important. Only the management that has confidence in human capacities and is itself directed toward organizational objectives rather than toward the preservation of personal power can grasp the implications of this emerging theory. Such management will find and apply successfully other innovative ideas as we move slowly toward the full implementation of a theory like Y.

Performance Appraisal

Before I stop, let me mention one other practical application of Theory Y which —while still highly tentative—may well have important consequences. This has to do with performance appraisal within the ranks of management. Even a cursory examination of conventional programs of performance appraisal will reveal how completely consistent they are with Theory X. In fact, most such programs tend to treat the individual as though he were a product under inspection on the assembly line.

Take the typical plan: substitute "product" for "subordinate being appraised," substitute "inspector" for "superior making the appraisal," substitute "rework" for "training or development," and, except for the attributes being judged, the human appraisal process will be virtually indistinguishable from the product inspection process.

A few companies—among them General Mills, Ansul Chemical, and General Electric—have been experimenting with approaches which involve the individual in setting "targets" or objectives *for himself* and in a *self*-evaluation of performance semiannually or annually. Of course, the superior plays an important leadership role in this process—one, in fact, which demands substantially more competence than the conventional approach. The role is, however, considerably more congenial to many managers than the role of "judge" or "inspector" which is forced upon them by conventional performance. Above all, the individual is encouraged to take a greater responsibility for planning and appraising his own contribution to organizational objectives; and the accompanying effects on egoistic and self-fulfillment needs are substantial. This approach to performance appraisal represents one more innovative idea being explored by a few managements who are moving toward the implementation of Theory Y.

Conclusion

And now I am back where I began. I share the belief that we could realize substantial improvements in the effectiveness of industrial organizations during the next decade or two. Moreover, I believe the social sciences can contribute much to such developments. We are only beginning to grasp the implications of the growing body of knowledge in these fields. But if this conviction is to become a reality instead of a pious hope, we will need to view the process much as we view the process of releasing the energy of the atom for constructive human ends—as a slow, costly, sometimes discouraging approach toward a goal which would seem to many to be quite unrealistic.

The ingenuity and the perseverance of industrial management in the pursuit of economic ends have changed many scientific and technological dreams into commonplace realities. It is now becoming clear that the application of these same talents to the human side of enterprise will not only enhance substantially these materialistic achievements but will bring us one step closer to "the good society." Shall we get on with the job?

A Funny Thing
Happened on the Way
to the Future
Warren G. Bennis

Analysis of the "future," or, more precisely, inventing relevant futures, has become in recent years as respectable for
the scientist as the shaman. Inspired by Bertrand de
Jouvenal, Daniel Bell, Olaf Helmer, and others, there seems
to be growing evidence and recognition for the need of a legitimate base of operations for the "futurologist." Writing in
a recent issue of the *Antioch Review,* groping for a definition
of the future I wrote:

> For me, the "future" is a portmanteau word. It
> embraces several notions. It is an exercise of the imagi-
> nation which allows us to compete with and try to out-
> wit future events. Controlling the anticipated future is,
> in addition, a social invention that legitimizes the
> process of forward planning. There is no other way I
> know of to resist the "tyranny of blind forces" than by
> looking facts in the face (as we experience them in the
> present) and extrapolating to the future—nor is there
> any other sure way to detect compromise. Most impor-
> tantly, the future is a conscious dream, a set of imagina-
> tive hypotheses groping toward whatever vivid utopias
> lie at the heart of our consciousness. "In dreams begin
> responsibilities," said Yeats, and it is to our future re-
> sponsibilities as educators, researchers, and practi-
> tioners that these dreams are dedicated.[1]

Most students of the future would argue with that definition, claiming that it is "poetic" or possibly even "prescien-
tific." The argument has validity, I believe, though it is
difficult to define "futurology," let alone distinguish between
and among terms such as "inventing relevant futures,"
scenarios, forecasts, self-fulfilling prophecies, predictions,

Reprinted from *American Psychologist* 25, no. 7 (July 1970):
595–608. Copyright 1970 by the American Psychological Association,
and reproduced by permission.

1. W. G. Bennis, "Future of the Social Sciences," *Antioch Review* 28
(1968): 227.

goals, normative theories, evolutionary hypotheses, prescriptions, and so on. Philosophers and sociologists, for example, are still arguing over whether Weber's theory of bureaucracy was in fact a theory, a poignant and scholarly admonition, an evolutionary hypothesis, or a descriptive statement.

However difficult it may be to identify a truly scientific study of the future, most scholars would agree that it should include a number of objectives:

1. It should provide a survey of possible futures in terms of a spectrum of major potential alternatives.

2. It should ascribe to the occurrence of these alternatives some estimates of relative a priori probabilities.

3. It should, for given basic policies, identify preferred alternatives.

4. It should identify those decisions which are subject to control, as well as those developments which are not, whose occurrence would be likely to have a major effect on the probabilities of these alternatives.[2]

With these objectives only dimly in mind, I wrote a paper on the future of organizations which was called "Organizational Developments and the Fate of Bureaucracy."[3] Essentially, it was based on an evolutionary hypothesis which asserted that every age develops a form of organization most appropriate to its genius. I then went on to forecast certain changes in a "postbureaucratic world" and how these changes would affect the structure and environment of human organizations, their leadership and motivational patterns, and their cultural and ecological values. A number of things have occurred since that first excursion into the future in September 1964 which are worth mentioning at this point, for they have served to reorient and revise substantially some of the earlier forecasts.

Perhaps only a Homer or Herodotus, or a first-rate folk-rock composer, could capture the tumult and tragedy of the five years since that paper was written and measure their impact on our lives. The bitter agony of Vietnam, the convulsive stirrings of black America, the assassinations, the bloody streets of Chicago have all left their marks. What appears is a panorama that goes in and out of focus as it is transmitted

2. O. Helmer, "Political Analysis of the Future" (Paper presented at the annual meeting of the American Political Science Association, New York, 4 September 1969).

3. W. G. Bennis, "Organizational Developments and the Fate of Bureaucracy" (Paper presented at the annual meeting of the American Psychological Association, Los Angeles, 4 September 1964). Published in *Industrial Management Review* 7(1966): 41–55.

through the mass media and as it is expressed through the new, less familiar media, the strikes, injunctions, disruptions, bombings, occupations, the heart attacks of the old, and the heartaches of the young. Strolling in late August 1969 through my own campus, lush, quiet, and sensual, I was almost lulled into thinking that nothing fundamental has happened to America in the past five years. Only the residual graffiti from last spring's demonstrations ("Keep the Pigs Out!" "Be Realistic—Demand the Impossible!"), hanging all but unnoticed in the student union, remind us that something has—though what it is, as the song says, "ain't exactly clear." One continually wonders if what has happened is unique and new ("Are we in France, 1788?" as one student asked), whether what is happening at the universities will spread to other, possibly less fragile institutions, and, finally, whether the university is simply the anvil upon which the awesome problems of our entire society are being hammered out. No one really knows. Despite the proliferation of analyses attributing campus unrest to everything from Oedipal conflicts (the most comforting explanation) to the failure of the Protestant Ethic, the crises continue relentlessly.

In his *Report to Greco*, Nikos Kazantzakis tells us of an ancient Chinese imprecation: "I curse you; may you live in an important age." Thus, we are all damned, encumbered, and burdened, as well as charmed, exhilarated, and fascinated by this curse.

In the rueful words of Bob Dylan:

> Come writers and critics
> Who prophesy with your pen
> And keep your eyes wide
> The chance won't come again.
> And don't speak too soon
> For the wheel's still in spin
> And there's no tellin' who
> That it's namin'
> For the loser now
> Will be later to win
> For the times are a-changin'.

Reactions to our spastic times vary. There are at least seven definable types:

1. First and most serious of all are the *militants,* composed for the most part of impotent and dependent populations who have been victimized and infantilized, and who see no way

out but to mutilate and destroy the system which has decimated its group identity and pride. Excluded populations rarely define their price for belated inclusion in intellectual terms, which confuses and terrifies the incumbents who take participation for granted.

2. The *apocalyptics,* who with verbal ferocity burn everything in sight. So, in *Supergrow,* Benjamin DeMott assumes the persona of a future historian and casts a saddened eye on everyone from the Beatles to James Baldwin, from the *Berkeley Barb* to Alfred Kazin, while contemplating the age of megaweapons. DeMott writes: "By the end of the sixties the entire articulate Anglo-American community . . . was transformed into a monster-chorus of damnation dealers, its single voice pitched ever at hysterical level, its prime aim to transform every form of discourse into a blast."[4]
These voices are hot as flamethrowers, searing all that get in their way and usually fired from a vantage point several terrain features away.

3. The *regressors,* who see their world disintegrating and engage in fruitless exercises in nostalgia, keening the present and weeping for a past: orderly, humane, free, civilized, and nonexistent. Someone recently recommended that the university insulate itself from outside pollutants—I suppose he meant students and the community—and set up, medieval Oxford style, a chantry for scholars which he warmly referred to as a "speculatorium."

4. There are the *retreaters,* apathetic, withdrawn, inwardly emigrating and outwardly drugged, avoiding all environments except, at most, a communal "roll your own" or a weekend bash at Esalen, longing for a "peak experience," instant nirvana, hoping to beat out reality and consequence.

5. The *historians,* who are always capable of lulling us to sleep by returning to a virtuous past, demonstrating that the "good old days" were either far better or worse. "The good old days, the good old days," said a Negro comedienne of the 30s, "I was there; where were they?" I learned recently, for example, that the university, as a quiet place devoted to the pursuit of learning and unaffected by the turbulence of the outside world, is of comparatively recent date, that the experience of the medieval university made the turbulence of recent years seem like a spring zephyr. It was pointed out that a student at the University of Prague cut the throat of a Friar Bishop and was merely expelled, an expedient that may

4. B. DeMott, *Supergrow* (New York: Dutton, 1969).

have had something to do with the fact that in dealing with student morals, university officials were constrained to write in Latin.

6. The *technocrats,* who plow heroically ahead, embracing the future and in the process usually forgetting to turn around to see if anybody is following or listening, cutting through waves of ideology like agile surfers.

7. And, finally, the rest of us, "we happy few," the *liberal-democratic reformers,* optimists believing in the perfectibility of man and his institutions, waiting for a solid scientific victory over ideology and irrationality, accepting the inevitability of technology and humanism without thoroughly examining *that* relationship as we do all others, and reckoning that the only way to preserve a democratic and scientific humanism is through inspiriting our institutions with continuous, incremental reform.

The 1964 paper I mentioned earlier was written within the liberal-democratic framework, and it contained many of the inherent problems and advantages of that perspective. The main strategy of this paper and its focus of convenience are to review briefly the main points of that paper, to indicate its shortcomings and lacunae in light of five years' experience (not the least of which has been serving as an administrator in a large, complex public bureaucracy), and then proceed to develop some new perspectives relevant to the future of public bureaucracies. I might add, parenthetically, that I feel far less certainty and closure at this time than I did five years ago. The importance of inventing relevant futures and directions is never more crucial than in a revolutionary period, exactly and paradoxically at the point in time when the radical transition blurs the shape and direction of the present. This is the dilemma of our time and most certainly the dilemma of this paper.

The Future: 1964 Version

Bureaucracy, I argued, was an elegant social invention, ingeniously capable of organizing and coordinating the productive processes of the Industrial Revolution, but hopelessly out-of-joint with contemporary realities. There would be new shapes, patterns, and models emerging which promised drastic changes in the conduct of the organization and of managerial practices in general. In the next 25–50 years, I argued, we should witness and participate in the end of bureaucracy as we know it and the rise of the new social systems better suited to twentieth-century demands of industrialization.

This argument was based on a number of factors:

1. The exponential growth of science, the growth of intellectual technology, and the growth of research and development activities.

2. The growing confluence between men of knowledge and men of power or, as I put it then, "a growing affinity between those who make history and those who write it."[5]

3. A fundamental change in the basic philosophy which underlies managerial behavior, reflected most of all in the following three areas: (a) a new concept of man, based on increased knowledge of his complex and shifting needs, which replaces the oversimplified, innocent push-button concept of man; (b) a new concept of power, based on collaboration and reason, which replaces a model of power based on coercion and fear; and (c) a new concept of organizational values, based on humanistic-democratic ideals, which replaces the depersonalized mechanistic value system of bureaucracy.

4. A turbulent environment which would hold relative uncertainty due to the increase of research and development activities. The environment would become increasingly differentiated, interdependent, and more salient to the organization. There would be greater interpenetration of the legal policy and economic features of an oligopolistic and government-business-controlled economy. Three main features of the environment would be interdependence rather than competition, turbulence rather than a steady, predictable state, and large rather than small enterprises.

5. A population characterized by a younger, more mobile, and better educated work force.

These conditions, I believed, would lead to some significant changes:

The increased level of education and rate of mobility would bring about certain changes in values held toward work. People would tend to (a) be more rational, be intellectually committed, and rely more heavily on forms of social influence which correspond to their value system; (b) be more "other-directed" and rely on their temporary neighbors and workmates for companionships, in other words, have relationships, not relatives; and (c) require more involvement, participation, and autonomy in their work.

As far as organizational structure goes, given the population characteristics and features of environmental turbulence, the social structure in organizations of the future would take

5. Bennis, "Organizational Developments and the Fate of Bureaucracy."

on some unique characteristics. I will quote from the original paper.

First of all, the key word will be temporary: Organizations will become adaptive, rapidly changing temporary systems. Second, they will be organized around problems-to-be-solved. Third, these problems will be solved by relative groups of strangers who represent a diverse set of professional skills. Fourth, given the requirements of coordinating the various projects, articulating points or "linking pin" personnel will be necessary who can speak the diverse languages of research and who can relay and mediate between various project groups. Fifth, the groups will be conducted on organic rather than on mechanical lines; they will emerge and adapt to the problems, and leadership and influence will fall to those who seem most able to solve the problems rather than to programmed role expectations. People will be differentiated, not according to rank or roles, but according to skills and training.

Adaptive, temporary systems of diverse specialists solving problems, coordinated organically via articulating points, will gradually replace the theory and practice of bureaucracy. Though no catchy phrase comes to mind, it might be called an organic-adaptive structure.

(As an aside: what will happen to the rest of society, to the manual laborers, to the poorly educated, to those who desire to work in conditions of dependency, and so forth? Many such jobs will disappear; automatic jobs will be automated. However, there will be a corresponding growth in the service-type of occupation, such as organizations like the Peace Corps and AID. There will also be jobs, now being seeded, to aid in the enormous challenge of coordinating activities between groups and organizations. For certainly, consortia of various kinds are growing in number and scope and they will require careful attention. In times of change, where there is a wide discrepancy between cultures and generations, an increase in industrialization, and especially urbanization, society becomes the client for skills in human resources. Let us hypothesize that approximately 40% of the population would be involved in jobs of this nature, 40% in technological jobs, making an organic-adaptive majority with, say, a 20% bureaucratic minority.)[6]

6. Ibid.

Toward the end of the paper, I wrote that

> The need for instinctual renunciation decreases as man achieves rational mastery over nature. In short, organizations of the future will require fewer restrictions and repressive techniques because of the legitimization of play and fantasy, accelerated through the rise of science and intellectual achievements.[7]

To summarize the changes in emphasis of social patterns in the "postbureaucratic world" I was then describing (using Trist's framework), the following paradigm may be useful:[8]

From	*Toward*
	Cultural Values	
Achievement	Self-actualization
Self-control	Self-expression
Independence	Interdependence
Endurance of stress	Capacity for joy
Full employment	Full lives
	Organizational Values	
Mechanistic forms	Organic forms
Competitive relations	Collaborative relations
Separate objectives	Linked objectives
Own resources regarded as absolutely necessary	Own resources regarded also as society's resources

I hope I have summarized the paper without boring you in the process. One thing is clear; looking backward, reexamining one's own work five years later is a useful exercise. Aside from the protracted decathexis from the original ideas, new experiences and other emergent factors all help to provide a new perspective which casts some doubt on a number of assumptions, only half implied in the earlier statement. For example:

1. The organizations I had in mind then were of a single class: instrumental, large-scale, science-based, international bureaucracies, operating under rapid growth conditions. Service industries and public bureaucracies, as well as nonsalaried employees, were excluded from analysis.

2. Practically no attention was paid to the boundary transactions of the firm or to interinstitutional linkages.

3. The management of conflict was emphasized, while the strategy of conflict was ignored.

4. Power of all types was underplayed, while the role of the leader as facilitator—"linking pin"—using an "agricultural model" of nurturance and climate building was stressed.

7. Ibid.
8. E. Trist, *The Relation of Welfare and Development in the Transition to Post-Industrialism* (Los Angeles: Western Management Science Institute, University of California, 1968).

Put in Gamson's[9] terms, I utilized a domesticated version of power, emphasizing the process by which the authorities attempt to achieve collective goals and to maintain legitimacy and compliance with their decisions, rather than the perspective of "potential partisans," which involves diversity of interest groups attempting to influence the choices of authorities.

5. A theory of change was implied, based on gentle nudges from the environment coupled with a truth-love strategy; that is, with sufficient trust and collaboration along with valid data, organizations would progress monotonically along a democratic continuum.

In short, the organizations of the future I envisaged would most certainly be, along with a Bach Chorale and Chartres Cathedral, the epiphany to Western civilization.

The striking thing about truth and love is that whereas I once held them up as the answer to our institution's predicaments, they have now become the problem. And, to make matters worse, the world I envisaged as emergent in 1964 becomes, not necessarily inaccurate, but overwhelmingly problematical. It might be useful to review some of the main organizational dilemmas before going any further, both as a check on the previous forecast, as well as a preface to some new and tentative ideas about contemporary human organizations.

Some New Dilemmas

The Problem of Legitimacy

The key difference between the Berkeley riots of 1964 and the Columbia crisis of May 1969 is that in the pre-Columbian case the major impetus for unrest stemmed from the perceived abuse or misuse of authority ("Do not bend, fold, or mutilate"), whereas the later protest denied the legitimacy of authority. The breakdown of legitimacy in our country has many reasons and explanations, not the least of which is the increasing difficulty of converting political questions into technical-managerial ones. Or, put differently, questions of legitimacy arise whenever "expert power" becomes ineffective. Thus, black militants, drug users, draft resisters, student protestors, and liberated women all deny

9. W. A. Gamson, *Power and Discontent* (Homewood, Ill.: Dorsey Press, 1968).

the legitimacy of those authorities who are not black, drug experienced, pacifists, students, or women.

The university is in an excruciating predicament with respect to the breakdown of legitimacy. Questions about admissions, grades, curriculum, and police involvement—even questions concerning rejection of journal articles—stand the chance of being converted into political-legal issues. This jeopardizes the use of universalistic-achievement criteria, upon which the very moral imperatives of our institutions are based. The problem is related, of course, to the inclusion of those minority groups in our society which have been excluded from participation in American life and tend to define their goals in particularistic and political terms.

Kelman[10] cites three major reasons for the crisis in legitimacy: (*a*) serious failings of the system in living up to its basic values and in maintaining a proper relationship between means and ends, (*b*) decreasing trust in leadership, and (*c*) dispositions of our current youth. On this last point, Flacks

> suggests the existence of an increasingly distinct "humanist" subculture in the middle class, consisting primarily of highly educated and urbanized families, based in professional occupations, who encourage humanist orientations in their offspring as well as questioning attitudes to traditional middle class values and to arbitrary authority and conventional politics. . . . Although this humanist subculture represents a small minority of the population, many of its attributes are more widely distributed, and the great increase in the number of college graduates suggests that the ranks of this subculture will rapidly grow.[11]

In short, as the gap between shared and new moralities and authoritative norms (i.e., the law) widens, questions of legitimacy inevitably arise.

Populist versus Elite Functions?

Can American institutions continue to fulfill the possibly in-

10. H. C. Kelman, "In Search of New Bases for Legitimacy: Some Social Psychological Dimensions of the Black Power and Student Movements" (Paper presented at the Richard M. Elliott Lecture, University of Michigan, Ann Arbor, 21 April 1969).

11. R. Flacks, "Protest or Conform: Some Social Psychological Perspectives on Legitimacy," *Journal of Applied Behavioral Science* 5 (1969): 127–50.

compatible goals of their elitist and populist functions? Again, the American university is an example of this dilemma, for the same institution tries to balance both its autonomous-elite function of disinterested inquiry and criticism and an increasingly service-populist-oriented function. This has been accomplished by insulating the elite (autonomous) functions of liberal education, basic research, and scholarship from the direct impact of the larger society, whose demands for vocational training, certification, service, and the like are reflected and met in the popular functions of the university. As Trow puts it:

> These insulations take various forms of a division of labor within the university. There is a division of labor between departments, as for example, between a department of English or Classics, and a department of Education. There is a division of labor in the relatively unselective universities between the undergraduate and graduate schools, the former given our largely to mass higher education in the service of social mobility and occupational placement, entertainment, and custodial care, while the graduate departments in the same institutions are often able to maintain a climate in which scholarship and scientific research can be done to the highest standards. There is a familiar division of labor, though far from clear-cut, between graduate departments and professional schools. Among the faculty there is a division of labor, within many departments, between scientists and consultants, scholars and journalists, teachers and entertainers. More dangerously, there is a division of labor between regular faculty and a variety of fringe or marginal teachers—teaching assistants, visitors and lecturers—who in some schools carry a disproportionate load of the mass teaching. Within the administration there is a division of labor between the Dean of Faculty and Graduate Dean, and the Dean of Students. And among students there is a marked separation between the "collegiate" and "vocational" subcultures, on the one hand, and academically or intellectually oriented subcultures on the other.[12]

To a certain extent, the genius of American higher education

12. M. Trow, "Urban Problems and University Problems" (Paper presented at the 24th All-University Conference, University of California at Riverside, 23–25 March 1969), p. 2.

is that it *has* fulfilled both of these functions, to the wonder of all, and especially to observers from European universities. But with the enormous expansion of American universities, proportional strains are being placed on their insulating mechanisms.

Interdependence or Complicity in the Environment

The environment I talked about in 1964, its interdependence and turbulence, is flourishing today. But my optimism must now be tempered, for what appeared then to be a "correlation of fates" turns out to have blocked the view of some serious problems. The university is a good example of this tension.

The relationship between the university and its environment has never been defined in more than an overly abstract way. For some, the university is a citadel, aloof, occasionally lobbing in on society the shells of social criticism. Both the radical left and the conservative right seem to agree on this model, maintaining that to yield to the claims of society will fragment and ultimately destroy the university. Others, for different reasons, prefer a somewhat similar model, that of the "speculatorium," where scholars, protected by garden walls, meditate away from society's pollutants. Still others envisage the university as an "agent of change," a catalytic institution capable of revolutionizing the nation's organizations and professions. In fact, a recent sociological study listed almost fifty viable goals for the university[13] (a reflection of our ambivalence and confusions as much as anything), and university catalogs usually list them all.

The role of the university in society might be easier to define if it were not for one unpalatable fact. Though it is not usually recognized, the truth is that the university is not self-supporting. The amount available for our educational expenditures (including funds necessary to support autonomous functions) relates directly to the valuation of the university by the general community. The extent to which the university's men, ideas, and research are valued is commensurate with the amount of economic support it receives.[14] This has always been true. During the Great Awakening, universities educated ministers; during the agricultural and industrial rev-

13. E. Gross, "Universities as Organizations: A Research Approach," *American Sociological Review* 33 (1968): 518–44.

14. T. Parsons, "The Academic System: A Sociologist's View," *The Public Interest* 13 (1968): 179–97.

olutions, the land-grant colleges and engineering schools flourished; during the rise of the service professions, the universities set up schools of social welfare, nursing, public health, and so on. And during the past thirty years or so, the universities have been increasingly geared to educate individuals to man the Galbraithean "technostructure."

Thus, the charge of "complicity" of the universities with the power structure is both valid and absurd; without this alleged complicity, there would be no universities, or only terribly poor ones. In the late 60s, the same attack comes from the New Left. The paradox can be blinding, and often leads to one of two pseudosolutions, total involvement or total withdrawal—pseudosolutions familiar enough on other fronts, for example, in foreign policy.

If I am right that the university must be valued by society in order to be supported, the question is not should the university be involved with society, but what should be the *quality* of this involvement and *with whom?* For years, there has been tacit acceptance of the idea that the university must supply industry, the professions, defense, and the technostructure with the brains necessary to carry on their work. Now there are emerging constituencies, new dependent populations, new problems, many without technical solutions, that are demanding that attention of the university. We are being called upon to direct our limited and already scattered resources to newly defined areas of concern—the quality of life, the shape and nature of our human institutions, the staggering problems of the city, legislative processes, and the management of human resources. Will it be possible for the modern university to involve itself with these problems and at the same time avoid the politicization that will threaten its autonomous functions? One thing is clear, we will never find answers to these problems if we allow rational thought to be replaced by a search for villains. To blame the establishment, or Wall Street, or the New Left for our problems is lazy, thoughtless, and frivolous. It would be comforting it we *could* isolate and personalize the problems facing the university, but we cannot.

The last two dilemmas that I have just mentioned, elitist *versus* populist strains vying within a single institution and the shifting, uncertain symbiosis between university and society, contain many of the unclear problems we face today, and I suspect that they account for much of the existential groaning we hear in practically all of our institutions, not just the university.

The Search for the Correct Metaphor

Metaphors have tremendous power to establish new social realities, to give life and meaning to what was formerly perceived only dimly and imprecisely. What *did* students experience before Erikson's "identity crisis"? Greer wrote recently:

> [But] much of our individual experience is symbolized in vague and unstandardized ways. There is, was we say, no word for it. One of the great contributions of creative scientists and artists is to make communicable what was previously moot, to sense new meanings possible in the emerging nature of human experience, giving them a form which makes communication possible. The phrase-maker is not to be despised, he may be creating the grounds for new social reality. (On the other hand, he may merely be repackaging an old product.)[15]

Most of us have internalized a metaphor about organizational life, however crude that model or vivid that utopia is—or how conscious or unconscious—which governs our perceptions of our social systems. How these metaphors evolve is not clear, although I do not think Freud was far off the mark with his focus on the family, the military, and the church as the germinating institutions.

Reviewing organizational metaphors somewhat biographically, I find that my first collegiate experience, at Antioch College, emphasized a "community democracy" metaphor, obviously valid for a small, town-meeting type of political life. In strong contrast to this was the Massachusetts Institute of Technology, which employed the metaphor (not consciously, of course) of "The Club," controlled tacitly and quite democratically, but without the formal governing apparatus of political democracies, by an "old-boy network," composed of the senior tenured faculty and administration. The State University of New York at Buffalo comes close, in my view, to a "labor-relations" metaphor, where conflicts and decisions are negotiated through a series of interest groups bargaining as partisans. There are many other usable metaphors: Clark Kerr's "City," Mark Hopkins's "student and teacher on opposite ends of a log," "General Systems Analysis," "Therapeutic Community," "Scientific Management," and my own "temporary systems," and so on, that compete with the pure form of bureaucracy, but few of them

15. S. Greer, *The Logic of Social Inquiry* (Chicago: Aldine, 1969), p. 46.

seem singularly equipped to cope with the current problems facing large-scale institutions.

Macrosystems versus Microsystems

One of the crude discoveries painfully learned during the course of recent administrative experience in a large public bureaucracy turns on the discontinuities between microsystems and macrosystems. For quite a while, I have had more than a passing *theoretical* interest in this problem, which undoubtedly many of you share, but my interest now, due to a sometimes eroding despair, has gone well beyond the purely theoretical problems involved.

My own intellectual "upbringing," to use an old-fashioned term, was steeped in the Lewinian tradition of small-group behavior, processes of social influence, and "action-research." This is not terribly exceptional, I suppose, for a social psychologist. In fact, I suppose that the major methodological and theoretical influences in the social sciences for the last two decades have concentrated on more microscopic, "manageable" topics. Also, it is not easy to define precisely where a microsocial science begins or where a macrosocial science ends. Formally, I suppose, microsystems consist of roles and actors, while macrosystems have as their constituent parts other subsystems, subcultures, and parts of society. In any case, my intellectual heritage has resulted in an erratic batting average in transferring concepts from microsystems into the macrosystem of a university.

An example of this dilemma can be seen in a letter Leonard Duhl wrote in response to an article by Carl Rogers which stressed an increased concern with human relationships as a necessary prerequisite for managing society's institutions. Duhl wrote:

> Though I agree with [Rogers] heartily, I have some very strong questions about whether, indeed, this kind of future is in the cards for us. I raise this primarily because out of my experiences working in the U. S. Department of Housing and Urban Development and out of experiences working in and with cities, it is clear that in the basic decision making that takes place, the values Dr. Rogers and I hold so dear have an extremely low priority. Indeed, the old-fashioned concerns with power, prestige, money and profit so far outdistance the concerns for human warmth and love and concern that many people consider the latter extremely irrelevant in

the basic decision making. Sadly, it is my feeling that they will continue to do so.[16]

The following examples from my own recent experience tend to confirm Duhl's gloomy outlook.

The theory of consensus falters under those conditions where competing groups bring to the conference table vested interests based on group membership, what Mannhein referred to as "perspectivistic orientation." Where goals are competitive and group (or subsystem) oriented, despite the fact that a consensus might rationally create a new situation where all parties may benefit—that is, move closer to the Paretian optimal frontier—a negotiated position may be the only practical solution. There was a time when I believed that consensus was a valid operating procedure. I no longer think this is realistic, given the scale and diversity of organizations. In fact, I have come to think that the quest for consensus, except for some microsystems where it may be feasible, is a misplaced nostalgia for a folk society as chimerical, incidentally, as the American search for "identity."

The collaborative relationship between superiors and subordinates falters as well under those conditions where "subordinates"—if that word is appropriate—are *delegates* of certain subsystems. Under this condition, collaboration may be perceived by constituents as a threat because of perceived cooption or encroachment on their formal, legal rights.

Or, to take another example, in the area of leadership, my colleagues at the State University of New York at Buffalo, Hollander and Julian,[17] have written for *Psychological Bulletin* one of the most thoughtful and penetrating articles on the leadership process. In one of their own studies,[18] reported in this article, they found that aside from the significance of task competence, the "leader's interest in group members and interest in group activity" were significantly related to the group acceptance of the leader. Yet, in macropower situations, the leader is almost always

16. L. Duhl, "Letter to the Editor," *Journal of Applied Behavioral Science* 5 (1969): 279–80.

17. E. P. Hollander and J. W. Julian, "Contemporary Trends in the Analysis of Leadership Processes," *Psychological Bulletin* 71 (1969): 387–97.

18. J. W. Julian and E. P. Hollander, *A Study of Some Role Dimensions of Leader-Follower Relations*, Technical Report no. 3, Office of Naval Research Contract no. 4679 (Buffalo: State University of New York at Buffalo, Department of Psychology, April 1966).

involved in boundary exchanges with salient interorganizational activities which inescapably reduce, not necessarily interest in group members or activities, but the amount of interaction he can maintain with group members. This may have more the overtones of a rationalization than an explanation, but I know of few organizations where the top leadership's commitment to internal programs and needs fully meets constituent expectations.

In short, the interorganizational role set of the leader, the scale, diversity, and formal relations that ensue in a pluralistic system place heavy burdens on those managers and leaders who expect an easy transferability between the cozy gemütlichkeit of a Theory Y orientation and the realities of macropower.

Current Sources for the Adoption or Rejection of Democratic Ideals

I wrote, not long ago, that

> While more research will help us understand the conditions under which democratic and other forms of governance will be adopted, the issue will never be fully resolved. . . . I. A. Richards once said that "language has succeeded until recently in hiding from us almost all things we talk about." This is singularly true when men start to talk of complex and wondrous things like democracy and the like.[19] For these are issues anchored in an existential core of personality.[20]

Today I am even more confused about the presence or absence of conditions which could lead to more democratic functioning. Somedays I wake up feeling "nasty, brutish, and short," and, other times, feeling benign, generous, and short. This may be true of the general population, for the national mood is erratic, labile, depending on repression or anarchy for the "short" solution to long problems.

Let us consider Lane's[21] "democraticness scale," consisting of five items: (*a*) willingness or reluctance to deny the franchise to the "ignorant or careless"; (*b*) patience or impatience with the delays and confusions of democratic

19. See G. Sartori, "Democracy," in E. R. A. Seligman, ed., *Encyclopedia of Social Sciences* (New York, Macmillan, 1957). "No wonder, therefore, that the more 'democracy' has come to be a universally accepted honorific term, the more it has undergone verbal stretching and has become the loosest label of its kind" (p. 112).

20. W. G. Bennis, "When Democracy Works," *Trans-action* 3 (1966): 35.

21. R. E. Lane, *Political Ideology* (New York: Free Press, 1962).

processes; (c) willingness or reluctance to give absolute authority to a single leader in times of threat; (d) where democratic forms are followed, degree of emphasis (and often disguised approval) of underlying oligarchical methods) (e) belief that the future of democracy in the United States is reasonably secure.

Unfortunately, there has been relatively little research on the "democratic personality," which makes it risky to forecast whether conditions today will facilitate or detract from its effective functioning. On the one hand, there is interesting evidence that would lead one to forecast an increased commitment to democratic ideals. Earlier I mentioned Flacks's[22] work on the "transformation of the American middle-class family," which would involve increased equality between husband and wife, declining distinctiveness of sex roles in the family, increased opportunity for self-expression on the part of the children, fewer parental demands for self-discipline, and more parental support for autonomous behavior on the part of the children. In addition, the increase in educated persons, whose status is less dependent on property, will likely increase the investment of individuals in having autonomy and a voice in decision making.

On the other hand, it is not difficult to detect some formidable threats to the democratic process which make me extremely apprehensive about an optimistic prediction. Two are basically psychological, one derived from some previous assumptions about the environment, the other derived from some recent personal experience. The third is a venerable structural weakness which at this time takes on a new urgency.

1. Given the turbulent and dynamic texture of the environment, we can observe a growing uncertainty about the deepest human concerns: jobs, neighborhoods, regulation of social norms, life styles, child rearing, law and order; in short, the only basic questions, according to Tolstoi, that interest human beings are How to live? and What to live for? The ambiguities and changes in American life that occupy discussion in university seminars and annual meetings and policy debates in Washington, and that form the backbone of contemporary popular psychology and sociology, become increasingly the conditions of trauma and frustration in the lower middle class. Suddenly the rules are changing—all the rules.

A clashy dissensus of values is already clearly foreshad-

22. Flacks, "Protest or Conform."

owed that will tax to the utmost two of the previously mentioned democraticness scale items: "impatience or patience with the delays and confusions of democratic processes" and the "belief that the future of democracy in the United States is reasonably secure."

The inability to tolerate ambiguity and the consequent frustration plus the mood of dissensus may lead to the emergence of a proliferation of "minisocieties" and relatively impermeable subcultures, from George Wallace's blue-collar strongholds to rigidly circumscribed communal ventures. Because of their rejection of incremental reform and the establishment, and their impatience with bureaucratic-pragmatic leadership, their movements and leadership will likely resemble a "revolutionary-charismatic" style.[23]

2. The personal observation has to do with experience over the past two years as an academic administrator, experience obtained during a particularly spastic period for all of us in the academy.[24] I can report that we, at Buffalo, have been trying to express our governance through a thorough and complete democratic process, with as much participation as anyone can bear. There are many difficulties in building this process, as all of you are undoubtedly aware: the tensions between collegiality and the bureaucratic-pragmatic style of administrators, the difficulty in arousing faculty and students to participate, and so on. I might add, parenthetically, that Buffalo, as is true of many state universities, had long cherished a tradition of strong faculty autonomy and academic control. Our intention was to facilitate this direction, as well as encourage more student participation.

When trouble erupted last spring, I was disturbed to discover—to the surprise of many of my colleagues, particularly historians and political scientists—that the democratic process we were building seemed so fragile and certainly weakened in comparison to the aphrodisia of direct action, mass meetings, and frankly autocratic maneuverings. The quiet workings of the bureaucratic-democratic style seemed bland, too complex and prismatic for easy comprehension, and even banal, contrasted to the headiness of the disruptions. Even those of us who were attempting to infuse and re-

23. H. A. Kissinger, "Domestic Structures and Foreign Policy," *Daedalus* 96 (1966): 503–29.

24. I am here reminded of Edward Holyoke's remark, written over 200 years ago on the basis of his personal experience: "If any man wishes to be humbled or mortified, let him become President of Harvard College."

inforce democratic functioning found ourselves caught up in the excitement and chilling risks involved.

Erich Fromm[25] said it all, I reflected later on, in his *Escape from Freedom,* but what was missing for me in his formulation was the psychic equivalent for democratic participants.

During this same period, I came across a paper by Argyris[26] which reinforced my doubts about the psychological attractiveness of democracy. Using a thirty-six-category group observational system on nearly thirty groups, in 400 separate meetings, amounting to almost 46,000 behavioral units, he found that only six of the thirty-six categories were used over 75 percent of the time, and these six were "task" items such as "gives information, asks for information," and so on. Almost 60 percent of the groups showed no affect or interpersonal feelings at all, and 24 percent expressed only 1 percent affect or feelings. These groups represented a wide cross section of bureaucratic organizations, research and development labs, universities, and service and business industries.

Argyris's data, along with my own personal experience, have made me wonder if democratic functioning can ever develop the deep emotional commitments and satisfactions that other forms of governance evoke, as for example, revolutionary-charismatic or ideological movements? The question which I leave with you at this time is not the one from the original paper ("Is democracy inevitable?"), but, "Is democracy sexy?"

3. The structural weakness in present-day democracy, using that term in the broadest possible political sense, is the 200-year-old idea first popularized by Adam Smith (1776) in *The Wealth of the Nations.* This was "the idea that an individual who intends only his own gain is led by an invisible hand to promote the public interest." The American Revolution brought about a deep concern for the constitutional guarantees of personal rights and a passionate interest in individuals' emotions and growth, but without a concomitant concern for the community.

In a recent issue of *Science,* Hardin, the biologist, discusses this in an important article, "The Tragedy of the

25. E. Fromm, *Escape from Freedom* (New York: Farrar & Rinehart, 1941).
26. C. Argyris, "The Incompleteness of Social-Psychological Theory: Examples from Small Group, Cognitive Consistency, and Attribution Research," *American Psychologist* 24 (1969): 893–908.

Commons." Herdsmen who keep their cattle on the commons ask themselves: "What is the utility to me of adding one more animal to my herd?" Being rational, each herdsman seeks to maximize his gain. It becomes clear that by adding even one animal, as he receives all the proceeds from the sale of the additional increment, the positive utility is nearly $+1$, whereas the negative utility is only a fraction of -1 because the effects of overgrazing are shared by all herdsmen. Thus, "the rational herdsman concludes that the only sensible course for him to pursue is to add another animal to his herd. And another, and another . . . ," until "Each man is locked into a system that compels him to increase his herd without limit . . . Ruin is the destination toward which all men rush . . . Freedom in a commons brings ruin to all."[27]

A recent, less elegant example along these lines occurred at my own campus where there is a rather strong commitment against institutional racism. A recent form this commitment has taken is the admission of at least double the number of black students ever before admitted. However, more disadvantaged students could have been accepted if the students had chosen to vote for "tripling" in the dormitories. It was voted down overwhelmingly, and it was interesting to observe the editor of the student newspaper supporting increased admission for black students and at the same time opposing tripling.

The democratic process as we know it, expressed through majority vote, contains many built-in guarantees for individual freedom without equivalent mechanisms for the "public interest," as Gans's[28] recent article in the Sunday Magazine section of *The New York Times* argues.

A character in Balchin's *A Sort of Traitors* expresses this structural problem with some force: "You think that people want democracy and justice and peace. You're right. They do. But what you forget is that they want them on their own terms. And their own terms don't add up. They want decency and justice without interference with their liberty to do as they like."[29]

These are the dilemmas as I see them now: the threat to legitimacy of authority, the tensions between populist and elitist functions and interdependence and complicity in the environment, the need for fresh metaphors, the discontinuities

27. G. Hardin, "The Tragedy of the Commons," *Science* 162 (1968): 1244.

28. H. J. Gans, "We Won't End Urban Crisis until We End Majority Rule," *New York Times Magazine*, 3 August 1969.

29. N. Balchin, *A Sort of Traitors* (New York: Collins, 1949).

between microsystems and macrosystems, and the baffling competition between forces that support and those that suppress the adoption of democratic ideology. All together, they curb my optimism and blur the vision, but most certainly force a new perspective upon us.

A New Perspective

These profound changes lead me to suggest that any forecast one makes about trends in human institutions must take into account the following:

The need for fundamental reform in the purpose and organization of our institutions to enable them to adapt responsively in an exponentially changing social, cultural, political, and economic environment.

The need to develop such institutions on a human scale which permit the individual to retain his identity and integrity in a society increasingly characterized by massive, urban, highly centralized governmental, business, educational, mass media, and other institutions.

The significant movement of young persons who are posing basic challenges to existing values and institutions and who are attempting to create radical new life styles in an attempt to preserve individual identity or to opt out of society.

The increasing demands placed upon all American institutions to participate more actively in social, cultural, and political programs designed to improve the quality of American life.

The accelerating technical changes which require the development of a scientific humanism: a world view of the social and humanistic implications of such changes.

The necessity of a world movement to bring man in better harmony with his physical environment.

The need for change toward a sensitive and flexible planning capability on the part of the management of major institutions.

The rising demand for social and political justice and freedom, particularly from the American black community and other deprived sectors of society.

The compelling need for world order which gives greater attention to the maintenance of peace without violence between nations, groups, or individuals.

A New Forecast for Public Bureaucracy

The imponderables are youth, and tradition, and change. Where these predicaments, dilemmas, and second thoughts take us, I am not exactly sure. However, by way of a summary and conclusion—and at the risk of another five-year backlash, there are a number of trends and emphases worth considering.

The Organization's Response to the Environment Will Continue to Be the Crucial Determinant for Its Effectiveness
Economists and political scientists have been telling us this for years, but only recently have sociologists and social psychologists, like Terreberry, Emery and Trist, Levine and White, Litwak and Hylton, and Evan,[30] done so. To quote Benson Snyder, concerning a recent trip to California universities:

> There is another consequence of this limited response to rapid change. The climate of society becomes suffused and distrait, positions ossified, and one hears expressions of helplessness increase, like dinosaurs on the plains of mud. Each in his own way frantically puts on more weight and thinks this form of strength will serve him. He doesn't know he has lost touch until the mud reaches the level of his eyes.[31]

Three derivatives of this protean environment can be anticipated: First, we will witness new ecological strategies that are capable of anticipating crisis instead of responding to crisis, that require participation instead of consent, that confront conflict instead of dampening conflict, that include comprehensive measures instead of specific measures, and that include a long planning horizon instead of a short planning horizon.

Second, we will identify new roles for linking and correlating interorganizational transactions—"interstitial men."

30. S. Terreberry, "The Evolution of Organizational Environments," *Administrative Science Quarterly* 12 (1968): 590–613; F. E. Emery and E. L. Trist, "The Causal Texture of Organizational Environments," *Human Relations* 18 (1965): 1–10; S. Levine and P. E. White, "Exchange as a Conceptual Framework for the Study of Interorganizational Relationships," *Administrative Science Quarterly* 6 (1961): 583–601; E. Litwak and L. Hylton, "Interorganizational Analysis: A Hypothesis on Coordinating Agencies," *Administrative Science Quarterly* 6 (1962): 395–420; W. M. Evan, "The Organization-Set: Toward a Theory of Interorganizational Relationships," in J. D. Thompson, ed., *Approaches to Organizational Design* (Pittsburgh: University of Pittsburgh Press, 1966).

31. B. Snyder, personal communication, 1969.

Third, and most problematical, I anticipate an erratic environment where various organizations coexist at different stages of evolution. Rather than neat, linear, and uniform evolutionary developments, I expect that we will see both more centralization (in large-scale instrumental bureaucracies) and more decentralization (in delivery of health, education, and welfare services); both the increase of bureaucratic-pragmatic and of revolutionary-charismatic leadership; both the increase in size and centralization of many municipal and governmental units and the proliferation of self-contained minisocieties,[32] from the "status-spheres" that Tom Wolfe writes about like Ken Kesey's "electric kool-aid acid-heads" and the pump-house gang of La Jolla surfers to various citizen groups. Ethnic groups organize to "get theirs," and so do the police, firemen, small property owners, and "mothers fighting sex education and busing," and so on.

Large-Scale Public and Private Bureaucracies Will Become More Vulnerable Than Ever Before to the Infusion of Legislative and Juridical Organs

These probably will become formalized, much like the Inspector General's office in the Army. In one day's issue of a recent *New York Times,* three front-page stories featured: (*a*) the "young Turks" within the State Department who are planning to ask the department to recognize the Foreign Service Association as the exclusive agent with which the department would bargain on a wide scale of personnel matters, (*b*) antipoverty lawyers within the Office of Equal Opportunity who have organized for a greater voice in setting policy, and (*c*) the informal caucus of civil rights lawyers in the Justice Department to draft a protest against what they consider a recent softening of enforcement of the civil rights laws.

I have always been fascinated by Harold Lasswell's famous analogy between the Freudian trinity of personality and the tripartite division of the federal government. Most bureaucracies today contain only one formal mechanism, that is, the executive or ego functions. The legislative (id) and the

---

32. Sometimes it is difficult to distinguish the reform groups from the reaction groups, except that the affluent, particularly the young, uncommitted affluent, have already begun to invent and manage environments, cutting across class and ethnic lines, that reflect unique life styles. And these begin and end as rapidly as boutiques on Madison Avenue, which in many ways they resemble, rather than the massive, more familiar conglomerates of yesteryear.

judicial (superego) have long been underrepresented; this will likely change.[33]

There Will Be More Legitimization for "Leave-Taking" and Shorter Tenure at the Highest Levels of Leadership

One aspect of "temporary systems" that was underplayed in my 1964 paper was the human cost of task efficiency. Recently, James Reston observed that the reason it is difficult to find good men for the most responsible jobs in government is that the good men have burnt out, or as my old infantry company commander once said, "In this company, the good guys get killed." Perhaps this creates the appearance of the Peter Principle, that is, that people advance to the level of their greatest incompetence. What is more likely is that people get burnt out, psychologically killed. Many industries are now experimenting with variations on sabbaticals for their executives, and I think it is about time that universities woke up to the fact that a seven-year period, for a legalized moratorium, is simply out of joint with the recurring need for self- and professional renewal.[34]

It may also be that leaders with shorter time horizons will be more effective in the same way that interregnum popes have proven to be the most competent.

New Organizational Roles Will Develop Emphasizing Different Loci and Commitments of Collegiality

Aside from consultants and external advisory groups, organizations tend to arrogate the full working time and commit-

33. The labor unions have been relatively unsuccessful in organizing either top levels of management or professionals. They have failed to do so, in my view, because they have operated at the lowest level of the Maslow hierarchy of needs, economic, physiological, safety, failing to understand the inducements of most professionals: achievement, recognition, intrinsic quality of work, and professional development. Ironically, this has provided more "due process" and, in some cases, more legitimate participation to nonsalaried employees than to higher level personnel. It is no coincidence that the cutting edge of last year's French revolution, in addition to the students, were middle-class professional employees and technicians.

According to William Evan ("The Organization-Set"), the lack of "due process" for the high-ranking managerial and professional personnel has led to or reinforced the "organization man."

34. At Buffalo, we have tried to develop a policy whereby all administrators would hold an academic appointment as well as an administrative post. They would be expected to return to their academic calling after no longer than five, possibly ten, years. The response to this formulation was less than positive, and I suspect that the basic reason for its unpopularity was the psychological blow to the self-concept which equates role-leaving (without manifest promotion) to failure.

ments of their memberships. One works for Ford, or the Department of Health, Education, and Welfare, or Macy's, or Yale. Moonlighting is permitted, sometimes reluctantly, but there is usually no doubt about the primary organization or where there might be a possible "conflict of interest." This idea of the mono-organizational commitment will likely erode in the future where more and more people will create pluralistic commitments to a number of organizations.

To use my own university as an example once again, we have set up one new experimental department which includes three different kinds of professors, different in terms of their relatedness and loci to the department. There is a core group of faculty with full-time membership in the department. There is an associated faculty with part-time commitments to the department, but whose appointment is in another department. And finally, there is a "network faculty," who spend varying periods of time in the department, but whose principal affiliation is with another university or organization. Similar plans are now being drawn up for students.

Similarly, a number of people have talked about "invisible colleges" of true colleagues, located throughout the world, who convene on special occasions, but who communicate mainly by telephone, the mail, and during hasty meetings at airports. I would wager that these "floating crap-games" will increase, and that we will see at least three distinct sets of roles emerge within organizations: those that are *pivotal* and more or less permanent; those that are *relevant,* but not necessarily permanent; and those that are *peripheral.* A person who is pivotal and permanent to one organization may have a variety of relevant and peripheral roles in others.

There are many reasons for this development. First and most obvious is the fact that we live in a jet age where air travel is cheap and very accessible. (A good friend of mine living in Boston commutes daily to New York City for his analytic hour and manages to get back to his office by about 10:30 A.M.) Second, the scarcity of talent and the number of institutions "on the make" will very likely lead more of the top talent to start dividing their time among a number of institutions. Third, the genuine motivational satisfaction gained from working within a variety of comparable institutions seems to be important not for all, but among an increasingly growing fraction of the general population.

We must educate our leaders in at least two competencies: (*a*) to cope efficiently, imaginatively, and perceptively with information overload. Marxist power was property. Today, power is based on control of relevant information. (*b*) As Michael says in his *The Unprepared Society:* We must educate for empathy, compassion, trust, nonexploitiveness, non-manipulativeness, for self-growth and self-esteem, for tolerance of ambiguity, for acknowledgement of error, for patience, for suffering."[35]

Without affective competence, and the strength that comes with it, it is difficult to see how the leader can confront the important ethical and political decisions without succumbing to compromise or to "petite Eichmannism."

We will observe in America a society which has experienced the consequences of unpreparedness and which has become more sanguine about the effects of planning—more planning not to restrict choice or prohibit serendipity, but to structure possibilities and practical visions.

Whether or not these forecasts are desirable, assuming their validity for the moment, really depends on one's status, values, and normative biases. One man's agony is another's ecstasy. It does appear as if we will have to reckon with a number of contradictory and confusing tendencies, however, which can quickly be summarized:

1. More self- and social consciousness with respect to the governance of public bureaucracies.

2. More participation in this governance by the clients who are served, as well as those doing the service, including lower levels of the hierarchy.

3. More formal, quasi-legal processes of conflict resolution.

4. More direct confrontations when negotiation and bargaining processes fail.

5. More attention to moral-ethical issues relative to technical efficiency imperatives.

6. More rapid turnover and varying relationships within institutions.

I think it would be appropriate if I concluded this paper with a quote from the earlier 1964 paper which still seems valid and especially pertinent in light of the new perspectives gained over the past five years. I was writing about the educational requirements necessary for coping with a turbulent environment:

> Our educational system should (1) help us to identify with the adaptive process without fear of losing our

35. D. Michael, *The Unprepared Society* (New York: Basic Books, 1968).

identity, (2) increase tolerance of ambiguity without fear of losing intellectual mastery, (3) increase our ability to collaborate without fear of losing our individuality, and (4) develop a willingness to participate in social evolution while recognizing implacable forces. In short, we need an educational system that can help make a virtue out of contingency rather than one which induces hesitancy or its reckless companion, expedience.[36]

36. Bennis, "Organizational Developments and the Fate of Bureaucracy."